Teaching with
The Norton Anthology
of Western Literature

EIGHTH EDITION

A Guide for Instructors

Teaching with *The Norton Anthology of Western Literature*

EIGHTH EDITION

A Guide for Instructors

Paula Berggren
BARUCH COLLEGE

Alex Purves
UNIVERSITY OF CALIFORNIA, LOS ANGELES (Ancient)

Jennifer Brown
UNIVERSITY OF HARTFORD (Medieval)

Mary Villeponteaux
UNIVERSITY OF SOUTHERN MISSISSIPPI (Renaissance)

Kenneth Watson
UNIVERSITY OF SOUTHERN MISSISSIPPI
(Eighteenth and Nineteenth Centuries)

Kim Herzinger
UNIVERSITY OF SOUTHERN MISSISSIPPI
(Modern and Contemporary)

Jonathan Barron
UNIVERSITY OF SOUTHERN MISSISSIPPI
(Modern and Contemporary)

W · W · NORTON & COMPANY
New York · London

ISBN 0-393-92746-6

W. W. Norton & Company, Inc., 500 Fifth Avenue, New York, NY 10110
www.wwnorton.com

W. W. Norton & Company Ltd., Castle House, 75/76 Wells Street, London W1T 3QT
1   2   3   4   5   6   7   8   9

Contents

The Ancient World

The Middle Ages

The Renaissance

The Enlightenment

The Nineteenth Century: Romanticism

The Nineteenth Century: Realism and Symbolism

The Ancient World

Backgrounds

The last chapter of *Gilgamesh*, Tablet or Book XI, is the culmination of the epic and also the resolution of the hero's quest for immortality. Gilgamesh, dreading his own death after seeing his friend Enkidu die, has located the sage who lives forever and who can—perhaps—teach him to evade this common human fate. Yet Utnapishtim, the "Distant One," first tells Gilgamesh a tale that has become a famous part of world literature: the story of the Flood, in which divine wrath nearly erased human beings from the face of the earth. Utnapishtim has survived the Flood and received immortality from the gods, and he challenges Gilgamesh to prove his own qualifications for immortality by staying awake for a week; when the hero fails this and a subsequent test, he is obliged to return home and resume his role as mortal ruler, made wise by his journey to the end of the earth and by the self-knowledge that it has brought him.

Tablet XI is unusual in that Gilgamesh's own story recedes temporarily into the background, a frame for the much more elaborate story of the Flood. Indeed, most critics believe that this tablet was written separately from the previous chapters, and that the difference can be attributed to the later writer's primary interest in telling the story of the Flood. Both this story and the story of King Gilgamesh, however, are intertwined. The king learns that heroic deeds will not stave off death and that human beings are limited to earthly accomplishments, while the story of the Flood illustrates the vastly separate destinies of gods and mortals.

The story of Gilgamesh moves through several distinct stages, almost like acts in a drama. The first begins with Gilgamesh himself, or rather, with the problem he poses for his people. In an ancient and legendary time, the gods of Mesopotamia have created the semi-divine Gilgamesh to be king of the great city of Uruk. He is perfect in beauty and strength, but his superiority makes him arrogant and he serves his people badly. He harasses the young men of the city in constant athletic competitions at which he excels, and he takes girls from their families and women from their husbands for his own pleasure. His subjects complain of Gilgamesh's oppression, and the gods hear them. On humankind's behalf they implore Aruru, the goddess of creation, to produce a second being equal in strength and ferocity to Gilgamesh who will serve as a counterbalance to him. The result is Enkidu, a creature who is half human and half wild animal, and who becomes king-protector of wild game, standing as much above them as Gilgamesh does above the people of Uruk.

Gilgamesh has already learned of Enkidu's coming through a dream that his goddess-mother interprets as portending that he will find a true companion. He tames the wild side of Enkidu by sending a temple prostitute to teach him the ways of men, after which the two heroes meet and battle in Uruk. Only with great difficulty does Gilgamesh throw Enkidu to the ground. Once he has established his superiority, however, his anger vanishes, and the two embrace as friends, united by a special alchemy into the first great male friendship in literature.

At Gilgamesh's urging, the two friends embark on heroic adventures in order to gain immortal fame. Their first adventure is the slaying of the monster Humbaba, but it is a hollow victory. The monster, who did not provoke the battle, is pathetic in defeat, begging for mercy and cursing them before he dies. In addition, Eulil, the god of wind and storm, is enraged by the staying of his creature and adds his curse to Humbaba's. A second adventure is provoked by Ishtar, the goddess of sex, love, and warfare. Gilgamesh has rejected her advances in insulting fashion, and she calls down the Bull of Heaven to ravage the people of Uruk. When the heroes save Uruk by destroying the bull, Ishtar demands vengeance and the gods grant that one of the two friends must die: Enkidu.

Enkidu's death is a terrible blow to Gilgamesh. Their heroic actions have come to nothing, and his friend's corpse lies decomposing before his eyes. Forced to confront his own mortality, he becomes panic-stricken, lets his hair grow matted, and ranges the steppe, killing and eating wild animals and wearing their skins. When he learns that one human being, Utnapishtim, has advanced beyond the limits of mortality, Gilgamesh decides to undertake a journey in search of him. The journey takes him out of the human realm into a region that seems to exist between his world and that of the gods. After passing through a dark mountain tunnel guarded by scorpion monsters—the same tunnel through which the sun returns during nighttime, so that the hero must literally outrun the sun over the course of one day—he emerges into a new region at the end of the world. Gilgamesh may be heartsick over Enkidu's death, but he has lost none of his assurance. He intimidates the tavern keeper at the end of the world and attacks the ferryman Ur-Shanabi (Utnapishtim's servant), breaking his stone charms, until Ur-Shanabi agrees to carry him across the waters of death. Meeting Utnapishtim on the farther shore, Gilgamesh explains his predicament:

> My friend whom I loved is turned into clay,
> Enkidu, my friend whom I loved, is turned into clay!
> Shall I too not lie down like him,
> And never get up, forever and ever? (X 264–67)

Utnapishtim does not respond as Gilgamesh had hoped: he chides him for his self-pity and emphasizes the impermanence of life.

> Dragonflies drift downstream on a river,
> Their faces staring at the sun,
> Then, suddenly, there is nothing. (X 312–14)

It is at this point that Tablet XI begins, with a disappointed Gilgamesh expressing (in Foster's translation) his surprise at the sage's ordinary appearance. "What made you so special?" he seems to ask. Utnapishtim does not respond to the implied criticism (at least, not until line 210: "who will convene the gods for your sake?"). Instead, he launches into the story of the Flood, explaining that he won immortality by following the commands of the god Ea to build an enormous boat in which to survive the coming deluge. It is this story, a "secret matter" and "mystery of the gods," that Gilgamesh brings back to Uruk, thereby gaining a reputation for great wisdom.

Utnapishtim does not mention the cause of the flood, but an earlier Babylonian narrative, called *Atrahasis*, explains that the gods were annoyed by the noise of an ever-multiplying humanity and decided to eliminate them all. At that time, Utnapishtim lived in the ancient city of Shuruppak on the bank of the Euphrates River; he was a favorite of the god Ea, to whom he prayed in a reed enclosure. Circumventing the divine agreement to keep the plan secret from human beings, Ea spoke to Utnapishtim's reed fence and ordered the sage to build an enormous cubical boat into which he would load himself and his family, as well as skilled craftsmen and every type of living creature, in order to keep human civilization alive through the coming flood. The storm arrives, so dreadful that the gods themselves are horrified and begin to weep. When the waters recede after seven days, Utnapishtim finds his boat stranded on Mount Nimush, and, after seven more days, he is able to emerge and make offerings to the gods—who, deprived of their customary offerings, have been feeling the pangs of hunger. All but Enlil are ready to forgive, and Ea finally persuades him to relent and moderate his punishment. Granting immortality to Utnapishtim and his wife—they will become "like us gods"—Enlil sends them to live at the end of the world.

With the end of his story, Utnapishtim challenges Gilgamesh to prove his own fitness for immortality by staying awake for six days and seven nights. Although the early Gilgamesh had rampaged "day and night," needing little or no rest, his experiences have changed the king and he drifts immediately off to sleep. The sage predicts that the "duplicitous" human being will try to cheat, and tells his wife to bake a loaf of bread each day to demonstrate how long Gilgamesh has slept. After the king awakes, Utnapishtim orders him and the ferryman to leave and never return. Another test ensues, however, for the sage's wife persuades him to grant the traveler a parting favor. The favor Utnapishtim bestows is the plant of perpetual rejuvenation, a gift close to the immortality originally sought by the hero. Gilgamesh obtains the plant from the bottom of the sea but carelessly allows a serpent to steal it on his homeward journey— the first literary occurrence of the snake as an enemy of human happi-

ness. The dejected hero returns to Uruk empty-handed but prepared to
make Uruk great.

> Full understanding of it all he gained,
> He saw what was secret and revealed what was hidden,
> He brought back tidings from before the flood,
> From a distant journey came home, weary, at peace,
> Engraved all his hardships on a monument of stone,
> He built the walls of ramparted Uruk,
> The lustrous treasury of hallowed Eanna! (16–12)

Gilgamesh's consolation is the knowledge that his worldly accomplishments will endure beyond his own lifetime.

Two translations of Tablet XI are offered so that readers may share in the latest attempts by poets and scholars to recapture the meaning of a poem lost for millennia and written in a language that still holds questions for linguists. A brief discussion of the manuscript's survival may be found in the anthology, p. 15, and each of our translators—the Near Eastern scholar Benjamin Foster, and the poet and translator Stephen Mitchell—finds his own way to reproduce (and occasionally to disagree about) the sense of this ancient narrative. Working from the same basic manuscripts, Foster retains every particularity of the fragmentary text, even indicating parts where the meaning is uncertain, while Mitchell modernizes, prunes repetitive passages, and occasionally rearranges material to create a unified impression. (For further linguistic particularities, see p. 17 of the anthology.) Differences of translation may also suggest differences in the interpretation of character. Whereas Mitchell portrays Gilgamesh hesitating to battle the sage Utnapishtim ("something is holding me back"), Foster shifts the personal reference and has the warrior point out the old man's unwarlike appearance ("your heart is drained of battle spirit"). A more striking discrepancy appears between lines 97–98 (Foster) and (Mitchell), and involves an action coming just after everyone has boarded the ark and the door has been sealed. Building on the original term *palace*—Assyriologists disagree as to whether it refers to the ark or to Utnapishtim's former home—Mitchell describes a sour joke played by Utnapishtim on one of his helpers: he leaves his splendid palace to the shipwright Puzur-amurri, knowing that it will soon be under water. Foster, on the other hand, has Utnapishtim bring the boatman Puzur-amurri on board to pilot the newly constructed edifice. The *literal* modern translation of *palace* implies an ironic gift (in a poem replete with double meanings); a sense of the term's potential *ambiguity* points to the presence on board of skilled craftsmen and suggests another interpretation.

Translation is always a negotiation, and the choices faced by Foster and Mitchell are not unique. Other new translations in this anthology show contemporary translators wrestling over linguistic, historical, and cultural meaning as well as ways to express an ancient text in modern

English without utterly deforming it from the shape expected by its original audience. Robert Alter, in his new translation of Genesis, insists on recapturing the different registers of biblical Hebrew, the physicality and "extraordinary concreteness" of its language, and the way that certain important biblical terms (such as "seed" or "hand") hold diverse meanings. He is specific about terms that are generalized elsewhere; Adam is not the first *man*, but "the human" throughout the first several books of Genesis: a literal translation of *'adam*, the generic term for human beings, that also emphasizes a common humanity rather than distinctions of gender. Raymond Scheindlin seeks to represent the poetic values specific to biblical Hebrew, and his new translation of the book of Job appears in carefully shaped verse lines rather than in the more usual prose. Charles Martin, in a new translation of Ovid's *Metamorphoses*, chooses to represent the Roman poet's "thoughtful lightness" in simple, direct language rather than reaching for poetic dignity. Such translators—and they are accompanied by many others in this anthology—build on our current knowledge of the remote past, knowledge won from texts and artifacts accumulating over time. They are also guided by their own readings, which stem not merely from factual information but from a more profound appreciation of the way that poetic structures create additional layers of meaning. At the same time, each translation is inevitably shaped by the translator's own historical situation. (For a more detailed discussion of this dialogical relationship with history, see the "Note on Translation" at the end of each volume.) In this negotiated attempt to correlate past and present, it is instructive to compare more than one translation—to get a second opinion, as it were—in order to triangulate a richer perspective on the distant past. The fact that each translator has provided a new artistic work only adds to our pleasure.

Classroom Strategies

1. Assign both translations and ask students to note passages that seem to differ. In class, focus on the story of the Flood.
2. Compare the two translations, focusing now on the character and quest of Gilgamesh.

Topics for Discussion

1. What is the knowledge brought back by Gilgamesh from the end of the world—the "secret matter" and "mystery of the gods"—and how does it establish his reputation for wisdom?
2. Gilgamesh fails the two tests: is this merely a sign of his personal weakness, or does it have broader significance? (Is eating the apple in the Garden of Eden merely a sign of frailty?)
3. The ending of *Gilgamesh* contains a description of the great city of Uruk, the king's legacy to future generations. (The passage is repeated from the prologue in Tablet 1, thus emphasizing its importance.) How are we to understand this achievement in the light of the hero's quest for immortality throughout the epic?

Topics for Writing

1. Discuss the differences between the Foster and Mitchell translations of *Gilgamesh*, comparing at least one passage from Foster with the corresponding passage in Mitchell. How do differences in translation intervene in our understanding of a character? Which translation, in your opinion, is more convincing in its representation of character?

2. Why is Utnapishtim called the "Distant One," and what do we know about his character? After considering the way the sage is portrayed in various circumstances throughout the story of the Flood, discuss whether the translation of lines 97–98 in Foster or the corresponding lines in Mitchell fit better with your overall impression of Utnapishtim's character.

Comparative Perspectives

1. *Gilgamesh* has the earliest version of the flood story that appears later in the Old Testament (Genesis 6–9). Discuss how each version has very different emphases and draws a different moral.

2. As the earliest human epic *Gilgamesh* also invites comparisons with later epics like the *Odyssey* and the *Aeneid*. Each provides a different goal as an organizing principle—the return home, the founding of a state, the search for immortality—and in each, the gods involve themselves in human affairs. Discuss the relationship of the gods to the protagonist's quest in each epic.

Further Reading

See also the reading suggestions in the *Anthology*, p. 2640.

Delaney, Stephanie. *Myths from Mesopotamia: Creation, the Flood, Gilgamesh, and Others*. 1989. Contains translations, with commentary, of a number of myths that illuminate the context of *Gilgamesh*.

Kirk, G. S. *Myth: Its Meaning and Functions in Ancient and Other Cultures*. 1970. Contains an extended discussion of both Mesopotamian and Greek mythology, and the similarities between *Gilgamesh* and some Greek myths.

Maier, John, ed. *Gilgamesh: A Reader*. 1998. Contains a broad cross-section of twenty-five essays by specialists and nonspecialists, ranging from discussions of the flood and the difficulties of translation to comparative readings with later literature.

THE HEBREW BIBLE

Genesis

[THE CREATION—THE FALL; THE FIRST MURDER; THE FLOOD; THE ORIGIN OF LANGUAGES]

Backgrounds

The Creation of the world in seven days: light and darkness on the first day; the sky (firmament) on the second; on the third, land and sea and also vegetation on the land; on the fourth, sun, moon, and stars; on the fifth, fish and birds; on the sixth, animals and man (Adam). On the seventh day God rested. Adam, in the garden of Eden, is given permission to eat the fruit of any tree except the tree of knowledge of good and evil. He is also given a mate, Eve, who, tempted by the serpent, persuades Adam to eat the forbidden fruit. They are punished by expulsion from the garden and must now work to live; they must also face the inevitability of death: "for dust you are and to dust you shall return."

In the next generation, violent death comes into the world: Cain murders his brother Abel. Their descendants become so wicked that God is sorry he ever created the human race and decides to destroy it. But one just man, Noah, is allowed to survive the Flood, with his family and specimens of all the animals, fish, and birds. So the Earth is repopulated, but humans, in their pride, begin to build a tower as high as Heaven. God prevents this by confusing their speech; before, there was one universal language, but now the builders of the tower speak different languages and cannot understand one another.

Though Genesis is traditionally assigned to the prophet Moses, it bears the marks of a document that has a long history of revision, addition, and reinterpretation over a period of time. (There are, for example, two different accounts of the Creation that do not agree in detail.) The book probably preserves ancient oral tradition but shows signs also of priestly revision at a later stage. Its original language is Hebrew, and Genesis and the next four books of the Old Testament from the Torah (the Law) of the Jewish faith.

Classroom Strategies

The selections are short but have matter enough in them to form one assignment. Refer students to the headnote in the anthology for some of the problems raised by these texts.

The main difficulties for modern students are the following.

- The concept of God that underlies the stories of Adam, Noah, and Babel. You should explain that the punishments inflicted by God are in each case just: Adam disobeys the one prohibition imposed on him, the Flood is sent to punish almost universal wickedness, and the builders of the tower are encroaching on God's space. But in every case, justice is tempered with mercy: Adam and Eve are not

destroyed, only expelled from the garden; Cain is not killed but condemned to be a wanderer on the face of the Earth; Noah and his
family are saved, to repopulate the Earth, and God makes a
covenant with him never to destroy the human race again; the
builders of the tower are not destroyed or even hurt, they are simply
divided by language. You can point out that these stories, like myths
in many societies, have an explanatory function: they answer questions. Why do we have to work to live and eventually die? Why don't
we all speak the same language? Why does the serpent crawl? And
why do we feel revulsion when we see it?
• The subordinate role of Eve and her responsibility for the Fall. A
difficult subject, but you can point out that this story is the creation
of a firmly patriarchal society in which sons were more highly regarded than daughters and authority was the prerogative of the
male. (We are told the names of Noah's sons, for example, but not
the name of his wife.) It can be pointed out, too, that the Hebrews
were not alone in this attitude; the Greek myth of Pandora has exactly the same moral: it's all the woman's fault.

Topics for Discussion

1. The significance of the fact that God forbids eating the fruit of the
   tree of knowledge. Why should the knowledge of "good and evil"
   be forbidden? *Are* there kinds of knowledge that it is risky for human beings to have?
2. The role of the serpent (refer ahead to *Paradise Lost*, where the serpent has become Satan). Is the serpent a way of passing the
   buck—of saying it's not *our* fault?
3. Cain and Abel, symbolic of two different ways of life, farmers and
   pastoral nomads.

Comparative Perspectives

What attitude toward city life is expressed in the story of the Tower of
Babel? Does this differ from the view of Uruk in *Gilgamesh*? How would
you compare the view of urban experience and architecture in other ancient works such as the *Iliad*, the *Odyssey*, or the *Aeneid*?

[ABRAHAM AND SARAH]

Backgrounds

Noah has three sons—one of them, Shem, is the ancestor of the Semitic peoples, including the Hebrews. Abraham, a descendant of Shem,
is called by God to leave his home and eventually settle in Palestine.
With the introduction of Abraham in chapter 12 (not in the anthology),
the focus of Genesis shifts from universal history to the beginnings of
monotheism. Abraham will be the founder of the Jewish people.

The first of the three Patriarchs of Jewish legend, Abraham, is married
to Sarah, who is childless. She gives Hagar, her female Egyptian slave, to

Abraham, and when Abraham is eighty-six years old he fathers his first son, Ishmael, by Hagar. In this section, we see God rename Abraham, who had been called Abraham (just as he also modifies Sarah's name from Sarai) and make a covenant with him that will affect the future of the Jewish people. For God tells Abraham that he will give him a son, Isaac, who will extend their lineage into a "multitude of nations," and that he will also give Abraham and his people the whole land of Canaan as "an everlasting holding." Then God commands Abraham to establish a new practice of circumcision, which will henceforth stand as a marker of the covenant between them.

In chapter 18, God visits Abraham again, in the form of three men, and informs him and Sarah for a second time that a son will be born to them in the coming year. In this scene, Abraham shows his pious nature by the hospitality he offers the men. As God is leaving, he looks over Sodom and tells Abraham that he will wipe out the city for its grave offense against him. Abraham persuades God to save the innocent in the region, even if only ten innocent men should be found there.

The destruction of Sodom unfolds in chapter 19, and the only innocents saved are Lot (Abraham's nephew) and his family. Again, the hospitality scene of chapter 18 is replayed, but this time it more explicitly serves as a test of Lot's piety. By the same token, the impiety of the other residents of Sodom is shown by an incident that occurs when the guests, God's messengers, have retired to bed. All the men of Sodom crowd around Lot's house and violently demand that the guests be brought outside. In pleading for his guests, Lot offers up his own daughters in their place. As the men of the city move to break down Lot's door, God tells Lot to escape with his family without looking back. As Sodom is destroyed, Lot and his family flee to safety. Only Lot's wife looks behind her, and is thereby turned into a pillar of salt.

Topics for Discussion

1. Laughter

   Laughter and joking play an important role in this section of the Bible. Not only does the new child's name, Isaac, mean "he who laughs," but both Abraham and Sarah separately laugh when God tells them they will have a child so late in life. Similarly, when Lot tells his relatives to flee because Sodom is about to be destroyed, they think he is joking. Note also that in the following section of Genesis, Sarah sends Hagar and Ishmael away, because she believes that they laugh at her (see Backgrounds to the Abraham and Isaac section). What does the use of laughter tell us about the relationship between men and God in this section?

   [In some ways, laughter acts as a bridge between God and men, offering them a way of communicating. But in another it only reinforces the difference between them. Man's laughter expresses amazement, and often disbelief at the power of God. At the same time, the element of laughter softens the imposing power of God as a figure in the text, and draws the story into a more familial and domestic context.]

2. Gender

Students are likely to express surprise that Lot offered up his virgin daughters to the impious men of Sodom to "do to them whatever you want" (19.9) for the sake of protecting two guests that Lot had never seen before. How can we explain such a decision in the context of Abraham and Lot's world? [see accompanying note in the text on the importance of hospitality customs]. Does Lot's wife's act of looking behind her have anything to do with her gender? [Compare the curiosity of Eve, of Pandora, and—in Ovid's well-known story of Orpheus and Eurydice (not in the anthology)—the reversal of the tradition, where Orpheus looks back and thereby seals Eurydice's death.] Finally, circumcision, God's covenant to Abraham, marks his family and descendants as a special race. But God offers no such mark to women. Does this leave them as "extras" in God's covenant with man? [Even woman's role as child-bearer is somewhat compromised by Sarah's inability to bear a child until God intervenes.]

[ABRAHAM AND ISAAC]

Backgrounds

A pattern adumbrated by the story of Cain and Abel is repeated in the history of Abraham's two sons, when the firstborn is found inadequate to serve the divine purpose. Hagar and her sixteen-year-old son are banished by Sarah, who believes that they laugh at her. In chapter 21 of Genesis (not in the anthology), Abraham follows God's instructions to grant Sarah's request, sending Hagar and Ishmael away, furnished with bread and water. As their supplies dwindle, it appears that they will die in the wilderness, and Hagar moves away from her son, lest he die before her eyes. At this desperate moment, God's messenger calls to Hagar, and she sees a well of water. They are saved, and God promises to make Ishmael (whose name means "God will hear") the founder of a nation.

In chapter 22 of Genesis, the obedient Abraham takes his "only son Isaac"—his only legitimate son, by the wife he loves—away from home. The narratives complement each other and in their different emphases denote the special burdens that the Covenant will impose on the Jewish people, the descendants of Isaac (the descendants of Ishmael will populate the Arabian peninsula; thus Muslims are also the children of Abraham).

Classroom Strategies

A close reading of this chapter famously demonstrates the narrative genius of Genesis. Three times Abraham speaks the same single word in Hebrew, *hineni*, which means "here I am" and signals not only his readiness but also his relationships toward Isaac, on the one hand, and God, on the other. For three days, he walks with two servants and his son (and the relentless repetition of "his son" insists on the terrible demand that God has made on Abraham, so ready to do His bidding).

In his influential comparison of the Hebrew Bible and Homeric epic, Erich Auerbach speaks of the silences and repressions in this text, "fraught with background." You may want to ask your students how the spareness of dialogue and description suggests what the impact of this journey on father and son must have been. Commentators note that Abraham is careful to carry the dangerous implements (the fire and the "cleaver," an instrument that implies the butchery that is to take place) himself, while he leaves the wood to Isaac. This protective instinct makes all the more agonizing the consciousness with which the father proceeds to fulfill his task, as the narrative carefully spells out the preparations for the sacrifice after being so laconic about everything that leads up to the moment of truth.

[JACOB AND ESAU]

Backgrounds

The wives of the three Patriarchs are the four Matriarchs, the second of whom is Rebekah. This strong-willed woman, Isaac's wife, plays the dominant role in deciding which of her children will gain the paternal blessing. Like Sarah, she is barren until her husband petitions God to give her children. In this second instance of two sons competing for favor, both are children of the same wife. The story of Jacob and Esau is consequently especially complex.

In chapter 25 of Genesis, Esau is portrayed as a coarse and unpromising person, not fit to fulfill the terms of God's Covenant with his grandfather. Hungry and careless, he "spurned the birthright." The narrative conveys this sense of his indifference with a rapid succession of verbs: "he ate and he drank and he rose and he went off." The description of Esau as a baby who came from the womb "ruddy, like a hairy mantle all over" recalls the description of Enkidu in *Gilgamesh*, a reminder that it is always helpful to consider the Mesopotamian sources behind the often problematic tales told in Genesis. (The commentaries in E. A. Speiser's edition of Genesis, the first volume in *The Anchor Bible* mentioned in the bibliography in the headnote, are particularly useful in this area.) As in the fates of Isaac and Ishmael, political motives can be discerned. Edom, a trans-Jordanian kingdom that springs from Esau, will rival the Kingdom of Israel. But the story of the stealing of Jacob's blessing cannot be reduced to a national allegory.

In chapter 27, the narrative sympathy lies with Esau; nevertheless, Genesis in its entirety demonstrates that the divine imperative transcends individual claims and personalities. Rebekah eavesdrops on the feeble Isaac's conversation with her first son and hastily arranges the ruse by which her favorite will prevail. The blind old man relies on his remaining senses to perceive the world, and Rebekah brilliantly foresees the need to transform her younger son into a physical simulacrum of his hunter brother. You will probably want to challenge your students to explain the superiority of Jacob's claim to the paternal blessing. Although Jacob is portrayed here as a trickster, later chapters of Genesis underscore why he is to become the progenitor of the Twelve Tribes of Israel (he later acquires the name Israel). For like all the great heroes of the Hebrew Bible, many of whom demonstrate serious moral flaws, he has tenacity and resourcefulness; above all, whatever his shortcomings, he is capable of intimacy with God and of intellectual and spiritual growth.

This chapter is worth reading for many reasons, not least that it prepares for the longer narrative of Joseph that follows. Rebekah helps Jacob trick his father with a change of garment and "the skins of the kids." Just so will Joseph's brothers bring his garment back to their father (the aged and infirm Jacob, or Israel), stained with the blood of a kid, so that he will believe his son has died. The Bible teaches that our actions have consequences. Only in experiencing these consequences and learning to accept them do human beings fully enact the meaning of free will.

The poignancy of Esau's response in chapter 27 of Genesis is quite contrary to his coarseness in the earlier one, and the significance of Jacob's name is more fully explained. Rebekah's second twin son, who emerged from the womb holding his brother's heel is called *Ya'aqob*, for the root of the word that means heel—*'aqeb*. But change one vowel and the word *'aqob*, or "crooked," also can be understood as the source of his name.

Topics for Writing

1. How important is primogeniture in Genesis? What evidence can you see that more than simple birth order determines the legitimacy of an heir?

2. The ordinary act of making stew takes on great significance in the story of Isaac and his sons, as it is through the preparation of dishes that Jacob wrests the birthright from his brother. In what other ways is food important in this selection? How are we to interpret Esau's hunger and his father's desire for a favorite dish?

   [Esau's other name, Edom, means "ruddy" like the "red red stuff" he calls the stew in his impatience to eat it. Presumably, Jacob's cooking of a stew reflects his competitive instinct, since Isaac prefers his first to his second son because of the venison he brings back from the hunt.]

Comparative Perspectives

1. When Abraham raises his knife against Isaac, a ram caught in a thicket is substituted and sacrificed. Compare the substitution of a human being for an animal in the events prior to the Trojan War that are described by the Chorus in *Agamemnon*. Why was sacrifice so important in the ancient world? Discuss the different views of divinity and the purpose of sacrifice expressed in the Greek and the Hebraic narratives.

2. Compare the brief biblical story of the binding of Isaac with *The Sacrifice of Isaac*, a twelfth-century poem by Rabbi Ephraim ben Jacob printed in the anthology's selection of medieval lyrics. How does the comparison clarify the importance of interpretation in reading biblical texts?

3. Like Isaac, Telemachus is the son of a great man. Contrast the tests by which Telemachus proves himself in the *Odyssey* with those by which Isaac is defined in youth and old age in chapters 22 and 27 of Genesis. What do the differences tell us about the values of the ancient Greeks and Hebrews?

   [Isaac essentially must obey and accept; Telemachus must learn to assert himself.]

[THE STORY OF JOSEPH]

Backgrounds

Jacob has thirteen sons; his favorite is one of the youngest, Joseph, to whom he gives an ornamented tunic, the proverbial "coat of many colors" (see note in anthology). Joseph has dreams that he interprets to mean that he will be the greatest of the brothers. His brothers are enraged and leave Joseph to die in a dry cistern in the outland pastures. They smear his coat with goat's blood and convince Jacob that his son has been killed by a wild beast.

But Joseph is rescued by passing merchants who sell him as a slave to Potiphar, the captain of the guard of Pharaoh, the ruler of Egypt. Joseph rises rapidly in his master's esteem and soon is entrusted with great responsibilities. Potiphar's wife tries to seduce him; rejected, she accuses him of an attempt at rape, and Joseph is sent to prison. There he interprets the dreams of fellow prisoners, and one of them, released and restored to his post as Pharaoh's butler, remembers Joseph when the Pharaoh has some disturbing dreams. Joseph interprets them as a prophecy of seven years of plenty followed by seven years of famine; he suggests storing food as a reserve. Pharaoh puts him in charge of the program; he becomes Pharaoh's chief minister.

The seven lean years begin as predicted; the Egyptians are provided for, but in Israel there is famine. Jacob sends his sons to Egypt to buy grain; they come to Joseph, whom they do not recognize. He denounces them as spies and tells them to come back, this time with the youngest of the brothers, Benjamin. Jacob is unwilling to let Benjamin go, but in the end he has to yield. Once in Egypt, the brothers are entertained royally; their sacks are filled with grain. But in Benjamin's sack Joseph has his servants, in secret, put his own silver cup. When it is found there after a search he tells the others to go home; he will keep Benjamin with him in Egypt. They beg him to let Benjamin go, saying that Jacob will die of grief. Joseph can conceal his feelings no longer and reveals his identity. He sends for Jacob, and so the Israelites settle in Egypt. After many years, when a later Pharaoh begins to oppress them, they escape from Egypt (the Exodus) led by the prophet Moses.

The story has some historical plausibility: for two centuries (1720–1550 B.C.) Egypt was under the domination of the Hyksos, a non-Egyptian people, and Semitic settlers were favored. Joseph's rise to power and influence could in such circumstances have happened. The sophisticated literary form of the story may owe something to a model: an Egyptian tale of a man who rejected the advances of his brother's wife, who then falsely accused him and almost caused his death at his brother's hands (see Thomas in "Further Reading"). The belief that dreams foretold the future, taken for granted in the Joseph story, is common to most of the civilizations of the ancient world; the teacher can refer forward, for example, to Penelope's dream in the *Odyssey* (XIX.604ff.). The basic mechanism of the plot, the hero in disguise (compare the scene between Joseph and his brothers), is also found on a larger scale in the *Odyssey*.

Classroom Strategies

One assignment. No special difficulties.

Topics for Discussion

1. Discuss Joseph's statement to his brothers: "And so, now it is not you who sent me here but God" (chapter 45).
2. "Here comes that dream-master!" Joseph as visionary and a man of action.

Topics for Writing

1. Discuss the function in the story of one of the following recurrent motifs: Joseph's clothes or dreams and their interpretation.
2. Recast the story as a play in five acts.
3. Why do you think Joseph put the silver cup in Benjamin's sack?
4. Does the "success story" of Joseph differ in any way from its modern counterparts in which an awkward, clumsy, ugly, or despised person makes good?
5. Genesis ends with the story of Joseph and begins with a story about free will, knowledge, and obedience. Discuss the importance and complexity of these three themes in the lives of the various biblical figures introduced in the anthology (Abraham, Jacob, Joseph). Does God want only obedience from those with whom He chooses to make His Covenant?

Exodus 19–20

[MOSES RECEIVES THE LAW]

Backgrounds

The story of Moses receiving the Law from God in the desert of Sinai, Exodus 19–20, is well known. While the Israelites are fleeing from Egypt, Moses goes up the mountain to communicate with God, and there receives from him the Law, which in this section take the form of the Ten Commandments. Moses' special relationship with God has already been explained in the earlier books of Exodus (not in the anthology), where we learn of his being found as a baby and raised by a daughter of the Pharaoh in Egypt. On reaching adulthood, however, Moses killed an Egyptian he saw beating a Hebrew, and so fled the country. But God spoke to Moses through a burning bush and commanded him to return to Egypt and lead the Israelites to Canaan.

The circumstances in which Moses receives the Law are noteworthy. He is explicitly placed as an intermediary between God and the Israelites, who wait at the bottom of the mountain. God sends Moses up and down the mountain to transmit certain messages to the people before he communicates the Law. He commands that the people must prepare themselves with certain ablutions and special rites before receiving the Law, and that they must stay away from the mountain while Moses receives the Law, for if they touch the mountain they are doomed to die. God then appears before Moses and Aaron in the form of a great cloud of thunder and smoke, and passes on the Law to them. The importance of the Ten Commandments that Moses receives from God in this section can scarcely be underestimated. They remain a central tenet of both Jewish and Christian thought today.

Classroom Strategies

1. The "law" that Moses receives from God is a translation of the Hebrew word *torah*, which really means teaching or instruction. It may be helpful to discuss with students the importance of the distinction between law and instruction. [For example, the ninth commandment, "You shall not bear witness against your neighbor" comes close to the idea of laws and courts with which we are familiar today.] How do the Ten Commandments compare with legal and moral codes in practice today? What is the extent of their influence in daily life, both as a religious document and as a social charter for the effective working of a community? How have changes in the translation of the Bible affected our understanding of God's Law? [For example, note the difference in meaning between the King James version's "Thou shalt not kill" and "You shall not murder," which is a more accurate translation of the Hebrew word *ratsah*.] Ask the students whether they can find patterns of organization in the Ten Commandments. The first three form a group that emphasizes that God's provenance over the Israelites is exclusive and absolute. He will entertain no divine rivalry. He is, as he says, "a jealous god." The next seven are harder to split into groups, but it is possible to find patterns. For example, the last five are all prohibitions. The fourth and fifth commandments appear to speak to the individual's place in a community, while the sixth, seventh, and eighth speak to how the acts of the individual can affect the community, and the last two seek to prevent divisions within

the community. But students should discuss in their own ways how they believe the commandments relate to the individual, to the family unit, or to the workings of society as a whole. Can we call the Ten Commandments complete and comprehensive? [Remember that these are not the only instructions that Moses receives from God—see headnote.]

2. Discuss how the deliverance of the Law to Moses—which amounts to little more than a list—is encased in a narrative frame. God is using Moses as a medium to transmit his commandments to the Israelites below, but at the same time he is also transmitting his laws to the reader of the Torah. As the notes to this selection observe, God uses the second person singular form in the Decalogue, not the plural as is more customary in formulations of law. The explanation usually given for this is that God is speaking to each person individually through his Law. The "you" of the commandments, therefore, is also a direct address to the reader. What narrative techniques does the Bible use to make the transmission of these laws more palatable to its readers or easier to remember? This section of the Torah is explicit in its role as "instruction," while other sections remain implicit or indirect (compare for example Eve's eating from the tree of knowledge, Joseph's dreams, the Book of Job, or the parables of Jesus in the Christian Bible). Or is it more accurate to say that the Torah is more concerned with imparting instructions than with constructing a narrative arc?

[Narrative techniques that might be considered here are God's delaying of the moment when he will give the Law, through the ordering of preparations, and the repetition of instructions (this builds suspense as the epiphany is continually deferred); the dramatic nature of God's appearance before Moses (smoke, trembling, flashes, and thunder); the added suspense created by the injunction that anyone who touches the mountain is doomed to die.]

[JOB]

Backgrounds

Satan—the Hebrew word means "the adversary"—challenges God to test the piety of Job, a rich and fortunate man famous for his devotion to the Almighty. How will his piety stand up in the face of calamity? God gives Satan permission to inflict any suffering short of physical harm on Job to see if, as Satan claims, he will curse God.

In the course of one day Job learns that all his servants, his flocks, and his sons and daughters have been killed, but he does not blame God. Satan demands and receives permission to inflict bodily harm; he covers Job's body with sores. Job's wife tells him, "Curse God and die," but he rebukes her.

Now three friends (Job's comforters) come to sympathize with him.

From this point on the story is cast in dramatic and poetic form until the short narrative conclusion.

Job wishes he had not been born, and the first of his friends replies: since Job has been punished, he must have sinned. Job's attitude is arrogant; he should show humility before God. The second friend suggests he may be paying for the sins of his children. The third returns to the theme of the first but more harshly: Job *must* be guilty or he would not be suffering. Job refuses to accept these arguments; the disasters inflicted on him are out of proportion to any sin he may unknowingly have committed. He appeals to God and wishes he could speak to him directly and learn the reason for his suffering: "Here is my desire: that Shaddai answer me" (chapter 31). His desire is fulfilled as God speaks from the whirlwind. His speech contains no justification for the suffering he inflicted on Job; it is a magnificent celebration of the power and greatness of God. Job accepts God's answer; he feels overwhelmed by God's personal intervention—now he has faith in him: "I knew you, but only by rumor; my eye has beheld you today" (42). God does not answer Job's question, but he does dismiss the beliefs of his friends: "you have not spoken rightly about me as did my servant Job" (42). And "Yahweh restored Job's fortunes . . . doubling everything Job had" (42).

The basis of the work is an oral folktale, the story of the patient sufferer. Onto a Hebrew version of the tale has been grafted a poetic dialogue between Job and three friends and also the voice of God speaking from the whirlwind. The text probably was set in its present form some time in the sixth century B.C.

Classroom Strategies

Ideally this should be one assignment, but if necessary, it can be divided: 1–14 and 15 to the end.

Satan is a problem for most people new to this text. He is not the Devil of later literature but one of the "sons of God" (chapter 1). His name means "the adversary"; perhaps he is a sort of loyal opposition. Students can be told to watch for the transformation of this figure in later texts (especially Milton), his identification with the serpent of Genesis and the Evil One of the New Testament.

Topics for Discussion

Job (in chapter 31) makes the claim that his life has been virtuous and devoted to the worship of God, and so he does not deserve the calamities that have fallen on him. He asks God for an answer, but the voice from the whirlwind does not deal with his question at all. Why does Job accept God's assertion of divine power (42) and not press for an answer to his question? Why is he satisfied with what he is given? Do you find the end of the dialogue satisfactory?

The answer should be along the lines that Job is content with the fact that the Almighty has condescended to speak to him in person. Even if his question is not answered, he has the assurance that God cares for him enough to speak to him directly. Before this, he has known of God only by hearsay, but now he has direct experience (42). The question of justice in the world, of apparently undeserved suffering (and its opposite, the prosperity of the wicked) is not resolved; it is a question, too, that will be debated by the Greeks (the *Odyssey* 1.37ff. and *Oedipus the King*, for example).

Topics for Writing

1. Recast in your own (plain) language the core of the arguments offered by the three comforters. How do they differ from one another?
2. Discuss the statement that although God does not answer Job's complaint he "reveals himself personally to him and shares with him the vision of his cosmic responsibilities."

Comparative Perspectives

Look carefully at the use of figurative language in a few passages from these texts and try to explain how Hebraic parallelism functions. What do the comparisons chosen tell us about the mode of life and values of the original audience? Chapter 29 offers some particularly good examples of metonymy and synecdoche. Give a moment to Job 7.6 ("My days are swifter than a weaver's shuttle; they end when the thread of hope gives out") if you expect to teach Villon's *Testament* which refers to this verse in lines 217–24) or Browning's *The Bishop Orders His Tomb* (see line 51). Depending on your choice of later texts, it can be useful also to point to differences between the more accurate modern translations and the King James Version, with which some students will be more familiar. For example, the oft-quoted King James line "Though he slay me, yet will I trust him" (13) gives exactly the wrong impression; the meaning can rather be translated, as here, "Let Him kill me!—I will never flinch," or even "Behold he will slay me; I have no hope." Other lines are hard to understand, such as "my feet washed with butter" (29). Compare the exquisite but confusing King James translation, "When I washed my steps with butter" (29) with Stephen Mitchell's vivid contemporary rendition: "when my feet were bathed in cream." How does each translation change our reading of the text?

Psalms

Backgrounds

Our selection offers five texts from what might be called the Hebrew hymnal, a collection of no less than 150 songs. (*Psalm* is a Greek word that describes the sound made by a plucked string, and many of these psalms have come down to us with musical directions attached—"for flutes," for example, or "with stringed instruments.") They are of various types; the selection offers specimens of hymns celebrating the majesty of

God (Psalms 8, 19, and 104), songs of trust in the Lord (Psalm 23), and laments (Psalm 137).

Hebrew poetry is not based on strict metrical pattern alone (as in Greek or Latin) or on metrical pattern and rhyme (as in English and many other modern languages); it works by what is known as "parallelism." A first statement is repeated or amplified in a different form —"The statutes of the Lord are right, rejoicing the heart: the commandment of the Lord is pure, enlightening the eyes" (19.8)—and this second form may echo the original thought, as in this example, build on it toward a climax, or contrast with it.

The Song of Songs

Backgrounds

The headnote offers a fine summary of different interpretive approaches to these astonishing poems, and it would be worth working through some of the possibilities with your students. If the overall idea of allegory seems plausible, the wildly imaginative metaphors of particular lines may seem quite a way from expressing God's love for the Chosen People, or Christ's for his church. If you want to emphasize their allegorical possibilities, you may want to read the Song of Songs with your students as part of your discussion of biblical texts. It may be equally useful to assign the poem as a companion piece to other love lyrics encountered later in the semester.

In any event, detailed elucidation of the figures of speech in the Song of Songs is infinitely rewarding. Note, for example, the comparison of the beloved "to a company of horses in Pharoah's chariots" (chapter 1). Robert Alter clarifies this perplexing reference: "a mare in heat, let loose among chariotry, could transform well-drawn battle lines into a chaos of wildly plunging stallions." The male celebration of female sexuality as landscape is familiar to readers of later love poems, but the violence of this pictorially evocative image is startling and unusual.

The Songs of Songs is also remarkable for the frequency with which the woman speaks. The description of her lover as a sachet of perfume between her breasts (1), for example, so specific, unexpected, and witty, gives some sense of the liveliness of the Song of Songs.

Topics for Writing

Choose examples of the techniques of parallelism and intensification in Job, the Psalms, and the Song of Songs, noting whether the imagery used seems traditional or innovative.

Comparative Perspectives

1. How do the metaphors in the Song of Songs draw on the geography of the land of Israel and the way of life of its people? Compare and contrast the range of metaphors in other early love lyrics, such as Sappho's "Some there are who say that the fairest thing seen."

2. Echoes of the Song of Songs resonate throughout later literature. Discuss the ways in which three medieval poets, Hildegard of Bingen, Judah Halevi, and Geoffrey Chaucer, borrow specific phrases from this biblical work to very different effects.

Further Reading

See also the reading suggestions in the *Anthology*, p. 2640.

Alter, Robert. *The Art of Biblical Narrative*. 1981.

———— *The Art of Biblical Poetry*. 1985.

———— *Genesis: Translation and Commentary*. 1996.

Bloom, Harold, ed. *The Bible*. 1987. This volume includes a number of provocative essays.

Eissfeldt, O. *The Old Testament: An Introduction*. 1965. Very full, authoritative discussion of every aspect of the problems posed by the Old Testament of the Bible by one of the greatest modern scholars in the field.

The New Oxford Annotated Bible (with the Apocrypha). 1977. The Revised Standard Version, which corrects misunderstandings in the Authorized and frequently translates a better text. It is equipped with helpful introductions to the different books and very useful footnotes. See "Characteristics of Hebrew Poetry" (pp. 1523–29) for help with the Psalms.

Olshen, Barry N., and Yael S. Feldman, eds. *Approaches to Teaching the Hebrew Bible as Literature in Translation*. 1989. Another useful volume in the MLA series.

Thomas, D. Winton, ed. *Documents from Old Testament Times*. 1961. Contains documents, translated by experts in the different fields from Babylonian, Egyptian, and other ancient Near Eastern texts that parallel or throw light on the biblical accounts. See especially the Babylonian creation myth, the flood story in *Gilgamesh*, the Babylonian *Theodicy* (a dialogue on divine justice and human suffering, comparable in theme to Job), and the Egyptian *Tale of Two Brothers* (for comparison with the story of Joseph and Potiphar's wife).

HOMER

The Iliad

Backgrounds

In the tenth year of the Achaean siege of Troy, a rich city in Asia Minor, Agamemnon, the most powerful king among the Achaean allies, quarrels with the bravest of them, Achilles. Agamemnon had taken as his concubine the captive daughter of a Trojan priest of Apollo; at the priest's request, the god had sent a plague to devastate the army.

Agamemnon agrees to give back the girl but demands compensation from the army for the loss of his share of the spoils of war. Achilles opposes this demand as unreasonable, and Agamemnon, at the end of a furious argument, announces he will take away Achilles' girl Briseis, whom Achilles had captured in a raid. Achilles draws his sword to kill Agamemnon but is dissuaded from violence by the goddess Athena, who promises that he will be amply recompensed for Agamemnon's insults at some future date. He goes back to his tent and pulls his men out of the fighting. But he also asks his mother, the goddess Thetis, to intervene. She is to use her influence with Zeus, the king of the gods, and ask him to inflict defeat and suffering on the Achaeans, so that they will turn against Agamemnon. She goes to Olympus and, in spite of the opposition of Zeus' wife, Hera (who favors the Achaean side), Zeus grants her prayer.

In books II–V (not included in the anthology) Agamemnon calls an assembly of the troops. In an attempt to test morale he suggests abandoning the war; the ensuing stampede for the ships is stopped only by Odysseus with the aid of the goddess Athena. The Achaeans then muster for battle and the poet describes each contingent in what is known as the Catalog of Ships; he then proceeds to list the Trojan forces. The two sides join battle, but Hector, the Trojan leader, proposes that the war be settled by a duel between Menelaus, the Achaean king, and Paris, the Trojan prince who had run off with Menelaus' wife, Helen. Both sides agree; Menelaus wins the fight and is about to kill Paris when the goddess Aphrodite, who protects Paris because he gave her the prize for beauty, rescues him and sends him to join Helen in Troy. Agamemnon tells the Trojans to give back Helen and all her possessions and also to pay an indemnity; it looks as if the two sides will make peace on those terms, but the gods, at the urging of Hera and Athena, prevent it. Athena persuades Pandarus to shoot an arrow at Menelaus during the truce. Menelaus receives only a light wound, but the truce is broken; the battle resumes. Zeus' promise is not fulfilled immediately; the Achaean hero Diomedes dominates the battle and the Trojans are hard-pressed.

In book VI Hector goes to Troy to organize prayers to Athena; the poet gives us a glimpse of the rich, civilized city that the Achaeans will in the end destroy. Hector meets his mother Hecuba; his brother Paris; and Helen, the cause of the war; he then sees, for the last time as it turns out, his wife, Andromache, and his infant son.

In books VII (not in the anthology) and VIII, the promise of Zeus is fulfilled. After an inconclusive duel between Hector and Ajax the Achaeans are driven back and the Trojans, who usually retire behind their city walls at night, camp out on the field, ready to deliver a decisive assault in the morning.

In book IX Agamemnon summons a council; they advise him to make amends to Achilles. He agrees and proposes not only to give a magnificent list of gifts but also to restore Briseis (whom he swears he has not touched) and to offer one of his daughters in marriage to Achilles after the war. This offer is made to Achilles by Odysseus, Ajax, and Phoenix, an old retainer of Achilles, but Achilles refuses outright. The insult to his honor is too great to be wiped out by gifts. He will go home, with all his men. Phoenix tries to persuade him, reminding him of the story of Meleager, who also withdrew from the fighting alliance in anger, was begged to return, and refused. When in the end he came back to the fighting, he had forfeited all of the gifts he would have been given if he had complied earlier. Achilles still refuses to fight, but he has been moved; he will stay at Troy. And the final appeal from Ajax moves him still more; he will not join the battle, he says, until Hector fights his way to the Greek ships and sets them on fire. Phoenix stays with Achilles; Odysseus and Ajax return to report the failure of their mission.

In book X (not in the anthology) Odysseus and Diomedes make a successful night raid on the Trojan lines, but this is the last Achaean success for some time. In books XII to XVII (not in the anthology, except for XVI), the tide of battle turns against the Achaeans. Paris wounds Diomedes with an arrow; Odysseus is wounded and withdraws; Machaon, the Achaean physician, is also wounded. Achilles, who is watching the fighting and rejoicing in the Achaean losses, sends his friend Patroclus to see if the wounded man he saw was indeed Machaon, and this, the poet says, "is the beginning of his evil." For Patroclus, moved to pity by the wounded men he sees in the Achaean camp and by Hector's assault on the wall the Achaeans have built to protect their ships, will appeal to Achilles on the Achaeans' behalf (books XIII–XIV). Achilles refuses to join the fighting himself but allows Patroclus, equipped with his own armor, to take the field. After driving the Trojans back, Patroclus is killed by Hector, who strips off the armor of Achilles and puts it on. After a desperate fight, the Achaeans recover the body of Patroclus and take it back to their camp (books XV–XVII).

When Achilles hears of the death of Patroclus, he resolves to avenge him by killing Hector, but he must wait until his goddess mother brings him new armor; it is forged by Hephaestus, the divine smith, and includes a marvelous picture shield. Achilles then (book XIX, not in the anthology) calls an assembly of the Achaeans, accepts Agamemnon's apology, and after mourning over the corpse of Patroclus, puts on the armor and goes into battle.

In the final battle (not in the anthology) even the gods take part, but Achilles drives all before him as he cuts the Trojan warriors down. He drives the Trojans inside the gates of the city but is distracted by the god Apollo, a protector of Troy who, taking the shape of a Trojan warrior, leads him on a futile chase. Hector, feeling responsible for the defeat of his people, stays outside the gate to face Achilles.

In book XXII the two great adversaries face each other at last. Hector is beaten but before he dies prophesies Achilles' imminent death. Achilles ties the corpse to his chariot and drags it out to his camp.

Book XXIII (not in the anthology) deals with the burial of Patroclus and the funeral games in his honor. Achilles distributes rich prizes to the winners of athletic events: chariot race, boxing, wrestling, foot race, armed combat, weight casting, and archery.

In the last book (XXIV) Priam, king of Troy and father of Hector, is led by a divine messenger, Hermes, to the tent of Achilles to offer a rich ransom for his son's body. Achilles has been told by Thetis that Zeus is angry with him for his desecration of Hector's corpse, and Achilles agrees to give it up. But he is not prepared to see Hector's father, king of Troy, a suppliant at his feet, and his pity for the old man puts an end to the inhuman fury that has ruled him since the death of Patroclus. He lets Priam take the body, gives him eleven days for the burial of Hector; on the twelfth day the war will be renewed. Hector's people lament for him and give him a magnificent funeral; the last line of the poem—"that was the funeral of Hector, breaker of horses"—reminds us that the fighting will begin again at once and that Achilles, in his turn, will face the death he has inflicted on others.

Nothing is known about Homer's life or personality. It has even been thought that there was no one poet who composed the *Iliad*, that it was the creation of many generations of illiterate bards, the product of an epic tradition. That it comes out of some such background there can be no doubt; not only does it contain linguistic forms and refer to customs that predate the Greek adoption of literacy in the middle of the eighth century B.C., but it also shows in its repetition of epithets ("Achilles, swift of foot"), phrases, lines, and even whole passages the characteristic features of oral composition. The products of such a tradition are, however, usually much shorter than the *Iliad* and *Odyssey*; further, they rarely display the masterly construction and internal cross-reference that distinguish the Homeric poems.

Critical opinion now tends to assume a poet who was a master of the oral techniques and repertory but who exploited the new resource of the alphabet (adapted from a Phoenician script) for the construction of large-scale epics. This does not mean that overnight the *Iliad* and *Odyssey* became poems for reading; they were still performed by professional reciters, but the poem was no longer the creation, from memory and improvisation, of an individual bard; it was the dramatic recitation of a known and admired text. By the late sixth century B.C. public recitation of the poems was a highlight of the great festival of Athena at Athens, and the poems were also studied in schools. Scholars of the library at Alexandria in Egypt worked on the text in the third century B.C. and from that time on written copies for readers were the almost exclusive medium for Homer's survival to our own day.

Classroom Strategies

Suggested assignments:

1. Book I
2. Books VI, VIII, and IX
3. Books XVI and XVIII
4. Books XXII and XXIV

The longer assignments, 3 and 4, are possible because in the first two the student will have become familiar with the style and character of the work.

One thing that may puzzle the student is the organization (if it deserves that name) of the Achaean army. Explain first that the poem does
not reflect any real historical situation; the oral tradition on which
Homer draws is not concerned with historical fact but with stories of heroes who surpass ordinary human standards of courage and martial
achievement. The Achaean army is an alliance of independent chieftains, each one in command of his own men, who have come together to
help Menelaus recover his wife and punish the Trojans and also to share
in the plunder that will result from the capture and destruction of Troy.
Agamemnon's overarching authority is uneasy, open to challenge (as we
see in book I), and based mainly on his being in control of the biggest
contingent of armed men. On every important decision he consults his
"council"—the chieftains of the separate bands; when he acts impul-
sively and without consultation, as in the quarrel with Achilles, he eventually comes to regret that action.

The political organization of the army is an imaginary, epic phenomenon, and the fighting is just as unrealistic. There are large numbers of
nameless infantry who presumably fight with spear and shield, but we
rarely hear about them; the poem concentrates on the duels of the chief
heroes. These heroes have horse-drawn chariots, but they do not use
them against the enemy infantry; they ride to the battlefield in them,
then dismount to fight. This is not the way war chariots were in fact
used, as we know from the art and historical literature of the ancient
Egyptians and Babylonians; the epic poets had kept the memory of the
chariots but forgotten how they were used. From the point of view of the
epic bard, the chariots would in any case get in the way of his story, for
time and time again he pits one hero against another not just in combat
but in verbal exchanges of threats, insults, taunts, and boasts, which
would not have been possible if they had been racing past each other in
chariots.

This does not mean that Homer's picture of war is totally unrealistic;
his descriptions of what happens when bronze weapons cut human flesh
are all too accurate. But the realistic wounding and killing are set in a
framework of single combat that allows the heroes to speak to each
other before, during, and after the fighting and allows the poet to create
dramatic tension out of these exchanges. See especially the speeches of
Hector and Achilles, XXII.277–298 and XXII.364–406.

Topics for Discussion

1. Freedom and responsibility. To what extent are the decisions made
   by the heroes independent, individual decisions? Discuss, along
   these lines, Agamemnon's decision to take Briseis from Achilles.
       Agamemnon's decision is presented in book I as completely in-
   dependent of divine persuasion or command (unlike Achilles' decision not to kill Agamemnon); his motives are anger (line 109),
   hatred for Achilles (lines 186ff.), a wish to assert his superiority
   (lines 195ff.). And when in book IX he regrets his action and

wishes to be reconciled with Achilles, he speaks of having "suc-cumb[ed] to a fit of madness" (line 124). It is noticeable, however, that he uses these words in a council from which Achilles is absent; the ambassadors to Achilles carry no apology from Agamemnon, only the offer of gifts. When finally, after the death of Patroclus, the two men meet, Agamemnon denies responsibility, claiming that his decision was not free. "But I am not to blame," he says (XIX.99); he blames his action on Zeus and Ruin, the daughter of Zeus, who took his wits away. In this case Homer shows us a man who evades responsibility for his free decision by blaming a god, but sometimes a god does affect human decision, as in book I when Achilles, after thinking over the alternatives, in-clines toward killing Agamemnon (line 203) but is dissuaded by the goddess Athena.

2. Discuss the statement "Morality is a human creation, and though the gods may approve of it, they are not bound by it."

   The fate of Troy depends on the will of the gods, and its final de-struction is a product of a power struggle among them: Hera, Athena, and Poseidon are inexorably hostile to Troy, Apollo is its champion, and Zeus is swayed now by one side, now by the other. The fact that Troy is a civilized city besieged by soldiers bent on its destruction, the massacre of its men and the enslavement of its women and children plays no part in the gods' decision, nor does the fact that, as Zeus says, Hector, the Trojan champion, wor-shiped Zeus with gifts and sacrifice ("Hector was dearest to the gods of all in Ilion," Zeus says, "At least to me," XXIV.72–74). Hera and Athena have no pity for Troy, even though the Trojans (in book VI) make offerings to Athena and pray for her help. They and their children will pay with their lives and freedom for the injury done to Athena's (and Hera's) pride when the Trojan prince Paris chose Aphrodite over them for the prize of beauty (XXIV.32ff.). However, in book XXIV, the gods (with the exception of Athena, Hera, and Poseidon) are appalled by Achilles' treatment of Hector's body and finally agree to order Achilles to give it up to Hector's father, Priam.

Topics for Writing

1. Aristotle said that the man who is incapable of working in com-mon, or who in his self-sufficiency has no need of others, is no part of the community, like a beast or a god. Discuss the figure of Achilles in the light of this statement.

2. In spite of the constraints imposed by the formulaic language of the oral tradition, Homer, according to one critic, "sees his people as individually distinct and makes us aware of their individuality." Discuss the ways in which Homer succeeds in presenting as differ-entiated individuals Hector, Nestor, Ajax, Odysseus, Agamemnon, Priam, and Phoenix.

3. Homer's preferred medium of poetic comparison is simile rather than metaphor, and his similes are "extended": the simile does more than establish a likeness between A and B; it goes on to describe B in great detail, some of the details not like A at all. Yet these details, the apparent development of B for its own sake, often do suggest points of comparison that lie below the surface, and often, too, they make significant comments on broader aspects of the situation in which they appear. Discuss the function of the extended simile in the following passages:

XVIII.219–25   XXII.178–240
XXII.33–37   XXIV.511–14
XVIII.339–43

Further Reading

See also the suggestions in the *Anthology*, p. 2640.

Cairns, D. *Oxford Readings in Homer's Iliad*. 2001. A valuable and accessible collection of some of the seminal articles in the scholarship on the *Iliad*.

Chadwick, John. *The Mycenean World*. 1976. An up-to-date and critical survey of Mycenean civilization (including full discussion of the Linear B tablets and the light they throw on the period). Chadwick concludes that the Homeric poems preserve very little of the real facts of the Mycenean period.

Dodds, Eric R. *The Greeks and the Irrational*. 1951. Chapter 1, "Agamemnon's Apology," deals with the problem posed in the first topic under "Topics for Discussion."

Kirk, Geoffrey. *Homer and the Epic*. 1965. A masterly survey of the whole field of modern Homeric controversy distinguished by its firm grip on the historical background, the fairness of its critique of the various theories, and the reassuring moderation of its conclusions.

Lloyd-Jones, H. *The Justice of Zeus*. 1971. Chapter 1 makes a case for the Homeric gods as dealing justly with humankind. Relevant to the second topic under "Topics for Discussion."

Lord, A. B. *The Singer of Tales*. 2000. Lord explains the background and methods of composition of Yugoslav oral epic and compares the results of his research to the Homeric text. Originally published in 1960, this remains the authoritative treatment of Homer as an oral poet. The updated version includes a new introduction and audio CD.

Luce, J. V. *Homer and the Heroic Age*. 1975. A survey of all the archaeological and historical evidence for the Mycenean and Dark Age periods, evidence that may have some bearing on Homer; Luce is much less skeptical than Chadwick.

Nagy, G. *The Best of the Achaeans*. 1998. Newly revised edition of Nagy's discussion of the concept of the hero as a figure both in Greek cult and in the tradition of Homeric poetics.

Slatkin, L. *The Power of Thetis*. 1991. Explores the figure of Thetis as a powerful goddess who nevertheless cannot save her son from his ultimate fate. Places the *Iliad* in its mythological context and discusses the differences between mortals and immortals.

Whitman, Cedric. *Homer and the Heroic Tradition*. 1965. Contains an excellent literary analysis of the *Iliad*.

Willcock, Malcolm M. *A Companion to the* Iliad. 1976. Based on the Lattimore translation. A detailed commentary that deals with difficulties in the text, explains mythological and historical details, and provides internal cross-references. An extremely useful volume for the teacher.

The Odyssey

Backgrounds

At a council of the gods on Olympus (book I), Athena pleads the case of Odysseus. It is now ten years since Troy was captured, but Odysseus, shipwrecked on his way home, is stranded on an island where the goddess Calypso keeps him as her mate. The sea-god Poseidon—angry with Odysseus because the hero had blinded Poseidon's son, the Cyclops Polyphemus—is absent from the council; Athena has her way, and Hermes, the messenger god, is sent to Calypso with the order to release Odysseus. Athena goes to Odysseus' home in Ithaca to encourage his son, Telemachus, whose household is occupied by the young and violent suitors of his mother, Penelope; they are convinced Odysseus is dead and demand that she marry one of them. Athena, taking the shape of Mentes, king of a neighboring city, advises Telemachus to visit old Nestor at Pylos and Menelaus at Sparta to see if they have any news of his father.

Encouraged by the goddess (book II), Telemachus calls an assembly of the people of Ithaca and assails the suitors for their unlawful occupancy of his house; he announces that he is off to find news of his father. The suitors realize that this is no longer a timid boy but a resolute and dangerous man; when they find out that he has actually left, they decide to set an ambush for him at sea and kill him on his way back. At Pylos (book III), Telemachus meets old Nestor and hears from him how Agamemnon was killed by his own wife when he came home from Troy and how Menelaus, blown by adverse winds as far as Egypt, came home in the seventh year after Troy's fall. Accompanied by Nestor's son Peisistratus, Telemachus goes to Sparta (book IV), where he is welcomed by Menelaus and Helen and told by Menelaus that, when last heard of, Odysseus was on the island of Calypso, without ship or crew, longing to return home.

Meanwhile, the god Hermes arrives (book V) to bring Calypso the command of Zeus. She accepts it with reluctance and when Hermes is gone makes one last attempt to keep Odysseus; she offers to make him immortal if he will stay with her. He refuses, and she helps him build a boat and sail off. The god Poseidon wrecks his boat, and Odysseus eventually crawls ashore naked and battered, on the island of Scheria, home of the Phaeacians. Here he meets the daughter of the king Alcinous, Nausicaa (book VI), who has come down to the shore with her retinue of girls to wash clothes. She is charmed by him and sends him off to the palace, where he is hospitably entertained (book VII). The next day, at a banquet in the hall (book VIII), Odysseus, moved to tears by a minstrel's tales of Troy, is challenged to reveal his identity. He does so (book IX) as he tells the Phaeacians (and us) the whole story of his wanderings since he left Troy (books IX–XII).

Rounding the southern cape of Greece on his way to Ithaca he was blown out to sea, southwest presumably, but from this point on his itinerary leaves real geography behind. His first landfall is the country of the Lotus Eaters, from which he rescues those of his crew who have tasted the Lotus and lost their wish to return home. From the next trial, the land of the Cyclops, he does not escape without casualties; four of his men are eaten by the one-eyed giant in his cave, and Odysseus would have been eaten, too, if he had not made the Cyclops drunk and then put out his one eye. After escaping from the cave, Odysseus, taunting the blind giant from shipboard as he prepares to leave, tells Polyphemus his name, and the giant prays to his father, Poseidon, to make Odysseus' homecoming a hard one. On the next island (book X) he reaches Aeolus, King of the Winds, who gives him a bag containing all the winds except the one that will take him home. But, in sight of Ithaca, his crew, thinking the bag contains treasure, open it and the winds, let loose, blow the ship back to where it came from.

At his next landfall he loses all his ships but one to the Laestrygonians, giants and cannibals. He goes on to the island of Circe, who turns his advance party into swine, but dominated by Odysseus, she restores their human shape and entertains them all in royal style. They stay for a year but before they leave, Circe tells Odysseus that he must go to the land of the dead and consult the seer Tiresias. There (book XI) he is warned by Tiresias not to eat the cattle of the Sun when he lands on the island of Thrinacia; speaks to the shade of his dead mother, who tells him what is going on in his house at home; sees a procession of famous women; and then meets; the ghosts of his companions at Troy— Agamemnon, Achilles, and Ajax.

Back on Circe's island (book XII), he bids farewell to her and passes the Sirens; who lure men to their doom by their song; makes the passage between the monster Scylla and the whirlpool Charybdis; and lands on the island of Thrinacia, where, in spite of his appeals, his men eat the sacred cattle of the Sun. Once again at sea, the ship is sunk in a storm, the crew lost; only Odysseus survives, to land at last on Calypso's island.

The Phaeacians take Odysseus home to Ithaca (book XIII); Poseidon, with the consent of Zeus, punishes them for helping his enemy. Odysseus meets the goddess Athena, and they plan a stealthy approach to his house in disguise: if he goes home in his own person the suitors may kill him. She transforms him into an aged, ragged beggar, and he goes to his swineherd, Eumaeus, for hospitality (book XIV). He tells his generous host a tall tale of wanderings in Egypt and the story of Odysseus at Troy. Meanwhile, Telemachus returns from Sparta (book XV), avoiding the suitors' ambush. While Eumaeus tells Odysseus how he was kidnapped as a child and sold to Odysseus' father as a slave, Telemachus makes his way to the swineherd's hut. Without letting Eumaeus know the truth, Odysseus reveals his identity to his son (book XVI); together they plot the overthrow of the suitors.

Odysseus and Telemachus make their separate ways to the palace (book XVII). As Odysseus comes into the palace yard Argus, his dog, on the point of death from old age, recognizes his master. Odysseus goes begging bread from the suitors; Antinous, the most violent of them, throws a stool at him. Odysseus is challenged by a real beggar, Irus (book XVIII), but beats him in a fight and wins the exclusive right to beg at the palace. Another prominent suitor, Eurymachus, insults Odysseus and throws a stool at him. Later that night (book XIX) Penelope sends for Odysseus to see if the beggar has any news; he tells her of meeting Odysseus on the nearby mainland and assures her he will soon return. The old nurse Eurycleia, told to wash his feet before he goes to bed, recognizes him by a scar on his leg, but he silences her.

Penelope decides to announce for the next day an archery contest that will decide which of the suitors may claim her hand. The suitors feast and revel (book XX); one more of them, Ctesippus, throws something at Odysseus, a cow's hoof this time. They all start to laugh hysterically; the tension is mounting. The archery contest is set up (book XXI); the bow of Odysseus is brought out, but none of the suitors can string it. Telemachus tells Eumaeus to give it to Odysseus, who strings it and kills Antinous (book XXII), Eurymachus, and then—with the help of Telemachus, Eumaeus, and some loyal servants—all the rest of the suitors. Only the poet-minstrel Phemius is spared. When Penelope is told the news she cannot believe it (book XXIII); she tests Odysseus' knowledge of a detail in their bedroom (the fact that the bed could not be moved since it was carved out of a standing olive tree) and accepts him as her husband.

But trouble is brewing in Ithaca. As Odysseus goes off to the country to see his father, Laertes, and the ghosts of the suitors go to the land of the dead (book XXIV) to be interrogated by Agamemnon and others, the relatives of the suitors gather to attack Odysseus and his family. But their attack is thwarted by the goddess Athena, and the two sides make peace.

There was a theory in the ancient world that the *Odyssey* was a work of Homer's old age and that this accounts for the more mellow tone and the happy ending. Modern scholars have claimed that it must be later than the *Iliad* on other grounds: they discern a closer connection between human morality and divine judgment (in, for example, the speech of Zeus in I.76ff.) and assume that a higher morality must belong to a later age. Others have based the same later dating on the wanderings in books IX–XII, seeing in them a reflection of the early days of Greek colonization. Since, however, the geography of the wanderings suggests fairyland rather than the real western Mediterranean, this thesis, like the other, is controversial. There have been many attempts to identify the island of the Cyclops and the land of the Lotus Eaters, but none of them has won general acceptance. The ancient critics were skeptical on this point: the great Greek geographer Eratosthenes of Alexandria (third—second centuries B.C.) said that you would be able to place the site of Odysseus' wanderings when you had found the cobbler who sewed up the leather bag containing the winds.

It is true, however, that the *Odyssey* takes for granted a knowledge of the *Iliad* on the part of the audience; it is remarkable that in all the tales told about Troy and the heroes of the war, by Odysseus, Menelaus, Nestor, Demodocus, and the ghost of Agamemnon, not one single episode is duplicated in the *Iliad*. Such a complete avoidance of the material treated in the *Iliad* suggests knowledge of it in something like its present form.

Classroom Strategies

The obvious assignments are I–IV (Telemachus), V–VIII (Odysseus and the Phaeacians), IX–XII (the wanderings), XIII–XVI (at the hut of Eumaeus), XVII–XX (the beggar in the palace), and XXI–XXIV (revenge and reunion). If you desire shorter assignments, take two books at a time.

If there is not time to read the whole poem, an Odyssean core (the wanderings) can be used: I, III–VI, VIII, IX–XII, XXI–XXIV. In this case, you will have to supply the bridge between VI and VIII, e.g., "Odysseus follows Nausicaa's instructions and is received as a guest in the palace by her mother, Arete, and her father, Alkinoös, who promises to help him return home."

Perhaps the main possibility of misunderstanding for today's students lies in the nature of the heroic ideal presented in the *Odyssey*. Odysseus is not an Achillean character (see the headnote), but he is bound by a heroic ethic just the same. Lies and stratagems are his natural weapons, since most of the time he is pitted against superior force; he is a survivor, one who fights "to save his life" (I.6), but there are limits to what he will do to save it. On Circe's island, for example, he will not abandon his advance party, which has not returned, even though the rest of his crew urge him to leave. He fights not only "to save his life" but also "to bring his comrades home" (I.9). In this he fails, but at least in the case of those who killed the cattle of the Sun, this is no fault of his.

In the famous contrast between Odysseus and Achilles in the lower world, many critics have seen a repudiation of the heroic ideal of the *Il-*

iad; Achilles would rather be alive and a slave to a peasant than a king over all the dead. Yet when told of the heroic achievements of his son Neoptolemus, he goes off "triumphant" (XI.615), and in book XXIV the shade of Agamemnon contrasts the glory of Achilles' funeral with the ignominy of his own death and burial. As for Odysseus, in the last books of the poem, he exemplifies one heroic ideal in spectacular fashion. The hero avenges insults to his honor, and Odysseus' slaughter of the entire younger generation of the nobility of Ithaca is a heroic revenge on a grand scale.

Topics for Discussion

1. The heroic ideal in the *Iliad* and the *Odyssey*. See "Backgrounds."
2. Hospitality as a criterion of civilization in the *Odyssey*. Polyphemus and Calypso as opposite extremes—no hospitality at all and too much; the Phaeacians as ideal hosts; courtly hospitality at Pylos (Nestor) and Sparta (Menelaus and Helen); hospitality abused (the suitors), and so on. Students should discuss the startling fact that the Phaeacians, the most civilized hosts in the epic, are punished for their hospitality by Poseidon and Zeus, who make sure they will not help travelers again. Does this conform to the picture of divine good intentions thwarted by human wickedness offered by Zeus in his speech in book I?
3. Telemachus' growth to manhood. Analyze the stages of his assumption of responsibility and the recognition of the fact by others. His mother's reaction is surprise; Nestor and Menelaus recognize him as Odysseus' son (whereas Athena in book I professes not to); the suitors recognize his attainment of maturity by planning to kill him—*now* he is dangerous. He helps Odysseus kill the suitors; does he risk becoming his father's rival?

Topics for Writing

1. Two ancient Greek critics, Aristophanes of Byzantium and Aristarchus, thought that Homer ended his poem on the lines "Rejoicing in each other, they returned to their bed, / the old familiar place they loved so well" (XXIII.337–38). In other words, they thought book XXIV unnecessary. What in fact does book XXIV contribute to the epic?

   [The ending at XXIII would have been a romantic ending: husband and wife reunited, nothing else matters. In fact there are still a great many problems to be solved, especially the consequences of Odysseus' slaughter of the suitors. Homer sees that Odysseus, who has established himself as master in his own house by violence, still has to be accepted by the community—the succession of his line depends on the community's goodwill. The epic ends with a reconciliation, engineered by Athena, but before the threat of conflict is removed, we are shown three generations of Odysseus' family—father Laertes, Odysseus, son Telemachus—standing side by side, ready for battle. Odysseus has been reintegrated in his family as he shortly will be in the community of Ithaca.]

2. Woman's role in the *Odyssey*.

   [Faithful consort (Penelope, Arete) or temptation (Circe, Calypso, the Sirens, even Nausicaa). Helen has been one and is now the other. How "female" is Athena?]

3. Odysseus and Athena. Compare their relationship with that of Job and God. What does this suggest about the religious attitudes of the Hebrews and the Greeks?

   [For Odysseus-Athena, analyze carefully the long interview between them in XIII.252ff.]

4. From the moment he hears from Athena in XIII how things stand in his own home, Odysseus, in his disguise as a beggar, puts everyone to the test, to see if they are loyal to him or even whether they are decent human beings. List the incidents in which he puts people to the test and the results in each case.

   [Eumaieus with the story of the cloak at Troy in XIV; the suitors by begging—Antinous in XVII, Eurymachus in XVIII, etc.]

5. List and differentiate the different recognitions of Odysseus, intended and unintended.

   [Intended: Telemachus in XVI; the suitors in XXII; Eumaeus and Philoetius in XXI; Penelope in XXIII; Laertes in XXIV. Unintended: Argus in XVII; Eurycleia in XIX.]

6. Penelope and Telemachus: a complicated relationship between mother and son. Analyze the process of Telemachus' assertion of independent manhood and Penelope's reluctant acceptance of it.

   [Telemachus' first action after Athena encourages him is to contradict his mother (I.409–14); "Astonished / she withdrew" (line 415). Telemachus forbids Eurycleia to tell his mother he is going to Sparta (II.413–16). Penelope is distressed when she hears he has gone: "Why has my child gone and left me?" (IV.792–800, 884–92). Athena inspires Telemachus with suspicions about Penelope's intentions—or does he have them anyway (XV.19ff.)? Telemachus is afraid she has already married one of the suitors (XVI.37). Their meeting after his return (XVII.40ff.). She reproaches him (XVIII.243ff.). Penelope on Telemachus (XIX.597–602); Telemachus on Penelope (XX.147–49). Telemachus sends her out of the hall (XXI.389–99). Telemachus berates her for not recognizing Odysseus at once (XXIII.111–18).]

Comparative Perspectives

1. Hospitality is one of the chief virtues of ancient and heroic cultures. Consider why this should be so, paying attention to the experience of Odysseus in his travels. How would you compare the nature and extent of the hospitality displayed in other narratives, including the *Aeneid*, which is consciously modeled on Homer's

poems, and those which are not, such as *Beowulf* and *Sir Gawain and the Green Knight*.

2. Compare the reasons that Odysseus visits the Underworld and what he experiences there with, as appropriate, Gilgamesh's visit to Utnapishtim, Aeneas's in book VI of the *Aeneid*, and Dante's in *The Divine Comedy*.

Further Reading

See also the reading suggestions in the *Anthology*, pp. 2640–41, and for the *Iliad* in this manual.

Auerbach, E. *Mimesis*. 2003. Translated by W. R. Trask, with a new introduction by Edward Said. Chapter one, "Odysseus' Scar," is justly famous for its reading of *Odyssey* 19 alongside Jacob's near-sacrifice of Isaac in the Hebrew Bible (included in the anthology). While much of Auerbach's reading of the *Odyssey* is too boldly stated, he still offers an invigorating and accessible reading of this short section of the poem.

Finley, M. I. *The World of Odysseus*, rev. edition. 1978. A historical-anthropological approach to Homeric "society" (in fact, to the "society" of the *Odyssey*) based on a study of the function of the gift in primitive societies. Stimulating, like everything Finley writes, and extremely good background for a discussion of the "economic" aspect of Homeric hospitality.

Goldhill, S. *The Poet's Voice*. 1991. See chapter 1 for a reading of language and representation in the *Odyssey*, particularly in relation to Odysseus' complex interaction with recognition, naming, and narrative voice.

Stanford, W. B. *The Ulysses Theme*. 1968. A rich and suggestive examination of the figure of Odysseus from Homer to James Joyce. Chapters II–V deal with Homer's hero. (Chapter V, "The Untypical Hero," is reprinted in Steiner and Fagles.)

Steiner, George, and Robert Fagles, eds. *Homer: A Collection of Critical Essays*. 1962. George E. Dimock's "The Name of Odysseus" is a brilliant discussion of the hero's identity, contained in a name he is proud to proclaim but must time after time conceal, a name that announces his nature and destiny. This volume also contains Erich Auerbach's famous but controversial essay on the scar of Odysseus (book XIX), which explores fundamental contrasts between Homeric and Old Testament biblical narrative, and W. B. Stanford's essay "The Untypical Hero," on the character of Odysseus.

SAPPHO OF LESBOS

Backgrounds

In some ancient texts Sappho is referred to as a teacher, and the girls whose names recur so often in her poems are said to be her pupils; a papyrus fragment published in 1974 (it was written in the late second century A.D.) speaks of her as "teaching in peace and quiet the noble girls not only from the local families but also from families in Ionia." A fragment of one of her poems, addressed, we are told by the writer who quotes it, to an "uneducated woman," begins with the words "But when you die, you will lie there in the grave and no one will remember you afterwards or long for you." The context of her poetry may have been a more or less formal circle of aristocratic girls whose same-sex bonding and instruction in music and dance prepared them for marriage.

Many of Sappho's poems were *epithalamia*, marriage songs, composed presumably for her favorite pupils; others were heartbroken laments for the loss of a loved companion. "I simply want to be dead," runs one fragment. "Weeping she left me / with many tears and said this: / Oh how badly things have turned out for us. / Sappho, I swear, against my will I leave you. / And I answered her: Rejoice, go and / remember me. For you know how we cherished you." And the second poem included in the anthology expresses a passionate reaction to the imagined sight of a beloved girl in conversation with a man. But Sappho's poetry is not always so tensely passionate; she can also treat the pangs of unrequited love with an ironic wit. The first poem in the anthology, for example, Sappho's invocation of the love goddess Aphrodite, starts out as a conventional appeal to a deity to come to the suppliant's help. It employs the usual formulas—"but come here if ever before / you caught my voice"—but then it departs sharply from the established pattern. Instead of dealing with the present occasion, Sappho's need for help, it gives a vivid account of the goddess's previous visit. And we are told what Sappho's "hard care" is all about: she has been crossed in love, someone is rejecting her suit. On that previous occasion Aphrodite was gracious and promised her aid; Sappho now asks for the same promise: "all my heart longs / to accomplish, accomplish. You / be my ally." The Greek for the final phrase means literally: "be my ally in battle."

The poem is a brilliant example of self-mocking wit. The whole religious terminology of a hymn, the appeal to a god, including the epiphany of the goddess concerned, is put in motion so that Sappho can win the heart of a recalcitrant girl, and furthermore, the poem shows us that this is not the first time Sappho has brought the goddess down from Olympus.

This ironic tone is, however, an exception; elsewhere Sappho is well aware of the awesome and terrifying powers of the goddess. One fragment speaks of the dramatic effects of desire upon the body: "tongue breaks and thin / fire is racing under skin / and in eyes no sight and drumming / fills ears / and cold sweat holds me and shaking / grips me all," and another speaks of love that shakes the heart "like a mountain wind falling on oak trees."

Comparative Perspectives

1. Compare Sappho's rhetorical strategies to those of Catullus and Petrarch. How does she view the competition for a loved one? Is hers a sentimental poetry? What moments in erotic relationships does she focus on in these few poems?

2. Sappho's poems show an exquisite awareness of the body. Compare her appreciation for somatic textures with similar details in other love poetry.

Further Reading

See also the reading suggestions in the anthology, p. 2642.

Campbell, D. *Greek Lyric*. Vol. 1 (Loeb Classical Library). 1982. Contains the complete text of what remains of Sappho's work, with an English translation.

DuBois, P. *Sappho Is Burning*. 1995. Reassesses Sappho's place in linear histories of the Classical corpus and in the history of Western thought.

Greene, E., ed. *Reading Sappho*. 1996. A collection of essays (all previously published elsewhere) by leading scholars in the field. Addresses Sappho's poetry as literature, in its social and performative context, and in relation to gender.

AESCHYLUS

The Oresteia

Backgrounds

The scene of the first two plays in the trilogy is the entrance to the palace of Agamemnon at Argos; the time is the tenth year of the Trojan War. A watchman on the palace roof sees the fire signal that announces the fall of Troy. A chorus of old men comes into the orchestra (the circular dancing floor in front of the stage area) and sings. They remember the departure of the army ten years before; adverse winds delayed the sailing, and at the command of the goddess Artemis, Agamemnon sacrificed his daughter Iphigenia to release the fleet. Clytaemnestra enters and tells the chorus the news—Troy has fallen. She describes the chain of signal fires across the sea from Troy and speculates about what is happening in that city now.

After her exit the chorus sings; the song begins as a hymn of victory for the Greek success but ends on a note of fear and foreboding. Enter a herald who has come to announce Agamemnon's arrival; he speaks of the suffering of the Greeks at Troy and also reveals that Agamemnon will come alone—Menelaus was blown off course and no one knows where he is. Another choral song begins with a meditation on the name and destiny of Helen but ends with a fearful vision of the recurrence of violence in one generation after another, as Agamemnon enters in a chariot. With him is a female figure who is not identified until later, but the audience knows, from Homer, that it is the Trojan princess Cassandra. Agamemnon, boasting exultantly of the destruction of Troy, is welcomed by Clytaemnestra in a speech full of menacing ambiguity. She invites him to walk into the palace on blood-red tapestries; at first reluctant, he eventually does so, after recommending Cassandra to her care. The choral song now is full of vague apprehension; they sense that something is wrong. Clytaemnestra comes on stage again to order Cassandra inside but meets only silence and departs.

Now Cassandra speaks. In a long exchange with the chorus she prophesies, at first in riddling images and finally in clear statement, all that is to come—her own death, the murder of Agamemnon, and even the death of Clytaemnestra at the hands of her son. She has been given the gift of prophecy by the god Apollo, who loves her. But when she refused him her love he added the proviso that though she could tell the future no one would believe her—as the chorus refuses to believe her now.

She goes off to her death, and almost at once the chorus hears Agamemnon's death cries from inside the palace. As they discuss what action to take, the doors open and the bodies of Agamemnon and Cassandra are brought out; over them, Clytaemnestra makes a triumphant speech of self-justification. But as the chorus, recovering from its initial shock, rejects her defense and prophesies retribution, she retreats from the high confidence of her opening speech and appeals to the "savage ancient spirit of revenge" (line 1534) that plagues the House of Atreus to let it end here, shed no more blood. At this point, its very embodiment, Aegisthus, enters, with an armed bodyguard, and threatens the chorus. Clytaemnestra prevents their coming to blows with her plea—"No blood-shed now" (line 1694)—and ends the play with her hope to "set the house in order once for all" (line 1713).

The second play, *The Libation Bearers*, treats the story of the next generation of the House of Atreus. It opens with Orestes, who had been sent away by Clytaemnestra as a child, returning in secret to the house of Atreus, having been instructed by Apollo to seek revenge for his father's murder. At the site of Agamemnon's tomb, Orestes hides to watch his sister pouring libations to her father with the chorus of libation bearers, as she laments and compares her position within the house to that of an outcast and a slave. To Agamemnon's grave too, we will later learn, Clytaemnestra has been sending libations, disturbed by a dream that a serpent she suckled at her breast will soon bite her and draw blood out with the milk. Through an artfully handled recognition scene, where Electra matches first hair and then footprints with Orestes, brother and sister, with the full cooperation of the chorus, hatch a plot to avenge murder with murder, and to take back control of their father's house.

The plot, as Electra states, is simple. Claiming to be an unknown traveler, Orestes approaches the house with news that he, Orestes, is dead. Once invited inside, he kills Aegisthus, and then comes face to face with his mother over the body of her lover. Wavering only once in his resolve,

Orestes resists Clytaemnestra's display of the breast that suckled him, and her warning of "a mother's curse," to kill her in much the same fashion as she had committed her own double murder in *Agamemnon*. The play brings little resolution, however. Apart from the fact that the murder is sanctioned by Apollo, there is scant suggestion throughout *The Libation Bearers* that this murder will cleanse the house of its bloodguilt. Rather, the play closes with Orestes fleeing in dread from the Furies, gruesome avengers of his mother's spirit.

The scene changes for the opening of *The Eumenides*: it is the temple of Apollo at Delphi. His priestess goes in to officiate but comes out terrified; she has seen, at Apollo's altar, a suppliant, Orestes, and the Furies sitting round him waiting. The audience now sees the scene she described: Apollo enters and sends Orestes off to Athens, where he will find "judges of [his] case" (line 84). The ghost of Clytaemnestra (or is she a dream in the Furies' heads?) spurs the chorus to action, and they exchange taunts and threats with Apollo before rushing off in pursuit of Orestes.

The scene is now Athens, where Orestes comes to clasp the statue of the goddess Athena; the chorus follows, and after singing a song designed to "bind" and paralyze him, they move on to take their prey just as Athena arrives. After hearing both sides she determines to summon judges and set up a court; she has shown such fairness that the Furies accept this decision. They sing of their ancient duties, the punishment of criminals who would otherwise escape; they are confident they will win their case.

As the trial begins, Apollo arrives to speak for Orestes. Under the skillful questioning of the Furies, Orestes breaks down and has to turn to Apollo for help. Apollo proclaims the priority of the father over the mother: Orestes' duty to avenge his father outweighed his link to his mother. Athena addresses the jury, stressing the importance of this "first trial of bloodshed" (line 696), and repeats a theme of the Furies: that without fear there can be no order. She herself will vote for Orestes, since as a goddess born directly from her father, Zeus, without the intermediary of a mother, she favors the male.

The votes are evenly divided, and this, under Athenian law, means acquittal; Orestes goes free, but the Furies now threaten to turn their rage against Athens itself. Athena finally wins them over by an offer of a home and worship in her city, and the Furies, who have been outcasts even from the gods because of their function as executors of blood vengeance, accept her offer and become kindly protectors of the institutions and lands of Athens.

Aeschylus (524?–456 B.C.E.) belonged to the generation that saw the establishment of democracy at Athens (in the last decades of the sixth century B.C.E.) and the heroic defense of that democracy against a Persian expeditionary force at Marathon in 490 B.C.E. as well as the decisive Athenian contribution to the defeat of a full-scale Persian invasion on the sea at Salamis in 480 B.C.E. and on land at Plataea in 479 B.C.E. Aeschylus fought as an infantry soldier at Marathon and, probably, in the naval battle at Salamis: on his tomb at Gela in Sicily, where he died, a verse inscription commemorated his combat service at Marathon and did not even mention his plays. Yet his plays so impressed the Athenian public that they were revived after his death, to compete with the offerings of his successors at the Dionysiac festival—an honor accorded to no other dramatist in the fifth century. In *The Frogs*, a comedy produced in the last decade of the fifth century, Aristophanes staged a contest in the lower world between the ghosts of Aeschylus and Euripides, old-fashioned patriotic virtue versus newfangled intellectual fashions, and of course, Aeschylus was the winner.

How closely this nostalgic vision of Aeschylus the Marathon veteran as an arch-conservative corresponded to the reality we have no means of judging, but he was certainly an innovator in the world of theater. Aristotle, in the *Poetics* (in a portion that is not included in the anthology), says that he was the first to increase the number of the actors from one to two, a move that "reduced the role of the chorus, giving first place to the dialogue." It also made possible dramatic confrontation instead of the predominantly narrative mode that must have been characteristic of performance with a single actor. Aeschylus was far from conservative, too, in his treatment of myth and especially in his manipulation of mythical material to give it contemporary resonance; in this field he had no equal.

The Eumenides, for example, put the court of the Areopagus on stage shortly after its status had been the key issue of a political struggle that threatened to lead to civil war. The Areopagus, its ranks filled by ex-magistrates, had become in the years after the Persian War a powerful political force, a sort of senate of elder statesmen that was an obstacle to reformists who wished to make Athenian democracy more radical and egalitarian. Just a few years before Aeschylus' play was produced, the reformers, led by Pericles and Ephialtes, had taken away all the court's powers except its legal right to try cases of homicide; feeling ran so high on both sides that Ephialtes was murdered. Hence when Aeschylus dramatized the foundation of the Areopagus by Athena he was treading on dangerous ground.

Modern critics are divided in their assessment of his position: was he acquiescing in the reform by emphasizing the solemn antiquity of the court's judicial function or was his reminder of the divine origin of the Areopagus a protest against the reforms? The fact that there is no agreement on this point suggests that in fact he did not take a position one way or another: the point he emphasized, in the song of the Furies and the speech of Athena (lines 526ff., cf. lines 711ff.) was moderation, the avoidance of extremes—"Neither the life of anarchy / nor the life enslaved by tyrants, no, / worship neither. / Strike the balance" (lines 538–41)—and the civil war that extreme measures are likely to lead to. "Brutal strife," the Furies sing, "the civil war devouring men, I pray / that it never rages through our city" (lines 991–93).

In *Agamemnon*, Aeschylus was dramatizing a story known to the audience from Homer (cf. *Odyssey* I.34ff., III.218ff., IV.573ff., XI.457ff.), but the climactic action of *The Libation Bearers*, Orestes' murder of his mother, is not explicitly mentioned there. The action of the last play, *The Eumenides*, has no Homeric model at all; in fact, it has been thought that Aeschylus may have invented the story of the trial of Orestes at Athens. Cassandra is mentioned in Homer (she is the first to see Priam coming back to Troy with Hector's corpse [*Iliad* XXIV.747ff.] and is killed with Agamemnon by Clytaemnestra [*Odyssey* XI.458ff.]), but in neither passage is there any hint of her prophetic powers. Aeschylus' adaptation of the standard version is very bold; the Attic dramatists, who worked almost exclusively with traditional tales, were allowed, perhaps even expected, to present the familiar figures and situation in a new light. Both Sophocles and Euripides, for example, wrote plays called *Electra* that present the same action as *The Libation Bearers*, but though in both of them Clytaemnestra and Aegisthus are killed by Orestes, everything else is changed. Both dramatists, in contrast to Aeschylus, make Electra the central figure of the play, on stage throughout; but in Sophocles she is a heroic figure, while Euripides gives her a near-criminal mentality and has her collapse in bitter remorse after the murders. The fact that the poets used familiar stories did not rule out innovation and the element of suspense. The fact that the dramatists had to work with three actors was also not as much of a limitation on creativity as might appear. A change of mask and costume enabled an actor to reenter as a different character. *Agamemnon*, for example, has six speaking parts (Watchman, Clytaemnestra, Herald, Agamemnon, Cassandra, and Aegisthus) and *The Eumenides* five (Pythia, Apollo, Orestes, the Ghost of Clytaemnestra, and Athena). In addition the leader of the chorus could play an important speaking part, as he does in the trial scene of *The Eumenides*.

But the main function of the chorus is not the spoken word; it dances and sings. The word itself in Greek suggests dancing above all (our word *choreography* preserves this emphasis), and the long choral sections of the texts must be imagined as delivered by fifteen dancers whose movements emphasized their words. This movement, however, could not have been as athletic or complex as that of the modern ballet, for the chorus also sang, in unison, and their words, unlike those of modern opera, had to be intelligible to the audience, for they are vital to the significance of the dramatic action. Unlike the actors, who by the time the *Oresteia* was produced were professionals, the chorus consisted of citizen volunteers, trained in their part, like the actors, by the playwright himself. The chorus is the onstage representative of the citizen audience; it observes and comments on the action and motives of the actors, reacts to their announcements and commands, opposes or supports them, and above all—and this is especially true of the chorus in *Agamemnon*—tries to understand, to interpret. It is rare to find a chorus that, like that of *The Eumenides*, assumes a decisive role in the action; this may have been a characteristic of Aeschylean drama, for we find it also in his *Suppliants*.

Classroom Strategies

Two assignments.

For the modern student, perhaps the most disconcerting feature of the trilogy is the trial scene in *The Eumenides*, particularly the argument put forward by Apollo and approved by Athena, that "the woman you call the mother of the child / is not the parent, just a nurse to the seed" (lines 668–69). This claim that the mother's role in the procreation of children is purely passive, that she is a mere incubator for the male seed, is the basis for Apollo's case that murder of a father is a more heinous crime than matricide.

This strange biology is not peculiar to Aeschylus; it appears also in the works of the philosopher Aristotle, who wrote a good hundred years after the death of Aeschylus. It is a theory that reflects the masculine bias of Athenian thought and feeling. The Greek city-state, and especially Athens, excluded women from political action and even in private life severely restricted their activities; they had no legal standing and were kept, in respectable families, out of sight in a special section of the house reserved for women and children. This male domination stemmed in part from the fact that most city-states, and especially Athens, were at war with their neighbors more often than they were at peace; treaties were always made with a time limit, and even so, it was rare for the truce to last the full term fixed in the treaty. War, which in the ancient world meant close combat in which physical strength was a crucial factor, was the exclusive business of men (cf. Hector's speech to Andromache in the *Iliad*: "Go back to the house now and take care of your work, / The loom and the shuttle, and tell the servants / To get on with their jobs. War is the work of men." VI.515–17.) As combatants who were often called on to risk their lives to save the city from destruction and its women and children from enslavement, men assumed the prerogatives of a ruling caste and developed an ideology of male supremacy to justify their dominance. (When Medea, in Euripides' play, makes her famous protest against a woman's subordinate position, she cites this military basis for male supremacy only to reject it.)

The goddess Athena explains her support for Apollo's position in mythological terms: she was born directly from the head of Zeus and had no mother. But it is understandable also in terms of contemporary realities. The goddess Athena, guardian and protector of Odysseus in the *Odyssey*, has another side to her nature: in the *Iliad* she is a relentless opponent of the Trojans, a warrior-goddess intent on the destruction of Troy and all its inhabitants. In Athens, the city that bore her name and worshiped her in the Parthenon on the Acropolis, she was thought of as the protector of Athens in war; her images in sculpture and painted on vases show her armed with a spear, shield, and helmet, sometimes actually in combat in the war with the Olympian gods against the Giants. "I honor the male," she says (line 754), as she casts her vote for Orestes, and later, when she urges the Furies to accept her offer of a home in Athens, she predicts a great future for her city: "As time flows on, the honors flow through all / my citizens" (lines 864–65). The source of such honor is made clear later in her speech: "Let our wars / rage on abroad, with all their force, to satisfy / our powerful lust for fame" (lines 874–76).

Topics for Discussion

1. The theme of conflict between the sexes dominates the trial scene of *The Eumenides*, but it is operative, sometimes openly, sometimes subtly, in *Agamemnon* and *The Libation Bearers* as well. Trace its appearance and discuss its significance in all three plays.

   [In the opening scene of *Agamemnon*, the Watchman calls Clytaemnestra "that woman" who "maneuvers like a man" (line 13), and later, when she persuades Agamemnon to walk on the crimson tapestries, we are shown how she works on his pride to bend him to her will. "Spoken like a man" (line 355), says the Leader of the Chorus to Clytaemnestra as she rounds off her vision of Troy's destruction with an ironic prayer for Agamemnon's safe return. Her lover, Aegisthus, plays the woman's part: "Coward," says the Leader of the Chorus, "why not kill the man yourself? Why did the woman . . . have to bring him down?" (lines 1680–82). Orestes repeats this sentiment in *The Libation Bearers*, when he calls Aegisthus "womanhearted" and claims that "my compatriots, the glory of men / who toppled Troy with nerves of singing steel, / go at the beck and call of a brace of women" (lines 308–11). In this play, in sharp contrast to the strong maternal instincts she claimed motivated her revenge of Iphigeneia, Clytaemnestra is unloved by her children and called a "reckless, brutal mother" (line 418) who secretly rejoices at the news of her son's death (cf. the two images of her as a mother suckling her child at lines 514ff. and 883–85). See also the chorus's description of woman as "frenzied, driven wild with lust" at 580ff. Apollo, the male god par excellence, supports the father's rights against the Furies, female deities, champions of the cause of Clytaemnestra.]

2. The question (which will recur in the discussion of *Oedipus the King*) of the independence of the characters: how far are their actions directed by the gods or by that Fate that seems even more powerful than the gods, until, at the end of the *The Eumenides*: "All-seeing Zeus and Fate embrace" (line 1062)?

   [The main question here is Agamemnon's responsibility for the sacrifice of Iphigenia. The goddess Artemis demands Iphigenia's death as the price for the release of the fleet from adverse winds. But, as in so many Greek stories of divine interference, Agamemnon is given a choice—he could abandon the expedition (indeed he mentions this possibility only to disregard it in *Agamemnon*, lines 213–16). Aeschylus, in a paradoxical phrase, characterizes Agamemnon's decision to sacrifice his daughter as a free acceptance of destiny: "He slipped his neck into the strap of Fate" (line

217). Once he took this step, however, his heart hardened, "he stopped at nothing, / seized with the frenzy" (lines 219–20) and gave the orders to gag his daughter and hold her ready for the knife in cold unfeeling words. Orestes too, in *The Libation Bearers*, acts under orders from the oracle of Apollo and the threat, if he disobeys, of dreadful disease and a miserable death. But he goes on to reveal that he has his own motives for action that would urge him to kill his mother even without the gods' command. There is not only "mounting sorrow for father" but—a revealing detail—"the lack of patrimony presses hard" (lines 306–7). His only route to the repossession of his father's kingdom and wealth lies through his mother's death.]

3. Many of the images of the *Oresteia* recur throughout the trilogy, gaining fresh significance with each new appearance (for an example see the discussion of the "net" imagery in the headnote). Trace through *Agamemnon*, *The Libation Bearers*, and *The Eumenides* the pattern of images connected with (a) lions or (b) dogs.

[*Lions.* The lion is the heraldic device of the house of Atreus, as the lion gate at Mycenae reminds us. The choral parable of the lion cub that, brought up as a pet, turns savage when full grown (*Agamemnon*, lines 713–32), prepared for by the choral reference to Artemis as "so kind / to the ravening lion's tender, helpless cubs" (*Agamemnon*, lines 140–41), is the nexus of a widespread pattern of references to lions. This cautionary tale is offered by the Chorus as a comparison with Helen and the destruction she will bring to the Trojans who welcomed her. But in *Agamemnon*, the lion is used to characterize other figures as well: Agamemnon, who boasts of the slaughter at Troy as the work of "the beast of Argos . . . our bloody lion lapped its fill, / gorging on the blood of kings" (lines 810–14); Clytaemnestra appears in Cassandra's vision as "the lioness" who "rears on her hind legs" and "beds with the wolf / when her lion king goes ranging" (lines 1276–78); even Aegisthus is "a lion who lacks a lion's heart" (line 1236). They all began as "a captivating pet . . . like an infant just born" (lines 717–20) and ended as "a priest of ruin" (line 731). But the real lion cub is Orestes. In *The Libation Bearers*, he and Pylades are referred to as "the double lion" after they have murdered Aegisthus and Clytaemnestra (line 925). In *The Eumenides*, when Apollo orders the Furies out of his temple he tells them where they should be: "your kind / should infest a lion's cavern reeking blood" (lines 192–93). To which they might have replied that the house of Atreus, whose last male descendant they are in pursuit of, is just such a lion's den.

Dogs. The Watchman on the roof in the opening scene of *Agamemnon* keeps his vigil "propped on my arms . . . like a dog" (lines 3–4). He is a faithful dog, loyal to Agamemnon; we remember him when Clytaemnestra falsely claims that she is a "watchdog gentle to him alone, savage / to those who cross his path" (lines 604–5) and salutes the king as "watchdog of the fold" (line 887) as she plans his death. When Cassandra sings of the crimes committed in the House of Atreus the chorus recognizes her as "a keen hound . . . trailing murder" (lines 1094–95); but when she foresees the king's death at the hands of "that detestable hellhound / who pricks her ears and fawns" (lines 1241–42), the Chorus cannot connect her word with Clytaemnestra. And Aegisthus, when the Chorus defies him in the final scene of *Agamemnon*, calls them "insubordinate dogs" (line 1702): "We'll see if the world comes dancing to your song, / your absurd barking—snarl your breath away! / I'll make you dance, I'll bring you all to heel" (lines 1667–69). In *The Libation Bearers* and *The Eumenides*, when we see the Furies they are hounds, trackers of the scent of blood (*The Libation Bearers*, lines 911 and 1054). Like hounds, they bay in their sleep (*The Eumenides*, line 133) and like hounds they follow the prey: "blood of the mother draws me on—must hunt / the man for Justice. Now I'm on his trail!" (lines 229–30). This is their exit line in the scene set at Delphi; their entrance speech, delivered by the leader of the chorus when they reenter now at Athens, uses similar language: "At last! / The clear trail of the man. . . . / He's wounded— / go for the fawn, my hounds, the splash of blood, / hunt him" (lines 243–47).]

Topic for Writing

Zeus, so the Chorus sings, "lays it down as law / that we must suffer, suffer into truth" (*Agamemnon*, lines 178–79). Trace the steps by which the Chorus of *Agamemnon* comes through suffering and a series of misapprehensions to a true vision of the situation.

[At the beginning of the play the Chorus believes that the war against Troy was just (lines 66ff.); the kings are sent by Zeus. Yet it is clearly disturbed by Agamemnon's sacrifice of his daughter (lines 210ff.) The Leader reacts with joy to the news of Troy's fall (lines 269–70), which will of course mean Agamemnon's return. In its second choral ode it begins a victory hymn to celebrate the Greek triumph, but as it describes the process by which men are led to tread "the grand altar of Justice / down" (lines 385ff.)—though it claims it is singing about the Trojan Paris—its words are reminiscent of its description of Agamemnon's change of mind that enabled him to kill his daughter. The Chorus returns to the theme of the righteous war with an indictment of Helen (lines 403ff.) and expressions of sympathy for the grief of Menelaus (lines 411ff.) but soon turns to the grief of mothers and fathers who have lost their sons at Troy, "all for another's woman" (line 444). The image of the war god as a broker who exchanges living men for funeral ashes is in flagrant contradiction with the opening of the ode. The Chorus goes on to speak of the "people's voice" that is "heavy with hatred" (line 451), and the victory ode ends with a wish to be neither victor nor vanquished. But the sight of the herald who brings news from Troy raises its hopes again; it returns to the illusion that Agamemnon's return will put an end to its doubts and fears. The herald's tale of victory renews its confidence, and the Chorus sings of Helen and the destruction she wrought on the Trojans who greeted her arrival with such joy (lines 683ff.). And when Agamemnon enters, it greets him with enthusiasm. The Chorus tells him it was against the war at first, "But now from the depths of trust and love / I say Well fought, well won" (lines 789–90). But when its king, whose sacrifice of his daughter it has almost forgotten in its joy at his return, goes into the palace treading the blood-red tapestries like some proverbial man of pride destined for a fall, it sings in fear of some unknown terror; it senses that something is badly wrong. Cassandra tells the Chorus, first in riddling and then in plain terms, what it fears but dares not face: that Agamemnon must die, that according to that standard of Justice it has often invoked itself (lines 374ff, 751ff.) Agamemnon must pay for the blood of Iphigenia and perhaps for the blood of all those who fell at Troy (lines 455ff.). Cassandra tells the Chorus the truth in plain terms, but it cannot accept it; only as she goes into the palace to her death does it dare ask the question: "now if he must pay for the blood / his fathers shed, and die for the deaths / he brought to pass" (lines 1367–69). The answer comes at once; it is Agamemnon's cry of agony from inside the palace. Confronted with the corpse of the king and the defiant boasts of Clytaemnestra, the Chorus tries to lay the blame on Helen (lines 1485ff.), a patent evasion that Clytaemnestra bluntly rejects (lines 1495ff.); it then casts the blame on the spirit of vengeance that plagues the house of Atreus from generation to generation, a view that Clytaemnestra accepts, for she sees it as absolving her of responsibility. To this the Chorus reacts violently, but reminded of the murder of Iphigenia, it loses its bearing: "The mind reels—where to turn?" (line 1563). In the end it recognizes, at last, Agamemnon's guilt: "None can judge between them. Justice. / The plunderer plundered, the killer pays the price. . . . The one who acts must suffer" (lines 1593–96). It has learned, through suffering, to see the truth. But by that same law Clytaemnestra too must pay, and stung to fury by the sight of Aegisthus lording it in the house of Agamemnon, the Chorus calls on Orestes as its only hope for justice; it now understands, too late as always, the full meaning of Cassandra's vision of the future.]

Comparative Perspective

Most of the world's great dramatic traditions have their roots in religious rituals, yet not all of the world's great religions have nurtured drama. What role do the Greek gods play in the *Oresteia*? Compare the way God in the Old Testament of the Bible and Allah in the Koran interact with human beings and try to explain why neither Judaism nor Islam gave rise to a classical theater.

Further Reading

See also the reading suggestions in the *Anthology*, p. 2642.

Aeschylus. *The Oresteia*. Trans. Robert Fagles. 1984. Contains a long and stimulating introductory essay by Robert Fagles and W. B. Stanford, as well as helpful explanatory notes on selected passages.

Kitto, H. D. F. *Form and Meaning in Drama*. 1956. In the first three chapters, Kitto discusses the trilogy in an attempt to answer a series of questions, for example: "Why in the *Libation Bearers* and the *Eumenides* are Agamemnon's sins entirely forgotten even by his adversaries? Why does Aeschylus so arrange *Agamemnon* that the event earliest in time, namely Atreus' feud with Thyestes, comes at the end of the play?" Kitto tackles these and many other puzzling aspects of the trilogy with probing analysis; his answers may not persuade everyone, but his great merit is to have recognized and explored the problems.

Knox, Bernard. *Word and Action: Essays on the Ancient Theater*. 1979. Contains the essay "Aeschylus and the Third Actor," which deals in some detail with the Cassandra scene and also with the way the chorus comes to understand and face, too late, the truth (see "Topic for Writing").

McCall, Marsh Jr., ed. *Aeschylus: A Collection of Critical Essays*. 1972. Includes an important article on freedom and its limitations by N. G. L. Hammond (see "Topics for Discussion") and a brilliant essay on symbolism in the *Oresteia* by R. F. Goheen. There is also an interesting survey of "tradition and method" in translating Aeschylus by Peter Green.

Sommerstein, Alan H. *Aeschylean Tragedy*. 1996. A comprehensive introduction and analysis of Aeschylean tragedy, with chapters on individual plays, the political and religious background, and major Aeschylean themes.

Taplin, Oliver. *Greek Tragedy in Action*. 1978. A book on the ancient staging of Greek tragedy by a scholar who has become perhaps the foremost expert in this field. The book proceeds by subject rather than play by play, but discussion of passages in the trilogy can quickly be located from the index.

Winnington-Ingram, R. P. *Studies in Aeschylus*. 1983. Contains interpretive essays by a recognized authority on Greek drama: "Agamemnon and the Trojan War," "Clytaemnestra and the Vote of Athena," "Orestes and Apollo," and "Zeus and the Erinyes."

SOPHOCLES

Oedipus the King

Backgrounds

The city of Thebes is ravaged by a plague, and in the opening scene of the play a delegation of its citizens comes to urge Oedipus, king of Thebes, to find some remedy. They have confidence in him, their efficient and benevolent ruler who many years ago, came to Thebes and rescued the city from the Sphinx, a creature with a bird's body and a human female head, which preyed on the city's young men. Those who encountered it and failed to answer its riddle were killed. Oedipus volunteered to face the Sphinx and answer the riddle correctly; the Sphinx died, and Oedipus was given, as a reward, the throne of Thebes and the hand in marriage of its recently widowed Queen Jocasta.

Her husband, Laius, had been killed on the way to Delphi in a quarrel over precedence at a junction of narrow roads; his killer was the young Oedipus, who does not realize that the man he killed in the fight was the former king of Thebes. Nor does he realize that Laius was his father and Jocasta is his mother. The play presents his discovery of this dreadful truth.

This situation is the result of a set of coincidences or perhaps the work of some power that guides the course of events. Laius and Jocasta heard a prophecy from the oracle of Apollo at Delphi that their son would kill his father and marry his mother. They told a shepherd to leave the newborn child on the mountainside; to make doubly sure that it would die, its ankles were pierced and fastened together. But the shepherd had pity on the child and gave it to another shepherd, one from the other side of the mountain range, the territory of Corinth. Knowing that his king and queen, Polybus and Merope, were childless, this shepherd took the baby down to them, and they adopted it. Because his ankles were swollen from the wounds, the boy was called Oedipus ("swollen-foot").

Oedipus grew up in Corinth, believing he was the son of Polybus and Merope. But rumors began to circulate about his legitimacy; to know the truth, he went to Delphi to consult the oracle, but all she said was that he would kill his father and marry his mother; appalled, he resolved never to return to Corinth and set out in the opposite direction. At a place "where three roads meet" he was crowded off the narrow road by a man in a chariot; a fight broke out, and he killed the man and (he thought) all of his companions. (One escaped and brought the news back to Jocasta.) Arriving at Thebes Oedipus defeated the Sphinx, married Jocasta, and became king. Apollo's prophecy was fulfilled.

Many years later, the plague rages in the city, and Creon, Jocasta's brother, comes back from Delphi, where he was sent by Oedipus to ask what to do. The answer: find the killer of Laius, then kill or banish him. Oedipus undertakes to find him. He puts a dreadful curse on the killer, cutting him off from all contact with his fellow citizens; he also sends for Tiresias, the blind prophet, who knows all things. He does in fact know the truth but refuses to tell Oedipus; the king reacts with fierce anger, accusing him of betraying the city and then of conspiring with Creon to overthrow him. His anger blinds him to the truth that Tiresias, now angry in his turn, begins to reveal, although in riddling terms; he speaks clearly in the end, but Oedipus leaves in a fury, paying no attention.

In the next scene, Creon is directly accused of conspiracy and sentenced to death; at the request of the Chorus and Jocasta, who now comes on stage, Oedipus reluctantly retracts the death sentence. Wishing to calm Oedipus, Jocasta asks the reason for his rage; he replies that Tiresias accused him of the murder of Laius. She tells him to pay no attention to prophets, they know nothing more than ordinary men. To prove it she tells him of the prophecy that her son would kill his father and marry his mother. In fact the child, she says, died on the mountain, and Laius was killed by a stranger at the junction of three roads.

This detail terrifies Oedipus; he now tells her the story of his encounter at such a place. He is afraid he may be the killer of Laius, the cause of the plague, the victim of his own solemn curse. (He does not connect the prophecy with the one given him by Apollo, for he is sure that his father and mother are Polybus and Merope at Corinth.) But he knows that he was alone, and Jocasta spoke of "robbers" as the assailants of Laius. He needs an eyewitness to reassure him, and there is one: the survivor of the fight, whom Jocasta has sent away into the country to be a shepherd. It is the same man who took the baby Oedipus to the mountains to die, and when he comes he will bear witness to more than the death of Laius.

But meanwhile a messenger comes from Corinth: Polybus is dead, and the Corinthians want Oedipus to come back to reign over them. The news of Polybus' death is a great relief; Apollo's prophecy at Delphi was wrong—Oedipus did not kill his father—but he will not go to Corinth, because the second half of the prophecy, that he would marry his mother, will best be falsified if he stays in Thebes. The messenger now tells him there is nothing to fear; Merope is not his mother. The messenger, when he was a shepherd, was given the baby by another shepherd; its ankles were pierced.

By this time Jocasta has realized the horrible truth; she tries to stop Oedipus, to make him give up the search. But he insists he will know the truth, whatever it is. Jocasta rushes off stage (to hang herself, as we find out later), and Oedipus waits for the shepherd Jocasta sent for in the previous scene. When he comes, the man from Corinth recognizes him, and Oedipus forces the whole truth out of him. Then Oedipus too rushes off stage as the Chorus sings a despairing ode about the nothingness of men.

A messenger comes on to tell of Jocasta's suicide and Oedipus' self-blinding; soon the blind king himself comes stumbling on stage. His laments turn to stubborn resolution as he demands that the Chorus obey the oracle of Apollo and drive him out to die, on the mountain where he now wishes he had died as a child. Creon, now king of Thebes, comes on to take charge. Oedipus is allowed to embrace his two daughters, Antigone and Ismene, and then is ordered into the palace; about his eventual disposition Creon will consult the oracle.

The oracle of Apollo at Delphi was, in Sophocles' time, a powerful religious institution that wielded considerable political influence. Greek states and foreign kings consulted it about the future, as did also private individuals; their sacrifices and offerings made it one of the greatest concentrations of art and wealth in the Greek world. Apollo, through his priestess the Pythia (cf. the opening scene of *The Eumenides*), answered requests for advice; his advice was treasured because he was believed to know the future. During the last three decades of Sophocles' life, Athens was at war with Sparta; before declaring war, the Spartans had consulted the oracle and had been told that they would win (as they did).

But this belief that the gods know the future was no longer universally held in Sophocles' day; like many other features of traditional religion it was subjected to critical examination by the new philosophers, who speculated about the atomic constituents of matter, and by the Sophists, who applied the canon of probability to religious myth. The attack on the belief in divine prophecy was in fact the most dangerous of all the new attempts to reject tradition; if the gods do not know the future, they are no more in control of the universe than we are.

This intellectual conflict is reflected in the play. Jocasta sums up her argument that Oedipus should disregard the oracles with a contemptuous rejection: "So much for prophecy. It's neither here nor there. / From this day on, I wouldn't look right or left" (lines 948–49). The reaction of the Chorus is to call on Zeus, the supreme god, to make the prophecies come true, horrible as that will be for Oedipus; otherwise, it says, there will be no point in worshiping the gods at all: "Never again will I go reverent to Delphi . . . or Apollo's ancient oracle at Abae . . . unless these prophecies all come true" (lines 985ff.). Prophecies are despised and "the gods, the gods go down" (line 997). Later on, when he hears of the death of Polybus, Oedipus echoes Jocasta's disbelief: "Why, why look to the Prophet's hearth" (line 1054), and "all those prophecies I feared. . . . They're nothing, worthless" (lines 1062–64). And Jocasta draws the ultimate conclusion, that human life is a meaningless chaos, a chain of mere coincidences: "What should a man fear? It's all chance, / chance rules our lives. . . . Better to live at random, best we can" (lines 1069–72). They do not know it, but the truth of prophecy is about to be revealed, to Jocasta before the end of this scene, to Oedipus in the next. The play uses the myth to present the most controversial religious and philosophical issue of the day; it comes down decisively on the side of prophecy, divine knowledge and design—even though the ruin of a good man is part of that design.

The Oedipus story was of course well known, but it is likely that Sophocles reworked it along lines suitable for his own artistic purpose (as all the Greek poets did when they handled mythical themes). In Homer's *Odyssey* the hero Odysseus sees, in the lower world, the mother of Oedipus (she is called Epicaste); she married her son, who had killed his father. The gods revealed the truth to humankind; Epicaste hanged herself, but Oedipus, though he suffered from the sorrows that the Furies of a mother bring to pass, lived on as king of Thebes (*Odyssey* XI.307–17).

There is no mention here of Oedipus' children, of his self-blinding and expulsion from Thebes, of Apollo's oracle, or of the Sphinx. All these details presumably came into the story later, in other epic tales or lyric poems, now lost. But we do know that Aeschylus produced a trilogy dealing with the house of Oedipus (we still have the final play, *The Seven against Thebes*); from that play and the fragments of the others we know that the Aeschylean trilogy referred to the story of the Apolline oracle and the exposure of the child, the encounter where three roads meet, the self-blinding of Oedipus, and the part played by the Sphinx. This suggests that Sophocles could rely on audience familiarity with the main elements of the story to ensure appreciation of this masterly use of dramatic irony in the first two-thirds of his play.

We have only a version of the riddle of the Sphinx that comes from sources much later than Sophocles' time, but there is good evidence that it was known in this form in the fifth century. It is in hexameter verse; here is a literal translation:

> There is a two-footed thing on this earth, four-footed (but only one voice) and three-footed. It changes its form and is the only thing to do so of all the creatures that move on land, in the air or in the sea. Now when it walks supporting itself on most feet, the speed of its limbs is at its weakest.

There may be an allusion to the text of the riddle where Creon says "The singing, riddling Sphinx / She . . . persuaded us to let the mystery go / and concentrate on what lay at our feet" (lines 147–49). In any case, the fact that the answer is "man" is singularly appropriate for a hero who begins the play as a representative of humanity as master of its environment and ends it as a blinded outcast.

Classroom Strategies

One assignment.

Modern students will probably find themselves in difficulty when they move from the dramatic exchanges in the spoken scenes to the sometimes meditative, sometimes excited lyric poetry of the choral odes. Yet the choral poetry is not only, for most of its length, a profound meditation on the moral and religious themes of the play but also a reflection of the Chorus's reactions to and interpretations of the dramatic action. As in *Agamemnon*, the attitude of the Chorus is not fixed; it varies as the song expresses the hopes and fears of the citizens of Thebes before the words and deeds of their rulers. But whereas in *Agamemnon* the Chorus learns through suffering to see, at last, the truth of the matter, the Chorus of *Oedipus*, oscillating wildly between overconfidence and utter despair, serves Sophocles as a dramatic instrument for the creation of suspense, irony, and contrast.

The opening song (lines 168ff.) is a desperate appeal to the gods for relief from the plague. The Chorus does not yet know the message Creon has brought to Oedipus; they await the word from Delphi with apprehension. The vivid description of the sufferings caused by the plague in lines 190ff. reinforces the dramatic effect of the opening scene: Oedipus must act quickly and decisively if he is to save his city. As he comes out of the palace he hears the closing lines of the choral prayer, and Sophocles gives him an opening line heavy with dramatic irony: "You pray to the gods? Let me grant your prayers" (line 245). He will indeed grant its prayers, but only at the price of his wife's death and the loss of his own eyes.

The second choral song (lines 526ff.) follows the scene between Oedipus and Tiresias. The first half of it develops a vision of the man responsible for the plague, the murderer of Laius, as a fugitive in flight from the gods' pursuit—an outcast in the wilds, in "bristling timber . . . rocks and caves" (lines 542–43). Evidently, the Chorus does not accept Tiresias' identification of Oedipus as the killer; as it goes on to discuss the prophet's charge, it confesses to bewilderment. For all its respect for Tiresias, it can see no reason that a prince from Corinth should quarrel with and kill the king of Thebes. It rejects this assault "without proof" on the reputation of the man who once before saved Thebes. Not that it rejects prophecy: "Zeus and Apollo know" (line 561). But a human prophet may err; it will not believe until it sees "these charges proved" (line 568).

But the next choral ode (lines 945ff.) comes after the quarrel between Oedipus and Creon (in which the Chorus intervened on Creon's behalf) and the revelations that followed; it has heard Oedipus tell how he killed a man at the crossroads and now fears that he may in fact be the killer of Laius—that Tiresias was right—and the Chorus has heard Jocasta reject prophecy altogether, including one that came from Delphi. It is deeply disturbed and sings of the immortal laws as it prays for reverence and purity; it denounces the tyrannical spirit that mounts too high only to crash in ruin. This seems to be a reference to political power (and so to Oedipus); the Chorus qualifies it immediately as it prays that the god will never put an end to the "healthy strife that makes the city strong" (line 969). But dark thoughts return: it sings now of one who has no fear of justice, no reverence for the gods, who "lay[s] hands on the holy things untouchable" (line 980). In that last phrase (and the suggestion is especially strong in the Greek) there might be a reference to incest. If such a man go unpunished, the Chorus asks itself, why join the sacred dance? The dance it is performing as it sings is such a dance; the theater is a place of worship of the god Dionysus. If such crimes go unpunished, the Chorus's words imply, why worship the gods at all? And it spells this implication out clearly in the final stanza. It will no longer go to Delphi or any other sacred site unless "these prophecies all come true" (line 989). They are ready to abandon their king if the condition of his survival is the failure of divine prophecy.

But the next choral song (lines 1195ff.) is a jubilant speculation about the birth of Oedipus. The Chorus knows now that he is not the son of the royal pair at Corinth; as it waits for the arrival of the Theban Shepherd who carried the baby Oedipus long ago to the slopes of Mount Cithaeron, it indulges in pleasing prospects: Oedipus may be the child of a god, of Pan by a nymph, of Apollo, Hermes, or Dionysus. It is not long before the dreadful truth is revealed, to Oedipus and to the Chorus, that now sings despondently of the fate of humankind: "generations of men . . . adding the total / of all your lives I find they come to nothing" (lines 1312–14). Oedipus is the example; in his rise and fall the Chorus finds the proof of this gloomy estimate of the human condition. Yet the last scene of the play suggests that just as it went too far before in joyful expectation, it has now gone too far in despair. For in the last scene, the blind Oedipus emerges from his initial abject misery to reassert himself as a man; he refuses to accept the Chorus's condemnation of his self-blinding: "What I did was best—don't lecture me" (line 1500). The imperious tone is certainly not that of a man who feels he is nothing, and he uses the same tone to Creon later: "I command you—I beg you" (line 1584). This return to self-confidence is based on a feeling that his cruel destiny marks him as unique and that, for some purpose undeclared, he has been singled out among humankind: "I have been saved / for something great and terrible, something strange" (lines 1597–98). That "something strange" is the subject of the last play Sophocles was to write, *Oedipus at Colonus*.

Topics for Discussion

1. The theme of sight and blindness; its importance in a play that turns on human ignorance of the truth.

   [Tiresias the blind prophet can see the truth (as Oedipus begins to fear, line 823). Oedipus, who has the use of his eyes, moves blindly toward the revelation of the truth. He sees clearly only when he is physically blind. Compare the emphasis on Oedipus' sight throughout the first part of the play (lines 17, 28, 70, 96, 119, 394, 427, 597, 830, 885, 1042, 1147, 1153, 1185, and 1190) and contrast the references to the vision of Tiresias (323, 359–60). Also Oedipus' sarcastic references to the blindness of Tiresias (lines 396, 423, 425ff., 440–42, and 469) and Tiresias' references to the blindness of Oedipus (lines 419, 470–71, 517ff.; cf. 879, 1082, 1095, 1360, 1406ff., 1567, and 1625ff.).]

2. Oedipus is a figure representative of human confidence that our intelligence makes us master of our world.

   [Oedipus is a man of action and experience (cf. lines 55–56), but he himself emphasizes that his action is based on thoughtful analysis ("groping, laboring over many paths of thought . . . painful search," lines 79–80). And he boasts that he alone was able to answer the riddle of the Sphinx: "the flight of my own intelligence hit the mark" (line 453). Here he prizes his own human intelligence above the prophetic skills of Tiresias, which are the gift of the gods. His intelligence is displayed in the frequent cross-questioning to which he subjects witnesses in the course of his investigation, an investigation that starts as a search for the murderer of Laius and ends as a search for his own identity. His questioning of Creon (lines 112ff.), Jocasta (lines 804ff.), the messenger (lines 1114ff.), and the shepherd (lines 1229ff.) are models of logical pursuit of the truth. And it is through these intellectual efforts that he finally brings about the catastrophe, learns the truth about himself.]

Topic for Writing

Trace the pattern and discuss the significance of the following images throughout the play: (a) Oedipus as hunter, (b) Oedipus as plowman, and (c) Oedipus as sailor-helmsman.

[All three of these images reinforce the central idea of Oedipus as the symbolic representative of human progress, for the conquest of the wild beasts, the discovery of agriculture, and the mastery of the sea are important stages in our long development from "savagery" to "civilization." (That the Greeks were conscious of this historical view of human progress is clear from the choral ode in *Antigone*, lines 376ff., where mastery of the sea, the soil, and the animals are the first accomplishments of "man the skilled, the brilliant.")

Oedipus as hunter. The investigator of the crime is easily seen as a hunter, and this image is pervasive throughout the opening scenes of the play. "Where to find it now," he asks when Creon tells him that Apollo demands the punishment of Laius' murder, "the trail of the ancient guilt so hard to trace?" (lines 123–24). "What stopped you," he asks Creon, "from tracking down the killer / then and there?" (lines 146–47). He will take up the chase himself and later claims that if he had been present at the time "there would have been . . . no long hunt / without a clue in hand" (lines 250–51). Later Tiresias will tell him "I say you are the murderer you hunt" (line 413), but it will be a long time before he realizes this is the truth. The Chorus envisions the murderer of Laius as a hunted animal: "that man who left no trace— / after him, hunt him down with all our strength!" (lines 540–41). It does not realize that Oedipus is both the hunter and the prey.

Oedipus as plowman. The agricultural images are heavily loaded with significance in this play, because in the Greek language such words as "plow" and "sow" are familiar expressions for the begetting of children (as they were in the seventeenth-century English of the Bible—"the seed of Abraham," "the fruit of the womb," for example). Quite apart from their clear reference to the incestuous begetting of children by the royal pair, these images are strikingly appropriate to the dramatic situation. For the plague in Thebes affects the products of the soil as well as human beings (cf. "The fruits of our famous earth, they will not ripen" and "the women cannot scream their pangs to birth . . . children dead in the womb," lines 196–98). This sympathetic relationship between the fruits of the soil and the fruit of the womb is reflected in the transference of agricultural terms to the pollution of the marriage of Oedipus and Jocasta; what this suggests is the responsibility of that unholy marriage for the stunted crops and the plague. Oedipus's first statement about his relationship with Laius is made in terms of this metaphor. Not realizing the hideous ambiguities involved, he says, "I hold the throne that he held then, possess his bed / and a wife who shares our seed" (lines 295–96). What he means is simply that he and Laius have had children by the same wife, but the words suggest to the audience the hideous truth. The same image recurs when Tiresias prophesies that Oedipus will be revealed as his father's murderer and his mother's son: "He sowed the loins / his father sowed" (lines 522–23). After the revelation of the truth, the Chorus asks in horror: "How, how could the furrows your father plowed / bear you, your agony, harrowing on / in silence O so long?" (lines 1339–41). When Oedipus bursts into the palace, he asks, the messenger tells us, for "his wife, / no wife, his mother, where he can find the mother earth / that cropped two crops at once, himself and all his children" (lines 1388–90). He explains his own polluted state to his daughters with this same image: "I fathered you in the soil that gave me life" (line 1627) and "Your father killed his father, sowed his mother, / one, one and the selfsame womb sprang you— / he cropped the very roots of his existence" (lines 1640–42). The plowman has reaped a dreadful crop, the sower is not only the sower but also the seed.

Oedipus as sailor-helmsman. Oedipus as helmsman is a natural image, for as king he is thought of as guiding the ship of state (a common metaphor in Greek as in English). The city is compared to a ship in the opening speech of the priest—"our ship pitches wildly, cannot lift her head / from the depths" (lines 29–30)—and Creon, bringing news from Delphi, speaks of the "plague-storm" (line 114) that afflicts the city; he also refers to Oedipus' rescue of Thebes in earlier days with the phrase "you came and put us straight on course" (118). The Chorus takes up and elaborates this image when it asserts its loyalty to Oedipus after his quarrel with Creon: "You who set our beloved land—storm-tossed, shattered— / straight on course" (lines 765–66). And it exhorts him to do the same thing now: "Now again, good helmsman, / steer us through the storm!" (lines 766–67). But its wish is not to be granted; after Jocasta's mention of the three roads, Oedipus is distraught. The citizens, in Jocasta's words, are "passengers in the grip of fear, / watching the pilot of the vessel go to pieces" (lines 1010–11). Oedipus has not yet discovered the full truth. When he does he will understand at last the riddling question Tiresias asked him. "What haven won't reverberate? . . . That day you learn the truth about your marriage? . . . the lusty voyage home to the fatal harbor!" (lines 480ff.). Oedipus, like a navigator, had plotted his course by the stars: "I abandoned Corinth, / from that day on I gauged its landfall only / by the stars" (lines 876–78). But it brought him to an unspeakable destination. "One and the same wide harbor," sings the Chorus, "served you / son and father both / son and father came to rest in the same bridal chamber" (lines 1336–39).]

Comparative Perspective

What kind of correlation exists between the time covered by the action of the play and the time it takes to perform? Compare the management of time and event in other dramatic traditions. Speculate on the extent to which cultural attitudes toward time and human life influence the presentation of dramatic action.

Further Reading

See also the reading suggestions in the *Anthology*.

O'Brien, Michael J., ed. *Twentieth-Century Interpretations of* Oedipus Rex. 1968. Contains an essay by Eric Dodds ("On Misunderstanding *Oedipus Rex*") that with admirable clarity and concision draws on a lifetime of brilliant scholarship and teaching to deal with the difficulties students usually experience on reading this play. There are also essays by Francis Ferguson (on the play as theater), G. M. Kirkwood (on dramatic form), R. P. Winnington-Ingram (on the Old Testament of the Bible and Greek archaic thought), and Bernard Knox (on the ending of the play). The volume also contains useful short quotations from critics ancient and modern, including, for example, Plutarch, Voltaire, Bowra, Freud, and Marshall McLuhan.

Sophocles. *Sophocles' Oedipus Rex.* R. D. Dawe, ed. 1982. This is an edition of and commentary on the Greek text of the play, but the introduction is an especially useful discussion of the problems raised by the intricacy of the plot.

Antigone

Backgrounds

Although produced considerably earlier than *Oedipus the King* (see headnote), Sophocles' *Antigone* continues the story of the fate of one family: the royal House of Laius at Thebes. In *Oedipus the King*, we saw Oedipus gradually come to the understanding that he had killed his father (Laius) and married his mother, and at the end of the play we saw him leave his children under the protection of his brother-in-law Creon and quit Thebes for a life of permanent exile (the story of his death is told in another Sophoclean play, *Oedipus at Colonus*). The children he leaves behind are two sons, Eteocles and Polynices, and two daughters, Antigone and Ismene. At some point in the intervening period between the action of *Oedipus the King* and *Antigone*, Oedipus curses his two sons, and they quarrel over the kingship of Thebes. When they are both unable to settle on a compromise, Polynices leaves the city and returns with an army of Argives. The resulting battle, fought at the seven gates of Thebes, leads to the demise of both brothers. Their joint deaths, each at the other's hands, fulfils Oedipus' curse and leaves no direct male heirs to rule the city. Creon therefore takes over as king of Thebes. *Antigone* opens in the aftermath of that battle, just as Creon has issued an edict that the "patriot" Eteocles will be awarded a hero's funeral, while the "traitor" Polynices will lie unburied.

The play opens at night, with the sisters Antigone and Ismene discussing the consequences of Creon's decree. While both are distressed, their reactions to the edict are very different. Ismene is practical, claiming that, as women, there is nothing that they can do but submit. Antigone, on the other hand, is defiant in her resolve to oppose the law and bury her brother, even if it brings her death. She is single-minded in her commitment to bury her brother, and immediately departs to do so. Antigone is fully aware that she is likely to be captured for her act, and it is not long before she is brought before Creon, whom we have seen furiously demanding that the culprit (whatever man he is) should be found. When the two come face to face, Antigone and Creon reveal themselves to be equally single-minded and resolute in their beliefs. Quick to anger, Creon calls Antigone proud, insolent, and disloyal, while Antigone claims that she answers to the laws of the gods over those of the city or of a tyrant obsessed with his own power. She calls upon Creon to hasten her arrest and execution, and, rather than try to excuse his niece, Creon attempts to condemn Ismene alongside her, bringing the other girl on stage and cross-examining her about her role in the crime. Although Ismene wishes to share in her sister's punishment, Antigone refuses to concede any part of it to her. Again, Antigone is resolute, underscoring the differences between them by claiming "You chose to live, I chose to die" (line 626).

Next, Ismene attempts to reason with Creon to spare her sister, and it is at this point that we are told that Antigone is due to marry Creon's son, Haemon. After an interlude in which the Chorus laments the curse of the House of Oedipus, Haemon enters and similarly attempts to reason with his father, gently implying that Creon is being too rigid, too simple-minded, and that he is disregarding the wishes of the citizens of Thebes. But with Creon's increasing anger the two are set at loggerheads, culminating in Haemon's rushing off stage with an ominous threat: "And you will never / see me, never set eyes on my face again" (lines 857–58). By this point in the play, it has become clear that Creon's unswerving adherence to his edict to leave Polynices unburied, despite the religious and political language he had used to justify it, is dividing him from the city he rules.

In the next scene, the idea that Creon may have offended against the religious rites of burial is reinforced by his further perversion of burial rites, as he reveals his decision to kill Antigone by burying her alive. Although he insists that such a death will free him of bloodguilt, since the girl would die of starvation rather than at anyone's hand, the following choral ode, which prepares for Antigone's procession to her death, is full of foreboding. The Chorus equates Antigone's death with marriage, and she appears in the bridal veils with which she will later be found hanging in the vault. Describing herself as a "stranger" who is without home or city (lines 941, 957, cf. 978), Antigone first laments her family's curse, and then explains that this is an ordeal she would have taken on only for a brother—not for a husband or a child, both of which can be replaced. Calling upon the citizens of Thebes to look upon her as "the last of a great line of kings" (line 1032), Antigone departs to her death.

Whether Antigone was right or wrong to choose to bury her brother is never made clear in the play, but it is evident that throughout she sees with unswerving clarity where her actions will lead her. Not so Creon, whose short-sightedness is highlighted by the next character to enter the stage, the blind seer Tiresias. The speech of the divine prophet offers the definitive proof that Creon's edict was wrong in the eyes of the gods, for they have brought a plague upon the city in response to its impious refusal to bury Polynices. Provoked by Creon's angry dismissal of his news, Tiresias then goes on to explain that there is still more to come: before the day is out one of his own children will have died, a corpse in return for a corpse (line 1186).

From here the course of Creon's tragedy is swift. He relents and attempts to save his son (in contrast to the unbending resolve of Sophoclean heroes like Antigone or Ajax, who never change their minds), but it is too late. A messenger describes to the Chorus and the silent wife of Creon, Eurydice, how Creon rushed in to the burial chamber to find Haemon weeping over the body of his "bride," and how Haemon then fell upon his sword, having unsuccessfully rushed upon his father. In the final scene of the play, Creon returns with Haemon's body, to learn that Eurydice has hanged herself at the news of her son's death. Left with nothing, Creon proclaims "the guilt is mine . . . I admit it all!" (lines 1442–45), and in the closing lines of the play both he and the Chorus refer to the crushing blows of fate, which "at long last . . . will teach us wisdom" (lines 1470–71).

Topics for Discussion

1. The Sophoclean Hero
   Sophocles' heroes are famous for their determination and single-minded perseverance, their privileging of the individual over the city or the community, and their force of character. Although Antigone gives her name to this play, Creon has by far the greater number of lines, and he is the one to suffer a tragic "reversal." Discuss what makes each of them tragic figures, and how fully they correspond to other ancient Greek heroes we have seen in both epic and tragedy. You may also wish to address the question of how Antigone's gender affects her role as a heroic figure.

   [Both characters are concerned with their status, and Antigone especially makes frequent reference to her glory and her royal blood. In her willingness to go to an early death for the sake of her honor and divine righteousness, she is reminiscent of Achilles in the *Iliad*, who chooses a short life for the sake of fame. Note her insistence to Ismene that she shout Antigone's act from the rooftops (lines 100–101) and her call for glory (her word is *kleos*, the same word used by Homeric heroes to describe the honor that comes from fighting on the battlefield) at line 561. Antigone is unlike Oedipus in that she willingly chooses her own fate; hers is a personal crisis that shows no regard for civic law or duty. Oedipus' choices, on the other hand, like Creon's, are bound up with his position as ruler of the city of Thebes (cf. the use of "helmsman-ruler" imagery to describe Creon's role at lines 180–82, 199, 212, 800–804). Like Oedipus in his determination to learn the truth, Antigone never swerves in her resolve, but, interestingly, Creon *does* change his mind two-thirds of the way through the play. Finally, although Antigone chooses a particularly female form of tragic death (hanging) in a female context (her "bridal vault"), she attributes to herself the "male" virtues of courage and glory, calls herself "the last of a great line of kings" (line 1032), and refuses to accept Ismene's claim that as women, they are powerless to act. Despite the frequent criticisms from Creon that she is not behaving as a woman should (lines 541, 593, 652), Antigone acts as a hero without being overly demonized for her status as a woman, as both Clytaemnestra and the "barbarian witch" Medea are in Aeschylus' and Euripides' plays.]

2. The City of Thebes

The city of Thebes plays a role of considerable importance in *Antigone*. Creon's first words are concerned with Thebes, and he identifies himself first and foremost as the ruler of a city. Should we understand his clash with Antigone as a conflict between the city and the individual? The city of Thebes is a constant backdrop to the action taking place on stage—what effect does it have on the actions and choices of the characters? [Creon tries to put the city first, before familial loyalties, and his refusal to bury Polynices shows how seriously he views the latter's crime as a "traitor" against the city. Antigone calls herself a "stranger" in the city (lines 941, 957, and see note at 978), and pays no heed to the commands of Creon its ruler, placing family and religion above civic law. Creon, on the other hand, cannot separate the identity of the city from himself. Although Haemon warns "It's no city at all, owned by one man alone" (line 824), Creon replies "What? The city *is* the king's—that's the law!"]

You may wish to expand this topic further to include

i. The role of Thebes in *Oedipus the King*.

[Oedipus is irrevocably drawn back to the city of Thebes, despite all the best efforts to keep him away from it, and although he saves the city by freeing it from the Sphinx, he also casts the whole of Thebes into plague by his unknowing actions. At the end of the play, Oedipus contrasts the city with the wild and isolated landscape of Mount Cithaeron, rejecting Thebes for this alternate birthplace far from civic structures.]

  ii. The production of *Antigone* in Athens, before the citizens of the
     Athenian democracy.
     [Although the word *tyrannus* in Greek simply means *king*, the
     negative associations of Creon's role as tyrant are highlighted by
     both Antigone and Haemon. (Cf. lines 566: "Lucky tyrants—the
     perquisites of power! / Ruthless power to do and say whatever
     pleases *them*"). The play thereby celebrates democracy by pre-
     senting the harmful effects of tyranny upon the greater good of
     the city. At the same time, however, Antigone's heroic actions
     are profoundly undemocratic, inasmuch as she places her own
     concerns, and her own royal bloodline, before the concerns of
     the city. See further the discussion in the headnote.]

Further Reading

   See also the reading suggestions under *Oedipus the King* and in the
Anthology, p. 2642.

Blundell, Mary Whitlock. *Helping Friends and Harming Enemies*. 1989.
   Contains a chapter on the ethical problems raised by *Antigone* (pp.
   106–408).

Griffith, Mark. *Sophocles Antigone*. 1999. A commentary on the Greek
   text with an excellent introduction, including a succinct survey of various critical approaches to the play.

Rehm, R. *Marriage to Death*. 1994. On the conflation of wedding and
   funeral rituals in Greek tragedy. Chapter 4 discusses the wedding-
   death in *Antigone*.

Winkler, J. J., and F. I. Zeitlin, eds. *Nothing to Do with Dionysos?* 1990.
   See Zeitlin's "Thebes: Theater of Self and Society in Athenian Drama"
   for further discussion on the role of Thebes in Greek drama.

EURIPIDES

Medea

Backgrounds

   The background for the events of the play is briefly sketched by
Medea's old nurse, who delivers the prologue. The romantic idyll of Jason and Medea (see lines 1–10 and the footnotes to those lines) has
long since come to an end; they are exiles in Corinth, and Jason has
married the daughter of the king, abandoning Medea and his two sons
by her. She is desperate, and the nurse is afraid of what she may do. The
boys' Tutor brings news that the king (his name is Kreon, but he has no
connection with the Creon of the Sophoclean plays) intends to expel
Medea and her children from Corinth; he is afraid of her.
   That his fears are justified is made clear in the next scene; Medea
wins over the Chorus of Corinthian Women by her famous speech
lamenting the subordinate position of women, and it promises not to be-

tray her plans for revenge. Kreon arrives to expel her but is talked into granting her one day's reprieve. That is all she needs, she says, when he is gone; she plans to kill him, his daughter, and Jason (lines 371–72). At this stage she has not yet thought of killing Jason's sons. Jason now comes in to try to offer her financial help in her exile from Corinth, an offer she refuses with contempt in a speech of violent denunciation; he makes a cynical defense of his conduct, but she sends him away with sarcastic wishes for his enjoyment of his marriage and with veiled threats.

One obstacle to her plan for revenge is the fact that if she does succeed in killing Jason and the king and princess of Corinth she will have nowhere to go for refuge; no city will take her in after that. The problem is solved by the chance arrival of Aegeus, king of Athens. He is childless and has been to the oracle at Delphi for advice, but Apollo's reply to his request was obscure and he is on his way to a wise man at Troezen to ask for an interpretation. Medea tells him her troubles and begs him for refuge in Athens, promising that through her knowledge of drugs she can cure his sterility. He offers her a home in Athens, and she makes him swear an oath to confirm this offer. (She does not tell him what she intends to do before leaving Corinth.)

Now she can plan her revenge. She will send the princess a wedding gift—a robe that will kill her and anyone that touches her. But she will also kill the children (line 776). Jason will be left wifeless and childless (lines 787ff.). She sends for Jason, and with feigned humility she plays the part of the submissive wife; Jason, deceived, leaves with the children, who carry the poisoned gifts for the princess. When the Tutor returns with the boys and announces that the gifts have been accepted, she prepares to kill her sons. In a famous monologue (lines 995–1054) she struggles with her own soul, changing her mind and then returning to her original resolution. After the messenger comes to report the hideous deaths of the princess and the king, she goes into the house to complete her revenge; she kills the children.

Jason comes on to save the life of his boys, for the king's friends will kill them otherwise (lines 1279–80), but Medea appears above the house in a chariot sent her by her grandfather the sun god. With her are the bodies of the children. She and Jason exchange reproaches and curses (she prophesies the manner of his death); finally, she leaves for Athens as Jason appeals to Zeus to bear witness to her slaughter of his sons.

Medea, with its concentration on the status of women, their sorrows and crimes, is not unique in Euripides' dramatic oeuvre; in fact he was famous (to some, infamous) for his emphasis on such themes. His *Hippolytus* deals with a stepmother, Phaedra, who falls in love with her stepson; in *Andromache* a barren, jealous wife plans to murder her husband's concubine and her son by him; the *Sthenoboea* had a plot similar to the story of Joseph and Potiphar's wife (see Genesis 39 in the anthology); *Aeolus* dealt with love of brother and sister, and *Auge* with a young woman who bore her illegitimate child in a temple. The comic poet Aristophanes, in his *Frogs*, staged a debate between Aeschylus and Euripides in the lower world (Euripides died just before the play was written) and had "Aeschylus" denounce "Euripides" for his *Phaedra* and *Sthenoboea* and some of his plots in the lines "His nurses go propositioning others / his heroines have their babies in church / or sleep with their brothers" (translated by Richmond Lattimore).

Long before Euripides produced *Medea* (in 431 B.C.), he had been attracted by the tragic possibilities of her story; his first offering at the festival of Dionysus (in 455 B.C.) included a play called *The Daughters of Pelias*, which dealt with Medea's role in the death of Pelias, king of Thessaly (*Medea*, lines 9–10 and the footnotes; lines 474 and 492). This incident was part of a long saga, the story of the Argonauts, which was well known to the audience that saw *Medea*; it is the background against which the drama of *Medea* is played out.

Jason's father, Aeson, was the rightful heir to the kingdom of Iolcus, in the north of Greece near Mount Pelion (line 3), but the throne was usurped by his half-brother, Pelias. Jason, who had been sent off to safety, came to Iolcus when fully grown to claim his rights. Pelias, who had been told by a prophet that his death would be brought about by one of his own kin, persuaded the young man to set off in quest of the fabulous Golden Fleece, which was guarded by a dragon in the eastern kingdom of Colchis (line 2), beyond the Hellespont, on the southern coast of the Black Sea. The king of Colchis, Aietes, was a son of Helios, the sun god (lines 403 and 930); he had a daughter, Medea, and a young son, Absyrtos.

Jason assembled a company of heroes (called Argonauts after the ship *Argo*, the first long-range ship ever built) and set off on his adventurous journey to the east; one of the many dangers he faced was a passage through the clashing rocks (the Symplegades, lines 2 and 423), which may be a mythical representation of the narrow passage of the Dardanelles, the entrance to the Black Sea. In Colchis, Jason had to face a series of ordeals before he could take possession of the fleece. He had to yoke a pair of fire-breathing bulls (lines 466–67), plow a field with them, and sow dragon's teeth. The crop would be armed men whom he would then have to fight. Medea, who had fallen in love with Jason, gave him an ointment that would make him invulnerable, and he came through successfully; he provoked the armed men into killing one another by throwing a stone that each side thought had been thrown by the other.

Aietes suspected Medea's complicity and planned to attack Jason and the heroes in the night. Medea came to warn them, led Jason to the dragon's lair, killed the dragon so that he could take the Golden Fleece (lines 468ff.), and embarked with Jason and the heroes in the night. When Aietes' ships came close in pursuit she killed her brother (line 165) and threw his limbs overboard one by one; Aietes' ships stopped to pick them up. After a long voyage Jason and Medea came to Iolcus, where Medea tricked the daughters of Pelias into killing their father. Jason did not, however, reap the rewards of Medea's action; Pelias' son drove Jason and Medea out of Iolcus, and they came to Corinth as refugees.

Classroom Strategies

One assignment.

Medea repeatedly refers to Jason as her husband (lines 227, 254, 259, 260, etc.) and herself as his wife (line 580), and Jason calls himself her husband (line 1312) and says she was married to him (line 1311). Yet he can abandon her and marry the princess of Corinth; though Medea protests passionately, Kreon and the princess find nothing objectionable in Jason's conduct, and there is apparently no violation of law on his part.

For the Athenian audience this would not have been seen as a contradiction; it was perfectly understandable as a reflection of conditions in their own society. At the time the play was produced, an Athenian citizen's sons could be recognized as citizens themselves only if born of an Athenian mother; "marriage" was a contract entered into by two Athenian families, the bride brought her husband a dowry (which had to be restored if he separated from her), and the purpose of marriage was officially defined as "the procreation of legitimate children." A marriage with a foreign woman was not a marriage in this sense at all; many Athenian men had, in addition to their legitimate wives, concubines who might well be of foreign birth and had no rights. What sort of a marriage ceremony Medea and Jason went through we are not told, but in the eyes of Athenian law it was not binding. Medea can call Jason to witness "the gods whose names you swore by" and "my right hand, and the knees which you often clasped / In supplication" (lines 481–85), but though it is true that he has broken his word, she has no legal hold on him.

Virgil will later make use of a similar situation in the *Aeneid*. Dido considers herself married to Aeneas by the pledge of his right hand (IV.409), but Aeneas does not recognize the bond as legal: "I never held the torches of a bridegroom, / Never entered upon the pact of marriage" (lines 443–44).

Medea has no legal recourse; she has to fall back on cunning and violence.

Topics for Discussion

1. Medea's plan for revenge is not clearly announced until fairly late in the play. Analyze the formation in her mind of the decision to kill the children.

   [The first formulation of Medea's revenge is vague; she asks the Chorus to aid and abet her by silence if she can find a means or devise any scheme "To pay my husband back for what he has done to me, / —Him and his father-in-law and the girl who married him" (lines 259–60). After she has won her day's grace from Kreon, she clarifies her intention: to kill all three of them, "father, the girl and

my husband" (line 371). She does not know how yet; she talks of
the sword (line 375) and of poison (line 381). But she cannot proceed without assurance of a refuge, a city to take her in after she
has killed her enemies. When she is sure of such a refuge at
Athens, promised by Aegeus and confirmed by an oath, her plan is
complete. "I shall tell to you the whole of my plan," she tells the
Chorus (line 756). She will pretend to give way, ask Jason to let the
children take gifts to the princess, poison gifts that will destroy her
and "all who touch the girl" (line 772). She hopes presumably that
both Kreon and Jason will do so. But her revenge now includes the
murder of the children. She speaks of this as specifically aimed
against Jason; Jason, she says, "will pay me the price. . . . For those
children he had from me he will never / See alive again, nor will he
on his new bride / Beget another child" (lines 786–89). Jason, that
is, will remain alive, to suffer the loss of his hopes—his sons who
would prolong his line and preserve his name and memory; he will
suffer also the loss of the hope of new children from his bride.

There has been no overt preparation for this drastic change of
plan; Medea gives no reasons nor does she explain, as Euripidean
characters often do, the psychological process by which she arrived
at this decision. Yet Euripides has in fact prepared the ground carefully, so that the audience can accept this new and dreadful resolve. Right at the beginning of the play, when the audience hears
her hysterical outbursts offstage, she wishes first for her own death
(lines 96ff.), but then, when she sees the children brought into the
house, she turns her despairing rage against them, Jason's sons. "I
hate you, / Children of a hateful mother. I curse you / And your father. Let the whole house crash" (lines 112–14). And the nurse
fears for the children's safety (line 118). When Medea speaks rationally and persuasively to the Chorus, her wild rage against the
children is forgotten.

In her fierce exchange with Jason, however, she hears him speak
with pride of his sons, of the plans he has for their future (which
do not, of course, include her). He has left her, he says, in her best
interests (and the children's). He wants to bring them up "worthy /
Of [his] position (lines 550–51), give them royal stepbrothers by
his new wife, a royal progeny to be brothers for the children he has
now, "a sure defense to us" (lines 584–85). Jason sees the future of
his house in these sons. The point is brought home sharply to
Medea and the audience by the appearance of Aegeus, an old man
who has no sons and who goes from the oracle at Delphi to the
wise man at Troezen in search of some remedy for his childless-
ness, who will promise Medea a refuge in Athens when she offers
to cure his sterility.

It is immediately after this scene that Medea announces her intention to kill the children. She will make Jason a man with no future in his line, a wreck of a man, like Aegeus. She does not
announce this motive; she speaks instead of her inability to save

the children after she has destroyed the king and his daughter (line 776). But when the Chorus asks her if she can really have the heart to kill them, she reveals her true motive: "Yes, for this is the best way to wound my husband" (line 801). In the false submission scene, the children's fate is sealed. For Jason shows how much he loves them, how much he counts on their future: "And of you, children, your father is taking care. / He has made, with God's help, ample provision for you. / For I think that a time will come when you will be / The leading people of Corinth" (lines 890–93). At this point Medea turns white and bursts into tears (line 898); Jason cannot understand why. "I was thinking about these children," she says (line 901).

We know what she was thinking. Jason's devotion to them, his rosy vision of their future career, to be men of influence and his support in old age—all this confirms Medea's feeling that this is in fact the best way to wound her husband. She wavers momentarily from her purpose (lines 1030ff.) but not for long; she kills the boys. And she savors her revenge in her last interview with Jason. She has left him childless, he says, (line 1301); "my life is over!" (line 1325). And she turns the blade in the wound: "The children are dead. I say this to make you suffer" (line 1345). And she reminds him that he will suffer more as time goes by. "I go," he says, "with two children to mourn for." And she replies: "Not yet do you feel it. Wait for the future" (lines 1370–71).]

2. Some critics (Denys Page, for example) refuse to see the play as, in part, a comment on woman's subordinate role in Athenian society; they point out that Medea is a dealer in supernatural poisons who escapes the consequences of her action on a magic chariot, that she is, in fact, an Oriental witch who cannot be regarded as representative of Athenian women. Is such a view justified?

[It is certainly expressed in the play; it is Jason's view: "There is no Greek woman who would have dared such deeds," he says (line 1314), and he calls her "a monster not a woman" (line 1317). It is true that she has at her disposal a poison that seems more magical than real and that she escapes in a chariot that flies through the air. It is also true that she swears by the goddess Hecate, "my mistress, / Whom most I honor and have chosen as partner . . . who dwells in the recesses of my heart" (lines 392–94). Hecate is the mistress of witches in Renaissance literature (she appears on the stage in this role in an interpolation made to Shakespeare's *Macbeth*, for example) and appears in Greek literature from the Alexandrian age (third century B.C.) on as the patron goddess of sorcery. But there is no text from Euripides' time or before to connect her with sorcery. She was a goddess particularly associated with women (and is often identified with Artemis, the protector of women in childbirth) and there was an image of her outside every Athenian house. Medea's invocation of Hecate carries no suggestion of witchcraft.

As for the robe and crown that burst into flames when put on, the audience is not likely to have read any hint of sorcery into it, since such devices are commonplace in mythical tales. In Sophocles' *Women of Trachis* the wife of Heracles sends him a similar robe (she does not realize its potency, but thinks it a love charm), which causes his death by fire, and in Euripides' *Ion* the Athenian princess Creusa uses a poison that is equally magical—a drop of the Gorgon's blood. Poison was in any case the natural recourse of a wronged wife driven to desperate action, for she could not hope to prevail in a contest of strength. The flying chariot is, of course, a gift from Medea's divine grandfather and points up the fact that the Odyssean figure with whom Medea is compared by the proponents of witchcraft, namely Circe, is not a witch at all but a goddess (cf. *Odyssey* X.233).

It is true that in other plays of the period, a lost play of Sophocles, for example, Medea is portrayed as a woman who works her will through drugs and poisons. But Euripides has been careful to avoid giving such an impression. It is noticeable that though his Jason, in the quarrel scene and in their final confrontation, pours out his contempt and loathing for her, he never uses this particular line of invective. Euripides did not want to undercut the effect of Medea's great speech on the position of women by any suggestion that she was not herself a wronged, abandoned woman. She tricks Kreon into giving her an extra day, Aegeus into offering her a refuge, and Jason into accepting the false gifts for his bride not through witchcraft but through purely human cunning and resolution.]

Topics for Writing

1. Medea is a woman, but Euripides has presented her as a figure previously thought of as exclusively male—a hero. Analyze her character in the play as an amalgam of the salient qualities of Achilles and Odysseus.

   [She expresses the heroic creed in lines 791–93: "Let no one think me a weak one, feeble-spirited, . . . but rather just the opposite, / One who can hurt my enemies and help my friends." Such a reputation ensures what Achilles values most—glory. "For the lives of such persons are most remembered," she says (line 794); so Achilles came to fight and die at Troy because his glory would be everlasting (*Iliad* IX.426ff.). When he goes to kill Hector even though he knows his own death will follow, he says: "But now to win glory!" (XVIII.130ff.). Like Achilles (I.181, IX.670), Medea feels dishonored ("slighted," lines 20 and 26; "scorned," line 1329; "insulted," line 591). Like Achilles (I.298, IX.263, IX.704) she reacts with "anger" and "rage" (lines 94, 99, 174), which makes her, like Achilles, impervious to advice, to appeals to reason, or to pleas for moderation (cf. Achilles in *Iliad* IX and Medea at lines 29ff.

and 827ff.). To others her rage seems like that of a wild beast ("wildness," line 103); she is "like a lioness guarding her cubs" (line 188). So Achilles makes his spirit "savage" (IX.648) and refuses to bend, "As savage as a lion bristling with pride, / Attacking men's flocks to make himself a feast" (XXIV.46–47). Both Medea and Achilles sacrifice the lives of their own people in their fury for revenge (Medea, the children; Achilles, his fellow Achaeans), and both become inhuman in their rage (Achilles: "I wish my stomach would let me / Cut off your flesh in strips and eat it raw," XXII. 384–5; Medea: "O your heart must have been made of rock or steel," sings the Chorus, line 1254, and "A monster not a woman, having a nature / Wilder than that of Scylla in the Tuscan sea," says Jason, lines 1317–18—cf. *Odyssey* XII.242ff.).

The resemblances between Medea and Odysseus are clear and abundant. She from the beginning of the play and he from the moment he loses his crew are absolutely alone, dependent on their wits and courage; no help comes from their protecting gods either, until Odysseus reaches Ithaca and is met by Athena, and until Medea, her purpose accomplished, is given the winged car. Both play on the guillibility of their enemies, who do not realize that they are being deceived; Odysseus fools the Cyclops as Medea does Kreon and Jason. Both assume humiliating disguises: Odysseus as the beggar in his own house; Medea, in her second scene with Jason, the role of fulsomely flattering obedient wife. Both of them triumph over their enemies in a bloody revenge that more than compensates for their sufferings—seems, in fact, to go too far.]

2. Medea is a foreigner, an Oriental princess, and Jason, as well as some modern critics, attributes the ferocity of her revenge to the fact that she is a "barbarian." How does the contrast between barbarian and Greek function in the play?

[The idea that Medea is a "barbarian" is in fact peculiar to Jason; even Kreon, who fears her, does not speak of her in such terms. Jason, in the quarrel scene, reminds her that she owes him the privilege of living in a civilized society: "instead of living among barbarians, / You inhabit a Greek land and understand our ways, / How to live by law instead of the sweet will of force" (lines 524–26). Medea, of course, has no reason to congratulate herself on living "by law," a law that allows her husband to abandon her; she later reproaches herself for trusting "the words of a Greek" (line 785). And Jason will later lament the day he brought her to Greece. "Now I see it plain, though at that time / I did not, when I took you from your foreign home / And brought you to a Greek house" (lines 1304–6). He should not have married a barbarian: "There is no Greek woman who would have dared such deeds" (line 1314).

The Chorus, however—who is appalled at her intention to kill the children (lines 795ff. and 827ff.) and prays to Earth and Sun to stop her (lines 1225ff.)—never for one moment speaks of her as a barbarian. When she makes her opening appeal for its sympathy (lines 212ff.) she speaks as a Greek wife addressing Greek women; her problem is the Chorus's. And though the Chorus rejects the murder of the children (but not that of the king and his daughter), it understands the desperate rage that prompts it. Far from saying that no Greek woman would have done what Medea did, it mentions one, Ino, who "laid her hands on her children" (line 1258). She was, it says, the only one, but the audience would have thought of others, too: Agave, of the royal house of Thebes, who, under Dionysiac possession, helped tear her own son Pentheus to pieces; Procne, who, to punish her husband for raping her sister, killed her son Itys and served his flesh to his father.

Medea, who sacrificed family and country to save Jason's life, is labeled a barbarian—called unfit for civilized Greek society—by the very man she tried to help. His cynical betrayal raises grave doubts about the civilization he claims to speak for.]

Comparative Perspectives

1. The protagonists of ancient literature often struggle with the decision to murder a child.

    a. Compare the motives that lead Medea to kill her children with those that impel Agamemnon to sacrifice Iphigenia. How does the Chorus in *Agamemnon* treat his decision? How does the Chorus in *Medea* view hers?

    b. Consider the motives that cause Abraham to prepare to sacrifice his son in light of Medea's deliberations, and contrast the different means by which (and degree to which) Euripidean drama and biblical narrative permit access to the thought processes of these tortured parental figures.

2. Compare Jason's abandonment of his wife and family with Aeneas's abandonment of Dido. What ancient views of sexual passion may be perceived in *Medea* and the *Aeneid*? How would you contrast these views with those that dominate medieval romances such as Malory's *Morte Darthur*?

Further Reading

See also the reading suggestions in the *Anthology*.

Bloom, Harold. *Euripides.* 2003. Assembles a number of brief critical views on *Medea* by leading scholars.

Conacher, D. T. *Euripidean Drama: Myth, Theme and Structure.* 1967. Pp. 183–98. A challenging analysis of the play, which is discussed as "realistic tragedy," as opposed to "mythological tragedy," that is concerned with "the individual in relation to the gods."

Mitchell-Boyask, Robin, ed. *Approaches to Teaching the Dramas of Euripides.* 2002. Ranges from essays on practical and theoretical consid-

erations, to classroom approaches, to specific Euipidean plays and issues (includes an article by Laurel Bowman on "Women and the
Medea").

Euripides' Medea. Introduction and commentary by Denys L. Page.
1938. This Greek text with commentary contains an eloquent introduction that puts the play in the context of its time and states the
classic case for Medea as barbarian witch (pp. xvii–xxi).

Schlesinger, Eilhard. "On Euripides' *Medea*." In *Euripides: A Collection
of Critical Essays*, edited by Erich Segal. 1968. Pp. 70–89. An essay
(translated from the German) that deals especially with the problems
posed by the ending and uses a comparative approach (Goethe,
Corneille, and Anouilh, for example, are cited) to throw light on the
Euripidean play.

ARISTOPHANES

Lysistrata

Backgrounds

Lysistrata, an Athenian wife whose name means "disbander of
armies," comes on stage expecting the arrival of other Athenian women
whom she has summoned to an important meeting. She also expects
some women from Sparta, a city with which Athens has been at war for
twenty years. When everybody has arrived she announces her plan: a sex
strike of the women on both sides to force the men to make peace. In
spite of their initial reluctance she persuades them to swear an oath to
refrain from sex with their husbands.

Meanwhile, another group of Lysistrata's women friends has seized
the Akropolis in Athens; the Athenian women on stage leave to join them
while the Spartan women go home to organize the strike in Sparta. A
Chorus of Men enters; it is on its way to the Akropolis to force an entry
or, if repelled, to smoke the women out with the timber and fire pots the
men are carrying. The Chorus is met, however, by a Chorus of Women
carrying water to put the fire out; the contest between the two choruses
is interrupted by a magistrate, who takes charge of the operations
against the Akropolis gates.

But Lysistrata comes out to parley, and in a spirited exchange with the
magistrate she gets the better of the argument. After another rowdy altercation between the two choruses, Lysistrata comes on again; her
troops are trying to desert under various pretexts—what they really want
is to go home to their husbands. She restores their morale, and they go
back to the Akropolis.

At this point, an Athenian husband, Kinesias, arrives; he is in a visibly
excited state and demands his wife, Myrrhine. In a ribald, comic scene
Myrrhine teases Kinesias with the prospect of sexual enjoyment but in
the end leaves him still frustrated. As he goes out, a Spartan Herald arrives, also visibly excited, looking for the Athenian Council of Elders; ev-

idently the Spartan women have not let the side down. The Athenian magistrate tells him Athens is ready to make peace; Sparta is to send ambassadors with full powers to negotiate.

After some more choral song, a delegation of Spartans enters; the Spartans too are in desperate condition. Under the guidance of Lysistrata, who prevents disputes over small points in the treaty from becoming major problems, peace is made and the end of the war celebrated with a banquet.

When this comedy was produced in 411 B.C. there was considerable war-weariness in Athens. The war, which began in 431, ended in a truce in 421, but this was not, in fact, the end of hostilities; Athens and Sparta fought each other indirectly through and sometimes directly with their allies, and in 415 Athens had launched a huge expedition westward with the aim of conquering the rich Greek colonies in Sicily. This expedition ended in disaster and inflicted huge losses in ships and men; the Spartans soon resumed hostilities against Athens as Athenian subject allies in the Aegean tried to secede from the empire.

This was not the first Aristophanic comedy to deal with the folly of the war and to express, in fantastically comic terms, a serious wish for peace. In 425 Aristophanes had produced a play called *The Acharnians*, in which a citizen who is fed up with the war makes a separate peace with the Spartans and proceeds to enjoy, in the midst of the Athenian war shortages, an abundance of luxury imports, not to mention exemption from military service. In *The Peace* (421), produced as the first ten years of hostilities came to an end, an Athenian citizen flies up to Heaven on a giant dung beetle to demand that Zeus put an end to the war. *Lysistrata* plays on the same wish, which must have been widespread in Athens, for a return to more peaceful days.

Nevertheless, the war went relentlessly on; even when the Spartans, on several occasions, proposed a truce on unexpectedly favorable conditions, the political leaders of the democracy rejected them and Athens finally went down to complete defeat in 404 B.C.

Aristophanes' comedies are not to be regarded as political propaganda on behalf of a particular group or party. It was the function of comedy to provide a momentary relief from everyday cares through fantastic visions of freedom, abundance, and self-indulgence. The action was always something that could not possibly happen in real life: the private citizen making a separate peace, a ride to Heaven on a dung beetle, or concerted political action on the part of Athenian women, who had no public function at all and played a subordinate role in private life as well. Athenian comedy did, however, comment freely and satirically on public affairs, and it used humor to make its audiences think. It embodied the energy of Athenian democracy.

Classroom Strategies

One assignment.

The sexually explicit jokes and action (the Kinesias scene, for example) should not mislead the modern reader into thinking of the play in terms of pornographic shows or "adult movies." Comedy in Athens was part of a religious festival; the low jokes and obscene gestures of the comic actors were just as much a part of the celebration of the god Dionysus as the dignified language and formal movements of the tragic stage. Dionysus was originally a god of vegetation (and not just of the vine); tragedy perhaps represented the flowering and inevitable death of all things, comedy the fertility of the natural world.

The comic actor wore, as part of his costume, the ancient symbol of fertility, the *phallos*, a leather replica of the male sexual organ. The joking remarks about the excited state of the Spartan ambassadors at the end of the play had their visual corroboration on stage, and it is not hard to imagine what a comic actor could do with this apparatus in the Kinesias scene. This kind of horseplay was native to the comic genre. In Aristophanes it is used with keen wit and to dramatic and thematic effect.

Topic for Discussion

Both *Medea* and *Lysistrata* deal with, among other things, a conflict between men and women and exploit the contrast between their situation and aspirations. But though the two dramatists develop many of the same major themes (and even sometimes coincide in choice of minor details) the two plays are worlds apart: the same basic material from which Euripides produces his shocking tragic effect serves Aristophanes for a series of comic scenes culminating in a happy ending—conciliation and a return to normality.

[Both protagonists are women of courage, determination, and keen intelligence. Medea's speech to the chorus, appealing to their consciousness of woman's unhappy condition, is as perfectly adapted to the situation as the repudiation of her reputation as a woman of intellect (lines 290ff.) in her plea to Kreon or as her assumption of the role of repentant wife in her deception of Jason. Lysistrata displays the qualities of a leader in her organization of the conspiracy in the opening scene and in her argument with the magistrate. Especially when she gives her recipe for managing the affairs of Athens and "cord[ing]" out the knots of the war (lines 602 ff.), she shows a statesmanlike intelligence beyond anything the fatuous magistrate she opposes could even imagine. Both heroines lament the subordinate lot of women—Medea in lines 229ff. and Lysistrata when she details the effects of war on the women of the city (lines 625–28)—but Medea's speech ends with her plea to the Chorus to abet her in her bloody revenge while Lysistrata's argument leads up to a ribald joke on the part of the magistrate, in return for which Lysistrata and the women's Chorus treat him like a corpse. Both Medea and Lysistrata speak of woman's nature as centered on love and sexual passion. "Once she is wronged in the matter of love," says Medea, "no other soul can hold so many thoughts of blood" (lines 264–65), and Jason sees woman's nature in the same terms: "You women have got into such a state of mind / That, if your life at night is good, you think you have / Everything; but, if in that quarter things go wrong, / You will consider your best and truest interests / Most hateful" (lines 557–61). He does not realize the meaning the audience will attach to these words: Medea will sacrifice her "best and truest interests"—her children—to punish him. In *Lysistrata* the same Greek cliché about woman's nature has no such tragic overtones, but is instead the base for coarse innuendo ("Is it a big one?" lines 20ff.), for the wholesale desertion on the part of Lysistrata's supporters when she tells them her plan, and for the series of preposterous excuses the women give as they try to escape from the Akropolis and go home to their husbands: "I've got some Milesian wool in the house, and the moths are chomping it all up," "the flax! / I forgot to shuck it," "I'm about to deliver a child!" (lines 743–62).

Each play has a scene in which the heroine administers a solemn oath. Medea makes Aegeus swear by Earth and Sun, repeating the words after her, that he will give her refuge in Athens when she leaves Corinth (lines 730ff.). Lysistrata binds the women, by an oath on a cup of wine, to repeat after her a series of promises to refrain from all manner of sexual enjoyment (lovingly described in detail, in lines 215–47) until their husbands consent to make peace.]

Topic for Writing

In an earlier comedy Aristophanes has one of his characters draw attention to the underlying seriousness of the action by claiming that even comedy (in spite of its buffoonery) can deal with questions of right and wrong. What serious issues are being explored beneath the ribald surface of *Lysistrata*, and how are they expressed?

[The main issue, of course, is the folly of continuing a war between Greeks that has gone on indecisively for so many years. There are serious obstacles to making peace and Aristophanes, right in the middle of the burlesque scenes of the women's oath-taking, brings them to the fore. The Spartan woman Lampito is sure that she and her friends can persuade the Spartans to make a fair and just peace. "But how do you keep Athenian rabble from acting like lunatics?" (lines 173–74), she says. It will be difficult, she says, to convince them: "as long as your battleships are afoot and your Goddess' temple have a bottomless fund of money" (lines 176–77). Lysistrata has already seen to the seizure of the Akropolis and the treasures stored there—the tribute from the subject cities of the Athenian empire. This, of course, is a joke; the fears of Lampito, however, do raise a serious issue.

Though Athens had been reduced to a position of military inferiority by its catastrophic losses of men and ships in Sicily, the Spartans on several occasions showed a willingness to negotiate a peace. The Athenian democratic leaders ("the rabble," as the Spartans thought of Athenian democracy) were unwilling to make the necessary concessions; they still considered their resources in ships and money sufficient to win them victory or at least a position in which they could negotiate from strength. It was in fact this attitude that brought them in the end to defeat and unconditional surrender. Later in the play Lysistrata answers the question—"Where do *you* get off taking an interest in war and peace?" (lines 513–14). She tells how the women would ask their husbands, " 'How did the Assembly go today? Any decision about a rider to the peace treaty?' " (lines 528–29). But all they heard was news of one stupid measure after another. The political content of all this is plain, and when Lysistrata is asked how women can stop all the confusion in the various states and bring them together, she makes her brilliant speech about "card[ing]" out the knots as if the war were a tangled ball of wool and then goes on to give a recipe for cleaning up Athenian politics, including "as for those who clump and knot themselves together to snag government positions, card them out and pluck off their heads" (603–606).

Toward the end of the play Lysistrata delivers a sermon to both sides, reminding them that they are all Greeks and that as they destroy each other, "there are plenty of enemies available with their barbarian armies" (lines 1178–80). And so negotiations for peace begin and, although the give and take of territory between Spartans and Athenians is made wildly and obscenely funny by a series of double entendres, the fact is that the comic stage is presenting to the audience an image of a negotiated peace—something that no politician dared do in the Assembly.]

Comparative Perspective

Although students tend to think they will enjoy a comedy more than a tragedy, they sometimes learn, to their chagrin, that comedy is in many ways harder to understand. Discuss some of the topical allusions in *Lysistrata* and compare them to those in other comic and satiric works (the *Satyricon*, perhaps, or *Gargantua and Pantagruel*). What is the connection between social detail and laughter?

Further Reading

See also the reading suggestions in the *Anthology*, p. 2641.

Easterling, P. E., ed. *Greece*. Vol. 1 of *The Cambridge History of Classical Literature*. 1985. Pp. 355–414. Contains a masterly assessment, written for the classical scholar and the literate general reader, of the whole genre; pp. 370–91 focus on Aristophanes.

McLeish, K. *The Theatre of Aristophanes*. 1980. This is "an attempt to examine the plays from the point of view of a dramatic critic and to try to discover . . . what their effect may have been on their original audience." The approach is by subject, not by individual play, but the index lists all the relevant passages under useful headings.

Whitman, C. H. *Aristophanes and the Comic Hero*. 1964. An analysis of Aristophanes' achievement as the creator of "a new kind of hero, the comic hero, who parodies his two solemn older brothers of tragedy and epic, but at the same time challenges their supremacy in expressing human aspirations in the face of the world's dilemma." Chapter 6 deals with *Lysistrata*.

PLATO

The Apology of Socrates

Backgrounds

Apology is the Greek word for "defense"; this speech is Plato's version of the one in which Socrates defended himself in court against the charges brought by his adversaries. It is divided into three sections, which correspond to the three stages of the trial. The first (17a–35e) is the defense proper; at that point the jury decides on a verdict. Socrates is guilty; it is now up to the prosecutors and the defendant to propose what they think an appropriate penalty. The jury will choose one or the other; no compromise will be made. The prosecution asks for death; Socrates, in the second part of his speech, instead of proposing exile or imprisonment for a few years, makes the outrageous suggestion that he be rewarded as a public benefactor. But he then offers a small fine. He is condemned to death. The last section of his speech (38cff.) is his final address to the court.

In the first and longest part of the speech he deals with the general prejudice against him: the widespread impression that he is a philosophical agnostic and that he is a "sophist"—one who teaches new ideas and rhetorical techniques for high fees. None of this is true. The real reason for his unpopularity, he suspects, is that he has confounded so many Athenians in argument, shown them up as confused and ignorant. In doing so he claims that he was simply trying to test the truth of the god Apollo's statement that Socrates was the wisest of men. He found that men who thought they knew something did not, and so he was wiser than they, since he knew that he knew nothing.

So much for the general prejudice; he turns then on his accusers, who have claimed that he corrupts the youth of Athens, disbelieves in the gods of the state, and introduces new divinities of his own. He cross-questions Meletus, his main accuser, and shows that the charges are invalid. He then announces that he will continue, as he has always done, to question the Athenians about justice and knowledge; this is, he says, his mission in life, imposed by Apollo. This announcement evidently causes an outcry in court, for he asks those present not to interrupt (30c); the jury brings in a verdict of guilty. Socrates' refusal to bargain about the death penalty leads to his death sentence. Socrates prophesies that the Athenians will silence him but will have to listen to younger men who will carry on his mission. He accepts his death calmly, secure in his belief that "no evil can happen to a good man, either in life or after death" (41d).

Plato belonged to an aristocratic Athenian family (he was related by his mother's second marriage to Critias, the leading spirit of the "Thirty Tyrants" who ruled Athens for a short time after the surrender to the

Spartans in 404); while still young (he was born in 429) he became one of the group of Athenian men who spent their time listening to and arguing with Socrates. Though Socrates did not, like the sophists, assume the role of teacher, Plato and his companions were in a real sense his pupils. The execution of his beloved teacher in 399 B.C. left an indelible mark on Plato's thought and writing; in all his philosophical dialogues except the last (*The Laws*) Socrates figures as one of the principals and, in most of them, as the protagonist. The *Apology* is Plato's version of the speech Socrates made before the Athenian court in 399. He was present at the trial (see 38b), and though his version is hardly likely to be a verbatim transcript of Socrates' remarks on that occasion Plato could not afford to make radical additions or subtractions; he was writing for an audience that included the crowds who attended the trial, not to mention the five hundred members of the jury.

The speech defies the conventions of Athenian legal procedure and the rules recommended by the sophists, the professional teachers of rhetoric. Instead of a speech "expressed in elegant language . . ., arranged in fine words and phrases" (17b), Socrates proposes to defend himself in his "accustomed manner"—in other words, in the deceptively simple but actually disconcerting manner that has made him so many enemies among those whose ignorance and intellectual confusion he has often exposed. In fact, after disposing of the popular caricature of him as an atheistic philosopher who teaches immorality for high fees—the Socrates of Aristophanes' comedy *The Clouds* (423 B.C.)—he proceeds to defend the very thing his audience finds most irritating about him: his habit of arguing with all the experts and proving them wrong. He knows that this has made him many powerful enemies but insists that it is a mission imposed on him by the god Apollo. So much for the actual charge brought against him by his accusers—that he does not believe in the gods the city believes in; to these charges he now turns, and in a skillful cross-examination of his chief accuser, Meletus, he demonstrates in his "accustomed fashion" that Meletus doesn't know what he is talking about when he claims that Socrates is corrupting the younger generation. From this point on, instead of trying to win the good graces of the jury, he alienates them by insisting, at great length and with unmistakable sincerity, that since what he has been doing all these years is by command of the god, he will continue to do so as long as he lives. To cease would be impious; it would also be dishonorable.

In the course of this defiant speech he also takes time to answer another unstated charge: that though he is so interested in other people's opinions he never speaks up in the Assembly, never plays his part, like a loyal citizen, in the discussion of public policy. His defense is that if he had done so he "would have perished long ago," for he would never have acted against his conscience, as a man in political life has to do. He cites two cases in which he had to defy in one case public opinion and in the other tyrannical power. Under the democracy, serving—as every Athenian had to sooner or later—on the steering committee of the Assembly, he refused to vote for what would otherwise have been a unanimous (and illegal) resolution, in spite of threats of impeachment. And under the dictatorial rule of the antidemocratic regime set up in Athens after the defeat in 404 he refused to obey an order to arrest a fellow citizen and escaped with his life only because the regime was overthrown soon after.

Plato does not mention the fact that there was a strong popular feeling against Socrates precisely on political grounds. Socrates mentions in his speech the fact that "young people . . . follow me around of their own accord, those who have the most leisure, the sons of the very rich" (23c); this innocuous phrase masks the fact that many of these rich young men were hostile to the democratic regime and one of them, Critias, was later the leading figure among the Thirty Tyrants, who, backed by the Spartan victors, imposed a reign of terror on Athens. This regime had been overthrown by the democrats in 403, but, to avoid a counterterror, the Athenians declared an amnesty (the survivors of the Thirty excepted); no prosecutions for political offenses committed before 404 were to be permitted. The resentment at what many saw as Socrates' responsibility for the education of such men as Critias could not express itself as a political charge; hence the vague indictment under a law against "impiety," which could be interpreted in more ways than one.

Socrates' defiance of the court in his apparently arrogant refusal to bargain by suggesting an acceptable penalty is not hard to understand, since the only penalty the court would have been likely to accept was exile: Socrates would leave Athens for some other city, and the Athenians would have been rid of him without having to put him to death (37c–e). This he refuses to do, just as later, in prison awaiting death, he will reject the offers of his friends to help him escape from Athens. He will remain true to his mission: "the difficult thing . . . isn't escaping death; escaping villainy is much more difficult" (39a).

Classroom Strategies

One assignment if possible; otherwise, divide at 28b, just before the paragraph beginning "But perhaps someone may say."

The student may well get the impression from the *Apology* that Socrates' philosophical contribution is purely negative, that all he does is convince people they do not understand the words they are using when they talk about morality; he himself has no definition to offer, but claims only to know that he himself knows nothing. In the other books of Plato that, unlike the *Apology*, are cast in the form of dramatic dialogues, Socrates emerges in a different light. It is true that he rarely proposes a solution to the dilemmas he uncovers by his questioning, but the dialogues show that his probing questions about the nature of piety, justice, bravery, and all the other moral qualities people think they know the nature of are the necessary preliminary to a definition. Previous philosophers have simply announced their doctrines to the world; the world could take them on or leave them, read them or not. Socrates insisted that true knowledge could not be simply proclaimed and accepted (or rejected); learner and teacher had to find their way, through hard-won agreement on point after point, to definitions they could both accept and act on. This process—*dialectic*, to give it its Greek name—is the so-called Socratic method, and it was, in its time, a startling contrast to the standard procedure of the sophistic teachers, who gave lectures and wrote books but did not expect to be questioned.

But Socrates' contribution was not merely a revolution in method. He was also responsible for a decisive shift in the area explored by philosophy, which had begun in the Greek city of Miletus as an attempt to understand the material universe (Thales, the first philosopher, thought that water was the basis of all matter). Some later philosophers had proposed more sophisticated and complicated answers (two philosophers almost contemporary with Socrates had in fact invented atomic theory), and others wrestled with the philosophical problems inherent in such concepts as being, becoming, and motion. But it was Socrates who brought philosophy to bear on the moral problems of human life, especially on the problem of justice in individual and collective conduct. Philosophy would after him still deal with cosmological, physical, and metaphysical problems, but the question of human conduct would bulk large in the works of Plato, Aristotle (author of the *Ethics*), and the later Epicurean and Stoic schools.

Though Socrates is no aristocrat (in fact his father was a stonemason and he himself, at the time of his trial, was penniless, 31c and 36d), he cites the example of Achilles for his refusal to be intimidated by the threat of death (38c–d) and, after his condemnation, looks forward to meeting, in the lower world, the heroes Palamedes and Ajax (41b). These epic figures seem at first glance strange company for a philosopher whose constant concern was to establish the primacy of justice and righteousness in human conduct, but in fact, in spite of the pride and violence such heroic names conjure up, they are not inappropriate in the context of the speech.

Palamedes was the cleverest of the Greek chieftains at Troy; he was credited with the invention not only of the alphabet and numbers but also of a game resembling checkers with which the Greeks amused themselves when all was quiet on the Trojan front. But he incurred the enmity of Agamemnon and Odysseus by speaking out against the long drawn-out war and calling for an immediate return home. Odysseus framed him: Trojan gold was buried in his tent while he was away and a forged letter from Priam produced to convict him as a Trojan agent. In spite of a brilliant defense at his trial, he was condemned and executed. The story was well known to Socrates' audience; both Sophocles and Euripides (and perhaps Aeschylus as well) had written tragedies on the subject.

The other sufferer from an unjust court cited by Socrates is, however, a very different case. Ajax was the best man among the Achaeans while Achilles was away, Homer tells us in the *Iliad*, and even his enemy Odysseus calls him the noblest of the Danaans after Achilles. When

Achilles was killed and the Achaeans decided to award his arms and armor to the bravest among them, Ajax naturally expected to be chosen, but the judgment went to Odysseus instead. After an unsuccessful attempt to murder Agamemnon, Odysseus, and others whom he regarded as responsible, Ajax killed himself.

When Socrates speaks of talking to Ajax in the next world he is of course recalling to the minds of his hearers the famous passage in the *Odyssey* XI, where Odysseus addresses Ajax but gets no answer. Socrates, as a fellow sufferer, will not be treated so contemptuously. Yet it is a little disconcerting to find the gentle philosopher, whose sharpest weapon was the cut and thrust of his dialectic, associating himself with the primeval violence of Ajax. Just as surprising is his citation of Achilles, whom he actually quotes as an example to follow. Achilles would not let the prospect of certain death deter him from his purpose, which was, of course, to kill Hector and avenge the death of Patroclus: "Let me die immediately . . . once I've given the wrongdoer his just deserts, so that I do not remain here . . . a laughing-stock" (28d). Socrates will not retreat in the face of death either: "wherever someone has stationed himself because he thinks it best, or wherever he's been stationed by his commander, there, it seems to me, he should remain, steadfast in danger" (28d). Socrates remained in his place as a soldier, obeying the orders of the generals elected by the Athenians; now he will remain steadfast in the place ordained for him by the god Apollo, or rather, since this depends on his interpretation of the word of Apollo, in the place that he has chosen himself.

The snub-nosed, poorly dressed old man of seventy, facing adversaries determined to drive him out of Athens or kill him if he will not go, defies them and sees himself, not without reason, as one of the company of heroes whose memory all Greeks held in respect and whose burial places they recognized as holy ground. When he refuses to follow the usual practice of defendants in Athenian courts, to beg for mercy, to produce weeping children and relatives, he speaks in heroic terms, as a man who must be true, like Odysseus, to his reputation, to what the world expects of a hero: "whether truly or falsely, it's firmly believed in any case that Socrates is superior to me by the majority of people in some way" (34e–35a).

Topics for Discussion and Writing

Behind the actual terms of the indictment lay a real prejudice against Socrates as an opponent of democracy, and this was not due solely to his association with such figures as Critias. Can you find in his speech any grounds for such a prejudice?

[His abstention from political activity under a democratic regime that encouraged and depended on full participation by all the citizens. In his defense on this point he actually uses clichés of the opponents of democracy: "The fact is that no man will be spared by you or by any

other multitude of people if he genuinely opposes a lot of unjust and unlawful actions" (31e).

Among the prominent figures he examined and found ignorant were
politicians (21c–22a), that is, the orators whose speeches in the Assembly shaped public policy (cf. Lycon who has a quarrel with Socrates "on
behalf of the rhetoricians," 23e–24a).

When he examines the craftsmen, he finds them, too, wanting: "because he performed his own craft well, each of them also thought himself to be wisest about the other things" (22d). In Athenian democratic
theory an artisan was supposed to have just as much understanding of
public policy and, therefore, just as strong a claim to direct it as, for example, a landed aristocrat.

When he proposes that he be rewarded instead of punished he speaks
of himself as the man who "didn't care about the things most people
care about—making money, managing an estate, or being a general, or
holding some political office, or joining the cabals and factions that
come to exist in a city" (36b). There is clearly a certain dislike for the
political life of Athens expressed in that list and in fact he continues:
"but thought myself too honest, in truth, to engage in these things and
survive" (36c).

Plato himself was no admirer of the democracy that had put Socrates
to death; his picture of Socrates may have been influenced by his own
feelings. But it is quite understandable that a man with Socrates' insistence on universal moral standards should have been disgusted with the
politics of Athens in the last years of the war; it must indeed have
seemed as if the politicians and the assembly that supported them were
bent on self-destruction.]

Comparative Perspectives

1. Socrates, as the headnote informs us, "wrote nothing," yet Plato's
   dialogues capture a defining moment in Greek culture, when oral
   traditions sustained by memorizing poetry like Homer's yielded to
   new styles of thought made possible by the writing of prose. What
   elements of Socratic dialectic seem, on the one hand, to reflect
   spoken discourse? What qualities of abstract thought expressed in
   that speech show, on the other hand, a shift away from the representation of thought through action characteristic of Homeric
   composition? [See, e.g., the opening of the *Iliad*, when the decision made by Achilles not to attack Agamemnon is attributed to the
   intervention of Athena, unseen by others, rather than to any
   process of internal rational analysis.]
2. Look at other philosophical texts of the ancient world (the Book of
   Job, the Sermon on the Mount, the Koran). Which seem primarily
   the record of oral discourse? How does the style of composition appear to affect the nature of the ideas being communicated?

Further Reading

See also the reading suggestions in the *Anthology*.

Guthrie, W. K. C. *A History of Greek Philosophy*, Vol. 4. 1975. Pp. 70–93. An authoritative discussion of the historicity, organization, and ideas of the speech. See also Vol. 3 (1969) on Socrates and the Delphic response (pp. 405ff.) and his political views (pp. 409ff.).

Havelock, Eric A. *The Muse Learns to Write: Reflections on Orality and Literacy from Antiquity to the Present*. 1986.

West, T. G. *Plato's Apology of Socrates*. 1979. A new translation with interpretation. A careful analysis of the speech section with helpful chapters on Socrates as a public man and Socrates as a private man.

West, T. G., and G. C. West. *Four Texts on Socrates*. 1984. Translations of *Euthyphro, Apology, Crito,* and Aristophanes' *Clouds*. The introduction deals with the *Apology*.

ARISTOTLE

Poetics

Backgrounds and Topics for Discussion

The short selection from the work deals with tragedy. It begins with the famous definition of tragedy (for an explanation of the term *catharsis*, see the text), which is explained, section by section, in the following paragraphs. Aristotle recognizes the importance of character in tragedy—the persons represented "must necessarily possess certain qualities of Character and Thought"—but places greater emphasis on the action, the plot. "It is not for the purpose of presenting their characters that the agents engage in action, but rather it is for the sake of their actions that they take on the characters they have." The plot has to have unity (which is not necessarily attained by telling the story of one individual) and the right "magnitude"—a length "sufficient to permit a change from bad fortune to good or from good fortune to bad to come about in an inevitable or probable sequence of events." Plots can be simple or complex; in complex plots the change of fortune involves a reversal or a recognition or both. (The prime example of change of fortune with both is the *Oedipus* of Sophocles.) Furthermore, the change of fortune should be from good to bad, and the victim of this reversal should not be a wholly bad man or a completely good one (for in the one case we would be pleased and in the other merely disgusted) but one "whose place is between these extremes . . . the man who on the one hand is not pre-eminent in virtue and justice, and yet on the other hand does not fall into misfortune through vice or depravity, but falls because of some mistake; one among the number of the highly renowned and prosperous, such as Oedipus." As a footnote explains, the word translated "mistake" is often referred to as "flaw," which suggests a moral defect.

Aristotle's *Poetics* is the first treatise ever written on literary composition (the Greek word *poietes*—poet—means, literally, "maker"); many before him, Plato especially, discussed the nature and effect of poetry but a systematic treatise on the subject was unprecedented. It has had an enormous influence on modern critical approaches to tragic drama; particularly influential in the European Renaissance was the idea of the "tragic flaw," derived from the Greek word *hamartia*, which James Hutton's translation more correctly renders as "mistake." A classic version of this doctrine can be found in Shakespeare, in Hamlet's speech about the Danish nation and their penchant for drink: "So, oft it chances in particular men, / That for some vicious mole of nature in them" (1.4.23ff.).

The *Poetics*, however, was written long after the deaths of the three great tragic dramatists of the fifth century B.C.E. And Aristotle's view of the tragic character as one who "falls by some mistake" is, in most cases, not easily applicable to the plays of Aeschylus, Sophocles, and Euripides. This is a possible theme of discussion with the class: how far does *Oedipus*, for example, Aristotle's famous example of the well-made tragedy, fit the definition? Is Oedipus a man "not pre-eminent in virtue and justice" who "on the other hand does not fall into misfortune through vice or depravity, but falls because of some mistake"? If so, what is the mistake? His whole life seems to be a series of mistakes. It is hard to see how Medea can be understood along the lines of Aristotle's formulation, or Clytemnestra either, but perhaps a case could be made out for Agamemnon. Orestes, who knowingly commits the crime of matricide, escapes this view altogether.

Also essential to Aristotle's conception of tragedy is the recognition, which in what he considers the best type of plot is identical to the reversal of the protagonist's fortune. Oedipus is the classic example: he recognizes himself as the murderer he is searching for and also as a patricide and incestuous son; but recognition plays a part also in the *Oresteïa*: when Clytemnestra recognizes her son's identity, her death is only moments away. Recognition of identity, though it frequently occurs in other Greek tragedies, plays no part in *Medea*; but in a metaphorical sense (one that Aristotle does not express but that he may have realized) recognition is essential to the tragic process. The tragic hero in the end is forced to dispense with illusions of power and claims to godlike superiority; in the reversal of fortune—often brought about, as Aristotle says, by his or her own actions, which produce the opposite of what is intended—he or she is forced to recognize the mortality and fallibility that are conditions shared with all humankind.

The class might also be asked to discuss the plays in the light of Aristotle's concept of unity—the avoidance of plots "in which episodes follow one another in no probable or inevitable sequence" in favor of a "plot so organized that if any one of [the events that are part of it] is displaced or taken away, the whole will be shaken and put out of joint." Many think that *Oedipus* has the most closely logical plot; comparison with *Medea* (how organic is the arrival of Aegeus?) should prove interesting, and all the plays can be examined to see if there is adequate motivation for new entries and developments.

Further Reading

See also the reading suggestions in the *Anthology*, p. 2639.

Aristotle. *Poetics*. Ed. D. W. Lucas. 1968. An edition, with commentary, of the Greek text. The introduction contains a survey of Greek literary theory before Aristotle and valuable appendices: "Pity, Fear and *Katharsis*" and "*Hamartia*."

Aristotle on Poetry and Style. Trans. G. M. A. Grube. 1958. A translation of the *Poetics* and selections from the *Rhetoric*. The introduction deals succinctly and clearly with the problems raised by the text.

Rorty, A. O. ed. *Essays on Aristotle's Poetics*. 1992. A large selection of essays by leading scholars, including examinations of catharsis, pity and fear, *hamartia*, and plot.

BELIEF SYSTEMS OF GREECE AND ROME

Backgrounds

The Greeks knew Homer very well, to the point of being able to recite large sections of the *Iliad* and *Odyssey* from memory, and his work formed the core of their belief system throughout the Archaic and Classical periods and beyond. At the same time, however, new voices were beginning to rise up, first among the Pre-Socratic thinkers and later among thinkers of all kinds, who sought either to challenge Homer's belief system directly or in other cases to modify it. One of the problems that some intellectuals had with Homer was his representation of the gods as capricious beings who were often not only petty and selfish in their actions but immoral as well. Hesiod's great work, the *Theogony*, which told of the origin of the gods and the evolution of the cosmos from Chaos, compounded this problem. Hesiod's gods are so debased as to castrate one another, swallow one another whole, and to attempt to suppress one another in their tyrannical aspirations for power.

Against this backdrop, the work of the Pre-Socratics emerged (not included in the anthology), a group of thinkers from the Ionian region of Miletus in the sixth century B.C.E. The Pre-Socratics were inquirers into the philosophical, scientific, and natural order of things, and their work was wide-ranging and immensely influential. They were the first to directly criticize Homer and Hesiod. One of their number, Xenophanes, wrote, "Homer and Hesiod attributed to the gods everything which in mankind is disgrace and reproach: stealing, committing adultery, deceiving one another," as well as the famous statement that "If oxen, horses, and lions had hands with which to draw and make works like men, horses would represent the gods in the likeness of a horse, oxen in that of an ox, and each one would make for them a body like the one he himself possessed." Although some of the Pre-Socratics, including Xenophanes, composed their treatises in verse, one of the most important breakthroughs for the Pre-Socratics was their use of prose as a form for recording their ideas. As prose developed within several different areas of Greek thought (such as medical writing, rhetoric, philosophy, historiography, and geography) it offered a revolutionary medium for expressing new arguments and belief systems.

Greek historiography began in the late sixth century but did not come to prominence until the work of Herodotus, known as the "father of history" for his monumental achievement in composing the *Histories*, a work that documents the war between Greece and Persia in the first decades of the fifth century B.C.E. Herodotus's work is much more wide-ranging than we would normally expect for historiography, since it encompasses large sections of geography and ethnography, showing a particular concern for the different belief systems and customs of the cultures it records. Herodotus plots his work according to a larger moral order, and he demonstrates how the patterns of history are played out through a series of connected episodes, rather like short stories. (A similar drawing of moral conclusions from history can be seen in the extract from Aeschylus' play depicting one particular aspect of the Persian war.) The next major historian to follow Herodotus is Thucydides, who adopted a markedly different style from his predecessor but who similarly used his work, the *Peloponnesian War*, as a vehicle to express larger theories about the patterns of history. The scope of Thucydides' work is limited to the Peloponnesian war, which he lived through and played a part in (see headnote). His role as an eyewitness of the events of his time are recorded with great care, and his work is a sensitive barometer of public feeling during one particular stage in the Athenians' history (as is particularly notable in his description of the plague).

At the time when Thucydides was writing, sophistry was also taking off in Athens. It is the sophists (itinerant teachers who worked for pay) from whom Socrates is most insistent to distinguish himself in Plato's *Apology* (see 18b, 19b–c, 33a–b). The sophists' inquiries into language and argument led them to be associated with a rejection of received values. They were also famous for postulating the opposition between nature (physis) and convention (nomos) in the Greeks' actions and beliefs. The debated conflation of sophistic thought with Socrates that took place in the fifth century can most clearly be seen in Aristophanes' *Clouds* (not included in the anthology, but mentioned in Plato's *Apology*—see references above). Plato, on the other hand, whose writings take the form of dialogues in which Socrates is the primary interlocutor, had a fixed system of beliefs that was based on the idea of a universal, transcendent good accessible through the practice of philosophy. His *Republic* is a formula for organizing mankind into the society best suited to bringing that "good" to light. Aristotle was a pupil in Plato's Academy for twenty years, but his own ideas depart from those of his teacher on a number of issues, especially in relation to ontology (the investigation into what really exists) and—as we see in this selection—in Aristotle's insistence that the soul cannot be separated from the body (see further discussion in the headnote). Aristotle conducted empirical investigations into the natural world and was a keen student of biology; his scientific outlook informed his approach to philosophy. Yet for both

Plato and Aristotle the idea of a higher form of happiness or goodness was linked to the search for knowledge and wisdom.

Philosophy thrived in the Hellenistic period and a number of philosophical schools developed in response to the earlier teachings of the Greeks. The most prominent of these were the Stoic and the Epicurean schools of philosophy. The best-known Roman Epicurean work is Lucretius's *De Rerum Natura* (*On the Nature of Things*), while the Stoics are well represented in the works of Cicero, Epictetus, Marcus Aurelius (not included in the anthology), and Seneca. Hellenistic philosophy bridged the gap between the thinkers of Greece and Rome, and much of it is a written in response to ideas set in motion not only by Plato, Democritus, and others, but also by Homer and the tragic poets. Through the strength of this movement, it is possible to see how important philosophy was for the ancients in the Classical, Hellenistic, and Roman periods as a medium for expressing their beliefs, and how, in all the selections provided here, the use of philosophy focused on the control of the individual over his emotions, his body, and ultimately his life through philosophical training and practice.

The Greek and Roman philosophers recast the questions that we have already seen emerge in Greek tragedy (can man control his life?; can wisdom save us from suffering?; why does the pious man suffer?) in their own language, and they set out to provide answers to the kinds of questions that Greek tragedy often left unanswered. The belief systems of the Greek and Roman philosophers are extensive in their range, encompassing a moral code by which one can lead one's life, take one's place in society, and (depending on the philosophy) also prepare for death. Lucretius and Cicero provide our earliest surviving examples of Roman philosophy written in Latin, and the Roman philosophers sought to integrate their philosophical beliefs into the social and moral practices of their daily life. Seneca exemplifies a prototypically Roman ideal of the philosopher as statesman and orator, an essentially public figure who practiced philosophy, among other arts like poetry, as part of a cosmopolitan aristocratic identity.

In the work of Apuleius, we see philosophy overlapping with an Egyptian mystery religion, the cult of Isis. In the final book of Apuleius's *Golden Ass*, Lucius's spiritual enlightenment take shape through his vision of an all-encompassing, divine figure whose domain reaches across the entire cosmos. Through the rites of initiation, Apuleius will adopt a wholesale belief system in the form of the religious worship of a single figure. It is important to stress that Isis' cult is one of several different religious systems available to the Greek or Roman in the late second century C.E., and its existence points to the continued diversification of Greek and Roman belief systems.

Classroom Strategies and Topics for Discussion

The readings can be divided into one and a half assignments. This is a large selection of texts which may be confusing and hard to keep straight for students who are unfamiliar with the ancient world. Separating the readings into a Greek and a Roman session should make it easier for them to find their bearings. Plato and Aristotle also form a good bridge between sessions 1 and 2.

Session 1: Hesiod to Aristotle

1. How the Greeks Established a Social and Religious Code
   In this session it is possible to draw on other readings from the anthology to discuss how we can define a set of Greek "belief systems" and where in ancient literature they can most easily be found. Is there anything close to the Hebrew Bible's Ten Commandments in the readings in this section? [This should lead into a discussion of the fact that the Greeks did not have a monotheistic religion, nor did they have anything that came close to a bible]. On the other hand, the Greeks did adhere to a number of strict social and religious practices, and these codes are reinforced in their literary texts. If you have just finished reading *Antigone*, discuss the importance of burial rites in Greek culture, and how their importance is emphasized in the *Iliad* (which ends with the burial rites of Hector), in the burial of Elpenor in the *Odyssey* (whose story is told at X1.48ff.), and in Thucydides' description of the moral chaos that ensues from the piling up of bodies during the plague (book 2). Both the *Odyssey* and *Antigone* use myth to reinforce the belief systems of the Greeks. Through stories that were told and retold from one generation to the next, the lessons of myth reinforced patterns of belief by showing how the failure to comply with religious or moral codes led to serious consequences. Elpenor will never rest until his body is buried; Creon will suffer divine retribution if he does not give the proper funeral rites to Polynices.
   Extending this idea further, discuss what the myths of Hesiod's *Theogony* might have taught the Greeks. [They reinforce the supreme power of Zeus; the divine succession and the story of Pandora justify patrilineal rule; the account of the first sacrifice works as an aetiological myth that explains why the particular customs of sacrifice are carried out.] With the movement toward science philosophy, and history, what replaces myth in the Greeks' ideology and belief system? [Herodotus uses the figure of the "wise man," Solon, to impart Greek (specifically Athenian) superior belief systems to the rich but ignorant barbarian king Croesus, and the events of history bear him out. Thucydides suggests that we can learn more readily from the events of history than we can from myth. Plato and Aristotle create their own world systems through philosophy, and Plato's parable of the cave is akin to several of the new "myths" he created in constructing his ideal city.]
2. Chance and Human Agency
   Discuss Solon's statement (Herodotus I.32) that "humans are the creatures of pure chance." Is this borne out by the other sections

of Herodotus' work and by the other selections of readings for this
assignment?

[Adrastus and Polycrates appear to be powerless to stop the course
of their fortunes, yet Croesus' misfortune, although preordained by
the Fates in recompense for the crime of his ancestors, was partly
brought on by his own actions, and partly mitigated by Apollo due
to the rich offerings Croesus had presented him (see the Pythian
priestess's speech at I.90). Xerxes' yoking of the Hellespont is so
sacrilegious as to strongly suggest that his actions predetermine his
suffering. Aeschylus presents Xerxes' downfall as his own fault in
the *Persians*, when he has Darius proclaim, "My son—young, impetuous, blind—brought these things about," emphasizing that because the Persians dishonored the gods by plundering their
temples, "their suffering matches the evils they did." In Thucydides' description of the plague, he offers only practical reasons for
its outburst (overcrowding and poverty in the city, rumor of well
poisoning, the fact that it had previously occurred in other places).
Although plagues are a recurrent motif in Greek literature as markers of divine displeasure (*Iliad* book 1, *Oedipus the King*,
Antigone), in Thucydides it is only after the plague has caused indiscriminate death that men stop fearing the gods and believing in
notions of right and wrong (paragraphs 52 and 53). In the Melian
dialogue, the two sides disagree as to the securing of divine goodwill (paragraphs 104, 105, and 112). The Melians will lose their
lives or freedom for placing their trust in "divine good fortune;" the
Athenians will eventually lose the war for their imperial arrogance
and disregard for notions of justice. Plato's philosophy adheres to
the principle that men who act wisely will achieve a higher good
(*Republic*, 517 b–c). Aristotle, in the *Nicomachean Ethics*, states
that "life according to reason is . . . the happiest" (1178a).]

Session 2: Lucretius to Apuleius

Topic for Discussion

Lucretius

It has often been noted that Roman literature and thought bear a self-
conscious relationship to their Greek ancestry. Discuss the ways in
which Lucretius seeks to differentiate his philosophy and belief systems
from those of the Greek poets. [Cf. book 1, lines 84ff. (the sacrifice of
Iphigeneia at Aulis. Compare with Aeschylus, *Agamemnon* 217ff.); book
III, lines 977ff. ("fairy-tale Tantalus" does not exist. Compare Homer,
Odyssey XI, 604ff.); book V, lines 1158ff. (the Origin of Religion, especially 1191ff: "Unhappy human race—to grant such feats / To gods, and
then to add vindictiveness!").]

Writing Assignment (all selections)

The Emotions

Using Seneca's *On Anger* as a starting point, discuss the role of the emotions in constructing the belief systems of the Greeks and Romans. You might wish to focus on one emotion, such as anger, or on a cross-section of emotions, such as pleasure, jealousy, pride, anger, fear, curiosity, or despair.

[A contrast should emerge between the philosophical ideal of rational, calm behavior and the emotion-driven responses of gods and men in Hesiod, Aeschylus, Herodotus, Thucydides, and Apuleius (before Lucius receives the vision of Isis). How important are the emotions in imparting a social or religious message? Seneca says there is "nothing useful in anger" and Lucretius claims that most of the things we fear are fabrications. Is this true for all the authors we have studied? Compare Aristotle's assertion that tragedy relied on the twin emotions of pity and fear to impart its message.]

Further Reading

See also suggestions under Aeschylus, Plato, and Aristotle.

Annas, J. *An Introduction to Plato's Republic*. 1981. A useful introduction to Plato's text. See ch. 10 on "Understanding and the Good: Sun, Line, and Cave."

Barnes, J. *Aristotle: A Very Short Introduction*. 2000. A clear and accessible guide to all of Aristotle's major theories and to his relationship to Platonic philosophy.

Braund, S., and C. Gill. *The Passions in Roman Thought and Literature*. 1997. Includes essays on anger, grief, pity, and fear in Roman philosophy and poetry. See the introduction for an account of the emotions in Greco-Roman philosophy.

Cartledge, P. *The Greeks: A Portrait of Self and Other*. 2nd ed. 1993. Intended for the nonspecialist, this book focuses on how the Greeks constructed their identity and ideology in relation to a non-Greek other. Includes important chapters on myth, history, and religion.

Lloyd, G. E. R. *The Revolutions of Wisdom*. 1987. Lloyd is one of the foremost experts on the emergence of Greek science. See chapter 1, "The Displacements of Mythology" on "the invention of the category . . . of the rational" in Greek thought.

Goldhill, S. *The Invention of Prose*. 2002. Divided into sections on Greek history, rhetoric and prose, with a useful introduction and bibliography.

Inwood, B. 2003. *The Cambridge Companion to the Stoics*. Up-to-date articles on all aspects of Stoic philosophy.

Lamberton, R. *Hesiod*. 1990. An accessible and informative guide to Hesiod's poetry.

Sharples, R. W. *Stoics, Epicureans and Sceptics.* 1996. An introduction to the major trends in Hellenistic philosophy.

Taplin, O., ed. *Literature in the Greek World.* 2000. See the essays on Herodotus and Thucydides by Leslie Kurke and on sages, sophists, and philosophers by Andrea Nightingale.

PLAUTUS

Pseudolus

Classroom Strategies and Topics for Discussion

You might want to begin by noting that the first two major comic works in the anthology are plays—*Lysistrata* and *Pseudolus.* It is important for students to understand how staging brings a verbal text to life and how funny Plautus's play is in performance. If you invite a small group of students to the front of the classroom to put on an impromptu short performance, you can make a serious point in the most natural and disarming way: without any prior rehearsal, even the most tentative enactment of a scene demonstrates the social nature of comic interaction. When a class becomes an audience, everyone experiences the power of comedy to bring members of a community together. Inevitably, one laugh begets more laughter, and you are launched on a discussion of why we laugh and why hearing someone else laugh makes us laugh more.

One reason we laugh, of course, is that we recognize the human reality that is exaggerated but not traduced by conventional type characters. Since Plautus, as the headnote points out, is the source of so many Western cultural conceptions about what is funny, you will probably want to examine why people who have no connection with ancient Rome continue to laugh at the definitions of behavior codified by Roman comedy. As always, it is a good idea to look both for the universal truths with which we can easily identify and for the culturally specific materials that require some contextualization. Some attention needs to be paid, therefore, to the satiric portrait of Rome that emerges from Plautus's work.

The play is dominated by the title character, and you should ask your students how they react to Pseudolus himself, perhaps by beginning with the detailed physical description that Harpax gives Ballio (4.7.215–18). Clearly, this is the Roman equivalent of a clown costume. It would be surprising if you have no natural clowns in your classroom, and it will be rewarding for everyone to consider why some people seem to be born with the gift of making others laugh. Why are some people good mimics? What gifts of observation seem to be required of a comic view of life?

This need not involve any profound delving; in fact, a point to make is that the stock figures of Plautine comedy demonstrate little in the way of individualized personality. Perhaps the most interesting psychological questions in this sort of drama involve the audience rather than the persons on the stage. Why does this scruffy-looking slave spend so much time talking to the audience? Pseudolus is only one of a long line of con artists who dare to take viewers into their confidence as they describe their mendacious plots and motivations. Audiences feel flattered by the implied compliment: you, the rogues seem to say, are smart enough to understand me; and, of course, I would never try to put anything over on anyone as smart as you!

In short, in the theater we become complicit with Pseudolus (whom in real life we would probably assiduously avoid) and root for him, even at the point when he is worried by the superior skills of Simia, whose virtuoso turn in Act IV is worth discussion. Other characters directly address the audience as well, notably Ballio in his whip-flourishing entrance. Your students should be asked why the audience is not seduced by the pimp's involving us in his contemptuous assessment of the members of his household—and why it is not offended. The genius of Plautine comedy is that it stylizes the seamy side of transactions such as these so that they do not threaten us.

Neither do the parents and children of the Plautine comic universe command the kind of audience interest or sympathy that we extend to the comic slaves. The *Pseudolus* actually offers rather an attractive version of the blocking father in Simo, not so much because of his paternal care but rather because of his amused acceptance of his clever slave's audacity. Calidorus is a sweetly hopeless youth, and perhaps the most remarkable fact about Phoenicium is that she can write.

It will be helpful to talk about the courtesan as a commodity in Roman comedy and Roman life. Although Plautine comedies center on sexual liaisons, *Pseudolus* contains no "love stories." Ballio is not simply a pimp but a slave trader. In threatening his stable of four "lovely ladies," he individualizes them only to the extent that three of them represent basic food groups: wheat, meat, and oil. Phoenicium, the fourth and the focus of desire in the *Pseudolus*, is identified simply with money. The real love interest of the play, then, is cash. If your students ask about the lines in which Ballio's teenage slaveboy wonders about homoerotic assaults (3.1), or note the way Ballio offhandedly assumes a sexual liaison between Harpax and his captain with the long name (4.7.145–46), you can simply note that these references show how relatively tolerant Rome (and Greece) were when it came to homosexual practices, which were understood as simply one phase of sexual expression rather than as an exclusive, self-defining carnal preference.

In fact, it could be argued that the most intense of bodily pleasures imagined in the *Pseudolus* involve food, not sex. Even in translation, the play's images emphasize gustatory preferences, from the Cook's celebration of spices to metaphors like "a lover who's been found / As empty as a rotten nut" (1.3.272–73) or "I'll bone and fillet him, the way / A cook prepares a slippery eel" (294–95). You may want to mention to your class that comic literature is full of characters whose whole existences, like the Cook's or the pimp's, seem penetrated by their professional activities, since one human foible at which we laugh seems to be tunnel vision. The comic protagonist generally possesses wide-ranging vision, sympathies, or resources; lesser characters are funny because they are stuck in one groove.

Food and sex are, of course, the staples of the rowdy, robust comedy that we associate with many of the authors in the anthology, emphatically including Aristophanes and Rabelais. We laugh at our appetites because we know how hard it is to control them and how they deflate our pretensions. In typical satiric style, bodily functions dominate the characters' experiences of themselves and each other. Ask your students what view of life emerges from the *Pseudolus*, with all its references to sweat, vomit, excrement, and fornication (the kind of references that are part of not only writers' but everyone's comic repertoire—we laugh at our bodies all the time).

Finally, you might consider with your students how the military is represented in the play and why a rigidly organized society like Rome's sanctioned the kind of festal rituals that produced the *Pseudolus*. How often do we get the chance to laugh at soldiers (even Ballio complains of the curtness of Polymachaeroplagides' epistolary manner)? What is the function of a safety valve? What does it mean to "let off steam"? After kicking up his big feet in the brilliant opening scene of Act V, Pseudolus heads "home," content to remain with his "old boss." Why?

In the end, the play is a tribute to the resourcefulness and sheer intelligence of two slaves. The dramatic medium makes it all the easier for Plautus to emphasize their wit. What is conveyed by the gusto with which they sing and dance and comment on their own performances? The headnote to the text provides a valuable discussion of the metatheatrical elements in this play, and you might conclude by asking your students to locate points in the text where they operate. In what sense is Pseudolus an artist? What kind of performer is required by this role?

Topics for Writing

1. Discuss the theatrical possibilities of Ballio's entrance with a whip, or of Pseudolus's final dance.
2. Food imagery in the *Pseudolus*.
3. The clever servant in classical comedy.

Further Reading

See also the suggestions in the *Anthology*.

Lowe, J. C. B. "The Cook Scene of Plautus' *Pseudolus*." *Classical Quarterly* 35 (1985): 411–16. This learned article discusses the Plautine additions to a Greek source, making the interesting observation that, unlike the Greeks, the Romans enjoyed convivial meals at tombsites (which may account for the Cook's advertising the life-prolonging virtues of his cuisine).

Wright, John. "The Transformation of Pseudolus." *Transactions of the American Philological Association* 105: 403–16

CATULLUS

Backgrounds

We know very little about Catullus; almost all that we do know is based on inference from the poems themselves. Luckily, the full collection of 116 poems that has survived the centuries contains many references to identifiable persons and events of his time. Many of them are addressed to men who were prominent in the cultural and political life of the Roman capital; it is clear that Catullus, though born in a provincial city, was well connected and fully at home in sophisticated society. He was also the leading figure in a literary movement, one of a group of young poets the orator and statesman Cicero refers to as "the moderns"; they turned their backs on what had so far been the characteristic media of Roman poetry, national epic, and tragedy, to produce shorter poems, modeled on the work of the Greek poets of Alexandria, full of learned allusions—elegant, witty, and compact. Catullus himself, however, surpasses his models; he can, on occasion, be learnedly allusive, even slightly pedantic, but he can also write about the humors and passions of everyday life with an energy and directness that have their equal only in the poetry of Sappho.

That the real name of his "Lesbia" was Clodia we know from the statement of a later writer, Apuleius (2nd century C.E.). What is not entirely certain is whether this Clodia was the famous—or rather, notorious—daughter of Appius Claudius Pulcher, a former consul and a member of one of the oldest patrician families of Rome. Clodia was married to another Roman aristocrat, Metellus Celer, but during his absence abroad as governor of a province her scandalous behavior was the talk of Rome. She took many lovers; there was even a rumor that she had an incestuous affair with her brother Publius Clodius Pulcher, who, in the last violent years of the Roman Republic's collapse into anarchy and civil war, distinguished himself as the most audacious and dangerous of the political gangsters who terrorized their opponents. When Clodia's husband died in 59 B.C.E. there were many who suspected she had poisoned him. Three years later she was instrumental in having one of her lovers who had broken with her, Caelius, prosecuted for a series of illegal actions. He was defended by Cicero, from whose speech in his defense, *Pro Caelio*, we know the details of the rumors that were circulating in Rome about Clodia's morals. Cicero was delighted to accept the case, since he was one of the principal targets of Clodia's brother and had suffered much at his hands. At one point in his speech he imagines that one of Clodia's most famous ancestors, Appius Claudius, has come back from the dead to reproach her. "Was it for this that I built the first aqueduct to bring water to Rome, so that you could use it to wash after your debauches? Was it for this that I built a road [the Via Appia] so that you could travel on it with packs of other women's husbands?" Cicero does not forget, either, to make good use of the rumors that one of her lovers was her brother.

This trial took place in 56 B.C.E.; Clodia's liaison with Caelius had lasted about two years. The latest event mentioned in Catullus's poems occurred in 55 B.C.E.; it seems probable that he died in that or the next year. His affair with Clodia must then have taken place before 54 B.C.E. Though we cannot be absolutely certain of the identification, some of the things Catullus says about *his* Clodia (for example, the adulterous emotions described in poem 83 and the accusations of promiscuity in poems 8, 11, and 58) correspond well with Cicero's picture of the woman. It remains open to debate, however, how much we should interpret Catullus's "Lesbia" as a real, historical person and how much she is a figure of poetic convention.

Topics for Discussion

1. Catullus had read and translated poems by Sappho. In what ways can one see evidence of a tradition of European love poetry in formation?
2. In poem 76, Catullus looks back on the pain of his love for Lesbia, using imagery of hunger and sickness, and tries to find some way to transcend his bitterness. In his own way, Catullus fuses convention and personal experience and produces verse that seems absolutely "sincere." What does this ability suggest about the function of poetry in Augustan Rome?

Further Reading

See also the reading suggestions in the *Anthology*, p. 2640.

Cicero. *The Speeches. Pro Caelio etc.* (Loeb Classical Library). 1958.

Contains a translation of *Pro Caelio*; for Clodia, see pp. 445–53.

Kenney, E. J., ed. *Latin Literature*: Vol. II of *The Cambridge History of Latin Literature*. 1982. Pp. 198–200.

VIRGIL

The Aeneid

Backgrounds

Aeneas, a Trojan prince in flight from the Greek sack of Troy with his father, his young son, and the statues of his household gods, sails west in search of the new home promised him by the gods in a score of prophecies. Virgil opens his narrative at a moment when Aeneas has almost reached his goal—the plain of Latium in Italy, where he will eventually found a city, Alba Longa, from which will come after his death the founders of Rome. Aeneas and his fleet are off Sicily, almost in sight of their destination, when Juno (the Roman equivalent of Hera), who hates even the survivors of ruined Troy, sends a storm to scatter the ships.

Aeneas, with his ship, is driven south to the African coast, to the territory of Dido, queen of Carthage, a new city for which Juno plans a glorious future as master of the Mediterranean world (the same destiny

Jupiter [Zeus] and Venus [Aphrodite] plan for Rome). While Juno attempts to thwart the Trojans' progress in book I, Venus attempts to help them. She ensures that Aeneas heads on the right path to Carthage (by appearing to him in disguise as a hunting girl) and later in book I she contrives to have Dido fall in love with her son. In conversation with Jupiter, Venus extracts from the leader of the gods a restatement of his promise to help the Trojans, who are destined to become "Lords of the world, the toga-bearing Romans" (I.379). But book I looks toward a Trojan past as much as it does to a Roman future. On the one hand, Aeneas's observation of the brand new city of Carthage (576ff.) foreshadows his own eventual founding of a city in Italy, but on the other, a mural on the new temple of Juno depicting the Trojan War draws his eye; he avidly follows the narrative of this mural (619–75), and even queen Dido's beauty cannot avert his gaze from it. Manipulated by Venus and her son Desire (Eros), Dido falls in love with Aeneas and offers him a partnership in the city that she is building. At a banquet she gives for them, Aeneas is prevailed on to tell the story of his wanderings since he left Troy. That story is told, in flashback, in books II and III.

Aereas begins (book II) with the fall of the city: the Greek stratagem of the wooden horse; the lying story of Sinon that tricks the Trojans into admitting it to the city; the fate of Laocoön, who warned against it; and the night assault of the Greeks, led into the city by the Greek warriors concealed in the horse. Aeneas fights but in a losing battle; he sees Priam killed at the altar of his palace by Neoptolemus, son of Achilles, and returns to his own house, where he collects his father, Anchisës, his wife, Creusa, and his son, Iulus, and leads them out of the burning city. On the way, Creusa is lost; her ghost appears to him, urging him on and promising him a kingdom in the west. From Troy, Aeneas sets sail and, after a series of adventures like those of Odysseus (one of them in fact is a meeting with a cyclops), reaches Sicily, where his father, Anchisës, dies. (These travels, the material of book III, are not included in the anthology.)

Book IV opens with Dido passionately in love with Aeneas; during a hunt they are overtaken by a storm and shelter alone in a cave. There they become lovers but, though Dido regards her union as a marriage, Aeneas will later insist that it is not binding. For meanwhile the gods who have imposed on Aeneas the responsibility for Rome's future have become impatient with his long stay at Carthage and his cooperation with Dido in the foundation of Carthage, a city that will one day be Rome's mortal enemy.

Jupiter sends Mercury (Hermes) to order him to put to sea. As he prepares to obey, Dido summons him, pleads with him, denounces him, and threatens him—all to no avail; he must obey the commands of Heaven, think of his son and the kingdom he is to inherit in Italy. As Aeneas puts out to sea, Dido, after cursing him and promising unceasing war between her descendants and his, kills herself. In book V (not in the anthology) Aeneas, back in Sicily, holds funeral games for Anchisës (like those Achilles held for Patroclus in the *Iliad*) and then sails for Italy.

There, in book VI, he is led by the Sibyl down to the realm of the dead, where he sees, as Odysseus does in book XI of the *Odyssey*, the great sinners and great men of the past but also, unlike Odysseus, the great men of the future, who will impose Roman dominion on the whole of the known world.

In books VII and VIII (not in the anthology) the Trojans become involved in a war with the Italians, who are roused to battle by Juno, anxious to forestall the foundation of the city that will be the rival and conqueror of her favored Carthage. At the end of book VIII Venus brings to her son Aeneas, as Thetis brought to her son Achilles in the *Iliad*, armor newly forged by Vulcan (Hephaestus); on the shield (cf. the shield of Achilles) Vulcan has depicted the glorious exploits of the Roman descendants of Aeneas. Books IX–XI (not in the anthology) follow the ebb and flow of battle, which end (Book XII) with the death of Turnus at the hand of Aeneas and Juno's acceptance of the Roman destiny. She accepts on the condition that the Trojans, whom she still hates, abandon their language and nationality and merge their identity in the new Roman nation that is to conquer the world.

In book XX of the *Iliad* (not in the anthology) the Trojan prince Aeneas, whose mother was the goddess Aphrodite, fights with Achilles; he is rescued from certain death by the god Poseidon because "it is destined that he shall be the survivor." He is to found a royal house that will reign over the Trojans in time to come. Later poets developed this mysterious prophecy into a story of Aeneas's escape from Troy, carrying his old father Anchisës on his back, and other poets made him the leader of a westward voyage with his family and his household gods in search of a place to found a new Troy. When in the third century B.C.E. the Romans came into contact with Greece, they admired and imitated its arts and literature, but had to subdue the Greek cities by force of arms. The Roman wish to find a place for themselves in the Greek epic and historical tradition without claiming kinship with the subjected and despised Greeks of their own day was granted by the creation of the legend that Aeneas the Trojan was the founder of the Roman nation. This story was given literary form in the epics (now lost) of the Latin poets Naevius and Ennius (third century B.C.E.) and was in Virgil's time the authorized version of Rome's origins. Augustus, the first Roman emperor and Virgil's patron, had the temple of Athena at Troy rebuilt on a magnificent scale.

Virgil was recasting the traditional Roman story in what was to be its enduring form, a restatement of national ideals, for the new age of peace and prosperity under the rule of Augustus, who had finally brought peace to a world that had been racked for over a century by civil war.

Augustus was intensely interested in Virgil's poem; we know that parts of book VI (the visit to the underworld) were read aloud to him by the poet himself and when Virgil, dying before he could put the last touches on the work, ordered his friends to burn it, Augustus intervened to preserve the poem.

The poem is, in a sense, officially inspired, but it does not read like propaganda. The sacrifices Aeneas has to make to fulfill his god-given mission are so great that some readers have even seen the poem as a muted repudiation of imperial Roman values. This is an exaggeration, but there is no question about the sacrifice the imperial mission involves, both for the hero and for the Roman people. Aeneas not only has to abandon the great love of his life but also will die before he has time to enjoy the promised reward, the city from which will come the founders of Rome. Dido's dying prayer to her gods will be answered. If, she says, he is indeed destined to land in Italy,

> yet all the same
> When hard beset in war by a brave people,
> Forced to go outside his boundaries
> And torn from Iulus, let him beg assistance,
> Let him see the unmerited death of those
> Around and with him, and accepting peace
> On unjust terms, let him not, even so,
> Enjoy his kingdom or the life he longs for,
> But fall in battle before his time and lie
> Unburied on the sand!
>
> (IV.823–32)

Aeneas does indeed find himself hard beset in war; books VII–XII are a Virgilian *Iliad* in which Aeneas and his Trojans fight against Turnus, a new Achilles. He does indeed have to leave his son, Iulus, and go begging for help from neutral Italian tribes. He loses allies in battle, chief among them young Pallas, for whose death he takes revenge on Turnus in the last lines of the poem. He accepts a peace that, if not unjust, is at least a compromise: the bargain made by Jupiter with Juno that the Trojan name will vanish in the fusion of Aeneas's people with the Latins. And after a few years at the head of his new kingdom he is to be killed in battle; his body will not be found. Greatness, Virgil is suggesting, calls for almost unbearable sacrifice. And the Romans who later carry on Aeneas' line will have to make sacrifices, too. Anchisēs, in the world of the dead, spells out the Roman destiny for Aeneas:

> Others will cast more tenderly in bronze
> Their breathing figures, I can well believe,
> And bring more lifelike portraits out of marble;
> Argue more eloquently, use the pointer
> To trace the paths of heaven accurately
> And accurately foretell the rising stars.
> Roman, remember by your strength to rule
> To pacify, to impose the rule of law,
> To spare the conquered, battle down the proud.
>
> (VI.848–57, not in the anthology)

The "others" who perfect the creative arts and sciences of peace are the Greeks; the Roman destiny is war and rule over peoples. The contrast is more emphatically expressed in the original Latin: the address to the Roman begins, *At tu romane memento* ("But you, Roman, remember"). The imperial destiny excludes the arts of peace. Virgil himself was an intellectual who studied philosophy, a poet steeped in the literature of Greece and Rome; his heart was with those "others," and he above all men realized what had to be given up if men were to become Romans.

Classroom Strategies

Suggested assignments:

1. Books I and II
2. Book IV
3. Books VI, VIII, and XII

or

1. Books I, II, and IV
2. Books VI, VII, and XII

Virgil, unlike Homer, thinks always in terms of history, of the rise and fall of nations and in particular of the rise of Rome. His characters and incidents have not only their dramatic present intensity, they are invested also with a wealth of symbolic correspondences to history, past and future. The student will need some background in Roman history to appreciate the significance, to take one example, of Dido's great curse on Aeneas. She appeals to her people, the Tyrians, the Carthaginians,

> besiege with hate
> His progeny and all his race to come:
> Make this your offering to my dust. No love,
> No pact must be between our peoples; No,
> But rise up from my bones, avenging spirit!
> Harry with fire and sword the Dardan countrymen
> Now, or hereafter, at whatever time
> The strength will be afforded. Coast with coast
> In conflict, I implore, and sea with sea,
> And arms with arms: may they contend in war,
> Themselves and all the children of their children!
> (IV.834–44)

Every Roman who read these lines remembered the history of the wars that, after threatening the existence of Rome itself, extended Roman power overseas from Italy and launched the city on the path to world empire. They were called the Punic (that is, Carthaginian) wars, and there were three of them.

The first began in 264 B.C.E. as a Roman attempt to restrain Carthaginian expansion in Sicily. To win the war, however, the Romans, who had never had a navy, found themselves compelled to become a seapower to deal with Carthaginian control of the sea between Italy and Africa. They did so and, in what was mainly a naval war ("Coast with coast / In conflict . . . sea with sea"), they eventually forced Carthage to evacuate Sicily and pay an indemnity.

The war lasted twenty-three years; a little more than twenty years later (218 B.C.E.) the Second Punic War began. In the interim, the Carthaginians had built up a base in Spain; when the Romans tried to check their expansion there, the Carthaginian general Hannibal led his forces through Spain and southern France, over the Alps, and down into Italy. He defeated one Roman army after another and laid waste Italy with fire and sword ("rise up from my bones, avenging spirit! / Harry with fire and sword the Dardan countrymen"). But he was unable to assault the fortified city of Rome itself, or to break the loyalty of the Italian fortified cities to Rome, and in the end, when the Roman general Scipio drove the Carthaginians from Spain and then invaded North Africa, Hannibal came home to Carthage, only to be decisively defeated by Scipio in 202 B.C.E.

Carthage was forced to give up Spain (which became a Roman province), surrender its fleet, and pay an indemnity. But in the next few decades it began to gain strength again, and in 149 B.C.E. the Romans began the Third (and last) Punic War. Carthage was invaded, the city stormed and then (146 B.C.E.) utterly destroyed; the Romans ran plows over the ruins of the city. Africa became a Roman province.

All this, and more besides, was evoked for the Roman reader by the lines of Dido's curse, and this is typical of Virgil's poetic practice throughout. Dido herself, for example, would recall to the Roman reader another African queen, Cleopatra of Egypt, who had ensnared with her love Mark Antony, Augustus's rival for supremacy in the Roman world. Aeneas, abandoning his mission and helping to build Dido's Carthage, would remind the Roman readers of Antony, who, reveling in the delights of Cleopatra's Alexandria, lost a world for love; this would deepen their sense of the danger Aeneas was courting by his delay at Carthage. The subdued reference comes clearly to the surface when, on the shield of Aeneas in book VIII, we see Augustus, the descendant of Aeneas, facing in battle Antony, the renegade Roman who marshals against Rome the power of the East "And in [whose] wake the Egyptian consort came / So shamefully" (VIII.106–7).

Topics for Discussion

Virgil deliberately models his poem on Homer; the first six books are Aeneas's *Odyssey*, the last six his *Iliad*. Sometimes specific incidents from Homer are imitated; yet though the relation to the model is in every case clear, Virgil makes the material serve his own, different purpose. Discuss the nature effect of the Virgilian adaptation of the following.

1. Odysseus's interview with Ajax in book XI of the *Odyssey* for Aeneas's interview with Dido in book VI of the *Aeneid*.

   [In both cases the hero makes an appeal for reconciliation with a suicide who has reason to feel wronged by him, but the appeal is rejected in silence. Odysseus, however, does not really admit that he was responsible; he wishes the Greeks had not given him the arms of Achilles as his prize but does not say that in fact they should have gone to Ajax. He blames the whole thing on Zeus ("Zeus sealed your doom," *Odyssey* XI.640). Aeneas too puts the responsibility on the gods (*Aeneid* VI.245), but in this case we know that he did indeed have direct orders from Jupiter, brought by Mercury, and furthermore that the fate and future of a great nation rested on his decision. For Odysseus the silence of the shade of Ajax is a minor matter: "Yet now . . . he might have spoken to me, or I to him, / but the heart inside me stirred with some desire / to see the ghosts of others" (*Odyssey* XI.646–49). Odysseus and Ajax in life were fellow soldiers, rivals for rewards and glory, but Aeneas loved Dido, and her silent, hostile rejection of his plea brings him to shed the tears he held back when they parted at Carthage. Unlike Odysseus, who let Ajax go, "Aeneas still gazed after her in tears, / Shaken by her ill fate and pitying her" (*Aeneid* VI.263–64).]

2. Homer's description of the shield of Achilles in the *Iliad* (XVIII.515ff.) for Aeneas's shield in the *Aeneid* (VIII.24ff).

   [The parallelism of the contexts is close; the mother goddess in each case brings armor made by the divine smith for her son to use against his enemy (Hector, Turnus), and each hero delights in the splendor of the arms. But the shields present two different worlds. Achilles' shield is an image of human life as a whole, of cities in war and at peace, of work on the land and the dance at the palace—a world that has no past or future, a human condition that will never change. On Aeneas's shield the god has figured episodes from the early history of Rome—the three generations of Ascanius (Iulus, Aeneas's son) and the wolf-suckling Romulus and Remus, the builders of Rome. On goes the historical procession, through the early kings, to the expulsion of Tarquin (the last king) and the heroic defense of the city against his Etruscan allies. An incident from times still further in the future, the Capitol attacked by the Gauls, is followed by scenes from the lower world, the conspirator Catiline in torment, the virtuous Cato giving laws. These two men lived and died not too many years before Augustus established his imperial regime; the prelude to that period of peace and reconstruction was the defeat of Mark Antony and his eastern allies at the Battle of Actium in 31 B.C.—the central scene on the shield. All this lies far in the future, and it is beyond the comprehension of Aeneas, though "He felt joy in their pictures, taking up / Upon his shoulder all the destined acts / And fame of his descendants" (*Aeneid* VII.165–67).]

3. Odysseus' story of his wanderings at the court of Phaeacia for Ae-

neas's account of the fall of Troy and his subsequent wanderings, at Dido's banquet.

[Odysseus at the court of Alcinous is alone, a shipwrecked naked sailor befriended by a princess and cautiously concealing his identity until, moved by the song of the bard Demodocus, his tears betray him as one of the heroes from Troy. His tale, a spellbinding story of encounters with giants, monsters, and hospitable goddesses, of visits to strange lands, even to the land of the dead, wins him rich gifts and a passage home, and though the princess Nausicaa, with her father's consent, would obviously like to keep him as a husband, he insists on returning to Ithaca. Aeneas does not conceal his identity but reveals it to Dido, as she offers his ships' crews the choice of passage to Italy or a share in the new city she is building in Africa. At the banquet where he tells his tale, the queen, through the machinations of Venus, is already falling in love with Aeneas, and the tale of his sorrows and adventures wins her heart completely. But Aeneas's story is very different from that of Odysseus. The first half of it is the account of the destruction of Troy, the hideous death of Priam, and the loss of his wife, Creusa. In what follows, he is wandering—not, like Odysseus, to find his way home but in search of a site to found a new city. His tale is not romance but the tragic history of a great defeat, the end of a civilization and of the painful search for a place in which it can be recreated. Nausicaa's gentle hints to Odysseus become, in the Virgilian version, Dido's passionate pursuit of Aeneas; and Odysseus' delicate rejection of Nausicaa's offer (*Odyssey* VIII.521–26), Aeneas's "marriage" with Dido in the cave. Odysseus on his travels becomes the lover of Circe and Calypso, but these are incidents with no consequences; Aeneas's love for Dido endangers the future of his race and of the world, and when he renounces it to follow his destiny he sows the seeds of the great Punic Wars of the future.

Topic for Writing

Discuss the character of Aeneas, which has often come in for harsh criticism. (Charles James Fox, the eighteenth-century English statesman, found him "either insipid or odious," and William Butler Yeats speaks of an Irishman who thought Aeneas was a priest.) The implied comparison is of course with epic heroes such as Achilles and Odysseus. How far is such an attitude justified?

[There is sufficient material in "Backgrounds" and "Classroom Strategies" to suggest an answer. The main defense of Aeneas is of course that, unlike Achilles and Odysseus, who have no responsibilities other than the maintenance of their own heroic reputations, Aeneas carries the burden of a nation's destiny. He is a man devoted to duty (this is the basic meaning of the word *pius*, which Virgil applies to him so often), and this does not make him as attractive a figure as the rebellious and wrathful warrior Achilles or the unscrupulous and calculating adventurer

Odysseus. It is particularly striking, in book 1, to see that the character who most resembles the *Iliad*'s Achilles is Juno, whose dramatic "anger" is repeatedly mentioned, and which drives the opening plot of the poem, while Aeneas is introduced with much more lackluster adjectives. Yet Aeneas can, on occasion, act with the wild passion characteristic of the heroic temper of an Achilles (or a Medea); in the last book, where everything leads us to expect that he will spare Turnus, his defeated enemy, the sight of Pallas's belt worn as a trophy by his killer inflames Aeneas with rage. The poem closes not on the note of reconciliation that the divine agreement seemed to promise but with a typically heroic act of revenge.]

Comparative Perspectives

1. The ghost of Hector comes to Aeneas in a dream to urge that he flee Troy and build another city, where he will salvage his household gods. Ghosts and dreams are familiar phenomena in early literature; the ghost of Clytemnestra, for example, asks the Furies at the beginning of *The Eumenides* to wreak vengeance on Orestes, her son and murderer, demanding that right and order be restored. How would you compare their roles?

   [If the motive for her ghostly visitation is fundamentally personal, Hector's motive seems more altruistic. It is not vengeance that he seeks but salvation for his people.]
2. Dido is one of many lovelorn women in the literatures of the world. Compare the emotions that contribute to her extreme reactions to her situation with those of Medea or Ovid's Myrrha.

Further Reading

See the reading suggestions in the anthology.

Commager, Steele, ed. *Virgil: A Collection of Critical Essays.* 1966. Contains the essays "Basic Themes" by Victor Poschl and "The Imagery of the Second Book of the *Aeneid*" by Bernard Knox, as well as a brilliant essay by Adam Parry, "The Two Voices of Virgil's *Aeneid*," which deals with the imperial theme and the contradictory theme of human suffering and sadness.

Kenney, E. J., ed. *Latin Literature.* Vol. II of *The Cambridge History of Latin Literature.* 1982. Pp. 331–69 (R. D. Williams). An up-to-date discussion for the modern reader. It covers the Augustan background, the literary background, composition and structure, the chief characters, destiny and religion, and style and meter.

OVID

Metamorphoses

Background

Ovid's account of "forms changed into new bodies" (I.1–2) runs, so his proem announces, "from the world's beginning to the present day" (line 5). The transformation that occurred in his own day was the meta- morphosis of the soul of Julius Caesar, assassinated in 44 B.C., into a star. Augustus was the adopted son of Julius Caesar, and the poem ends with a compliment to the reigning emperor, which is deftly capped by the wish that many years may elapse before Augustus too ascends to Heaven and becomes a god (not in the anthology).

Ovid starts with the creation of the material world, the origination of form and shape from the "shapeless, unwrought mass" of Chaos (I.10). Just as in Hesiod's *Theogony*, it is through the separation of earth and heaven that the "disentangled elements" (I.32) of the cosmos are given form. An unnamed god gives the globe limits by dividing it into zones and kingdoms, assigning different creatures to each (constellations and the gods to the heavens, fish to the sea, beasts to the earth, and birds to the air). Man is born last, and two stories are given of his origin. Ei- ther the same god (the "fabricator" of the world) created him out of di- vine substance, or Prometheus molded him out of a clod broken off from the aether, modeling him after the shape of gods (I.109–17). The selection ends by explaining that man differs from all other earthly crea- tures, because he looks "directly up into the vaulted heavens / and turn[s] his countenance to meet the stars" (I.122–23). Man, therefore, seems to connect the immortal and mortal spheres, and Ovid claims that the earth was "rude and formless" until it took on the shapes of men.

After a history of the four ages of man (not included in the anthol- ogy), Ovid describes how Jove (Jupiter) decides to wipe out the human race with a flood. When life finally comes back to the world, we embark upon the stories of mostly human transformations at the hands of the gods. The story of Daphne and her transformation into a laurel tree is typical of many metamorphoses in the poem, because it combines the elements of attempted rape, flight, and an appeal for help at the mo- ment of transformation. Apollo is made to fall in love with Daphne by Cupid, whom he had provoked. She, however, is a virgin huntress who flees the god's advances. About to be overtaken, she prays for help to her father, the river god, who changes her into a laurel tree. The rivers of Greece come to console Peneus, all except Inachus, whose daughter Io is missing; he does not know whether she is alive or dead.

She has, in fact, caught the roving eye of Jove, who has pursued and caught her. When Juno catches him in the act, he changes Io into a white heifer. Juno, pretending not to know what has happened, begs for the heifer as a gift, and Jove must give way. Juno puts Io under the sur- veillance of Argus, who has a hundred eyes. Io finds her father and man- ages to identify herself by scratching her name in the dust, but there is nothing he can do. Jove takes pity on them and sends Mercury to kill Argus. He first lulls Argus to sleep with his magic wand, meanwhile playing on his reed pipes and telling a story.

It is the story of Syrinx, pursued by the god Pan but rescued from his embraces by being changed into a reed. Once Argus falls asleep, Mercury kills him. Jove takes his hundred eyes and sets them in the tail of the peacock. Juno also sends a fury to drive Io all over the world. Io's prayers to Jove induce him to swear to Juno that he will never touch the girl and Juno changes Io back again to human shape.

Ovid, whose reputation as a poet had been built on his playful, witty, and at times licentious love poetry, turns in the *Metamorphoses* to the epic genre; the meter of his verse, the hexameter, is the same as that of Virgil's *Aeneid*, and the opening lines of the poem announce the theme in solemn strains. This dignified tone is maintained through the account of the creation and the four ages, the account of the flood and the recreation of humankind; but with the episode of Apollo and Daphne we are back in Ovidian territory.

But it is not only the subject matter that has changed; though the stories still deal with gods, the style modulates toward the playful wit that will be characteristic of Ovid's narrative for the bulk of the poem. The dialogue between Apollo and Cupid, for example (I.634ff.), makes no attempt at epic seriousness. Apollo's detailed appreciation of Daphne's charms as he pursues her (lines 686ff.) recalls the poet of the *Art of Love*. The embarrassment and subterfuges of Jove when caught redhanded by Juno (lines 840ff.) suggest social comedy rather than epic grandeur. Daphne is rescued from what she feared most, and Io is restored to human shape.

Ovid's poem pursues its course through more than twelve thousand lines; this "epic of the emotions," as it has been called, rings the changes on all the genres—comedy, tragedy, pastoral, didactic—as it creates a brilliant anthology of mythological tales (most of them Greek). Most of the mythical stories that have become household words in Western culture through their re-creation in later art and literature—Pygmalion and Galatea, Midas and the golden touch, Pyramus and Thisbe—owe their form to their appearance in Ovid's *Metamorphoses*.

Classroom Strategies and Topics for Discussion

Ovid's treatment of the gods may puzzle some students. In the *Aeneid*, the gods, though subject to human passions—Juno's hatred of Troy, for example—are figures of immense dignity. Virgil's Juno may be simply jealous, but she is also terrifying in her wrath; Venus may trick Dido into falling in love with Aeneas, but her purpose is serious and the fate of empires is involved. In Ovid, however, these same gods are treated with lighthearted humor; even Jove himself appears in the likeness of an embarrassed husband caught philandering by his wife. Ovid's attitude toward the gods is not really a religious one at all. In his *Art of Love*, in fact, Ovid had expressed a cynical view: belief in the existence of gods is advantageous for society, so, he says, let us believe in them (*Expedit esse deos, et, ut expedit, esse putemus*). In that same passage, however, he goes on to recommend conformity with ritual—incense should be burned and wine poured on the altars. For Ovid the Olympian gods had become material for poetry, and lighthearted poetry at that; but there is no reason to think that his attitude was unusual. Pagan religion, in the early centuries of the Roman Empire, was for most people a question of conformity to custom, not of belief. It had little spiritual force with which to confront the new religions, Christianity in particular, which commanded fervent belief in its new visions of divine power and humanity's life in this world and the next.

Students will have little trouble perceiving how abundantly clear Ovid makes his skeptical view of the gods, since so many of the selections in the anthology show them intent on rape and, in their zeal to ravish, often memorably ridiculous. As you examine Apollo's pursuit of Daphne, ask the class how desire for Daphne undermines Apollo's vaunted divine attributes (the god of oracles can't predict the future; the god of medicine can't heal himself). As the headnote suggests, the poem openly invites us to laugh at Jove himself when he transforms himself into a bull: "Majestic power and erotic love / do not get on together very well" (II.1161–1162).

When Jove undertakes a metamorphosis, of course, he assumes a new form temporarily; once he achieves his mission, he resumes his grandeur, and if he decides to become a bull, he becomes an adorable bull. Rarely do the gods' intended victims have the opportunity to return to their previous forms. The sufferings of Io, so poignantly detailed, are partially assuaged, but she never can be herself again. By elaborating on a process that is, at its most serious, about the eradication of identity, the poem responds subtly to a complex array of moral and psychological issues.

Ovid invests this long poem's repeated descriptions of "forms changed into new bodies" with finely judged detail, appropriate to each individual case. Jove's transformation is never shown; he just becomes a bull, feeling no pain. Mortals, even when they welcome their metamorphoses, seem more pathetic as they pass from one form to another, as does Daphne (I.754–62). Myrrha, in her guilty exhaustion, hastens her metamorphosis (X.579–600) and Arethusa's sweating abets hers (V.810ff.). When they struggle against punitive metamorphosis (as in the changing of the daughters of Pierus into magpies at the end of book V), the poem, like the process it illustrates, can seem cruel.

Read in its entirety, the poem's own transitions rival the transitions of those bodies, as topic leads to topic and a finely ironic sense of order is dimly revealed. The story of Ceres and Prosperina, for example, is told by the Muse Calliope. Embedded in a sequence of stories that involve impious human challenges to the power of the gods. Calliope's convoluted story bests the narrative efforts of the "simpleminded sisters" (V.446)—like the Muses, nine in number—who are turned to magpies for their insolence. Thus cruelty is an important theme throughout. Embedded in the story of Cere's heroic quest for her lost daughter, for example, is the episode in which she angrily transforms a young boy into a lizard because he laughs at her thirsty drinking of barley water proffered by his grandmother. (V.621–28) Similarly, Venus will turn Hippomenes and Atalanta into lions tethered to Cybele's chariot for failing to show their gratitude for her assistance (X.795–820).

Ovid's range is also notable for the way he interweaves familiar mythological materials, such as the aetiological story of Ceres and Prosperina that "explains" vegetation cycles, with others that he embroiders or invents to comment on fundamental human experiences. Books IX and X examine a group of stories about "impossible love" (a term used by Galinsky in his book mentioned in the headnote). The story of Iphis and Ianthe should particularly interest students, since (as noted in the headnote) its understanding of the way gender identity is shaped by environment seems extremely modern. At the same time, the last-minute sex change undergone by a resolutely heterosexual Iphis is a staple of literary history. (The story of Fiordispina, Bradamant, and Richardet in Ariosto's *Orlando Furioso*, which borrows from the Iphis-Ianthe story and elsewhere in the *Metamorphoses* as well, will give your class an opportunity to see a good example of Ovid's influence on later poets.)

In the same sequence of stories is the tragic tale of Myrrha, whose forbidden love of her father leads to incest. Preceding this story, which has many affinities with classical and neoclassical tragedy (note especially the nurse as confidante to the lovesick heroine, a relationship to be studied as well in *Medea* and in Racine's *Phaedra*, which is itself based, of course, on another play by Euripides, the *Hippolytus*), is the even better-known story of Pygmalion and Galatea, one that rewards extended inquiry in its richly ambivalent approach to another erotic dilemma.

As the headnote indicates, Pygmalion's inability to love a woman he has not created seems pathological. Linked to Myrrha's story in a typically Ovidian transition (the child of Pygmalion and Galatea is Myrrha's grandfather), Pygmalion may be considered another practitioner of incest. He is also, of course, an artist, and art is a central concern of Ovid's poem. Like Calliope and Minerva, gods who assert their artistic superiority to the efforts of mere mortals, Venus and not Pygmalion is the true creator in this story. Without her granting the sculptor's prayer, the statue would have remained ivory. The power to transform, to shape experience, is granted to the gods; the *Metamorphoses* begins, after all, with a creation story. But it is also the vehicle by which lesser beings express their passions—ask your students how Io manages to communicate with her father (I.899–901) or how Syrinx is transformed into a musical instrument (I.973–78).

The Ovidian narrator weaves in and out of his long poem, ceding to other narrators as will Shahrazad in *The Thousand and One Nights*, and as she might, he concludes by boasting that the power of his words will confer upon him immortality. When Venus turns Adonis into an anemone, the flower's evanescence is recalled. Yet your students will find evidence at every point along the literary continuum that follows of the longevity of the fragile, shifting forms that populate the *Metamorphoses*.

Topics for Writing

1. Ovid drew on the rich mythological literature for his stories of transformation, but he added a new element to these tales of changed forms. "By . . . fleshing out the story, by inspecting the emotions and psychological problems of the characters, . . . by weighing the reasons for the metamorphosis and the feelings of the human spirit inside the changed body, Ovid gave new life and meaning to the myth" (W. S. Anderson). Discuss this analysis of Ovidian technique for the transformation of Daphne, Io, Iphis, or Myrrha.
2. Pygmalion "falls in love with his own work." How would you evaluate him as an artist and a man? What implications does this episode have for our understanding of the nature of artistic creation?

Comparative Perspectives

1. Compare and contrast the involvement of the gods in human life in *Gilgamesh*, Genesis, the Homeric epics, and the *Metamorphoses*. What do the deities want from human beings? How do they treat them?
2. Ovid's narrative technique, as well as his narrative content, is metamorphic. Look closely at the way he manages transitions from one story to the next. How does this resemble the technique of other anthologies of popular stories, such as the tales of *The Thousand and One Nights*?
3. This is the third account we have now seen of the origins of the cosmos (the other two are Genesis I and the opening of Hesiod's *Theogony* [lines 115–210]). How do these three accounts differ? [Genesis and the *Metamorphoses* both describe the world as created by a single god with a master plan; in the *Theogony*, no reason is given for the emergence of Gaia from Chaos. All three accounts contain a version in which man (or woman) is created from an earth-like substance, and fashioned after the shape of God or gods. Ovid's account, with its separation of the world into climactic zones, owes more to science and natural philosophy than the other two.]

Further Reading

See also the reading suggestions in the *Anthology*, p. 2641.

Anderson, W. S., ed. *Ovid's* Metamorphoses, *Books* 6–10. 1972. An edition of the Latin text with introduction and commentary. Although it does not deal with the books printed in the anthology, the introduction gives many useful insights into Ovidian style and technique.

Duff, J. Wight. *A Literary History of Rome from the Origins to the Close of the Golden Age.* 1909. Pp. 598–605. A venerable but still suggestive discussion of the *Metamorphoses* and its place in Latin and European poetry.

Hardie, P. *Ovid's Poetics of Illusion.* 2002. See his chapter on Pygmalion for a wide-ranging discussion on the nature of art and illusion.

Smith, R. A. *Poetic Allusion and Poetic Embrace in Ovid and Virgil.* 1997. The discussion of Pygmalion is particularly good.

Tissol, Garth. *The Face of Nature: Wit, Narrative, and Cosmic Origins in Ovid's* Metamorphoses. 1997. A close reading of the poem, emphasizing Ovid's puns. Even teaching from a translation, one can profit from this discussion of the tightly woven wordplay of several episodes, including that of Myrrha.

Wilkinson, L. P. *Ovid Recalled.* 1955. Pages 190ff. discuss the gods; pp. 203ff., mortals in the *Metamorphoses*.

PETRONIUS

The Satyricon

[DINNER WITH TRIMALCHIO]

Backgrounds

The selection in the anthology is an account of a dinner given by a vulgar profiteer, a freedman (ex-slave) called Trimalchio; the narrator, Encolpius, is an educated man, a student of rhetoric. The dinner proceeds with one wildly extravagant course after another as the guests, most of them tradesmen with Greek names, talk business and cheap philosophy in language that has a scurrilous vitality unequaled in all Latin literature. Trimalchio tells the story of his life, and with the late arrival of Habinnas (a man in the funeral monument business who is building Trimalchio's tomb according to his specifications) the party gets wild: Fortunata, Trimalchio's wife, arrives and shows off her jewelry, but when Trimalchio makes a pass at a handsome boy slave, she bawls him out and is treated, in turn, to a vicious stream of vulgar abuse from her husband. Finally, maudlin drunk, Trimalchio orders his burial shroud to be brought in for the guests to admire; the band he has ordered to play a funeral march makes so much noise that the neighborhood is aroused and the fire brigade, thinking Trimalchio's house is on fire, breaks in with water and axes, thus giving Encolpius and his friend Giton a chance to escape in the confusion.

The *Satyricon* has come down to us as a collection of fragments (the banquet of Trimalchio is the longest); we have only remnants of what was originally an immense narrative of perhaps twenty books (the fragments included in the anthology seem to come from books XIV–XVI). It was a sort of picaresque novel: the amorous and disreputable adventures of its young narrator, Encolpius. He is a penniless student of rhetoric, living by his wits (and occasionally by the lightness of his fingers) in the cities of southern Italy. He has a young companion-lover, Giton, who is a perpetual bone of contention between Encolpius and another of his shady companions, Ascyltus, who from time to time takes his place in Giton's affections.

The literary origins of such a work are hard to seek. The *Satyricon* may have drawn on licentious Greek narratives (the so-called Milesian tales) and does owe much to Roman satire (in one of his *Satires* the Augustan poet Horace, for example, describes a rich upstart's banquet much like that of Trimalchio), but the vitality and realism of Petronius's fiction is something new in ancient literature.

Its author was almost certainly an aristocratic member of the court of Nero (emperor, A.D. 54–68), Titus Petronius, whose life and death are described by the historian Tacitus, writing some fifty years after the events he records (*Annals* XVI, chapters 18–19). Petronius, he says,

> was a man who spent his days sleeping and his nights working or enjoying himself. . . . He was thought of as a refined artist in extravagance. His conversation and actions had a freedom and an air of carelessness which appealed to people by its lack of affectation. Yet as governor in Bithynia and later as consul he showed that he was a man of energy and fully equipped to deal with business. Later, returning to loose habits (or perhaps pretending to do so), he became a member of the inner circle of Nero's companions where he was known as the Arbiter of Elegance; Nero's jaded fancy would find charm and finesse only in what passed Petronius' scrutiny.

This position of influence aroused the jealousy of the powerful commander of the praetorian guard, and as a result of his intrigues, Petronius was arrested on suspicion of treason. Rather than wait for Nero's sentence, he committed suicide by cutting his veins. But his suicide was a spectacular event:

> He had the veins, once severed, bandaged up, when he felt like it, and then opened them again, meanwhile talking to his friends, not on a serious note or with any intention of winning a reputation for a brave end. The conversation was not concerned with the immortality of the soul or philosophical doctrines but consisted of amusing songs and frivolous verses. Some of his slaves he gave rewards to, others he had whipped. He sat down to a banquet, drowsing a little, so that his death, though forced on him, would look natural. In his will he did not follow the usual routine of flattering Nero; instead he listed the names of Nero's sexual partners male and female, and followed that with detailed descriptions of the emperor's activities, specifying the novel features of each sexual encounter. This document he sent to Nero.

Classroom Strategies

One assignment.

The student may wonder about the social position of slaves in Roman imperial society; on the one hand Trimalchio owns a great many of them—there are at least forty "divisions" of slaves in his household—but he himself was a slave once, and so were some of his rich friends (one of them takes it on himself to reproach Ascyltus for laughing at Trimalchio [p. 1068] and proclaims his pride in his status of "freedman," that is, liberated slave). There seems to be a certain social mobility in this society, and this does correspond to the facts of Roman history.

In Greece we hear very little about the transition from slave to free status; the one thing we do know is that a freed slave remained an alien in the city—he could not acquire citizenship. In Rome, however, he did. His status as *libertus*, "freedman," gave him citizen rights, and in the next generation his son would be not even a freedman but a citizen on a level with all comers. The Augustan poet Horace was, in fact, a freedman's son, and yet he moved easily in the exalted circle of the emperor Augustus.

Trimalchio's account of his rise from rags to riches (p. 1080), though Petronius's satiric intent is plain, has a ring of truth to it. He came from Asia—probably a Greek city in the Middle East—and was a slave for fourteen years, during which time he was the sexual favorite of his master (and incidentally obliged his mistress too). He became, as he says, "boss in the house"; he learned accounting and became steward—the indispensable servant manager. He was left, at his master's death, not only his freedom but a fortune. He bought freedom for his wife, Fortunata, too (p. 1079), and went into business in the wine trade. With the proceeds he bought back all his master's old estates, built a house, and invested in slaves. Trimalchio's emancipation by his master's will was in fact a common occurrence; common enough that the imperial government collected a tax on it.

Topic for Discussion

Although the *Satyricon* is unlike any other literary work that has come down to us from antiquity, it is nonetheless influenced by and conscious of its predecessors. In particular, since it is a long narrative, it frequently compares and contrasts itself with the noblest and most monumental narrative form in antiquity, the epic. The references are, of course, ironic; the business of the inhabitants of Trimalchio's world emerges in sharp relief from the implied comparison with Achilles and the heroes of the Trojan saga.

The name of the rhetoric teacher, Agamemnon, is one among the many deliberate references to the heroic past; the point is emphasized by the name of his assistant, Menelaus. But this Agamemnon is a flatterer who dignifies Trimalchio's inane remarks by admiring their wit (p. 1074). The mural in Trimalchio's house includes representations of "The *Iliad*, and *Odyssey*, and the gladiatorial show given by Laenas" (p. 1067), and in the conversation of the guests that goes on when Trimalchio has left to go to the toilet, the heroes of past time who are held up to admiration are not warriors but, for example, Chrysanthus, who "started out in life with just a penny" and "left a solid hundred thousand" (p. 1070), and Safinius, who kept the price of bread down by terrifying the bakers: "he used to wade into some of them—no beating about the bush" (p. 1071).

As for the heroes of the present day, chief among them is Titus, who, his friend Echion the rag merchant says, is about to give a gladiatorial show that will be "the best ever . . . cold steel, no quarter and the slaughterhouse right in the middle where all the stands can see it" (p. 1071). Echion's son is "ahead with his Greek, and he's starting to take to his Latin," but his father wants him to pick up some legal training for home use: "There's a living in that sort of thing" (p. 1072).

Trimalchio too has pretensions to culture; he has "two libraries, one Greek, one Latin" (p. 1074), but he doesn't seem to have read the books. He remembers a story of Ulysses (Odysseus), "how the Cyclops tore out his thumb with a pair of pincers" (p. 1074)—which he claims to have read in Homer. The only time he gets an allusion to the great literature of the past even remotely right is when he calls Fortunata, who has objected to his dalliance with a boy slave, a "Cassandra in clogs" (p. 1079).

Topics for Writing

1. Discuss the following statement:

   Trimalchio is a complex character; he now wallows in luxury and self-deception, but was once resilient and faced a hard world on its own terms. For all his coarseness and ostentation, he is not utterly unlikeable.

   F. D. Goodyear

2. The same critic says of the characters who speak at the banquet when Trimalchio is absent: "they are characterized by what they say as well as by the way they speak." Discuss with specific examples.

Comparative Perspectives

1. What view of life emerges here? What cultural developments seem to precipitate this kind of satiric vision? Compare the elements of life emphasized in Rabelais's account of life in Paris or by Gulliver when he looks at the way the Yahoos live.

2. *Dinner with Trimalchio*, like the *Aeneid* and the *Metamorphoses*, shows how Roman writers had constantly to deal with the example set for them by the Greeks and how complicated were their attitudes toward their precursors. In both the *Aeneid* and the *Satyricon*, wall paintings take Homeric texts for their subjects. The one Aeneas sees in Carthage evokes an interpretation that would not be out of place in Petronius's work: what is satiric about the way he describes Achilles (I.85–86)?

Further Reading

See also the reading suggestions in the *Anthology*, p. 2641.

Kenney, E. J., ed. *Latin Literature*. Vol. I of *The Cambridge History of Classical Literature*. 1982. Pp. 635–38 (F. D. Goodyear). A short discussion of the *Satyricon* as a whole, with some perceptive remarks on the banquet of Trimalchio.

THE CHRISTIAN BIBLE: THE NEW TESTAMENT

Backgrounds

The selection in the anthology (from Luke and Matthew) begins with the birth of Jesus (from Luke) and the famous story of the "good news, great joy" brought by the angel of the Lord to the shepherds in the fields. This selection ends with the picture of the twelve-year-old Jesus questioning and answering the learned interpreters of the scriptures and the laws. There follows Matthew's account of the Sermon on the Mount, which contains Christ's basic doctrines and also the words of the Lord's Prayer. The next selection (from Luke) contains the famous parables of the lost sheep, the lost piece of silver, and the prodigal son, along with Jesus' account of why he speaks in parables. The rest of the selection, also from Matthew, narrates the Last Supper, the agony in the garden, the betrayal and arrest of Jesus, his denial by Peter, and then the trial before Pontius Pilate and the Crucifixion, ending with the Resurrection and Christ's command to the disciples to "instruct all the nations."

When Alexander died at Babylon in 323 B.C. after conquering the whole of the immense land empire of the Persians, his generals divided the spoils between them; Ptolemy took Egypt (his descendants ruled it until the last of them, Cleopatra, went down to defeat with Mark Antony in 31 B.C.); and Palestine, together with most of the Middle East, came under the control of Seleucus and his descendants the Seleucids. Over the whole area Greek became the language of administration, and in the cities, at any rate, Greek culture took firm hold; the ruins of its typical buildings—temple, theater, and gymnasium—still testify to its wide dissemination.

In Palestine, however, the attempts to impose Greek culture ran into the stubborn resistance of the Jews, who after a long war succeeded in retaining the right to practice their own religion and observe their own laws. Eventually, in the first century B.C., the area came under Roman control; it was before a Roman official, Pontius Pilate, that Jesus was tried and condemned to death.

While the governing officials conducted their business in Greek or Latin, the Jewish population spoke a Semitic dialect called Aramaic (though the scriptures that their rabbis expounded were written in classical Hebrew). Jesus' native tongue was Aramaic (some of his last words on the cross—*Eli Eli lama sabachthani*—are in that language), but he must have learned classical Hebrew to be able to dispute with the rabbis in the temple, and it is quite likely that he knew enough Greek to speak to and understand Roman and Greek officials. But his preaching to the crowds that came to hear him was in Aramaic, and when he died on the cross in A.D. 30 it must have been in that language that his disciples remembered and perhaps began to record his words.

He had given them the mission, however, to "instruct all the nations," and if his message was to go outside the narrow confines of Aramaic-speaking Palestine, it would have to be in a Greek version. And it is in that language, the "common" Greek of the Middle East (not the highly wrought literary Greek of the Athenian writers), that the four Gospels were written, probably in the last third of the first century A.D. In that language the message was accessible to anyone in the Middle East and mainland Greece who could read at all; later, as Latin versions were made, the Gospels (the word means "good news") could be read all over the Roman Empire.

Classroom Strategies

One assignment.

One aspect of the Gospel narratives, especially that of Matthew, that may puzzle students is the frequency of reference to the Old Testament, often to cite a prophecy that is being or is about to be fulfilled. Many of these references are made by Jesus himself, as, for example, when he predicts that his disciples will desert him in his hour of need and cites the prophet Zechariah (13.7: "For it is written, I will smite the shepherd and the sheep of the flock shall be scattered abroad"), or by the narrator, as in the case of the potter's field bought with the thirty pieces of silver paid to Judas—a fulfillment, says Matthew, of a prophecy made by Jeremiah (in the text it is in Zechariah 11.13: "And they took the thirty pieces of silver, the price of him that was valued, whom they of the children of Israel did not value, and gave them for the potter's field").

The purpose of these references is to establish Jesus' claim to be the promised Messiah, a Hebrew word that means "anointed" (the Greek word for which is *christos*, hence our word *Christ*). A king was anointed with holy oil (a king or queen still is in the British coronation ceremony), but this king, the Messiah, was to be one appointed by God to deliver his people, the Jews, and establish his kingdom in righteousness. Jesus' claim to be that Messiah was one of the reasons for the hostility of many of the Jews, for they expected the Messiah to deliver them from the Romans, while Jesus, announcing that his kingdom was not of this world, renounced violent action of any kind. It is with reference to this claim to be the Messiah that the Roman magistrate Pilate, not understanding its theological nature, can ask Jesus, "Are you the King of the Jews?" (Matthew 27.11) and that the mocking legend can be fixed to the cross: "THIS IS JESUS, THE KING OF THE JEWS" (27.37).

By the end of the Book of Matthew (the one that is clearly aimed especially at a Jewish, as Luke's is at a Greek, audience), the mission of the Messiah has become worldwide. The resurrected Jesus tells his disciples: "Go out therefore, and instruct all the nations" (28.19).

Topic for Discussion

All three of the parables in the selection—the lost sheep, the lost silver piece, and the prodigal son—emphasize the lesson that the redeemed sinner is more precious to God than the righteous person who never sinned. This implies a conception of God unlike that found in the Old Testament (cf. the Genesis stories of the Garden of Eden and the Flood) or in Greek literature and thought (cf. the gods of the *Iliad*, the *Odyssey*, and the *Oresteia*). The parables emphasize the entirely new emphasis that Christian doctrine was to place on human repentance and divine mercy.

Topic for Writing

Compare the recommendations for human conduct offered in the Beatitudes (Matthew 5.3–11) and those that are implied in the Greek texts you have read.

[The contrast is striking in the case of the heroic values of an Achilles or Odysseus; perhaps the only one of Jesus' commands that one can imagine Achilles accepting is "Blessed are the pure in heart" (which he would probably have understood as meaning "Blessed are they who speak the truth and hate a liar," cf. *Iliad* IX.317ff.). With Socrates, on the other hand (who was also put to death), many of the commands of Jesus seem perfectly compatible.]

Comparative Perspectives

1. Although Jesus was a Jew, the religious institutions created in his name proved difficult for Jews to embrace but attractive to Greeks. What elements in the Nativity and the Passion narratives seem particularly acceptable and culturally familiar to a pagan audience? Compare, if appropriate, references in the Koran to "The People of the Book," the Christians and Jews whom Muslims acknowledge as sharing previous prophetic revelations.
2. Teaching in parables, as Jesus explains to his disciples, puts a burden on the audience that straightforward instruction does not. Why does this method of communication particularly suit a religious or spiritual subject?

Further Reading

See also the reading suggestions in the *Anthology*, p. 2640

Barrett, C. K. *The New Testament Background: Selected Documents.* 1961. Documents illustrating the period of the origin and rise of Christianity translated from Greek, Latin, Hebrew, and other languages.

Cook, Stanley. *An Introduction to the Bible.* 1950. Useful chapters are 1, "The English Bible"; 5, "The Books of the Bible: The New Testament"; and 6, "The Messiah and the New Age."

May, H. G., and B. C. Metzger. *The New Oxford Annotated Bible*. 1965; reprinted 1977. Besides presenting an annotated edition of the Old and New Testaments in the Revised Standard Version, this volume contains excellent chapters on modern approaches to biblical study (pp. 1519ff.), literary forms in the Gospels (pp. 1530ff.), and a historical account of Palestine during "the invasion of Hellenism" and the rule of Rome (pp. 1543ff.).

Metzger, B. C. *The New Testament: Its Background, Growth, and Content*. 1965. An up-to-date survey of the historical and doctrinal problems presented by the New Testament, written for the nonspecialist by one of the most prominent biblical scholars of our time. Especially recommended are chapter 4, on the sources of our knowledge of the life and teachings of Jesus, and chapter 6, on his teachings.

LUCIAN

A True Story

Classroom Strategies and Topics for Discussion

A True Story is one of the comic gems of the ancient world: like *The Satyricon*, another comparatively late work that makes fun of the masterpieces of ancient Greek culture, Lucian's self-conscious tour de force provides a wonderful opportunity for you to pause retrospectively at the end of the first major sequence in the anthology. If your students have already read Homer, they are ready to appreciate Lucian's deft allusions to the heroic tradition, a feature of this text that he advertises prominently at the beginning of his second paragraph.

You should make sure your students understand that allusion depends on an audience's ability to "get" references that the author does not flag or explain—you could point out that many of the anthology's footnotes have been provided precisely to elucidate allusions. You may also find it worthwhile to distinguish between the complementary but essentially different literary approaches that we categorize as *satire* or *parody*. Satire, which exposes folly and pretension, can be serious or comic and may inhabit any genre: it is a point of view rather than a static form and its targets are generally social and behavioral. Parody, on the other hand, requires an exquisite sense of form, since it is based on stylistic imitation. The better the parodist's eye, the more successful the parody. It combines affectionate tribute with debunking (broader, less precise imitations that intend mainly ridicule verge into burlesque or travesty). As the headnote makes clear, *A True Story* uses parody to entertain even as it raises fundamental questions about the nature of literature as an art form and as a human enterprise.

Baldly announcing that all writers lie, Lucian then turns on a dime to deploy a full range of technical tricks by which authors feign truth. For example, he highlights the artificiality of a familiar Homeric convention that gives an illusion of verisimilitude by specifying precise details. Your students should be able to recognize that Lucian's "fifty acquaintances" and his telling us that on the eightieth day at sea "the sun broke through" parody Homer's tendency to use fifty to suggest plenitude (as in Priam's fifty sons) and to announce that the ninth, or eleventh, day yields to some decisive action on the tenth, or twelfth. By its very title, of course, A True Story skewers a wide range of devices that historians and natural philosophers use to create a semblance of truth.

Fans of science fiction will have a background on which to draw in analyzing why A True Story propels its reader to one imaginary setting or another. What impulse prompts writers to depict what they demonstrably cannot have experienced, like life on the moon or some further intergalactic destination? Comic satire abounds in examples that your students will recognize and perhaps go on to read as the year progresses: Voltaire in Candide and Swift in Gulliver's Travels satirize their own societies by their invention of fictional places that absurdly exaggerate tendencies at home. Fantasy worlds in romances like Ariosto's Orlando Furioso tend to be places where wishes that would be denied in the ordinary world can be fulfilled.

With such comparisons in mind, you might ask your students to identify the preoccupations of the traveler in part I: he directly participates in warfare with a variety of grotesque hybrid formations, observes unusual sexual practices, and comments on the local diet (note the ubiquity of beans, a staple of ancient—and many modern—cuisines, and of farce—given their effect on the digestion—in every period as well). Students will have no trouble enumerating the mortal appetites being held up for critique or ridicule here. As much of the first part of A True Story has to do with the logistics of waging war, you might have your students look back over the readings they've done elsewhere in the anthology: in how many does the battlefield dominate events? In what ways does Lucian show how ridiculous, rather than heroic, war really is? Even more does Lucian make fun of the tall tales brought back by travelers and historians, particularly through his vivid descriptions of oddly constructed creatures. Travel writers seem always to have reported on the monstrous forms to be found beyond the boundary lines of the civilized world (this is a point you may want to return to when you reach Othello's stories of "men whose heads / Do grow beneath their shoulders" and Gulliver's encounters with the Houyhnhnms). The allegorical implications of centaurs and minotaurs are not hard to discern. What are we to make, however, of Flounderfoots and Lobstertails, of Crabhands and Tunaheads, "bound to each other by a military pact as well as emotional ties"?

It appears that something about our experience of our own bodies leads writers to populate their works with beings who violate the species divide. In some contexts, hybridity is a source of horror—your students will be well versed when it comes to werewolves and vampires, among others. But in A True Story, in cartoons and in caricatures, hybridity gives rise to humor. Lucian's method of draining a potentially serious theme of emotive content leaves us with absurdities that require a reexamination of received values and assumptions.

He introduces us to his gallery of monsters early in part I, with the comparison of the grapevine women to Daphne turning into a tree. Although Lucian, who chose Greek over Latin, may not be alluding to Ovid's *Metamorphoses* here, your students are most likely to recognize the myth from its Ovidian treatment, and a comparison between the two writers is instructive. Even so ironic an artist as Ovid tends to give psychological interest and pathos to the transformations of his tortured human subjects. Lucian's approach is more parodic, turning familiar myths on their heads in the deadpan references to the freaks of nature encountered throughout *A True Story*. Ovid's Daphne is the victim of the predatory Apollo, whereas Lucian's aggressors are the females in the case. The old myth becomes a dirty joke as the hapless men who surrender to these clinging vines undergo an unusual early penile transplant.

It is worth mentioning that Lucian's parallel universes are overwhelmingly male; one productive critical approach to *A True Story* is to examine it in terms of the assumptions about gender that permeate the works of Greek antiquity. Like Zeus, who bears two of his own offspring (Athena and Dionysus), the males on the womanless moon do their own childbearing. Lucian's offhand description of perhaps the most fervent male fantasy, the dream of self-generation, is substantiated by a fabulously specific and wild description of the lunar bodily experience. His disclaimer reiterates the power of his double-sided attitude toward truth: "Any person who doesn't believe that all this is so need only go there himself."

Part II of *A True Story*, set among the "celebrities" of Greek culture, offers particularly rich ground for your students to discover examples of parody. You might take the opportunity to talk here about the kind of humor that fuels American popular culture, which is awash in burlesques like *Naked Gun* or *Scary Movie*, and to compare their broad strokes with the minutely observed detail of Lucian's narrative. How does a knowledge of Odysseus' escape from Polyphemus's cave, for example, enrich our appreciation of the carefully laid plans for escaping from the belly of the whale that Lucian describes in the beginning of part II of the narrative?

Getting free of the whale leads us to the Isle of the Blest and to the literary references which your students will most immediately "get." Lucian gives us the inside story on Socrates, who seems to be having a fine time in the afterlife. Ask your students why Lucian makes a point of noting that Plato and the Stoics aren't among the Blest: what is he saying about the importance of a sense of humor? Or consider why he announces that Homer was born in Babylonia: what personal amusement may Lucian, a native of Samosata, situated "on the west bank of the Euphrates River," derive from so settling the vexed question of the origin of the greatest of Greek authors?

Your retrospective exercise could conclude with Lucian's portraits of characters encountered earlier in the semester, while you may point the way ahead by encouraging your students to remember Lucian's treatment of the afterlife when they move on to read Dante or Ariosto later in the term. And if you read *The Trial of Renard* or *The Wife of Bath's Tale*, you will have further opportunity of looking closely again at parody, in these cases of medieval epic and Arthurian romance.

Topics for Writing

1. Survival skills in *A True Story*: how may the dangers that Lucian encounters and the way he addresses them comment on ancient Greek literature and society? What equivalent dangers and responses could be invented by the writer of as true a story set in the contemporary United States?
2. How does Lucian comment on topics already covered in your syllabus, including perhaps the morality of the Trojan War, the pursuit of academic philosophy, or the governance of nations?
3. Write a letter to be sent by one of your favorite figures in Greek literature in the style of the one Odysseus smuggles past Penelope to send to Calypso. Some suggestions: Achilles to Peleus, Helen to Clytemnestra, Sappho to Lucian.

Comparative Perspectives

1. Lucian apologizes for having "nothing true to record—I never had any experiences worth talking about." Does a writer have to write about personal experience? What kinds of "truth" can fiction convey?
2. Why do nations at peace return obsessively to narratives of war? How would you contrast the absurd series of conflicts recounted in a *A True Story* with the significance of war in epic works like the *Iliad* or the *Aeneid* or *The Song of Roland*?
3. In the beginning of *A True Story*, Lucian talks about the "tomfoolery" of travel narratives like the *Odyssey*. Consider the ways in which parody can simultaneously discredit and pay tribute to the works it imitates.

Further Reading

See also the reading suggestions in the *Anthology*, p. 2641.

Hall, Jennifer. *Lucian's Satire*. 1981. A monograph that demonstrates that the weird creatures and events described in *A True Story* differ in degree but not in kind from those in the texts (many now lost) that Lucian parodies.

Marsh, David. *Lucian and the Latins: Humor and Humanism in the Early Renaissance*. 1988. Discusses the rediscovery of Lucian in the early 1400s, with comments on the influence of *A True Story* on Rabelais.

AUGUSTINE

Confessions

Backgrounds

Augustine begins with a reconstruction of the first months of his childhood, based on the "word of others," then describes his own earliest memories; they include a fascinating analysis of the process of learning to understand his parents' speech. He continues with an account of his boyhood, his education, and later his adolescence; one incident from this period, his participation in the theft of fruit from a pear tree, remains in his memory as an example of malice—"my soul was depraved" (p. 1119).

At Carthage, where he was a student, he fell victim to the lusts of the flesh; he also frequented the theater and was one of a gang of rowdy and rebellious students at the university where he studied law and rhetoric. He read for the first time the Gospels (in Latin) but found the style inferior to that of Cicero and was "repelled by their simplicity" (p. 1123). He became professor of rhetoric at Milan in the north of Italy, at that time (late fourth century A.D.) the administrative center of the Western Roman Empire.

His mother, Monica, came to live with him and was distressed to find that he was not yet a Christian. He had great worldly ambitions (conversion would have interfered with them) and was also living with a mistress by whom he had a child. He did not wish to give her up and so resisted the force that drew him toward Christianity but was finally converted when a voice he heard in a garden said: "Take and read" (p. 1129).

He took up the Bible that was on his knees, opened it at random, and found the words of Paul that begin, "Not in rioting and drunkenness" (Romans 13.13). He went in and told his mother he had made up his mind; he left his mistress, resigned his professorship at Milan, joined the church there, which was headed by St. Ambrose, and eventually became a priest. His mother died as she was about to return home to Africa; Augustine records what she had told him about her early life and paints an affecting picture of a simple but devoted woman who lived in the Christian faith through all the trials of a hard life and a difficult marriage.

Augustine wrote his *Confessions* around A.D. 397, a few years after he had become bishop of Hippo, a town second in importance only to Carthage, the capital city of the Roman province of Africa. Although no other example of autobiography survives from classical antiquity, we know that he had predecessors; the Roman statesman Sulla, for example, had written his memoirs in the first century B.C. But, judging from the examples of Greek and Latin biography that have survived—the lives of the famous Greeks and Romans by Plutarch, for example, or the lives of the Roman emperors of the first century A.D. by Suetonius—Augustine's book must have been very different from any of its predecessors.

The biographers, for example, hardly mention the childhood and youth of their subjects; they are concerned with the public career and, though they may give lurid details of the subject's private life (especially in the case of Suetonius), they do little to explore the psychology behind the virtues and vices they chronicle.

Augustine's work, however, is a spiritual biography, an account of a man's long and troubled journey toward his final conversion to the Christian faith that his mother had lived by and was to die in, an account, furthermore, pervaded by that sense of sin that is the particular contribution of Christianity to the Western mind. Augustine's genuine regret and shame for his part in the robbery of a neighbor's pear tree is something a classical Greek or Roman would have found incomprehensible.

This concentration on the spiritual life, rather than on the life of activity or the intellect, is the real novelty of the work, and from that stem many of its most remarkable innovations. The account of his childhood, for example, the first in all ancient literature, with its remarkable analysis of the process by which babies learn their parents' language, owes its genesis to Augustine's conviction of the basic sinfulness of man, even children. "In your sight," he says to God, "no man is free from sin, not even a child who has lived only one day on earth." This conviction that sin is innate in human nature and that without God's grace human beings cannot hope for salvation is a world away from the Greek anthropocentric vision of humanity's capacity for heroic action, as warrior, inventor, legislator, or poet, with or without and sometimes in defiance of the gods who are like us in shape as well as in their passions, different only in their overwhelming power.

Classroom Strategies

One assignment.

See "Backgrounds" for a discussion of the main difficulty the modern student will encounter—Augustine's sense of sin. You might add to the discussion of this subject the relevance of the form Augustine employs. The work is not presented as an autobiography; the title *Confessions* is accurate, since all through the work Augustine is speaking directly to God, confessing his sins. This, again, is something unparalleled in the ancient world, one more sign of the transition from the ancient to the medieval world that is visible in the pages of Augustine's book. No Greek or Roman would "confess" to a god; prayers, sacrifice, worship by hymns or dance, consultation by oracle—these were the pagan approaches to the gods. The very idea that a god would be interested in an individual's confession of wrongdoing is alien to the ancient mentality; the gods, for one thing, are not so closely concerned with human feeling and conduct. Augustine's sense of sin is oppressive, but, on other hand, his conviction that God is interested in him is a comfort that the pagan could not enjoy.

Topic for Discussion and Writing

Compare Augustine's evaluation of his own conduct with that offered by Socrates in the *Apology* and the complete lack of self-criticism or evaluation by Achilles in the *Iliad* (until, in book XXIV, he does for a moment see himself through the eyes of others).

Comparative Perspectives

1. Augustine is ashamed of having wept for Dido. What does he think is wrong with reading imaginative literature? How would you compare the attitudes of Lucian toward classical epic?
2. Look closely at Augustine's tribute to his mother, Monica. What virtues does he particularly commend in her? Would you want to see her conduct of family life emulated by women today? Compare her view of marriage and a woman's responsibilities to her husband with that of Rebekah in Genesis or Homer's Penelope.

Further Reading

See also the reading suggestions in the *Anthology*, 2639.

Marrou, H. *St. Augustine and His Influence through the Ages.* n.d. An introduction to the life and works, lavishly illustrated, with selections (translated) from other works than the *Confessions* and an estimate of his importance for later centuries.

The Middle Ages

Students may groan at the thought of reading and studying literature from the Middle Ages. They often have preconceived notions about what that literature entails—archaic language, long discourses about nobility, and most difficult to grasp, religion as a focal point. A good way to begin a unit on medieval literature would be to ask students what they expect of what they will read, what they think they know about the people and life of the years that span the millennium between 500 and 1500. You will probably find that while students have high opinions of the learning and culture of the ancient worlds of Greece and Rome and the period of renaissance in Europe that will bring us everything from Shakespeare to Michelangelo, they view the Middle Ages as a kind of wasteland—the "Dark" Age in every sense of the word.

It may be useful to start with the idea of "Middle" and why this long period is identified as such. When the Renaissance came into full bloom and its humanists looked back to the Ancient Worlds for its inspiration and ideas, they deemed the period in between as *medium aevum*, from which we get both the terms "medieval" and "Middle Ages." As far as many of those living in the sixteenth and seventeenth centuries were concerned, the Middle Ages was just a bridge and not in itself a moment of cultural production or change. This, however, is not at all the case, and it is important to point out to your students that the aspects of the Renaissance that they know and love so well would be virtually impossible without the learning, art, and writing that happened during the medieval period.

While the "Dark Ages" is often used a synonym for the Middle Ages, this is an unfortunate misunderstanding. In many ways, what historians have deemed the "Early" Middle Ages (roughly 300–1000) *is* "dark" to us. It is not that there was no cultural production or writing during those seven hundred years, but most of it is lost to us today, leaving us in the "dark" about what exactly was being produced. The few remnants that we have, like the writings of Augustine, *Beowulf*, and *The Song of Roland*, show that the time was indeed one of great imaginative growth and cultural production, but it seems that much of the culture was an oral one and many written and artistic documents from the era have long since been destroyed.

The "High" Middle Ages usually incorporates the years 1000–1200. In this period many of the oral stories and texts from the Early Middle Ages are finally recorded, like the Arabian tales in *The Thousand and One Nights* and the Breton *lais* of Marie de France, and the Western world makes a crucial transition into vernacular culture. Where Latin had ruled almost all written works, vernacular writers begin to use the predominant language for all things secular, as well as some theological texts. This is also the period when real creative literary work begins. Chretien de Troyes, for example, incorporates Arthurian and Celtic legends into his texts but is really creating his own story and characters as he does so.

The "Late" Middle Ages (1200–1500) is one of high production and yields most of the literature with which your students will be familiar: Chaucer, Boccaccio, Dante. You can have your students trace themes and ideas as they move from Early to High to Late Middle Ages and talk about what may come next in the Renaissance. One important point to stress to your students is that the Middle Ages encompasses a huge expansion of both time and place. While today is certainly the most "global" culture the world has ever known, things were not as isolated in the Middle Ages as people often believe. There was trade all over Europe and the Middle East, making a person in England just as likely to be familiar with silks and spices from Italy as from Palestine. In addition, the primacy of Christianity in Western Europe made pilgrimages the first tourism industry. Pilgrims came from all over Western Europe to places as far as Jerusalem (there were many travel guides for such a purpose). The fact that Latin was a widely known and used language made contact between cultures more common than we can imagine, allowing men from one country to preach or study in another with relative ease.

The fact that Latin was so widely known and used points to the centrality of Christianity in Western culture during the Middle Ages. Until Martin Luther, virtually all rulers in Europe were in some ways beholden to the papacy in Rome and there was no real separation of church and state the way the American government is conceived. It is important to point out to students that there were Jewish communities all throughout Europe, and although they participated in the life and culture of their countries, they suffered quite a bit of ostracism and prejudice (this can be seen in Chaucer's *Prioress' Tale*, for example). In parts of Spain, Islam was a major religious force and influence. Further, the pagan past of Europe would not be too far behind. While the Church ruled the practices and lives of many people, pagan religious practices still had their place in daily life (evidenced in harvest or carnival celebrations, for example). Texts like *Beowulf* show that its writer was still reconciling the pagan heritage of his culture with the Christianity he evidently believed and practiced. Students need to recognize that while Christianity was the governing religion of the time in Europe, both the rulers and the inhabitants would have been aware of (if not truly tolerant of) other religious beliefs.

As powerful as Christianity was in the governing and practices of medieval people, it was not wholeheartedly believed and accepted by all.

Students tend to be a bit reductive of people "back then" and not give them the same sense of agency or thought that they feel modern people possess. A medieval person would have been just as likely as a modern one to be critical or skeptical of things he or she was told to believe, and this shows in the literature of the time—both religious and secular. The consistent accusations of heresy throughout the Middle Ages demonstrate that the Church and government were both aware of the dangers of public dissenters and were always alert to those who did not toe the party line.

Of course, the literature will speak to this for itself. Although Christianity is ever-present (even if only in the character of a monk or priest), it is not always praised. These conflicting views are particularly evident in the tales of Chaucer and Boccaccio, but virtually every medieval European text will show some conflicts. If the Church is not the central focus, students will find conflicting views on other issues that they may have at first believed to be cut and dried. For example, the definition of codes of behavior like chivalry and nobility is constantly addressed and can be traced from texts as early as *Roland* and *Beowulf* through to *Perceval* and *Gawain and the Green Knight*.

Another marker of medieval literature is the blending and mixture of genres. Students will be tempted to identify pieces as bawdy humor, morality tales, epics, or romances, but they will soon see that any piece can have elements of all of these things and other genres as well. Writers in the Middle Ages are exposed to a variety of media—oral, literary, religious, visual—and these will all be reflected in their literature. Indeed, what students often find the most frustrating is the difficulty in "reading" a text the way they are used to—finding the beginning, middle (and climax), and the end. This kind of linear and set storytelling process is not part of the medieval mind-set, and it shows as texts begin in the middle, digress, throw in some poetry, return to the story, and maybe end in a satisfying way (but usually not so neatly). It is interesting to note that this kind of narrative nonlinearity (as in *Beowulf*) and the notion of stories within stories (like *The Thousand and One Nights*) is back in vogue and considered highly postmodern in its conception.

In the end, your students should find that the Middle Ages, far from "dark," is a period of imagination with a breadth and depth of creativity and cultural production that allows the Renaissance to follow. At the end of the unit, you may want to inquire how your students' perceptions of the time period have been altered and reshaped, and see what they expect to come next and why.

THE KORAN

Backgrounds

About the year 570 C.E. a young man was born into the Quraysh tribe of Mecca. He was given the name Muhammad, and since his father had died before his birth and his mother died while he was about six, he was raised first by his grandfather and then by his uncle, Abu Talib. In his early twenties he was married to the wealthy widow Khadija, who was some years older than him. The marriage was prompted by convenience—he was a poor orphan, she a middle-aged widow—but by all appearances it was a happy and loving one. He had been trained as a merchant by his uncle and had a talent for commerce. Their affairs prospered.

Muhammad had a serious, spiritual bent and often withdrew to meditate. One day in the year 610, while he was meditating in a cave outside Mecca, the Angel Gabriel appeared to him, ordered him to "Recite," and revealed to him the first verses of what became the Koran. Other verses followed, and Muhammad gradually gathered a circle of believers around him. The first was his wife, and the second his nephew, Ali. (Ali was married to Muhammad's daughter, Fatimah; became the fourth caliph, or successor, to him as leader of the community; and through his marriage to the Prophet's only surviving child, was the focus of the legitimist claims of the Shi'ite community.)

Others followed, and the success of this fledgling community threatened the established order of Mecca. Mecca's success as a trading center rested on its importance as a center of pilgrimage. Muhammad's God demanded the destruction of the idols that were the objects of pilgrimage. He also challenged the tribal basis of the society, saying that faith was more important than blood. He even went so far as to say that all the Meccans' ancestors who had not worshiped God were suffering the torments of damnation. Eventually, he was disowned by his own tribe, a virtual sentence of death, because it left him without protection from his enemies since there was no civil government outside of the tribal alliances. He survived by being adopted into another tribe. His situation was perilous, and some of his followers fled to temporary refuge in Ethiopia. Eventually, in 622, he and his community made a flight (Arabic *hijra*) to the oasis center of Medina at the invitation of the local residents. There he established a Muslim community, which he led until his death in 632. During this period, he attracted many converts from all over Arabia. He also forced out the Jewish tribes that had been resident there so that Medina became wholly Muslim.

In 624, Muhammad initiated a war with Mecca that ended with a complete Muslim victory in 630. All the Meccans converted to Islam, and the remaining tribes of Arabia followed their example in short order. Mecca became the center of the new religion, and a few months before his death, Muhammad returned to Mecca to make a pilgrimage to the Ka'ba—now emptied of idols—a journey that established the pilgrimage ritual that is followed to the present day.

Shortly before his death, Muslim expeditions were sent against Islam's neighbors to the north. There was a brief pause after the Prophet's death while the question of his succession was settled, but then the Muslim conquests continued to the north, west, and east with astonishing success. Within a century, Islam stretched from the Atlantic in the west to central Asia in the east, and from northern Syria to the southern shore of Arabia.

Classroom Strategies

One assignment.

Classroom Discussion

For those familiar with the Bible, the Koran is a hard book to get used to. It lacks the narrative thread of the Old Testament and is poor in the vivid stories and the rich variety of characters and incidents that reading the Bible has taught us to expect in a book of revelation. And despite the fact that "the Merciful," (ar-rahmân) and "the Munificent" (ar-rahîm) are the two commonest epithets given to God by Muslims, the revelations that make up the Koran more often speak of God's wrath and the punishments He inflicts on unbelievers than of His mercy and generosity.

While acknowledging where one's personal tastes lie, however, it can be self-defeating to read the Koran simply as an inferior version of the Bible. Whatever else it is, the Koran is a work of revelation that has inspired and continues to inspire Muslims throughout the world. Even today, Islam is the fastest-growing evangelical religion and one that has hundreds of millions of adherents in the Middle East, Asia, and Africa as well as large and increasingly influential communities in Europe, the U.K., and the United States. Indeed, it now seems likely that Muslims will displace Jews as the largest religious minority in the United States sometime early in the twenty-first century. Islam has served as the basis for a world civilization that in its golden age was the equal of any that existed before the modern transformation of Europe. The Koran has also provided the foundation for rich and varied literatures in a great many languages. For these reasons alone it merits careful study.

Examining the differences between the Koran and the Bible obliges us to read the Bible from a new perspective. It illuminates, for example, the extent to which the Bible is embedded in the story of a single nation, the Jews, and is the product of a lengthy historical process. Although the Koran is deeply linked to the Arabs by reason of its language, it does not explicitly elevate that nation over any other or designate it as chosen by God for special greatness. The Bible evolved over many generations, and many voices contributed to its composition. The revelations that make up the Koran were all mediated by a single personality, Muhammad, and in a single, brief historical moment. Despite differences in tone and emphasis, the Koran has a coherence and singleness of vision that makes it unlike the Bible. However, texts of revelation all seem to have some features in common—the exhortative tone of divine authority, an insistence on the transcendental meaning of human history, an oracular style that invites interpretation while inveighing against it, and the resistance of the heedless human community to the warnings of its prophets.

The most familiar portions of the Koran, and so the most accessible, are probably the prophetic tales. Sura 5 (The Table) indicates an awareness of at least portions of the story of Christ's birth from the Gospels (*anjil*). But Islam rejects the divinity of Jesus and the idea of the Trinity (which seems to have been understood to include God the Father, Jesus, and Mary), as Sura 5 makes clear in its concluding paragraphs. There are few other allusions to the teachings of Jesus Christ and none to indicate an awareness of the other portions of the New Testament. It seems, in short, as though the source was oral, not written, and might have resulted from conversations with Christians that Muhammad met in his travels north to Syria. But having said that, we enter the uncertain ground of speculation about whether or not Muhammad was the "author" of the Koran or simply the agency by which it was revealed. Christians and Jews are obliged by their faiths to assume that he was the author, and Muslims by theirs to reject any suggestion that words of the Koran are anyone but God's. In the Muslim view, the Koran's revelations were sent to correct and complete all prior revelations.

The Koran's relation to the Old Testament is both more obvious and more problematic. The Koran does not refer to the Old Testament, but it does to the books of the Torah, which are described as a single book of revelation, like the Koran—a revelation that Jesus was sent to confirm. The tales of the prophets that appear in both the Old Testament and the Koran are inevitably the focus of efforts to understand the relation of the two texts. They appear in the Koran as allusions or illustrations in a number of Suras, but are not gathered into independent narratives as they are in the Old Testament. Even when the scattered parts are gathered together, however, the versions are significantly different. Sura 12 (Joseph), which ignores completely Joseph's role as leader of the Jews, illustrates these differences most obviously. This famous Sura, the single long continuous narrative in the Koran, differs from the biblical treatment of this story (which Muhammad almost certainly had never read) by ignoring Joseph's role as leader of the Jews and by stressing the involvement of Allah in every significant human decision. As the headnote points out, much is made of Joseph's extraordinary beauty (p. 1149), which became proverbial in Islam; thus this telling of the story shows a sympathetic understanding of the motives of the Prince's wife. Moreover, Sura 12 tells us that Joseph "would have succumbed to" Potiphar's wife "had he not seen a sign from his Lord." By contrast, Genesis emphasizes Joseph's resourcefulness and his morally informed refusal to abuse his master's trust.

Other brief vignettes in Sura 5 (The Table) illustrate the same tendency in the Koran to glorify the power of Allah and blunt the struggle of the individual conscience; free will is not so important as the all-embracing protection Allah extends to believers. The abbreviated version of the murder of Abel by Cain (significantly, the names of "Adam's two sons" are not given) does not include the tense dialogues between Cain and Abel and then between Cain and God that readers who know the story from Genesis will remember. Rather, the Koran stresses the swiftness of the murdering son's repentance when he recognizes that Allah has sent him a sign.

Narrative chronology is also unimportant in the Koran. The prophets are connected to each other principally by their prophetic role, and there is little concern to link them by genealogy or much concern for historical sequence. A retelling of the story of Jesus and Mary may immediately precede a brief excerpt from the story of Abraham.

Koranic references to the prophets seem sketchy and incomplete in comparison with the more detailed biblical versions. Early Muslims seem to have been puzzled by these stories, too, and sought information about the prophets from Christian and Jewish converts to Islam. However, this material from outside the Koran was suspect at the same time that it was informative. It is an article of faith for Muslims that the Koran is perfect and self-contained. From the Muslim point of view, the fuller biblical versions of the prophetic tales distort and undermine the original intention of these stories. What appears as allusiveness to us is the divinely sanctioned style of revelation.

Topics for Writing

1. Compare the accounts of Cain and Abel, Joseph, Moses, or Noah in the Koran with those in the Old Testament of the Bible. How do the narrative strategies of these versions alter both their "message" and their relation to the larger discursive fabric in which they appear? Could you write an Islamic critique of the Old Testament versions of the prophetic tales?
2. What is the Koranic attitude toward women as revealed in Sura 12 (Joseph)?
3. How do Islamic perceptions of Heaven and Hell differ from those of Christianity and Judaism?
4. How does the Koran make the case for itself as an immortal work, the actual words of God?

Comparative Perspectives

1. Compare the Koran's many descriptions of paradise and the rewards that the righteous will enjoy there with Dante's vision of Paradise at the end of *The Divine Comedy*. How much in these perfect worlds seem culturally specific?
   [Note gardens, carpets, and fountains.]
2. Compare the emphasis on the purity required by pilgrimage in the Koran with Chaucer's treatment of pilgrimage in *The Canterbury Tales*.

Further Reading

See also the reading suggestions in the *Anthology*, p. 2643.

Arberry, A. J., trans. *The Koran*. 1955. The most poetic translation.

Esposito, John L. *Islam: The Straight Path*. 1988. Both useful and up to date.

Fisher, Michael J., and Mehdi Abedi. *Debating Muslims*. 1990. There is a thoughtful discussion of the dialogic nature of the Koran in part 2.

Gibb, H. A. R. *Islam*, 2nd rev. ed. 1962. This classic is still lucid and insightful.

Peter, F. E. *Children of Abraham: Judaism, Christianity and Islam*. 1982. Contains an excellent brief introduction to the comparative study of these three religions.

Schuon, Frithjof. *Understanding Islam*, 3rd ed. Translated by D. M. Matheson. 1972. An explication of Islamic beliefs and an impassioned defense of them. Chapter 2 is especially useful on the logic of the Koran.

BEOWULF

Backgrounds

Although *Beowulf* is now firmly placed in the canon of Western literature in general and English literature specifically, your students may not be familiar with how tenuous that position almost was. Many pieces of literature become canonical because of their popularity during their own time or their extensive influence on ensuing literature, but *Beowulf* cannot lay claim to either of these events. For one thing, *Beowulf* was preserved in only one manuscript (now housed in the British Library), so we have no sense of its contemporary popularity—at least in its written form—as it seems clear the work was in some ways circulating orally throughout England and Scandinavia. For another, that one manuscript was nearly lost in a fire in 1731 (in fact, some of the poem *is* lost to us, having been burned in that fire). Not until the nineteenth century did the poem enter our literary landscape.

The epic poem, probably written in the tenth century, is one of the earliest pieces of literature in English that we have. It seems to have been influenced—at least tangentially—by Scandinavian *sagas*, other epic poetry like the *Odyssey*, folklore, and oral legends. It is written in Anglo-Saxon, or Old English, a language that will seem to modern eyes very far from the English of today, as it was heavily influenced by the Norman invasion in 1066 that forever changed our vocabulary and syntax. It also may seem an odd kind of "poetry" to your students, who probably associate old poetry with rhyme schemes and iambic pentameter. Seamus Heaney's new translation gives the flavor of Anglo-Saxon words and poetic devices, and you should have your students look for alliteration—the major technique employed by Anglo-Saxon poets that survives well into the late Middle Ages—as well as the "caesura," a pause in the middle of each line. Another poetic device that Heaney translates well into our modern tongue is that of the "kenning," an Anglo-Saxon technique of combining two words to convey a new one, so that the ocean becomes "whale-road" and bodies are "bone-lockers."

It is also useful to look at the narrative structure of the poem in detail. While the main narrative plot follows Beowulf and his exploits against Grendel, Grendel's mother, and the dragon, the poem is constantly leading the reader off into narrative asides, telling stories within stories.

Some of these seem strange digressions to the modern reader, but they would probably have held great significance to the poem's original audience and show how legends and oral stories were most likely interlinked and led into one another. They also serve as foils for the dominant narrative, reminders of what had been or could have been depending on fate.

There is also an interesting tension throughout the epic between Christian and pagan sensibilities and beliefs. The poet is obviously writing in a Christian time and very possibly even a Christian place, like a monastery. However, the poem is from another time, when pagan beliefs ruled. It is easy to see where these tensions arise—for example, Beowulf does not seem to have any of the values dear to Christian heroes, like humility, but often swears his allegiance to a Christian God. Grendel, too, is a strange amalgam of Christian and pagan beliefs; he is described as a descendant of the Old Testament Cain. At the end of the poem, students may grapple with the seemingly depressing closure after Beowulf's death, indicating that all he worked for and achieved will eventually come to naught. It may help to explain that the Anglo-Saxon worldview is one that understands the power of fate and how the "wheel of fortune," as it was conceived, keeps turning (again at conflict with the Christian concept of free will).

No divisions are specifically indicated in the poem, but scholars seem to agree that it falls into either two or three parts. In the latter division, part one would encompass Beowulf's fight with Grendel, part two would be his fight with Grendel's mother, and the third part would be the fight with the dragon. Considered in two parts the first would deal with both Grendel and his mother, while the second part would be Beowulf's fight with the dragon. You may find an outline listing the sequence of topics (or groups of topics) helpful. Such an outline may be especially appropriate in view of the poet's fondness for including brief narratives not actually a part of the main story. These are sometimes called "digressions," but this term is inaccurate as well as unfriendly. The poet never loses sight of his theme and purpose; rather, a situation or event in the story of Beowulf often reminds him—by similarity or contrast—of a figure or an incident from Germanic tradition. The "included narratives" (as we shall call them) are sometimes closely related to the central plot: thus Beowulf's account of the swimming feat shared with Breca both refutes Unferth's disparaging remarks and reinforces his fitness to undertake the contest with Grendel. (It is a substantial item of his résumé!) And near the end of the poem, the gloomy forecast of a Geatish spokesman—now that the great king Beowulf is gone—is justified by references to earlier wars between the Geats and foreign nations. Nevertheless, it may prove helpful to recognize the distinction between Beowulf's exploits (and their context) and the other topics in the poem. The included narratives are enclosed in brackets in the following list.

1. Pp. 1180–81: The ship burial of the Danish king Scyld; his royal descendants down to Hrothgar, who builds the splendid hall named Heorot. (Includes the *Prologue* to the poem.)

2. P. 1183: Heorot ravaged by the monster Grendel; arrival of Beowulf, a Geatish prince; entertainment in Heorot; offer to await Grendel in the hall. [Included narrative: the swimming feat of young Beowulf and Breca.]

3. P. 1197: Beowulf's victory over Grendel; celebration with speeches and gift giving. [Included narratives: Sigemund, the dragon-slayer; the story of Hnaef and Finn.]

4. Pp. 1208–10: Heorot invaded by Grendel's mother, who kills Aeschere; Beowulf's fight with her in the underwater room, and return to Heorot.

5. Pp. 1215–27: Renewed celebration in Heorot; Beowulf's farewell to Hrothgar; return voyage of the Geats to Hygelac's kingdom. [Included narratives: Heremod's disastrous career as a warning to Beowulf; the taming of Modthryth.] Beowulf's report to King Hygelac, his uncle, marks the end of part 1. [Included narrative: Ingeld and renewal of a Danish-Heatho-Bard feud—represented as a prophecy by Beowulf.]

6. Pp. 1227–33: Beowulf and the dragon. [Included narratives: Hygelac's expedition against the Frisians and Franks, in which he was killed, his death avenged by Beowulf, who killed Daeghrefn, the slayer of Hygelac; Beowulf supports young Eofor and succeeds him as king of the Geats when Heardred is killed in a battle with Swedes;
Beowulf's autobiographical speech recounting earlier Geatish wars.]

7. Pp. 1237–43: With Wiglaf's help, Beowulf finally kills the dragon; the hero gives directions for his funeral pyre and memorial mound; Beowulf's death. [Included narratives: the herald's prophecy of wars between Geats and Swedes, Frisians, and Franks; he recounts episodes from times past, notably the deeds of the Swedish king Ongentheow.]

Classroom Strategies

Assignments will naturally depend on the length of time devoted to the poem. The list above may serve as a flexible outline of the possibilities: the area covered in each item could provide enough material for a single class period. In the event of time restrictions, combinations of these sections are possible.

The range of emphases in teaching *Beowulf* is wide indeed; each instructor is free to decide which focus is best suited for the course. The editor's view is indicated, more or less, in the headnote in the anthology and in "Topics for Discussion and Writing," below. Judicious use of visual aids—slides, photographs, etc.—have proved especially valuable in any approach to the poem.

Approaches to Teaching Beowulf, edited by Jess B. Bessinger Jr. and Robert F. Yeager (from the Masterpieces of World Literature series, MLA, 1984) is a rich mine of materials and information. Donald K. Fry (pp. 144–49) offers an extensive list of visual materials. The book also contains, as its primary content, groups of essays by experienced scholars arranged according to particular focus: undergraduate and graduate classes in Old English, in translation, mixed undergraduate and graduate classes, and so on. Along with the books mentioned in the anthology, this volume provides abundant guidance in both teaching focus and further reading.

Topics for Discussion and Writing

1. Do you find Beowulf more or less attractive than Homer's Achilles or Odysseus?

   [You should defend your preference by citing acts, situations, and speeches from the poems. Then try to form a comprehensive but concise statement of your view.]

2. Which is the more dangerous antagonist for Beowulf: Grendel or Grendel's mother?

   [Discuss specific features of each contest, for example, the killing of Hondscioh, the escape of Grendel from Heorot, the fearsome head of Grendel, which Beowulf brings back to Heorot; and the fierceness of Grendel's mother's struggle with the hero, the lucky discovery of a sword at the essential moment.]

3. The poem has been described as a portrait of the ideal ruler, "a mirror for princes" of the age. What do you think of this view?

   [Consider the traits of character shown in the narrative—the motives of his acts; his treatment of Unferth, Hrothgar, Wealtheow, Wiglaf, Hygd, and Hrethric; including the similarities and contrasts suggested by reference to other figures of Germanic tradition.]

4. In a speech after the hero's death, Wiglaf expresses regret that his friends could not persuade Beowulf to leave the dragon alone. What do you think of this view?

   [Consider such aspects as these: what the dragon was doing; the apparent absence of anyone else to cope with the dragon; the hero's motives (the glory and the gold); the responsibility of the king for the welfare of his people. (If you have read Sophocles' play *Oedipus the King*—in the anthology—you might compare Oedipus' refusal to follow the advice of others, especially Tiresias.)]

Comparative Perspectives

1. What happens to women in the world of Beowulf? Compare gender roles and relations in heroic narratives of other cultures in the Middle Ages.

2. What does the hero's choice of weapons in this poem tell us about him as a fighter and as a human being? Compare the weapons and the means of dealing with their enemies chosen by other heroes, looking for evidence about them in the same way.

   [Consider Achilles, Odysseus, Roland.]

Further Reading

See the reading suggestions in the *Anthology*, p. 2643.

THE SONG OF ROLAND

Backgrounds

In 777 C.E. Charles, king of the Franks, later known as Emperor Charlemagne, concluded an agreement with a rebel faction of the Saracen rulers of Spain. In return for sending an army in support of that faction, Charlemagne was to be acknowledged sovereign of the entire country. But things did not work out as planned. The great city of Saragossa, which by the agreement was to welcome Charles's entry, kept its gates closed against him, and following a fruitless six-week siege, he decided to withdraw. On August 15, 778, as it made its way home through the Pyrenees, his army was set upon in the manner described in the following passage from a life of Charlemagne, written about fifty years after the event:

> It happened this way: as the army was proceeding, stretched out in a long thin column because of the narrowness of that defile, the Basques [*Wascones*] lay in ambush on top of a mountain—the place is thickly covered with woods and therefore well suited for such covert attacks; and they rushed down upon the end of the baggage train and upon those troops in the rear guard who were protecting the main army ahead, forced them down to the bottom of the valley, engaged them in battle and killed them to the last man; then they looted the baggage, and protected by the gathering night they scattered in every direction with all the speed they had. In what took place the Basques were favored by the lightness of their arms and the terrain in which they fought; and the Franks were put thoroughly at a disadvantage by the great weight of their arms and the unevenness of the ground. In this battle were killed Eggihardus, seneschal of the royal table; Anshelmus, count of the palace; and Hruodlandus [i.e., Roland], prefect of the marches of Brittany, among many others.

It is on this incident, altogether transformed by storytellers' imaginations, that the *Song* is based. As the poem presents it, Charles's withdrawal from Saragossa is brought about by a trick. The Saracen king of Spain, Marsilion, seeing his country laid waste by seven years of French invasion and even Saragossa about to fall, sends Charles a deceitful message promising to surrender sovereignty if he and his forces will return to France. Marsilion and the other Arab leaders will, they promise, speedily follow him there, confess his rule, and convert to Christianity.

To Charles and his barons, worn by years of war, the offer looks attractive and is accepted, though one of their number opposes it: Roland. Now word of their acceptance must be sent to Marsilion, and the question is who shall go? The last time ambassadors were sent to the Arabs, they were executed. Various stalwart heroes volunteer—Roland, Oliver, Turpin, and others—but Charles is unwilling to risk them. At last Roland nominates his stepfather, Ganelon, a choice all immediately approve. All, that is, except Ganelon, who is outraged and plans revenge. Reaching Saragossa as Charles's ambassador, he tells Marsilion and the other Arab leaders that the surest way to be rid of the French forever is to kill their stoutest fighting men—Roland, Oliver, and the Twelve Peers—by a sortie against the forces that will be left behind to protect the army's rear as it makes its way through the mountain passes. He, Ganelon, will see to it that Roland and the rest are in that rear guard.

Returning to the French camp, Ganelon announces that the Arabs will behave as promised. Naturally, a rear guard will have to be established for security's sake, and who so suitable to command it as Roland and his dauntless friends? In the great battle that follows, twenty thousand French soldiers are slain with their leaders until only Roland remains—dying not because any Saracen has bested him but because he has burst his temples by his efforts to recall Charles's armies with mighty blasts upon the oliphant, the ivory horn.

Summoned, too late, by Roland's trumpet, the emperor Charles returns with his main army and destroys Marsilion and his allies. There follows a long episode telling of his later victory over the great Saracen leader Baligant, after which the scene changes to the headquarters at Aix. Ganelon is brought to trial; his claim that his acts against Roland involved no treason against Charles is finally disallowed. There ensues a "judicial combat" between the emperor's champion Tierri and Ganelon's representative Pinabel; victory was left in the hands of God in the traditional view of such affairs. Pinabel is defeated, and Ganelon is executed.

The poem itself offers abundant evidence that it has a background in the "oral" tradition of poetic composition. First, there is a pattern of repetition; for example, the idea that Charles will, or may, or should leave Spain and return to his capital at Aix is stated at lines 36ff., 51ff., 134ff., and 187ff. The scene and the participants vary, or course, but the thought is expressed again and again in very similar phrasing. Entire scenes are often closely parallel: Charles and Marsilion hold assemblies, receive ambassadors, listen to counselors, and render decisions essentially in the same manner. The battles are series of single combats between notable fighters and the action as well as the language describing it is often much the same from one encounter to the next. And since the deeds and the skills remain essentially identical, it is natural that the words and phrases that describe them should do so as well. The result is a large number of more or less uniform phrases or short sentences. In the *Roland* and in the Greek epics and in the Old English *Beowulf* also the result is a body of *formulaic* diction (differing from one language to another) conspicuous in poems deriving from a background of oral tradition. These poems were meant to be listened to by an audience, rather than read by a solitary individual in silence. Hence the recurrence of set phrases, like the repetition of scenes, would reinforce the narrative and reassure (rather than annoy) the public for which the poems were composed.

Roland is by general consent the finest example of a popular genre of narrative poetry known in French as the *chanson de geste*. Poems of this kind dealt typically with great deeds done in war or warlike adventure; normally love is absent or unimportant, and this especially differentiates the *chanson de geste* from the romance (French *roman*). Again typically, *Roland* has a tenuous relation to actual history; the central background figure is Charles, king of the Franks (crowned emperor by the pope in the year 800, the first head of the Holy Roman Empire). But comparison of the historical kernel, given on earlier pages, with the poet's narrative will indicate the extent of the transformation.

As intimated in the headnote in the anthology, the attitude of the poet is emphatically "positive"; the story as he tells it is filled with enthusiasm for king, Charles, whom all his feudal vassals extol with complete sincerity; for country, "sweet France," almost a refrain in many a *laisse*; and for the Christian religion. Indeed, Charles feels an obligation either to annihilate the heathen religion of the Saracens by destroying or by converting its adherents. Neither the poet nor any of his Christian characters expresses the least doubt as to the rightness of this purpose. It may seem a bit strange to us that they know so little about the faith they oppose; the poem makes them polytheists, worshipers, oddly enough, of the Greek god Apollo as well as the Arabic prophet Mahoun (Muhammad). Historically, of course, they have always been strict worshipers of one god, Allah, whose prophet was Muhammad. In short, the poet is an ardent partisan untroubled by qualms of any kind. Once the modern reader understands and accepts this fact, he or she should be free to enjoy the unremitting energy deployed in the narrative, to delight in the brilliant pageantry of its assemblies, to "identify" with Roland and his comrades in the procession of military duels.

But *Roland* is not simply a narrative of straightforward action; the plot is complicated by the treachery of Ganelon and later by the disagreement between Oliver and Roland. The poet carefully shows us how Ganelon sets about his object, the destruction of Roland. This is no easy task. First, he must convince King Marsilion that Roland, not Charles, is an implacable enemy of the Saracens, and he must begin by convincing Blancandrin, the envoy who has come from Marsilion and who will return with Ganelon himself. Then he must persuade Marsilion to send hostages and false promises of submission to Charles and then to attack with overwhelming force the small army that Charles will leave behind as a rear guard under Roland's command. If we dwell for a moment on the several uncertainties in this plan—the number of things that could go wrong—we realize what a skillful diplomat Ganelon must have been. Thus his initial harshness in stating Charles's (alleged) terms is designed to anger Marsilion and his court, to get them in the mood to fight. Once that is done, the anger can be directed against Roland. The poet's lines make it clear that Ganelon took a deliberate risk; there were two moments at which he might have been struck down by an enraged Saracen. (This topic could be a focus of class discussion or written assignments.)

Oliver, whose sister has been promised in marriage to Roland, is also his closest friend and, apparently, second only to him in valor. From the beginning onward the poet calls attention to the difference between these devoted friends. When Roland offers himself as the envoy to Marsilion, it is Oliver who protests at once (lines 255–57):

> "No, no, not you!" said Oliver the Count,
> "that heart in you is wild, spoils for a fight,
>   how I would worry—you'd fight with them, I know."

Later, when both see the huge Saracen army approaching the rear guard, Oliver pleads with Roland to blow the trumpet, which will bring Charles to the rescue; Roland is adamant in his refusal. Finally, after the rear guard has suffered total defeat and death stares the survivors in the face, Roland wants to sound the horn; now Oliver objects, and his anger is evident when he breaks off the marriage arrangement between his sister and Roland. His reply to Roland, who asks why Oliver is angry with him, is important for the poet's characterization of Roland: it is judgment, not madness, that makes a good vassal; Roland had rejected (good) judgment when he refused to sound the horn while there was time. The reply occupies an entire *laisse* (no. 131). The relationship between the two men (which need not be further rehearsed here) is one of the major foci of the narrative; it should receive due attention in the classroom. Nowhere else in the poem is there a relationship of friendship, then alienation, then misunderstanding, and finally reconciliation at death. As for the attitude of the poet, it seems clear that he uses the contrast of the two men to point to a flaw in the character of Roland. Immediately after Roland's rejection of Oliver's repeated pleas that the horn be sounded (before the battle), we find the line (1093), "Roland is good, and Oliver is wise." (The word translated *good* is the French *proz*, which may best be rendered "valiant.") The distinction, made incidentally in this passage, is confirmed and developed in *laisse* 131.

But Roland's defect does not lead the author to "prefer" Oliver or to treat him as of comparable importance to Roland. It is clear that Roland is the central figure in the poem as a whole and especially in the first half—until his death. He is the only man who declares that Marsilion does not intend to keep his promise of submission to Charles; now the poet has already told us (readers or listeners) the same thing. This weights our sympathy in advance on Roland's side. Then, while Oliver's deeds in the battle are heroic, like those of all the leaders of the French, Roland's are superheroic (but never treated as incredible or ridiculous). After the death of all the rest—except Turpin, and again after *his* death—Roland and Roland alone holds the stage for many a *laisse*. (A good topic for oral discussion or an essay assignment might be found here.)

The fighting archbishop, Turpin, proves, at least, in the poet's view, that the crusading zeal of Charles and Roland is righteous. He promises paradise to the French warriors; the penance he assigns for their confessed sins is to fight bravely! His prominence in the story is indicated by the fact that he dies last of all—except Roland. In this war, church and state are indeed united.

Classroom Strategies

You will, of course, divide the poem for class assignments according to the time available, but here are a few convenient breaks in the narrative to the death of Roland:

1. *Laisses* 1–27: Charles chooses Ganelon as envoy to Marsilion.
2. *Laisses* 28–53: Ganelon and Marsilion plot treachery.
3. *Laisses* 54–71, 79–95, 104–15, and 125–27: destruction of the rear guard.
4. *Laisses* 128–76: the last great deeds and death of Roland.

Topics for Discussion

1. The poet's attitude toward Roland.

   [Take account of the passages cited in item 3 under "Topics for Writing"; then note that Roland dominates the action of the poem both before and after the disagreement with Oliver; overall as well as piece by piece Roland is paramount; note his well-nigh superhuman exertion after the rest of the French are all dead and the enemy either dead or fled, and so on. He is a flawed hero but nonetheless the hero of the poem.]
2. Archbishop Turpin and the Crusaders' attitude.

   [Turpin's prominence as both fighting man and priest; his hearing the confessions of the French and assigning the penance of valor in battle; the final blessing of the slain leaders whose bodies Roland brings to Turpin; the repeated assertion that Christians are right and pagans are wrong (in the course of the poem).]
3. The supernatural and the superhuman elements in the poem.

   [Omens; dreams; the angel Gabriel; the exertions of Roland in the final scenes. Does all this amount to a miscellany of the incredible, tacitly ridiculed by the poet? Or is it so handled that the reader accepts it without demur, with no distress over its improbability in our prosaic, workaday world?]
4. Elements of oral poetry in *Roland*.

   [The frequent pattern of repetition of incidents or situations or items of dialogue—for example, Oliver's three requests that Roland blow the horn (lines 1051–92) and Roland's three refusals, matched by Roland's later declaration that he will now blow it and Oliver's dissent, both stated twice (lines 1702–21). In climactic situations like these such repetition is still effective for the modern reader, though the partial repetition of identical phrasing shows that we have here a relic of oral practice.]

Topics for Writing

1. How does Ganelon persuade King Marsilion to plan an attack against Roland and the rear guard?

   [Begin with the talk between Ganelon and the Saracen envoy

Blancandrin during their journey from Charles's headquarters to Marsilion's. Then Ganelon states Charles's message in the harshest, most offensive terms possible; and, acting as his surrogate, draws Marsilion's hot anger on himself. But with Blancandrin's help this anger is diverted from Ganelon (and Charles) and directed at Roland. They now plan the destruction of Roland by means of the attack on the rear guard.]

2. The poet's parallel treatment of the courts and entourage of Charles and Marsilion.

[Each is shown presiding over a group of leaders and advisers of the ruler; each has a select group of warriors (the twelve—*douze*—peers) distinguished above the mass; and heading these groups are Charles's nephew, Roland, and Marsilion's nephew, Aelroth. The peers do battle with peers on the opposing side; nearly all are spectacular fighters, though the French are (individually) superior (the Saracen victory is due to overwhelming numbers). Students' papers should quote or cite specific passages of the poem, usually moving from the first assemblies onward.]

3. Oliver's attitude toward Roland.

[Begin with Oliver's protest when Roland offers to go as Charles's envoy to Marsilion (lines 255–57). Go on to Oliver's urging Roland to blow the horn that will call Charles to the rescue (lines 1049–92: Oliver asks three times and Roland refuses three times); then to Roland's wish to blow the horn when it is clear that the French will be destroyed, whereupon Oliver dissents— and breaks off the betrothal of his sister Aude to Roland (line 1702–21); then to Oliver's answer to Roland's question, "Why are you angry at me?" (lines 1722–37), "I will tell you what makes a vassal good: / it is judgment, it is never madness." Finally there is an implicit reconciliation just before Oliver's death (2010–23).]

Comparative Perspectives

1. Heroic literature shows reverence for kings even while it reveals their human limitations. What gesture repeatedly describes Charles the Great? How does this link him with Beowulf's Hrothgar?

[See the opening of *laisse* 15 of *The Song of Roland*, in which "The Emperor held his head bowed down with this, / and stroked his beard, and smoothed his mustache down, / and speaks no word." In these narratives, kings may be ineffectual, malign, or wrong, but their right to rule is never challenged.]

2. The attitudes toward Islam in *The Song of Roland* demonstrate how the Saracens threatened medieval Christians. Compare the view of the Christian world in the Koran.

[Cf. references to "The People of the Book" in the Koran.]

Further Reading

See the reading suggestions in the *Anthology*, p. 2644.

MARIE DE FRANCE

Lanval *and* Laüstic

Classroom Strategies and Topics for Discussion

With Marie de France, a leading figure in the Renaissance of the twelfth century, medieval literature moves decisively from the heroic to the romantic. The headnote's reference to romances as "novelistic narratives" is a good point from which to start a discussion of the lai, the genre with which Marie is primarily identified. Much briefer than the romance (variously represented in the anthology by Sir Gawain and the Green Knight, The Wife of Bath's Tale, and Malory's Morte Darthur), lais are distinguished by their intensity, their use of symbols, and their frequent appeal to the supernatural. Although the narratives are pared down, by invoking the symbolic and the supernatural they offer surprisingly acute insights into motive and personality. In their penetration of her human actors and the scenes that surround them, Marie's lais do indeed prefigure the novel as we know it today.

In introducing their work, the translators of *Lanval* and *Laüstic* point out that the "*lai* . . . generally starts from a position of lack and crisis" and moves swiftly to a moment of happiness that is then severely tested. The topic is generally love, and in this respect as well Marie sets a pattern that is to define much of the great narrative fiction written by women down to the present day. Looking at the way individuals are revealed by the choices they make in love and marriage, she is a precursor of writers like Jane Austen and George Eliot and the lesser authors of romances that many of your students doubtless cherish. Like these novelists, Marie is an astute recorder of manners. Today's students often think of "good manners" as phony, externalized poses. Reading the fiction of manners should prove otherwise.

Without saying so explicitly, in *Lanval* Marie undercuts the Arthurian court (as Chaucer's Wife of Bath will do from a very different vantage point two centuries later) by emphasizing the good manners of Lanval, which put to shame the unexplained neglect that he suffers at the hands of knights who are supposed to have perfected good behavior. In *Laüstic*, her keen eye for the physical circumstances in which her characters live allows for a different critique of manners and the way they express the truth of human nature.

By beginning the action of *Lanval* in late spring, Marie de France appeals to the same seasonal expectations that set the mood for so many of the love lyrics in the anthology: spring and summer are times when mind and body can flower into romantic radiance along with fields and trees. You might ask your students why Marie specifically mentions Pentecost and St. John's Day—festival days that offer a hiatus from the everyday responsibilities of the workaday world by reminding believers of their ties to another, higher world in touch with the miraculous. The appearance of the otherworldly to the unhappy hero is heralded by a detail your students will probably recognize—Lanval's trembling horse resembles the sensitive animals who populate vampire and werewolf movies and always know well before their human owners that the supernatural has invaded the ordinary world. (According to Malory, Pentecost was also the occasion for an annual oath sworn by the Knights of the Round Table to defend ladies and gentlewomen "upon pain of death." If Marie was familiar with this tradition, her reference to Pentecost compounds the ironies of Lanval's difficulties, since his impetuous defense of his lady both defies her explicit orders and enrages the queen.)

The generosity and kindness of the extravagantly outfitted and alluringly beautiful ladies show up Arthur's unexplained denial of gifts deserved to a lonely foreigner. Although the lady is clearly supernatural, she is never called a fairy; surprisingly, her attractions are described in highly material terms. Even her clothing seems paradoxical: in warm weather, she wears white ermine that reveals more than it conceals. Likening her to Semiramis and Octavian may be yet another stab at Arthur, who never approaches the imperial sway associated with these famed rulers, but Semiramis in particular, legendary for her incestuous lust, is a curiously compromised figure of comparison. However capricious the lady might turn out to be, Lanval—"neither foolish nor ill-mannered"—behaves perfectly with his unearthly lover and graciously with those in need. His lavish charity reveals his moral superiority to the court that has withheld its rewards from him.

Marie paints a compelling picture of the society that first snubbed and then tries Lanval: note the introduction of the queen "reclining by a window cut out of the stone," indolent and watchful at once, and the ferocity with which she strikes out at Lanval when he rejects her. It is typical of medieval narrative that it declines to explicate moments so fraught with drama. Marie's great gift for suggesting interiority comes through in the crisis that this scene between lady and vassal precipitates, with both retreating to their bedchambers, hurt and angry. Poor Arthur, happily returning from a day in the woods to a demanding wife, is faced with a catastrophe at once domestic and political.

The failure of King Arthur's court is carefully delineated; the legendary companionship of the Round Table has been flawed from the start. The emphasis on Gawain and his ever-present entourage and the comment that "a hundred" would have liked to see Lanval acquitted remind us of how estranged the foreign knight has been from the group activities that prevail throughout this tale. Whose fault is it that there is no place for this sensitive, alienated soul in this public realm? At the very end, Marie implies that the martial concerns of the Arthurian world have deformed the good manners for which it has become legendary. Perhaps the heavy marble block that supports armed warriors about to mount their chargers symbolizes the crudity that has infected the chivalric world. The alienated hero has no real choice but to follow his unearthly lover, who bears him away to the mystical land of Avalon rather than to battle. If you plan to move on to read the *Morte Darthur*, you will want to call your students' attention to this moment, for the dying Arthur himself will be gathered to the Vale of Avalon, the only place where he can finally escape the conflicts that brought his kingdom down.

In turning to *Laüstic*, you may want to spend a few moments discussing the authorial self-consciousness that leads Marie to address her audience directly and refer to her own tale-telling. She pays attention to her titles and prides herself on her linguistic range, for words count in her poetry. Although she is a writer, she probably functioned as an oral performer as well, perhaps offering her *lais* to the court as an evening's entertainment. References to her literary situation seem most appropriate as they frame the very brief *Laüstic*, which is, as the headnote points out, much like the jeweled reliquary that contains the nightingale and by extension its song, the essence of poetic art.

It would be rewarding to ask your students to locate the center of narrative consciousness in both *Lanval* and *Laüstic*. Marie de France displays unusual interest in her female characters and the drives that motivate them, matters about which the headnote provides helpful guidance. Yet she is no special pleader for her heroines. Lanval himself is very much the center of his tale, the cynosure of two powerful women. *Laüstic*, on the other hand, begins with the friendship of the two knights of St. Malo, and only focuses on the lady when the love triangle has been established. The suggestion that the bachelor falls in love with his married friend's wife out of a sense of rivalry rather than for any good qualities possessed by the lady herself qualifies our response to this ultimately failed love affair.

The real interest here seems to be in the adjoining houses that create the proximity that brings the lovers together but also rest on the wall that keeps them apart. It is perhaps not too distant a digression to spend some time talking about the importance of architecture in the frequent tales of adulterous passion that distinguish medieval European literature. Ask your students to think back to the mead-hall of *Beowulf*, where Hrothgar's warriors congregate; only the king and queen seem to have private accommodations. Look ahead to a bawdy tale like Boccaccio's Sixth Story of the Ninth Day, which, like many a fabliau, derives its humor from the complex geography of the shared bedroom. Adulterous love is a theme primarily in aristocratic literature because a person needs time and privacy to indulge it. The two knights of St. Malo have up-to-date homes, it would appear, but they are crammed together in limited urban space. Without a luxurious, self-standing castle, adultery on a grand scale appears hard to sustain.

Marie de France can be quite direct about cruelty and pain, as in her depiction of the husband's obsessive pursuit of the nightingale. He correctly understands that the bird represents his wife's personal freedom, whether or not he suspects her of adulterous love. Marie implies that this need to assert her separate being is the real source of the love the wife feels for her neighbor; perhaps she is spared a direct attack because the love never takes a material form. The spatter of blood on her breast is a mild rebuke, hardly a scarlet letter.

Keeping other materials in the anthology again in mind, you may want to assign *Laüstic* in tandem with Boccaccio's Ninth Story of the Fourth Day, which seems to be an elaborate variation on the basic plot of *Laüstic*. The symbolism of the cherished nightingale, an emblem of a love that never really transgressed the bounds of marriage, is transformed to the brutal reality of a lover's heart served up to the unsuspecting lady, who consumes it and then kills herself. The casual horror inflicted by the husband in Boccaccio's story does not belong in the Breton *lai*, a more delicate genre suited to the first great woman writer in England.

Topics for Writing

Detailed observation of the material world in Marie de France's lais gives substance to a genre that shows the importance of transcending the material world.

1. Discuss the physical details that describe the regal elegance and sexual attractions of the otherworldly lady in *Lanval*. How is she shown to possess qualities that diminish Arthur's realm and his jealous queen?
2. Show the significance of the adjoining houses and the jeweled casket in *Laüstic*.

Comparative Perspectives

1. Marie de France flavors her poetry with allusions to oral performance. Compare her self-reflective comments on her art form with the traces of oral formulaic in the early epic poems of the medieval period, like Beowulf and The Song of Roland.
2. Compare and contrast the response of Lanval to the queen's advances and accusation with those of Joseph to Potiphar's wife in Genesis and/or the Koran. Why in each case does the man refuse the lady's offer of herself? How is the lady treated by the narrator?

CHRÉTIEN DE TROYES

The Story of the Grail

Backgrounds

Writing toward the end of the twelfth century, Chrétien de Troyes is one of the earliest and most influential authors of Arthurian romances, one of the most popular genres of the Middle Ages that will be reinvented for centuries to come. At first glance it may seem strange that de Troyes was French and wrote in French about an English hero, Arthur, but after the Norman invasion in 1066 French was the language of the educated and the nobility in England and was the language of choice for most literature. There is much evidence that de Troyes had English readers. There is also some evidence that de Troyes probably spent some time in Britain and was familiar with both places and customs. De Troyes is the first author to put the Arthurian legends and oral histories into romance form. His sources, however, are mainly lost to us today save for Geoffrey of Monmouth's pseudo-historical account of the Kings of Britain.

Many parts of the Arthurian legends that we consider most basic— Guinevere's love for Lancelot, for example—are de Troyes's inventions and part of his collection of romances concerning Arthur. His texts are also the first place where the grail is mentioned—but not in the context with which we normally associate the grail, as a quest Arthur and his knights pursue. Here, Perceval is a naïve but noble rural man turned knight who witnesses the grail at the home of the Fisher King. The grail here is a plate, not a chalice, and has no overt link to the life or death of Jesus Christ, the idea that later becomes its main distinguishing characteristic. Students may be somewhat disappointed that the intrigue and conspiracy theory surrounding the grail in today's popular culture (mainly thanks to *The Da Vinci Code*) is utterly absent from its early appearance in Arthurian lore. While grail legends certainly existed and circulated throughout Celtic culture, they had never been explicitly linked to the Arthurian legends that seem to have been circulating separately.

While the title implies that the story is about the grail, it is quickly obvious that the narrative is actually about Perceval's journey—from being naïve to having knowledge, from being a country boy to becoming a knight, from being uncouth to becoming chivalrous. Finally, the story ends with Perceval's transition to a place of real salvation and penance. For students of modern literature, the transition may seem more abrupt than what they may be used to in later coming-of-age narratives, but for medieval literature this kind of sustained adventure story is relatively new. Of course, in the Middle Ages any transition into maturity necessarily encompasses a more mature relationship with God and one's own sins and penance, making what may seem at first a puzzling ending more understandable within the context of the time.

De Troyes is writing for an audience that is probably familiar with many of the different Arthurian legends and characters circulating throughout France and Britain. Many of de Troyes's allusions and details may seem tedious or uninteresting to modern students, but for his original audience they would have meant more and enhanced the storytelling experience. Unfortunately, most of these are now lost to us, or are at least are not readily evident for the scholar or student who is encountering an Arthurian tale for the first time. If your students find some details irrelevant or parts of the narrative a bit tedious, it may be helpful to point out that these things may have meant a lot more to the first audience (just like many modern movies reference current products and events in ways that may seem strange or unimportant to future spectators).

Classroom Discussion

Students will be somewhat familiar with Arthur and his knights from the myriad modern films and books on the subject—*The Sword in the Stone, Excalibur, Mists of Avalon, First Knight*, and others. One way that you can have students approach the text is by deciding what is familiar and known to them and what seems particularly strange or foreign. For example, the stories of both the Fisher King and the grail have taken on lives of their own in Arthurian literature and lore. Today, these are probably some of the major features of Arthurian legend and film (as is Guenevere's relationship with Lancelot, also de Troyes's invention in another romance), and it may be interesting to ask your students why they think these particular aspects have gripped the popular imagination for so long.

De Troyes is one of the first authors to describe his characters' setting in detail. One exercise may be to have students comb the text for descriptive images of armor, clothing, halls, and other things and discuss what they tell us about medieval life and people. For example, Perceval's initial refusal to take off his mother's clothing is accompanied by rich descriptions of what he is wearing and what he is offered. The clothing very clearly represents the two worlds that are colliding here: the countryside and the court. Perceval believes his clothes are very suitable and fine, but the knights find them ill-fitting and representative of his uncouth Welsh upbringing.

Chivalry is a concept that will repeatedly be defined and discussed in Arthurian literature, although what it encompasses seems to be different according to each author who tries to shape its characteristics. De Troyes is very concerned here with both chivalry and chivalric code and the way that these things manifest themselves in Perceval and in the other knights he encounters. Students will be interested in the different ways that chivalry is expressed throughout the text, both in words (for example, Gornemant de Gohort attempts to give Perceval some guidelines of chivalrous behavior) and through the deeds of some of the knights (like the defeated knights staying true to their word and handing themselves over to Arthur).

Chivalry is also defined by the things that are not chivalrous—Perceval is decidedly not chivalrous toward the beginning of his journey when he demands to be knighted or practically assaults the maiden in the woods for a kiss, and it is clear that in many ways Arthur's knight Kay is not chivalrous, although he is a capricious character throughout the other de Troyes romances. The discussion may include whether chivalry exists today at all, or if there are different codes of behavior that need to be followed. There are no longer knights, but is a certain expectation of speech, dress, and action required of politicians? Or celebrities? If we were to write a code of chivalry today, what would it look like?

At the end of the romance, Perceval is heralded as the quintessential knight. He is exceedingly chivalrous to the maiden who was slapped by Kay, he is unmatched by the bravest and strongest knights, he saves countless maidens in distress (even though he was the cause of it in one case), he shows mercy to those who ask for it, and he recognizes his sins and resigns himself to a life of penance and salvation. However, de Troyes certainly gives Perceval his share of faults. Indeed, he is rash and boastful, and he causes the death of his mother. Many critics argue that these things are ultimately excusable and can be chalked up to Perceval's naïveté, but the text does not explicitly say that and many of Perceval's actions (like leaving his mother after she has fainted) seem unsettling when they happen. Students may want to discuss the character of Perceval and what makes him such an acclaimed knight in the end, and whether this praise is deserved.

Gender plays an interesting role here, as it often does in Arthurian romances, and a fruitful discussion would examine the women that Perceval encounters, loves, and saves. There are three main female characters—the laughing maiden slapped by Kay whom Perceval vows to avenge and continues to think of throughout the story, the beautiful Blanchflor who deftly manipulates Perceval into defending her kingdom and who becomes his lover, and the maiden that Perceval kisses forcefully who is then punished excessively by her own lover until Perceval can later avenge that wrongdoing. You may want to ask your students what these women are doing there and how they both add to and advance Perceval's own journey toward maturity and chivalry.

Another fruitful discussion may approach why this text was so well received in its own era. The popularity and dissemination of medieval texts is judged by the number of surviving manuscripts. Your students may be interested to know that the romances of Chrétien de Troyes were obviously popular, found in several different manuscripts and collections, but some great pieces of literature, like *Beowulf*, exist in only one surviving manuscript—indicating that they probably never had a wide audience at all. Ask your students to speculate on what was so appealing to the initial audience of *The Story of the Grail* that it would be so copied and distributed. This can lead into a discussion about why its popularity has remained so strong, making it still one of the most widely read texts of medieval literature.

The Story of the Grail is an unfinished text and no one is certain why. It may be that de Troyes felt he could not satisfactorily resolve the story of his hero who now seeks penance; possibly other things may have prevented him from returning to the text; and it is also a possibility that the narrative is intentionally unfinished (that is—that it *is* finished), and that this is the only way de Troyes wanted his romance to end. Ask your students why they think the story has this open ending. An interesting creative assignment may be for students to write their own finish to Perceval's tale (a task that many other writers have attempted).

Classroom Strategies

The text unfortunately does not fall along clear natural divisions. I've outlined below the best way that the text can be divided, depending on how many days and how much time is to be spent on *The Story of the*

Grail. There are three main divisions, corresponding to the beginning, middle, and end of Perceval's journey toward understanding and maturity, and inside these three parts there are smaller ways that the narrative can be parsed out, divided along the lines of his individual adventures and encounters.

The first part would last until Perceval arrives at the Fisher King's castle. This is Perceval's most naïve, least chivalrous time and also foreshadows much of what is to come (his mother's faint from grief, the maiden who is slapped, his encounter with the maiden in the forest, and so on). Smaller divisions may go from the beginning to Perceval's defeat of the Red Knight at Arthur's court, when he receives his armor. The next section would include his time spent at Gornemont's home through Anguingueron's defeat. Finally, a third section would begin with Clamadeau's arrival at Blanchflor's castle through to his submission at Arthur's court.

The second section would be primarily taken up with the Fisher King episode, the turning point in the text when Perceval should be relying on his own instincts but instead takes Gornemont's advice too literally and to his own detriment. The section would end when Arthur defeats the Haughty Knight. Smaller sections would be Perceval's stay with the Fisher King, the following morning when he discovers the castle deserted and learns from the maiden of the mistakes he has made, and finally his encounter with the maiden he had wronged and his fight with the Haughty Knight.

The third section will be Arthur's pursuit of Perceval (directly following the Haughty Knight's presentation at Arthur's court) through to the end of the romance. It is here that Perceval resolves his anger with Kay by defeating him in battle and then ultimately gives himself over to a life of penance, even though the other knights continue to pursue adventure at Arthur's side. In two smaller sections the story would begin when Arthur and his knights set off in search of Perceval through to his defeat of Kay. The next section would begin when Gawain encounters Perceval through to the end of the tale.

An excellent way to get students to understand and discuss the text is to bring in visual representations of knights and maidens in the Middle Ages. How are they depicted? What qualities do they seem to embody? Clips from some Arthurian-themed movies may also be helpful in discussing how modern audiences understand Arthur and ways in which that may differ from a medieval understanding of the king and his legendary knights.

Topics for Writing

1. Many characters try to give Perceval advice about what chivalry is and means. Who speaks about chivalry and what do they say? Is their advice good? Why or why not? Do you think Perceval needs to hear what to do or would he have arrived at chivalrous behavior on his own?

2. Trace the development of Perceval's character throughout the romance. What events lead him toward his ultimate destiny as one of Arthur's knights? What are the crucial moments in his journey toward maturity?

3. Look at the four major women characters in the story (Perceval's mother, the maiden who is slapped by Kay, Blanchflor, and the woman who is a lover to the Haughty Knight). What role do they play in Perceval's education? How does gender play into the idea of chivalry in the Middle Ages?

4. We never know what the grail is exactly, why it's in the Fisher King's home, and where it goes. Perceval only sees the procession pass him by. In this creative assignment, follow the grail into the next room and write what happens next.

Comparative Perspectives

1. At the end of *The Story of the Grail*, Perceval is an ultimate hero. Compare him to other heroes that you have seen, such as Odysseus and Beowulf. Has the idea of heroism changed since these earlier works? Are there elements that remain?

2. Arthurian romances were so popular in the Middle Ages that they really are their own genre. *Sir Gawain and the Green Knight* and *The Wife of Bath's Tale* are both Arthurian tales. Compare one or both of these to *The Story of the Grail*. What makes them Arthurian? Are there common elements you can expect from them?

3. Perceval is always on a quest in *The Story of the Grail*. First, it is to become a knight, then to find his mother, and finally to seek penance for his sins. The quest has always been and continues to be a central theme in literature. Compare the *Story of the Grail* to another piece that you consider a quest. What is the protagonist questing for and why? How is this quest different from Perceval's?

Further Reading

See also the reading suggestions in the *Anthology*, p. 2643.

THORSTEIN THE STAFF-STRUCK

Backgrounds

The events of the story take place in northeastern Iceland, near the coast and mostly at Thorarin's farm in Sunnudale or at Hof, the homestead of Bjarni, the head of a household including his wife, Rannveig; his brothers, Thorhall and Thorvald, who are his dependents or subordinates; and his chief servant, Thord. Our story is a pendant to a longer saga (Vopnfirdinga saga) in which Bjarni is the principal figure; hence the allusions to his acts at Bodvarsdale, as well as the account of his descendants at the end of the story. The protagonists in Thorstein the Staff-Struck are old Thorarin and his son, Thorstein, on one side and Bjarni, with his family and household, on the other. But it is important to note the mixture—sometimes amounting to conflict—of motives within the several characters. Thus Thorstein, who surely knows that Thord's blow was intentional, would prefer to avoid further violence; one motive, implied rather than spelled out, is his aged father's precarious physical and economic condition. If Thorstein should be killed or forced to go into exile, old Thorarin would be left destitute and helpless. Knowing the old man's bellicose disposition, Thorstein tries to keep him from hearing of Thord's act; but he does learn about it and hence goads Thorstein to action by accusing him of cowardice. Now note the contrast between Thorstein and Thord. Thord, who surely knew that he had been the unjustifiable aggressor, is offered a way out: he can declare the injury unintentional and pay a fee. According to the code of that age and country, this would be an honorable settlement for both men. But it does not appeal to Thord, whose foolish arrogance costs him his life.

In this situation, Bjarni, the master and necessarily the protector of Thord, has no easy alternative to the step he takes, namely prosecution of Thorstein for homicide, ending in a sentence of exile. We must remember that Iceland in the tenth century had no public means of enforcing judicial decisions; the plaintiff when victorious had to step in and see that the verdict was carried out. When Bjarni does nothing in this direction, malicious gossip, shared by the brothers Thorhall and Thorwald in his own household, ridicules him as a coward. It is a nice touch on the author's part to have Bjarni *overhear* this kind of talk; and the reader will think it a fit response when Bjarni sends Thorhall and Thorvald to kill Thorstein—if they can! When he kills them instead, Bjarni is once again forced into the position of reluctant avenger. But now the major protagonists, Bjarni and Thorstein, must face each other. You should point out the abundant detail with which their encounter is narrated—with time out for shoe-tying and a word with old Thorarin back in the house. All this enables us to understand the characters of the two men better; and a near-final surprise comes with the hopeless attempt of Thorarin to beat Bjarni (who has told him that he has killed Thorstein). Then the final reconciliation satisfies protagonists and reader alike.

Topics for Discussion

1. The authors of Icelandic sagas do not overtly declare their attitudes toward the characters. Usually much can be inferred, though sometimes a measure of doubt may remain. Students might be asked to attack or defend such a conclusion as this: "The author approves of Thorstein, admires Bjarni, holds Thorhall and Thorvald in contempt, enjoys Thorarin with reservations, is amiably amused by Rannveig and the other (unnamed) female character."
2. The role of Rannveig, wife of Bjarni.
   [She goads Bjarni into going after Thorstein and then seems to discourage him from the act, at any rate without her help. Their two conversations dramatize the conflict in Bjarni's own mind (al-

though in the sagas women traditionally incite their kinsman to vengeance).]

Topic for Writing

The reluctant avengers.

[Thorstein would prefer to treat Thord's blow as an accident both because he is "even-tempered" and because he fears for his aged father's welfare if he (Thorstein) should be killed. Bjarni is not eager to avenge Thord because he believes that Thorstein never attacks anyone without good reason. Yet both Thorstein and Bjarni ultimately feel compelled to fight in order to maintain their reputation as men of courage (essential to a satisfactory life in that civilization). Their final confrontation provides a happy solution in the form of reconciliation.]

Comparative Perspectives

1. Compare this story's treatment of shifting attitudes about the need for vengeance (embodied in the contrast between Thorarin and Thorstein) to the treatment of the same theme in the Oresteia. How important is Bjarni's conversion to Christianity to the development of the theme? What spiritual change plays a similar role in the end of *The Eumenides*?
2. Compare and contrast the portrait of a marriage in this short narrative with that in *The Tale of the Merchant and His Wife* in *The Thousand and One Nights*. What view of women do these texts seem to share?

Further Reading

See also the reading suggestions in the *Anthology*, p. 2644.

Byock, Jesse L. *Feud in the Icelandic Saga.* 1982.

MEDIEVAL LYRICS: A SELECTION

Classroom Strategies and Topics for Discussion

This rich trove of chronologically organized lyric poems offers a variety of teaching opportunities. One mode of organizing your materials is to select lyrics according to the categories enumerated in the headnote. You could have your students read an apparently homogeneous group of poems that explore seasonal celebrations, with their embroidery of birds and flowers, say, or several of the spiritual effusions representative of the three great monotheistic traditions that shaped the European medieval sensibility. Close study of a sequence of such thematically related poems will reveal, of course, that they are not genuinely homogeneous at all but reflective of very different authorial sensibilities, as the discussion below will suggest.

If you have not yet concentrated on the short lyric as a distinct genre, you could choose a few of the more complex poems in this selection and work through them with your students in great detail, examining the way idiosyncratic speaking voices capture the play of mind as they twist and turn through their subjects. You might also consider using a single poem to complement another work you are studying, either to indicate how widespread certain conventional assumptions were within medieval culture itself, or to juxtapose works from different periods with each other, to show your students how certain thematic preoccupations may be treated differently in different times and places. Many of these themes will recur in the second volume, most obviously in Continental Romantic Lyrics: A Selection, but elsewhere as well, and some notable foreshadowings are mentioned here, so that you can alert your students and take advantage of echoes and connections that can help you shape a year-long course.

Here are a few suggestions for each of these approaches. It is hard to overstress the constant revisiting of nature as a dominant lyric concern in century after century and culture after culture. At some point in your discussion you may want to ask your students to write a few lines of verse themselves, to articulate a personal response to the turn of the seasons, the song of a bird, the color of flowers, the patterns of clouds in the sky—one has to be hardened indeed not to have felt a sense of wonder in the presence of great natural beauty. Models may be found in a grouping of spring and summer poems that might include any or all of the following: Song of Summer, The Singing Lute; Spring Song; Judah Halevi's Summer, Jaufré Rudel's Love Song, Hadewijch of Brabant's The Cult of Love, Guido Cavalcanti's An Encounter. You might ask your students to single out the details typical of this subgenre. Keenly observed pictures of flora and fauna express the intimacy with which human beings lived in the natural world until very recently; at the same time, such references quickly became conventional tropes, expressing a sense of literary community as much as any genuine encounter with the natural world. The catalog, a literary device students may remember from classical epic, unites both the natural and the artificial by simultaneously evoking a sense of nature's plenitude and literature's variety.

The anonymous Song of Summer, a virtuosic accounting of Western poetry's favorite birds and their attributes, is a good point at which to begin. Here, as so often with these medieval lyrics, there is no strict dividing line between secular and sacred (indeed, perhaps the hallmark of the period is the effortless interweaving of the two, an acknowledgment of the divine in every aspect of created life). Here, the catalog of birds yields to the poet's initially surprising elevation of the diligent, unglamorous bee. You may wish to explain that bees became symbolic of the Virgin Mary because it was thought that they did not physically reproduce their young but instead gathered them up—immaculately, as it were—from the flowers they visited.

Ibn Arfa' Ra'suh's The Singing Lute illustrated the special role of the garden trope in Islamic poetry. The Koran, as the penultimate verse of The Table (p. 1162 in the anthology) demonstrates, abounds in references to the gardens of paradise. Here, too, an apparently secular poem interweaves sacred motifs—neither world is intelligible without the other. Wine (forbidden, of course, to Muslims in this world) promotes the inebriation sought by the Sufis as the mystical means to know the divine. (You may want to make a note about returning to *The Singing Lute* if you plan to teach Naguib Mahfouz's wonderful short story *Zaabalawi* in the second semester of your course.) As the headnote suggests, the garden here is also a place of high culture: the fragile gazelle, covered in elegant embroidered silks, is almost an advertisement for a sophisticated union of nature and commerce. A connection may be made here to the garden imagery in The Song of Songs. (Note that Hildegard of Bingen in *A Hymn to St. Maximus* and Judah Halevi in *Summer* explicitly refer to the biblical poem; without being specifically indebted to the same source, *The Singing Lute*'s use of garden imagery indicates how profoundly these paradisal images are embedded in the shared inheritance of the Middle East.) The gazelle then gives way to a tribute to the patron, the great ruler of the East (the source of silks) and the West (the place of the poet). Finally, the poem doubles back around itself to become a song of unrequited love (again, a familiar equation of God and the beloved is available to the interpreter). The powerful ruler deigns to greet his servants; the disdainful beloved, by contrast, ignores the poet-suitor.

One might conclude this grouping with *Spring Song* of William IX, duke of Aquitaine. Here, the little birds are themselves poets, "each in their own language" knowing participants in what is clearly a well established genre. This sense of emotions both fresh and time-tested recurs in the delicate early spring setting of a real human relationship, fragile but already rooted. Not for this poet the "strange talk," the vaunting that turns into gossip and destroys new love. The bold final image proclaims the solidity of love, food into which the poet and his lady have cut with a knife, not a tremulous emotion that might melt with the frost on the leaves.

The ever-changing interplay of society, religion, psychology, and natural imagery to be observed in this trio of early poems emerges in almost all the selections in this unit. These concerns similarly color every one of the more extended narratives available among *Masterpieces of the Middle Ages*, making for another valuable way of using these poems in the classroom. Rather than devote an entire session to lyric poetry per se, consider using individual poems as an establishing point for discussion of a major text: from Judah Halevi's *Summer*, for example, one may jump directly into the opening lines of *The Canterbury Tales*, in which April's sweet showers penetrate dry March. From Christine de Pizan's *Alone in Martyrdom*, an autobiographical poem that uses familiar pastoral imagery (the young widow resembles "the turtledove without her mate" and "the ewe that the wolf seeks to kill"), one might move ahead in the anthology to the work of Marguerite de Navarre and consider the opportunities open to women who wished to write in the early modern period, or to Petrarch, whom Christine acknowledged as her master. All three incorporated and transmuted personal experience into their art, raising again the question of the relationship of nature to art. Most obviously, perhaps, one may want to teach Dante the lyric poet as a way of introducing Dante the poet of *The Divine Comedy*. Recall the imagined literary symposium among lovers and friends in *Love and Poetry* in relation to canto IV of the *Inferno*, where Dante and Virgil join the great poets of classical antiquity for a short seminar, a kind of busman's holiday on the way down to hell.

Less capacious than Dante's great work, the religious lyrics in this selection tend to concentrate on heaven, and they show the influence of liturgical forms. Students familiar with biblical poetry and antiphonal church music will appreciate the reason why Notker's *Hymn to Holy Women* is laid out in parallel stanzas on the page. For a precise reading of this intricate poem, you may want to consult Peter Dronke's magisterial survey, *The Medieval Lyric*, in which he explains the genesis of Notker's poem in a pair of dream visions. It is not necessary to go into such detail, however, to appreciate the vivid visual imagination at work in this text and to grasp the familiar tribute to women, who, through Mary, as the headnote points out, were empowered to redeem the Edenic fall. The address to the serpent and the embrace of feminine bravery (on the part even of courtesans) could lead to a discussion of other strong women in fictional medieval texts you will discuss.

Or it could lead equally to an account of the remarkable Hildegard of Bingen, whose genius has recently been celebrated on the nine hundredth anniversary of her birth. One of the great medieval visionary artists and writers, a scientist and a memoirist, author of one of the first medieval dramas (*Ordo virtutem*) and composer of liturgical songs in honor of the Virgin Mary (*Symphonia*), Hildegard (like her work) is now accessible as she has not been for hundreds of years. In *A Hymn to St. Maximus*, as in Notker's *Hymn*, we are in the presence of an imagination deeply influenced by the visual arts. The ladder of Notker's poem, based ultimately on Jacob's ladder, describes an avenue linking human and divine as do the vertical images used to describe St. Maximus. Note the word "Lucent" that begins stanza 3B. Behind both poems is the tradition of illuminated manuscripts and stained-glass windows. Hildegard begins her visionary prose work *Scivias* with these words: "It happened that, in the eleven hundred and forty-first year of the Incarnation of the Son of God, Jesus Christ, when I was forty-two years and seven months old, Heaven was opened and a fiery light of exceeding brilliance came and permeated my whole brain, and inflamed my whole breast." This brilliance infuses Hildegard's hymn, subject of another one of Dronke's learned analyses, with its helpful synthesis: "the saint is masterpiece of both nature and art," captured in the Latin pun on the word *gemma* (line 8), "both bud and jewel."

To the rich sensory trappings of Catholic worship captured in both of these remarkable poems, one might contrast the tragic Hebrew poem here called *The Sacrifice of Isaac*, another masterpiece of liturgical style. At the age of thirteen, Ephraim ben Jacob, a native of Bonn, lived through the massacre of the Jews in the Second Crusade (1146). Years later, he commemorated that event in this poem and various learned biblical commentaries. As the headnote points out, the stanza that begins with line 61 takes as its point of departure a tradition that Abraham—"the alert one" (line 29)—responded to God's command so swiftly that he did actually did sacrifice Isaac once. The source of this tradition is unclear; in *The Last Trial*, Shalom Spiegel speculates that it would have received terrible confirmation in the massacres of the Jews of Germany during the First and Second Crusades. One Hebrew chronicle describes the pile of corpses that greeted the Crusaders after the townspeople had committed suicide rather than endure forced conversion. Sifting through the bodies, the Crusaders came upon still-breathing bodies and offered to save these survivors if they would convert. When these half-dead Jews refused, the text says "they proceeded to torture them some more, until *they killed them a second time.*"

Literally, the poem's title means *The Binding of Isaac*: lest he squirm involuntarily from the knife, becoming a blemished and thus unacceptable sacrifice, Isaac (the legend teaches) requested to be tightly bound. Notice that the poem ends with a sequence of references to binding and prayer that the bonds separating God from His people be broken. Indirectly, though its learned allusion, Ephraim's poem asks, How long oh Lord?

Despite their differing subjects, these three religious lyrics share some characteristics that students may ponder: in their ease of biblical reference, the complexity of their emotional range, and their recognition of the sublimity of struggle that informs true faith, they are hallmarks of the deep and serious spirituality of an era that is, as the headnote reminds us, "an age of faith"—but not only an age of faith.

The suffering but obedient father who is called upon to bring his child to the point of the knife may raise parallels with the Virgin Mary, brought into new prominence by medieval Christianity. Alluded to in several poems already mentioned, she is directly the subject of two more poems in this selection, each of which might profitably be read in tandem and in conjunction with Notker's *Hymn*. The four lines of *Calvary* express the intense pity of the speaker for the mother whose child is on the cross; the *Lament of the Virgin* speaks for Mary, evoking in graphic physical detail the bodily pain that so many of the great Northern painters of the era made palpable to view.

If the writers of these powerful religions poems tend to submerge themselves in their visions, others among these selected lyrics bristle with the restless intelligence of strong individual personalities. It would be interesting to teach as a group some of the poems in which the speakers are physically in motion, like those of Walahfrid Strabo or The Archpoet, whose journeys both provide the organizing scheme for the poems discussed below and embody the quest motif that gives shape to so many medieval narratives.

It helps students new to lyric to think of each poem as a small, self-contained drama. You might examine Walahfrid Strabo's poem of exile, asking students to identify the speaker's motives for leaving the "happy island" that he cannot put out of his mind. Driven out by "Shameful penury," lonely and cold, this traveler seeks "heart-felt wisdom" that seems to elude him. The headnote gives important biographical information about Walahfrid; college students on a bad day may recognize themselves in this sad portrait of a homesick wanderer and take courage from the ultimate success that he seems to have made of his life.

To Walahfrid's Penseroso one might juxtapose the dashing Archpoet, an Allegro who prefers not "to sit firm upon a rock." This portrait of a questing vagabond (line 23) who comes to rest in a tavern presents a type in which college students taking off on spring break might wish to recognize themselves. It appears that readers through the centuries have identified with this wanderer, for Peter Dronke call the *Confession* "perhaps the best-known poem in Medieval Latin." Dronke cautions against reading it as sincere autobiography, however. Certainly it seems to be uttered outside the confessional. Taking the opportunity to remind students that not all lyrics unlock the poet's heart, you might ask them to trace the progressive lightening of this poem, which starts with "fierce indignation" in which the speaker compares himself to a "withered leaf," and explain why so many writer like to pose as free spirits even if, as Dronke suggests, they are actually dutiful civil servants.

Motion, both physical and mental, is at the core of Walther von der Vogelweide's *Dancing Girl*, which begins with the troubadour offering a garland to a pretty girl, turns into a dream, and ends with him looking at another group of dancers, trying to find that girl again. The circular image of the garland opens and closes the poem, but the speaker's quest is open-ended. In Guido Cavalcanti's sophisticated version of a similar encounter, the poet makes a definitive foray into the woods for an idyllic embrace with the god of love looking on; the minnesinger's artless dancing girl becomes a glamorous shepherdess. Dronke calls this *pastorela* "perhaps the highest expression of the Arcadian ideal in medieval lyric."

Another kaleidoscopic poem, Alexander the Wild's *Strawberry Picking*, begins with a memory of children racing across the meadows and of a group of dancers, like Walther's, crowning the prettiest girl with a garland. Shifting patterns of movement adumbrate the loss of childhood and the fall into adult experience that this poem seems to trace. By the fifth stanza, genial reminiscence has yielded to monitory allegory: in the enigmatic cry "Children, right here there was a snake! / he has bitten our pony" (lines 31–32), Dronke hears an allusion to the prophetic vision of Dan, one of the twelve tribes of Israel:

> Dan shall be a serpent in the way,
> An adder in the path,
> That biteth the horse heels
> > So that his rider shall fall backward.
> > (Genesis 49.17)

The children have been ambushed; they must "make haste" now to exit the forest. The aimless freedom of the opening gives way in the last stanza to uncertain "loitering" and unexpected violation. Childhood is forever gone.

Repeated scenes of everyday life like the garland dance are worth noting, especially if one can reinforce them with period illustrations from some of the wonderful facsimile Books of Hours easily available in libraries these days (or digitized images increasingly accessible from different museum sites on the Internet). With the writings of the Middle Ages, we have access to the sights and sounds that gave them being. The melody for *Strawberry Picking* can be found on p. 245 of *The Medieval Lyric* and sung today; Hildegard of Bingen's music can be heard on numerous recordings. Almost a thousand years after real people left their mark on the material world, we can make contact with the vibrancy of their experience through their art and their music.

Asking your students to look at the sources of the metaphors in the poetry they read gives them a window into the concerns of a time and a place as well as a reference point by which to judge what we mean by the timelessness of great literature. You might conclude a discussion of the medieval lyric by noting that several of these poems mirror the increasing mercantilization of the material world. In *The Scorpions*, for example, Alfonso X finds no comfort on the traditional pastoral images with which so many of the earlier lyrics concern themselves. The earth on which this monarch works seems scorched; he is beset by traitors, symbolized by the scorpions of his title. Being a king is not as satisfying as being the pilot of a merchant ship, "selling vinegar and flour."

To contrast Alfonso's imagery with the use of commercial terms in the charming *Balade* of Charles d'Orléans or with the netherworld of the decaying shopkeepers in Villon's *Testament* underscores how complex the medieval period was (and how complex, by extension, is all human experience). The wonder of lyric poetry is that it manages to make the Helmet-seller's pitiless catalog of her physical features as compelling as the lover's catalog of birds.

The chronological organization of this section makes it possible to trace a world in flux. Despite the stereotyped notion of the poet removed from earthly concerns in some isolated ivory tower, to which some of your students may initially subscribe, these lyrics (like all the poems in the anthology) demonstrate the tangibility of their subject matter. Part of the pleasure of reading poetry is to imagine what private impulses and public experiences spurred the poet to write. Poetry reaches out into the world, and yet it is ultimately more than the sum of its contents, even in translation, as any survey of the selections included here can immediately show.

Topics for Writing

1. Link one of the poems in this selection to a longer work that offers a contrasting perspective on its subject matter:
   a. Compare the complicated vision of the fox in Dafydd ap Gwilym's *The Fox* to the portrait of the animal as trickster in

The Trial of Renard; or to the hunting of the fox as victim in *Sir Gawain and the Green Knight*.

b. Compare the tenor of the conversation between Gawain and Sir Bercilak's lady with the tone of *A Lover's Prize* by Beatrice, countess of Dia.

c. Compare the dancing girl who captures Walther von der Vogelweide's imagination or the shepherdess who entrances Guido Cavalcanti in *An Encounter* with Griselda in Boccaccio's Tenth Story of the Tenth Day. How important is the social status of the girl who attracts the male admirer? In what ways does the girl stand for qualities beyond herself?

d. Compare the admiring tone of *The Ruin* with the speech of the Last Survivor in *Beowulf* (p. 1246).

e. Compare the conflation of sex and war in *In Battle* with Othello's greeting to Desdemona in Act II of Shakespeare's play or with the alternation of episodes in Ariosto's *Orlando Furioso*.

f. Evaluate the terms offered by Charles d'Orléans's *Balade*, in which the speaker proposes buying kisses at a discount and giving his heart on deposit in return, and investigate the tonal difference between Charles's use of commercial imagery and the investigation of the economics of marriage elucidated by Chaucer's Wife of Bath in her *Prologue*.

2. Link one of the poems in this selection to a later work that alludes to the poet:

a. What qualities expressed in Bertrand de Born's *In Praise of War* seem consistent with Dante's consigning him to the Inferno?

b. Dante called Arnaut Daniel "*il miglior fabbro*" (a term that means "the better craftsman" and was later appropriated by T. S. Eliot in gratitude to Ezra Pound for his editorial assistance with *The Waste Land*). Daniel's *The Art of Love* begins with the image of the poet as craftsman. Describe the hard labor he devotes to this "usurious" lover's demand. What is there especially to admire in Daniel's facility with metaphor (as, for example, in the melodramatic last stanza)?

c. In *The Wife of Bath's Tale*, how does Chaucer dramatize the debate on "gentilesse" launched by Guido Guinizelli in *Love and Nobility* and taken up by Dante?

3. Link one of the poems in this selection to a prior work that influenced it:

a. How does Rabbi Ephraim ben Jacob's poem *The Sacrifice of Isaac* give tragic currency to the biblical story that is its source?

b. Christine de Pizan and Petrarch.

4. Medieval literature can be brutally detailed. Choose a poem that confronts the reality of physical suffering and decay and discuss the degree to which rhetorical devices can turn cruelty into art. (Good choices includes Villon's well-known and unsparing *Testament*, for the sheer virtuosity with which it shapes ugliness into el-

egant stanzas; *The Sacrifice of Isaac*, for reiterating a determination to trust the divine will through its constant reference to biblical verses; *Lament of the Virgin*, for underscoring the redemptive purpose of Christ's Passion.)

5. The language of poetry can help transmute grief so that it becomes bearable. Discuss the voice in Meir Halevi Abulafia's *A Letter from the Grave*, in which Abulafia offers comfort to his father, and compare the success of his efforts with those of Hadewijch of Brabant in *The Cult of Love*, in which the speaker contrasts herself with the birds, whose laments are short-lived, and finds no use for telling about her pain.

6. Assign a variety of readings in conjunction with an Internet assignment, a museum visit, or listening to or attending a musical or theatrical performance, and ask students to imagine life in the medieval world and to draw specific examples of everyday experience from the music, art and literature of the period.

Further Reading

See also the reading suggestions in the *Anthology*, p. 2643.

Wilson, Katherine M. *Medieval Women Writers*. 1984. A useful compilation of short biographies, with discussions of Hildegard of Bingen and Christine de Pizan.

MEDIEVAL TALES: A SELECTION

Classroom Strategies and Topics for Discussion

These lively short narratives provide an extraordinary variety of opportunities for classroom discussion, but one unifying theme they seem to share is a concern for the proper relationship between the individual and the community. A good starting point, then, would be in every case to ask students to reconstruct the social assumptions that these tales take for granted and frequently subvert. The following comments will treat each sequence individually, since all of the tales can stand on their own. At the same time, since you most likely will want to draw connections among them and other assignments, attention will be paid to some of the many possible combinations that work well in the classroom.

An overview of the eight separate tales contained in this unit suggests that they move from simplicity to complexity. Yet even the shortest of them is far from simple-minded; all of these tales can challenge students even as they are almost guaranteed to amuse and surprise them. You may wish to raise at once the question of community in introducing the two brief exampla by Petrus Alfonsi that begin the selection. Why are we going to Mecca in a short Latin piece written for Christian readers by a converted Jew? How do we account for its praise of an exemplary camel? Many of the great European medieval romances demonize the Saracen infidel, yet these selections from *The Scholar's Guide*, like a number of the medieval lyrics in the anthology, bespeak the often comfortable and intimate relations of the three monotheistic cultures, especially as they came together in al-Andalus.

Should your students read selections from *The Thousand and One Nights*, Boccaccio's *Decameron*, or Chaucer's *Canterbury Tales*, they will recognize evidence of the stockpile shared by medieval storytellers. *The Two City Dwellers and the Country Man* appears to be a distant and rudimentary analogue of the narrative at the core of *The Pardoner's Tale*, for example. Setting it within the context of a Meccan destination, which hints of pilgrimage (the experience that continues to unify the far-flung adherents of Islam), presupposes a community that puts a premium on hospitality.

Both of Petrus Alfonsi's exempla revolve around the refusal to distribute food fairly. We also see in the two city dwellers themselves a mistaken notion of their own urban superiority; outwitted by the country man, they are the first characters in this selection of tales to see a reversal of the expected social order. In *The King's Tailor's Apprentice*, with the apprentice called Nedui and the supervising eunuch, we are again in an essentially Islamic cultural milieu, but the universal application of the story transcends any one creed. These benign celebrations of a swift intellect, told within a frame that emphasizes the orderly transmission of values from parent to child, conclude on one more ecumenical note, with the father implicitly chastening his son for the pleasure he seems to feel in seeing others punished. In citing the teaching of Moses (more commonly attributed to Rabbi Hillel), Petrus Alfonsi honors his own origins and complicates the revenge motif that lies on the surface of these two small exempla.

With the four thirteenth-century fabliaux, we move on to another country and another sensibility. Revenge is simply the nature of the world in these old French tales; nevertheless, hospitality continues to be an important virtue, and cleverness to earn its just rewards. Although it would be delusory to read fabliaux in quest of moral improvement, you may certainly ask your students to investigate the moral universe that motivates the genre. The eponymous butcher of Abbeville, for example, as Thomas C. Cooke points out in the study cited below, seems "almost the ideal man" on the evidence of the poem's second stanza. Like so many of these stories, his begins with a need to spend the night in somebody else's house. If the butcher eventually sleeps with his host's women and sells him his own sheep, the tale has made it clear that the priest (not coincidentally, of course, the deserving victim of such depredations in many fabliaux) has richly earned his comeuppance.

The tellers of these tales, with their keen eye for domestic detail and disdain for snobbish pretension, appreciate competence (in butchery as in bed and many another place) and skewer hypocrisy. Many fabliaux are inhabited by exceedingly well-dressed women who don't quite protest enough. (Note the detailed description of the deacon's lady's pleated green gown and her halfhearted objection to the butcher's proposition, good points to raise if you plan to read *The Miller's Tale*, whose teenage village heroine boasts a smart black and white ensemble and succumbs remarkably quickly to the handy Nicholas's approach.) The real hyp-ocrites, however, tend to be the selfish priests, whose way of life betrays their absolute indifference to their churchly duties, and the victims are often ill-advised old husbands, like the hunchback in the selection in the anthology or the rather more pathetic John of *The Miller's Tale*. (These character types are staples of comic satire, of course—you may want to recall them if you go on to teach *Tartuffe* later in the course.)

Although *The Butcher of Abbeville* has a far more pleasant tone than does *The Three Hunchbacks*, both stories offer fascinating windows on daily life in the real world. One of the delights of teaching these tales is to train your students to read with an archeologist's attention to minu-tiae. Without neglecting the many rural scenes typical of the genre, Charles Muscatine notes that "the flourishing of the fabliaux, the rise of the cities, and the emergence of an urban middle class are equally visi-ble symptoms of the same social and spiritual climate." Ask your stu-dents to characterize the standard of living in the fabliaux' world. The delicate cuisine (peas with bacon are a feature of many a medieval tale, to judge from the selections in the anthology) and the rich interiors of the priest's "manse" in Abbeville and the hunchback's townhouse in Douay bear witness to an atmosphere of such wealth that we happily ex-cuse the efforts of those who are less well-off to take advantage of this plenty.

Discuss with your students the importance of furniture and real estate location in *The Three Hunchbacks*: were it not for an intricate three-drawered bed and its two-story situation on a canal, the hunchback's house would not be the scene of this remarkable story. You will not be able to avoid the question of cruelty in many of these medieval works; in this case, it's important to notice the improvisatory nature of events that are the product of chance, not careful plotting (again, a contrast with *The Miller's Tale* would be instructive). The situation of the hunchback's beautiful young wife is deftly sketched. From one angle, she seems a sympathetic figure: starved for entertainment, she invites the three hunchbacked minstrels to return to their house in her husband's ab-sence (and gives us a glimpse of the life of the strolling players who sang and told stories in private homes, illustrating the point made in the headnote about the performative nature of much medieval literature). Still, it's important to note, rather more cynically, that she is quite happy to exploit the porter and sheds not a tear on account of the accident that frees her.

Adding to the macabre humor of the story is the casual use of disabil-ity as a comic trait in itself. The weird disposal of the three dead hunch-backs is almost a textbook illustration of Henri Bergson's famous definition of comedy as a defense against the dehumanizing effects of standardization and regimentation: when one is reduced to a body that looks exactly like another's, can one be an individual deserving of sympa-thy? The shock comes with the fourth hunchback, the man of property who presumably has an individualized identity, but who is doomed by the porter's mechanized response to yet one more misshapen body. In farce, where dehumanization is the rule, one rarely feels sorry for flat characters caught in automatic routines. Indeed, in the cheerfully amoral climate of the fabliau, the offered lesson of the story seems misplaced, as the narrator appears to acknowledge. While he dutifully quotes Durant's conclusion, "everything on earth's for sale," this has little to do with the husband's death. Prefiguring Alison's fate in *The Miller's Tale*, the wife here escapes unscathed. And despite disposing of a few inconvenient corpses at a good price, she does seem relatively blameless.

If Bergson seems the tutelary genius of *The Three Hunchbacks*, perhaps Freud would smile on the efficacious work accomplished by *The Wild Dream*. Both here and in *The Ring That Controlled Erections*, the fullblown bawdiness for which the fabliaux are famed takes center stage. Students are generally amazed by the explicit detail of such stories, and it is appropriate to ask why these obscene anecdotes should have been such a staple of popular culture. One route is to inquire what, if anything, is wrong with describing genitalia and their propensities? (If your students have read the selections from Genesis in the anthology, you might ask them to recall the first result of eating the fruit of the tree of knowledge of good and evil: what attitudes make nakedness shameful?) Another profitable avenue is to explore the coexistence during the Middle Ages of bawdy fabliaux and romantic tales of chivalry, classic examples of the way popular and elite forms "correct" and feed off each other.

You might also point out that these particular tales show none of the mean-spirited pleasure in other persons' pain or discomfort that many fabliaux and *The Trial of Renard* do demonstrate. Instead, in this quartet of stories, there is a satisfied sense of bargains well struck, of getting what one pays for—and paying for what one gets.

That equilibrium is missing from the wild lawlessness at the heart of *The Trial of Renard*, a genuinely subversive narrative. Though the Renard stories owe their form to the animal fable, they are emphatically not themselves such fables, since they have no uplifting moral lessons to teach. You may want to spend some time talking through the interpretive possibilities created by the employment of animals as characters. Your students may be familiar with some of Aesop's fables, and it will be helpful to discuss how the Renard stories differ from them; you may also ask them to react to the headnote's citing of cartoon characters like the Road Runner and Wile E. Coyote. In fact, a brief investigation of the humor in cartoons is a very good way to talk about comedy in general: if your class deplores the cruelty of some of these tales, as noted above, ask them why we laugh at people who slip on banana peels. The speaking animals in the twelfth-century Renard sequence mock the heroic pretensions of chivalric culture, another example of a "low" form deriving its power from the existence of a "higher," idealized genre. The late twentieth century has seen cartoons that mock contemporary genres that define another kind of honor, like the detective story. *The Trial of Renard*, however, finds humor but little that seems heroic or admirable in its central character's amoral predation.

That the collective title for the group of stories to which it belongs is the *Romance of Renard* attests to their parodic power. There may be something noble about King Noble, who shows flashes of the grand beneficence of both Charlemagne and King Arthur. Little in the behavior of the feral aristocrats who inhabit his court, however, seems humane; deplorably, perhaps, a great deal of it is human. Although you will want to be sure that your students understand the historical specifics of the political burlesque in *The Trial of Renard*, the eternal relevance of its mordant depiction of government in action should not be missed. If King Noble the Lion represents in some ways the twelfth-century monarch, Louis VII, who, as the headnote indicates, imposed a truce upon the fractious nobility, the poem's generally disenchanted view of hypocrisy among the powerful also deserves careful consideration in the classroom.

As the poem starts, Noble recommends that Ysengrin give up his vendetta against Renard, since "nowadays one sees all sorts / Of cuckolds, even ruling courts!" How timeless and timely this worldly-wise counsel seems (some commentators believe that medieval audiences would have recognized this as a swipe at the scandalous Eleanor of Aquitaine, whose marriage to the pious Louis was annulled in 1152). Bruin the bear, not the brightest member of Noble's court, says out loud what many a favor-currying politician less publicly puts into practice: "We will hate anyone you say." While the guardians of absolute morality, led by Clamor the bull, seems obsessed by the sexual misconduct of which Renard is accused (this in itself is a joke, of course, since bulls traditionally embody virility rather than *pudeur*), Grinbert the badger, Renard's cousin, undercuts their righteous objections. In the animal as in the human world, rape cases are always notoriously hard to win; with marvelous deftness, the author reminds us that Hersent is, after all, a wolf, whose "fur stood on end" when she hears her innocence questioned. Her offer to undergo trial by ordeal seems heroic, but to rich ironic effect; for Hersent here echoes Iseult, one of the great heroines of tragic romance, to be sure, but also compromised, adulterous, and untrustworthy. Only by cheating did Iseult pass her trial; for his part, Ysengrin is wise enough to know that testing his wife's honor can lead only to his humiliation.

In this story, Renard is the center of attention for many reasons. The narrative begins with a murder charge leveled against the fox by the bereaved hen Pinte. Given the occasion by this rather unsurprising event (as the headnote should remind your students, all this means is that a fox has eaten a chicken), *The Trial of Renard* finds targets for satiric commentary on every side. The body of Pinte's tragically deceased sister turns out to have miracle-working properties, like the relics of so many medieval saints. The author's knowing glance at the conspiracy of the wolf and the dog, who falsely testify to having been cured of earaches on the martyr's grave, takes aim at the religious establishment that profited from such testimony, much as his allusions to Charlemagne and Iseult parody the world of chivalric romance. Nowhere, according to the translator, Patricia Terry, is the voice of the author more prominent than in Renard's explanation of his failure to answer the king's summons (lines 498–537): the poor are badly treated at table when they venture into the courts of the mighty, who let themselves be robbed by their cooks and stewards. Through this falsely pious comment, of course, Renard segues into his masterstroke, an apparently casual reference to the fresh honey that he just consumed to complete his delicious meal of peas and bacon.

Bruin, who has happily ventured to Renard's den, is now "on the hook." With feigned reluctance, the fox shows the bear an enormous tree that purportedly houses a store of honey. Trapped in the oak, the credulous, greedy Bruin must run for his life, leaving much of his muzzle behind, to escape from the enraged villagers who "swarm through the trees," human beings who intrude on the animal world and act like animals in the process. It is a mark of the author's skill that he can move easily between the two realms, satirizing all manner of human foibles by looking at animals and at people, without losing his bearings.

As in *The Butcher of Abbeville*, the corruption of the priesthood is simply a given. The parish priest, "Father of Martin de la Tour," wounds the suffering bear in the side (one wonders just how sacrilegiously this reference was intended, especially since at the sight of the mangled bear, King Noble vows to avenge his wrongs "by the death of Christ"). Of the young Martin, himself destined for Holy Orders, we shortly hear when Renard tricks Tibert the cat, another rogue who would have been ready to collaborate with the fox, into tripping the noose set to catch Renard when he next tries to raid the henhouse. The dizzying pace of the narrative reaches an apogee as one event triggers another. Awakened by the commotion, Martin's parents race from their bed to catch the predator, whom they assume to be the fox; but the cat manages to defend himself by unmanning the priest, who has run outdoors *en deshabille*, to the horror of his concubine.

Neither the animal nor the human community can take much more of Renard's anarchic will. When Grinbert summons his cousin to court, Renard manages a confession of sorts before leaving his family. Prostrating himself in what looks at first like a gesture of humility (soon revealed by the author to be merely the posture required to exit from his lair), Renard goes before the court and delivers a proud speech to King Noble (now called the "emperor," presumably to remind the well-read audience of Charlemagne listening to Roland). Self-serving and arrogant, Renard nevertheless raises some troubling questions; this remarkable comic parody seems deeply serious as well when Renard asks whether his victims share no responsibility for their own fates. Even Noble, however, whose predisposition to favor Renard is clear in the earlier parts of the poem, is outraged as the fox appeals for sympathy: "It's a sin to drag me here to speak, / Old as I am, before this court." Taken out to the gallows, Renard escapes again. He will expiate by sailing to the Holy Land, a promise that is accepted, although Noble remarks that pilgrims usually return more corrupt than when they set out. Incorrigible, impenitent, and free, Renard escapes his pursuers, managing to grab the cowardly rabbit for dinner along the way (although the hare himself escapes when Renard stops to boast—see lines 1525–32). As the poem ends, we know that his story is not over: miraculously rejuvenated after a good meal and a bath, Renard lives on in the bosom of his loving family.

Renard, a ruthless rogue, lives on in other guises too, not all of them in the Saturday morning cartoons. How many movies make us complicit with ruthless gangsters who have happy homes? You will want to ask your students why we take pleasure in the gratuitous cruelty and outrageous duplicity of outlaws like Renard. Do we all wish we had the courage to express the contempt he so gleefully displays for social pieties? Why do we laugh at his obscene gestures?

Finally, the selection returns to the exemplum, but, as the headnote says, a very mysterious one. What is the lesson that we are to learn from *The Cursed Dancers of Colbeck*? Ambiguities abound in this short narrative, beginning with the title of the handbook in which it appears, *Handling Sin*. As Mark Miller suggests in the excellent article listed at the end of the headnote, we are always handling sin—we cannot escape it; and so we must learn to deal with it. Robert Mannyng's manual addresses the seven deadly sins and a host of others. This selection begins on a seemingly puritanical note, warning against "carols, wrestling, or summer games," but quickly limits their potential for sacrilege to the venue in which they are performed. While at first glance one is hard pressed to understand why dancing and singing carols at Christmas time should be considered sacrilegious, we soon see that, by pursuing such activities in the church or churchyard, the participants are competing with the holy services conducted by the priest, putting their own pleasures before God.

The conflict between the individual and society that underlies all of these medieval tales is heightened here by the nature of the offending carolers, who are called "fools" in the text but should be understood, in Miller's words, as "a group of wandering madmen." Somehow these alien beings, whose names Mannyng carefully lists (as if to assure us that this all really happened, although he has already hedged by noting that "most of" what he says is "the gospel truth"), have made contact with the priest's daughter and recruit her to join in their rivalry with her father's Mass. (That a priest should have a family is here again taken for granted. It is not the occasion for satire, as in the fabliaux or *The Trial of Renard*, but seems just one more troublesome sign of the difficulty that the Church had in enforcing its dictates, in this case, clerical celibacy.)

When Robert the priest curses the dancers, the focus of the story changes. The priest becomes the principal offender, and his son his accuser. His daughter Ave (presumably a form of "Eve," another disobedient female) has paid the price for her father's wrath. The dancers have been frozen into robotic motion, a parody of a parody, and the unholy nature of their unauthorized dancing is forgotten in the general horror at their loss of humanity. Even the Emperor tries to ameliorate the situation, to no avail.

When the term of the curse expires, the dancers resume their activities, although no longer in solidarity. The loss of Ave's arm reenacts the

fragmentation that has divided the mad dancers of Colbeck from themselves and from the Christian community. Ironically, her severed arm is
treated like a holy relic, confusing the moral of the story even more;
Robert the priest dies too, while nothing else seems to have changed. At
the end, Mannyng almost admits he doesn't know what to make of this
exemplum: "some hold it an idle story." The tale ends with too many
statements of its moral lesson for us to know which one to follow. The
article by Miller provides a sophisticated summation: "Their ossification
in a parody or perversion of Christian community is replaced, not by
their incorporation into the body of the faithful, but by their fragmentation into solitary versions of the dance." Your students' reactions will
likely not be so elegant, but you can profitably work with whatever lingering confusion they may feel. The deepest value of these assorted medieval tales is that they demonstrate the diversity and inventiveness of an
era that too many think of as hidebound and moralistic.

Topics for Writing

1. What do we, can we, or should we learn from fiction?
   [The focus of this assignment may shift according to the works
   you ask your students to discuss. Like the novel, which was a vehicle for "news," many of these short medieval tales provide pleasure
   by giving us information about how people live; others, especially
   the exempla, teach lessons, although the lessons are not always
   clear. And sometimes, what we learn is simply to admire the keen
   eye and fertile imagination of authors, both high and low. As always, the challenge for student writers is to present textual evidence that will persuade the reader of the truth of their claims.]

2. Consider the attitudes toward the body in medieval narrative: the
   hedonistic celebrations of pleasure in the fabliaux, where the body
   and its needs and self-expression reign supreme; or the graphic descriptions of punishment in *The Trial of Renard*, where the natural
   cruelty of the animal world seeps into the sense of what is normal
   in human affairs as well; or the dismembered arm of Ave in *The
   Cursed Dancers of Colbeck*, perhaps a sign of the perverse difficulty
   we have in coordinating our actions in harmony with those of others and the expectations of the community.
   [This topic will link well with the work of Boccaccio and
   Chaucer, too, particularly perhaps the Ninth Story of the Fourth
   Day and the Eight Story of the Fifth Day of the *Decameron*, *The
   Wife of Bath's Prologue*, and *The Pardoner's Tale*.]

3. Consider the question of human agency and responsibility: What
   is the source of the greed seen in the tales of Petrus Alfonsi or the
   fabliaux? Can Renard stop himself? Should he? Why do those mad
   dancers dance? Why does the priest curse them?

Comparative Perspectives

Discuss the techniques by which farce encourages us to laugh at situations that would not be so funny in "real life," using literary examples from the three time periods covered in Volume 1 of the *Anthology*: from the ancient world, Lysistrata, Pseudolus, The Satyricon, and A True Story; from the medieval world, the fabliaux, The Trial of Renard, and the Miller's Tale; from the Renaissance, Gargantua and Pantagruel.

Further Reading

See also the reading suggestions in the *Anthology*, p. 2644.

Cooke, Thomas D. *The Old French and Chaucerian Fabliaux: A Study of Their Comic Climax.* 1978. Some helpful comments about a few of the fabliaux in the anthology.

DANTE ALIGHIERI

The Divine Comedy

Backgrounds

The headnote provides a general view of *The Divine Comedy* as a whole as well as a more detailed account of the Inferno and the parts of the *Purgatorio* and the *Paradiso* included in the anthology. The headnotes and footnotes to the individual cantos offer ample guidance and abundant information about the persons, places, and thoughts encountered along the way.

Many people know—or know of—the *Inferno* but not the *Purgatorio* or *Paradiso* and hence infer that Dante was exclusively or at least unduly preoccupied with evil. We should point out that only one-third of *The Divine Comedy* is focused on the bad, one-third shows people in pursuit of the good (*Purgatorio*), and one-third describes the enjoyment of the good (*Paradiso*).

Some people in our time are alienated by the doctrine of eternal punishment; why not redeem everybody, after suitable reformation? The first answer, of course, is that Dante was following orthodox Christian teaching. But there are other answers philosophically and aesthetically more satisfactory to our age. Do we want to see every villain in every serious film reformed? Could we believe in the repentance of Iago in Shakespeare's *Othello* or of Goneril and Regan in *King Lear*? The (psychological) truth about such men and women—and innumerable others who have actually lived in this world—is that they do not want to reform. They would be unhappy in Heaven. What the *Inferno* reveals to us is the final state or consummation of the people who have chosen one of the various kinds of wrong conduct. The range is from the illicit lovers of the fifth canto to the figures enclosed in ice at the center of the Earth in the final canto. Lawless passion was the lovers' choice—rather than reasonable restraint; now they are blown about by the winds; they have no hope of *peace*. The people in the ice endure the cold—the lack of feeling that enabled them to betray and kill their kindred on the Earth.

It is worth noting that moral criteria may have changed since Dante wrote his poem. Homosexuality is apparently the only reason why Brunetto Latini is in Hell, and the Florentine usurers also on the burning sands might now be regarded as respectable bankers. Dante was a conservative in economics.

The *Purgatorio* has been called the most *human* of the three parts of the poem—the part that comes closest to the experience and attitudes of most of us. For we are not hopelessly sunk in evil or infallibly committed to good, but we should like to avoid the one and attain the other—if only we knew how to do it. The *Purgatorio* dramatizes and exemplifies the Christian teaching about the way. The front page of a newspaper or the daily telecast of news indicates that things are far from all right in our world today. The same was true in Dante's time. Conflict, violence, cruelty within and between families and nations are evidence that the human situation is not satisfactory. According to Christian teaching, the ultimate source (on Earth) of these bad things is the uncontrolled passions and appetites of the individual human being. Long before Dante, the Church had described these excesses as the Seven Cardinal (or Deadly) Sins: illicit love, gluttony (any undue concern about food), avarice (and its opposite, reckless spending), sloth (idleness as a way of life), selfish and unjustified anger, envy (the wish for another person's loss or failure), and pride (not proper self-esteem but haughtiness and aggression). Each of these stems from a vice or fault, a flaw in the moral character of the man or woman. In Roman Catholic practice—modern as well as medieval—he or she should confess to a priest, ask God's forgiveness, repent sincerely, and promise to mend. The priest might also assign a penance, which, especially in medieval times, might be painful or burdensome. It was assumed that most people would not have completed the process of purgation before death; hence the doctrine of Purgatory as an interval of purification (for a true Christian) between the end of earthly life and entry into Heaven.

Dante's *Purgatorio* is based quite clearly and directly on Church doctrine and practice. But he is careful to assign self-discipline—or discipline gladly accepted—in a rationally appropriate manner. Thus his penitents exert themselves to the utmost in practicing the virtue opposite to the vice under correction at the time; so the proud behave humbly (symbolized by the heavy weights they carry on their backs—in a canto not included in the selections); and Pope Adrian, who had been too fond of material wealth, is literally brought down to bare earth. The suffering of the soul in Purgatory would be meaningless if it were permanent, if it served no purpose. It is important to remember that Purgatory is an interlude, a preparation for Heaven. Moreover, Dante intended his readers to apply the example of his poem to the amendment of their lives while still in this world.

It is worth remarking that there are no terraces on the mountain of

Purgatory for such specific crimes as murder or robbery. The reason is that all crimes are motivated by one or more of the Seven Cardinal Sins; when the man or woman has got rid of the inclination to evil, there will be no temptation to kill or steal. On the other hand, murderers and robbers are classified as such in the *Inferno*—because a vice, or flaw of character, may have variable consequences. It may amount only to self-indulgence without direct harm to another person; or it may lead to the worst imaginable crimes.

Classroom Strategies

The reader's immediate experience of the poem should come first; then that experience can be integrated in an increasingly wide range of events, ideas, and horizons. As to class assignments, obviously they must depend on the amount of time available for the segment (Dante) as a whole; two or three cantos might be average.

In our time it cannot be taken for granted that most students will be familiar with the basic doctrine and belief of organized Christianity, that is, the Church. But Dante, like Chaucer and every other medieval and Renaissance writer, could assume this knowledge and hence allude to it with confidence that he would be understood. Indeed, it was condensed in capsule form in the Creed regularly recited in many services of worship. The following is one version, known as the Apostles' Creed:

> I believe in God, the Father almighty, creator of Heaven and earth. I believe in Jesus Christ, his only Son, our Lord. He was conceived by the power of the Holy Spirit and born of the Virgin Mary. He suffered under Pontius Pilate, was crucified, died and was buried. He descended to the dead. On the third day he rose again. He ascended into Heaven, and is seated at the right hand of the Father. He will come again to judge the living and the dead. I believe in the Holy Spirit, the holy Catholic Church, the communion of saints, the forgiveness of sins, the resurrection of the body, and the life everlasting.

Of course, it is not suggested that the Creed be taught systematically, but an occasional reference to one or another of the statements in it may clear up many a passage in the anthology.

The teacher should take full advantage of the episode of the grafters in cantos XXI and XXII. Students who are turned on by nothing else will enjoy this crude, malicious, sly, malevolent cartoon comedy once it becomes clear to them. The milieu of low-level corrupt office holders has not changed much since Dante's time; we still talk about "sticky" fingers, and cartoonists often wield the tar brush or its equivalent. Furthermore, the poignance of Virgil's rescue of Dante at the end of this sequence provides a good opportunity to discuss the relationship between the two: how it changes and deepens in the course of the journey. The conclusion of the topic must await the *Purgatorio*: Virgil's farewell and Dante's sudden awareness that Virgil is no longer at his side.

Topics for Discussion

1. The suitability of the penalties to the sins in the *Inferno*.

   [This is relevant throughout, including the area outside the nine circles; thus those in the ante-Hell—those sometimes called the moral neutrals—are plagued by annoying *little* things, such as unpleasant insects. The "virtuous pagans" in the first circle are not actively punished; they live without the good of participating in God, as Christians must do by definition. The poet does not usually explain why the various conditions in Hell are appropriate; hence we can profitably think about the matter. Fire, in sundry form, is familiar to us as a punishment; ice, which Dante makes the ultimate penalty, may seem strange to us at first. Reflection may well change our view.]

2. The differences between upper and lower Hell.

   [Basically, the people in the upper Hell were guilty of (excessive) self-indulgence. They loved not wisely but too well—other persons, material goods (thus either as misers or spendthrifts), food and drink, or their own aggressive impulses (anger). Primarily, they did not deliberately seek to injure other persons. Those in the lower regions (violence and fraud) did precisely that—in a great variety of ways.]

3. Possible differences between Dante's perspective and ours.

   [It has been suggested that one category of the angry in the *Inferno*—the incorrigibly morose—might now be treated as patients in a mental hospital. Similarly, most modern views of homosexuality do not regard it as either a sin or a crime, and the same can be said of suicide. Dante's view depended on the idea that we belong to God as our Creator; He has prescribed the manner and set the limits of our lives in definite ways; we dare not interfere.]

4. Mini-tragedies in the *Inferno*.

   [It has been said that Dante's portrayal of a number of the most notable figures in the *Inferno* amounts to a series of microscopic tragedies: Paolo and Francesca in canto V, Pier della Vigne in XIII, and Ulysses in XXVI are notable examples. These are people very attractive in personality, intellect, or even character, but they knowingly made the wrong decisions and so decided their own fate.]

Topics for Writing

1. For some of the major figures of the poem, personality and character are indicated by the speeches that Dante puts in their mouths.

   [Thus in canto V of the *Inferno*, Francesca's good manners are indicated by her courteous greeting of Dante; her romantic temperament by the tercet in which she tells of her homeland; her adherence to the "doctrine" of courtly love by the three tercets each beginning with the word *love*; her habit of blaming something besides herself shows through in the reference to the book about

Lancelot; and perhaps her vindictiveness in the single verse in which she foretells the punishment of her slayer (lines 106–7).

In canto XIII the lawyer-poet Pier delle Vigne may seem to play—seriously—with words as he contrasts and pairs "locking and unlocking," "inflamed" (verb, then past participle, then verb again), all in a severely logical and antithetical account of his unfortunate experience (lines 58–78).

2. The method of contrasting pairs of persons.

[In *Inferno* X the Florentine aristocrats Farinata and Cavalcante (the elder) rise to talk with Dante from their shared tomb among the unbelievers. Farinata is proud, haughty, disdainful of unknown characters like the present visitor (Dante)—"he looked at me, and half-contemptuously / he asked 'And *who* would *your* ancestors be?' " (lines 41–42). Their ensuing dialogue is interrupted by Cavalcante, who asks about his son, Dante's closest friend at one time. Distressed at Dante's uncertain answer, he is overcome by grief and sinks down into the tomb. Thereupon Farinata resumes his remarks just as if there had been no interruption.

In the Circle of Evil Counselors (*Inferno* XXVI–XXVII), we come to the Greek Ulysses, deviser of the Trojan horse, and to an Italian politician of the thirteenth century. Virgil conjures the flame that is Ulysses to utterance remote, detached, impersonal (so far as its auditors are concerned), but in itself lofty and splendid. After a bit the flame that the soul of the politician has now become (Guido da Montefeltro) addresses Dante, asks for news of Italy, and telling Dante he is sure the story won't get out, indulges his urge to tell how he was tricked into a final sin that accounted for his present situation. Thus this garrulous old gossip is juxtaposed to the sublime Homeric hero.]

3. The grafters and the demons of popular lore (*Inferno* XXI, XXII, and XXIII.1–54).

[The more or less grotesque and comical names of the demons who have charge of the grafters in their ditches and pools of pitch; the tricks they play on sinners trying to escape momentarily; their readiness to deceive the travelers with barefaced lies, solemnly spoken; the rough handling of the sinners, like bags of stuff, carried on a demon's shoulder. The crouching, fearful, utterly undignified figure of Dante the traveler in this episode; its biographical counterpart in his being charged with misuse of funds while an office holder in Florence.]

Comparative Perspective

Discuss the imagery invoked in Dante's vision of the punishment of "Mahomet" in canto XXVIII of the Inferno. How does it reflect the medieval Christian fear of Islam? What other Western works have you read in which this fear is echoed? Do you find similar preoccupations with rival religions in the Koran?

Further Reading

See also the reading suggestions in the *Anthology*, p. 2643.

Clements, R. J., ed. *American Critical Essays on Dante*. 1969.

Slade, Carole, ed. *Approaches to Teaching Dante's* Divine Comedy. 1982.

GIOVANNI BOCCACCIO

The Decameron

Backgrounds

Boccaccio's introduction (not in the *Anthology*) is the counterpart, with some differences, of Chaucer's General Prologue. Each provides the setting for a long sequence of tales. There is a measure of chance or coincidence in both groups of storytellers. Boccaccio's seven young ladies, happening to meet in a church (though they are already friends or acquaintances), decide to leave plague-ridden Florence and live with more safety on their country estates; they invite three young gentlemen, also well known to them, to share their plans. Chaucer's twenty-nine pilgrims—traveling alone or in twos or threes or even more—all happen to have come for a night's lodging to an inn or tavern in Southwark, across the Thames from London, on the route to Canterbury. Boccaccio's company decide to spend part of each day in telling stories and agree that on the first day each of the ten is to tell a tale on a topic of his or her own choosing. In Chaucer's account the innkeeper takes charge of proceedings; he plans four tales to be told by each traveler; the order is to be determined by lot, and he says the Knight is due to tell the first tale.

Chaucer has no real equivalent of Boccaccio's extended and vivid account of the plague in Florence (not in the anthology). Boccaccio knew the Italian plague of 1348 from his own experience. His description of the mode of life of the company of young folk in the country, though idealized, is perhaps not too far from actuality. The physical comforts, the apparent abundance of food and other necessities, the ease with which the people move from place to place, all these reflect what was possible or even usual among the wealthy class of Italians in the fourteenth century. They also have the pleasing manners of gentlefolk; they treat one another with courtesy and consideration—from which good-natured jest and humor are not excluded. It may seem idyllic to us, but it was probably nonetheless realistic.

[THE FIRST STORY OF THE FIRST DAY]

The storytelling proper begins with Panfilo's announcement that God's infinite grace descends upon people not "through any merit of their own" and that God attends to "the purity of the supplicant's motives." These general truths will take on interpretive significance at the conclusion of this story of a bad man who becomes a kind of saint. The First Story of the First Day, then, might be treated as a parody of a

Saint's Life; certainly, the elaborate introductory strategies suggest that the audience is being prepared for a weighty and important narrative.

After telling us that God works in mysterious ways, Panfilo moves to an account of the network of financial and political relationships that bind Ser Cepperello and Musciatto, for one of the mysteries of this story is why so bad a man should honor those obligations "in a gentle and amiable fashion that ran contrary to his nature." How evil that nature is has been abundantly documented with great rhetorical flourish, with Panfilo devoting considerable energy in the long paragraph on p. 1433 to explain what a great sinner Ciappelletto is (ask your students to note every use of *great* here), at the point where hagiographers establish the credentials of their subjects.

Even the name Ciappelletto is a lie, since the French among whom this Florentine notary spends much of his time mistake *Cepperello*, which means, as the footnote indicates, "little stump," for the far more elegant *Ciappelletto*, "little garland." This substitution of a flattering name for an ignoble one prefigures the plot of the story. And yet this evil man does a great favor for his hosts and then for the multitudes who visit and profit by their visits to his tomb.

The power of words attested to in the aside on naming suggests that Boccaccio has decided to begin the *Decameron*'s narratives with a tribute to language and its power. Ser Ciappelletto, after all, reinvents himself through his words in the course of the brilliant false confession he makes to the credulous friar, who will see to it that he is entombed in a holy chapel (and not thrown into a "moat like a dog," as his perturbed hosts had feared). The ruse is undertaken because of words overheard (Ser Ciappelletto engages to save the honor of the Italian bankers in whose home he is lodging when he hears their agitated discussion of the effects his death might have on their reputation and safety). The brothers station themselves "behind a wooden partition"—almost a false confessional in itself—to eavesdrop on Ser Ciappelletto and the friar, in order to satisfy themselves that their reputations will be safe when their guest dies. And, it might be noted, the "sin" that this master liar saves for his final challenge to God's mercy is that once, when he was a little boy, he cursed his mother. In sum, Ser Ciappelletto is a great storyteller, but God puts this greatness to unintended uses.

The narrative concludes with Panfilo reiterating his hymn to God's powers, which can find the good in the bad, and with a recognition of the ways in which speaking and hearing and telling stories can promote the divine purpose: "let us praise [a verbal counteraction of the curse] the name of Him with whom we began our storytelling, let us hold Him in reverence, and let us commend ourselves to Him in the hour of our need, in the certain knowledge that we shall be heard." Boccaccio has the last word: "And there the narrator fell silent."

[THE NINTH STORY OF THE FOURTH DAY]

The Fourth Day's topic is love stories with unhappy endings. As the footnote indicates, the story of the eaten heart was well-known in medieval Europe; this macabre incident is based on the life of the troubadour Guillem de Cabestaing, and Marie de France tells an analogous *lai* in *Laüstic*. Although so different in plot from the story of Ser Ciappelletto, this tale too pays tribute to verbal art. In appropriating his source material, it appears, Boccaccio suppresses the poetic identity of the tragic male protagonist, but he also brusquely turns away from the fate of the butchering husband, whose punishment is an important part of the Provençal original. Instead, the story (again, the comparison to *Laüstic* is suggestive) reaches its highpoint with the magnificent pronouncement and suicide of the lady and the verses commemorating the lovers in their shared tomb (a theme to pursue in relation to Ser Ciappelletto's).

[THE EIGHTH STORY OF THE FIFTH DAY]

The Fifth Day is devoted to love stories that end in happiness after a period of misfortune. The strange story of Nastagio degli Onesti, a critique of obsessive love, echoes two of the other tales in the anthology, which have been selected in part to demonstrate how Boccaccio orchestrates his one hundred stories as variations on a series of themes. We have already noted the repeated motif of the tomb. Here, we find another use of the heart torn from the body. The horrific vision that Nastagio sees has this brutal act at its center; the gruesome spectacle of which it is the climax alludes to the depiction of such punishments in Dante's *Inferno*, perhaps to prod the audience into reflection on the harshness of Dante's unsparing view of crime and punishment.

The theatricality of presentation in this story is worth pondering: to satisfy his friends' urging that he abandon his fruitless and expensive quest of the haughty lady who refuses him, Nastagio makes a show of setting out on a long journey. He instead organizes a lavish camping expedition just three miles out of town, and there he finds himself witness to another deceptive show, on a far grander scale, enacting a routine even more obsessive than his own unrewarded pursuit of love. The Sisyphean horrors that he witnesses and then turns to his own advantage are the sort of forest nightmare that will in turn be taken up by Ariosto in his *Orlando Furioso*, a comparison that you may want to exploit later on, to aid your students' understanding of the aura of tinsel about this entire episode and throughout Ariosto's great poem.

Staying with Boccaccio, you should be able to convince your students that the Eighth Story of the Fifth Day is another self-conscious comment on the power of storytelling. Nastagio's lady is smart enough to "read" the *grand guignol* she has witnessed correctly, as if it were a moral exemplum that works its desired end. Interestingly, this tale is told by Filomena, one of the seven women who decide to flee plague-ridden Florence in the introduction to the book. She is described as "prudent," or "discerning," when she deprecates their ability to take care of themselves in such difficult circumstances and initiates the decision then taken collectively to include men in their retreat. While the *Decameron* is notable for its sensitivity to women's concerns, Filomena's story emphatically does not approve of Messer Paolo Traversari's high-handed daughter, who clearly lacks prudence and makes her own decisions without parental or manly guidance throughout. Perhaps Filomena wishes to correct the excessive cruelty of the lady celebrated in the courtly love tradition. Watching the punishment of the hard-hearted naked fugitive is enough to make the ladies of Ravenna "much more tractable to men's pleasures than they had ever been in the past." Your students, perhaps especially the women among them, may wish to debate whether the story fits the day's agenda: how happily does it end?

[THE SIXTH STORY OF THE NINTH DAY]

The topic for the ninth day, as for the first, is open. If you have read *The Butcher of Abbeville*, your students will recognize the tale of Pinuccio as a *fabliau*. If you are limited to situating it within the *Decameron* selections, you can point to it as another example of the way Boccaccio's narratives revise each other as the days go on. Pinuccio may be viewed as a less exalted cousin of Nastagio degli Onesti, as the maiden he goes in quest of is frankly lower-class (and therefore more malleable than the daughter of the Traversari family). Like Nastagio, Pinuccio sets out on a phony voyage. Where the nobleman "mustered an enormous baggage-train" to make his three-mile foray into the forest, the Florentine gentleman feigns a voyage by loading a pair of saddlebags "probably with straw" and reversing direction so that he can plausibly ask the genial host to give him—and his indispensable sidekick—overnight lodgings.

The headnote explicates the significance of the cradle within the mercantile world in which the story is set; you may also want to note the prominence given to the surprised wife, who is so much more intelligent than Pinuccio the schemer but no more resourceful than her daughter, Niccolosa, who—unlike the Traversari lady—does not end up with a husband, but seems satisfied nevertheless.

[THE TENTH STORY OF THE TENTH DAY]

The final story in the *Decameron* culminates a day dedicated to examples of "magnificence," or the performance of generous deeds that have won fame for the doers. The famous tale of Gualtieri and Griselda matches the First Story of the First Day for its complexity and for the controversy it has generated. Another Saint's Life, it features a heroine who may be as problematic a subject as Ser Ciappelletto. Dioneo's irony, however, is reserved for Gualtieri (what, for example, does the reference in the opening paragraph to the Marquis's intelligence actually mean?).

One fruitful approach to this story is to view it as a fairy tale; Griselda reacts to the attendant instructed to take her first child from her with a request that the little girl not be left "to be devoured by the beasts and the birds" (p. 1637) unless he has been expressly told to do so. Your students will probably recognize this as a motif from *Snow White*, among other such folktales, and it is worth exploring the fears of abandonment in a cruel world that such stories exploit. But the *Decameron* version of the story of Griselda, which was recast by Petrarch as an allegory of the love between God (as represented by Gualtieri) and the Church (Griselda) insists on establishing a biblical frame of reference as well. Have your students identify the biblical allusions in Boccaccio's version, and then ask them how these allusions should be interpreted. Note details of Gualtieri's selection of his bride (he had "been casting an appreciative eye on the manners of a poor girl from a neighboring village," not unlike Pinuccio in the Sixth Story of the Ninth Day, whose "eye" had been caught by the honest host's daughter). Having made preparations for a wedding without nominating the bride, Gualtieri meets Griselda "as she was returning with water from the fountain" (p. 1635). This is a repeated motif in Genesis; it is how Isaac, for one, meets Rebekah and decides to marry her (and in Christian typology, this union represented the love of Christ for the Church).

More striking and upsetting are the allusions that make Griselda a figure of Job, whose beautiful response to God's trial she embodies: "Naked came I out of my mother's womb and naked shall I return thither: the Lord gave and the Lord hath taken away; blessed be the name of the Lord" (p. 1638). This is footnoted in the *Anthology*, and you might inform your class that the suffering of Job was frequently invoked during the time of plague in which the *Decameron* is set. Why is Griselda being tested? Why are human beings subjected to such cruel trials by a divinity who is supposed to love his creatures?

The footnotes also cite an echo of Mary's answer to Gabriel in the Annunciation. What mysterious purpose is Griselda serving here? The allusions suggest that Griselda in her imperturbable acceptance exemplifies the generosity that is the day's theme. But the community within the story views Gualtieri in theses terms as well, regarding him "as the wisest and most discerning man on earth" (p. 1636). In the concluding paragraph of the story, Dioneo unequivocally judges Gualtieri as a tyrant, remarking on his good luck to have found a "celestial spirit" to dwell in his house, while he "would be better employed as [a swineherd]."

Some critics see a political motive in the republican Boccaccio's description of a despotic Marquis. Whether this is true or not, it can be said with certainty that, like the First Story of the First Day, this final story turns expectations inside out. Although the story is set up as the last in a sequence of celebrations of the magnificence of the ruler, Dioneo explicitly announces that the Marquis disproves the theme. Instead he celebrates the magnificence of the ruler's victim. Or does this story really warn us against the kind of martyrdom that the faithful Griselda seems ready to accept? "Who but Griselda" would be so masochistic as to endure the public humiliation that her husband visits upon her?

In asking questions such as these, today's readers join the interpretive community that Boccaccio's ten fictional storytellers form as a refuge against death and disease. The most perfectly shaped of the framed tales in the *Anthology* (*The Thousand and One Nights*, *The Canterbury Tales*, and the *Heptameron* are all unfinished), the *Decameron* continues to be an inexhaustible source of inspiration.

Topics for Writing

1. Discuss the internal narratives contained in the First Tale of the First Day or the Eighth Story of the Fifth Day: how does Ser Ciappelletto's confession or the spectacle of horror that Nastagio degli Onesti comes upon embody the power of fiction?
2. Among Boccaccio's ten storytellers are seven women, and the *Decameron* as a whole is addressed to women. Comment on the depiction of gender relations in the stories you have read. Are the female narrators more sympathetic to women's concerns than the males? Do you think women are favored in the way they are portrayed? Give examples to support your argument.

Comparative Perspectives

1. Does the repeated scene in the forest that Nastagio degli Onesti witnesses fit the theory of the contrapasso that governs punishment in Dante's Inferno?
2. Compare the frame tales in the *Decameron*, *The Thousand and One Nights*, *The Canterbury Tales*, and/or the *Heptameron*. In each case, what is the reason for telling stories? Do the stories accomplish the purpose for which they are intended? How important is the relationship between the tale and the teller in the selections you choose to discuss?
3. Is Griselda the ideal woman? Explain your answer and compare her behavior with that of other highly praised literary wives, to be selected from possibilities that include Rebekah in Genesis, Penelope in the *Odyssey*, Shahrazad in *The Thousand and One Nights*, Desdemona in *Othello*.

Further Reading

See also the reading suggestions in the *Anthology*, p. 2643.

Potter, Joy Hambueden. *Five Frames for the* Decameron: *Communication and Social Systems in the* Cornice. 1982. Helpful review of the social situation behind the tellers, who are described as on "a retreat . . . during which they both learn and reassess the value of their society."

Seung, T. K. *Cultural Thematics: The Formation of the Faustian Ethos.* 1976. Contains interesting analyses of the "sovereign will" displayed in the first and the last stories of the *Decameron*.

Sir Gawain and the Green Knight

Backgrounds

[Part I]

The poet quickly tells how, after the fall of Troy, various of the surviving Trojan warriors migrated to the west and founded new nations; among them Brutus came to Britain; later Arthur ruled as king in Camelot. This will be a wondrous tale of events during a Christmas–New Year's holiday there. Arthur; his queen, Guinevere; and Gawain, his nephew, are at a high table or dais; many other knights sit at other tables; all await the feast; but Arthur has vowed not to begin until someone comes to tell him of a "wonder." Suddenly a huge horse and rider, both covered in green, dash into the hall and approach the dais; the visitor has neither spear nor shield but carries a branch of green holly in one hand and a large ax in the other. He asks who is in charge here; Arthur answers and invites him to dismount and be treated as a guest. He declines, saying he has heard of the prowess and courtesy of Arthur's knights; he comes in peace to propose a Christmas game. Arthur assents, and the Green Knight offers his head to be stricken off with the ax—on condition that a return blow be accepted a year and a day hence. When all the company remain silent, he taunts them harshly, whereupon Arthur in anger and shame steps forward to accept the challenge. But now Gawain intervenes, asking that he be allowed to take over in place of the king; Gawain modestly says he is the weakest of all in body and mind and of no consequence except for his kinship to the king. This folly, he says, fits not a king. His request is granted, and now the Green Knight, repeating the conditions of the challenge, dismounts, lies down, uncovers his neck, and is neatly beheaded by Gawain's blow with the ax. But the Green Knight rises, catches his head up from the floor, mounts his horse, and tells Gawain to come next year and look for the Knight of the Green Chapel, who will be ready with the return blow. He then rides rapidly out of the hall; the company resume their feasting.

[Part II]

The seasons pass in due course until All Hallows Day (November 1), when Gawain is ready to start on his journey in search of the Knight of the Green Chapel. He bids king and friends farewell; he is richly armed, as his horse, Gringolet, is handsomely caparisoned; the pentangle (five-pointed star figure) on Gawain's shield includes in its symbolism his devotion to Mary, queen of Heaven and all his moral virtues. As Gawain departs, some of the court regret that the affair was not better handled: it is a shame that he is likely to lose his life, "Beheaded by an elf-man, for empty pride" (line 681). In the course of Gawain's solitary journey, he is threatened by wild animals and wild men and hampered by winter cold and sleet; he prays to Mary for guidance. Presently, he catches sight of a splendid castle and surrounding grounds, approaches, and is

greeted by the porter, who lets down the drawbridge. The lord of the castle welcomes Gawain, and he is finely entertained, wined, and dined.
There are two ladies in the host's family, one comely and beautiful, the
other ugly and graceless. After the visit has lasted from Christmas Eve
till St. John's day (December 27), Gawain says he must continue his
search for the Green Chapel; his host assures him that it is close by, and
so Gawain can stay on as a guest for three more days. The host then proposes a game: he will go hunting each day, while Gawain rests (after his
tiring journey) in the castle; each evening the host will give Gawain
whatever he has got on the hunt and Gawain will give him whatever he
has received in the castle.

[PART III]

As noted in the headnote, the same narrative sequence is maintained
for all three days: first, the start of the hunt; then the visit of the lady, the
host's wife, to Gawain's bedchamber; then the conclusion of the hunt,
the evening meal, and the exchange of gifts. On the first day the host and
his company hunt deer and bring home many carcasses, duly presented
to Gawain; he duly gives the host a single kiss. On the second day comes
the boar hunt; and Gawain correctly gives the host two kisses. The third
day the quarry is a fox; and Gawain correctly bestows three kisses on the
host but silently withholds the silk belt that the lady had given him, with
the promise that it would ensure the wearer against death.

[PART IV]

Early on New Year's morning Gawain sets out to keep his rendezvous;
the young guide whom the host assigned to him warns him of the great
danger facing him at the hands of the savage Knight of the Green
Chapel and says he (the guide) will keep silent if Gawain avoids a meeting; Gawain says he must keep faith, and trusts to God. Proceeding,
Gawain soon comes to a sort of mound; he hears nearby, but out of
sight, someone sharpening a blade on a grindstone. Gawain calls out,
giving his name, and the Green Knight comes over the crest of a hill carrying a huge Danish ax. Gawain duly prepares to receive the blow, but
twice the Green Knight feints, bringing the ax down but not touching
Gawain; the third time he lets the blade graze Gawain's neck, drawing a
few drops of blood. Thereupon Gawain leaps up and offers to resist any
further blows. But the Green Knight now explains that he was the host
in the castle (of Bercilak); the two feints correspond to the two days on
which Gawain carried out the exchange faithfully and in full; the slight
scratch made by the third blow was Gawain's due because he kept back
the silk belt—but only because it might save his life. Gawain quickly
gives back the belt and reproaches himself bitterly for cowardice and
covetousness. But the Green Knight declares Gawain, who has confessed the fault and suffered the penance (of the third stroke), as pure
as the day he was born; and invites him to return to the castle, where his
wife (the lady who had visited Gawain in his bedchamber) will be glad to

see him. The host also gives the belt once more to Gawain, who must keep it as a reminder of the event; Gawain says he will keep it as a warning of his spiritual weakness and peril. In answer to Gawain's question, the Green Knight says that the old, ugly lady in the castle is Morgan le Faye, King Arthur's half-sister; she is an enchantress and an enemy of Guinevere, and hence was responsible for the visit of the Green Knight to Camelot. Gawain makes his way back to Arthur's court, where he tells the whole story; the belt is used as a model of a baldric to be worn by knights of the court.

The earliest extant literary treatment of the "beheading game" is in the Irish prose narrative *The Feast of Bricriu* (*Fled Bricrend*), dated approximately in the eighth century. Cuchulainn, the great warrior of the Ulster cycle of tales, is engaged in a contest with other fighters for the right to the "hero's portion" at a feast. A rough-looking figure of magical powers invites each of them in turn to an exchange of blows in the manner of Gawain and the Green Knight, but the time interval is one day instead of a year. The others fail to keep the appointment for the return blow, Cuchulain alone is faithful, and he receives an entirely harmless blow and is declared the winner of the contest. (The Irish episode is translated in Kittredge, *A Study of Sir Gawain and the Green Knight*.) The Irish plot was taken over by French and perhaps other medieval storytellers; the anonymous author of the selection probably knew it in *The Book* (*Le Livre*) *de Caradoc*, which appears among the "continuations" of the Old French Percival romance. (For discussion and summaries, see Larry D. Benson, *Art and Tradition in Sir Gawain and the Green Knight*, 1965.) The temptation plot was also familiar from various romances (see Benson); of course, it has an ancient history, e.g., the story of Joseph and Potiphar's wife in Genesis 39.7–20 as well as the deeply tragic Greek tale of Hippolytus and Phaedra. The author of the English romance may have been the first to combine the two plots.

In his descriptions and characterizations he also makes abundant use of tradition. Thus the knight in green costume, carrying a bough of holly, was a familiar figure representing the verdure of spring in the new year. Not combined with this but rather juxtaposed is the green color of his skin; this, along with the enormous shock of hair covering his shoulders, may well have reminded medieval listeners or readers of the figure of the Wild Man, the uncouth stranger who often erupts in royal courts (in romances). Both traditions are doubtless related to prototypes of ultimate (pre-Christian) ritual significance; one thinks of spring festivals and sacrifices, the renewal of the waste land at the end of winter—though it is unlikely that the fourteenth-century audience made conscious connections of this kind.

In the portrayal of Gawain, the poet makes an independent use of tradition. In this poem Gawain is a brave, spotless Christian knight, imbued with the five chivalric virtues and devoted to the Virgin Mary, his heavenly patroness; he is, of course, keenly sensitive in any matter of truth or honor. But, while making him also peerless in courtesy (conduct as a cultivated gentleman), the poet definitely does not attach to Gawain the habits of a medieval Casanova. But that is just the reputation that Gawain had acquired in romance tradition by the late fourteenth century. What the poet does is to have the temptress—the wife of the Green Knight—pretend to believe that Gawain had well earned this latter reputation and ought to have no hesitation about living up to it. She is playing a game, of course; with the resources of a magic household and entourage and a shape-shifter for a husband, she incurs no risk, however Gawain may respond to her overtures. Thus she is free to deploy the whole gamut of invitation, including praise, entreaty, pretended unhappiness at his rejection, disbelief that he can really be Gawain—no holds need be barred and none are. This is a hilariously comic situation, and the author takes full advantage of it.

Gawain, on the other hand, is deterred by his situation as a guest of the lord of the castle and the agreement to exchange winnings at the end of each day; by the fact that such an intrigue is a sin; and by his preoccupation with the approaching rendezvous with the Green Knight. Yet we can see that he feels deeply the obligation to behave always with courtesy (good manners and consideration of the lady's emotions). Nevertheless, the poet indicates that Gawain was genuinely moved, at least on the third day; we are told at the beginning of the visit that he delights in the lady's company—and there is a reminder that Mary had better look after her knight.

The parallel patterning of the hunts and the lady's visits has been noted. Probably it is significant that the third hunt, of the fox—regarded in that age as vermin—is paired with Gawain's breach of faith in not giving the belt to his host, a reprehensible act even if extenuated by the circumstances.

The humor of the situation after the Green Knight has delivered the final stroke must not be missed. Gawain instantly springs up ready to defend himself (against further attack, beyond the terms of the agreement); and the Green Knight quietly stands there, doubtless laughing to himself. Presently he explains the whole design. But the amused reader can sympathize with Gawain in his chagrin at the deception that has been practiced on him; he has been under such pressure for so long! Even the most ardent feminist should forgive his outburst against the wiles of women. Indeed, the art and skill of the poet maintain the reader's sympathy with and esteem for Gawain through the many scenes in which he inevitably becomes a figure of comedy.

Classroom Strategies

You must see to it that students discover the many and various delights of the romance. Once they get into it, they will see how much fun it can be—as well as being a serious treatment of important issues. Early on, some of the vivid descriptive and "action" passages might well be read aloud in class. Later, some of the dialogue between Gawain and the lady should receive oral dramatization, with parts appropriately assigned to members of the class.

Topics for Discussion

1. Reasons for Gawain's chagrin and self-disgust.

   [When he throws the girdle at the Green Knight, he realizes that he has been made a fool of, but that it is his own fault; but it is also true that he has been obliged to play a game without knowing the rules, and he has shown a flaw by not returning the girdle earlier (as promised by the terms of the agreement)—a fault that he *need* not have committed—as he has just discovered. In his view—at the moment, at least—the flaw cancels out his persevering resistance of the other temptations that the lady had pressed on him.]

2. What is the verdict of others (than Gawain) on his conduct?

   [Sir Bercilak (the Green Knight himself) lets the ax barely scratch the skin of Gawain's neck and afterward declares him wholly absolved and invites him to return to the castle for more festivity. Arthur's court adopts the girdle as a badge of honor—rather than shame or disgrace. The reader is likely to see the narrative as a series of extreme tests imposed (without his full knowledge) on a superlative knight, courtier, and man of scrupulous honor. He passes them all with flying colors—with one slight exception, and there he believed his life was at stake. Since the author leads the reader to this conclusion, it must have been his also.]

3. Does the author indulge in too much descriptive detail?

   [There is certainly a rich abundance: the festivity at Arthur's court, the elaborate clothing and arming of Gawain for the journey, the details of the three hunts, etc. But is the description static? Or is something happening all the time within the descriptions? And could there be a difference between the spontaneous interest of the fourteenth-century listener and the twentieth-century reader?]

Topics for Writing

1. Characterization of the Green Knight.

   [To some extent a dual personality: the outlandish visitor at Arthur's feast and Sir Bercilak, Gawain's host at the castle. How are these necessarily somewhat different? Is there an underlying unity?]

2. The story as a Christmas "game"—in two parts.

   [The initial setting at Arthur's court; the wait for a wonder; the Green Knight's challenge (which is noted as a "folly" but nevertheless must be taken seriously); the Christmas season a year later at Bercilak's castle; the triple exchange of gifts; the happy conclusion of both plots on New Year's morning.]

3. Gawain as a graceful naysayer.

   [A close look at Gawain's part in the dialogue with the lady on the three mornings; how he maintains his (attributed) reputation for courtesy but still remains modest about himself; how he avoids involvement without giving offense; the details of his acceptance of the girdle.]

Comparative Perspectives

1. Gawain's quest for the Green Knight is accompanied by detailed descriptions of the changing seasons of the year. How does this attention to weather and landscape complement the figure of the giant knight, who appears both in green and, as Sir Bercilak, with a beard "of a beaver's hue"—that is, a deep brown? How would you compare the role played by seasonal change in the characters' lives here with that in other poems and narratives you have read?
2. Gawain is introduced as a nephew of King Arthur. What features of feudal and aristocratic societies make this an important relationship? How do similar family ties put subtle pressures on the young heroes of other heroic tales you have read?

Further Reading

See the reading suggestions in the *Anthology*, p. 2644.

GEOFFREY CHAUCER

The Canterbury Tales

↝ GENERAL PROLOGUE

The Knight, his son the Squire, and their servant the Yeoman make up a group of three traveling together. The account of the Knight is representative and typical, rather than based on any individual actual person. He is a professional soldier of notable experience and exemplary character. It has been shown that various English knights took part in most or all of the campaigns mentioned. Such a young soldier as the Squire might well have served with English armies in France in one or more campaigns of the Hundred Years' War.

Next comes another group of three: the Prioress, another nun who serves as her secretary, and an accompanying priest; neither the secretary nor the priest is described in the *General Prologue*. Chaucer's attitude toward the Prioress has been much discussed among scholars. It has been pointed out that she has many of the qualities expected in a fashionable lady of the period but not necessarily in a nun: meticulous table manners, graceful costume, the use of (insular!) French. The "love" emblematic on her brooch may be ambivalent—religious or ordinary earthly; her tenderness about the pet dogs—not monastic—seems to be an individual trait. Chaucer seems amused by the various items *not* generally approved for nuns, yet fully appreciative of an exquisite person.

Chaucer's treatment of the Monk is rather difficult. He does not merely tell us that the Monk is an ardent hunter and that he is often away from his monastery, and so on; he repeatedly notes that these things were contrary to monastic "rule" and precedent. Consequently, when Chaucer declares his approval of the Monk's way of life, some kind of irony must be involved. One view is that, in *The Canterbury Tales*, there are two Chaucers—one is the sophisticated author, the other is the simple, suggestible pilgrim—and that sometimes we hear the voice of one, sometimes of the other. Thus Chaucer the author painted the portrait of the Monk, but Chaucer the pilgrim liked and approved of his way of life. Without making so sharp a division as this, we can at least agree that Chaucer occasionally pretends to say what would contradict other clear positions or attitudes; he enjoys a moment of make-believe.

Unlike monks, friars were expected to leave their "house," to go out into the world and serve, especially, the poor and helpless—after the example of St. Francis and other founders. But Chaucer makes it evident that this Friar had all the traits of an expert salesman and used them assiduously for his own enrichment and enjoyment—leaving the poor to themselves.

The next several pilgrims require no comment here; then we come to the Parson, who, like the Knight, receives a full and entirely favorable treatment. Later still, there is the Summoner, a thoroughly unsavory and corrupt but also comic figure. He is not a member of the clergy; instead, he is a kind of policeman or constable attached to the Church court presided over by an archdeacon. The Summoner is apparently an associate of the Pardoner, who comes next in Chaucer's list. The latter's occupation is discussed in the headnote. Here it may be added that the Pardoner has often been regarded as a eunuch *ex nativitate* (by birth, congenitally); it has also been shown that Chaucer's description and language might apply to homosexual characters. There may thus be innuendo in the mention of the association between the Summoner and the Pardoner. And the present account should be kept in mind when the reader comes to the bitter altercation between the Pardoner and the Host at the end of *The Pardoner's Tale*.

◦ THE MILLER'S PROLOGUE AND TALE

The Prologue: When the Knight has told his tale—a romance of chivalry and of courtly love (not included in the anthology)—the Host invites the Monk (next in social rank to the Knight) to continue with the storytelling. But the Miller, partly drunk, insists on telling his tale at once. It is in some ways a parody of high romance, but primarily it is a very fully developed *fabliau*.

The Tale: John, a comparatively rich old carpenter of Oxford, has a pretty young wife, Alison; and there are two young servants, male and female. They have a boarder living in the house, Nicholas, who is a student at the university and a semiprofessional astrologer. He and Alison plan an (uncourtly!) intrigue, but they will have to be cautious—the husband is jealous. Meanwhile the parish clerk, Absolom, is infatuated with Alison (who has no interest in him) and likes to serenade her under the window at night.

Nicholas shuts himself up in his room for a time; John, who likes the young man, comes to his room to inquire. Nicholas explains that he knows from his astrology that a flood greater than Noah's is in the offing; but they can save themselves if they keep the news a secret. The carpenter must hang huge baskets from the ceiling or loft and he, Alison, and Nicholas will climb up and bed down, each in one of the baskets. (The servants have been sent out of town.) Then Nicholas and Alison—the weary John has gone to sleep—climb out, go downstairs and so to bed. Presently Absolom comes singing and pleading for at least a kiss from Alison. She sits on the windowsill, her rear projecting outward; Absolom's kiss chills all his amorous itch and inspires him with a plan for revenge.

Obtaining a colter or plowshare well heated at one end from a late-working blacksmith, Absolom returns and asks Alison for another kiss. This time Nicholas projects over the window; Absolom is ready with the hot iron. When Nicholas yells "Water! Water!" the carpenter wakes up and instantly cuts the rope holding his basket (expecting that form of navigation during the flood), falls to the floor, and breaks his arm. In the aftermath Nicholas and Alison insist that only the foolish John believed a flood was imminent.

♦ THE WIFE OF BATH'S PROLOGUE AND TALE

The Prologue: The Wife of Bath has the longest prologue in *The Canterbury Tales,* an apology for her life that threatens to overwhelm her (slightly) more succinct tale. Apparently rambling, the *Prologue* is in fact quite well organized, according to the principles of medieval argumentation. From her opening announcement, she contrasts the claims of experience with those of authority. In her *Prologue,* she draws amply on both as evidence for her views on sexuality and marriage. She manipulates her frequent biblical references and quotations to bring objective authority to justify her many marriages (Solomon is a favorite) and to demonstrate that virginity is a self-limiting ideal not to be universally imposed (Paul is undercut).

When the Pardoner interrupts her well-argued defense of heterosexual activity, the Wife of Bath turns to personal experience (which, as the headnote suggests, is actually as much rooted in the misogynist texts of literary authority as in any authentic life experience that this fictional character can claim). Her first three husbands were "good," inasmuch as they were old and she could control them, and she shows off the aggressive ways in which she attacked before they could chastise her.

At the midway point in her *Prologue,* when Alison comes to her fourth husband, she momentarily falters (note the repeated effort, at lines 454 and 483, to explain her life with the first man to have cheated on her). Rather than inquire too deeply into this humiliating experience, she launches into the great defense of her own charms and the poignant recognition that they are fading.

Boasting of the pain she dealt the man who had pained her, she moves on quickly to the story of her life with husband number five, the young clerk who made this eager conversationalist deaf in one ear and over whom she eventually triumphed. Here again, she becomes the mouthpiece for the antifeminine tirades of her clerkly husband, a technique aptly captured in a telling detail: to stop him from reading at night when she wanted to go to bed, she tore three pages out of his book (line 787). Shortly after losing that final battle with a wife twice his age, Jenkin died (one might well ask what killed him), and the Wife of Bath is on pilgrimage, as we learn in the *General Prologue*, to see if she can find her sixth husband.

The Tale: Interrupted again by the Friar, a nefarious charmer who preys on widows, the Wife of Bath pays him back in the brilliant prelude to her Tale. In her story about one of King Arthur's knights, a singularly ignoble rapist, she takes us back to the world of fairies and elves, stopping to compare the dull contemporary world to this charmed past, maliciously noting that the incubi of the old (pre-Christian) world who impregnated innocent women have been replaced by the friars of the new dispensation, who may try to force themselves on women but to no avail—they are, she implies, an impotent bunch (line 23).

In the *Tale* itself, she seems to identify more with the questing knight than with his victim, for the question the queen and her ladies put to the knight is the Wife's own question as well (not to mention Sigmund Freud's): "what is the thing that most of all / Women desire" (lines 39–40)? Searching for the answer provides another opportunity for a literary-historical review; notably, Dante is cited as the authority on the importance of true gentility, as opposed to mere family inheritance. The knight answers correctly because listening to his unattractive old wife has led him (and the Wife herself, we feel) to see that every human being must understand how little we actually can control. To gain sovereignty is to give it up; typically, Alison disclaims this moral truth almost as soon as it is affirmed, returning in her concluding lines to her aggressive, self-protective stance.

ⓞ THE PARDONER'S PROLOGUE AND TALE

The Prologue: In this exuberant address to his fellow pilgrims the Pardoner boasts about his skill in getting money from the simple, rustic people who listen to his preaching. His text, "The root of evil is greed," serves to loosen their wallets and fill his own. His fake relics, he assures them, will cure ills of domestic animals, prevent suspicion of wives by husbands, increase the yield of crops—if a suitable offering is made. But note this: it won't work if the person making the offering is guilty of any really serious unconfessed sin. (Thus he intimidates anyone who did not come forward with an offering.)

The Tale: The Pardoner offers this tale as a specimen of his preaching. First, he briefly sets a scene: three young men are in a tavern; they eat and drink to excess, indulge in much profanity, and roll dice. Here the Pardoner inserts a long denunciation of gluttony, drunkenness, profanity, and gambling, with allusions to the Bible, examples from secular history, and a lively imitation of the snoring of a person who has taken too much alcohol—"Samson, Samson"—yet Samson never drank wine! Resuming the story, the revelers hear a bell outside the tavern. Learning from the waiter that it is rung for a man recently slain by this thief Death, they (are just intoxicated enough to) resolve to go immediately in search of this Death, intending to kill him.

Before long they meet a mysterious old man whom they question roughly. Without saying who he is, he describes himself as a hopeless wanderer who would welcome Death; but Death won't have him. The revelers then demand, with threats, that he tell them where Death can be found. He directs them to follow a crooked road to a grove nearby; they will find Death waiting under a tree. They do as he says, but what they find is almost eight bushels of fine gold coins.

After this they forget all about Death and set about ways of guarding the money for themselves. It is decided by lot that two will stay with the gold while the third goes into town to buy food for the (overnight?) wait that they must count on for safety. While one is away, the other two plan to kill him as soon as he returns; and he buys poison to put in one of the jugs of wine that he carries back to the grove. Both designs succeed, and soon all three are dead.

Apparently carried away by his own eloquence, the Pardoner, having quickly concluded his sermon, invites his fellow pilgrims to come forward and make offerings; that is, he tries to treat them like his rural congregations. When he suggests—playfully or not—that the Host should begin, being the most involved in sin, the latter answers him angrily and abusively; finally the Knight insists on a reconciliation, and the incident passes.

Topics for Discussion

1. Of the Lawyer, the Franklin, and the Physician in the General Prologue, what remarks by Chaucer might indicate something less than total approval of each? Try to relate the qualifications to the portrait as a whole; bear in mind that these men are neither scoundrels nor saints.

2. In *The Miller's Tale*, how does the overall characterization of John, Alison, Nicholas, and Absolom make it plausible that each would act in the way the story tells it? Take into account such things as John's credulity and (qualified) respect for Nicholas's learning, Alison's youth and beauty, and Absolom's naive taste in love songs.

3. Is *The Miller's Tale* pornography?

   [This would involve an effort to define pornography or at least to decide its essential feature(s). Is Chaucer's story ever suggestive or

prurient? Or is it instead honest and forthright? The same questions might be asked in the discussion of Boccaccio's tale of Brother
Alberto and Lisetta.]

4. The variety of aspects and settings in which death is referred to in
The Pardoner's Tale.

[Consider: the bell heard by the three young men in the tavern
(line 182), the waiter's talk about "a sly thief" (line 193), the resolution of the young men (lines 210ff.), the talk of the mysterious
old man (lines 238ff.), his directing them to a grove (line 280), the
pile of gold (lines 288ff.), the apothecary's drug (lines 362ff.), and
the (pretended) bit of friendly wrestling. When and where is there
personification? (The use of a capital *D* is a clue.)]

Topics for Writing

1. Men and women of the Church.

[The Prioress, the Monk, the Friar, the Oxford student, the Parson, and the Pardoner are described in the *General Prologue*. The
Priest accompanying the nuns is characterized in the *Prologue* to
his tale. The Oxford student is a devoted cleric and serious scholar;
the Parson is a diligent and faultless servant and moral guardian of
his parish. Chaucer's account of the Prioress is ambivalent: is it basically sympathetic? He admires the skill of the Friar and the Pardoner, but what is his judgment of them otherwise? After noting all
these, come back to the Monk and try to assess Chaucer's estimate. Finally, dispose of the question, Was Chaucer in favor of the
Church or opposed to it?]

2. Chaucer's pilgrims in Dante's *Inferno*.

[The headnote to Chaucer suggests that some of the rascals
among them might have found a place in one or another of the
subdivisions of the Eighth Circle, devoted to Fraud, or dishonesty.
Choose several characters and discuss their fitness for such a category. Use both plain statements and indirect indications of both
poets.]

Comparative Perspectives

1. As in much Western medieval literature—including Dante's Inferno and Sir Gawain and the Green Knight—and in the Chaucerian selections in the anthology, punishment for transgression is a
concern. Compare Dante's formulation of apt punishments with,
as appropriate, the punishments inflicted—or not inflicted—on the
characters in The Miller's Tale and The Pardoner's Prologue and
Tale. How does the prevailing vision of punishment here measure up against the punishments suffered by characters in non-
Christian narratives of roughly the same period?

[Cf. *The Thousand and One Nights*.]

2. From the way even the least educated of Chaucer's characters
speak, it is clear that the rhetorical traditions of the Middle Ages

were available to listeners as much as to readers. Select a passage that shows evidence of popular styles of argumentation and discuss their effect on the tone of Chaucer's tales. Compare the tone of voice in works like *The Book of the Courtier* and the *Heptameron*, which reproduce the conversational style of a highly literate aristocratic culture.

3. How does Chaucer, in *The Wife of Bath's Tale*, take up the debate on *gentilesse* launched by Guido Guinizelli in *Love and Nobility* and continued by Dante in his lyric poems?

Further Reading

See also the reading suggestions in the *Anthology*, p. 2643.

Gibaldi, Joseph, ed. *Approaches to Teaching Chaucer's* Canterbury Tales. 1980.

THE THOUSAND AND ONE NIGHTS

Background

The Thousand and One Nights begins with a lengthy prologue. Two brothers have ruled their respective kingdoms in equity and peace for ten years. The elder, Shahrayar, desires to see the younger, Shahzaman, and sends for him. Shahzaman appoints a deputy to rule in his stead and sets out. Returning unexpectedly before he has traveled far, he discovers his wife committing adultery with a kitchen boy and executes them both summarily. He arrives in Shahrayar's court depressed but unwilling to tell his brother why. By chance, Shahzaman witnesses the extraordinary infidelity of Shahrayar's wife and attendants with black male slaves from her husband's court. His depression lifts on seeing that even so powerful a monarch as his brother can be wounded as he is. His brother notices the improvement in his spirits and asks the reasons. Eventually Shahzaman must tell him, with the result that Shahrayar secretly witnesses a repetition of his wife's carnival of infidelity. Now he becomes depressed. He and his brother resolve to abandon the court and wander the world seeking someone who is even more afflicted than they are. They discover such an unfortunate in an enormous black demon who stands as much above Shahrayar in power and authority as he does the slave who has cuckolded him. Moreover, this demon has protected his woman by means that should even be more secure than the walls of Shahrayar's palace. Yet she has managed to betray him with a hundred men, including Shahrayar and Shahzaman. Now convinced of the impossibility of finding a virtuous woman, Shahrayar returns to court, slays his wife and her maids and begins an insane and murderous policy designed to ensure that he will never be betrayed again. He marries a new wife each evening and murders her the following morning. Shahzaman returns to Samarkand and is heard from no further.

The people of his realm are outraged and pray to God for deliverance. Shahrayar's vizier is incapable of finding a solution, but the elder of his two daughters, Shahrazad, is uncommonly wise, well read, and exceptionally brave. She plans to save the people, but it requires that she be married to Shahrayar. Her father tries to dissuade her by telling her two stories. He is unsuccessful, and, indeed, his stories seem irrelevant to his purpose. Shahrazad's plan is to use her skill as a storyteller to manipulate Shahrayar into deferring her death endlessly. That is, each night she tells him stories to while away the long hours of the might, and stopping each sunrise just before some crisis. As she expected, Shahrayar's eagerness to hear the end of the story is stronger than his desire to have her executed. She continues this way until he at last pardons her, marries her, and abandons his policy. This lengthy prologue is the frame in which all the tales are set. In the various manuscripts and many printed editions of *The Thousand and One Nights*, the formulaic interruptions at dawn are usually retained. In the translations they usually are not.

Classroom Strategies

The reading can be easily divided into two or three sections. The first section would include the *Prologue* and *The Tale of the Ox and the Donkey*, the second section would begin with *The Tale of the Merchant and His Wife* and go through to *The Third Old Man's Tale*, the final section would begin with *The Story of the Fisherman and the Demon* and go through to the end (*The Tale of the Enchanted King*). If two sections are preferable, the first section would begin with the *Prologue* and encompass all of the readings listed above in the second section. The second section would be the same as the third section listed above.

Topics for Discussion

The theme of justice or the relation of crime to punishment is a central one in this portion of the Nights. The young women whom Shahrayar married and murders are innocent of any crime against Shahrayar whatsoever, and by punishing the innocent Shahrayar changes himself from a just ruler into a monster of indifference, a ruler who makes war on his own people. The merchant is equally innocent of evil intent toward the jinn or his son. There is, to our eyes at least, an absurd or comical element to this encounter that undermines any inclination to sympathize with the jinn in his loss. As pointed out in the headnote, the tales the three travelers tell offer further variations on this theme; moreover, they provide very attractive examples of women who are virtuous and obedient to their fathers or husbands—the herdsman's daughter, the merchant's magical wife, and the butcher's daughter.

The most provocative question raised by the *Prologue* are those of the morality of women and racial discrimination. All too often the story is read through Shahrayar's eyes, and he, his brother, and the demon are seen simply as victims of evil and designing women. The key to a reading that does more justice to the woman's point of view is in the relation of the demon to his captured bride. He is the villain here, not the young woman whom he has stolen away from her husband and home on her wedding night and kept imprisoned at the bottom of the sea solely for his own pleasure. That Shahrayar and Shahzaman don't see this suggests that they are insensitive husbands although they may be just rulers. Shahrayar's assault on the young women of the realm is the height of insanity since by it he, the king, is making warfare on his own people. It suggests that he is angry with them, not just the young women, perhaps because he feels they have shared in his wife's secret and not told him. After all such astonishing performances, which involved so many of the palace staff, can hardly have been a secret to anybody in the palace but Shahrayar.

The selection of black partners for Shahrayar's queen and her attendants may reflect Muslim stereotypes about black male potency, but it is not necessarily invidious for that reason. Islam was not completely color blind, but there have been eminent and distinguished Muslims of African origin in every profession since the time of Muhammad. The demon who is the most powerful figure in the story, and whose misfortune is seen by Shahrayar and Shahzaman as greater than their own, is also black.

Beginning with *The Story of the Fisherman and the Demon*, the tales open up like nesting dolls, with tales within tales within tales. The overall frame is that of a fisherman who fishes out a bottle and, upon opening it, liberates a demon that had been held captive for hundreds of years. When the demon declares that he will kill the fisherman, the fisherman begs for mercy and tells him that his death would only bring destruction on the demon. Then, cleverly, the fisherman—as a last request—says that he doesn't believe the demon could ever have fit in the bottle in the first place. The demon proves that this is possible by returning to the bottle, which the fisherman quickly closes. Here is where the story within story structure begins.

The demon begs to be released, and the fisherman tells him that he is reminded of *The Tale of King Yunan and the Sage Duban*, and he begins to tell the tale. In this story, King Yunan is cured of leprosy by the Sage Dubon, whereupon he showers him with wealth of all kinds. A jealous vizier tells the king that the sage is plotting his death and should be killed. The king tells the vizier that he is lying, as in *The Tale of the Husband and the Parrot*, in which a husband wrongly puts a parrot to death because of the deception of his wife. The vizier responds that really it is more like *The Tale of the King's Son and the She-Ghoul*, in which an unfaithful vizier leads a prince to near death, but the prince's prayer saves him and he is able to kill the vizier before there is another attempt on his life. The king then agrees with the vizier, summons the sage, and orders his death. The sage says this is just like *The Story of the Crocodile*, but no story follows because he declares he is too upset to tell a story. There are a few "false leads" like this, which are humorous moments in the tales.

Finally, the sage agrees to be killed, but tells the king that if he looks in the sage's book, *The Secret of Secrets*, after the wise man is decapitated, the dismembered head will be able to answer the king's questions.

The king thinks that this is fantastic and kills the sage, and upon turning the pages of the book, he is poisoned and dies. Here, we return to the story of the fisherman and the demon. The fisherman says he is like the vizier, and that the demon is like the king. You may want to ask your students about the multitude of comparisons and parallels up to this point. Why do the characters keep referring to other stories and people for analogies to their own situation? How effective is the tale within a tale structure for keeping the audience interested? (After all, this is Shahrazad's main concern!)

The fisherman finally agrees to release the demon, who in return leads him to a magical lake with multicolored fish. In bringing the fish to the king (for which he receives a great sum), the fisherman unwittingly leads the king into another mystery and to the kingdom of the ruler who is the protagonist in the last story in this section, *The Tale of the Enchanted King*. Here, under a spell, the king has become half flesh, half stone; his kingdom has been enchanted (and his subjects turned into the multicolored fish); and by day he must witness his evil wife's constant infidelity and scorn. The first king (ruler of the fisherman's kingdom) breaks the spell, kills the wife and her black lover, and earns the trust forever of the enchanted king. Ultimately, everyone is happy—even the fisherman, whose daughters marry the two kings and whose son becomes a member of the court.

Many of the earlier themes will recur here and will make terrific discussion topics for your students. Have them trace the characteristics of demons and their powers; of liars and their comeuppances; of jealousy, infidelity, and honor. Does a good tale necessarily need a magical element to entertain? Finally, have your students discuss the wider frame within which all of these stories are taking place—Shahrazad's desire to stay alive and break the king of his wish to kill his wives after one night. Why is her storytelling effective? Why does she choose the tales that she does?

Topics for Writing

1. Shahrazad is a better storyteller than her father. She convinces her audience; he doesn't. Is the fault in the tales or the tellers?
2. How are we to understand Shahrayar's madness? Does it make sense to you? That is, are male egos in macho societies that frail or is his a special case?
3. How are women portrayed in these stories? Does "good daughters bad wives" about cover it? What are we to make of that?
4. Shahrayar and Shahzaman are appalled by the actions of their wives. Should we be as well? Can you write a revisionist interpretation that lifts some of the blame off the wives' shoulders?
5. Both the vizier and his daughter, Shahrazad, tell tales that surround their human characters without important animals, but the animals play different roles in the imaginative worlds of father and daughter. Compare and contrast the powers attributed to the ani-

mal world in *The Tale of the Ox and the Donkey* and *The Tale of the Merchant and His Wife* with those described in *The Story of the Merchant and the Demon*. How may these differences reflect the contrasting visions of gender relations so central to *The Thousand and One Nights*?

6. How do all of the tales relate to each other under the umbrella of *The Story of the Fisherman and the Demon*? Does the tale within a tale structure work to enhance the main story, or is it confusing? Is there more suspense because of all of the interruptions for other tales?

Comparative Perspective

Like Ovid's *Metamorphoses*, Shahrazad's tales feature metamorphosed human beings who are mute in animal form. Compare Ovid's depiction of Io, a maiden turned into a heifer, with Shahrazad's description of circumstances in which family members become deer and dogs. What details does Ovid stress that Shahrazad overlooks? How do the outcomes of their narratives differ? What is the connection between those differences and the details each prefers to emphasize?

You may also want to look at the intersection of the supernatural world with that of the natural world, a theme your students will have encountered in Chaucer, Dante, Boccaccio, and *Sir Gawain and the Green Knight*. Are there indications that you are moving from one to the other?

[For all the violence that they contain, the basic optimism of Shahrazad's tales contrasts strikingly with Ovid's witty, urbane despair. Students might be asked to reflect on the essentially amoral Ovidian cosmos and the ultimately just and merciful world that the brave and buoyant Shahrazad shows to Shahrayar.]

Further Reading

See also the reading suggestions in the *Anthology*, p. 2644.

Hamori, Andras. *On the Art of Medieval Arabic Literature*. 1974. Several chapters are devoted to the *Nights*.

Malti-Douglas, Fedwa. *Woman's Body, Woman's World*. 1991. See the first chapter.

EVERYMAN

Backgrounds

The longer form of the title is given early in the speech of the first character, the Messenger: "The Summoning of Everyman" to a final reckoning with God. The play is not divided into acts and scenes, but lines 1–183 serve as a framework and may be considered the equivalent of a first act. After the Messenger's announcement, God in a speech of sixty-two lines declares his disappointment with humankind: his redemptive sacrifice on the Cross is generally ignored, and the human situation seems to grow steadily worse. Hence He calls on Death to summon humankind to judgment. Everyman comes on stage and is given the summons by Death, who cannot be begged or bribed to delay Everyman's answer; instead, Everyman must prepare at once to go. Here Death leaves the stage and does not return.

Now Everyman asks a long series of his companions for their help; they begin with ready promises, only to renege when they learn where Everyman must go—so much for Fellowship, Kindred, and Goods (riches, wealth). Now (Everyman's) Good Deeds is willing to go with him but has been bound to the Earth by Everyman's sins; she calls on Knowledge, who directs Everyman to Confession, who recommends Penance; after Everyman's earnest prayer of repentance and acceptance of Penance, Good Deeds is released and now free to accompany Everyman. (That is, Everyman is now absolved of his sinful condition.) Strength, Discretion, Beauty, and the Five-Wits will now assist Everyman (as long as he lives on Earth)—that is, the natural endowments of human nature can now be directed rightly instead of sinfully. Five-Wits lectures Everyman on the importance of the priesthood; it is the priest who dispenses the seven holy sacraments of the Christian life. Everyman goes briefly offstage to receive Holy Communion and extreme unction. Soon Everyman grows weak; he learns that Strength, Discretion, Beauty, and the Five-Wits (our familiar five senses, touch, sight, etc.) will not go with him into the cave of death; only Good Deeds will do so and thereby ensure his acceptance in Heaven—which is announced by an Angel (probably a voice offstage).

Everyman is a supreme example of a literary work with allegorical characters, that is, not individual men and women but personified abstractions or genetic groups such as Fellowship or Kindred or Goods or Good Deeds. As we have seen in other pieces, allegory was a favorite pattern of literature in the Middle Ages. The headnote shows that the abstract characters of *Everyman* may speak on stage very brisk, crisp, sharp dialogue. The action also moves rapidly and purposefully. It is clear, on reflection, that the play dramatizes the central moral or spiritual situation of the Christian believer, or at any rate, the medieval Christian. Absorbed by the business and pleasures of earthly life, he (or she) may not often remember the inevitability of death and the certainty of divine judgment. A sudden reminder may alarm and presently disillusion; there follows a genuine realization that "you can't take it"—or "them" (other persons with whom your own life seems inseparably involved)—with you. The desertion of Everyman by one after another of his cherished companions is a poignant experience shared by the reader or spectator.

Topics for Discussion and Writing

1. The role of Strength, Discretion, Beauty, and Five-Wits.
   [It is noted immediately after Everyman's reorientation that they will now direct and assist him on his journey. But when he ap-

proaches the cave of Death, they too, like his earlier companions, depart and leave him. What realities of human life do the two stages of their relationship represent? In what sense can it be said that Good Deeds, alone, goes with Everyman into the grave?]

2. Why are Fellowship, Kindred, and Goods effective figures in the play?

    [They at first cheerfully promise to go with Everyman on his projected journey—without bothering to ask where he must go. When they learn his destination (Death and the Judgment of God), they promptly renege, one after the other. This desertion is a poignant experience for Everyman—and for the reader or spectator as well.]

3. Compare *Everyman* with the twentieth-century play (or film) *You Can't Take It with You*.

    [In both there is a withdrawal from the usual pattern of life in the world. The cause or motivation is different, but the result is a readjustment in both cases, and the two are not entirely dissimilar. The defense of the new perspective in the dialogue of the modern piece might correspond to the (religious) reordering in Everyman.]

Comparative Perspectives

1. The bracketed stage directions and much of the dialogue in this text hint at a strong pictorial style of presentation aimed at an audience used to interpreting stained-glass windows (for example, the first lines spoken by Goods, which imply that the personified figure may be represented by a money sack, or the gradual strengthening of Good Deeds, who can hardly move until Everyman undergoes penance). Discuss one or two of these moments and compare the dramatic means employed here with those in Greek or Renaissance drama.

2. God appears on stage as a character in medieval morality and mystery plays. In what other cultures do gods take roles on the stage? In what religions would this be impossible, and how does that impossibility inhibit the development of a dramatic tradition?

    [There are no ancient Jewish and Islamic plays, for example, perhaps because both religions prohibit pictorial representation of the unseeable God—cf. Moses and the burning bush, and the power of the voice of God in the Old Testament of the Bible and in the Koran.]

Further Reading

See the reading suggestions in the *Anthology*, p. 2643.

CLUSTER: MEDIEVAL WOMEN

Backgrounds

All too often students and academics alike dismiss the idea of women in the Middle Ages. They believe that women were so utterly repressed and suppressed that there couldn't possibly be anything of value to study there. However, the Middle Ages is a vast and rich period in which women played a vital role and gender was a category constantly discussed and debated. The introduction to the cluster describes important sets of dichotomies that governed the literature and discourse surrounding gender; male and female represented reason and emotion, intellect and body, culture and nature, self-control and disorder, among others. Some of the writings here, particularly those of Tertullian, Chrysostom, and Capellanus, demonstrate how many male thinkers of the time argued that they held the first half of these binaries, and women the second. Later texts, like Christine de Pisan's and Joan of Arc's testimony, show how medieval women tried to combat these stereotypes.

Sometimes students want to dismiss misogyny and its effects by claiming that people were less intelligent then or vastly different today, but it is important that they not do so. It is far more fruitful to discuss motivations and consequences of these authors' ideas and uncover the inherent complexities and contradictions therein than to gloss over them as "medieval" and therefore dismissible. Students can also discuss which ideas still may have a hold on today's society, even if not overtly, and which ones clearly have fallen away from popular thought.

Tertullian is one of the early Church Fathers, and although he writes only in the second century, his words will be reworked and echoed throughout the Middle Ages and even into the Renaissance. Your students will probably be both amused and appalled at what he writes in his essay *The Appearance of Women*; it will seem so utterly foreign and blatantly misogynistic to them. However, it may be helpful to ask students how women's appearances are critiqued and judged today—from annual Best and Worst Dressed Lists to speculations on which celebrities have had plastic surgery to epidemic proportions of eating disorders among young women. Indeed, Tertullian's *focus* on how women appear, if not his critique, is still an obsession of society.

Tertullian believes that women sin twofold by adorning themselves (or caring about their appearance). On the one hand, they are exhibiting their own sinfulness (and closeness to Eve) by their dress. Tertullian claims that "the desire to please through appearance does not come from a sound conscience," so that even if the women to whom he writes (his "most beloved sisters") claim chastity and a desire to remain chaste, they belie this outwardly. On the other hand, Tertullian writes that the women have also sinned on behalf of the men who are stirred by how they look. If the man sins in thought or deed because he has looked at a beautiful woman, she is the real sinner for tempting him in the first place. This second aspect is reflected time and again in later Church writings. One thirteenth-century writer, the anonymous author of *Ancrene Wisse*, makes the analogy of someone who digs a pit and allows a dog to fall into it. The person who dug the pit is the real sinner (the woman who shows her beauty), not the dog (the man who sins as a result). Tertullian takes this message to an even more extreme point—that women who have natural beauty (even without adorning themselves) are responsible for "concealing and neglecting it" so this beauty will not unwittingly be dangerous.

If these comments were not misogynistic enough, Tertullian's last words of advice are perhaps the most enraging to modern women and men alike. He offers what he considers an appropriate alternative to adornment for women: that they should "bow [their] heads" to their husbands who will serve as enough "ornament" and keep busy by spinning (sewing) and staying at home. An interesting way to get your students engaged in this essay, and to not dismiss it as completely backward, is to ask them why they think Tertullian felt the need to write such a piece. What was he witnessing with the women around him, and the wives of the men he knew, that such a missive had to be written? It is important that students realize women were *not* doing what Tertullian advised or acting in the way he espoused; if that were the case, he would not have felt the need to write this at all. Indeed, women were clearly interested in how they looked, were *not* bowing their heads to their husbands, and were not completely occupied with spinning and with home. As much as this upset Tertullian, he could also not control it, as is evidenced in the vitriol of his language. This will be a useful concept for students as they read through this cluster and try to uncover the motives and agendas behind the various pieces represented here.

John Chrysostom (347–407 C.E.) was widely translated and disseminated in the Middle Ages and his opinions, like those of Tertullian, will be hard for your students to swallow. Where Tertullian focused on dress, Chrysostom focuses on women's speech. He writes that women should not speak in church or ask questions publicly, but rather speak only with their husbands in their homes. Chrysostom reinforces the dichotomy that Tertullian has set up of public (the church and male domain) and private (the home and the woman's). These attitudes can be found reflected just as strongly in later Victorian texts where women are named the "angels of the house" and the public/private spheres are defined as distinctly gendered and separate. Like Tertullian, Chrysostom bases his theories on Eve and her actions in Eden. Again, students may want to discuss women's speech within today's context (are women silenced publicly? How? Where? What does society think of an outspoken woman?).

Theophrastus is speaking to men in his essay *On Marriage*, but counterparts for women also exist in the Middle Ages—an important point to stress to students. But the reasons for dissuading men and women from marriage are very different, and that may be a fruitful point of conversation. Women's texts warn against the dangers of childbirth and the demotion in heaven for not remaining a virgin. Theophrastus argues that marriage is a risky prospect all around—generally the man does not choose his wife, she is chosen for him, and chosen women may have "a temper, [be] foolish, malformed, proud, [or] smelly." He goes on to remind his audience that most things bought can be returned or tested before they are kept, but that a wife is a "purchase" you are stuck with.

But this scare tactic is not Theophrastus's main point. Indeed, he says he is most concerned with a man's mind and capacity to study and practice philosophy. Marriage impedes that pursuit in many ways—through the wife's demands and vices (shopping, predominantly) and through the stress the wife puts on the husband and the time she takes away from him. Ultimately he claims that no wife is a safe bet—pretty ones attract other men; ugly ones are, well, ugly. Her chastity is always at risk because of the dangers of all the men around her and because she herself is so weak that she will of course fall prey to any man who tries to take advantage of her. Even if, Theophrastus argues, in the rarest of rare cases a good and kind wife is found, she is still more trouble than she is worth. He writes, "when she is in danger, we, too are tortured with her," and that is ultimately not good for the study of philosophy! In the end, Theophrastus suggests that a servant is a far safer investment than a wife.

The idea of women as property is clearly outlined here, and because that notion will persist in Western culture until the modern era (and still persists in some Arab nations), this will be a good discussion point with your class. This text is also part of *The Book of Wicked Wives* that Chaucer's Wife of Bath discusses in her prologue—a great point of discussion, demonstrating again what real medieval women probably thought of the text and how they reacted to it! After all, the Wife of Bath steals the book from her husband's hands and rips it to shreds.

It will be interesting for students to see the ways that women both incorporated and resisted the stereotypes and conflicts that are so clearly outlined in the texts so far. Heloise is the perfect example of how these things play out. Theophrastus would not have approved of Abelard's courtship of and subsequent marriage to Heloise because he was the exact sort of philosophical thinker Theophrastus had in mind when he warned against marriage. Even though Heloise and Abelard were properly married, Heloise's uncle had him castrated thinking that she was pregnant out of wedlock (which initially she was, but the marriage had changed that). Abelard and Heloise were planning to live in a "chaste marriage," a concept foreign to us today but not uncommon in the Middle Ages, in which a couple would be married but live separate and religious chaste lives.

Heloise's letter shows all of the conflicts that she is feeling about her relationship with Abelard as well as her position as a woman in this particularly misogynistic time. Ask your students what conflicts they can see in the text. For example, Heloise points out some obvious contradictions she feels and the irony that she was happy and felt God's love when they were having an affair, but upon doing the proper thing and marrying she was thrust into despair and God's wrath. She says that when she was in love she felt higher than all women (because he had preferred her to all others), but that their separation and his punishment have made her feel the lowest of the low. And of course Heloise's point is that they were unpunished while "fornicating," but punished in chastity. But some of these conflicts are more subtle—Abelard has been punished by castration, but Heloise feels that she deserved the punish-ment. He was the older, wiser party involved (he was, after all, her teacher), but she believes that both are equally to blame.

The text is most interesting where Heloise directly engages some of the kinds of misogynistic and insidious texts that have been in the clus-ter. She reminds us of Eve and what her temptation of Adam means for all women, she writes about the biblical warnings against women, and she argues that Satan ("the cunning arch-tempter") knows that men will be "brought to ruin" through their wives. Here, Heloise is careful to set herself apart from the women she's been describing, even while placing herself among them: "the tempter did not prevail on me to do wrong of my own consent, like the women I have mentioned, though in the out-come he made me the instrument of his malice." Heloise is a literate and educated woman, and this separation from Eve is a crucial point she makes. Although it was her uncle who afflicted Abelard, Heloise is not directly responsible for his troubles.

Students will most likely be surprised by Heloise's confessions toward the end of her letter to Abelard. She writes that she is not truly penitent for her sins, because that would involve real regret for her actions. How-ever much she regrets how her actions have led to Abelard's situation (or *their* actions, since Heloise never claims sole responsibility), she writes that she does not at all regret the affair that they had or the affection they shared. Again, Heloise is revealing a doubleness and a contradiction within the text itself. On the one hand, she *is* being completely honest and truthful, refusing to admit regret where there is none, but on the other hand by not regretting she is in a constant state of sin. She says, "I should be groaning over the sins I have committed, but I can only sigh for what I have lost."

Although your students might rightly see the intelligence and strength of character that Heloise shows in this section through her intense hon-esty and the admission of her carnal desires for Abelard, point out to them that she is at the same time reinforcing medieval views of women as tied to their flesh and unable to separate themselves from lust. She is a nun, living a chaste life, but still admits that she is haunted by her memories with Abelard and the desire that she has for him, and she also writes that this is because she is a woman and weaker of will than men. Students may want to debate whether Heloise truly believes the things that she writes about women in general, or whether she is simply pan-dering to the social views surrounding her.

At the end of her letter, Heloise honestly admits that she has no inter-est in the religious life of piety that she lives, but only does it because it was at the behest of Abelard and continues to earn his praise. The rela-tionship between Abelard and Heloise is one of the greatest love stories of the Middle Ages even though the ending is so tragic, and students may want to discuss the nature of that love (particularly the tricky ethics involved—even then—with a teacher and a student), and whether it is still "romantic" despite its ending, or simply sad. In any event, one value of the letter is to show that even in the twelfth century women were educated and aware of their lives and feelings in ways that seem to contradict how they are understood and depicted. As much as students may have the temptation to say "well, back then women didn't know any better," Heloise shows them that yes, they certainly did.

Andreas Capellanus is most famous for defining the idea of "courtly love," a concept students should be familiar with if they read *Sir Gawain and the Green Knight*. He wrote in the late twelfth century and his satirical treatise *On Love* had a great impact on court culture. Here, Capellanus talks about a characteristic of women already familiar to readers of the cluster—their speech. First, he writes that women are always in a state of envy and because of this are given to slander, no matter what the consequences. He appears to argue that gossip is specifically a woman's problem and is not something that men do or suffer from. Likewise, women's tongues get them into other problematic positions because they cannot keep a secret. This characterization of women is also clearly outlined in the Wife of Bath's prologue and tale. Capellanus writes that women are physically incapable of keeping a secret and this defect cannot be changed, so the only solution is to never share something secret with them.

A nice counterpart to some of the antiwoman and antimarriage rhetoric will be found in Guillaume de Mailly's thirteenth-century sermon. He writes that there are three things needed for a marriage to be right in the eyes of God: that both husband and wife have the right intention before entering it, that both maintain a faithfulness and mutual respect within it, and that a husband and a wife live together. These three things may seem unremarkable to an audience of twenty-first-century students, so it may be helpful to talk about what things might have gone into marriage in the Middle Ages. The primary of these is that a formal ceremony was *not* required for a marriage to be legal or sanctioned by the Church, so it was easy for people to be secretly married (or married off to people). Marriage in the Middle Ages was more a decision between two people or, more often, between two families.

Marriage most often served as a contract between families, especially among the wealthier classes. People were married because the union increased land, wealth, or prestige. This is why Mailly feels the need to state the first thing needed—"a right intention in contracting it." Students may notice that within his description of a "right intention," Mailly never discusses *love*, what is surely considered the most important basis of marriage today. For Mailly, a right intention means the desire to procreate and then educate the fruits of that procreation in the Church. The second two reasons may also seem odd ones to underscore to the modern student. Reminding them that most medieval marriages are not based on love (indeed, not even the ones that Mailly espouses) may make it easier for students to understand why fidelity and living together may not be the status quo. Overall, Mailly is writing in support of a marriage union that is more than just a business contract and that respects all parties involved—women included.

This thirteenth-century English work is excerpted from a text called

The Southern Passion, a metrical depiction of Christ's life. Many narratives of Christ's life and Passion circulated in the Middle Ages and were considered a common form of devotional meditation for lay and religious people alike. Interestingly, women were particularly known to read Passion narratives and make them a focus of their religious devotion. This may be a fact you would like to share with your students as they consider the author's description of Mary Magdalene, the only major female character in the New Testament besides the Virgin Mary.

What begins as the author's defense of Mary Magdalene becomes a defense of women in general, particularly against the accusation that women are controlled by lust and cannot separate themselves from their flesh (a stereotype demonstrated in Heloise's letter here in the cluster, but also present in *The Thousand and One Nights, Sir Gawain and the Green Knight*, and of course The Wife of Bath's prologue and tale). The author's comments will seem logical to your students and demonstrate one important fact—that people in the Middle Ages were capable of understanding the fallacies that they put forth and seeing the truths of their society, despite what texts like *The Book of Wicked Wives* stated repeatedly. A text like this one that challenges the common stereotypes and perceptions about women make things like the court cases presented next even harder to understand.

The first case takes place in fifteenth-century York and involves two women, Emma and Agnes. Although Emma seems to be the one truly under accusation here—she called the "good" and "honest" Agnes a whore and a thief publicly outside of the parish church—the excerpt ends with the news that Agnes is the one who has lost her social standing and been ostracized. Emma clearly embodies the vicious woman's tongue described in Capellanus, while Agnes demonstrates the fragility of a woman's reputation and how easily people will believe ill if a woman is the target. The second excerpt, also from the fifteenth century, takes place in Hereford and shows the fate that can befall women who are accused of misdeeds. Here, the town's ordinance lists a variety of "crimes" for which women can be subjected to punishment and humiliation. These include "quarrelling" and "discord . . . between neighbors." Ask your students to imagine what their town would look like if such offenses were worthy of public censure! Note that these cases involve women only. What would the results be if men were the perpetrators? Would they have been prosecuted for their crimes? Would the behaviors even be considered crimes?

Christine de Pizan is a very interesting woman for her time. She was the first woman to support herself entirely from her own writing, and her texts were decidedly feminist in their arguments. Her books include the famous *Book of the City of Ladies* as well as a collection of letters that argue vehemently against the popular misogynist texts of the time, particularly the popular *Romance of the Rose*. In this text, *The Letter of the God of Love*, Christine writes in response to the kind of misogyny that is apparent in this cluster—from the early Church Fathers down to the court cases and excerpts. Christine makes several important attacks and points in her essay: she writes against men who seduce and slander women, she writes against misogynist texts (like those we've seen here), and she writes about the inherent good nature of women despite the accusations against them. Christine is the first woman to systematically respond to these stereotypes and accusations, and your students may want to discuss the education and talent that allow her to do so.

Christine first addresses men who lie and deceive women in order to get them into bed. This alone is not what angers Christine most; it is the lying that takes place afterward—particularly if a man has been rejected by a woman. Note that after so much discussion of women's speech and the consequences of their slander and gossip, Christine is making it clear that men are just as guilty of these crimes (if not more so) as women, but still it is the women who suffer the consequences, not the men who have lied and deceived. She reminds men that their mothers are women and that they dishonor them by slandering any of her sex.

Then Christine attacks the texts that have given rise to these assumptions and falsities about women. She chides the women who give their sons these books to read when they are young and then complain about the attitudes they contain. All of the texts that Christine discusses here are veritable "best sellers" of the Middle Ages (Ovid particularly) and familiar to all educated men and women. She is brave in opposing them and exposing the misogyny inside. Christine makes a point also made by Chaucer's Wife of Bath—women did not write these books; if they had the stories would be vastly different. She then takes familiar stories portraying the woman as the sinner or the downfall of the man involved, and turns them around. She discusses Medea and Dido as heroines, not villains, and reminds her audience of true and faithful women of literature who are often not discussed—like Penelope, Ulysses's wife.

Christine also turns to the Bible (which, as we've seen, is often used as fodder for misogynist statements and beliefs) and again uncovers what is often ignored. She looks at the three Marys who kept vigil at Jesus' tomb and reminds her readers that Jesus had been abandoned by everyone except the women in his life. She also talks of the ever-present Eve, but even places her in a positive light. She writes that Eve repeated the words she had been told by the devil, but never approached Adam with an intent toward deception or malice, and reminds the audience that Eve was created in Paradise, not Adam. Christine has taken the single most cited example of woman's treachery, Eve, and made her a kind of heroine rather than the ultimate sinner.

Finally, Christine says women generally do not have it in their nature to do battle or kill people, alluding no doubt to the multitudes of wars waged by men in the Middle Ages. Women are not cruelly natured, she writes, but "mild, very piteous, fearful and hesitant, humble, sweet, calm and very charitable, lovable, devout, modest in peace, fearful in war, unpretentious and pious, with an anger that is quickly appeased, [and] unable to bear the sight of cruelty or suffering." Your students may note that this is just another extreme. Here, Christine has most women lined up for sainthood in her discussion of their "inherent goodness." A good point of discussion may be whether it's necessary to have the pendulum swing so completely in the opposite direction in order to undo some of the damage done by hundreds of years of misogynistic beliefs and writings. Could Christine have written a more moderate view of women to the same effect?

The last piece in the cluster is the transcript of Joan of Arc's interrogation when she was put on trial in Rouen as a heretic. It truly could be read as everything that embodies the male authority of the Middle Ages (the Church, literacy, etc.) putting everything threatening about a woman on trial, and it may benefit your students to analyze the transcript in this light. Joan is threatening for several reasons: she is a visionary and claims to have authority from God and through his intermediaries, Archangel St. Michael and St. Margaret and St. Catherine; she wears men's clothing and was dominant in a male domain (war and battle); also, she is very smart in her answers to the charges put before her, never falling prey to traps that the judges keep trying to set in order to get her to admit to charlatanism or witchcraft.

The saints that Joan claims to hear are not arbitrarily chosen. St. Michael cast Satan out of heaven in a battle, and Joan feels that she has done the same under God's guidance with the English. St. Margaret protected her virginity by dressing as a man and entering a monastery and Joan also dresses as a man because she has been instructed to by God. Finally, Catherine of Alexandria was a young visionary who also confronted the political forces at work around her under divine instruction.

It is easy to see why visionary women would have been troublesome and problematic to the Church hierarchy. They were a relatively common phenomenon from the end of the twelfth century through to the fifteenth (when Joan testified), and the main question was one of validity. What if the voices a woman claimed she was hearing were actually demonic? Or if there were no voices at all? The Church was worried that any woman who claimed to be a visionary could do heretical or suspect things in the name of God. Have your students go through the description of the trial and find all the places where the questioners are trying to judge the source and the validity of Joan's voices and the visions. Along with this, the judges are very concerned that Joan may actually be a witch and in league with devils and the supernatural. This shows the Church's discomfort not only with Joan's visionary status but also with the broader question of pagan worship and how it conflicts with the Church. Students can look for these moments of unease—particularly in the questions about the significance of woods near Joan's home and the existence of fairies.

Joan's clothing is another important theme throughout the questioning. The judges are very concerned with why and under whose authority Joan wears men's clothing. This cross-dressing may seem like no big deal to a modern-day student when much of women's and men's clothing is virtually the same, but it is against the law in the Middle Ages. Of course, it should be easy for your students to pinpoint that this is not merely about clothing but all that it represents. Joan is crossing gender boundaries constantly and her clothing is just the most outward manifestation of that blurred line. Why can't that line be blurred? Because it would threaten all the misogynist beliefs and arguments about women's inherent faults. It's important to the maintenance of the status quo in the Middle Ages that Joan's position as a woman, and therefore weak and inferior, is carefully maintained.

The most compelling aspect of Joan's testimony is how incredibly savvy and careful she is with the questioner's remarks. She knows exactly what statements will get her into trouble and is particularly careful in her word choice and answers. She never claims that the "voice" will do anything on her command or that she has special protection from God (both possible markers of heresy), and she is consistent in her story, never contradicting herself. She also consciously distances herself from anything that may smack of witchcraft. For example, when the judge asks her about mandrake root—often considered to be used by witches—she claims she does not know anything about it and the voices too have never mentioned it. Whenever there is clearly an attempt to trap Joan into somehow admitting supernatural knowledge or power, she always answers in an orthodox manner. Even when she is pressed to tell her own revelations about her fate, she says "That does not concern your trial. Do you want me to speak against myself?" demonstrating her knowledge of court procedures and the fact that she would be trapped no matter what her response.

Despite Joan's exceptional intelligence and her clear ability to maneuver around the exhausting questioning of the judges, she is ultimately sentenced for heresy and burned at the stake. The Church later admitted this was an error and Joan was canonized in 1920. You may want to have your students surmise why Joan was convicted—what could she have done differently (if anything)? Was the trial decided before she even began? Could such a trial exist today? Or, even more interesting, what would we do today with a woman who claimed to get her direction from God? Students might also want to consider why the Church later reversed its position on Joan and made her a saint so long after her terrible death.

Although the end of the cluster is somewhat discouraging, with Joan's brave testimony and disappointing death, students may want to trace how attitudes about women have changed through the centuries. There is something inspiring about medieval women like Christine de Pisan and Joan of Arc who, despite all of the obstacles facing them and discourse intended to suppress them, still manage to find a voice that remains with us over half a millennium later. Everyone is familiar with the twentieth-century women's movement, but this shows that women have always been fighting for their own place from which they can be heard. Ultimately, women like Christine, Joan, and Heloise show that the Middle Ages was home to many intelligent, thoughtful, and courageous women—like today. A true study of the Middle Ages takes all of its inhabitants into account, and that is the real importance of this cluster and the texts within it. Women could not be brushed aside and dismissed because of their gender then, despite all of the ways in which writers and thinkers attempted to do so.

The Renaissance

The introduction characterizes the Renaissance in terms of change: scientific discovery, religious upheaval, and global exploration all contributed to a mood of excitement but also uncertainty. In fact, ambivalence may be the hallmark of Renaissance literature: systemic changes brought simultaneous exhilaration and anxiety; the promise of fulfillment in earthly life competed with a strong religious sense of worldly renunciation; human potential and achievement were both celebrated and denigrated. You might ask your students to look for this ambivalence as they read. Certainly the travel narratives embody both excitement and anxiety, as does the era's most famous play, *Hamlet*, whose protagonist memorably describes man as "like an angel . . . like a god," yet ultimately asks, "What is this quintessence of dust?" Such ambivalence about human accomplishments may also be found in the section on metaphysical poetry, where we read poems that simultaneously display human virtuosity and register human depravity: Herbert's "Easter Wings" represents man's inevitable decay unless he gives himself over to God; Huygens's "Good Friday" depicts a speaker whose heart is so hard that he must be destroyed by God in order to live.

The introduction also comments on the theatricality of Renaissance life and art: social roles that must be "played" are both liberating and confining, and nowhere is Renaissance theatricality more apparent than in court life, the opulence and danger of which fascinated writers of this period. The excerpts from Castiglione's *Book of the Courtier* should probably be read early in your exploration of the Renaissance; they will provide your students with a sense of the idealism as well as the conscious theatricality that accompany the court life that is the setting or context for much of the literature in this section: *Hamlet*, *Orlando Furioso*, *Don Quixote* with its ironic use of the courtly context, the courtly Petrarchan love lyrics, and of course *The Prince*, which in its pragmatism makes an interesting counterpoint to *The Courtier*. (*Orlando Furioso* and *Don Quixote* can also be profitably read as counterpoints to one another.)

Along with aristocratic ideals and struggles, scholarly energies inform Renaissance literature. As the Introduction explains, the Renaissance was imbued with the languages, philosophies, and artistic values of classical antiquity. Histories and characters from ancient Greece and Rome comprise a common cultural medium shared by all educated Europeans in this period. Scripture is another common medium; one of the most fundamental, often-cited characteristics of the Renaissance is the fusion of classical and Christian, seen in Erasmus's *Praise of Folly*, in Montaigne's *Essays*, and most dramatically in Milton's *Paradise Lost*, where the Genesis story of the creation and fall of man is cast as a classical epic. Your students should be prepared to encounter literary works that speak an allusive language that most of us cannot fully appreciate without some apparatus to explicate the many references to classical works as well as the Bible.

Finally, the Renaissance world is also concerned with the ideal order of things: social structure and political systems are much discussed and contested during this period. Though much of the literature in this section is by and about an elite—male aristocrats and scholars—some of these works speak for and about other groups, such as women and commoners. Marguerite de Navarre's *Heptameron* stories depict various faces of love and feature women as the central characters (these stories would make a nice counterpoint to the Petrarchan and carpe diem lyrics). Lope de Vega's *Fuente Ovejuna* is about a popular uprising in an oppressed village and includes peasants, male and female, among its protagonists. It is good to remember that theater in the Renaissance was a popular medium; literacy and education are not required for appreciating a play, and theater audiences included commoners as well as nobility. Even *Hamlet*, though its setting is the court at Elsinore, gives voice to the common gravediggers.

The Introduction asserts that the Renaissance represented a true departure from the values and attitudes of the Middle Ages and cites Rabelais as evidence that Renaissance humanists perceived themselves as standing in contrast to an earlier era: Gargantua compares the "murky, dark time" of his youth to the present time, which has seen the return of "light and dignity" to humanistic studies. But, as the Introduction also notes, to see the Middle Ages as an age of ignorance and denigration of earthly life is a gross oversimplification. Your students might like to argue this issue for themselves. If they have also read literature from the Middle Ages, they can finish their study of Renaissance literature by considering whether these two bodies of work truly differ in theme, tone, scope, and attitude.

FRANCIS PETRARCH

Backgrounds

Petrarch's collection of lyric poetry is known as the *Canzoniere* ("Song Book") and sometimes also as the *Rime sparse* ("Scattered Rhymes"), a title taken from line 1 of the introductory sonnet. Neither of the two is Petrarch's title; his own had been, significantly, in Latin—*Rerum Vulgarium Fragmenta*, "fragments" written in the "vulgar" tongue, that is current poetic Italian as opposed to Latin.

The main image of Petrarch, as it has been through the centuries and justifiably remains, is that of the author of sonnets written in honor of his beloved Laura or somehow related to that central experience. The selections in the *anthology* belong mainly to that category. It should be noted, however, that the *Canzoniere* comprises in all 366 poems numbered by the poet himself; and though an overwhelming majority of these are sonnets (317), many are written in other forms, notably the much longer and the metrically varied *canzone*, of which there are 29. Still other forms represented in the collection are the sestina (9), the ballad (7), and the madrigal (4). Excellence in the poetic art was closely identified in Petrarch's day with technical skill in handling a number of verse patterns and in achieving variety within strict metrical norms. It was also closely identified with music. "Lyric" poetry is named for the "lyre," a musical instrument; *canzone* is the Italian for "song"; and the root of the word "sonnet" is in the Latin *sonus*, "sound." Musical accompaniment was regularly a part of the "performance" of a poem; in fact, sonnets by Petrarch have been set to music up to our own century.

The ordering of the *Canzoniere* was made by the poet himself; to see it exclusively as a poetic diary of his love for Laura from its inception through its countless modulations to her death and to the continuing celebration of her image is to forget that not all of the *Canzoniere* is devoted to Laura. Sonnets 136–38, to give a particularly extravagant example, are invectives against the papal court at Avignon; and the *canzone* numbered 78 (not to be confused with Sonnet 78, printed in the *Anthology*)—one of the most famous poems in the Italian language—is a lament on politically divided Italy, with an exhortation to peace, in what we may call the mode of "cultural patriotism." (A significant quotation from this poem will be found in the Machiavelli selections in the *Anthology*, at the very close of *The Prince*.) These exceptions allowed for, however, it is fair to say that poems in praise of Laura alive make up the larger part of the collection, and poems commemorating her after death most of the rest.

During his life Petrarch was in contact, professionally and otherwise, with courts, the most memorable being that of the pope at Avignon, in Provence. That region also provides the physical landscape against which Petrarch's love for Laura is imagined. His sonnets can be partly described as courtly love poetry in the sense that they originated in an aristocratic milieu.

Love poetry has, of course, a long tradition from remotest antiquity on. Petrarch's immediate and obvious antecedents are Dante and poets such as Guido Cavalcanti (cf. Dante, *Inferno* X.52–72, and *Purgatorio* XXIV.19ff. [not included in the *Anthology*]), Guido Guinizzelli, and the Provençal "troubadours" (see their poems in Medieval Lyrics: A Selection). Apart from quotations in Latin, the only non-Italian lines in *The Divine Comedy* are spoken by the poet Arnaut Daniel in his native Provençal tongue (*Purgatorio* XXVI.140–47). Petrarch was also steeped, of course, in the culture of antiquity; and the major Latin love poets—Ovid, Tibullus—figure prominently among his sources.

Equally evident in his work are manifestations of the Christian tradition. One is the insistent connection that he makes between his love and the Passion of Christ, as shown in Sonnets 3 and 62. Another is his sense of love as guilt, in the expression of which he initiates the now-familiar Romantic image of the poet as lamenting sufferer. Closely related to both of these is his framework of repentance and confession as if after a sinful life. This, as found in the *Canzoniere*, has its chief source in the *Confessions* of St. Augustine, probably the most important influence in Petrarch's intellectual life. It would not be amiss, in fact, to think of the *Canzoniere* as Petrarch's own Confessions.

The prose selection in the *Anthology*, the letter to Dionisio on the ascent of Mount Ventoux, is an allegory of the sinner's repentance and contrition under the decisive Augustinian influence.

Classroom Strategies

Undoubtedly the least useful strategy is to take the selections from the *Canzoniere* as parts of a poetic diary and follow the many failed attempts to reconstruct the work as an autobiographical love story. Petrarch had practical experience in matters of love—had, in fact, some illegitimate children by a mistress. But it is equally clear that his poems are not only a purification of love in its usual terrestrial senses but are also conscious models of literary convention. The persons of the speaker and his beloved have almost as little historical identity as those of the author and the object of any popular love song. A practical way to cope with this problem, if the Dante selections in the *Anthology* have been previously studied, is to attempt a comparison and contrast between the strictly unearthly view of Beatrice and whatever is earthly in the image of Laura. Also, as already mentioned, a complete "execution" of a Petrarchan sonnet is probably best imagined with musical accompaniment. At the very least, emphasis should be placed on the musicality of Petrarch's language; and it would be a good idea to have some of the poems read out loud in the original, vowel-rich Italian. (Italian pronunciation is easy to learn; and a colleague conversant with Italian may be available on campus.)

Topics for Discussion and Writing

1. The figure of the speaker of the poem and his varied attitudes between elation and despair.
2. The Petrarchan sonnet and its structure in comparison with the Shakespearean pattern. In particular, compare the endings of the sonnets and the relative effectiveness of Petrarch's closing lines, in Sonnet 90 for example, and that of the closing couplet in the Shakespearean form of the sonnet.
3. Choosing an appropriate passage from the *Paradiso* selections and one of the sonnets on Laura in death, indicate specific differences in the handling of the two feminine images.
4. Petrarch was a public man, a diplomat, and an extremely influential poet. So was, for example, Sir Thomas Wyatt, who introduced the Petrarchan sonnet to England. (Of Wyatt's thirty sonnets, pub-

lished in *Tottel's Miscellany*—the *Anthology* of English poems published by Richard Tottel in 1557—ten are translations from Petrarch, including the famous *My Galley*, based on sonnet 189.) Would such a multidimensional individual be conceivable today?

5. Although we read Petrarch in translation, there is no reason that a topic for discussion shouldn't be (with possible comparisons to the situation in other national literatures) the part that a literary language may have in establishing or indeed creating the identity of a country.

Comparative Perspectives

1. The *Letter to Dionisio da Borgo san Sepolcro* describes an experience that surprises Petrarch, who had begun the ascent of Mount Ventoux eager "to see what so great an elevation had to offer." Unlike the Romantic poets of the nineteenth century, who also were assiduous ascenders of mountains, Petrarch brings his copy of Augustine's *Confessions* with him on his journey, and reading it convinces him that it is more important to look within than (to put it crudely) to go sightseeing. Describe the tension between nature and belief that both Petrarch and Augustine reflect on in their writings. Compare it, if appropriate, to the view of nature in the poems of Bécquer, Leopardi, or Wordsworth, in Volume 2 of the *Anthology*.

2. Discuss Petrarch's facility in appropriating classical and biblical imagery in comparison with the treatment of such references in his sources or in earlier poems in any of the examples listed below. How does Petrarch's way of combining his sources justify considering him a Renaissance writer, although he was a contemporary of Boccaccio's?
   a. The use of The Song of Songs in Canzone 126.
   b. The treatment of Calvary in the medieval lyric on p. 1903 and in Sonnet 62.
   c. Ovid's description of Apollo's pursuit of Daphne and her subsequent metamorphosis and the quasi-metamorphosis in the vision of Laura in the last line of Sonnet 34.
   d. The meaning of Scylla and Charybdis in Virgil and their transformation in Petrarch's Sonnet 189 (see the helpful guidance in the footnote).
   e. The use of classical allusion in Sonnets 34 and 78.

3. Looking forward to one of the many ways that later poets used Petrarch, discuss the creation of the pastoral scene surrounding Laura in sonnet 126 and compare the treatment of pastoral in canto I of *Orlando Furioso* or in book IX of *Paradise Lost* (see especially lines 385–454).

Further Reading

See also the reading suggestions in the *Anthology*, p. 2646.

Bergin, Thomas G. *Petrarch*. 1970. A useful study by the Yale Italian scholar and translator of Dante, Petrarch, and other authors.

Bergin, Thomas G., ed. *Selected Sonnets, Odes and Letters*. 1966. With introduction, principal dates in the life of Petrarch, and selected bibliography. A good source for further readings from Petrarch's works.

Bloom, Harold, ed. *Petrarch: Modern Critical Views*. 1989. An excellent collection that includes the essay by John Freccero mentioned in the headnote, as well as an intricate analysis by Robert M. Durling, "The Ascent of Mount Ventoux and the Crisis of Allegory."

Donadoni, Eugenio. *A History of Italian Literature*. 1969. See the chapters on Petrarch's life and on his Italian works. A standard, reliable account of the history of Italian literature, widely used as a textbook in Italian schools.

Harrison, Robert Pogue. *The Body of Beatrice*. 1988. Chapter 5 is "The Death of Dante's Beatrice and the Petrarchan Alternative."

Trinkaus, Charles Edward. *The Poet as Philosopher: Petrarch and the Formation of Renaissance Consciousness*. 1979. Examines how Petrarch's "poetic mentality penetrated and shaped his thought."

Wilkins, Ernest Hatch. *History of Italian Literature*. Revised by Thomas G. Bergin. 1974. Chapter 10 is dedicated to Petrarch. One of the best among the few histories of Italian literature written in English. Professor Wilkins is also a renowned Petrarch scholar.

LYRIC POETRY: AFTER PETRARCH

Backgrounds

The question that comes to mind once we recognize the dominance of Petrarchan discourse in the Renaissance is: Why? Why did Petrarchism become the distinctive lyric genre of the Renaissance? What accounts for the extraordinary popularity of Petrarch's *Rime*, its attitudes, themes, and metaphors? This popularity flourishes not immediately after Petrarch's death (1374) but roughly a century and a half later. The sixteenth century is indeed the age of the sonnet. Statistics support this assertion: roughly 3,000 writers produced approximately 200,000 sonnets between 1530 and 1650.

As they contemplate the immense popularity of this genre, students might like to ponder what correspondences, if any, exist between the features of Petrarchan discourse and the features of the Renaissance itself. The performance of the self, a heightened sense of individualism, the tension between valuing and rejecting the pleasures of this world, a fascination with the mechanisms of power, even the exaltation of classical antiquity—all these qualities of the Renaissance world, it might be argued, are reflected in the Petrarchan lyric. Less easy to answer is the question of why any age would fixate upon a genre that has at its heart frustration and failure. Granted, not all the poems included here reflect this mood, but many of them—poems of Wyatt and Sidney most notably—do indeed give voice to the impossibility of obtaining the object of one's desire.

In considering the individual poets represented here, a sense of context might be helpful. Several of the poems, for instance, are excerpts from complete sequences with narrative frames like that of Petrarch's *Rime*. Sceve's *Delie*, for example, was the first complete *canzoniere* in French and records the poet's love for Delie as a deeply spiritual quest. Sceve uses mythological allusions, symbols, and repeated pairs of images—darkness and light, separation and union, life and death—to explore love's possibilities. Sidney's poems are taken from his sonnet sequence *Astrophil and Stella*, in which the speaker Astrophil self-consciously performs various roles in order to win "grace" from the lady he desires, Stella. Astrophil, though he claims at one point to have won Stella's heart, never gets closer than a stolen kiss to the (married) woman he desires and ends in a state of isolation, hopelessly vacillating between elation and despair. Spenser's sonnet sequence, *Amoretti*, is perhaps the most radical narrative revision in that the poet-speaker woos not with the aim of seduction but in order to "knit the knot that ever shall remain." The speaker is eventually accepted by the lady (Elizabeth), and in Spenser's original edition the *Amoretti* sonnets are followed by a wedding poem, *Epithalamion*.

Obviously, not all Petrarchan lyrics are part of a complete sequence; not all the poets even speak in the voice of a desiring male. Women sometimes wrote Petrarchan lyrics, too (see Louise Labe, Gaspara de Stampa, and Mary Wroth, for instance). But Veronica Franco is unusual because of who she was and what she wrote about. A *cortigiana onesta* (intellectual courtesan), Franco wrote terza rima verses that are responses to poems by an anonymous author who may have been an aristocratic member of a literary salon with which she was associated. Clearly the *capitolo* 13 included here offers rich ground for reevaluating Petrarchism. Franco challenges the objectified status of woman; by claiming for herself a strong sense of personal honor, she appropriates a masculine stance, as she does also when she imagines herself dueling the other poet. But by imagining herself fighting to the death because of love, because of words, Franco replaces typical Petrarchan immobility and stasis with violent action. She also brings to the surface the sexuality of Petrarchan discourse, displaying rather than submerging the sexual meaning of "to die" in her vision of a martial struggle transformed into "a love match in bed." Petrarch never lets us forget that love is war—in poem 3 he describes himself as a disarmed warrior wounded by an arrow in a surprise attack—but in her poem Franco takes that trope and makes it dramatic and explicit. Her bold verse violates conventional expectations that women should be chaste and silent, but of course as a courtesan she was already in violation of conventional mores. Something of Franco's ambiguous position in sixteenth-century Venetian society is indicated by the fact that she associated with aristocrats, was visited by the King of Poland, but was also accused of being a whore and a witch before the Inquisition court. Her precarious social position and vulnerability to powerful men and institutions is not unique among the Petrarchan writers studied here, though her position as a woman sets her apart. But Petrarchan discourse played an important role in European courts and was often a vehicle for courtiers to both promote themselves as well as reflect on the difficulties and dangers of courtly life.

Wyatt's poetry may serve as the best example of Petrarchism as an expression of courtly discontent. Wyatt implies that both the lady's favor and the court's favor are transient; and trying to hold on—to the beloved or to one's courtly position—is like trying to hold the wind in a net. The fact that Wyatt was twice imprisoned in the Tower of London, yet twice managed to extricate himself and regain Henry VIII's favor, indicates that Wyatt's position, like Veronica Franco's, was precarious. Wyatt is usually credited with introducing Petrarch to sixteenth-century England, though some of his English translations are only loosely based on the Petrarchan originals. One of the most effective ways to contrast Petrarch's and Wyatt's visions is to have students read Petrarch's poem 190 alongside its "translation" by Wyatt, "Who So List to Hunt."

The idealized feminine object of devotion undergoes many revisions during the Petrarchan era: Michelangelo (and Shakespeare) idealize a young man rather than a woman; Berni and Shakespeare challenge the ideal in comic parodies, but Wyatt deflates the ideal entirely. His woman is not chaste but soiled, not remote but fickle, not a flowering laurel branch but a rotten bough, not a dreamlike white doe but a common hind hunted by many men. Audience is an important concept in teaching Petrarchan poetry; clearly some of our poets directly address the object of their desire, but others address an audience of other men—in Wyatt's case, men at court who circulated their poetry in manuscript or performed their lyrics as part of courtly entertainment. Castiglione wrote that the ideal courtier should be a poet (and a dancer, artist, philosopher, musician); one context for poems such as Wyatt's and Sidney's, as well as Michelangelo's and Berni's, is a courtly world where displays of artistic achievement were part of the courtier's self-presentation. The Elizabethan poets such as Sidney and Spenser wrote in an atmosphere especially conducive to Petrarchan discourse, since their sovereign was an unmarried woman. "Political Petrarchism" is the name given to the rhetoric sometimes used by Elizabeth I's courtiers to address their queen. A typical example is found in a letter from one of the queen's courtiers, Sir Christopher Hatton. Forced to be away from court and concerned that a rival might replace him in Elizabeth's favor, he wrote:

> Madame, I find the greatest lack that ever poor wretch sustained. No death, no hell, no fear of death shall ever win of me consent to so far wrong myself again as to be absent from you for one day . . . to serve you is a heaven, but to

lack you is more than hell's torment. . . . Passion overcometh me. I can write no more. Love me; for I love you.

Given the prevalence of this rhetoric at court, it is not surprising that the poetry of Sidney, Spenser, and the other Elizabethan sonneteers is sometimes read as encoding political rather than sexual and romantic desires. In fact, Spenser in one of the *Amoretti* sonnets openly conflates his beloved Elizabeth with his queen.

Along with considering differences among these lyrics—different contexts, different voices, different approaches—students might also want to examine similarities. These selections make it possible to trace certain motifs, and see, for example, how several different authors treat the metaphor of the ship used in Petrarch's poem 189. Not only tropes but also techniques recur. The blazon—body parts represented metaphorically, as in "her eyes are like suns, her lips like roses"—seems to be the aspect of Petrarchism that inspired the most parody. The poems herein by Berni and Shakespeare are good examples; both mock the false idealizing of the lady's beauty by the Petrarchan lover. Other parodic approaches to the blazon are available for students to consider. In Shakespeare's *Twelfth Night*, Olivia responds to remarks about her beauty ironically, and in part she is mocking the artificiality and insincerity of her wooer's Petrarchism:

> I will give out divers schedules of my beauty. It shall be inventoried, and every particle and utensil labell'd to my will: as, *item*, two lips, indifferent red; *item*, two grey eyes, with lids to them; *item*, one neck, one chin, and so forth.

Students might also enjoy seeing one of the visual parodies of the Petrarchan blazon popular in the sixteenth century—for instance, the painting of "La Belle Charite" reproduced in *The Icy Fire*. This "portrait made of metaphors" mocks the extravagant language of the Petrarchan poets in its depiction of a woman whose cheeks are literally roses, whose eyes are literally suns, and so forth. Of course, there is no surer mark of a form's popularity than the existence of parodies.

DESIDERIUS ERASMUS

The Praise of Folly

Backgrounds

The Praise of Folly is divided into four sections; the selections in the *Anthology* are from the first, second, and fourth parts. The work, originally written in Latin, is a satire for which the author has adopted, with tongue in cheek, the structure and manner of a public oration. The "goddess" Folly, after giving her own jocose genealogy as the illegitimate daughter of the god of wealth and plenty (part 1), describes the manner of her birth and identifies the symbolic persons who attend her as she appears before a varied assembly of listeners. She proceeds to declare herself (part 2) the true life-giving goddess on the ground that every man in the act of procreation inevitably makes a fool of himself—hence the very conception of life is Folly's doing. From this premise follows the conclusion that all truly human activity must necessarily contain the life-giving element of folly/foolishness. Folly conducts this argument colorfully, relying on such classic devices of oratory as rhetorical questions, apt quotations, and, above all, vivid anecdotes. Prominent among the targets of her satire are the Stoic philosophers, whose attempt to "eliminate from their wiseman all emotional perturbations" she naturally scorns. What could such a regimen result in but a "marble statue of a man" unfit for any responsible position ("What army would select him for their general? Indeed, what woman would consent to marry him or put up with him as a husband?")?

Not unaware of life's pains and disappointments, Folly prescribes as remedy a good measure of "foolish" self-love and self-deception. Here again, in a sequence of quick satirical strokes she celebrates the foolish and happy victims of deceit along with their deceivers. Among physicians, for instance, "the more ignorant, bold, and thoughtless one of them is, the more he is valued by these high and mighty princes. Besides, medicine . . . is nothing but a subdivision of flattery, just like rhetoric." As deceivers, lawyers rank next to doctors:

> In fact, I wonder if they don't hold the highest rank of all, since their profession—not to speak of it myself—is universally ridiculed as asinine by the philosophers. Still, all business transactions, from the smallest to the greatest, are absolutely controlled by these asses. They acquire large estates, while a theologian who has carefully read through whole bookcases of divinity nibbles on dried peas, waging continual war with bedbugs and lice.

Asses, in other words, wait upon other asses, and "everyone is all the happier the more ways he is deluded." Other categories of foolish but happy maniacs are listed and illustrated in as many brilliant little sketches—hunters, gamblers, nobility buffs, the superstitious.

At this point the speaker—quite transparently a mouthpiece for Erasmus the Christian humanist—shifts to religious "superstitions," to "absurdities . . . so foolish that even I am almost ashamed of them," such as the belief in the specific powers of particular saints: "One offers relief from a toothache, another helps women in labor, another restores stolen goods. . . . Some saints have a variety of powers, especially the virgin mother of God, to whom the ordinary run of men attribute more almost than to her son." Further on, in the same vein: "Likewise, if any saint is more legendary or poetic—for example, think of George or Christopher or Barbara—you will see that such a saint is worshiped with far more devotion than Peter or Paul or Christ himself."

The culminating association between religious piety and Folly occurs in the final section, where the character of the "Christian Fool" is depicted. Showing in familiar scriptural quotations Christ's preference for the meek and simple-minded, Folly claims among her followers the Savior himself, who, "though he was the wisdom of the Father, became somehow foolish in order to relieve the folly of mortals." Along this line, in the grand finale of her oration, Folly vividly describes the experience of the mystic and defines it as that portion of folly that will not be taken away by death and as "something very like madness," a "madness" that is only "a faint taste, as it were, of that future happiness." She realizes at this point, however, that she has forgotten who she is and has " 'gone beyond the pale,' " and comes to the gracefully ironical and self-deprecating conclusion of her "torrent of jumbled words."

The Praise of Folly, though it is far and away Erasmus's most popular work, occupies a very small place within the wide range of his activity as a writer, scholar, translator, editor, theologian, and polemicist. He is said to have completed it in a week (citing the quotations from memory) while he was the guest of Thomas More at Bucklersbury in the autumn of 1509 and possibly for this reason is also said to have ascribed little value to it. Whatever the truth may be in this regard, the piece is as impressive in its learning and as sober in its implications as anything he ever wrote. There is no doubt either about its literary merits, the elegance and liveliness of its language, the gusto of its author's droll inventions. Behind the humorous façade, Erasmus's familiarity with the great texts of the ancient and the medieval worlds—with the Greco-Roman as well as the Judeo-Christian traditions—is fully visible. More particular models may also be cited: from the ancient world, the Greek satirist Lucian, some of whose work Erasmus had translated into Latin, and from Erasmus's own time, Sebastian Brant's *Ship of Fools* (*Narrenschiff*, 1497), of which there was a Latin translation in 1500, an English one in 1509.

Classroom Strategies

Our selection can be managed in one assignment. As with Petrarch and most other authors in this section, it may be advisable to explore first the degree to which the class is acquainted with the main elements of the Greco-Roman and the Judeo-Christian traditions. Questions on mythological concepts and themes, such as "Zeus/Jove, father of the gods," or on the historical conflicts between Roman Catholic and Protestant churches in the period of the Reformation will yield information on how to proceed. A basic point to be stressed is that at the time Christianity was also rampant politics, religious divisions and doctrinal controversy being everywhere. Discussions of the meaning of the Reformation and Counter-Reformation may need to be elicited together with class views of the function of satire—both in that era and in our own. Ensuing discussion should bring out the point that Erasmus favored direct contact with Scripture and a return to a simpler purified ritual. Passages about "superstitious" Christian practices show that he had particularly the Roman Catholic Church in mind. Unlike the extreme reformers, however, he wished to preserve the unity of the Church and to improve it from within, so he was also well received in papal circles. Under the polemical, flippant surface, it is important to detect the wise and conciliatory nature of Erasmus's piety. At the same time, beneath that surface, it is important to note the home thrusts at absurdities still very much with us today.

Topics for Discussion and Writing

1. Take what seem to be the most memorable objects of Folly's mockery (the Stoics, the Roman Catholic Church, various categories of fools and maniacs, etc.) and ask the class to explain by what means the satirical effects are obtained.
2. Satire may work in two opposite directions at the same time—that is to say, both criticize and undercut the criticism; both praise and undercut the praise. Work on specific passages to see how this happens. Give special attention to the handling of wisdom versus foolishness.
3. The presence of the author is sometimes more, sometimes less detectable under the mask of Folly. With particular emphasis on the selection from part 4, identify passages where the author's presence shows clearly.
4. Satire has been described as presupposing, in the object satirized, some sort of deviation from an accepted or even ideal norm. Discuss what norms can be inferred from a reading of *The Praise of Folly*—what kinds of acts and attitudes, in other words, does the author value?

Comparative Perspective

Folly distinguishes between two different kinds of madness. Explain what she means. From your reading this semester, give examples of both sorts. Given the evidence you cite, do you agree that some forms of madness are to be desired?

[The figure of the vengeful cuckold or Orlando are examples of the first kind; the duped husband of the fabliaux exemplifies the second.]

Further Reading

See also the reading suggestions in the *Anthology*, p. 2645.

Bainton, Roland H. *Erasmus of Christendom*. 1969. An illustrated biography, with emphasis on Erasmus as a Christian philosopher. With notes and bibliography.

Huizinga, Johan. *Erasmus and the Age of Reformation*. Trans. F. Hopman. 1957. A thorough, illustrated study, originally published in 1924, of Erasmus's life and career by the famous author of *The Waning of the Middle Ages*. Chapter IX deals with *The Praise of Folly*.

Olin, John C. *Six Essays on Erasmus*. 1979. Essay 4 is on *The Praise of Folly*.

Thompson, Geraldine. *Under Pretext of Praise: Satiric Mode in Erasmus' Fiction*. 1973. A study of Erasmus's fiction with emphasis on Erasmus as an educator and on his use of irony. Chapter II deals with *The Praise of Folly* as a parody as well as a moral indictment of European society in Erasmus's time.

Tracy, James D. *The Politics of Erasmus: A Pacifist Intellectual and His Political Milieu.* 1978. Erasmus's place in European intellectual history as a political philosopher, with emphasis on the "national matrix" of his political opinions.

Zweig, Stefan. *Erasmus of Rotterdam.* 1934. By an eminent novelist and biographer.

Niccolò Machiavelli

The Prince

Backgrounds

The Prince in a very general sense belongs to the same category as *The Book of the Courtier*, presenting sets of instructions and ultimately the description of an ideal type (the "employer" of the courtier, as it were). Yet from the very first brief chapter (not in the *Anthology*), a briskly didactic tone differentiates it unmistakably from Castiglione's work:

> All the states and governments that ever had or now have power over men were and are of two sorts: either republics or princely states. And princely states also are of two sorts: either hereditary . . . or else new. And the new ones are either brand-new . . . or they are like grafts freshly joined to the hereditary states of a prince. . . . New acquisitions of this sort are either accustomed to living under a prince, or used to being free; they may be acquired either by force of other people's arms or with one's own, either by fortune or by strength [*virtù*].

To each of the twenty-six chapters of *The Prince*, Machiavelli gave a strictly undecorative explanatory title, originally in Latin, then the standard language of scholarly communication. The style of the work makes it one of the supreme examples of vigor and originality in the history of Italian prose. The general distribution of the material is announced in chapter 1. Chapter 2 takes up hereditary princedoms. Chapters 2 and 3 deal with the conquest and maintenance of new provinces by a state already possessing its own structure and form of government. Chapters 4 and 5 concentrate on how best to annex cities or princedoms that had previously lived in freedom under their own laws. Chapters 6 through 9 handle newly formed princedoms acquired by the force of arms (6–7), by crime (8), or by the choice of fellow citizens (9). Chapter 10, as a kind of corollary, discusses the military defense of such newly formed states. Chapter 11 moves to "ecclesiastical states," that is, the dominions of the pope, their unusual nature, and the vast current power of the papacy. Chapters 12 through 14 examine what to Machiavelli and to most modern statesmen is the major problem in the government of a state—the organization of its armed forces. According to Machiavelli, the prince must not enlist mercenaries but rather have his own armies, the art of war being the only one that pertains to a sovereign. Chapters 15 through 23, in turn, concentrate on the qualities and codes of behavior that should characterize an efficient ruler and inspire his conduct. The uses of praise and blame, of liberality and stinginess, of cruelty and clemency, and finally of keeping or not keeping promises are expressed in a form so definitive and lucid they can hardly be summarized. For a specimen, see the second paragraph of chapter 18, which is possibly the most famous and controversial passage in the history of political writing.

Criteria of efficiency and political expediency pervade the advice given to the prince in chapters 19 through 24. These treat such diverse matters as how to avoid contempt and hatred (19); the utility of protecting the city-state with fortresses (20); the means to acquire a prestigious reputation, the dangers of neutrality, and the recognition to be granted artists and men of talent (21); the way to select and judge private counselors (22), with a corollary on avoiding flatterers (23). Chapter 24 concentrates on the present situation of Italian princedoms and prepares for the last two chapters, where, as indicated more elaborately in the headnote, the "realistic" and the "poetic" methods are mingled.

The origin of *The Prince* is best described in Machiavelli's letter to Francesco Vettori. Vettori, a prominent public figure under the Medici, was a friend and frequent correspondent of Machiavelli's, in spite of political divergencies; he had been instrumental in obtaining from Pope Leo X (Giovanni de' Medici) Machiavelli's release from imprisonment, followed by his confinement to the small estate he owned near Florence, where he wrote *The Prince*. From early in 1513, Machiavelli had begun the writings that were eventually to become his *Discourses on the First Ten Chapters of Livy*, the culminating result of his meditations on Roman history and of his passionate interest in its teachings. In Machiavelli's case, as we know, the strict meaning of Renaissance as the "rebirth" of ancient culture has a particularly concrete validity; for him, the Romans offered supreme models in all areas of human endeavor, most particularly as examples of that political and military competence that in the princes of contemporary Italy he found wanting.

The reasons generally given for Machiavelli's interruption of the *Discourses* to write *The Prince* between July and December of 1513 are highly speculative. Possibly, once launched on the task of political analysis, he felt an understandable urge to draw on his own experiences as a political man and observer of political events in his own time and place. Possibly, too, he hoped that his political sagacity as shown in *The Prince* would capture the attention of the dominant Medici family and bring him a new employment with them.

Machiavelli's sources are mainly his readings in ancient history and his own political experience. Though *The Prince* has resemblances, as noticed earlier, to the established genre of the manual of instruction, its matter, manner, and impact put it beyond easy classification. In Castiglione, our other instance of this kind of literature, apparent similarities of content and conception only put the differences in sharper focus. Castiglione was not unaware of the uses of power, and his courtier's highest manifestation of loyalty is the service of his prince on the battlefield. But his accent falls on the esthetic aspect of human actions, on "style" in performance, and on government of the inner man rather than government of other men. In Machiavelli, on the other hand, even the final "Roman dream" has its roots in his practical notion of Roman political competence, efficiency, and military preparedness.

Classroom Strategies

The Prince offers no special textual difficulties. Its statements, however startling, are as cuttingly clear as anything in political writing. The examples drawn from history may be puzzling inasmuch as they refer to particular and often obscure episodes; yet the contexts in which they are presented, plus the footnotes provided in the *Anthology*, should suffice to suggest the types of situations and the themes they illustrate. Maps may be helpful, not to teach geography or history, but to create in the student's mind some concrete idea of the location and respective sizes of such political entities of the day as the Kingdom of France, the Papal States, and the larger Italian city-states. As for the "moral" aspects of Machiavelli's teachings, a look forward to the "devilish" Machiavelli image through the centuries and particularly to the Elizabethan stage "Machiavel" may be in order. Finally, here as always, reading significant passages aloud will help bring out the dramatic aspect of Machiavelli's prose.

Topics for Discussion and Writing

1. Granted that Machiavelli's own historical context is remote, how far does his pattern of contrasts between political ideals and concrete realities apply today? What do modern rulers of states mean by *realpolitik*?

2. Attempt to define in specific passages the borderline between "realism" (practical advice, emphasis on military preparedness, etc.) and "myth" (the ideally equipped leader, the mirage of a unified Italian state). A close analysis of the last chapter, or even only of its last two paragraphs, may be one of many ways to see how the terms of that contrast can coexist, as it were, in the same breath.

3. Taking specific passages from *The Prince*, identify the characteristics that make Machiavelli's style effective.

4. Discuss the extent of Machiavelli's "amorality," and his basic alibi that "if man were good . . ."

5. Compare and contrast Machiavelli's idea of Fortune with the religious idea of man's free will and, on the other hand, with the meaning of "luck" when we refer to a contemporary political leader as being lucky.

Comparative Perspective

How would Machiavelli judge the actions of some of the rulers depicted in the works you have been studying?

[Candidates for discussion include Agamemnon in the *Iliad*, Oedipus in *Oedipus the King*, Hrothgar in *Beowulf*, Guzmán in *Fuente Ovejuna*.]

Further Reading

See also the reading suggestions in the *Anthology*, p. 2645.

Anglo, Sydney. *Machiavelli: A Dissection.* 1969. A study of Machiavelli's works and political thought through analysis and quotations from his works; with bibliography. Hale calls this book "refreshingly iconoclastic but somewhat too tart."

Bondanella, Peter E., and Mark Musa, eds. *The Portable Machiavelli.* 1979. A good general introduction to Machiavelli's life and works. The introduction is brief and cogent and includes sections on the historical context of *The Prince*, politics and history in Machiavelli, and on Machiavelli today. A good *Anthology* with ample possibilities for further readings.

Hulliung, Mark. *Citizen Machiavelli.* 1983. Separates Machiavelli from the tradition of "civic humanism" and describes him as "the first and one of the greatest subversives of the humanist tradition."

Mazzeo, Joseph Anthony. *Renaissance and Revolution: The Remaking of European Thought.* 1965. See the chapter on Machiavelli.

Pitkin, Anna F. *Fortune Is a Woman: Gender and Politics in the Thought of Machiavelli.* 1984. A study of Machiavelli "in terms of ambivalence about manhood."

Pocock, J. G. A. *The Machiavellian Moment.* 1975. See particularly chapter VI, B, "Machiavelli's *Il Principe*." An attempt to "selectively and thematically define . . . the moment, and the manner, in which Machiavelli's thought made its appearance within the specific historical context of the Florentine republic."

Wilkins, Ernest Hatch. *A History of Italian Literature.* Revised by Thomas G. Bergin. 1974. Chapter 23 deals with Machiavelli and Guicciardini.

Ludovico Ariosto

Orlando Furioso

Classroom Strategies and Topics for Discussion

In approaching Ariosto's *Orlando Furioso*, perhaps your first task is to establish how adding romance to epic transforms the heroic tradition with which students have become familiar. Placing Ariosto's introductory verses alongside those of Homer and/or Virgil, students should immediately see the difference between the classical poet's conventional deference to the Muse and the Renaissance poet's bolder announcement of his mission. Working in the shadow of many predecessors, including the medieval accounts of Roland and Boiardo's more recent treatment of that same hero in love, Ariosto will nevertheless set "down what has never before been recounted in prose and rhyme." To the somber Virgilian formula, the writer of romance epic adds new themes, not the least his own identification with his hero: like Orlando, once renowned for "his great prudence," the narrator struggles under the burden of an apparently ruthless mistress. Instead of an omniscient Muse, he addresses himself to a patron (yet later on in his long poem, Ariosto will make a number of sly, if apparently complimentary, references to the Este family that he served, of a sort that Virgil could never have dared). To launch their narratives, the classical poets appeal for an informed elucidation of divine motives. Ariosto's declarative self-assurance is a mark of the secularity of the *Orlando Furioso*.

A look at Ariosto's references to armor will underscore his burlesque handling of serious martial themes. The discomfiture of walking around fully armed is frequently noted, especially when one is intent on raping a lady. Ferrau's preoccupation with his lost helmet typifies the petty concerns of these paladins, accentuated by the lineage of their helmets; to demonstrate the debased treatment of the Matter of Troy (and the Matter of France) in this poem, have your students recall the emotional power in the ancient references to Hector's helmet and compare it to Ferrau's concerns.

With the introduction of Angelica, it will be helpful to define the topography of romance epic. As the headnote makes clear, the *Orlando Furioso* covers most of the known world, but no one would consult this poem for information about the real places it mentions. Close attention to the description of Angelica's flight in the opening section of canto I shows how the poem's pastoral terrain mirrors shifting psychological states even as it embodies presumably stable allegorical meanings. If you have taught *Gilgamesh* or Dante's *Inferno*, your students have already been in dark forests; the *Orlando* allows urban and suburban readers familiar with sanitized camping grounds to reconsider why the woods have figured in so much great literature of the past as the site of mental anguish and spiritual crisis.

Angelica's flight is rendered as nightmare, and the telling epic simile that likens her to "a baby fawn or kid who has watched through the leaves of the wood where he was born, and has seen the leopard's fangs close on his mother's throat" will resonate throughout the poem. Her (dubious) virginity is conventionally but significantly imagined in similar terms: once the rose "is plucked from her mother-stalk," she loses all. Callously deciding to use Sacripant as a protector in the dark forest, Angelica announces herself to him, with this result: "Never was such joy, such amazement to be seen in a mother's eyes when she lifted them to look on her son whom she had bewailed and lamented for dead as she heard the troops return without him: such, though was the Saracen's joy,

such his wonder on suddenly beholding her angel's face." Three different figures of speech in close succession have identified Angelica as an
abandoned orphan. Taken seriously, they seems to suggest that, in the
dark wood of life, human beings are existentially alone.

In the same breath, of course, you need to instill in your students
an appreciation of Ariosto's exquisitely balanced seriocomic tone. The
pathos is (often) real; so (always) is the ridiculousness of the overblown
rhetoric. When the narrative shifts to Ruggiero and the rugged hero's
unruly mount starts tearing trees apart, other facets of the European
pastoral tradition come to the fore. Astolfo is caught in—not by—a tree.
You and your students may want to debate how sorry we should feel for
Astolfo. From a serious perspective, this image of the Christian soul
trapped in the material world might conjure up memories of Dante's
Pier delle Vigne; from an entirely different vantage point, Astolfo, who
lacks the dignity of this literary precursor, may be closer to Bruin the
Bear, farcically entrapped in a tree by Renard the Fox, who has lured
him there with visions of a honeycomb. And Alcina's garden evokes
other, more ironic pastoral antecedents, drawing both on Ovid and the
allegorical geography of the medieval romance.

Without losing sight of Ariosto's way of adapting prior writers' themes
and images, you might ask your students to characterize that which is
distinctively Ariostan. His treatment of sexuality should be an easy way
to introduce this discussion. On the one hand, the poem titillates with
surprisingly graphic details: note, for example, the poet's readiness to
cede his descriptive office to Alcina and Ruggiero in bed, "the more so as
they frequently had a second tongue in their mouth," or to Richardet,
who is the narrator when Fiordispina is led to discover the proof of his
sex. This soft porn reaches its apogee in the extraordinary description of
the impotent hermit's "flop-eared nag." On the other hand, Ariosto's
symbolic universe takes sexuality, and (as the headnote indicates) the
horse as its embodiment, seriously.

One useful way into a discussion of horses and the control of sexual
energy is to ask students what term the Orlando Furioso uses for
"knight." Someone is sure to know the word "cavallo," which opens up
an inquiry into the equine vocabulary of "chivalry." Why do we build
equestrian statues? Why is horsemanship so central to the idea of
knighthood in the Romance languages, while the Germanic languages
stress instead apprenticeship and service ("knecht" derives ultimately
from the Old High German word for "boy")? A comparative view of the
heroic values represented by Beowulf (and embodied in Chaucer's latter-
day very perfect knight) would be illuminating here. There is a hint of
glamor, if not outright self-aggrandizement, built into the notion of the
cavalier (even the use of the word in English to mean "disdainful" or
"offhand" suggest this) that the humble knight eschews.

Ariosto's concerns differ from those of the old oral poets in many
ways, of course. If time permits, the Orlando Furioso offers a good introduction to the complexity of Renaissance attitudes toward reason.
Alcina's sister, Logistilla, stands for Reason in one of the clearest alle-

gorical details in the poem. How logical human action can ever really be remains a question, however. Ruggiero backslides after his immersion in Logistilla's realm, and neither human reason nor human strength can solve all problems. When pressed, even the bravest must turn to magic. Of the implements most frequently mentioned in the selections available in the *Anthology*, it is notable that both the shield of Atlas and the ring of Angelica solve dilemmas by transcending reason. The shield gives its bearer power because it dazzles when uncovered, blinding one's opponent's eyes, the locus of sight and understanding. Similarly, the ring of Angelica confers invisibility when the bearer takes it in the mouth, the locus from which speech—the word, the Logos—emerges.

Another quintessential Renaissance concern is addressed in the poet's many self-conscious references to his own artistic method. He compares himself to a musician selecting "different strings, fresh harmonies, as he seeks effects, now muted, now strident." Too vigorous a quest of variety, of course, threatens to leave an audience disoriented and destabilized. You might want to ask your students why Ariosto's narrative so often breaks off in the middle of an episode. A ready answer, which is not to be despised, is "for the sake of suspense."

Recent criticism of romance epic prefers to cite psychoanalytic explanations for the displacement, condensation, interpolation, and fragmentation of narrative in the *Orlando Furioso*. Without discoursing on critical theory, you may refer your students to the rapid succession of events in Orlando's dream, which is no more dreamlike than the episodes that enmesh the poem's many characters when they are awake. At base this narrative method illuminates the identity crises through which so many of Ariosto's characters pass. Like most Renaissance texts, his poem is not conceived in terms of the realistic development of character that students expect, having been brought up on late-nineteenth-century prose fiction. It nevertheless provides a variety of subtle nonlinear depictions of personality development and, more typically, of neurotic individuals' failure to establish a secure sense of self.

Adapting the epic simile to such concerns, Ariosto manages to endow a stock character like Angelica with a modicum of internal life. When we first meet her, she is adamantine in her scorn for her suitors. Her fate, fittingly enough, is to be chained to a rock and all but mistaken for a statue. Likened in the first frenzied canto to a ewe lamb, as we have seen, she is recalled by Orlando in this mode again. The narrative suggests, however, that Angelica fell in love with Medor because he needed her—because for him she served a maternal role. If this is a sign of female maturation, it also is the point at which the poet essentially loses interest—he leaves his characters when they become domesticated and, presumably, boring.

Psychological complexity is also hinted at in romance literature by the doubling of characters. Students familiar with Shakespeare's *Twelfth Night* will see in the twins Bradamant and Richardet precursors of Viola and Sebastian. The unfulfilled yearning so endemic in the *Orlando Furioso* is crystallized in the story of Fiordispina. Significantly, the Spanish princess comes upon shorn, armor-clad Bradamant "asleep in the tender grass." On the one hand, her appearance declares her masculinity; but on the other, her posture and surroundings betray her underlying softness. Bradamant quickly explains that she is a woman, and Fiordispina has no recourse but to dream. With the appearance of Richardet, who invents an Ovidian metamorphosis to explain "Bradamant" 's new accoutrements, Ariosto suggests how complex are the links between gender and identity, mischievously skirting the porous boundaries of sexual orientation.

The longing for completion that drives men and women to seek for their lost other half (as expressed in the parable of the separated egg in Plato's *Symposium*, to which, you may want to note, reference is made in the debate following Story Eight of Day One of the *Heptameron*) is further complicated when twins mirror each other. The martial woman, like Bradamant, is a figure out of a dream, almost hermaphroditic and supernaturally desirable. Typically, it should be emphasized, Ariosto's poem is conscious of the delicacy of Bradamant's sensibility; yet in detailing Fiordispina's earthier needs, it also coarsens the love theme in the bawdy bedtime scene between Richardet and the disbelieving Fiordispina.

This episode can also lead into a discussion of the fragility of the self in Ariosto's world. Bradamant and Richardet seem to be two versions of the same person; how much worse for two versions to coexist within one frame, as they do in the case of mad Orlando. If flux is frightening, so can stability be a horrifying state in this poem. Too firm a constancy, as Orlando's case makes clear, can be a danger; certainly students should be asked to comment on the brutal physicality of the naked, demented knight. Is every human being capable of acts that we would like to consider subhuman?

Another instance of constancy that leads to brutality may be found in the fate of Isabel. In choosing to die by his hand rather than to be raped, she elicits from Rodomont a definitive enactment of the self-centered attack on her person that he had been planning all along. Even here, in an episode that Ariosto takes as an occasion for a compliment to Isabella D'Este that seems to be deeply felt, he allows himself a moment of comic deflation that inspired no less a satirist than W. S. Gilbert in *The Mikado*: "Her head bounced thrice: from it a voice could be clearly heard pronouncing the name of Zerbin, to follow whom she had found so novel a way to escape from the Saracen."

In the midst of flux, both personal and narrative, Ariosto is acutely sensitive to the need to provide some sense of continuity, however mockingly. One of the devices that links the poem together, the brilliant introductory stanzas that shift from one set of concerns to another, increasingly deal with the poet's identification with Orlando mad for love. Interestingly, he links Orlando to Ceres in quest of Proserpine, the mother searching for her daughter, as he is searching for the Angelica he views as a motherless ewe lamb. Disabused of the notion that Angelica needs him, he runs mad, and at this point Ariosto forcibly reiterates his kinship with Orlando. This link between the poet and his titular hero suggests how much the human experiences of love and desire depend on literary conventions. Orlando, the most desperate of the poem's lovers, is also the most literate and linguistically gifted of its heroes. Indeed, if not for his command of languages, he would be incapable of deciphering Medor's ecstatic verses, which give the evidence of Angelica's desertion of all other men for this Saracen peasant.

In his very madness, Orlando becomes a link in another literary chain. Rejecting the life of reason and of courtly responsibility, dragging a dead mare in his wake, Orlando (as the headnote suggests) defiles the *cheval* at the root of chivalry. World literature has always found in the distracted hero a powerful sign of the folly of human ambition and pretension; at the same time, it is always the gifted who run mad, thereby accentuating the ironic sense of what is lost when reason and measure become impossible for the human being to maintain. To gauge the range of meanings that may be gleaned from the spectre of talent run amok, you might point to one of the earliest plays of Sophocles, *Ajax*, which explores the suicidal rage of that Greek hero (see the headnote to *Oedipus the King*), and all his dramatic descendants—which include virtually all of Shakespeare's tragic heroes. If you've read Lucian's *A True Story*, remind your students that "a dose of hellebore" has been prescribed to rehabilitate Ajax and earn him a place at "the Heroes' banquet" on the Isle of the Blest.

Lucian is a powerful presence in the ending of the *Orlando Furioso*, when Astolfo takes over the poet's role in the concluding movement of the poem by going to the moon and restoring the feckless hero with whom Ariosto has too fully identified himself. Having fallen under Alcina's spell because he mistook a whale for an island (another motif that echoes Lucian's story), misreading flux for stability, Astolfo can finally be trusted to rescue Orlando's missing wits. He alone, perhaps, may have profited from his experience.

Astolfo's literary critical chat with St. John the Evangelist, author of the Apocalypse, provides a fitting ending for a discussion of Ariosto's long poem. Consigning "verses written in praise of patrons" to what one critic has dubbed the "lunar junkyard," and commenting on the power of poets to burnish a hero's reputation beyond merit, Ariosto indulges in one more self-reflective set piece. In the end, anticipating postmodernism, the Renaissance writer seems to say that poetry is really about poetry. Fully clothed in Hector's armor, Ruggiero concludes the narrative by defeating Rodomont, the embodiment of "*rodomontade*," and the poem comes to its terse, abrupt end, imitating Virgil at its conclusion as it had in its beginning.

Topics for Writing

1. Landscape description in *Orlando Furioso*.
2. Angelica as a Petrarchan heroine.
3. The evolution of Ruggiero.
4. The role of the poet in *Orlando Furioso*.

Comparative Perspectives

1. Roland / Orlando: what distinguishes the hero as he appears in
   The Song of Roland? How does Ariosto redefine him in *Orlando
   Furioso*? How does the difference between the two tell us about
   the different concerns of the early medieval and the high Renaissance periods?
2. Poets and patrons, writers and courts: Ariosto and the Este family,
   Virgil and Augustus, Machiavelli and the Medici, the *Book of the
   Courtier*, the *Heptameron*.
3. Defining knighthood and chivalry—compare Ariosto's knights to
   any of the following: Beowulf, Gawain, Lancelot, Don Quixote.
4. The hero mad for love: how does a comparison of the circumstances that drive Orlando and Othello to distraction clarify the
   difference between romance fiction and psychological drama?

Further Reading

See also the reading suggestions in the *Anthology*, p. 2644.

Giamatti, A. Barlett. *Exile and Change in Renaissance Literature*. 1984.
   A magisterial discussion of the horse motif, with a probing analysis of
   Orlando's madness.

Quint, David. "Astolfo's Voyage to the Moon." *Yale Italian Studies* I
   (1977): 398–408. On the "lunar junkyard" and the impossibility of
   transcendent meaning in Ariosto's epic.

Reynolds, Barbara, trans. *Orlando Furioso*. 2 vols. 1975. A contemporary
   English verse translation, with excellent apparatus, including maps,
   charts of characters and devices, and genealogical tables.

Wiggins, Peter DeSa. *Figures in Ariosto's Tapestry: Character and Design
   in the* Orlando Furioso. 1986. Particularly interesting on Ariosto's female characters, whom Wiggins sees as more than cardboard caricatures.

LYRIC POETRY: CARPE DIEM POEMS

Backgrounds

These poems share thematic rather than stylistic similarities. The poets represented here belong to different schools of poetry: Donne is of
course the most famous of the Metaphysical poets, while Ben Jonson is
sometimes regarded as his stylistic opposite, the "father" of a school of
poets, by some called the "Cavalier" poets, who were writing at the same
time as the Metaphysicals. Marvell is usually categorized as Metaphysical; Herrick as Cavalier; Opitz as "Baroque," and so on. If these poems
don't share a style, what they do share is a topic. All of them voice desire, though they speak in diverse tones, from joyous to desperate. Most
of these poems issue an invitation, usually an invitation to erotic love.
Many of the poems focus on the delights of the natural world, many

sound a note of urgency, many raise the specter of time passing, some treat the invitation to physical bliss ironically—but no one statement characterizes all the poems in this section. A good way to approach these poems may be to ask students to recognize stylistic and tonal differences even as they identify frequently occurring themes in the section.

Nature's beauty is an important topic in many of these poems. Students might like to analyze the different ways that images from the natural world are used by these poets. Poliziano, Tasso, and Marvell describe a world of natural beauty that seduces by reflecting the joys of love. The "wild banner" of May, the cool shade of the trees, the beasts and birds burning with love, the flowers and garlands—Poliziano's "Welcome to May" creates a world that demands a loving, generous response from the young girls whose love is so ardently desired by their sweethearts. In fact, nature's cyclic quality is used by Poliziano to suggest to these maidens that by surrendering, they will be renewed like the grass rather than withering away like the cut branch. Tasso uses nature to reflect the lover's sadness at his love's departure; but he also uses it seductively, when the absolute silence and stillness of the woods, rivers, and winds at night reflect the sweet, silent joys of the lovers when they are together. Marlowe's shepherd turns roses into beds; flowers into caps; the sheep's wool into gowns and slippers, straw, and ivory; coral and amber into a belt, using charming images of nature to literally house and clothe the lover he invites to live the pastoral life with him. Raleigh's poem answers with the observation that winter does indeed come to the sheepfold—there is no such thing as perpetual springtime, in the natural world or in lovers' hearts. Other poets make similar observations about the natural cycle of age and death, not to refute a plea for love but to persuade in a different way. Jonson, Marvell, Herrick, and Opitz use the setting sun, the withering flowers, and the fading of youthful beauty to suggest that the lady should indeed seize the day, since that day will be short and the chance for happiness soon lost. Thus, for your students, a rich discussion of nature in these poems might lead to the insight that images from nature can be used for opposite effects: they might reflect the beauty of love or urge love upon us by reminding us that beauty is fleeting.

It might surprise your students that this poetry of sweetness contains so many references to old age, loss, suffering, and death, but it is the inevitability of these things that often seems to inspire the most intense desire to experience the pleasure of the moment. Marvell's "To His Coy Mistress" in the most obvious example of the way mortality inspires the passionate desire to seize the moment. This poem will repay intense discussion. It begins in a lighthearted vein, but the bantering tone changes abruptly at line 21 with the introduction of "time's winged chariot," and the poet envisions a future, an eternity, of deserts, worms, decay, and dust. Many would argue that the tone of this poem becomes desperate as reflected in the violent—and rather unpleasant—image of the two lovers as birds of prey who will "devour" time, and "tear our pleasures with rough strife/ Thorough the iron gates of life." Opitz's "Ah, Dearest,

Let Us Haste" is less violent in imagery but no less pessimistic about a future in which fair cheeks turn pallid and snowy hands decay. But some poems that continually remind us of future woe maintain a far lighter tone, as does Lorenzo de Medici's "Triumph of Bacchus and Ariadne," which, though its refrain is "There's no certainty of tomorrow," still celebrates even old age in the figure of Silenus and love's failure in the figure of Ariadne who, though she was adandoned on Naxos by her lover Theseus, still found happiness with the god Bacchus.

Your students may notice that all the writers in this section are male, and that all the threats of time's decay are directed at women. How do we react to these warnings to women: your beauty will fade with age, so you'd better take advantage of your present attractiveness by captivating a man now? Ask students for their reaction to Herrick's warning to the virgins: "Then be not coy, but use your time, / And while you may, go marry; / For having lost but once your prime, / You may for ever tarry." An interesting discussion might ensue about the different options and expectation for women today as compared to Herrick's day (mid-seventeenth century).

Appeals to the natural world and warnings about time's passage are not the only means of persuasion in these poems. Your students should notice the variety of means these poets use to lure the objects of their desires. Inspiring a fear of age, decline, and death is one tactic, as is appealing to natural beauty and delight. But the poets also employ wit, logical argument, and flattery in order to persuade. Compare Donne's, Johnson's, and Marvell's use of flattery as they address the beloved: Donne compares her to an angel, Jonson asserts that she is "a drink divine," sweeter than Jove's nectar, and Marvell agrees that the lady's beauty deserves centuries of praise devoted to each part. What effect does this hyperbole have on the reader? The two Donne poems in this section contain wonderful examples of metaphysical wit and might be read equally well as part of the section on Metaphysical Poetry. Considering them in the tradition of carpe diem, we might think about how that wit functions to persuade. How might the auditor, the assumed woman listening to the speaker's persuasion in Donne's Elegy 19, react to the witty wordplay? When the poet asks at the end, "What needst thou have more covering than a man?" for instance, he means both that the woman should not need to cover herself more than he does himself—and he is naked—but of course he also suggests that his body will be her "covering" in lovemaking. The poem is full of such puns, which we might recognize and admire for their wit—but do they play a part in persuading his audience? How?

One last aspect of these poems that repays attention is the sense of self that is conveyed by the speaker. Admittedly some of the poems are less personal than others. Lorenzo de Medici's "Triumph of Bacchus and Ariadne," for instance, is a poem that may have been intended as an accompaniment to a public procession or *trionfo*, as the visual directions imply. When the poet says, "Here are Bacchus and Ariadne," or "Midas comes after these," he may have been pointing out figures on a float or in a procession. (Your students might enjoy the illustration of "The Triumph of Bacchus and Ariadne" in Dempsey's "Portraits and Masks," p. 10). But many of the poets speak in the first person. While we cannot necessarily assume that a first-person narrator "is" the poet himself, we should be attentive to the sense of self developed in the poem, whether it is the self of the poet or of a persona that he fashions as speaker of the poems. Sidney's poem 71 from *Astrophil and Stella* is a good example of the latter. The speaker in this Petrarchan sonnet sequence is a character, "Astrophil," who in poem 71 is trying to banish sexual desire from his relationship with the married Stella, who has agreed to give him the "monarchy" of her "high heart" as long as he maintains a virtuous course (poem 69). In the poems that follow, including 71, Sidney depicts an Astrophil who struggles to repress his desire and to view Stella, as he does in this poem, as "that virtuous soul" rather than as that alluring body. But Astrophil's Platonic meditation on Stella as an "heir to heavenly bliss" who leads others to salvation is interrupted by the raucous cry of Desire, "Give me some food!" While Sidney's Astrophil struggles with contending forces within himself, Spenser's poet-persona depicts himself as a theatrical figure, performing a variety of roles rather than expressing some essential and authentic selfhood in his quest to win the lady (sonnet 54 from *Amoretti*; see the introduction to "The Lyric after Petrarch."). Finally, Opitz alludes to the possibility of self-annihilation as a by-product of love when in the final stanza of "Ah, Dearest, Let Us Haste Us."

> As thou thyself then lovest,
> Love also me;
> Give me, that when thou givest
> I lose to thee.

By predicating the woman's love for him upon her own self-love, Opitz suggests that the self survives through love, but his final statement, "I lose to thee," carries connotations of self-effacement or loss of identity, the same sense expressed by several of Shakespeare's characters, such as Claudio in *Much Ado* who tells Hero when he proclaims his love for her, "I give away myself for you."

Even as these poets tell us, in one sense or another, to "seize the day," many also register a strong sense of loss. We are reminded that youth and beauty will fade and the body will decay, and are warned that union with another may erase some of our self-contained identity. But we are also lured by pleasure as it is inscribed in the many concrete details of these poems: Poliziano's wild banner of May, Herrick's rosebuds, Donne's mine of precious stones—even the olives, capers, and mutton of Ben Jonson's "Inviting a Friend to Supper."

Further Reading

Cheney, Patrick, and Anne Lake Prescott, eds. *Approaches to Teaching Shorter Elizabethan Poetry*. 2000.

Dempsey, Charles. "Portraits and Masks in the Art of Lorenzo de Med-
    ici, Botticelli, and Politian's *Stanza per la Giosta*." In *Renaissance
    Quarterly*. Spring 1999.

Ulmer, Bernhard. *Martin Opitz*. 1971.

Warnke, Frank J. *European Metaphysical Poetry*. 1961.

BALDASSARE CASTIGLIONE

The Book of the Courtier

Backgrounds

The Book of the Courtier is a book of etiquette meant to be useful to
gentlemen (and ladies) who lived and worked at court in the service of
aristocratic rulers of states. Its form, traditional in Renaissance literature, is that of a dialogue, or more precisely, of a conversation. Even
more specifically, it is a transcription, formalized but nonetheless brilliant and sometimes witty, of after-dinner talk among people well versed
in the customs and requirements of court life. Its style in the original
has long been regarded as a model of proper Renaissance Italian, classically formal and yet supple and graceful. Its larger setting is one of the
states that composed the mosaic of the then-divided Italy, the duchy of
Urbino. Its narrower setting may be imagined to be one of the halls in
Urbino's splendid ducal palace. The conversationalists, or dramatis personae, are assembled from different parts of Italy and represent some of
the most illustrious families in their respective city-states: a Gonzaga
from Mantua, a Bembo from Venice, a Medici from Florence. The local
ruler, the duke of Urbino, Guidobaldo da Montefeltro, is irremediably ill
and has the habit of retiring early. Hence the evenings at court, with
their conversations and games, are ruled over by the authoritative but
gentle Duchess Elisabetta, who often delegates her authority to the
Countess Emilia, née Gonzaga, one of her ladies-in-waiting. One such
evening is imagined by Castiglione to have been the origin of his famous
work. Various forms of entertainment are suggested by different members of the party; the one chosen, somewhat unexpectedly, is a purely intellectual "game" proposed by a Count Federico Fregoso from Genoa.
The "game" will consist in composing, through well-regulated debate, a
description of the qualities and functions of a worthy courtier, or indeed
of "forming with words a perfect Courtier."

The work is divided into four parts corresponding to the four evenings
of the debate. Book I, after the exordium and the choice of the "game,"
describes the qualities and capacities required of the model courtier,
from the indispensable nobility of his birth to his dexterity in his major
profession—the handling of arms in war, in dueling, and in peaceful
tournaments. There follow rules and recommendations concerning
physical and moral virtues, speech, manners, generosity, the ornaments
of culture and the arts. Book II (not in the *Anthology*), partially elaborates on and perfects some of the theme of book I, adding details on

music, dance, gracefulness, benevolence, humaneness, and the art of conversation, including counsel on how to handle, in the proper measure, wordplay, jokes, irony, witty repartee, and *burle* (practical jokes). Book III (not in the *Anthology*) discusses the *Donna di Corte* or *Donna di Palazzo*, that is, the lady-in-waiting or other female member of the court. The qualities, education, and norms of behavior appropriate to her are elaborated on in their similarities to and their differences from those of the male courtier. Examples of feminine excellence are taken from all ages and praised; immodesty and ostentatiousness are blamed.

The first part of book IV deals with the ways in which the courtier, who is not only a loyal subordinate but also a wise counselor to his prince, may conquer the latter's good graces by advising him wisely on such varied matters as war and peace, the active and contemplative life, justice, magnanimity, religion without superstition, and the respective merits of different forms of government. The latter part of the book centers on the sentiment and practice of love by the courtier, in youth and in old age, and finds its culmination in Pietro Bembo's discourse on earthly love transforming to divine love, just as the work itself moves from matters of civilized behavior to concerns of the soul. The selections in the *Anthology* contain the most classic and influential passages on the nature and accomplishments of the courtier. Of the "Words" that, according to the announced purpose, shall "form" the ideal picture of the courtier, some are key terms, particularly "grace" and *sprezzatura*, a Castiglione coinage usually translated as "nonchalance." (For further definition, see below.)

The "courtesy book" as a genre was common in Renaissance culture. The form goes back to Plato's dialogues, and "Platonism" in a generic sense is to be found also in Castiglione's aiming at an ideal form (the *perfect* courtier). But the major source of Castiglione's treatise is, of course, his own experience as a courtier. Though much of that experience in its practical results was negative and disappointing (see the biographical data in the *Anthology*), Castiglione continued to pursue his established aim through his long years of labor on the book with an ever-increasing tendency to idealize what was rarely ideal.

Classroom Strategies

A major difficulty in teaching Castiglione is the remoteness of the society and customs he depicts. On the other hand, *The Book of the Courtier* offers a splendid opening for discussions of the practical usefulness of utopias in establishing an ideal, however unattainable, and of the other kinds of "how-to" books that abound in our own age. The *Courtier*'s own description of its courtly milieu may be enhanced by obtaining from your art department illustrations of the place (the ducal palace at Urbino) and some of the participating characters (e.g., the portrait of Castiglione himself by Raphael or Piero della Francesca's portrait of the duke of Montefeltro). You may also bring the participants closer by reminding the class that they are, in their way, simply government officials in an age when aristocrats had the responsibilities of public office.

The other possible stumbling block—the artificiality of Castiglione's dialogue—should not be exaggerated. The custom of orchestrated conversation survives even in modern times, not only in the society represented, say, in the first chapter of *War and Peace* but also in such contemporary institutions as the panel or roundtable or the television talk show. Moreover, since a large part of our selections concerns the courtier's achieving such expertise in the arts of dueling and dance that he can exercise them without apparent effort—that is, with *sprezzatura*—Olympic sports activities offer a wide range of comparisons.

Topics for Discussion and Writing

1. Discuss the individual qualities given to the main characters in *The Book of the Courtier*, considering also such matters as differences in age and personal history.
2. Attempt a definition of *sprezzatura* more detailed and inclusive than the simple, approximate translation as "nonchalance."
3. How many writers whom you have studied this semester would agree with the Count that the artist's goal is "to conceal art"?

Comparative Perspectives

1. If the students have read the Boccaccio selections in the *Anthology*, a clarifying discussion can center on the characters in the *Courtier* as compared and contrasted with those who take turns telling each other tales in the *Decameron*.
2. A parallel topic can center on the function of the "frame" story as an organizing element in both works.
3. If the students have read Machiavelli, a discussion can center on the likenesses and differences in the ideal of the Renaissance man as presented in *The Prince* and the *Courtier*.
4. Compare the aspects of Achilles praised by three masters of political and philosophical discourse to those emphasized by Homer: see the references in *The Book of the Courtier*, *The Prince* and/or *The Apology of Socrates*. What do their different views of the Greek hero reveal about the values espoused by these writers?

Further Reading

See also the reading suggestions in the *Anthology*, p. 2645.

Hanning, Robert W., and David Rosand, eds. *Castiglione: The Ideal and the Real in Renaissance Culture*. 1983. Among the ten excellent essays in this collection, the following are perhaps of greatest relevance to our discussion: chapter 1 (Thomas M. Greene, "*Il Cortegiano* and the Choice of a Game"), chapter 4 (Eduardo Saccone, "*Grazia, Sprezzature, Affettazione* in *The Courtier*"), chapter 7 (Robert W. Hanning, "Castiglione's Verbal Portrait: Structures and Strategies"), and chapter 10 (Louise George Clubb, "Castiglione's Humanistic Art and Renaissance Drama").

Wilkins, Ernest Hatch. *History of Italian Literature*. Revised by Thomas G. Bergin. 1974. See chapter 24, "Castiglione and Other Prose Writers."

Woodhouse, J. R. *Baldesar Castiglione*. 1978. A "reassessment of *The Courtier*," the book opens with chapters on life at court and the courtly educational ideal. There follow individual analyses of the four books of the *Courtier* and the subjects with which they deal.

Marguerite de Navarre

The Heptameron

Backgrounds

For an account of the "frame story" as given in the prologue of the *Heptameron*, see the headnote. A definitive text of Marguerite de Navarre's collection has not been established and probably never will be, owing to the situation of manuscripts (seventeen of them exist, not at all identical in the numbering and ordering of the stories included) and of early printed editions. The first printed edition appeared in 1558, nine years after Marguerite's death, edited by a prominent scholar, Pierre Boaistuau, under the title *Histories of Fortunate Lovers*. The present title appeared a year later in *Héptaméron des Nouvelles*, a printed edition done by Pierre Gruget, who divided the stories into "Days" with ten stories each and gave more space to prologues and dialogues, although he censored some names and passages, as well as three entire stories that had to do with the corruption of Franciscan monks. Among the manuscript texts, the one produced by the scholar Adrien de Thou in 1553 is of particular interest; oddly enough, it "calls itself *Le Décaméron* of Marguerite, and seems to leave empty pages for missing tales to complete the hundred implied in the title" (P. A. Chilton).

Even from these sketchy notes it is clear that a definitive canon of the stories does not exist. Details are available in Chilton's introduction to his translation, which is based on the best available scholarship and contains seventy-two stories, ten for each of seven days and two for a barely started eighth day. Each "Day," in addition to its prologue, has a long title that summarily indicates the type of stories it contains. The First Day, from which the selections in the *Anthology* are taken, announces "A Collection of Low Tricks Played by Women on Men and by Men on Women." It is generally thought to be the most finished of the sequences, and it introduces the narrators well.

Marguerite de Navarre presents a peculiar type of storytelling, as each story is followed by a discussion of its moral and social implications among the storytellers themselves; thus we have something of a mixture of two genres, the short story and the treatise in the form of a dialogue or conversation. A major example of the latter is Castiglione's *Book of the Courtier*. For the short story as Marguerite handles it, three precedents can be indicated: the medieval *fabliau*—a short tale in verse form, typically with a humorous and bawdy subject; the *lai*, a longer narrative in verse form, exemplified by the work of Marie de France; and most importantly the *novella*, of which the major medieval exponent was Boccaccio. Boccaccio's *Decameron* had first been translated into French by Laurent Premierfait in 1414; a new translation, mentioned in the prologue to the *Heptameron*, was commissioned by Marguerite herself and done by a member of the court of Francis I, Antoine Le Maçon; it came out in 1545.

Classroom Strategies

Marguerite's stories present no difficulties in terms of plot development and narrative sequence. As for their content, particularly with regard to the codes implied in the characters' behavior, it may be in order always to keep in mind some basic facts. This is a group of people who belong to the higher echelons of aristocratic society, indeed to the inner circle of royalty, at a time of kings "by divine right" and of extremely classified societies; whether they tell stories about their peers (which sometimes verge on the "juicy piece of gossip") or about characters of inferior social status, they act as people who do not feel bound by common standards of judgment but who have established standards that are valid for persons of their own rank.

Hence the literary qualities of the stories, the naturalness with which they handle potentially shocking situations such as overt matrimonial infidelity, rape, or the bawdiness of the clergy. This general attitude is reflected in the relative simplicity and directness of Marguerite's narrative manner. Discussion of this attitude may present good opportunities to familiarize students with such notions as objectivity in fiction, point of view, and authorial comment. Actually, Marguerite's manner and technique may prove to be more subtle than they appear at first, especially in the relationship between the stories themselves and the commentary that follows each of them. It could be pointed out that the conversations among the characters, all of them narrators in turn, ultimately create a variety of "voices" or "points of view" for the same fictional material; hence Marguerite's narrative, however deceptively simple, may turn out to be quite sophisticated and "modern."

To a significant degree, these debates seem modern because they address serious moral question in regard to sexual behavior. In the *Decameron*, Boccaccio balances three men and seven women, and his book frequently elevates women's concerns to a level of dignity not always typical of the age. Maguerite balances five men and five women, and since many of the women argue against what one might consider feminist perspectives, the tenor of the discussion often undermines the accomplishments of the female characters in the stories.

Consider, for example, the conversation that follows Story Ten.

Though Oisille and Parlamente regard Florida as one who "was tried to the limits of her endurance" by Amador, who twice tries to rape her, the male characters defend him, Hircan even going so far as to criticize Amador for being "so easily put off" by Florida. The final word on Amador is Geburon's tribute to him as "the most noble and valiant knight that ever lived." By contrast, at the end of Story Eight a woman gets the last word when a wife scolds her errant (and ironically compromised) husband, and the ensuing conversation is focused around Dagoucin's lack of sympathy for men who have every reason to be content and yet stray.

Topic for Discussion and Writing

The characters of Parlamente and Hircan are generally identified with Marguerite herself and with her second husband, Henri de Navarre. Take these two characters' words as they appear in the prologue and in the conversation following Story Eight and attempt to describe the implied notions of what constitutes a rational, successful matrimonial relationship in the world of the *Heptameron*. Also use contributions from other characters surrounding this central couple.

Some Comparative Perspectives

1. Compare the handling of "bawdy" materials in the selections from Day One and in Boccaccio's Sixth Story of the Ninth Day (see p. 1631 in the *Anthology*).
2. Compare the attitudes toward cuckoldry in Story Three with those in Chaucer's *Miller's Tale*, or canto V of Dante's *Inferno*, or the frame of *The Thousand and One Nights*. How does each author handle the reasons for and moral consequences of adultery?
3. Referring to Plato's *Symposium*, Dagoucin describes the ideal love: "if she whom you love is your true likeness . . . then it will be your own self that you love, and not her alone." Adam's love for Eve in *Paradise Lost* uniquely illustrates this situation; compare the conversations about love in Milton's poem with the discussions in the *Heptameron*.

Further Reading

See also the reading suggestions in the *Anthology*, p. 2646.

Cholakian, Patricia Francis. *Rape and Writing in the* Heptameron *of Marguerite de Navarre*. 1991. A useful feminist analysis.

Gelernt, Jules. *World of Many Loves: The* Heptameron *of Marguerite de Navarre*. 1966. Views the work as a "Renaissance treatise on love" and traces in its background the "idealistic" line from courtly love to Renaissance Neoplatonism and the "realist" tradition of the *novella*.

Kinney, Arthur F. *Continental Humanist Poetics*. 1989. See chapter 4 on the *Heptameron*.

Meijer, Marianne. "The *Héptaméron*: Feminism with a Smile." In *Regionalism and the Female Imagination*. 1977–78. A short article from a contemporary point of view.

FRANÇOIS RABELAIS

Gargantua and Pantagruel

Backgrounds

Gargantua and Pantagruel, as we know it now—whatever the history of its composition, the dates of its parts, and the authenticity of its final part—is an immense and seemingly chaotic work of fiction, divided into five books. It is possible, however, to extract an intelligible "story line" from the seemingly haphazard movements of its narrative course. The necessary premise to any successful encounter with it is that it operates on two levels—fantasy and realism—which are variously balanced and merged. The locale at the opening of book I is a kingdom, for which Rabelais borrowed from Sir Thomas More the name of Utopia, but it is at the same time a large French country estate. The gigantic king-squire is Grandgousier. He and his queen, Gargamelle, beget a giant-son, Gargantua, who enters the world from her left ear while she is lying in a meadow and who calls immediately for wine. After this comes the story of Gargantua's education in Paris. It is a story told in semifantastic, often comic terms, but tracing what was then a highly controversial transition from medieval scholasticism (a term whose meaning students should be asked to look up) to the subjects and methods of the "new" learning: see the selections in the *Anthology* from chapters 14–24.

Later on in book I Gargantua will leave Paris, answering the summons to war from his father the king. The so-called Picrochole War is a mock-heroic version of a country brawl between people of two neighboring estates, with, however, many of the characteristics of wars between nations. The cake-peddlers of nearby Linne ("King" Picrochole's domain) have refused to sell their wares to Grandgousier's shepherds, one of whom knocks down a Picrochole baker. The "incident" is used by Picrochole as an excuse to invade Grandgousier's territories, but his overblown "imperialistic" designs are thwarted by Gargantua's gigantic physical stature and power. (There are such vaguely pre-Swiftian details as his combing cannon balls out of his hair and inadvertently eating several pilgrims in his salad.) Another valiant and picturesque war hero is the monk Friar John of the Funnels; after the enemy is conquered and pardoned, he is allowed as a reward to build the monastery of his dreams, the Abbey of Thélème (see chapters 52–57).

Book II is Pantagruel's book. Like his father, Gargantua, Pantagruel is sent to Paris to study. The new learning now happily dominates, and Gargantua's letter to Pantagruel is a kind of manifesto of the proud intellectual achievements of the period. Shortly thereafter, a major new character makes his entrance—Panurge, the still-familiar type of student who grows in age without ever getting his degree: poor but generous, astute and malicious, an erudite and practical joker, and as much a proverbial figure in French literature as Pantagruel himself. The two young men become inseparable; their most significant adventure in book II is the war against the Dipsodes (not included in the *Anthology*)—the root of *Dipsodes*, the same as in "dipsomania," is Greek for "thirst"—who are conquered, Pantagruel becoming their king.

Book III (not included in the *Anthology*) introduces a question that pervades the rest of the work: should Panurge marry? To find out, Panurge and Pantagruel make several fantastic journeys to consult a sibyl, a poet, a magician, a doctor, and a philosopher. Finally a madman, Triboulet, advises them to seek the Oracle of the Holy Bottle. For that purpose, they go on further fantastic voyages, which take them, among other destinations—again in a pre-Swiftian manner—to the island of the Papefigues (Protestants or "Pope-snubbers") and the island of the Papimanes (Catholics or "Pope-enthusiasts"). Finally in book V (also not in the *Anthology*), taking a shortcut through the frozen ocean north of Canada, Panurge and Pantagruel reach Northern India and the subterranean location, under a vineyard planted by Bacchus, of the Holy Bottle. Its oracular response is the single word TRINCH ("DRINK!"). The assuaging of thirst, actual and also symbolical, physical and intellectual, proves to be the cultural metaphor of the entire work.

Before Rabelais made them heroes, raising them to a high place in the literary culture of France, Gargantua and Pantagruel existed as characters in French folklore. In other words, they already had the kind of household popularity now enjoyed by some of our comic-strip heroes endowed with exceptional muscle and superhuman powers. In French folk tradition, Gargantua was a gigantic figure famous for his exceptional voracity, while Pantagruel was a pleasant little devil whose favorite work was making men thirsty. It was Rabelais who, among many other innovations, made them father and son. The composition of *Gargantua and Pantagruel* was as leisurely as the work itself. The first of its parts to see the light was what is now book II. This was published in 1532 under the pseudonym Alcofribas Nasier, an anagram of Rabelais's own name, with a long title, as was then the fashion: *The Horrible and Fearful Facts and Brave Deeds of the Renowned Pantagruel, King of the Dipsodes, Son of the Great Gargantua*. It was intended as the continuation of a preceding anonymous book, *The Great and Inestimable Chronicles of the Great Giant Gargantua*. Rabelais's own and quite different *Gargantua*, the present book I, was published two years later. Books III and IV and the spurious book V were published with considerable intervals between them (1547, 1552, 1564).

Rabelais's characters, apart from their folksy lineage, may be related to such previous literary giants as Morgante and Baldus, respective heroes of mock-heroic poems by Luigi Pulci (1432–1484) and Teofilo Folengo (1491–1544). Their attribute of longevity is, of course, traceable as far back as the heroes of Genesis. More generally, the disparate elements assembled in Rabelais's work are a reflection of his unique life experience, his multiple occupations, and his extraordinary learning.

Even a summary biography of the man throws light on the sources of the
work: for the Abbey of Thélème, his experience with monastic life; for
the education of the giants, his knowledge as a scholarly humanist and
practicing physician; and so on.

Classroom Strategies

Like *The Praise of Folly*, Rabelais's work can help your classes learn
how to detect serious ideas in comic and, in this case, particularly extravagant garb. The new reader may have some difficulty with the twists
and turns that the author gives to such august texts as the Holy Scriptures—typically, for instance, in his handling of the biblical pattern of
"begats" in tracing the genealogy of his heroes. The idea to be suggested
and elaborated upon in such cases is that a humanist must be well at
ease in a tradition (in this case the Judeo-Christian tradition: Rabelais,
in however unorthodox a fashion, was a monk) before he can take the
liberty of twisting and parodying that tradition. Laughter does not necessarily indicate disrespect, but often an affectionate familiarity. With Rabelais's mixture of realism and fantasy there should be no problem.
Young audiences have long been trained in that area by science fiction
and films. The selections in the *Anthology* are intended to emphasize
both the fundamental seriousness of Rabelais's purpose and the sheer
fun to be derived from his method.

Topics for Discussion and Writing

1. In the course of the story Rabelais often seems to forget the gigantic size and superhuman nature of his characters. Find specific examples of this "oversight" and attempt to explain its significance
   (for instance, in Gargantua's letter to Pantagruel, we hardly think
   of father and son as supernatural giants).
2. Describe the implications of the name of Pantagruel's kingdom:
   Utopia. Discuss the idea that utopias are useful in showing the way
   to an unattainable perfection.
3. Discuss the idea that the Abbey of Thélème's orderly, pleasant life
   depends on an aristocratic sense of honor.
4. Although Rabelais wouldn't have known the phrase, *Gargantua
   and Pantagruel* can be called in part a "generational novel." What
   are possible similarities and contrasts with the generation gap as
   we experience it in our own time? Discuss the role of one single
   humanistic or scientific change in altering the outlook of our own
   period.

Comparative Perspectives

1. Discuss possible comparisons between Rabelais's and Erasmus's
   views of religious practices, comparing passages in which both
   seem to oppose pompous, exhibitionistic piety.
2. Compare Rabelais and Castiglione on the mental and physical ed-

ucation of a gentleman. Keep in mind that Pantagruel is also a
prince, and receives the traditional education for his rank.

3. Pantagruel is born "as hairy as a bear," a feature that leads to a pre-
diction of a great future. Heroic characters, serious as well as
comic, are often supposed to have been marked at birth in similar
ways. Compare the births of Enkidu or Esau, or the appearance of
Orlando when mad. What attributes are linked to the hirsute male
in each of these cases?

4. The English scholar Thaumaste and Panurge conduct an argument
through signs rather than words. Panurge wins because he has a
repertory of (obscene) gestures far more imaginative than Thu-
maste's: obviously, Rabelais intended this scene to be great fun,
and it is. In today's "visual culture," however, the power of nonverbal signs is taken very seriously. Discuss the wit of pictorial description in *Gargantua and Pantagruel* (for example, the landscape
of Pantagruel's mouth in book II, chapter 32) and in works like *A
True Story* (in the belly of the whale, perhaps), which influenced
Rabelais, or in the serious iconography of medieval religious poetry
(like *A Hymn to Holy Women* or *A Hymn to St. Maximinus*). Why
did images have such power when a large part of the population
could not read? Why do they have so much power today, when a
large part of the population does not read? How would you contrast the signs typical of earlier centuries with those that are current today?

Further Reading

See also the reading suggestions in the *Anthology*, p. 2646.

Bowen, Barbara C. *The Age of Bluff: Paradox and Ambiguity in Rabelais
and Montaigne*. 1972.

Coleman, Dorothy G. *Rabelais: A Critical Study in Prose Fiction*. 1971.
An in-depth study of "the richness of Rabelais's vocabulary and the
galvanizing dynamics of his style," as well as of "some of the general
orientations of his work," his characters, choice of form, and so on.

Cruickshank, John, ed. *French Literature and Its Background*. Vol. 1,
The Sixteenth Century. 1968. Chapter 2, by G. D. Josipovici, is dedicated to Rabelais.

Febvre, Lucien Paul Victor. *The Problem of Unbelief in the Sixteenth
Century: The Religion of Rabelais*. Trans. Beatrice Gottlieb. 1982. A
thorough treatment of the question of Rabelais's religious ideas in relation to the time in which he lived, by an important French scholar.

Losse, Deborah N. *Rhetoric at Play: Rabelais and Satirical Eulogy*. 1980.
Quite specialized, with quotations in the original French.

Screech, M. A. *Looking at Rabelais*. 1988. An Oxford lecture by an eminent Rabelais scholar.

MICHEL DE MONTAIGNE

Essays

Backgrounds

Montaigne's *Essays* are divided into three books, each containing a different number of essays of widely varying lengths and, of course, subjects (fifty-seven in Book I, thirty-seven in Book II, thirteen in Book III). The essays are designated as "chapters," a term that can be misleading, not only because a collection of essays is not a work of fiction but also because of the ostensibly haphazard way in which the "chapters" follow one another. Each essay, therefore, would lend itself to individual mention and description. Yet some sense of progression and development can be detected.

Montaigne began to work on what was to become his famous collection of essays when he was thirty-eight years old and had already had considerable experience of the world. Retired now to the library of his castle, he had a private purpose in his writing—not, however, of keeping a chronological diary but rather of assembling a scrapbook in which to record passing thoughts and memorabilia. Thus the work began as a collection of rambling observations and meditations on Montaigne's readings, on events past and present, on general human attitudes, foibles, qualities, oddities. Many of his chapter or essay titles start with "Of" followed by the name of a human virtue, vice, or custom. "Of" sorrow (I, 2), idleness (I, 8), liars (I, 9), fear (I, 17), pedantry (I, 24), friendship (I, 27), sleep (I, 44), smells (I, 55), drunkenness (II, 2), conscience (II, 5), the affection of fathers for their children (II, 8), riding post (II, 22), anger (II, 31). Such titles, as well as those featuring maxims or proverbs—*That the Study of Philosophy Is to Learn to Die* (I, 19), *That We Laugh or Cry for the Same Thing* (I, 37), *That Our Desires Are Augmented by Difficulties* (II, 15), *Cowardice, the Mother of Cruelty* (II, 27), *All Things Have Their Season* (II, 28)—introduce essays showing the same qualities of casual progression as the work as a whole and coming to the justification of their titles in comfortable, roundabout ways. A selection from book I, for instance, the famous essay *On Cannibals*, opens with a little episode from Roman history, then mentions the unnamed friend who had spent a long time in a section of Brazil and relates to the author some observations made there; gradually, but only gradually, the focus shifts to the main subject, cannibals, and to the personal acquaintance of the author with one of them. The author seems able to maintain a detached, often ironical attitude throughout, however bizarre or horrible his material.

That such an attitude may be ascribed to the influence of a particular philosophical system is doubtful; many not entirely successful attempts have been made to formalize Montaigne's thought, usually in terms of a progression from the Stoicism of his much-admired Seneca and an initial confidence in the authority of human reason, to a more balanced, temperate "natural philosophy" and a deep albeit undramatic contemplation of the limits of human judgment. The thirteen long chapters of book III, written at a more advanced age and after new private and public experiences (such as Montaigne's four years as mayor of Bordeaux), would then be the ultimate statement of that wise "natural philosophy," not without touches of "Epicureanism." Though there is some truth in this, Montaigne remains a striking example of his own idea of the changeable nature of man; he has "slipped through the fingers of even the most daring critics," as he himself says of the Emperor Augustus. Hence the safer, simpler, and most obvious way to trace a line of development in the three books of the essays is to see it in terms of increased focusing on the individual self. Our selections, however sketchily, exemplify such a progress, from Montaigne's early eclecticism to a consideration of mankind's "presumption and littleness," to the overtly central purpose of analyzing the exemplar at hand, himself.

The originator of the "essay" as a literary genre, Montaigne can hardly be said to have had predecessors in that form. His mode of writing can be related, however, to a kind of book very fashionable at the time: collections of informative bits of knowledge and wise sayings in all areas from grammar to geography, from mathematics to history, of which Erasmus's *Adagia* is perhaps the best surviving example. One of the major purposes of such collections, besides moral teaching, was to enable one to display one's familiarity with antiquity. They also exemplify a view of history, and particularly of Roman history, as a source of teachings and models of behavior—a view that in his own different way Montaigne entertained as enthusiastically as Machiavelli. Ancient Roman archetypes of the genre were found in such works as *Memorable Deeds and Sayings* by Valerius Maximus, a writer of the first century C.E., or in Aulus Gellius's *Attic Nights* (second century C.E.). In the shaping of Montaigne's thinking in the earlier parts of the *Essays*, a similar role may be attributed to the philosophical writings of the Stoic philosopher Seneca (ca. 50 B.C.E.–40 C.E.), while the way Montaigne handles historical characters testifies to his knowledge of and professed admiration for Plutarch (45 C.E.–ca. 125 C.E.). Montaigne's deep familiarity with an enormous number of other possible "sources" is shown in the very abundance of his quotations from, and his opinions on, a wide range of writers. Naturally his most obvious source remains the observation of life and of himself.

Classroom Strategies

Readers new to Montaigne may be disturbed by the large number of quotations from texts with which they are unacquainted. The best way to cope with this reaction is to demonstrate the fitness of the quotation to its context. It should also be remembered that the passages Montaigne quotes were as familiar and commonplace to him as proverbs; memorizing well-turned sentiments from the classics was a normal school exercise at the time, and keeping a notebook of striking aphorisms was the habit of every educated adult male. The quotations supply a further coloring of universality to Montaigne's themes, most of which belong to all times and are demonstrably still very much with us—the relativity of the ideas of civilized and uncivilized behavior; the position of man in an ever more widely explored and yet mysterious universe; the complex, self-contradictory nature of human intelligence; and so on.

Analysis of Montaigne's texts also offers good ground for the discussion of literary style. Montaigne's great influence is due not only to his subject matter but also to his "tone of voice," the gait of his prose, and his tempered, ironical manner, which is both detached and yet very personal. It is an influence that extends even to such writings of our own day as the newspaper feature article and syndicated column, but no contemporary journalist has the range of reference and the elliptical intelligence that particularly distinguish these essays. *Of Coaches* offers an excellent opportunity for classroom analysis; ask your students to outline Montaigne's arguments here, noting especially the way the titular coaches appear, vanish, and then suddenly draw the essay together in its concluding paragraph.

Topics for Discussion and Writing

1. Granted that it is impossible to extract from Montaigne's view of the world a well-organized philosophical "system," examine closely the meanings he attaches to any one of the following: nature, reason, justice, courage.

2. Montaigne writes of the "disorders of our poor country" and elsewhere states that "it is no slight pleasure to feel oneself preserved from the contagion of so depraved an age." Our present world can hardly be seen as free from tumultuousness and corruption. Discuss whether, and to what degree, Montaigne's position as we deduce it from our readings and from the main elements of his life, would be conceivable and morally justifiable in our own age.

3. Discuss the quotation as a rhetorical device to support an argument and give it authority. Examine five to ten particular quotations in Montaigne and discuss their effect. What examples can you think of in electoral oratory of our own day in which references to respected national figures of the past and quotations from their utterances are used for similar objectives? Discuss, of course, differences as well.

4. Examine Montaigne's attitude toward scientific discoveries and the idea of progress. Make possible comparisons with Rabelais's notions of the betterment of humankind through education.

Comparative Perspectives

1. In urging caution when we presume to judge others, Montaigne offers an important critique of the comparative method of thought. Explain the sensitivity he shows to cultural difference in *Of Cannibals* and the significance of noting that we "are all of patchwork" in *Of the Inconsistency of Our Actions*. Can you think of any occasions

during this semester's reading when either of these essays would have been a useful critical guide?

2. Augustine's *Confessions* is the first autobiographical work of the Western world. Montaigne, in *To the Reader*, declares, "I am myself the matter of my book." Yet his *Essays* are not autobiographical. Examine his reasons for writing and compare them to Augustine's.

3. Ovid was an early favorite of Montaigne's, and a line from the *Metamorphoses* caps a discussion of spontaneous sex change in *On the Power of the Imagination*. Discuss the psychological insights that this essay provides into the nature of sexuality, comparing and contrasting them with fictional examples in Ovid, Ariosto, or other writers whose work you have studied this term.

Further Reading

See also the reading suggestions in the *Anthology*, p. 2646.

Bencivenga, Ermanno. *The Discipline of Subjectivity: an Essay on Montaigne.* 1990. By a philosopher specializing in language analysis.

Cruickshank, John, ed. *French Literature and Its Background.* Vol. I. 1968. One chapter, by C. R. Baxter, is dedicated to Montaigne.

McGowan, Margaret M. *Montaigne's Deceits: The Art of Persuasion in the Essays.* 1974. By a student of French Renaissance aesthetics and rhetoric.

Sayce, R. A. *The Essays of Montaigne: A Critical Exploration.* 1972. A thorough, detailed analysis, with quotations in French.

MIGUEL DE CERVANTES

Don Quixote

Backgrounds

Don Quixote is divided into two parts (the first of fifty-two chapters, the second of seventy-four), published separately with an interval of ten years between. Like *Gargantua and Pantagruel, Don Quixote* mixes realism and fantasy, but with the obvious difference that the fantasy is not here external but located in the mind of the hero. He is an impoverished gentleman who owns a small country estate in the Spanish province of La Mancha. As the whole world today knows from the innumerable films, plays, paintings, and sculptures inspired by his story, he is so infatuated with the reading of romances of chivalry and particularly with the image of the knight-errant and his code—heroic adventurousness, helpful generosity toward the weak and the needy, the service of justice, acts of valor for valor's sake and as an offering to a beloved lady—that he decides to equip himself in the proper manner and single-handedly revive the profession of knight-errantry. Quixote's spear and shield are old relics, his horse is the lean nag Rozinante; he leaves home at dawn, unnoticed, through a secret door. To complete his credentials as a knight-

errant he chooses for the object of his devotion a peasant girl, whom his
imagination transforms into the Lady Dulcinea del Toboso. Stopping at
an inn, which he sees as a castle, he compels the crooked innkeeper, in
a scene accompanied by much jesting and slapstick comedy, to dub him
knight.

After he leaves the inn, Don Quixote's first actions are his pathetically
futile defense of a farm boy being lashed by his master, and his unsuccessful attempt to force a group of merchants from Toledo to perform an
act of faith, that is, to swear to the incomparable beauty of Dulcinea
without having seen her. In the ensuing brawl Quixote is unhorsed and
badly mangled. A fellow villager finds him in this condition and takes
him back home on a donkey (chapters 1–5). Since Quixote's troubles are
attributed to his mad infatuation with the chivalry books in his library,
the local curate and barber proceed to burn them; but this proves to be
a futile action, for he resumes his wanderings (chapter 7), now with his
newly appointed squire, Sancho Panza. Their first adventure—probably
the most famous of them all—is a fight against windmills, which
Quixote declares to be giants; their second, an encounter with two
Benedictine monks on their mules, whom Quixote sees as enchanters
abducting a lady. The consequent scuffles culminate in Quixote's battle
with a choleric attendant in the lady's retinue (chapters 8–9).

After the significant exchanges between Quixote and his squire in
chapter 10, chapters 11–17 (15–17 not in the *Anthology*) take us to a
pastoral world. There follow some of the more legendary Quixotic exploits: the attack on a flock of sheep, which the Don sees as an enemy
army, and the disastrous effort to liberate a chain of galley slaves (chapters 18 and 22).

Chapters 23 through 32 (not in the *Anthology*) are the Sierra Morena
chapters. In that region of woods and forests Quixote decides to spend a
period of retirement and penance, in imitation of his knightly models;
from there he dispatches Sancho to his lady Dulcinea with a letter for
her. The squire never delivers the letter but returns to the Sierra Morena
with the curate and the barber, their aim of course being to bring the
Knight of the Mournful Countenance back to his senses and his home.
In the interval between departure from Sierra Morena and return to the
village, they spend a period, long and full of incidents (chapters 32–46,
not in the *Anthology*), at the place they had left in chapter 17, the
inn/castle of which Sancho has dire memories.

Both the Sierra Morena and the inn sequences are enriched by exemplary cases of romantically difficult loves, presented through the technique of the story-within-the-story, of which Cervantes originated the
fashion. In the intimate setting of the inn, the intricate vicissitudes
of the two major couples—Cardenio and Lucinda, Fernando and
Dorotea—have their happy endings. Their connection with the main
Quixote plot is made through the character of the beautiful Dorotea,
who on the urging of the curate and the barber has persuaded Quixote
to leave Sierra Morena and return to the inn—to him an enchanted castle—by playing the part of Princess Micomicona, a "damsel in distress."

To the outside world (when Quixote and Sancho are in danger of arrest for their attempt to liberate the slaves) Quixote's rescuers use as a plea his insanity, but in dealing with him they use his own visionary notions and convince him that he is himself the victim of enchantments as they carry him back to his village (chapter 52, the last of Part I). Of the curate's and the barber's two aims—to bring Quixote home and to "cure" him—the first has been achieved, but not the second.

The most important thing that happens to Quixote and Sancho at the beginning of Part II is the realization that their adventures have been narrated in a book. Quixote, of course, is not cured (in the first chapter of Part II he has declared to the curate and the barber: "A knight-errant I shall live and die"), nor is Sancho less desirous of becoming "governor of an island," as his master has promised him. It is Sancho who tells Quixote that they have been put into a book, the source of that information being the young Sansón Carrasco, just back from the University of Salamanca, where he has received his bachelor's degree. Chapter 3 is the point at which Cervantes, through Quixote conversing with Carrasco, amiably glorifies the popularity of his book (i.e., Part I) in other countries as well as Spain and debates the objections of the critics as reported by Carrasco.

From chapter 8 on (chapters 8–11 are not in the *Anthology*), the two adventurers are on their way again. In the country around El Toboso, Sancho saves himself from trouble by assuring Quixote that his failure to recognize the beautiful Dulcinea in the country wench confronting him comes from devilish spells and enchantments. As they move on toward Saragossa, there is a troublesome encounter with a company of players in their costumes—strange apparitions including "the Devil"—on their way to a performance of *The Parliament of Death*. The two most memorable encounters follow (chapters 12–17).

The first is with Sansón Carrasco. Carrasco, having joined the ranks of the would-be rescuers of Quixote from his folly, tries to do something decisive about it by meeting Quixote on his own terms: as a knight (first called the "Fearless Knight of the Mirrors," then the "Knight of the Wood"), Carrasco plans to challenge and defeat Quixote in a duel. The plan fails as the Knight of the Wood is himself unhorsed and vanquished by the fury of the mad Don. Quixote's other significant encounter is with a kind, wise gentleman, Don Diego de Miranda, who witnesses Quixote's courage as he provokes a lion to come out of its cage and fight. Appropriately placed after Quixote's victorious interlude, this episode—a pivotal instance of Quixote's idea of gratuitous valor—has a semicomic ending, which is fully balanced by Quixote's speech on "the meaning of valor," one of his most movingly eloquent speeches. Aroused to a puzzled admiration, Don Diego invites Quixote to be his guest. Chapters 19 through 21 (not in the *Anthology*) consist once more of a story-within-the-story. It tells of the planned marriage between the fair Quiteria, loved by the poor shepherd Basilio, and the rich Camacho; on the day of the wedding Quiteria is abducted by Basilio, her true love, much to her delight and with Quixote's wholehearted support.

From this point on, the four main narratives of *Don Quixote*, Part II, treat the hero's descent to the cave of Montesinos (chapters 22–23, not in the *Anthology*); Quixote's and Sancho's long stay at a castle as the guests of a duke and duchess (chapters 30–63, not in the *Anthology*); their stay in Barcelona, the scene of Quixote's last duel and lamentable defeat (chapters 64–65); and the hero's return to his village and his death (chapters 73–74). The peculiar character of the Montesinos sequence is that it is narrated by the hero himself to his incredulous listeners after he has been lifted from the cave; to all appearances it is a dream in which Quixote has been granted visions of ancient kingdoms and of his enchanted Dulcinea. A dreamlike atmosphere also pervades the long scenes at the castle, but now it is a manipulated illusion, the result of theatrical pranks played by the duke and duchess and their retinue of idle jesters on the knight and his squire, who are now famous everywhere for their drolleries. One of the castle scenes concerns Dulcinea: a prankster, dressed as Death and pretending to be the magician Merlin, reveals as the harsh condition of her disenchantment that Sancho must submit to 3,300 lashes, a sentence that of course will never be carried out. Another scene involves Sancho. Conducted, blindfolded, to a nearby village that he supposes to be the island of Barataria, he is given the promised governorship. Sancho's victory consists in the fact that he will prove to be a good "governor," beloved by the villagers. The crucial Barcelona episode (chapters 64–65) is staged by Sansón Carrasco, who turns up in a new disguise as the Knight of the Moon and this time defeats Quixote. The Don, after flirting with the idea of a new life enacting a pastoral play instead of a romance of chivalry, returns to his village to sicken and die (chapters 73–74).

Three literary traditions make their presence felt in *Don Quixote*: the epic or romance of chivalry, the adventure story of the *picaro* or vagabond, and the pastoral narrative of shepherds and their loves. The qualities of the chivalric epic may be sampled by the student in the selections in the *Anthology* from *The Song of Roland*, and those of the chivalric romance in the tales of King Arthur and his knights of the Round Table, especially such episodes of courtly love as that of Tristan and Isolde or that of Lancelot and Guenevere. The latter, it will be recalled, is so moving to Dante's Paolo and Francesca (*Inferno*, canto V) that it inspires their sinful love and leads to their destruction. The two collections of stories—that centering on Roland and his uncle, the great king Charlemagne, and that centering on Arthur—are combined and subjected to new twists in the major Italian Renaissance poems, *Orlando Innamorato* (Orlando in love) by Matteo Maria Boiardo (ca. 1441–1494) and *Orlando Furioso* (Orlando gone mad) by Ludovico Ariosto (1474–1533). Both of these poems were well known to Cervantes, and the latter is possibly the immediate source of the Sierra Morena episode and other passages in *Don Quixote*.

The "picaresque" tradition is named from the *picaro*, the stock rogue-hero of many popular tales dealing with life in the undergrounds of society, where robbers, tramps, and various eccentrics meet. This tradition contributes to the "realistic" or "Sancho" aspects of Cervantes's story. Its major literary formulation is the anonymous novel *Lazarillo de Tormes* (first published in 1554), the influence of which was enormous at the time and indeed may be traced through eighteenth-century English fiction and down to our own time.

As for the pastoral romance, this tradition has its roots in Greek and Roman antiquity from Theocritus to Virgil and flourished during the Renaissance in such works—known to Cervantes and cited by him—as the *Arcadia* of Jacopo Sannazzaro (1457–1530) and most particularly the *Diana* of Jorge de Montemayor (ca. 1520–1561).

What matters for us, of course, is what Cervantes made of these backgrounds: a work so new and absorbing it is impossible to lay it down, and peopled by two creations, Quixote and Sancho, who have become part of our everyday mental furniture.

Classroom Strategies

Our selections from *Don Quixote* are best handled in three assignments. A first can center effectively on the figure of Don Quixote as a blind hero, fool, and ultimately wise fool, with the contributions of successive attitudes to our complex of feelings about him. A second can focus in similar ways on Sancho and his functions in the story. And a third can deal with the nature and development of the relationship between the two.

Analysis and discussion of *Don Quixote* call for some use of the terms "parody" and "satire." Parody is ordinarily a magnification of the characteristics of a particular style to the point at which its absurdity becomes unmistakable—in the case of *Don Quixote*, the inflated highfalutin style of the chivalric romances. Yet apart from the early quotations from Quixote's readings, obviously inserted to parody that style, his own speeches in the course of the story and the general nature of his eloquence move increasingly away from parody toward a speech that registers both his delusion and the idealism that feeds it. The term "satire" is equally inadequate for describing Cervantes's tone. Satire, in its usual sense, aims to expose an object or a person to ridicule and censure with implicit reference to a higher standard of conduct. In Cervantes the case is more complex. The argument can be made, in fact, that Quixote, far from being an object of satire, unconsciously becomes the satirist—of, say, crooked innkeepers or aristocratic pranksters—by exposing their cruelty, childishness, and vulgarity. In addition, and more generally, Cervantes's complex attitude toward the world of medieval chivalry can hardly be considered unmitigated satire. The serious interest and the underlying importance of Quixote's actions and speech can be demonstrated by observing their effect on other characters, particularly Sancho, whose warm response to Quixote's genuine chivalry of heart should correct any tendency to identify the two men with a superficial polarity between idealism and realism.

Topics for Discussion and Writing

Don Quixote is perhaps unparalleled as a starting point for broad discussions of the art of fiction in general and its place in a literate society. Our first three suggestions are along those lines.

1. We may grow attached to a fictional character in such a way that the character becomes a solid point of reference, something "truer than life." Granted that Quixote and other characters in the novel have acquired that kind of "reality," take any number of examples, major and minor, and analyze by the verbal devices Cervantes uses to produce our perception of them. Discussion may be interestingly extended to the differences between our perception of a character in fiction and one on stage or in a film.

2. *Don Quixote* has been and still is held to be "great" literature. Yet one of Cervantes's most respected contemporaries, Lope de Vega, considered it trash. There is evidence of a similar duality of attitude toward the romances of chivalry in Cervantes's time, some readers regarding them with a mixture of overt contempt and secret fascination. Can you think of forms of writing in our own time that are similarly both admired and condemned?

3. What constitutes the hero of a piece of fiction? One way to put it is that he is the one who determines and qualifies the actions and attitudes of the other characters. Show with specific evidence that Quixote is a hero in this sense, examining the characters of Sancho, the curate and the barber, Don Diego de Miranda, Sansón Carrasco.

4. Don Quixote has become a world figure not only as the hero of a celebrated novel but also as one of the main emblems of Spain. Discuss ways in which he can be compared, in his popularity and representativeness, to heroes of ancient epics on the one hand and to modern heroes of fiction, film, and comics on the other.

5. Take the passage in part I, chapter 4, where Don Quixote confronts the merchants from Toledo; the general effect of the episode may be comic or pathetic, yet the underlying pattern of Quixote's speech is nothing less than the theological virtue of Faith. Choose and analyze other passages of Quixote's eloquence where serious concepts raise an apparently comic situation to importance and significance (e.g., the concept of valor in II, 17).

6. Quixote has been described as the most "autonomous" character in literature—a supreme example of the phenomenon by which a fictional character acquires a life of its own, independent of its inventor. See how this paradoxical situation is consciously dealt with by Cervantes, not only in the first selection from part II, but more generally in the way in which the narrator "reports" on his hero to the reader.

Comparative Perspectives

1. *Don Quixote* is the supreme example of the attachment to books exhibited in so many of the Renaissance texts in the *Anthology*. How do writers as different as (to name only a few) Montaigne and Cervantes and Milton turn their reading into original forms that then in turn became reading matter for others? How would you compare the concerns of these hyperliterary eras with those of earlier, essentially oral cultures?

2. Discuss episodes in your own experience that suggest how much of the way we feel—or think we ought to feel—derives from what we read (or see on television or in the movies). In societies like ours, heavily influenced by the media that are the contemporary equivalent of the books that drove Don Quixote, can we have "authentic" emotions? (What makes Don Quixote need to challenge so many of the people he meets to a duel: what is the source of his "violent behavior?")

Further Reading

See also the reading suggestions in the *Anthology*, p. 2645.

Bjornson, Richard, ed. *Approaches to Teaching Don Quixote*. 1984. Contains background, critical appraisals by various expert hands.

Brenan, Gerald. *The Literature of the Spanish People*. 1951. Chapter VIII is devoted to Cervantes's life and works. Brenan, who is not only a renowned scholar but also a brilliant writer, has a vast knowledge of Spanish culture.

Madariaga, Salvador de. *Don Quixote: An Introductory Essay in Psychology*. 1961. A famous view of the novel, by an outstanding Spanish writer.

Mann, Thomas. *Cervantes, Goethe, Freud*. 1943. Individual appraisals by one of the major fiction writers and essayists of the twentieth century.

Nelson, Lowry, Jr., ed. *Cervantes: A Collection of Critical Essays*. 1969. Besides Nelson's enlightening introduction, includes two essays by authors of great literary stature: Thomas Mann ("Voyage with Don Quixote") and W. H. Auden ("The Ironic Hero: Some Reflections on Don Quixote"). Also includes essays by some of the most outstanding literary critics: Harry Levin ("The Example of Cervantes"), Leo Spitzer ("On the Significance of Don Quixote"), and Erich Auerbach ("The Enchanted Dulcinea").

Predmore, Richard L. *The World of Don Quixote*. 1967.

Riley, E. D. *Cervantes' Theory of the Novel*. 1962.

Unamuno, Miguel de. *The Life of Don Quixote and Sancho According to Miguel de Cervantes Saavedra*. Trans. Homer P. Earle. 1927. (Originally published 1905.) A famous view of the novel, by an outstanding Spanish writer.

LOPE DE VEGA

Fuente Ovejuna

Classroom Strategies and Topics for Discussion

One excellent way to begin your discussion is to ask about the title of this play. Why is *Fuente Ovejuna* not called by the name of its protagonist; or is it? Lope de Vega's emphasis on the community rather than on a single outsized hero anticipates a trend that will become increasingly common, and you may want to ask your students to name some post-seventeenth-century plays that they have read or seen. Like *The Cherry Orchard* or *Six Characters in Search of an Author*, *Fuente Ovejuna* has an idea rather than a person at its center.

Before exploring the play itself in detail, it's helpful to look at its broad outlines in order to contrast classical and Renaissance drama. The theaters of Elizabethan England and Golden Age Spain had neither proscenium arches nor architecturally defined backdrops. Eschewing the palace façade and altar of the ancient Greek theater, or the street scene of Roman comedy, Lope (like Shakespeare) confidently shifts the action back and forth from country to city, from royal palace to public square. Verbal clues and portable props suffice to indicate the scene. The resulting juxtapositions encourage audiences to recognize parallels in apparently unlinked situations, a device that typifies popular Renaissance drama.

Although Lope does not observe the classical unities, the structure of *Fuente Ovejuna* deserves attention for its economy. Character is firmly established, but often quite allusively, in fleeting strokes to which you will want to call your students' attention. The dominant figure in the play is the villain, Guzmán, and like Shakespeare's Iago, he sets the terms of the action. Lope begins by focusing on Guzmán's self-serving disquisition on courtesy. Putting the spotlight on the Comendador's multifarious discourtesies, made immediately perceptible in the short, swiftly shifting scenes of this three-act play, shows that he is unfit to rule. You might point particularly to the momentum against the Comendador's power that builds throughout Act II: in one scene, set in Esteban the mayor's house, we see the Comendador "lose" Laurencia to Frondoso; in the next, set in a meadow, we learn that the Order of Calatrava loses Ciudad Real to Ferdinand and Isabella. The act ends as Guzmán reasserts himself by violating agreements that bind persons together: he arrests the groom as his marriage is performed, he wrests the mayor's staff from his hands, and it looks as if he has won.

This pitting of the one against the many defines the pace and emphasis of *Fuente Ovejuna*; capitalizing on the point made in a consideration of the play's title, you may wish to contrast Lope's celebration of community with Shakespeare's dramatic focus, in *Hamlet*, on a singular tragic hero. In *Fuente Ovejuna*, the public backdrop against which personal strife stands out in both cases reflects a crucial historical moment. Europe's obsessive struggle with Islam took a significant turn with the unifying rule of Ferdinand and Isabella: in 1492, under their leadership, the Moors (and the Jews) were expelled from Spain. By the time in which the play is set (1476), the Order founded in 1158 to defend Calatrava from Moorish incursions had become an outlaw power, personified by Fernan Gomez de Guzmán. The Moors are no longer the real enemies. Flores, the more cynical of the Comendador's servants, dryly mentions that men in Holy Orders, "if they wear the Cross upon their breast, they are obliged, though they be friars, to take up arms against the Moorish infidel." For Guzmán, the cross is an occasion for shedding, rather than a symbol of, innocent blood (see his inciting of the young Maestre to fight, ll. 48–102). He is in fact an infidel.

You might have students enumerate the many references to his barbarity: he is compared to pagan tyrants like Heliogabalus and corrupts the good; witness his transforming the medically useful enema into an instrument of pain. Make sure that your students understand that Guzmán is not simply a gallant womanizer, as his inventory of women may lead the casual reader to believe. When he brags of compelling "Pedro Redondo's wife" to surrender to him, we may initially think he has artfully charmed a good woman in the manner of Don Juan; but he later says to her, "You shan't be mine. You shall become my soldiers' baggages," and he turns her over to the soldiers' bestial treatment.

Given the villain's sordid brutality, your students may wonder why *Fuente Ovejuna* is, as the headnote points out, a comedy. Explain that this generic distinction is based not on the evidence of a laugh meter but on the outcome of events; Dante, too, wrote a "comedy." The offstage rape and torture of peasants are graphically represented; indeed, whether Laurencia herself has been raped remains problematic. Certainly her shocking entrance, "disheveled," a conventional stage sign of madness and disgrace, along with the great diatribe against the men, whom she calls "timid hares" and "clucking hens," who have failed to protect their women, leads the audience to assume the worst. One measure of the play's comic status is the relief that comes at the final moment, when Frondoso praises Laurencia to Ferdinand and Isabella, saying that she "fought him [Guzmán] off and showed how virtuous she is." If some of your more skeptical students wonder whether we should believe what Laurencia has told Frondoso, so much the better—skillful actors can easily suggest that Laurencia has told Frondoso a face-saving lie. Mulling over the question, you can lead your students to the conclusion that in comedy, characters get on with their lives, however they can.

Such doubts notwithstanding, Lope is sophisticated enough to imply that true purity transcends physical assault. In its pastoral setting and its treatment of the progress of its central couple's love, *Fuente Ovejuna* draws on many traditional features of romantic comedy. Indeed, the strength of Laurencia's and Frondoso's union is clearly proposed as a match for that of Ferdinand and Isabella themselves, who are actually represented on stage. Daringly, the echo of Laurencia's query "Is that the King and Queen?" by Isabella's "Are these the villains?" at least momentarily equates the peasant lovers with the royal pair. The dialogue between Frondoso and Laurencia has a cleansing effect on *Fuente Ovejuna*, and in their early exchanges they conduct a merry war somewhat in the style of Shakespeare's Beatrice and Benedict. Students will recognize in their initial gambits a standard model for romantic comedy, for Hollywood as well as for Renaissance playwrights: boy loves girl, girl insults boy, boy wins girl with one heroic gesture.

They, and several of the other rustic characters in this play named for a village, command a rather exalted rhetoric. This marks them as traditional pastoral lovers in a traditional pastoral setting (you can remind your students that Fuente Ovejuna means Sheepwell—as "pastor" means shepherd). If you have read *Orlando Furioso*, recall the obsessive carving of "Medor" and "Angelica" on the bark of trees. This is a textbook illustration of the absurd attribution of poetic inspiration to woodland lovers that gives pastoral romance so much of its fantasy and charm. In her first long speech, Laurencia, promoter of linguistic probity and delicacy of expression, makes the authenticity of simple cuisine a metaphor for the decent life. When Frondoso joins the scene, he deplores the meretricious language of false courtesy ("Nowadays your schoolboy's called a graduate, your blind as a bat, myopic; your cross-eyed man has just a squint"). In her riposte, Laurencia exposes the opposite fault, a language that scorns virtue: "Be constant and they call you boring, . . . be kind and you're a hypocrite, a Christian's someone seeking favor."

Among these curiously eloquent peasants is Mengo, an important character who may be a bit difficult for your students to place. In examining his role, reassure students who have had problems understanding him—in a staged performance, Mengo is precisely the kind of figure who comes alive, who does not need explanation because a good actor, well costumed, embodies his whole nature. Reconstructing his pastoral credentials from the details scattered through the printed text, ask your students why he values his boxwood rebec more than a barn. This piece of information virtually defines Mengo as a pastoral icon, the shepherd who loves music and philosophy (although he disclaims the title of philosopher). At the first, in witty dialogue with the play's two principal women, he reduces love to self-interest:

> MENGO. I'm no philosopher and, more's
> The pity, I can't read. But if
> The elements are always in
> A state of war, and our bodies—blood,
> Phlegm, melancholy, choler—draw
> Their sustenance from them—where
> Is love?
>
> PASCUALA.   So what's the point
> You want to make?
> MENGO .   That we love ourselves
> And no one else.

By the play's end, as he triumphs over his torturers, Mengo's self-abnegating courage disproves his defense of self-interest. Experience, as opposed to theory, shows that individuals can love their community more than themselves.

Fuente Ovejuna further defines its pastoralism by giving dramatic form to a variety of traditional metaphors, most markedly by turning that staple of love poetry, the hunt for the deer, into the crisis that brings Act I to a stunning conclusion. When Frondoso takes up the Comendador's bow, he not only defends the hunter's quarry, Laurencia, but he directly challenges both the masculinity and the rank of a dangerous opponent. Act II begins with a contrasting scene of communal life in which the mayor and the village scholar, in separate conversations, seem to digress on the wisdom of simplicity. You will want your students to see, however, that in denigrating the pompous pronouncements of "these forecasters who, knowing nothing, claim that they can tell the future" and inveighing against the flood of false learning generated by the new invention of "a German, a certain Gutenberg from Mainz," Esteban and Leonelo are actually continuing Frondoso's attack on those who abuse positions of authority. This is another instance of how Lope uses scenic juxtapositions to link expressions of personal concern to the social, political, and religious issues they mirror.

Finally, as always when teaching a play, ask your students to think about what performance would add to the literary text. The many songs, some of them actual popular ballads of Lope's day, are choral efforts; what is the impact on an audience of the sound of massed voices? How do these songs give auditory force to the central thematic idea of *Fuente Ovejuna*, that proverbial site of human solidarity? Similarly, have your students imagine the visual power of the various flags displayed on stage, from the defiled red cross to the improvised banners of the rebellious villagers, braver than any "Cid or Rodomonte," to the scutcheon with the royal arms of Aragon and Castile. The shapes and colors of these physical signs help define the location of the action; their content bespeaks the seriousness of the comedy of *Fuente Ovejuna*.

Topics for Writing

1. What is the importance of Mengo, Jacinta, and Pascuala—the figures who really suffer in the play?
2. Where do you see signs that Lope has incorporated literary conventions and/or folk material into staged drama? How do these elements enrich the dramatic power of the play?
3. Are Frondoso and Laurencia overidealized? Why does Lope give a peasant woman a love sonnet to speak?

Comparative Perspectives

1. Contrast the heroic ideals embodied in "Cid or Rodomonte" with the kind of heroism demonstrated in *Fuente Ovejuna*.
   [Perhaps especially fruitful for classes that have read *Orlando*

Furioso as well as a serious heroic work like *The Song of Roland*, or a skeptical review of the tradition like *Don Quixote*.]

2. In *Lysistrata*, Aristophanes finds comedy in a women's revolt against men and warlike Establishment values; compare and contrast the treatment of women and the power of the disenfranchised in *Fuente Ovejuna*.

3. In comparing Guzmán to Heliogabalus, Lope joins the many Renaissance writers who draw on their knowledge of the ancient world to veil or justify their criticism of contemporary political wrongs. In *Of Coaches*, for example, Montaigne slides from a depiction of Heliogabalus in his coach to a general reflection on the "pusillanimity in monarchs, and evidence of not sufficiently feeling what they are, to labor at showing off and making a display by excessive expense." Discuss the conclusion of Lope de Vega's play in these terms: does the murder of Guzmán solve the larger political problems that *Fuente Ovejuna* uncovers? How does Lope's attitude toward the relationship between rulers and those they rule compare to, say, that of Montaigne in the passage referred to above, or of Machiavelli in "The Roman Dream," at the conclusion of *The Prince*?

Further Reading

See also the reading suggestions in the *Anthology*, p. 2645.

Yarbo-Bejerano, Yvonne. *Feminism and the Honor Plays of Lope de Vega.* 1994. Interesting comments on "the construction of gender" in Laurencia's scornful Act III speech to the men who have abandoned their masculinity.

WILLIAM SHAKESPEARE

Hamlet, Prince of Denmark

Backgrounds

Hamlet, Prince of Denmark—even in the title the play's hero is presented within the framework of a country and a royal court. He is, in fact, the most eminent member of that court; and the court as a setting and organizing structure is as typical of Renaissance drama as of the drama of antiquity. In *Hamlet* we soon realize that this setting is not a Denmark remote and medieval, but a modern state, of the kind described and studied by such political writers as Machiavelli; and that this kingdom is undergoing a crisis caused by inner corruption and foreign threats.

The previous king of Denmark—Hamlet was his name, too—has been assassinated by his brother Claudius, who has inherited the throne (through a partly elective procedure) and married his brother's widow—his sister-in-law, Gertrude. In certain social codes, one of which Prince Hamlet obviously accepts, this is marriage within the forbidden degrees—is, in short, incest. But there is also trouble from without. On the ramparts of the castle at Elsinore, sentinels stand guard against a foreign threat of invasion, embodied in Fortinbras, prince of Norway. The ghost of the murdered king appears there, seeking to be avenged. Hamlet promises to obey, and while seeking evidence that the apparition was in fact his father's ghost and spoke truth, puts on an appearance of insanity to avoid suspicion that he may be planning to kill the king. For the time being the court interpretation of his insanity is that its cause is love for Ophelia, daughter of the lord chamberlain Polonius. Hamlet "loved" Ophelia "once" but now treats her with cruel sarcasm.

When a group of traveling players visits Elsinore, Hamlet devises a plan, his "mousetrap": he has the actors perform a play, *The Murder of Gonzago*, about a royal fratricide similar to the one committed by Claudius, and Claudius's visible reaction when he sees it performed confirms the ghost's truthfulness. In an immediately following scene with his mother, whom he accuses of complicity in the murder, Hamlet suddenly suspects that the king may be listening behind a curtain. Actually it is Polonius; and when Hamlet thrusts his sword through the curtain Polonius is killed. The king, now aware of danger, sends Hamlet on a mission to England accompanied by two courtiers, Rosencrantz and Guildenstern, with the instruction that he be executed there. By a ruse, Hamlet turns the king's trick back on to Rosencrantz and Guildenstern, and returns to Denmark to complete his mission as avenger of his father's death. There, soon after, he encounters the funeral cortege of Ophelia who has gone mad and drowned herself. Her death and Polonius's bring Laertes (her brother and Polonius's son) back to Denmark on a similar avenging errand. An elaborate show is planned—a sort of counterpart to Hamlet's "mousetrap," but more complex and devastating—by the king and Laertes, allied in their desire to liquidate Hamlet. Laertes will challenge Hamlet to a duel in which they will fight as if in sport, but secretly the point of Laertes's foil will be poisoned. A cup of poison to be administered when Hamlet is thirsty will also be ready as a possible last resort. During their encounter Hamlet is hit and thus mortally wounded, but by an exchange of weapons manages to give Laertes a mortal wound also. The queen in ignorance of the plot drinks from the poisoned cup. Laertes, dying, confesses his and the king's plot to Hamlet, and Hamlet kills the king. In his own dying speech he urges his friend Horatio to live on to report truthfully on the past tragic events and gives his vote to Fortinbras for the succession to the throne.

Hamlet constitutes all by itself an important area of Elizabethan scholarship, but the main lines of what we know about its sources and composition are relatively clear. The plot of *Hamlet* originates in the account given of Prince "Amleth" in Books III and IV of the *Danish History* (*Historia Danica*) written by the Danish chronicler Saxo in the late twelfth century and first printed in 1514. The story reappears in Book V of *Tragic Histories* (*Histories Tragiques*) by the French historian François de Belleforest (1530–1583), first printed in 1576. In all probability Shakespeare knew neither of these two sources—the *Hystorie of Hamlet*, an English adaptation of Belleforest, was published only in 1608, and indeed seems to have been influenced by Shakespeare's play rather than vice versa. What Shakespeare did know was an earlier play on the same subject, now lost, but mentioned in several places, including the *Diary* of Philip Henslowe, the most important theatrical manager of the time. That play was being performed during the late 1580s and early 1590s. The likelihood is strong that its author was Thomas Kyd, whose *Spanish Tragedy* (first printed in 1594) is the best-known example of what was then a very popular genre, the "revenge play." Of course, the starting point of any class study of *Hamlet* should be to consider how far it surpasses the simple idea of a "revenge play."

Classroom Strategies

One profitable strategy is to trace the aspect of mystery that Shakespeare seems to have built into the play—its riddling language, its continual questions, the obscure motivations of the characters (why *does* Hamlet chide himself for delaying? how much does the queen know? on what account does Ophelia go mad and drown?)—from its first words ("who's there?") to its last. Does this stress on mystery affect your response to the play? If so, how?

Useful too is consideration of the range of idioms in the play: those of the soldiers on guard; of the ghost; of Claudius; of the Player King and Queen; of Ophelia in madness; of the queen in describing Ophelia's death; of Osric; of the grave-diggers; of Hamlet. What suggestion do we find that Hamlet speaks all these idioms, and how does this affect our estimate of him? Hamlet praises Horatio for being steadier than he—but would one choose to be Horatio rather than Hamlet? Why and why not?

A third and most important strategy is to avoid putting all the emphasis in class discussion on the motivation of the prince. The play bristles with an exciting variety of incident, mood, imagery, and (as noted above) personalities depicted through their speech. The surest way to bring out these qualities is to ask successive teams of students to read aloud, or even try to act out a few of the multitude of encounters and confrontations that the play provides.

Topics for Discussion and Writing

1. Compare the character of Polonius—his behavior and speech—to that of the ideal courtier, and of the dialoguing courtiers "forming him with words" in Castiglione's book. Do likewise for Osric.
2. Consider Hamlet's "antic disposition" in the light of the themes of folly and madness in Erasmus and Cervantes.
3. Hamlet has been described (by Rebecca West) as a "bad man," and it has been argued that he is even more of a politician than the king, his uncle. Drawing specific evidence from the play, do your best to support this proposition. Then, again using specific evidence, do your best to refute it.
4. Imagine yourself a director and then describe as accurately as you can your ideal handling of the play's opening scene. Or of the

closet scene between Hamlet and his mother (III.4). Consider especially what you wish the scene to contribute to the tone and effect of the play as a whole.

Comparative Perspectives

1. Compare the character of Polonius—his behavior, speech, and position of power in Claudius's court—to that of the ideal courtier in Castiglione's book. Compare his use of his daughter to that of Genji's father-in-law in *The Tale of Genji*, or to the Vizier's in *The Thousand and One Nights* (as appropriate).
2. Compare Osric to the ideal courtier in Castiglione's book, and imagine his type in some of the different courts you have read about. How would Sei Shōnagon react to an Osric figure?
3. In an essay called "Shakespeare in the Bush," the anthropologist Laura Bohannan describes her frustration when she attempts to explain the plot of *Hamlet* to a group of West African elders who challenge at every turn the cultural assumptions that govern Hamlet's despair. For example, they approve Claudius for having the good sense to marry Gertrude: "In our country also, the younger brother marries the elder brother's widow and becomes the father of his children." What else that disgusts Hamlet might seem quite normal in other cultural milieux?
4. Distinguish between the motives that impel the ghost of Hamlet's father and those that create the demons and ghosts of Japanese literature and drama. What do the differences suggest about the deepest fears within the cultures?

   [Japanese ghosts and demons tend to represent passions that the society works hard to repress. They intrude upon a world that seems orderly and ordinary. *Hamlet*, by contrast, opens in a state of terror—"Who's there?"—and the ghost's appearance only confirms the sense of dislocation with which the play begins. Old Hamlet's ghost, a Senecan convention, has a political and a domestic agenda intended to restore rather than ravage the status quo.]

Further Reading

See also the reading suggestions in the *Anthology*, p. 2646.

Aldus, P. J. *Mousetrap: Structure and Meaning in* Hamlet. 1977. With bibliographical note. An analysis of Shakespeare's tragedy as literary myth, focusing on "Aristotelian criticism of dramatic structure" and Platonic concepts of metaphoric form in literary myth.

Bloom, Edward A., ed. *Shakespeare 1564–1964: A Collection of Essays by Various Hands*. 1964. Seventeen essays, including two on *Hamlet* and one on Shakespeare criticism from 1900 to 1964.

Cohen, Michel. Hamlet *in My Mind's Eye*. 1989. This deals also with a production of the play.

Gatti, Hilary. *The Renaissance Drama of Knowledge*. 1989. Chapter 4 is on *Hamlet*.

Harbage, Alfred. *William Shakespeare: A Reader's Guide*. 1971. A guide to Shakespeare's language, verse, and style. Works are described chronologically, scene by scene, followed by a brief analysis of each.

Hoy, Cyrus, ed. *Hamlet*. A Norton Critical Edition, Second Edition. 1992. Contains sections on the text of *Hamlet*, intellectual backgrounds, sources, and essays in criticism. With notes and bibliography.

Knight, G. Wilson. *The Wheel of Fire*. Revised 1948. The section on *Hamlet* ("The Embassy of Death") is well-known for its "positive interpretation" of the character of the king.

Wilson, John Dover. *What Happens in* Hamlet. 1959.

TRAVEL AND DISCOVERY

Backgrounds

In a book about Mandeville, Columbus, Cortés, Díaz, and others, Stephen Greenblatt asserts, "The authors . . . were liars—few of them *steady* liars, as it were, like Mandeville, but frequent and cunning liars none the less, whose position virtually required the strategic manipulation and distortion and outright suppression of the truth" (7). The question of veracity is one that students will doubtless find interesting as they read these narratives. How plausible is Alvise Da Mosta's depiction of the silent trade in Mali? What discrepancies do we notice in Cortés's and Díaz's depictions of the conquistadors' dealings with the Aztecs? Las Casas's passionate protest against the Spanish treatment of New World natives will—and should—color the students' perception of the accounts of Columbus, Cortés, and Díaz. Especially after they have read the entire cluster, students may have questions about the overt and implied contradictions in these accounts.

To delve deeper into the question of truth, one might ask why the explorers and conquistadors found it necessary to lie. What does Greenblatt mean when he asserts that their position *required* that they manipulate, distort, and suppress the truth? Ask students to consider the audience for these accounts and the ostensible purpose for the Europeans' presence in Africa, the Caribbean, the Americas. Christopher Columbus's celebrated letter, though we are not certain of the intended recipient, seems aimed at those who might have a vested interest in his voyage. The letter itself was quickly disseminated throughout Europe, appearing in print in eleven different editions in 1493. One Latin translation of the letter, published in Rome in 1493, identifies the original recipient as King Ferdinand's treasurer, Raphael Sanxis, suggesting that the general intended audience was Ferdinand's court. Keeping in mind the audience, ask students to discuss how the details of Columbus's narrative characterize his purpose and his success. In the first paragraph he

says of the Caribbean islands he found, "of them all I have taken possession for their highnesses." Later he will advertise his own good treatment of the natives, asserting that he "gave [the natives] a thousand
handsome good things," by which he hoped they would "conceive affection" and "might become Christians." Yet in the same breath he also acknowledges his hope that they "might be inclined to the love and service
of their highnesses and of the whole Castilian nation." Las Casas says
that the Spanish are motivated by pure greed, yet Cortés writes about
his desire to turn the Aztecs away from idolatry as well as his aim of obtaining the Aztec loyalty to the Spanish monarchs. Cortés's own motives
were complex, since he had not originally been sent into the Aztec Empire by the Spanish king but rather by Diego Velásques, the Spanish governor of Cuba, against whom he in effect rebelled. Cortés wanted and
needed support from the Spanish crown for his independent decision to
attempt a full conquest of Mexico. A good classroom strategy is to ask
your students to identify both the implied audience for these accounts
and the motives the writers impute to themselves, as well as reflecting
on how we, a twenty-first century audience, might respond differently
from the original readership.

As the introduction asserts, the discovery and exploration of the New
World changed forever Europeans' self-concept. Many of these accounts
reveal a fascination with the order of things. Hierarchies and boundaries
fundamental to the worldview of Europeans of the Middle Ages and Renaissance were sometimes challenged by what the explorers found. In
his fantastic description of the world, Mandeville is deeply concerned
with violations of the boundaries that for Europeans define categories
such as male and female, human and animal, even the category of kin or
family. So in his *Travels* Mandeville describes Amazonia, a mythical land
of "Feminye" that is "all women and no man," where men's traditional
roles as governors, warriors, even sexual pursuers, are all taken by
women. An even more radical undermining of gender boundaries can be
found in Mandeville's description of the "folk that be both man and
woman." Boundaries between human and animal are shaken by his account of folk with horses' feet or people with animal skins and feathers
who go upon their hands and feet "as beasts." Even the bond of kinship,
regarded as basic and "natural" by Europeans, is revised in Mandeville's
story of the cannibals who kill and eat their own family members. An interesting classroom strategy might be to compare Mandeville's entirely
fictitious account with Columbus's real one. Columbus remarks that he
has not found the human "monstrosities" he expected, yet he goes on to
repeat reports of an Amazonian society and an island peopled by ferocious cannibals. Since he has not actually witnessed these phenomena,
why does he mention them? Hans Staden's story of capture by actual
cannibals makes for an interesting contrast with Mandeville's and
Columbus's accounts of reported cannibals. Staden's captors, cannibals
though they may be, display responses and attitudes (often humorous
ones) that seem much more recognizable than those of some of the Europeans depicted in these stories.

When reading these histories, your students should also consider the important role played by religion, both that of Europeans and that of native peoples. Ask students to respond to Cortés's attempt to appropriate Aztec temples for Christian worship. Cortés reports Montezuma's response very blandly. Here's an instance where we might doubt the truth of his account, especially given what we know about the absolute centrality of religion to Aztec life.

Knowing something about the history of European contact with these new worlds and about the cultures they describe is imperative for teaching this unit. For example, Da Mosto's role as an explorer for Henry the Navigator must be understood by students in its larger context in order for them to recognize the historical importance of his account. Da Mosto's exploration of West Africa in the second half of the fifteenth century was part of Portugal's early efforts in West Africa that led eventually to a heavy slave trade in that region. Though the earliest Portuguese explorers were interested in gold (an interest reflected in Da Mosto's narrative), they quickly discovered the profit to be made in trading and transporting slaves. The first African slaves were brought to Prince Henry in 1441; within a hundred years thousands of African slaves were being sold annually in the slave market of Lisbon. The island of Cape Verde that Da Mosto "discovered" became a Portuguese base for receiving slaves from mainland Africa. The long history of Portuguese involvement in West Africa, of which Da Mosto's account is one early voice, had devastating repercussions for much of that region. The history of the Spanish conquistadors' activities in Latin America, and the history of the English Jamestown colony are similarly important to a full appreciation of the texts in this section.

Both the texts themselves and the larger histories toward which they gesture often challenge our received notions of these events. Your students are likely to be familiar with an idealized version of Christopher Columbus's "discovery" of America, for example. They are also likely to know children's versions of the story of Pocahontas (from Disney) and even perhaps have seen the animated *Road to El Dorado* (2000) and its version of the history of the conquistadors. One classroom activity you could use would be to have your students reflect (in writing or aloud) on their impressions of, say, the Pocahontas story, before they read Captain John Smith's narrative. You can augment the rather brief selection from Smith with other related historical texts: William Strachey's accounts of the Jamestown settlement that make mention of the ongoing hostilities with the Algonquin Indians; even Smith's epitaph, which offers a radically different view of his relationship with Pocahontas's father Powhatan and the Algonquins than we are accustomed to by recounting how Smith "made those heathen flee, like smoke / And made their land, being so large a Station / An habitation for our Christian Nation." Comparing our popular versions of these people and events with the original texts produced by them and their contemporaries should lead to a rich discussion.

Many resources are available that will help teachers of this particular section. A number of critical studies of European exploration and colonization have been written in the past thirty years, as is discussed in the introduction. But there are also numerous valuable websites on these topics. The University of Calgary has a wonderful series of online interactive teaching modules on the European Voyages of Exploration that are very helpful and provide not only narratives but also maps and other visual aids. The Newberry Library also has maps suitable for classroom use on their website. Fordham University's Internet Medieval Sourcebook provides resources on Mandeville and Columbus. The Jamestowne Society's extensive website offers portraits and text about John Smith and Pocahontas. One final context that teachers might want to use is that of art produced both in Europe and in the cultures Europeans were encountering during this period. *Circa 1492* is a book about art from Europe and the worlds "new" to the Europeans around the time Columbus navigated the globe. And the Metropolitan Museum of Art's website offers a timeline of art history that includes a special page on the Portuguese in Africa 1415–1600. Teachers will find a rich array of materials to complement this cluster of travel narratives.

Further Reading

Fleck, Andrew. "Here, There, and In-Between: Representing Difference in the *Travels* of Sir John Mandeville." In *Studies in Philology*. Fall 2000.

Greenblatt, Stephen. *Marvelous Possessions: The Wonder of the New World*. 1991.

Levenson, Jay A. *Circa 1492: Art in the Age of Exploration*. 1991.

JOHN DONNE

Backgrounds

The bulk of Donne's poetry first appeared in print in 1633, two years after the poet's death. Until then Donne's poems, with very few isolated exceptions, had circulated only in manuscript form, as was more often than not the custom of those days. Problems of dating and chronological sequence are thus very difficult in Donne's case, but fortunately this scarcely matters. His most characteristic qualities are present throughout his career.

Certainly Donne knew the classics, such as the Latin love poets; and he was aware of the Petrarchan tradition. (He used a line from a Petrarch *canzone* as his *ex libris*.) That tradition continued to be felt in England to Donne's day as well as on the European continent where it originated. (Scholars have calculated that in Italy and France alone, during the sixteenth century, no fewer than 200,000 sonnets in the Petrarchan manner were printed, the large majority of them being love sonnets.) There are "certain Petrarchan features in some of Donne's lyrics," as Theodore Redpath has pointed out (see below in "Further

Reading"), yet the majority of his poetry "is quite divergent from Petrarch in spirit." In fact, there seems to be agreement on the general
idea that Donne's manner implies a reaction to the mannerisms and
clichés of "Petrarchism."

Like other poets of his generation, Donne wrote poetry that was nourished by the extraordinary diverse experiences and activities that his
time, country, and historical circumstances offered to a man of his education, gifts, and social position—hence, the variety and the up-to-
dateness of his materials and his imagery. His poetry presupposes an
equally varied audience of scholars, courtiers, wits, and also of voyagers,
merchants, soldiers, judges, lawyers. Finally, in the framework of literary
history as exemplified in our *Anthology*, Donne's treatment of the
man–woman relationship can be placed at the opposite end from the
canons and formalities of "courtly love."

Classroom Strategies

Possibly the best way to introduce students to the reading of Donne's
poems is to attempt with them a definition of the "speaking voice"—its
tone, its character, its function. Reading out loud will be helpful. So will
be some reference to Petrarch sonnets as the simplest way to bring
about a feeling of Donne's difference and novelty. From the Petrarch
sonnets we draw the image of a lover in isolation. His voice, as he addresses the beloved, distant lady (or speaks of her in the third person)
may present a considerable variety of tones, from joyful celebration to
lament and nostalgia; yet it persistently maintains the quality of a lover's
confession, or of a meditation on his present state and on the evoked
past. On the other hand, the speaking voice in the typical Donne poem
resounds in the present; it is a voice in action. Its function is to set up a
dramatic situation. While the Petrarchan kind of poem, even when addressing the lady, suggests isolation, the Donne poem, instead, sounds
like the speaker's side of an animated, voluble exchange on an imaginary
stage.

Even the newest reader will easily see the significance of the basic differences in poetic forms between the two poets. The Petrarchan sonnet,
with its established structure, is the proper vehicle for events and emotions recollected from memory, or in any case ordered into regular
shape, metrics, rhyme. The characteristic unit of Donne's love poems is
a stanza, sometimes single but often repeated (five times in "The Canonization," three in our other selections). There is, however, variety among
stanza patterns, so that each seems created to fit the tone of the particular poem.

We may hold on to the theatrical metaphor when we approach individual love poems by Donne. The speaking voice is that of the principal
actor who all by himself is staging a variety of situations where the main
business is the rapport between man and woman, clearly in a society
where the game of sensual love is played with both passion and intellectual sophistication. Although the speaker's voice is fairly consistent in its

quality and originality, situations and moods change, so that the central character can be compared to a frequently typecast actor performing in a variety of plays.

Using our selections as models, there is for example a particularly obvious kinship between the central characters in such poems as "The Good-Morrow" and "The Canonization," in which the speaker enacts the philosophical wooer, fashionably demonstrating (cf. Bembo in Castiglione's *The Courtier*) the power of love to transcend mortality. Yet the implied audiences and dramatic situations differ, as do the verse forms; the philosophical wooer performs his role in a variety of contexts.

It is particularly obvious in such cases, of course, that imagery, metrical patterns, unusual and circuitous ways of conveying the main idea of the poem—all the ways of "staging" the situation—make all the difference, and that true experience of the poems can be attained only through explication and exchange in the classroom.

Obvious as it may be that "dramatization is all," the student should not be allowed to forget that the main "idea" of a poem may be a cliché, consecrated by centuries of love poetry, Petrarchan and otherwise. There is no need to go into detail on the endless conventions and formalities of that tradition to realize that "Donne's originality is bound up with his use of common positions" (A. J. Smith [see "Further Reading"]), a fact that is evident, for example, in "The Ecstasy," which is an extraordinary elaboration of a commonplace idea in devotional writing: that the soul contemplating God is transported out of the body. The idea also exists in Neo-Platonic discussions of love such as Bembo's description, in Book 4 of *The Courtier*, of the lover's souls leaving the body to be united with each other and the divine. An even greater power of renovation is apparent in Holy Sonnet 14, where the traditional ideas are no less than the highest verities of Christian faith. (For an interesting and provocative discussion of the quality and religiosity of these poems, see Sanders in "Further Reading.")

Topics for Discussion and Writing

1. Discuss and define the differences between a Petrarchan and a Donne love poem, considering such elements as imagery, the implied character of the speaker, and the greater or lesser awareness of the "presence" of the person whom the speaker is addressing and of other possible "presences" and "voices," as the case may be.
2. Compare and contrast the religious element in Petrarch and Donne (see Petrarch's sonnets 3 and 62, and Donne's "The Canonization" and, of course, Holy Sonnet 14).
3. Compare and contrast the stanza pattern of "Song" to that of "The Apparition" and their respective appropriateness to the matter of the two poems.

Further Reading

See also the reading suggestions in the *Anthology*, p. 2645.

Gardner, Helen, ed. *The Divine Poems*, by John Donne. 1978. A basic edition, with critical and textual introduction and notes.

Gardner, Helen, ed. *The Elegies and the Songs and Sonnets*, by John Donne. 1965. A standard edition, with commentary and critical and textual introduction.

Grierson, H. J. C., ed. *The Poems of John Donne*. 1912. The classic modern edition, with critical and textual introductions and commentary.

Redpath, Theodore, ed. *The Songs and Sonnets of John Donne*. 1983. Contains a lengthy introduction on the status of the Songs and Sonnets in English poetry and on the "psychological" and "literary" features of the poems, and on their relation to the Petrarchan tradition (the latter is discussed at length on pages 47–88). Each of the poems is followed by explanatory and critical notes.

Sanders, Wilbur. *John Donne's Poetry*. 1971. The discussion of the Holy Sonnets comprises pages 111–39.

Smith, A. J. *Donne, Songs and Sonnets*. 1964; reprinted 1975. A short and very useful study from the series Studies in English Literature.

LYRIC POETRY: OTHER METAPHYSICALS

Backgrounds

According to the introduction, these poems have in common the label "metaphysical" or "baroque," so you might want to help your students arrive at a definition of these terms by examining what the poems have in common besides their religious concerns. There is no consensus on the definition of metaphysical, the definition of baroque in poetry, or the difference between the two terms. As Frank J. Warnke says, "Metaphysical poetry is associated in the minds of its readers with the work of one man, John Donne. Yet . . . one cannot simply make a touchstone of Donne's style in determining what poetry is Metaphysical." The poems in this section might be profitably read alongside those of Donne, and students might want to discuss what features, if any, these poems have in common with each other and with Donne's lyrics.

Metaphysical poetry is partly characterized by its intensity, though there is a world of tonal difference between the serenity of Herbert's "Prayer ("something understood") and the passion of San Juan de la Cruz's "Song of the Soul in Union with God" ("Oh so desired pain!"). When we read the poems in this section alongside those of Donne, we notice that he writes of erotic love with an intensity that is directed toward spiritual love in most of the poems in this section. Of course, some of the authors represented here were, like Donne, priests or ministers: George Herbert was an Anglican minister; San Juan de la Cruz a

Carmelite monk and famous mystic. Agrippa d'Aubigne was an artist and soldier but also a theologian who fought for the Protestant cause. Francisco de Queveda was a public figure who served the Duke of Osuna, later became royal secretary in the Spanish court, but also studied theology. Thus many of these authors not only wrote about religious experience but lived religion-centered lives. Teachers of this poetry might want to address the question of religious belief with their students. The religious passion expressed in these poems might be quite foreign to some or all of your students, but the emotions expressed in the poems can still be accessible if the students think in terms of human relationships. For example, Herbert's beautiful and deceptively simple poem, "Love (III)," depicts a speaker who both desires and resists union with a beloved, and who feels guilty and unworthy in the face of the beloved's generosity and forgiveness. While your students may not have had these feelings in the context of a spiritual relationship, they will be able to talk about similar dynamics in human relationships. Reading Donne's poems of erotic love suggests many parallels between religious and erotic love that students might enjoy discussing.

Many of these poems express passionate emotions about God, whether love, fear, or awe. Another quality shared by many of the poems is that God is the assumed audience. The Dutch poet Constantijn Huygens provides a good example, though Sor Juan de la Cruz and Herbert do the same thing. They address questions, complaints, pleas to God as their listener—and in Herbert's case, even presumes to provide God's answer in the poem "The Collar." Students can compare poems by Donne, Herbert, San Juan de la Cruz, and Huygens in terms of what is implied about God and the nature of the speaker's relationship with the divine in these poems. Huygens is the one continental Metaphysical poet who was directly influenced by Donne, and his poem "Good Friday" can be compared in interesting ways to Donne's Holy Sonnet 14.

Nearly all of these poems have at their heart strange and extreme metaphors—"metaphysical conceits"—that are one of the salient features of metaphysical or baroque poetry. These metaphors can work on an emotional level but must sometimes be analyzed intellectually before their impact is experienced. Students often need help unpacking all the implications of these metaphors but can truly come to appreciate and enjoy the complexity of this figurative language.

Many of the representations employed by these poets are quite commonplace: God as the sun; love as a flame; temporality as a flower; mortality as dust. Yet each traditional metaphor is presented in new and startling ways. Boderie's ray of sun remains whole as it passes through glass which is also intact, and this phenomenon becomes a metaphor for the incarnation. Mary is like the glass, a vehicle for the sun, God, who remains entire in Jesus, the son whom Mary bore without a "break" in her "crystal," that is, without a break in her hymen, as she retains her virginity. God-as-the-sun takes on a new and complicated meaning that we have to work out intellectually, and Boderie actually presents this metaphor as a kind of proof to unbelievers: if we can believe this happens in Nature—a ray of sun passing whole through a glass, breaking neither the glass or itself—why can we not believe that God did the same with Mary?

While these poets might take an ordinary metaphor and find unusual meanings in it, they sometimes create bizarre metaphors, the best known being Donne's lovers imagined as a compass in "A Valediction: Forbidding Mourning." Some of the conceits your students will encounter in this section are similarly strange or even startling: Herbert's description of prayer as a "Christian plummet" is odd if students know that a plummet is a ball of lead on a string used to measure depths or set straight vertical lines, though it can also mean a metal weight on a line used as a weapon or a scourge. Some of the conceits, or metaphors, used by these poets are simply carried to an extreme, whence comes their bizarreness. For example, imagining one's chest as a tomb or vault is not terribly unusual (see, for example, the last poem in Sidney's "Astrophil and Stella"). Yet Agrippa D'Aubigne will take that conceit to extremes when he envisions his cleft heart, blackened blood, and dried-out bones on display when his "tomb," or breast, lies open.

A poem like "Prayer (I)" offers a list of metaphors for prayer, each one of which repays close consideration. "God's breath in man returning to his birth": what are the implications of the phrase "God's breath"? The metaphor suggests so many things: that prayer is the divine aspect of humans, that it is life-giving, that it is God speaking through us. Because these poets speak in such a dense language, students can benefit from using the Oxford English Dictionary as they read these poems. For example, when Herbert says "if I imp my wing on thine" in "Easter Wings," he is using a term from falconry that means "to engraft feathers in the wing of a bird so as to make good losses or deficiencies," as students researching "imp" in the OED will learn. But "imp" has other suggestions both as a verb, and also as a noun, when it can mean a young shoot of a plant or tree, but also a scion of a noble house. Similarly, in the next line, when the poet says that "Affliction shall advance the flight in me," the OED entry for "affliction" will inform students that this word means not just misery or distress, but in its earliest uses had the specific meaning of the self-infliction of religious discipline. While exercises in using the OED to enrich our understanding of this dense poetic language will work well for Herbert and Donne, the other poets in this section wrote in languages other than English, so we are reading translations.

An exercise that students enjoy is the creation of their own metaphysical conceits. Working alone or in groups, they take a common comparison (love is like a rose, for example) and try add new correspondences to that figure: In what ways is love like a rose? Traditionally because it is beautiful or sweet, or maybe even because it is thorny. But students trying to spin out the metaphor might decide that love is like a rose because it is difficult to grow, or requires light and space, or maybe even because it can often be found dried up and resting in mothballs. Or they can try to create a startling comparison (love is like a Honda Accord) that they will have to explain and draw meaning from. This exercise may increase your students' appreciation for the poetry they are reading as well as allowing you to see how well they understand the use of figurative language in these poems.

A final suggestion for teaching the concept of "baroque" poetry: use the art of this period to develop a context for the poetry. Though you may not be able to establish one-to-one correspondences between particular works of art and particular poems, students might come away from contemplating the sculpture of Bernini or the painting of Caravaggio with a deeper appreciation for the intensity and complexity of these poems.

JOHN MILTON

Paradise Lost

Backgrounds

Milton's epic *Paradise Lost* is divided like Virgil's epic, the *Aeneid*, into twelve books. Its great theme is announced in the proemium as that of man's transgression and fall and the promise of redemption. Actually, the scope of the poem is vaster. Using a device common to both the Greek and the Roman epic—the *Odyssey* and the *Aeneid* in particular—that is, a flashback in the form of a tale told by one of the characters in the poem (in this case the Archangel Michael in his speech to Adam and Eve in books V–VIII), *Paradise Lost* encompasses the story of the rebellious angels and *their* fall, the creation of Hell as their eternal abode, and of man and his earthly habitation surrounded by its celestial universe. Thus Milton, through Michael, has also undertaken the Dantean task of "delineating" events occurring in the Empyrean heaven, and in created Hell, "by likening spiritual to corporeal forms" (V.573, not included in the *Anthology*).

Immediately after the proemium and the invocation to the Muse, the curtain rises on the vision of Hell, where the former Lucifer, now Satan, tells his legions of "a new kind of Creature to be created" and summons them to a council in his palace, "Pandemonium," which has suddenly risen from the depths of surrounding Chaos. In book II, the infernal parliament debates whether it should engage in a new battle against God, or whether it should first verify the news of His having created a new world and a new being, man, possibly susceptible to Satanic influence. The latter plan is accepted, and Satan leaves on his exploratory mission. Book III (not in the *Anthology*), shifts to the vision of Heaven, where God sits on His throne, the Son on His right side. Here Milton takes up the task of presenting in poetic language the doctrinal problems of God's foreknowledge, man's free will, and his redemption. The omniscient God knows that man will fall, but clears Himself of "all imputation," having endowed man with free will; He declares His "purpose of grace," provided that someone is found who will "answer for" man's offense and undergo his punishment. The Son offers Himself and is exalted as the Redeemer.

The last part of book III shifts back to Satan, who in book IV—after being torn by the passions of fear, envy, and despair—"confirms himself in evil." His first attempt on Eve, in the form of a dream, is frustrated by the intervention of the Archangel Gabriel, and he is chased from the Garden. In book V, after Eve's account of her dream to Adam, Raphael as God's messenger descends upon Eden; he warns Adam of the imminent danger of temptation by the fallen angel, thus beginning his long flashback, which will end in book VIII with Raphael answering Adam's questions on the celestial bodies and their movements. Adam in turn confides to Raphael what he remembers of his own creation and tells of God's warning about the Tree of Knowledge. At the end the two discourse on appropriate relationships between man and woman, and the archangel departs.

Book IX and the second part of book X are the climactic selections in the *Anthology*. Raphael has gone, and the poet announces a change in tone from "venial discourse" to the tragedy of the transgression and fall. This is the section that deals with the poet's theme and purpose as announced in lines 1 and 26 of book I: "Man's first disobedience," and the justification of "God's ways to man." It ends, at the close of book X, with the prospect of life on Earth—life as we know it—and with the first sinners recommending themselves as supplicants to the Son of God, who in book XI (not in the *Anthology*) intercedes for them with the Father. God decrees their expulsion from Paradise and sends Michael with a band of Cherubim to announce the sentence. Before executing it, the archangel from a hilltop sets before Adam a vision of the future life of man up to the Flood; his revelation continues in book XII up to the coming of the Messiah and His incarnation, death, resurrection, and ascension. They descend the hill, and Adam awakens Eve from gentle dreams (p. 2256); the two are led by Michael out of Paradise.

Scores of plays and poems on sacred subjects, in English and in Italian (during his visit to Italy, Milton had known local poets and even wrote poems in Italian) have been mentioned as possibly inspiring Milton's conception; such relationships in general belong to the area of specialized curiosities. Milton was extraordinarily well read in several languages; and there may be, for example, generic echoes from Dante (whom Milton greatly admired) in such early lines of *Paradise Lost* as ". . . sights of woe, / Regions of sorrow, where peace / And rest can never dwell, hope never comes / That comes to all, but torture without end . . ." (I.64–69), or of Tasso's *Jerusalem Delivered* in Milton's conception of the infernal council in book II. Or Milton may practically translate a line from Ariosto's *Orlando Furioso* ("Things unattempted yet in prose or rhyme," I.16) and effectively use it in a totally different context, much as Dante does when on his first meeting Beatrice he uses a line (*Purgatorio* XXX.46) that in Virgil's *Aeneid* is spoken by Dido as she is falling in love with Aeneas. This is one of the minor ways in which the "great tradition" works.

More important, quite early in life Milton had conceived of a great work (at first, apparently, imagined as a drama) on the central story of the Judeo-Christian tradition. This was to constitute the crowning achievement of his variedly active life—an indication of the supreme place that he reserved for his activity as a poet. Thus Milton's main inspiration for *Paradise Lost* was the very awareness of the magnitude and height of his task. The significant lines 20–47 of book IX also express his notion of the superiority of his poetic material (to him, accustomed to religious meditation and doctrinal debate, "chivalry" materials were not only inferior, they were "tedious") and implicitly of his own poetic power. And perhaps also those lines signal the feeling that he is the last in a tradition of poetry on a grand scale, which had begun with the Homeric epics and continued through Virgil and through Virgil's Christian "pupil," Dante.

Classroom Strategies

Experience would indicate that in Milton's case as in others (cf. the notes on teaching Erasmus) a useful first measure is to test students' knowledge of the biblical events that constitute his material. There may be surprises in either direction. Specifically for the selections in the *Anthology*, a supplementary reading and explication of the relevant passages in Genesis may be in order. Young people possessing superficial knowledge and mental images of the story of the fall and its meaning as a *felix culpa* may find in that notion as dramatized by Milton a source of considerable intellectual stimulation and enlightenment. Attention should be drawn to Milton's poetic handling of the story of the temptation, fall, and promise of redemption, in a poetic style alternating between solemn discourse and lively drama. The ideal student should be able to discover that there is fascination in the Adam–Eve dialogue, conducted as it is by the poet both as doctrinal argumentation and as human drama. Also, as in other previous cases, it should be observed in detail how the poet incorporates Greco-Roman material and uses it in handling his biblical story. The footnotes in the *Anthology* attempt to be helpful on all these levels.

Topics for Discussion and Writing

1. Analyze, in specific passages from the selections in the *Anthology*, the ways in which the concept of the fall as a *felix culpa* (a "happy fault") is dramatized by Milton.
2. If the last selections from the *Purgatorio* have been read, compare the scene and function of the Earthly Paradise in Dante and in Milton.
3. Choose and analyze passages in which pagan and Christian imagery are fused in Milton.
4. In his description of "chivalry materials" in book IX.27–41, Milton seems to ignore the fact that this material also had a Christian world as its background and that the "battles feigned" were also between Christians and infidels. Contrast with the revitalization of that same material in Cervantes. Discuss whether the differences

may be due to the diversity in cultural and religious backgrounds
of the two writers.

Comparative Perspectives

1. Discuss the way Eve and her flowers are interwoven, and compare
   the intimate links between other heroines and the natural world.
   How might we account for this widespread tendency to identify
   women with the landscape?
2. Compare the attitudes toward epic expressed in the Invocation to
   book IX with those of Lucian and Petronius in the ancient world,
   or of Ariosto, to whom Milton pays a kind of backhanded homage
   in line 16 of book I.

Further Reading

See also the reading suggestions in the *Anthology*, p. 2645.

Broadbent, J. B. *Some Graver Subject: An Essay on* Paradise Lost. 1967.
With illustrations and index. A thorough, detailed analysis of *Paradise
Lost*, perhaps somewhat extravagant.

Demaray, John G. *Milton's Theatrical Epic: The Invention and Design of*
Paradise Lost. 1980. A critical interpretation of *Paradise Lost* with a
view to its origins and development, Milton's theories and techniques,
influences, and its relation to Renaissance dramatic forms.

Emma, Ronald David, and John T. Shawcross, eds. *Language and Style
in Milton: A Symposium in Honor of the Tercentenary of* Paradise Lost.
1967. Eleven essays on the linguistic background, theological language, spelling and pronunciation, Aristotelian notion of ethos and di-
anoia, grammar, imagery, and style of *Paradise Lost*. With selected
bibliography.

Le Comte, Edward S. *A Milton Dictionary*. 1969. A dictionary including
"hard" words from Milton's works, entries on the individual works,
and biographical data.

Leonard, John. *Naming in Paradise: Milton and the Language of Adam
and Eve*. 1990. Particularly appropriate to the selections in the *Anthology*.

Lieb, Michael. *Poetics of the Holy: A Reading of* Paradise Lost. 1981. A
religious interpretation, with illustrations and bibliography. Deals with
the basic religious context of *Paradise Lost*, the esthetic dimensions of
that context, and the aspects of sacral phenomena in the work.

Summers, Joseph H. *The Muse's Method: An Introduction to* Paradise
Lost. 1962. Broadbent says that this is the most complete study of its
kind.

Wittreich, Joseph Antony. *Feminist Milton*. 1987.

The Enlightenment

Jean-Baptiste Poquelin Molière

Tartuffe

Classroom Strategies and Topics for Discussion

The biggest problem for students who are reading *Tartuffe* for the first time is likely to be the expectations they bring to the play. If they anticipate characters with realistically conceived psychologies and events closely resembling what might occur in ordinary life, they will be bewildered and irritated. It is important, therefore, to explain in advance that the play depends on the particular forms of artifice we call convention.

In the first place, it relies on the set of *dramatic* conventions associated with the comedy of manners. These conventions include the use of type characters, figures differentiated by role rather than by psychology. Students can probably identify many of the types in *Tartuffe* themselves, once alerted to the presence of type characters: the hypocrite, the clever maid, the blustering young man, the foolish but tyrannical father, the naïve young girl, and so on. Equally conventional is the structure of the plot, dependent not on plausibility but on the design of providing pleasure (including particularly the pleasure of surprise) by its ingenuity and of demonstrating the restoration of a just social order and the punishment of deviants from that order.

The play also assumes a set of *social* conventions. These have to do with the kind and degree of authority exercised by the father of a family. A father, for instance, has absolute power over his daughter's marital choices; he may be argued with but not refused. A wife's chastity is of paramount importance to her husband. A son's economic status depends entirely on his father. Thus the father's role in the family resembles the king's in the country—a point of some importance to the ending of *Tartuffe*.

It is especially useful in teaching this play to read aloud sequences, with different members of the class assuming different roles. Only thus will students realize the brilliance of the verse, the wit of the language (e.g., "You deserve to be tartuffified") and rhymes (e.g., "fossil" and "docile")—effects approximating in English the dramatist's achievement in French—the speed and economy with which Molière conveys necessary information and moves the plot along, the sheer *fun* of language and event. The first scene is a good place to start, both for reading aloud and for analysis. Mme. Pernelle's initial haste ("Come, come, Flipote, it's time I left this place": students should think about how the entrance would be staged, with everyone rushing to keep up with Mme. Pernelle), when contrasted with her leisure for denunciation, extending to everyone in the household except Tartuffe, of course creates comedy. One might ask whether it has also a serious point. It announces a theme that runs through the play: the degree to which people are driven by their own obsession to be blind to the needs of others. If students are asked for examples of this pattern, they will probably mention Tartuffe and Orgon (perhaps the brilliant scene in which Orgon hears of his wife's illness but concerns himself only with "poor Tartuffe"), but Damis, Mariane, and Valère are also relevant. What else does the first scene accomplish? It introduces the presence of Tartuffe as a potential problem. Students might discuss the impression of Tartuffe they get from this scene; later in the discussion, they might pursue the ways that this impression is elaborated and modified as the play goes on. And the scene sketches, mainly from Mme. Pernelle's distorted point of view, characteristics of the play's persons. What notion does one get of each? It introduces Dorine as a young woman exceptionally willing to state her own opinions. Does one trust her view or Mme. Pernelle's more fully? What aspects of their accounts of other people make them seem more or less trustworthy?

Many individual scenes of the play reward similar analysis. Particularly rich are the farcical scene between Valère and Dorine (II.4) and the seduction scene, with Orgon under the table (IV.5). Analysis of almost any scene can lead to investigation of the play's larger issues. A few general points worth pursuing: *Is* this comedy in fact antireligious, or does it only attack corruptions of religion? (Opinions may differ here; the point is to get students to support their opinions by reference to the text.) In Act IV, Scene 3, Elmire remarks, "My taste is for good-natured rectitude." Is "good-natured rectitude" the implicit value advocated by the play? How does the concept of rectitude relate to the common sense consistently exemplified by Cléante? (Cléante's role is worth extended discussion. What, exactly, does his common sense involve? What sort of view of human nature does he seem to have? Why does Orgon refuse to pay attention to him?) How serious a criticism of society does this play offer? In other words, is its purpose only to entertain, or does it aspire to educate as well?

In working out answers to such questions, it is worth thinking about what causes characters to be deluded. The ridiculous misunderstanding between Valère and Mariane comes partly from the wish of each to have the other acknowledge need or desire first. If Valère proclaimed his love when Mariane was actually willing to marry someone else, he would appear weak; conversely, if Mariane says she won't marry Tartuffe because she loves Valère, she gives him the upper hand. Similar issues of power emerge in every situation. Orgon feels himself powerful in his role of benevolent patron to Tartuffe; he must believe in Tartuffe's goodness in order to believe in his own magnanimity. Tartuffe, to take the most obvious example, gains power by proclaiming his weakness and humility. This common element in the characters' motivation is worth emphasizing because it calls attention to the way the play lights up issues of perennial concern, not simply those inherent in a society with religious and political structures quite different from our own.

Some time should be spent on the question of plot and how it works here. Tartuffe's will to power (including the power of wealth) and Orgon's determination to indulge him are the motivating forces producing an intertwined sequence of events that seem inevitable, given the premises. Students might be asked at what points in the play they were surprised by what happened next. Any answers to this question would be worth pursuing, to try to ascertain whether surprise reflects a real failure of plausibility or a failure of expectation. The most likely moments of surprise are Tartuffe's attempt to seize the house, after he is unmasked and one expects all problems to be solved, and the final intervention of the king. Both are particularly useful to discuss. The first surprise derives from our expectations of comedy: we anticipate no really serious problems, and we assume that difficulties will be readily resolved in a comic scheme. Molière's extra twist serves as a reminder that the problems announced in this play *are* in fact serious—and perhaps as a reminder that in the real world they are not so easily solved.

The matter of the king is more complicated. To twentieth-century sensibilities, this may seem an arbitrary intervention or a piece of gross flattery; and perhaps it cannot be fully justified. But it can at least be argued that the introduction of the king as a force in the action serves as a reminder that the family is a microcosm for larger patterns of social organization. Order must be restored in the family for order to operate in the kingdom; and it is only by the exercise of authority, in this play, that order exists.

Topics for Writing

1. The function of the mother-in-law (Mme. Pernelle).
2. The importance of seeing in *Tartuffe*.
3. The voice of reason in *Tartuffe*.
4. What kinds of emotion are important in the play?
5. Secrets and secrecy in *Tartuffe*.

Comparative Perspectives

1. Compare the kinds of conventions employed by Molière and by Brecht in *The Good Woman of Setzuan*. How do characters speak? Is either play aiming for "realism"? How would you describe the relationship between the reality of a stage performance and our perception of actual events in our own lives?
2. Who possesses "common sense" in Molière's theater and other literary works of the Enlightenment that you have read? Compare the way class status contributes to the experience of passion in literature of the ancient world.

Further Reading

See also the reading suggestions in the *Anthology*, p. 2538.

Gaines, J. F., and M. S. Koppisch, eds. *Approaches to Teaching Molière's* Tartuffe *and Other Plays*. 1995. A volume in the MLA series.

Gossman, L. *Man and Masks*. 1963. Looks at Molière in his historical situation, with emphasis on his continuing relevance to the present as well as on the way he embodies ideas important in his own time.

Guicharnaud, J., ed. *Molière: A Collection of Critical Essays*. 1964. Exemplifies diverse approaches and includes a particularly valuable group of seven essays under the rubric "The Art of Comedy."

Hubert, J. *Molière and the Comedy of Intellect*. 1962. Particularly useful for teachers: studies the playwright's "achievement as a creator of dramatic and poetic forms," emphasizing the inner coherence and the moral vision of Molière's work as a whole. The chapter on *Tartuffe*; "Hypocrisy as Spectacle," is rich in insight.

Jagendorf, Zvi. *The Happy End of Comedy*. 1984. Treats Molière's comedies in relation to Shakespeare's and Ben Jonson's.

McBride, R. *The Sceptical Vision of Molière*. 1977. Organized around the idea of paradox, with an introductory section about the relation between Molière as moralist and as comic artist, followed by a detailed study of how the playwright's thought is embodied in his comedy.

Walker, H. *Molière*. 1971. This introductory volume in the Twayne series provides a brief biography, thematically organized analysis of the plays, and valuable bibliography.

MARIE DE LA VERGNE DE LA FAYETTE

The Princess of Clèves

Classroom Strategies and Topics for Discussion

This short novel lends itself readily to division into two assignments, with the first one ending at the end of the brief paragraph on p. 93. The text, so different from the realistic novel with which most students are familiar, presents some obvious problems for the beginning reader. The class should perhaps be warned in advance not to expect the kind of circumstantial detail and leisurely narrative typical of more recent fiction. Instead, the story proceeds by a series of rather flat, rapid summaries of events, focusing attention on characters' inner responses rather than their external behavior. If students have been prepared to take note of the work's psychological complexities, they may have an easier time reading it.

Particularly if they have been told that this is a psychological novel however, undergraduates are likely to be troubled by its stress on political detail. The first few pages, crammed with historical and political data, are therefore a good place to start the discussion. The question of how the political relates to the personal has considerable immediacy for twentieth-century readers: de La Fayette's apparent assumption that the two cannot be separated challenges belief in the possibility of an altogether "private" life. It is easy enough to see that in a court, love might be mingled with politics and politics with love; as the novel develops, however, the reader begins to understand that love *is* politics. The opening pages' stress on beauty, wealth, and status as publicly accepted values prepares for the gradual revelation that the same values operate in private relationships as well. Students may be interested in discussing how romantic entanglements in the novel are revealed to involve balancings of power. Even the princess's genuine concern with virtue becomes a means for her to dominate both husband and lover, although she has no apparent wish to dominate. Discussion of politics as the science of power, and of how private and public politics reflect one another, can help students see that the remote historical setting and formal diction of the novel only slightly disguise its preoccupation with issues that still concern us.

A specific episode useful to discuss in this connection is the story of Mme. de Tournon (pp. 94ff.), told by M. de Clèves to his wife. This tale of love, deceit, and misunderstanding epitomizes the mistaken trust in appearances, the misdirected passion, the intertwining of public and private concerns that pervade the novel as a whole. (Students may find it interesting to trace other occurrences of these themes.) It also emphasizes processes of reinterpretation likewise typical of the entire work— and of students' everyday experiences with their classmates. Sancerre is forced to understand his relation to his beloved in new ways; Mme. de Clèves reinterprets both Sancerre and Mme. de Tournon; Mme. de Clèves enlarges her comprehension of possibilities of female deceit. The telling of stories about other people is an insistent activity in this fiction; typically, these episodes (the story of Mme. de Tournon is exemplary in this respect too) remind their immediate hearers as well as the reader of the fact that what happens to a single member of a coherent society affects everyone else as well, if only by changing understanding. The past keeps changing as people find out new things about it; neither public nor private history remains static. The tale of Mme. de Tournon can provide a starting point for examining the reiteration of these points in *The Princess of Clèves*.

With the second assignment, discussion might turn to psychological issues: those suggested by the headnote and others as well. A possible starting point would be the princess's act of deception in rewriting from memory the lost letter. Why, despite her virtue, is she willing without urging to engage in this deception? The act, which involves her in close association with her would-be lover, suggests her desire for such association; it hints a weakening in her rigid moral code, since she allows herself an interlude of pure pleasure with M. de Nemours; it illustrates the way the past keeps encroaching on the present and demanding reinter-

pretation. To think about the princess's feelings here and how they are
expressed leads readily to discussion of how those feelings develop in the
course of the novel, from premarital repression through this brief interlude of expansion and back finally to postmarital repression.

Talking about the princess's emotional development may involve
awareness of how much this novel emphasizes not the feeling conventionally associated with romantic love but rather such emotions as fear,
embarrassment, and anxiety. It is worth discussing both the plausibility
of such emotions in the society evoked, and the nature of their importance. Among other things, the kind of embarrassment and anxiety here
typical reflect the novel's assumption that the pressures of other people
largely determine much individual experience. (A more abstract way of
putting the same point would be to say that society is of the utmost importance to every person in it; there is no way to avoid its force.) To
think about how people impinge upon one another in this fiction may
lead to understanding of the princess's final choice: she has removed
herself from the arena of social pressure, thus ultimately declaring her
individuality even when she seems to be suppressing it.

A question particularly likely to engage contemporary students is that
of the novel's female authorship. Is there anything in the work that declares the sex of its author? Answers to such a question must necessarily
remain highly speculative, but it is perhaps worth considering how characteristically the action here proceeds by indirect rather than direct
means. People overhear one another, spy on one another, watch in mirrors, learn things by accident, rely on rumor and gossip, withhold crucial
information. Another possibly "female" aspect of the fiction is its stress
on pain as something to be concealed rather than displayed (compare
Racine). Does the great attention to appearance have anything to do
with the author's sex? Does this author's way of setting a private drama
in a public context have the effect of subverting the importance of the
public? Such unresolvable questions of course persist for modern authors as well.

Topics for Writing

1. The importance of propriety in *The Princess of Clèves*.
2. The character of the prince of Clèves.
3. The princess's relation to her mother.
4. The significance of paintings.
5. The happy ending.
6. The unhappy ending.

Comparative Perspectives

1. Where would the princess fit in the spirit world of Pope's *Rape of
   the Lock* (see canto I, lines 46–66)? Would she be attended by a
   Sylph, a Salamander, a Nymph, or a Gnome? To answer this question, it will be helpful to compare and contrast the ethical views of
   the French heroine and Pope's raisonneuse, Clarissa.

2. If you have read the selections from Marguerite de Navarre's *Hep-tameron* or Castiglione's *Book of the Courtier* in Vol. 1, compare the court and the conversation depicted in *The Princess of Clèves* with those in either of those works. What characteristics do they all share?

Further Reading

See also the reading suggestion in the *Anthology*, p. 2537.

Beasley, F. E., and K. A. Jensen, eds. *Approaches to Teaching Lafayette's* Princess of Clèves. 1998. A volume in the MLA series.

Gregorio, L. *Order in the Court: History and Society in* La Princesse de Clèves. 1986. A sound historical investigation.

Haig, S. *Madame de La Fayette.* 1970. Of the scanty literature in English on the novel, this is probably the most useful. It follows skillfully the usual Twayne formula of biographical introduction, critical analysis, and bibliographical survey.

Kuizinga, D. *Narrative Strategies in* La Princesse de Clèves. 1976. A highly specialized treatment, with its focus indicated by the title.

Showalter, E. Jr. *The Evolution of the French Novel, 1641–1782.* 1972. Places de La Fayette in the context of the developing tradition of realism.

Turnell, M. *The Novel in France.* 1951. Includes biographical information and speculation and a short critical analysis of *The Princess of Clèves.*

JEAN RACINE

Phaedra

Classroom Strategies and Topics for Discussion

Even if they have already read Molière, students may have trouble with the artifice and formality of Racine. To encounter characters who make pronouncements about their feelings in blank verse, with none of the comic relief familiar from Shakespeare, often proves a forbidding experience. The problems that preoccupy these characters seem remote from modern life; the personages on the stage do not invite easy identification from the audience. But all is not lost. Although students should probably be told at the outset enough about seventeenth-century tragic convention to understand that they are to look at and learn from these characters, not instantly perceive them as analogues for the self, in fact it is possible to find in the long run important points of contact between the constructed world whose inhabitants concern themselves with conflicts of love and virtue and our own time and experience.

To achieve such a result demands attention to the play's detail. Although it is possible to read the entire drama as a single assignment, it lends itself well to a two-part division: the first three acts, and then the final two. A good place to start discussion is with Phaedra's first important speech, her explanation to Oenone, in Act I, of the source of her distress. Reading this speech aloud facilitates talk about the function of the play's sonorous verse. Even in translation, one can feel how the dignity and control of language and meter provide a counterpoint for the chaotic emotion they render. The dramatist is always in control, although the characters are not necessarily able to keep a sense of mastery, and the poetic authority of Racine's voice (behind Phaedra's) affirms the possibility of restored human order—that possibility clearly announced at the play's ending.

But the content of Phaedra's speech also deserves attention. Her initial characterization of her love for Hippolytus as "My ills" sets the tone for her utterance as a whole, with its emphasis on evil, pain, and misery. Students might be asked to find the metaphors in this passage. The imagery emphasizes war and sickness: metaphors that run through the play. Where else do such metaphors occur, you might ask; the answers will help students see how imagery creates and emphasizes unity. This speech also brings up the large question of Phaedra's responsibility for her own and other people's suffering. She sees herself as helpless ("Venus fastens on her helpless prey"); is she? This is not, of course, the kind of question that has a preestablished answer, but students should be urged to find evidence for their position on either side. If they believe that Phaedra's love has overcome her with no possibility for her to resist, is she to be held responsible for her further acts, for confessing her love to Hippolytus and condoning Oenone's terrible lie about him? How does one determine human responsibility in a world governed by gods and goddesses? Are we to take these deities simply as projections of human feelings? If so, Phaedra *is* responsible. In that case, does she become villain rather than victim? The problem of moral responsibility is a powerful issue in the play, as in our lives. One way of understanding Phaedra's insistence that Venus is to blame is to recall our modern tendency to see criminals as "sick" rather than wicked, ourselves as formed by our heredity and environment rather than our wills. But no matter how much we blame our parents for what's wrong with us, we are left with a residue of feeling that it's all our fault. So is Phaedra. Discussion of the final two acts of the play should obviously involve attention to how Phaedra's suicide modifies our sense of her disclaiming responsibility.

Oenone's speech in response to Phaedra's revelation (after the interruption of Panope) brings up further large issues. The nurse speaks, typically, in a voice of common sense. She invokes public opinion, a mother's obligation to her child, tactics for appealing to Hippolytus. Of course her advice proves fatally wrong. Does this fact suggest anything about the value attached to "common sense" in the play? Why does common sense seem altogether irrelevant to the characters' real problems? To investigate such questions leads one to understand the insistent claims within the play that human dilemmas must be comprehended first of all in moral rather than in pragmatic terms. Oenone does not think primarily about right and wrong; Phaedra tries to, but often fails. Yet right and wrong remain the crucial issues of this drama.

To speak of "right and wrong" brings up the whole matter of "virtue," allegedly Hippolytus's defining characteristic. Why is Hippolytus so completely vulnerable, a teacher might ask. The answer must surely involve the character's claim to virtue. He knows himself to be good and believes goodness to be sufficient protection; the innocent, he fancies, must triumph. But he is wrong—not only mistaken because he inhabits a corrupt world, but mistaken because his smugness about his own virtue involves ignoring the claims and the feelings of other people. Oenone observes to Phaedra, "You must give up, since honor is at stake, / Everything, even virtue, for its sake" (III.3); she values the reputation of virtue more highly than the thing itself. She is wrong too: neither honor nor virtue is sufficient in itself.

Such general formulations are less important than the means of reaching them: by close attention to the language of the text, which provides material for many kinds of formulation. Other large questions that discussion might engage include why and how the past is important in this play. The past figures as both public history (the history of rulers and governments) and private (the history of families, frequently and emphatically alluded to). It is also involved in allusions to gods and goddesses: in the background is a history of relations between deities and mortals. Such stress on the past emphasizes the fact that here no act occurs in isolation. People cannot act independently of other people, as Hippolytus must tragically learn, and they cannot cut themselves loose from what has happened before them. Why is there so much stress in the play on Theseus' womanizing? Sometimes this seems an aspect of his heroism; sometimes it seems a flaw. Hippolytus' attitude toward it emphasizes both his own inadequacy and his moral superiority. It underlines the whole problem of sexual feeling that lies at the heart of the drama. Sexuality appears to be the primary source of human vulnerability: it gets Theseus into trouble; it kills Phaedra and Hippolytus; it makes Aricia miserable. It seems to lie outside the control of reason—a fact that must be taken into consideration in any discussion of the function of reason as an ideal in this action. How do issues of power become part of issues of love here? Private politics reflects public. Not only do actual and potential sexual alliances literally affect government, but they too involve complex patterns of dominance and submission that can be traced through the play. And finally, what about the play's ending? Does one believe in the reconciliation that Theseus proposes? How does one feel about Phaedra's final "purity" (the last word she speaks)? Again, there is no "right" answer, but discussion of such problems calls attention to the fact that the play demands, and usually receives, complicated emotional responses from its readers. Such responses reveal that the problems it engages remain dilemmas that concern us all, even though we typically put them in less elevated terms.

Topics for Writing

1. The role of Oenone.
2. The meaning of Hippolytus' death.
3. Theseus as a father.
4. The emotional effect of any single speech and how it is achieved (for example, Phaedra's speech to Hippolytus, II.5.90–131, Hippolytus to Aricia, V.1.11–47).
5. Phaedra as a strong woman.
6. Phaedra as a weak woman.

Comparative Perspectives

1. Hippolytus fears Phaedra, "the child of Minos and Pasiphaë." Show how her heritage is linked to the treatment of sexuality in this neoclassical play, and discuss the way it expresses an Enlightenment view of irrational desire. Contrast the imagery associated with another seductive female, Keats's Belle Dame sans Merci.

   [Racine, like his model, Euripides, treated Phaedra's passion as a derangement, typified by the imagery of monsters, bulls, and dragons. Keats's beautiful lady is no less fatal, but a figment of the Romantic imagination recycling the conventions of Arthurian romance, she is a creature of fairyland enchantment rather than brute passion. If your students have read Malory's *Morte Darthur* or Marie de France's *Lanval*, comparisons would be instructive.]

2. Theseus, Phaedra, and Hippolytus are the actors in a tragic triangle oddly like the one that traps Melville's Captain Vere, Mr. Claggart, and Billy Budd. Discuss the roles played by the key figures (choose any pair or write a long essay discussing all three): the paternal Theseus/Vere; the predatory Phaedra/Claggart; the innocent Hippolytus/Billy. How does an analysis of their motives and personalities clarify the difference between Racine's view of good and evil and Melville's? How are subtle psychosexual conflicts addressed by each author?

   [Racine draws on the ancient classical tradition, Melville on the biblical; their moral universes differ, although their plots share many assumptions. Venus has Phaedra in her clutches; what impels both Claggart and Vere in their fixations on the Handsome Sailor is not so clearly delineated or, perhaps, understood.]

Further Reading

See also the reading suggestions in the *Anthology* p. 2538.

Burnley, A. M. *Lilith Raging: The Gender Crisis and Alienation in the Theatre of Jean Racine.* 1989. Strong feminist interpretation.

Cloonan, W. *Racine's Theatre: The Politics of Love.* 1977. A study of the conflict between the personal emotion of love and the socially accepted ideal of glory that examines the "quest for reconciliation between personal needs and the legitimate obligations which society must impose upon its members."

Goldmann, L. *Racine*. Trans. A. Hamilton. 1972. A Marxist analysis that reviews biographical data and studies the development and structure of Racine's drama.

King, R. *Racine: Modern Judgments*. 1969. Includes pieces on structure, detail, style, and tradition.

Turnell, M. *Jean Racine, Dramatist*. 1972. A thorough and illuminating study of the "dramatic experience" Racine provides, with attention to versification and staging as well as theme and structure.

Weinberg, B. *The Art of Jean Racine*. 1963. An investigation of Racine's dramatic development that demonstrates how the art of each play builds on that of its predecessors.

JEAN DE LA FONTAINE

Classroom Strategies and Topics for Discussion

La Fontaine (1621–1695) is the most important poet of the French Enlightenment. All the virtues of Enlightenment aesthetics are displayed in his verse. The eight fables by which his work is represented, published between 1668 and 1694, are largely adaptations of Aesop. To base work in materials from classical antiquity is a central Enlightenment impulse, and to locate in such materials qualities highly valued in the later seventeenth century is one of La Fontaine's great talents. The style is graceful, harmonious, and decorous, balanced and restrained, even a bit severe. The treatment is cool, ironic, economical, sharp, and witty. The matter is potentially explosive with taut social, political, and ethical implications. Students will probably already be familiar with some of these fables, perhaps from other versions of Aesop—"The Cicada and the Ant," for instance, has appeared as a cartoon, and has become proverbial nigh unto cliché. It is one of La Fontaine's singular virtues to show what is fresh, vital, and even troubling in these somewhat hackneyed fables.

The Cicada and the Ant

The story of the frivolous grasshopper and the pragmatic ant is well known. It is usually taken to be a fable about the desirability of deferring gratification and making careful preparations while it is possible against the inevitable hard times ahead, and something along these lines can probably be elicited from students. La Fontaine's version will bear this reading, but it also has other possibilities. However the ant—or the reader—may judge the cicada, La Fontaine's fable also judges the ant: stingy, grasping, and opposed to pleasure. If from the point of view of the ant the cicada is frivolous, La Fontaine offers us the cicada-as-artist, "singing night and day / For the pleasure of anyone whom chance/ Sent my way." The ant has a worldly contempt for art and artists: art is not useful, artists are not practical. Some students are likely to agree with the ant on this score. They can be asked to defend their position, and then stand self-accused as Philistines.

The Crow and the Fox

A beloved figure of French folklore, the fox is a trickster figure who offers instruction and is not infrequently instructed himself. This fable spells out its moral: "That all flatterers live / At the expense of those with a credulous ear to give." Students might be asked if there's anything more to it. Their attention can be called to the terms in which the fox flatters the crow: "a veritable Romeo," "phoenix," "gorgeous." To be sure, Romeo is a beautiful young man, but the story in which he figures doesn't end well, and the phoenix, though also beautiful, has a kind of immortality that involves periodic death and immolation. To this equivocal praise the fox adds a harsh challenge: "But how well can you sing?" Since his aim is to get the crow to open his mouth, these barbs are to the point, but a reader might suppose the crow does so for other reasons than "to show off." He has been abused as much as flattered, and abuse can be as effective as flattery for getting what you want.

The Wolf and the Lamb

This fable, too, spells out its moral, and students can be encouraged to question it. The head note has some useful things to say about might, right, the powerful, and the powerless. It can be added that the argument as presented has a taint of legalism, and La Fontaine gestures in that direction: "verdict," "appeal." Absolutist France of the later seventeenth century, like Nazi Germany, was awash in lawyers, judges, and courts, and this fable is dangerously satirical. The wolf, acting as judge, prosecutor, and jury, levels charge after charge. The lamb defends himself ably against the first charge, but is declared guilty of it nonetheless (l.18). The lamb has an alibi as his defense against the second charge, which the wolf brushes aside by leveling a third charge, one which seems scarcely to the point (l.22), and which, as the lamb testifies, isn't true anyway. The wolf, less and less interested in legal argument, grows more and more irrational, pronounces his verdict, and attacks and devours the lamb. Farces of trials with pre-arranged conclusions were extremely common in La Fontaine's time. Except perhaps to make himself feel better, one wonders why the wolf even bothers, and students could be questioned about this.

The Oak and the Reed

This fable also concerns itself with power relations, but with a rather different outcome. The oak offers his condolences to the reed, on the score of his own great size and strength and the reed's comparative smallness and weakness. The oak's pity has more than a touch of bragging about it, but the reed receives it courteously, and then points out to the oak that great size and strength are not inevitable advantages: "I bend, but I never break." The next storm uproots the oak, but the reed is unscathed. Because of the oak's iconic connection with royal and state power, this fable carries a considerable satiric charge. Students should be able to see that relative weakness and insignificance can be a source of protection in the social and political arena, whereas great power exposes its wielder to much greater threats. They should also be able to see that the falling oak crushes reeds.

The Lion and the Rat

Like the oak, the lion has an iconic connection with royal and state power. State power depends to at least some extent on the consent of the governed. If state power is exercised mercifully that consent can be maintained more easily, and can even be transformed into active and useful support. Something along these lines can probably be elicited from students. Though the bearing of this fable is explicitly ethical, and has to do with social relations, its subtext is clearly political. The tale is also equipped with two morals, and students can be asked which one they regard as more applicable.

The Fox and the Grapes

This fable apparently recommends an attitude rather than an action. If we fail in the accomplishment of a desirable end, we can always waste our time complaining. Alternatively, we can declare the end not so desirable after all. What the fable doesn't recommend is that we seek better means to attain our goals rather than giving up, and this option seems the more conspicuous by its absence. Students might be asked what other possibilities are open to the fox. It can be pointed out that in the large body of French folklore about the fox, his wiles are such that he often figures out how to get what he wants. The Norman–Gascon dispute featured in this fable emphasizes its implicit derision of lazy resignation in the face of failure, and students can be pointed in that direction using the regional rivalry as a tool.

The Two Pigeons

This is a lover's fable, though students might resist this conclusion because the two pigeons in question are of the same gender. One of the happy pair wants to fly off in search of adventure; the other worries the adventurer will come to harm. The adventurer responds in closely reasoned verse that he'll return quickly, and that his adventures will provide a rich source of conversation. His adventures prove perilous, but he returns safely, if battered. Then the fable turns to its application: "Fly, then, but never far away / Fly to a world of beauty fixed between you two." The speaker goes on to say that he too has been a lover and wouldn't have left his beloved for anything. But that affair is in the past; apparently he *did* leave his lover, or his lover left him, and they never returned to each other. He worries that he'll never love again. This poem is unexpectedly personal. Its irony, as students can probably be brought to see, is that the speaker has been unable to follow his own advice.

Topics for Writing

1. Write your own Fontainean fable, in prose.
2. Discuss the irony inherent in some of these poems.
3. Discuss the political satire inherent in some of these poems.
4. Discuss some of these poems as exemplary of Enlightenment literary aesthetics.

Further Reading

See also the reading suggestions in the *Anthology*, p. 2538.

Richard Danner. *Patterns of Irony in the Fables of La Fontaine*. 1985.

Marc Fumaroli. *The Poet and the King: La Fontaine and His Century*. 2002.

SOR JUANA INÉS DE LA CRUZ

Reply to Sor Filotea de la Cruz

Classroom Strategies and Topics for Discussion

Perhaps the most interesting aspect of Sister Juana's polemical Reply, from the point of view of modern readers, is its use of autobiography as an element of argument. A class discussion of the work can profitably be organized around this topic.

Such a discussion might start with a question about what the author is arguing for in the essay as a whole—or, as usefully, what she is arguing against. Students may conclude that she wishes to defend the right of women to learning; alternately, that she wants to defend herself against charges of presumption, impiety, or unwomanliness. Other formulations of the grounds of argument are possible, but all will probably fall into one or the other category: arguments about Sister Juana's own role, arguments about the position of women in general. The relation between the two categories—women in general, Sister Juana in particular—provides a way to focus discussion.

The first few pages of the *Reply* consist mainly of apologies, couched in a tone of extreme deference ("my clumsy pen"; "your most learned, most prudent, most holy, and most loving letter"). What purpose do they serve in the piece as a whole? Whether or not they are asked to make such a judgment, students are likely to volunteer that Sister Juana does not sound "sincere." Such a comment supplies a useful opening. Is it possible that Sister Juana doesn't *wish* to sound sincere, that she is heavily ironic in her insistence on her own comparative inadequacy and she wants the irony to show? She thus dramatizes the posture of humility expected of women and suggests her own discontent with it. Increasingly as her essay continues, the reader is forced to realize the discrepancy between her elaborate pose of ignorance and her rhetorical skill.

The autobiographical section of the *Reply* begins with Sister Juana's assertion of her "vehement . . . overpowering" inclination toward learning. It concentrates mainly on her intellectual life—but the intellectual and the emotional merge for this writer, and in a sense that merging is the subject of the autobiography. Students can be asked to locate the various ways and places in which the writer conveys her intense feelings about learning. Does she also communicate emotions about other matters? What is she trying to establish in her "autobiography"? Most autobiographies dwell on a sequence of experience; Sister Juana appears less concerned with experience than with character. She primarily wants us to know not what she has done or what has happened to her but what kind of person she is. What kind of person *is* she? If students disagree on this matter, the disagreement can be made the starting point for detailed discussion not only of what kind of character emerges from this narrative but of the strategies Sister Juana uses for conveying character.

Autobiography in effect merges with argument at various points—for example, in the paragraph in which Sister Juana speaks of the inspiration she has found in books and lists the gifted women who appear in the Bible. Such a passage not only tells us of Sister Juana's reading and her reaction to it; it also contributes to a larger argument about the capacities and rights of women. You might invite your students to locate other passages in which the writer's personal experience—particularly her experience of books—is recorded in ways suggesting her views about the nature of women.

Sister Juana's career is obviously an unusual one, and she presents herself as a phenomenon among women. What makes her "special"? The question is worth considering in some detail: perhaps one might conclude that her intellectual enthusiasm and capacity are no more remarkable than is her relative lack of interest in the ordinary social life of the convent. Her revelation of genuine passion also helps to define her specialness: the sheer intensity of her feeling, and her willingness to make it known, differentiate her from other women.

But if Sister Juana differs dramatically from others of her sex, the question recurs: How does her autobiography relate to her argument about the status of women in general? A remarkable aspect of the *Reply* is its combination of assertions of uniqueness with the implication that many women, given the opportunity, might display comparable capacities. Indeed, the repeated allusions to the author's inadequacies emphasize her insistence that many women, despite social restrictions, have demonstrated their ability to rule, to teach, to write. She narrates her own struggles to learn as part of an argument that women should routinely receive opportunities for education. What makes her "special," she implicitly argues, is not her intellectual gifts so much as her will to develop them. Her desire for learning—which she alludes to as a "torment" and as an "ungovernable force"—drives her to surmount the limitations imposed on women.

The *Reply* makes a powerful case for the value of learning in itself—a value equally great for men and for women. Love of wisdom, Sister Juana maintains, constitutes a ground for persecution: people hate the person who claims intellectual authority, who demonstrates intellectual vitality. But the writer herself has been willing to endure obloquy for the sake of her endless mental activity. How does she make the reader feel that the pleasure of thought and writing is worth the pain of social disapproval? It might be worth drawing attention to the passages in which children are playing spillikins. Both provide instances of Sister Juana's indefatigable spirit of inquiry; they exemplify the nature of intellectual inquiry in general at the same time that they tell us of this woman's special ways of pursuing it.

Topics for Writing

1. Examine Sister Juana's use of specific detail as an element in her argument.
2. What is Sister Juana's attitude toward the power of language? How does she convey this attitude? How important is it in her argument as a whole?
3. What is the dominant emotion of the *Reply*? Self-pity? Pride? Anger? Write a paper maintaining the primary importance of one emotion in Sister Juana's essay.
4. Discuss the functions of biblical allusion in the *Reply*.
5. Write an essay in which you use some elements or elements in your own experience as the foundation for a serious argument.

Comparative Perspectives

1. As a child, Sor Juana reports, she asked her mother to dress her in boy's clothing and send her to study at the university. How did she manage to acquire her education? Compare the fate of the fictional sister of Shakespeare in Virginia Woolf's *A Room of One's Own*. How does Woolf's motive differ from Sor Juana's? Why did Woolf prefer not to document the few remarkable women who gained knowledge by their own efforts?
2. Sor Juana cuts off her hair to force herself to learn more quickly, although she knows that among young women, "the natural adornment of one's hair is held in such high esteem." Finally, she enters the convent (where women had their heads shorn). What other works have you read that emphasize the importance of a woman's hair? Why does it seem to have so much symbolic value in such a range of cultures and times?
   [Examples include *Paradise Lost*, *Hedda Gabler*, *The Love Song of J. Alfred Prufrock*.]

Further Reading

See also the reading suggestions in the *Anthology*, p. 2537.

Apart from the Twayne volume cited in the *Anthology*, virtually all the available English-language material on Sor Juana occurs in the context of broader discussions.

Anderson-Imbert, Enrique. *Spanish-American Literature: A History*. Revised by Elaine Malley. Vol. 1. 1969. Sets Sor Juana's writing in its historical context.

Henriques-Urena, Pedro. *Literary Currents in Hispanic America*. 1945. Given as the Norton Lectures at Harvard, these essays offer a good introduction to Sor Juana in relation to her contemporaries and her successors.

Montross, Constance M. *Virtue or Vice?: Sor Juana's Use of Thomistic Thought*. 1981. A fairly technical study of Sor Juana's theological position.

Torres-Rioseco, Arturo. *The Epic of Latin American Literature*. 1942. Another general treatment, which sets Sor Juana in her literary context.

CLUSTER: THE SITUATION OF WOMEN

Classroom Strategies and Topics for Discussion

Ranging from the end of the seventeenth century through the end of the eighteenth, and including materials from England, France, and Germany, these excerpts show the impact the Enlightenment had on an increasingly prominent question, that of the social position of women relative to men and to their own supposed innate capabilities. The Enlightenment's guiding principle of free-ranging rational inquiry made it inevitable that this question should be raised, though it may surprise students that the side of the question favoring women was raised relatively infrequently and by sometimes little-known figures. First-time readers of this material might be encouraged to reflect on what they already know about the Enlightenment, and what its principles might predict about any approach to the question of the position of women. The answers are not hard to find. Although from Locke onward progressive Enlightenment thought could easily have been extended to include the equality of women with men, it seldom was. Too many other currents of mostly conservative thought operated against this result, and in both theory and practice women remained firmly subjugated to men in almost all social arrangements. There were very few educational opportunities for women, and conservatives often argued that there should not be. Marriage and property laws were weighted against women in a way that will seem inconceivable to students. Women had no franchise in any of the developing representative democracies of Europe (nor, at the end of the eighteenth century, in the newly established United States or in the short-lived First Republic of France). Deprived of education and of the franchise, women could not hold public office and had no access to the legal, medical, ecclesiastical, military, or academic professions, and only limited access to the mercantile professions. Given these facts, it will seem less surprising to first-time readers that the arguments on the behalf of women were raised so infrequently.

The first excerpt, from "An Essay in Defense of the Female Sex" (1696), is attributed to Judith Drake, of whom nothing whatsoever is known. Whoever she may have been, plainly she had achieved a considerable level of education against formidable odds. She knows Locke's and Descartes's basic cognitive theories, even if she declines to enter into a full-scale discussion of them. She knows how to mount a systematic rational argument, and she commands an occasionally vituperative rhetoric in which irony and sarcasm play important parts. The central question Drake raises, whether or not the company and conversation of women, for a well-educated and well-disposed man, is a waste of time, she answers in the affirmative, because women have been barred from the education that would make their conversation either instructive or entertaining. Students can be asked to speculate on the causes of this situation.

The second writer excerpted is pseudonymous and has never been identified, but she deserves her pseudonym "Sophia" (i.e., "Wise Woman") in both its senses. Writing in 1739, she rejoins the theme taken up by Drake, insisting that lack of education alone has rendered women ill-equipped to contend with men on an equal footing. "Sophia" goes a step further than Drake when she argues that only prejudice, and the consequent lack of educational opportunities, keeps women from professional and public pursuits. Students should also note the zest with which she proceeds, and be asked whether and where her humor has a bitter cast.

Rousseau, one of only two men represented in this section, takes up the question of women's education in his novel/treatise *Emile: On Education* (1762). Unlike the other writers in this section, he believes women to be "naturally" dependent and inferior. First-time readers should think about his evidence for this belief. But unlike more conservative thinkers, Rousseau does not think that women's subordinate position should be the cause of denying them any educational opportunities. Instead, he argues that women's education should be designed to suit their position and function in society: to be pleasant companions to men, to manage a household properly, and to conduct the early education of children. The system of education he outlines will purportedly produce the ideal woman, whom he names "Sophie" (students will probably find this ironic, given the pseudonym of the preceding author). Students should be asked to evaluate this system, which does have some progressive tendencies, and to speculate on the likelihood of its producing the results Rousseau envisions.

The far more radical writings of Olympe de Gouges, represented by her "Rights of Women" (1791), was produced as a feminist counterpoint to the revolutionary declaration of "The Rights of Man." It is couched as a decree to be enacted by the National Assembly and is a thoroughgoing declaration of the equality of women in all social, legal, and political arrangements, much more detailed and pointed than the torpedoed American "Equal Rights Amendment" of the 1970s. Students can be asked to debate its enactment and possibly put it to a vote. This is by far the most clear-cut assertion of women's equal status in this section. De Gouges also communicates with great clarity an analogy handled by many of these writers: equating the status of women and slaves. Students can be asked to evaluate this analogy: Is it accurate? What are its weaknesses? Students should also be reminded that De Gouges was executed by the Jacobins in 1792 and that her proposals never came before the Assembly.

The German writer Theodor Gottlieb Von Hippel, whose *On Improving the Status of Women* (1792) is excerpted in this section, followed the developments in revolutionary France carefully, and in all probability read De Gouges's "Rights of Women." His legal training and his career as a public official orient his remarks, and he has no hesitance in recommending that women should be educated for and encouraged to assume a fully equal role in public life. In his view this would only serve the interests of the State, which under then-current arrangements was deprived of the services of half the population. Von Hippel is a formidable controversialist, and his rhetoric is often indignant with those who would deny women equal worth and status with men. This note of indignation, rising sometimes to exasperation, is often met with in this section, in apparent contradiction to Enlightenment ideals of measured rational dispute by people of good will in the pursuit of truth or of the right course of action. Students can be asked if this contradiction as it appears here and elsewhere in this section is more apparent than real, and also questioned as to its motivations.

This problem comes squarely to the fore in the excerpt from Mary Robinson's *Letter to the Women of England, on the Injustice of Mental Subordination* (1799). First-time readers are likely to see little but outrage in this excerpt. Robinson's culminating image for the position of women in her culture is Tantalus, "placed in a situation where the intellectual blessings she sighs for are within her view; she is conscious of possessing equally strong mental powers; but she is obliged to yield." In classroom discussion, this image, implicit in most of the materials in this section, can be usefully evaluated for its accuracy.

Another of the writers in this section is the well-known Hannah More, whose contribution is the "Introduction" to her *Strictures on the Modern System of Female Education* (1799). More was a conservative evangelical Christian, and her evident target is the corrupting triviality of the kind of ornamental education young women of the middle and upper classes typically received. However, her solution is not to recommend equality of educational opportunities or any genuine intellectual preparation for women that would fit them for public life. That is the last thing she has in view. Rather, she wants young women to receive the

kind of serious religious instruction that will fit young women for a lifetime of faithful domestic subjugation and child rearing. With this excerpt the first-time reader comes full circle; Drake did not recommend
the preparation of women for public life, but rather for useful private
companionship with men.

Topics for Writing

1. Women and slavery.
2. Women's intellectual capabilities.
3. The Enlightenment and women's rights.
4. The French Revolution and women's rights.

Further Reading

There is very little available in English on the subject of eighteenth-
century feminism or on the authors represented in this section. Beyond
the materials mentioned on pp. 2537, 2538, and 2539 in the *Anthology*,
consult the following two books.

Erica Harth. *Cartesian Women: Versions and Subversions of Rational Discourse in the Old Regime.* 1992.

Katharine Rogers. *Feminism in Eighteenth Century England.* 1982.

JONATHAN SWIFT

Gulliver's Travels

Classroom Strategies and Topics for Discussion

Students may well be bewildered by the sometimes bland, sometimes
ferocious tone of *Gulliver's Travels*, part IV, and by such questions as
What is Swift attacking? Why? What does it have to do with us? and,
most troubling of all, How can we be sure?—exactly the questions that
have disturbed generations of critics. It may be useful at the outset to
point out that a minimal definition of satire is "attack by indirection"
and to discuss the possibility that one important satiric function, often,
is to generate just the kind of trouble the students are presumably experiencing. *Gulliver's Travels* creates uncertainty partly because of society's
constantly changing assumptions about what is important, what is good,
for human beings. Swift concerns himself with such fundamental values. If he can make his readers inquire about their own assumptions, as
well as about how matters should be, he has achieved part of his aim.
His kind of satire does not produce certainties; it produces difficulties.

One can profitably organize discussion around a series of large and
obvious questions, with special attention to the need to support hy-
potheses from the text. First of all, what is the relation between the Yahoos and humankind? In answering (or attempting to answer) this
question, one must consider the development of Gulliver's attitude toward them. At the outset, he says, "I never beheld in all my travels so

disagreeable an animal, or one against which I naturally conceived so strong an antipathy." This response suggests that the Yahoos belong to an alien species. But Gulliver's convictions change, influenced partly by the assumptions of his Houyhnhnm hosts, who believe him to be of the Yahoo kind. The episode in which the young Yahoo girl pursues Gulliver with lustful intent might suggest that they belong to a single species. By the end, Gulliver believes all the rest of humanity to be Yahoos, but appears to exempt himself. He is, at any rate, a Yahoo educated in a way no other human being has enjoyed. If we accept Gulliver's view, we must understand this volume of *Gulliver's Travels* as constituting an unrelenting and total attack on humankind.

The problem of how far we can accept Gulliver's view must be dealt with fairly early in the discussion; it will certainly come up in the course of considering the Yahoo question. Evidence for Gulliver's state of mind after his sojourn with the Houyhnhnms comes from the book's final chapters and from the prefatory letter to Gulliver's cousin Sympson (which students should be urged to read, or to reread, *after* reading the narrative proper). The question can be formulated as one of delusion: Is Gulliver deluded after his journey? Does his attack on pride only conceal his own pride, his overweening desire to escape the limits of the human situation? In trying to decide how far we can accept his judgment (e.g., his judgment that human beings are Yahoos), one must try to assess the forces possibly operating to distort his judgment: for example, the pressures inherent in the master-slave relationship in which he finds himself.

The obvious corollary to the Yahoo question is the Houyhnhnm question. Whether or not people and Yahoos are the same, do Houyhnhnms represent an ideal for humanity? Considering this matter implies not only further speculation about Gulliver's dependability but direct assessment of the evidence. What are the characteristics of this race? Most salient, of course, is their allegiance to reason. They believe that reason is sufficient guide for a reasonable being. Is this conviction relevant to the realities of human existence? How does one respond to their lack of literature, to their difficulty in finding subject matter for conversation (Gulliver provides useful material for their talk), to such activities as their threading of needles, to their attitudes toward their young? If one has negative responses to any of their manifestations of commitment to reason, do such responses declare something wrong with them or something wrong with us?

The part of the book dealing with Gulliver's activities and responses after leaving the Houyhnhnms deserves particularly close attention. What does it mean, in Swift's satiric structure, that he is wounded by the arrow of savages? Certainly this fact suggests that man in the state of nature is brutal and far from being governed by reason and benevolence. But the character of the Portuguese captain also demands attention. Here is civilized man, acting with generosity and sympathy in the face of Gulliver's boorishness. Does the existence of such a man refute the identification of humanity with the Yahoos? What differences does it suggest between humanity and the Houyhnhnms? If Gulliver seems wrong (misguided) in his response to the captain's kindness, how does this fact bear on our assessment of his judgments?

The answers for this series of questions are largely indeterminate, and this fact itself must become an issue for discussion. It brings up a historical problem: does our difficulty in ascertaining where Swift stands come simply from the time that has elapsed since he wrote? One must suspect that shifts in general assumptions between the eighteenth century and the twentieth century help to account for the problematic aspects of this satire, but the difficulty in determining the exact scope of the attack is also partly built into the text. The historical problem, however, also creates an opportunity to raise the question of how far Swift's satire remains relevant to our own time, in which wars and lawyers and doctors and politicians continue to provide manifestations of folly and vice and in which questions about the human capacity for reason and virtue continue to present themselves.

One problem about teaching *Gulliver's Travels* (it's a problem in teaching everything, of course—but particularly here) is time. The general issues sketched above are peculiarly compelling, and they are *essential* to minimal understanding of the narrative. But Swift's local effects also deserve attention. If time permits, it is useful to take up such episodes as Gulliver's early conduct toward the Houyhnhnms (his assumption that they are to be won by bracelets and mirrors) and his recital to his master about the nature of civilized life. Students need to understand that in the structure of the narrative, Gulliver's account demonstrates considerable distortion and exaggeration, attributable to his desire to impress his master in various ways; and also that, in the structure of the satire, it exemplifies exactly the kind of distortion that generates emotional power. If it is not always clear what designs *Gulliver's Travels* has on the reader in the most general sense, it *is* clear that it attacks specific corruptions of eighteenth-century English society in a way that makes it relevant to our own.

A Modest Proposal

Classroom Strategies and Topics for Discussion

Virtually every teacher has at least one anecdote about trying to teach *A Modest Proposal* to a class whose members insisted on taking it straight, unable to comprehend the nature of Swift's irony. As the horrors of the twenty-first century multiply, it becomes harder and harder to appeal to universal standards of decency, to insist that of course we all know that no one would really think of eating children. Human skin has been made into lampshades; why shouldn't babies be made into meat? The problems of teaching this work, then, are clear-cut: to help students find the clues to Swiftian irony, and to make them understand what as well as how the satirist attacks.

One way to start is with the character of the speaker. What sort of person does he seem to be? Undergraduates can readily be brought to recognize his self-image as a practical, sensible man, fond of statistics ("three, four, or six children") and of economic solutions ("a fair, cheap, and easy method"), not devoid of vanity (he would like to have his statue set up as a preserver of the nation), both self-confident and ambitious (see the third paragraph). Students should be asked to read the opening paragraphs with particular care, and asked what is the first word that begins to make one suspicious about this projector. For most readers, it is "dam," in the fourth paragraph, with its suggestion that the speaker thinks of human beings, if they are poor, as identical with lower animals. One can trace further evidence of the projector's inhumanity, his incapacity to imagine the poor (or at least the Irish poor) as beings like himself, throughout the satire.

The speaker objects to his friend's proposal of butchering starving adolescents on the grounds that it might be censured as "a little bordering upon cruelty." Why does he not think of his own proposal as cruel? This topic is worth extended consideration. One can examine the various ways in which the projector demonstrates the need for drastic measures; the cruelty of the existing state of things, he implicitly and explicitly argues, far exceeds that of his scheme for remedying the situation. Particular attention should be paid to the italicized paragraph of "other expedients" that Swift would in fact advocate. What are these expedients like? It should be noted that they combine the practical and the moral; that they demand clear perception, concerted action, and steady moral awareness. The speaker's doubt that there will ever be a sincere attempt to put them in practice therefore suggests Swift's criticism of the Irish people as well as of their English oppressors.

This text of course provides abundant opportunity for talking about the classic problems of satire. Students might be interested to discuss the question of whether such writing as this implies any real purpose of reform or whether it constitutes only attack; and they might wish to talk about how the satire makes them feel, and why. (Indeed, such an apparently naïve approach to the work might be a profitable way to start.)

Topics for Writing

1. The importance of Gulliver's initial situation (how he is cast ashore) to the narrative.
2. How Gulliver sees himself.
3. A specific object of attack and how it is criticized.
4. Why are horses (rather than some other species) made creatures of pure reason?
5. A definition of a Yahoo.
6. A modest proposal for our time.
7. Has Swift any hope for Ireland?

Comparative Perspectives

1. Like the readers of this *Anthology*, Gulliver constantly finds himself in contact with strange worlds. What marks of cultural differ-

ence does he distinguish in the Houyhnhnms and the Yahoos that make them unlike their counterparts in England? How good an observer is he? Do you find yourself confronting similar signs of difference in any of the works you have been reading this semester? Give some examples and compare your criteria for evaluating what you have discovered with those used by Gulliver.

2. "The Houyhnhnms have no letters, and consequently, their knowledge is all traditional," Gulliver declares in the middle of chapter IX, but he praises their poetry. Writing in the 1700s, Swift may very well have had an opinion of this critical pronouncement quite different from ours. What works of oral cultures prove that poetry can exist without "letters"?

3. Impressed by the truthfulness of a society that lacks a word for "lie," Gulliver takes great pains in his conclusion to set himself apart from other travelers whose descriptions of their voyages "impose the grossest falsities on the unwary reader." Is factual accuracy always the best measure of truth? Have you read any travel accounts in this *Anthology* that challenge Gulliver's strictures here? Why do their writers sometimes say *the thing that is not*?

[If possible, compare Lucian's *A True Story*, as well as Voltaire's *Candide*.]

Further Reading

See also the reading suggestions in the *Anthology*, p. 2539.

Donoghue, D. *Jonathan Swift: A Critical Introduction.* 1969. An interpretation that seeks to avoid relying on irony as the governing mode of Swift's work. Offers a detailed exegesis of *Gulliver's Travels* as "an anatomy of human pride."

Ehrenpreis, I. *Swift: The Man, His Works, and the Age.* 3 vols. 1962–83. The definitive critical biography. Vol. 3, *Dean Swift*, contains detailed treatments of *Gulliver's Travels* and *A Modest Proposal:* accounts of their composition and publication as well as critical analysis.

Quintana, R. *The Mind and Art of Jonathan Swift.* 1956. An accessible introduction to Swift. Provides both biographical data and a critical survey of thought and technique.

Reilly, E. J., ed. *Approaches to Teaching Swift's* Gulliver's Travels. 1988. Immensely useful, pedagogically focused collection of essays.

ALEXANDER POPE

The Rape of the Lock

Classroom Strategies and Topics for Discussion

This fanciful narrative of trivial pursuits uses its account of a belle's pleasures and conflicts to suggest the moral flaws and the aesthetic values of early eighteenth-century English social life. Its allusions to epic imply intent to comment on the preoccupations of a society—not, of course, "society" in its largest sense, the community of humankind, but the limited aristocratic society of eighteenth-century London, concerned with appearance and with luxury rather than with genuine accomplishment, cut off from realities of human suffering, yet miniaturizing the same desires that drive the heroes of the *Aeneid* or the *Iliad*. One problem you face is to ask students to discover connections between eighteenth-century London society and its twenty-first-century American counterpart.

The glittering smoothness of Pope's verse, concealing complexities of thought, sometimes creates the illusion that the poetry is easy to read. It isn't, of course, given its density of meaning, but first-time readers have to be shown that it's worth struggling with. You might find it useful to spend time working on a single short passage: for example, the toilette scene at the end of canto I (lines 121–48). By exploring in depth the implications of such a phrase as "the sacred rites of Pride" (line 128), you can demonstrate what close attention Pope's language demands and what rewards it offers. Why are these rites "sacred"? And why, for that matter, are they "rites"? As students begin to realize how completely Belinda (and her society, and ours, and we ourselves) has ritualized everyday procedures, they come to understand why the trivial receives so much emphasis in the poem and in our own lives. The necessity for putting on makeup is never questioned in Belinda's world, as the order of religious rituals is never questioned. The sequence of rouge and powder and eyeshadow is unvaried, unchallenged. Like other "rites," this one of makeup provides a stay against confusion, an assertion of continuity and of power. Such rites are "sacred" because they participate in a religion of self-love belonging not only to Belinda herself but to the community in which she participates. And they are *called* "sacred" in the poem to remind us of other more significant rites that they trivialize.

If it is possible to spend two class hours on this poem, students might be asked to read it in its entirety for the first meeting, which could concentrate on close reading of a relatively short sequence; the class might read the poem again for the second meeting, and then engage in a more general discussion of the poem as a whole.

Students often find the couplet structure monotonous and uninteresting. The best way to disabuse them of the notion that Pope engages in a kind of automatic writing is to ask each to compose a single couplet. The experience of trying to condense meaning into two rhymed pentameter lines usually proves both chastening and enlightening.

Sometimes students assume that *The Rape of the Lock* is as trivial as its subject matter. But of course the trivial can be highly revealing, in Pope's time and in ours. A character who mingles Bibles and love letters on her dressing table bears some resemblance to the student who reads Milton while listening to rock music: incompatible commitments jostle in all our minds. To call attention to such jostling does not imply the commentator's frivolity, but it's usually necessary to spend a good deal of time demonstrating how Pope enforces his criticism of a group that has lost its sense that some values are preferable to others, as well as time talking about why mere "silliness" matters in the moral scheme.

Students can become quite involved in the problem of how to ascertain the poet's precise targets of attack. The famous couplet, "The hungry judges soon the sentence sign, / And wretches hang that jurymen may dine" (III.21–22) provides an obvious example of satiric attack, in which the extreme discrepancy between the motivation of judge and jury and the fate of the "wretches" they condemn calls attention to something wrong in society. Discussion might move from this sort of obvious satiric instance to other kinds of discrepancy: between staining one's honor and one's dress, for example, or between the stately elephant and the comb to which its tusks are converted. Pope's discrepancies typically alert the reader to "something wrong"; figuring out just what is wrong and why often proves a valuable enterprise.

One more difficulty troubling many readers of Pope is ascertaining positive value in *The Rape of the Lock*. What does the poet believe in? This is by no means a simple question to answer, but it is a useful one to confront. Clarissa's counsel of good sense provides one standard by which to judge the deviations from the sensible that pervade the poem, but it is not the only standard. Why is the lock taken up into the heavens, why does the poem conclude with stress on its own permanence, and why is Belinda's world evoked with such poetic beauty? The answers to all these questions are surely related: the poet, too, appears to believe in the aesthetic, in the necessity and the lastingness of the art that transforms the trivial into the stuff of poetry (or of constellations).

Topics for Writing

These develop readily from the kinds of discussions suggested above. A few possibilities.

1. The function of Clarissa's speech.
2. The importance of the Sylphs.
3. The concept of manhood in *The Rape of the Lock*.
4. What's wrong with Belinda?
5. Why the Cave of Spleen?

An Essay on Man

Classroom Strategies and Topics for Discussion

Students—like other people—often have trouble with the very idea of a philosophic poem: the notion of the "philosophic," they seem to feel, opposes that of the "poetic." The teacher's problem, then, is to demonstrate (or to help the class discover) how Pope reconciles the two modes—a task made more difficult by the fact that *An Essay on Man*, unlike *Paradise Lost*, presents no sustained characters.

As usual, a good place to start is at the beginning, with the introductory section. Students can be asked to locate Pope's images: maze, wild, garden, field, "Nature's walks," "Folly" and "Manners" as birds to be hunted. Then they can discuss how the images' implications expand. Why, for example, is the garden "tempting with forbidden fruit" (line 8)? The world is thus made analogous to Eden, and humankind, by implication, is in danger of recommitting the original sin of Adam and Eve. Thinking about the rest of epistle I, students might speculate about what this sin constitutes, how it might be repeated. As the epistle develops, it increasingly emphasizes the human tendency to pride (and the degree to which this tendency often seems inherent in the very act of presuming to philosophize). Eve too, as readers of *Paradise Lost* may remember, was victimized by pride: the desire to assume a place closer to that of Deity. The introductory section of *An Essay on Man* thus foretells the epistle's argument in specifically metaphoric terms. Reminded of the particular allusion to *Paradise Lost* in line 16, students may wish to reflect about how *vindicate* differs from *justify*, Milton's word: what a different (more combative, more skeptical) universe the change of a verb implies. Enough time should be spent on this section (the development of the hunting metaphor, with its casual tone and purposeful rhetoric, also repays attention; and the conversational, almost joking tone of the opening couplet) for the class to realize that Pope has established a situation and an atmosphere not at all predictable for philosophic verse, and that he has done so by relying on traditional poetic devices.

Students will probably be eager to discuss, even to argue about, the nature of Pope's thought. It is valuable to trace the argument as it develops, section by section, through the epistle, pausing on the question of how connections are made between one point and the next. A useful way to link Pope's method with his subject is to look for persuasive devices. How does the poet seek to convince his audience of the rightness of his view? Aspects of the poem likely to attract comment in this connection include the use of example, both brief images ("die of a rose in aromatic pain" [line 200]) and more extended vignettes (the poor Indian, or the lamb licking the hand of its slaughterer), and of the sheer power of sound and rhythm as persuasive devices (the concluding passage, for instance). Discussion of the poem's shifting tone would also be appropriate. If asked, after talking about such matters, whether Pope relies more heavily on intellectual or on emotional arguments, students are likely to agree at least that emotional persuasion forms an important part of his agenda: that he works, in this respect, more like what they might expect of a poet than what they might expect of a philosopher.

Another fruitful subject for discussion is the relationship, or series of relationships, established between the narrator and the reader. The section numbered I, for instance, begins in a measured, reasoned tone suggesting the opening of a set of intellectual propositions. By the end of the eighteen-line section, the narrator is beginning to insult the reader ("Is the great chain, that draws all to agree, / And drawn supports, upheld by God, or thee?" [lines 33–34]) by calling attention to that reader's insignificance in the universe; the next section, emphasizing humankind's pettiness, begins, "Presumptuous Man!" Alternations of didacticism, insult, a kind of cooperative reasoning (see section V), and inspirational rhetoric (section VIII) continue through the poem, shifting with bewildering rapidity. Asked to think about this technique in relation to Pope's purposes here, students might conclude that the poet's rhetorical agility calls attention to exactly the problem the epistle's title announces: "The Nature and State of Man, with Respect to the Universe." The dilemma about humanity's nature and state involves the poet as speaker and the reader as listener: neither poet nor reader, it seems, can securely know his or her position. Sometimes the poet appears to understand everything; sometimes he shares the humility he enjoins for the reader; sometimes he substitutes awe for comprehension. Always he dramatizes the human position.

Specific passages worth special attention include the short sequence on the passions (lines 165–72), interesting to discuss as exemplifying Pope's emotional and ideological commitment to necessity for action: the passions may be good or bad in themselves, but they *function* for good because they make things happen. The lines beginning "All are but parts of one stupendous whole" (lines 267–80) are important for defining Pope's view of the universal scheme in terms that will be useful if you teach Wordsworth.

Topics for Writing

1. Why the poor Indian?
2. How the satiric impulse is expressed in *An Essay on Man*.
3. A specific image and how it works.
4. What does Pope mean by "order"?
5. The function of animals in the poem.

Comparative Perspectives

1. Although Pope goes back to the classical tradition in these works, he also invokes a vernacular world. How would you compare his treatment of domestic and everyday life with Dorothy Wordsworth's in *The Grasmere Journals* or Flaubert's in *Madame Bovary*? What kinds of details do they single out? Do they view ordinary life as laughable, serious, or dull?
2. How committed are Pope and Dr. Johnson to the traditional values and sense of order (classical and Christian) against which their characters are measured? What balance of ancient and modern does each seem to prefer?
3. Compare Pope's attitude toward evil with that expressed by Machiavelli in *The Prince* by discussing the reference to Cesare Borgia in *An Essay on Man* (line 156) in relation to "New Princedoms Gained with Other Men's Forces and through Fortunes," in which Machiavelli describes Cesare Borgia's political and military tactics (Vol. 1).

Further Reading

See also the reading suggestions in the *Anthology*, p. 2538.

Griffin, De. *Alexander Pope: The Poet in the Poem.* 1978. Uses biographical data to help explain the positions taken by the speakers in Pope's poems.

Guerinot, J., ed. *Pope: A Collection of Critical Essays.* 1972. Provides a survey of critical approaches useful to the student.

Jackson, W. and R. P. Yoder, eds. *Approaches to Teaching Pope's Poetry.* 1993. A volume in the MLA series, with several relevant articles.

Spacks, P. *An Argument of Images.* 1972. Interprets Pope's imagery in comparison with his poetic predecessors and successors.

FRANÇOIS-MARIE AROUET DE VOLTAIRE

Candide, or Optimism

Classroom Strategies and Topics for Discussion

Its combination of metaphysical and social satire makes *Candide* both exciting and problematic. What is the connection between pointing out the barbarities of war and of organized religion (themes also of Swift in *Gulliver's Travels*) and calling attention to the possible fatuities of philosophic optimism (by exaggerating and simplifying ideas like those in *An Essay on Man*)? How does Voltaire persuade us to tolerate, and even to laugh at, recitals of incredible horror? If such questions are too large and forbidding for students (or anyone else), answers to them can at least be approached by discussing specific aspects of *Candide*.

To begin with the first chapter: a useful exercise is to try collectively to separate sentences with satiric bite from those (like the first) that seem intended quite seriously. There will probably be dispute about at least a few examples—a development that can profitably lead to questions about how one decides. Even if everyone agrees about everything, the group can discuss how they know what is straightforward and what satiric. Such discussion should include consideration of the matter of assumed common standards. We all agree, presumably, that for a woman to weigh three hundred and fifty pounds is not sufficient reason for her to be respected, and that the congruity of noses and spectacles is not part of the order of nature. What is worth emphasizing is that we share these assumptions, and many others, with Voltaire, and that he can and does draw on them in constructing his satiric fiction: moreover, that without at least some vestige of such shared standards, we would be unable to recognize satire. This point is important for students to understand, both because it helps them to realize that the gap between the eighteenth and twenty-first centuries is not in every respect so great as they imagine and because it is absolutely fundamental to an understanding of satire.

Candide's experiences in the Bulgar army typify central patterns of

Voltaire's work. You might call the class's attention to the enormous speed of the narrative (other sequences of the fiction would of course work equally well to demonstrate this aspect of Voltaire's technique). Detailed discussion of effects generated by this speed is likely to prove profitable. For instance, it's worth pointing out that the failure to linger over gruesome details helps to suggest that they are not too serious after all. Their lack of apparent "seriousness" of course depends on their emphatic fictionality: because the narrator himself seems unconcerned, seems to think these things don't matter much, we are reminded that they belong to the realm of imagination. If they had really happened, they would horrify the narrator and the reader alike. The speed of movement also has a comic effect: the sheer incongruity between the dreadfulness of what allegedly happens and the gusto and rapidity with which reports of the dreadful pile up makes us smile. Consideration of this sort of effect enlarges understanding of the workings of satire, which typically depends on exaggeration and unmistakable distancing from the actual to enforce its comments. In this connection, it is perhaps worth inquiring whether the literal horrors of twenty-first-century war, far in excess of anything Voltaire has imagined, have any effect on our response to Voltairean satire.

A large question that will both interest students and draw them closer to the workings of this fiction concerns the functions of sex in the narrative. What purpose does the stress on sexual feeling and action serve? As in *Phaedra*, although of course with tonality as different as possible, sexuality makes people vulnerable. It is a form of feeling all men and women share, a defining aspect of animal nature but also, in some of its specific expressions, of human nature. The relation between animality and humanity is a recurrent theme of *Candide*; students might be asked to find examples of it. In this respect and others, the sexual expressiveness of men and women epitomizes kinds of paradox that interest Voltaire. Sexuality involves both weakness and strength, pleasure and pain, physical disease and psychic health, human connection and violation, and so on. Students can find instances of apparently contradictory values associated with sex, and can move from these to realization of how *Candide* constructs a notion of humanity far too complicated to be contained in a Panglossian scheme of things.

What keeps one reading this narrative? Voltaire generates genuine suspense, not so much about his characters as about the workings of his imagination. What will he think of next; what further excess will he conjure up? What explanation will he find for the fact that the old woman has only one buttock? Our interest in the operations of the satirist's fancy intensifies satiric effect: as we realize that we are enjoying images of rape, murder, treachery, violence, we are presumably led to reflect on the real occurrences of such phenomena in our own world, on how we respond to them (when, for example, they are reported on TV), and on the implications of our capacity to tolerate horrors when they happen to other people.

But another point that should be discussed is the incursions of realism into this text. In what ways, to what extent, does Voltaire rely on realistic insights? In chapter 14, Candide laments, "Cunégonde, brought from so far, what will ever become of you?" Cacambo responds, "She'll become what she can . . . women can always find something to do with themselves; God sees to it; let's get going." Cacambo's kind of practicality accepts the limitations of a fiercely competitive world and acknowledges the need for dealing with the given. (His attribution of women's instinct for self-preservation to God is another matter, more closely related to Voltaire's satiric pattern.) The kind of comment we might call "realistic" is here typically a general observation on human nature or habits drawn from the exaggerated experience of the protagonists. Students can easily multiply examples. In this way—by offering generalizations of which we recognize the cogency—Voltaire keeps his satire rooted in truths we can acknowledge. (Again, the matter of shared assumptions between author and reader is relevant.)

Increasingly toward the end of the tale, the narrative dwells on human corruption (e.g., the shooting of admirals, the deposing of kings, the various operations of avarice, lust, envy, competitiveness). In the last chapter, "Pangloss asserted that he had always suffered horribly; but having once declared that everything was marvelously well, he continued to repeat the opinion and didn't believe a word of it." By the time we are told directly that Pangloss doesn't believe his own philosophic contentions, we have been brought to realize that philosophic optimism (here parodied as the view that everything is for the best in this best of all possible worlds) itself amounts to one of the constructions human beings make to protect themselves from reality—like Pococurante's belief that nothing is of value, Candide's declarations of love for Cunégonde; and like the human propensity for war, thievery, and rape, all of which constitute modes of asserting or acquiring power and importance. Political arrangements and philosophic beliefs, the work has shown, have a good deal in common.

Topics for Writing

1. Could Voltaire satirize Hitler?
2. An exercise in Voltaire satire (i.e., student attempts in the mode).
3. What Candide learns.
4. A moment of comedy and how its effect contributes to the satire.
5. The function of some minor character.
6. The relation of the conclusion to the beginning.

Comparative Perspectives

Like many of the travelers depicted in this *Anthology*, Candide has an entourage. What literary purpose is served by making a traveler one of a group? How does the tone of a travel narrative differ when the protagonist forges on alone, as in the case of *Gulliver's Travels*? See also comparisons suggested to Frederick Douglass, *Narrative of the Life of an American Slave*; Camus, *The Guest*.

Further Reading

See also the reading suggestions in the *Anthology*, p. 2539.

Aldridge, A. *Voltaire and the Century of Light.* 1975. The biographical treatment emphasizes both personality and thought, "combining the methods of comparative literature and the history of ideas."

Torrey, N. *The Spirit of Voltaire.* 1938. Provides a biographical treatment with emphasis on Voltaire's intellectual life and development.

Wade, I. *The Intellectual Development of Voltaire.* 1969. Supplies an exhaustive examination of Voltaire's intellectual life.

Waldinger, R., ed. *Approaches to Teaching Voltaire's* Candide. 1989. This collection of essays by many authors, published by the MLA, is designed to help teachers in the classroom.

SAMUEL JOHNSON

The History of Rasselas, Prince of Abissinia

Classroom Strategies and Topics for Discussion

What often makes *Rasselas* puzzling to modern readers is the nature of its status as fiction. On the one hand, it offers a fanciful setting at the outset, a kind of latter-day Eden, and presents a series of clearly imaginary characters traveling and having diverse experiences in a way familiar to any reader of picaresque fiction. On the other hand, the characters all sound roughly the same—their voices are not really differentiated—and nothing that happens to them makes much difference: it only provides material for elaborate semiphilosophical reflection. Perhaps the best way of tackling this problem is to confront it directly, to ask students to think about what kind of fiction this is. The terminology doesn't matter (to explain that this is a "philosophical tale" only obscures the difficulty of reading it); what matters is trying to figure out what Johnson is doing here and why.

So a good place to start is to ask how the characters are distinguished from one another. It's useful to read aloud, say, a speech by Nekayah and one by Rasselas, and to inquire how one tells the difference. In some instances (as when Nekayah investigates private life and Rasselas public), difference in immediate experience produces differences in what they say, but there is little contrast in the way they say it. Similarly, Imlac differs from the others in having had more experiences before the escape from the Happy Valley, but only in that respect. One has little sense of distinct personality in any of the travelers. What degree of interest do their adventures generate? The only real suspense concerns their efforts to find out what they should do in life, and it comes as little surprise that they reach no firm conclusion.

Once a group agrees, as it almost certainly will, that Johnson's characters all sound alike and that their adventures elicit no suspense to speak of and little excitement, the next obvious question is what Johnson is trying to accomplish here. He does not appear to have conventional fictional purposes; it is not hard to decide that his intent is didactic. But what is he trying to teach, and why does he choose this particular method of instruction?

These large questions may be announced fairly early, but they will only be answered by close attention to what is going on in the text. The Happy Valley section offers some interesting problems. Does one feel that Rasselas is wise or mistaken in wanting to get away? How does the language generate a feeling of uneasiness about this idyllic setting? Students can be asked to find the words that suggest something wrong here—words like *imprisonment* and *tediousness*. It's useful to call attention to the degree of effort that seems to be involved in making the place attractive for its inhabitants. Rasselas's experience of boredom is convincingly rendered. But if one sympathizes with the young man's desire to escape his benign environment, what does such sympathy mean? Is the point that humankind, in its imperfection, cannot be happy with perfection? Or is there really something wrong with the Happy Valley? Perhaps the best answer to these questions is Imlac's observation, in relation to his own life, that "some desire is necessary to keep life in motion."

Imlac's narrative of his past experience is worth close attention. He reaches the conclusion, in one of Johnson's best-known formulations, that "Human life is every where a state in which much is to be endured, and little to be enjoyed." Although the actual events of his earlier life bear little relation to those the travelers will undergo, it can be argued that his brief autobiography is a miniature version of what happens later in the narrative. Students can be asked to support or refute this contention by reference to the text. A specific point worth attending to is the famous dissertation on poetry. How does that relate to what happens later, to the argument as a whole? It announces the discrepancy between the imagined and the actual that the rest of the story will reiterate in many different ways; when students see that point, they will begin to see how ingeniously Johnson has enforced a consistent vision of life.

To substantiate that vision is, of course, the didactic function of the tale. If class discussion does not arrive at the conclusion that *Rasselas* is primarily concerned with exploring the power and the danger of the imagination, the instructor can suggest this view as a hypothesis. Then the group can look at any single episode, or any group of episodes, to see how the idea is embodied (the philosopher unable to face the death of his child—he has constructed a set of theories with no relation to actuality; the mad astronomer, who has a vision of himself equally unrelated to the real; the pyramids, which show the imaginative boldness of an ancient people vainly trying to surmount the limitations of mortality; and so on). Even at the narrative's end, when the protagonists are disillusioned, they retain shreds of their own imaginative compulsions. (Any adequate discussion of this tale will of course confront the problem of the ending: what does it mean that the travelers return to Abyssinia? Are they going back to the Happy Valley? If so, why?)

But the final question remains: if this is in fact a treatise on the imagination, why cast it in the form of a fiction? If earlier discussion has concluded that characters are differentiated largely on the basis of their experience, the matter of experience is worth returning to at the end. Johnson's differentiations imply that experience is essential to the making of a human being. Experience is an important value in *Rasselas*; the gaining of experience—experience of events and of other people—appears to be the only way for people to combat in themselves the hunger of imagination. The mad astronomer, after all, loses his delusion only by associating with others. Johnson's use of a fictional form, a form dependent on the idea of characters if not of individually distinguished character, declares his conviction that abstract truths have no meaning: they mean only as they are experienced. He demonstrates (or at least outlines) the process of learning in his characters; he hopes to induce a comparable process in his readers, who have the benefit of vicarious experience through the fictional model.

Topics for Writing

1. Johnson's arguments against the pursuit of happiness.
2. Rasselas as an idealist.
3. What does Rasselas learn?
4. The importance of the pyramids in the narrative.
5. How happy is the Happy Valley?

Comparative Perspectives

1. Among the many similarities between Candide and Rasselas is the choice of an Eastern, or Islamic, venue in which the protagonists pursue their quests for understanding and truth. Compare and contrast Voltaire's depiction of Constantinople with Johnson's portrait of that city's murderous politics in chapter 24 of *Rasselas*; and consider the way in which each author reflects on European concerns from the vantage point of his protagonist's travels. Cite examples from each text that characterize the satiric weight of these narratives. Is Johnson as interested in reforming institutions as Voltaire seems to be?
2. Nekayah, a keen observer of domestic conflict and marital unhappiness, utters one of Dr. Johnson's most famous percepts: "Marriage has many pains, but celibacy has no pleasures" (end of chapter 27). Many of the texts in this section of the *Anthology* are devoted at least in part to an exploration of the nature of marriage: Drawing your evidence from any of them (*Tartuffe, The Princess of Clèves, Phaedra, Gulliver's Travels, The Rape of the Lock*), try to construct an image of the ideal Enlightenment marriage and evaluate its features from a contemporary point of view.
3. Johnson died just as Romanticism was about to overturn many of the assumptions he had made about the function of literature. (He loathed pastoral poetry, for example, yet he allows Nekayah to con-

fess a tendency "to play the shepherdess in my waking dreams.")
Using Imlac's ideas about "the dangerous prevalence of imagination" (chapter 43) as your base, explain how any one of the Romantic poets would respond to Imlac's pronouncements that "all
power of fancy over reason is a degree of insanity." What views of
insanity and imagination become prevalent in nineteenth-century
literature?

Further Reading

See also the reading suggestions in the *Anthology*, p. 2537.

Anderson, D. R., and G. W. Kolb, eds. *Approaches to Teaching the Works of Samuel. Johnson.* A volume in the MLA series.

Bate, W. J. *Samuel Johnson.* 1977. Likely to remain the best biography since Boswell, exhaustive in critical exploration of Johnson's work as well as supplying data about the life. Also, Bate's earlier *The Achievement of Samuel Johnson* (1955)—shorter and more concentrated on locating general themes in Johnson.

Greene, D. *Samuel Johnson.* 1970. Provides a somewhat quirky but thorough and stimulating introduction; Greene also edited *Samuel Johnson: A Collection of Critical Essays* (1965), which contains good general essays on Johnson, though nothing centrally concerned with *Rasselas.*

Korshin, P. J., ed. *Johnson after Two Hundred Years.* 1986. Essays by many writers, offering contemporary reassessments.

McIntosh, C. *The Choice of Life: Samuel Johnson and the World of Fiction.* 1973. The most valuable work on *Rasselas* in particular. Places Johnson's fiction in the context not only of the eighteenth-century novel but of other forms of contemporary fiction, by Johnson and others—satire, periodical essays, Oriental tales, and others.

The Nineteenth Century: Romanticism

JEAN-JACQUES ROUSSEAU

Confessions

Classroom Strategies and Topics for Discussion

The aspect of Rousseau's autobiographical writing likely to interest students most, even in a fragmentary selection, is the author's determination to create a mythology of the self. Class time can profitably be occupied in tracing elements in Rousseau's systematic development of a self-image that coincides with his notion of what a man should be. Most important, perhaps, is his emphasis on his "passions" as defining a central aspect of his nature. You might ask students to locate occurrences of the word and the concept of passion. The writer claims for himself "unique" knowledge of the passions as a child-reader; he celebrates his own passion for music; he characterizes himself as "a man of very strong passions," which take total command of his personality; he suggests that no one has ever possessed passions "at once more lively and purer" than his own; he boasts his "lively and tumultuous passions"; and so on. Everyone has passions (meaning strong feelings), of course; why does Rousseau believe his own feelings so important? As students speculate about this question, it would be worth suggesting that they think back to the eighteenth-century texts they have read, and the very different valuation of the passions expressed or hinted in them. In *Phaedra*, for example, passion is the enemy of reason and of civil order; in *Gulliver's Travels*, part IV, it belongs only to Yahoos. If *An Essay on Man* indicates that passion generates action, it also suggests the need for restraint. Such reminders will emphasize that Rousseau's self-glorification on the basis of his own intense and uncontrollable passion implies a new value system. Possible answers to the question about why Rousseau assigns such importance to his passions include the hypothesis that strong feelings are associated with "naturalness" and with authenticity. Even when Rousseau says of himself that he is marked by "sluggishness of thought" along with his "liveliness of feeling," he describes himself as a man whose thought readily becomes inextricably mixed with feeling; the resulting "agitation" testifies once more to his status as a being uncorrupted because uncontrolled.

Other aspects of his personality that Rousseau emphasizes include his imagination, his attachment to nature, his commitment to impulse, his interest in the common people. Each of these characteristics could also become subjects of discussion that might dwell on how this writer differs from his eighteenth-century predecessors. Possibly even more fruitful would be an examination of the idea of uniqueness in the *Confessions*. The book opens, of course, with the author's claim of absolute distinction ("If I am not better, at least I am different"). In book II, however, Rousseau observes, "I have been reproached with wanting to pose as an original, and different from others. In reality, I have never troubled about acting like other people or differently from them." And in book VI, instead of asserting his difference, he *wonders* about whether others share his ideas. Is it possible to reconcile these claims? One can, of course, emphasize the verb "pose" in the second sequence: Rousseau doesn't want to *pose* as an original; he simply *is* one. But the question of posing or acting is a useful one to bring up in connection with the *Confessions*. Is all Rousseau's self-presentation perhaps a form of posing? His wondering about other people acknowledges the mystery of uniqueness. In fact, no one can possibly know whether he or she is different from everyone else. So to claim difference, as Rousseau does at the outset, necessarily involves a kind of posing. But is that necessarily a bad thing? Such questions can obviously lead to consideration of the perplexing problem of what autobiography as a genre implies.

Rousseau himself directly brings up the problem of autobiographical narrative in the selection quoted from book VI. He suggests the difficulty of communicating the source of feeling, the impossibility of making narrative equivalent to memory. Students may be asked to assess the degree to which he in fact solves these problems. Does he convincingly evoke feeling and memory? If so, how?

Topics for Writing

A useful paper assignment is to ask students to write a fragment of their own "confessions." Other possibilities:

1. The place of imagination for Rousseau.
2. Rousseau's evocation of Paris.
3. A description of Rousseau as a child.

Comparative Perspectives

1. As self-contemplating wanderers and lovers of nature, Rousseau, Wordsworth, and Whitman share many personal preferences, but their cultural backgrounds are quite distinct. How important to each of these three gigantic figures are other people? How fully does each identify with his country and its principles? Is Rousseau a "Swiss" or "French" writer in the sense that Wordsworth is "English" and Whitman "American"?
2. Rousseau wishes to "dispose of Nature in its entirety as its lord and

master," and exults in his power to express the sensations he draws
from it. How does his pleasure in appropriating the natural world
for his own delectation compare with the approach to nature observed in the lyrics of some of the later Romantic poets, such as
Bécquer or Leopardi?

Further Reading

See also the reading suggestions in the *Anthology*, p. 2538.

Crocker, L. *Jean-Jacques Rousseau*. 2 vols. 1963. An exhaustive and perceptive treatment of Rousseau's life and works.

France, P. *Rousseau*, Confessions. 1987. A critical study entirely focused
on the *Confessions*.

Gremsley, R. *Jean-Jacques Rousseau: A Study in Self-Awareness*. 1961.
Provides psychological analysis of Rousseau's personality.

Guéhenno, J. *Jean-Jacques Rousseau*. Trans. J. and D. Weightman. 2
vols. 1966. Another excellent critical biography (its treatment of the
Confessions is confined to Vol. 2).

Havens, G. *Jean-Jacques Rousseau*. 1978. In the Twayne series. A rather
pedestrian but useful general introduction.

JOHANN WOLFGANG VON GOETHE

Faust

Classroom Strategies and Topics for Discussion

As the "type characters" in Molière are likely to create problems for
student readers, so are the personages of Goethe's *Faust*. You can sim-
plify the task of reading this work (probably in two assignments, the first
one ending just before the first appearance of Margarete, l.2396), by explaining that Faust can best be read as a philosophic poem. Its characters exemplify positions rather than developed personalities. Such
positions, however, can be very complex indeed; a good place to start
discussion of the play is by trying to elucidate together the set of attitudes and assumptions that Faust himself embodies.

What, first of all, about his attitude toward knowledge? Those who
know Marlowe's *Doctor Faustus* or other versions of the Faust legend
may anticipate that the protagonist will seek intellectual grasp or comprehension of the universe. In fact, it is Faust's rather foolish and obtuse
assistant, Wagner, who aims "at knowing everything." Faust, on the
other hand, proclaims that "nobody knows, or ever can know, the tiniest
crumb!" He adds immediately, " I feel completely undone" (l.129). Does
he mean that the knowledge he has gained all seems irrelevant to his
purposes? or that none of it means anything? or what? Detailed analysis
of his first speech will announce the chief problems of his role. *Why* can
he not presume to make use of his learning, or open his mind to improve

humankind? No answer is immediately given in the text; students should be urged to support speculations based on later passages and actual textual evidence. They may well conclude—even on the basis of the first speech as a whole—that Faust cannot use his learning or improve humankind because learning has nothing to do with reality and because people exist only in individual isolation.

As the first speech continues, it becomes ever clearer that Faust wishes not to gain more knowledge but to escape the knowledge he has acquired. He wants to leave his "books, worm-eaten, covered with dust," to unite himself with nature, to "escape outdoors! Breathe the fresh air," to participate in the world rather than deal with "skeletons" (books and theories). A useful question is how the concepts that seem important to Faust compare with those apparently important to Rousseau. Nature and imagination are key ideas here too; the common people are valued (in the scene where Faust walks in the village), and so is feeling. But Faust dwells on these ideas in more meditative and detailed fashion than does Rousseau. Rousseau assumes their authority; Faust comes closer to arguing it. The question of his heroic stature is perhaps best postponed until students have finished reading the entire play, but it is worth inquiring even at the outset what kind of impression his passionate investment in his own convictions makes on first-time readers.

An important early piece of action is Faust's near-suicide. What impels him to kill himself? One way of answering this question (there are of course others, and students should be encouraged to find them) is to say that he cannot tolerate the gap between his capacity to imagine and his capacity to act. He can conceive of great possibilities for himself, but the realities of experience and of other people keep frustrating them. (This source of pain is best articulated in the soliloquy beginning "How such fellows keep their hopes up is a wonder" (l.377). The choir of angels he hears saves him from self-destruction; why? Its meaning seems concerned less with religion than with memory—"yet all's familiar from when I was young, and back to life I feel myself summoned" (l.544). Memory involves reminiscences of past faith and, perhaps, of past community.

Faust, like Rousseau, considers himself unique, superior to others. Mephistopheles presents himself as "the spirit that says no, no always," and Faust, accepting him, implicitly denies himself association with his kind. An important issue for class discussion of the first reading assignment is Faust's pact with the devil. Why does he voluntarily accept death and damnation if ever he stretches himself on a bed of sloth? This is a complicated and important question. In assessing why Faust in effect equates sloth and death, students should be urged to think, for example, of the scene in which he amends the Bible, denying the power of the Word as originating force, replacing Word with Mind, then with Force, then with Act. As Faust says shortly after making his compact, "To be always up and doing is man's nature." A little later, he makes it clear that he desires "the realization of all human possibility, that crown my soul so avidly reaches for." The class should consider such statements (and others) as evidence for the high value Faust attaches to *effort* and *force* and *action* as defining characteristics of the truly human. His aspiration involves the need constantly to *do*, without much regard for what the doing specifically involves.

When Margarete enters the play, its emphasis changes. Discussion of the second assignment might begin with the figure of Margarete. In her first appearance, she seems rather spunky ("I can find my way unaided" [l. 2400]), but once Mephistopheles begins plotting on Faust's behalf to get her, she loses obvious force of character. What is her function in the play? Neither great beauty nor great intelligence is assigned her; she epitomizes virtue but falls easily to Faust. One way of understanding her (students may generate this hypothesis themselves, or be asked what they think of it) is as a projection of Faust's desires. What does he want in a woman? He rhapsodizes over the neatness of her room; he praises her as an "angel." If he himself wants to act and desire without ceasing, he appears to wish for a woman who will do neither except in response to him. Margarete fills his needs because she so readily makes him the center of her universe (he is already the center of his own). But at the end of Part I, she transcends his construction of her. Is her refusal of his rescue attempt psychologically and morally plausible? The question admits of much debate. One can at least argue that her reaffirmation of the moral authority of her religion and her community both fits with her previously demonstrated need for self-subordination and shows how, in the play's logic, a sense of guilt (which Faust is only beginning to develop) can be liberating. Certainly the voice from above that pronounces her "redemption" suggests that her misery results in a happy ending.

Obviously important to the structure and the argument of *Faust* is Mephistopheles, worth attention both for the way that his moral position is established and elaborated and for the relation of that position to Faust's. A crude way to put the contrast between him and Faust might be to suggest that he always takes a cynical view of experience and Faust often takes an idealistic one. Discussion of this point might begin with investigation of the dialogue just before the scene in Marthe's garden, where Faust, and Mephistopheles spar about truth, deception, cynicism and choice. One brilliant aspect of this play is the way it demonstrates the partial accuracy of many points of view. Faust's conviction of the absolute authenticity and authority of his own feelings is from one viewpoint naïve and self-centered; from another, it affirms the value of the emotional capacity that presumably helps to differentiate humanity from the lower animals. Conversely, Mephistopheles's cynicism is entirely too easy—everything in experience is obviously susceptible to his kind of criticism; the value of feeling and aspiration can in the nature of things never be proved. But it also calls attention to the equivalent "easiness" in Faust's protestations. Students can be led toward an understanding of the relationship of cross-commentary between Faust and Mephistopheles by beginning with an apparently simple but engaging question: How do you feel toward Mephistopheles? The next question, obviously, is: Do your feelings change? If so, when, and why? The various answers generated by such questions will lead the group back to the text to look particularly at the various sequences of dialogue between Faust and his betrayer.

Other issues worth attending to include the importance of the supernatural in the play—What is gained by casting this drama in terms of God and devil? Could the same story be told as well in other terms?—and the functions of the various minor characters.

Topics for Writing

1. Why the witches?
2. How does the figure of Marthe clarify that of Margarete?
3. Is Faust a hero?
4. How does Margarete affect Faust?
5. The importance of feeling.
6. The importance of imagination.
7. What nature means in this play.

Comparative Perspectives

1. Goethe draws on many works in the Western literary tradition in shaping the issues he raises in Faust. Compare his treatment of the relationship between God and Satan in conversation with the opening chapters of Job; compare Goethe's Mephistopheles with Milton's Satan; or review the medieval lyrics in Vol. 1 to show how Goethe re-creates the late-medieval world in his Faust.
2. Goethe (in a passage not included in the *Anthology*) prefaces *Faust* with a Theatre Prologue. (Note the appearance of the Stage Manager in the "Walpurgis Night's Dream," a reference to a play by Shakespeare.) What do dramatists achieve when they expose the workings of the theater to their audiences in devices such as these?
   [Compare, as appropriate, *Six Characters in Search of an Author* or *Endgame*.]
3. Why is Gretchen shown at her spinning wheel? Note the conversation "at the well" about Barbara, who used to stay out late while other girls stayed home "spinning the whole day, and mother didn't let us out at night." How do nineteenth-century musical settings of this moment, most notably Schubert's song "Gretchen am Spinnrade," illuminate the girl's state of mind by mimicking the undertone of the relentlessly spinning wheel? Compare Leopardi's *To Sylvia*.

Further Reading

See also the reading suggestions in the *Anthology*, p. 2541.

Dieckmann, L. *Johann Wolfgang Goethe*. 1974. In the Twayne series. Particularly good, "intended as a guide to close reading," and offering a chapter on *Faust*.

Fairley, B. *Goethe as Revealed in His Poetry*. 1932; reprinted 1963. Includes two chapters on *Faust*, one arguing that the entire play rather than merely its hero must be understood as dramatizing a process of development, the other on *Faust* as a manifestation of Goethe's lyricism.

Friedenthal, R. *Goethe: His Life and Times*. 1965. Concentrates on the poet's life and his social and historical context rather than on his works.

McMillan, D. J., ed. *Approaches to Teaching Goethe's* Faust. 1987. Varied and useful essays.

Stearns, M. Goethe: *Pattern of Genius*. 1967. Predominantly biographical in emphasis, also offers detailed analysis of *Faust*.

CLUSTER: REVOLUTIONARY MOMENTS

Classroom Strategies and Topics for Discussion

The revolutions in North America and in France during the last quarter of the eighteenth century were events of such magnitude that they can scarcely be overemphasized. The brief selections here are by some of the principal participants in these events; a few are testimonies from more minor actors, or excerpts from histories of the two revolutions written in their immediate aftermaths.

Hutchinson's address provides the opportunity to discuss royalist and conservative resistance to the cause of independence from Great Britain. A significant minority remained loyal to the Crown, often fearing lawlessness and chaos, and consequent disruption to agriculture, commerce, and legal and financial arrangements that a protracted war for independence would be likely to bring. Hutchinson, last royalist governor of Massachusetts, is one of their chief spokesmen. He speaks as a member of the governing elite to other governing elites, and his arguments against the revolutionary experiment, though they have practical implications, are based in what he took to be the principles of British constitutional law. He is measured and rational rather than emphatic, but once students understand that his opposition is founded in convictions as deeply held as those of the revolutionary party, his address should serve the useful purpose of displaying the seldom examined American resistance to the revolution and some of the arguments often used by the usually condemned and dismissed royalists. Students can be asked to speculate on the results of any violent overthrow of political authority. Hutchinson has been called the American Burke, after the British statesman whose *Reflections on the Revolution in France* (1790) urged great caution in the face of any lure to violent revolution, predicted bloodshed and military tyranny as the revolution's likely result, and recommended the stability and order promoted by submission to properly constituted traditional authority. Hutchinson's address dates from 1773, seventeen years before Burke's pamphlet, but it takes many of the same positions.

The letters between John and Abigail Adams are from 1774 to 1776, when the Continental Congress was contemplating a declaration of independence, the armed insurrection that would be necessary to sustain it, and the political arrangements that would take the place of British colonial control. These documents, alternatively domestic and national, intimate and political, should be immediately appealing. The long months of separation, with Adams in the midst of planning and negotiating with representatives from other colonies in Philadelphia, and his wife, Abigail, presiding over their large family and their farm in Braintree (close to Boston), was a source of hardship for both. An eighteenth-century farmstead in New England was exceptionally challenging to wring a living from, requiring constant diligence and a small army of agricultural laborers. Adams was a well-regarded lawyer as well as a farmer, but his presence in Philadelphia meant that his law practice was in abeyance and his family was deprived of its principal source of income. The sacrifices involved underline the depth of this couple's unwavering commitment to the revolutionary cause. Further, Boston and the surrounding townships were under continuous British threat; armies and navies were already maneuvering to assert British rule, and military violence or rumors of it were a part of Abigail Adams's daily life. Students can be brought to see how she minimizes the hardships and dangers she and the family confronted, and that nonetheless John Adams was fully cognizant of what they were undergoing. Another issue that arises in this correspondence is their mutual concern for the education of their children. Prevailing conditions had disrupted the usual arrangements for this purpose and were likely to continue to do so. Abigail Adams is especially concerned that not only her sons but also her daughters be accorded the benefits of adequate educational opportunities, foreshadowing Mary Wollstonecraft's proto-feminist polemic on women's education, A Vindication of the Rights of Women (1792). Meanwhile the absorbing and important affairs in Philadelphia were of paramount interest to them both, and John Adams tells his wife as much about them and the people involved as he can. Many of the negotiations in which he took part were held in secret, and there was the additional fear that his letters might fall into British hands, thus compromising the safety of his family. So Adams's letters from Philadelphia are written at a certain level of generality, and students need to understand why this is so. Only after the Declaration of Independence is ratified and about to be publicly promulgated does he permit himself to write a letter of uncensored revolutionary fervor (July 3, 1776). As one of the signatories to the Declaration, he was then a very public traitor to the Crown.

The excerpts from Mary Otis Warren's History (1805) provide the conclusion to these readings on the American Revolution. Warren's work, written in the immediate aftermath of the war and the establishment and implementation of the constitution of the new republic, is understandably triumphalist in tone. Her political theory brings her work into counterpoint with Hutchinson's. Whereas he asserts the duty and consequent benefits of submission to traditional authority, she asserts the rights of political equality as an outgrowth of natural law. In her view, the military struggles of the revolution were devoted to the defense of these rights—although women and slaves are not accorded them. In fact, the vexing issue of slavery is only implicitly raised in this excerpt. She quotes the seventh article of the treaty between Great Britain and the newly established United States, which declares that the British armies and navies will withdraw forthwith, "without carrying away any negroes or other property of the American inhabitants." This contradiction of the natural law of equality goes unremarked. However, students can usefully reflect on this contradiction and its consequences.

The opening phases of the French Revolution began in 1789, only six years after the signing of the treaty that concluded the American Revolution. Many of the French revolutionists looked to the American experience as a model. Although the contexts were hugely different, nonetheless a monarchical government had been overthrown and a representative democracy of a highly rationalized form was taking its place. A more moderate faction looked to Great Britain's constitutional monarchy controlled by a representative legislature as a desirable political arrangement for France. It took most of the next century, with a series of monarchs, emperors, and republics, for a stable polity to emerge—more along American lines than British.

Germaine de Staël's *Considerations on the Principal Events of the French Revolution* (1818) was published shortly after the final defeat of Napoleon by Great Britain and the Allied Powers in the midst of the short-lived restoration of the Bourbon monarchy. De Staël is a moderate, opposed to fanaticism of any stamp, whether revolutionary or reactionary, and to her the British system seems to be *the* desirable middle course between extremes. Another feature of the arguments excerpted (a commonplace of the discourses surrounding both the American and the French revolutionary experience) is the appeal to the republics of classical antiquity. The heroes of both revolutions were often represented in togas and laurel wreaths for this reason. However, De Staël condemns the ancient republics for their limited franchise and their practice of slavery, which in her analysis eventually transformed them into despotisms. Her tracing of the evolution of political forms will bear close examination. It is conducted on a high level of abstraction, but students can be drawn into it if they are supplied with some of the relevant contextual detail. De Staël's overview of the evolution of political forms can be framed usefully with Hegel's on the one hand and Marx's on the other, and it is markedly similar to both.

This excerpt is supplemented by a short article by De Staël, "The Superiority of Moderation over Extremism." Here she argues once again against fanaticism, and in favor of the moderate course of a constitutional monarchy controlled by a representative legislature. This was essentially the system envisioned in the constitution imposed by the revolutionists on Louis XVI in 1791. In 1792, shortly after this article appeared, the monarchy was decisively overthrown, a republic inaugurated, and the king tried and executed. Because of her support of a constitutional monarchy, De Staël was forced into exile.

Thomas Paine stands in useful contrast to De Staël, although his is by no means the most radical position among the revolutionists. Well known for his eloquent propaganda on behalf of both the American and French revolutions, he was made an honorary citizen of France and elected to the National Convention in 1792. His open letter of thanks emphasizes the continuity between the two revolutions. Republican and antimonarchical in his views, Paine further thought that reasonable people the world over would be persuaded of the sagacity of his position by the successful establishment in the United States and in France of representative democracies. However, he was not thought radical enough by the Jacobins and was imprisoned by them in 1793. This letter provides an opportunity to direct student attention to the connections Paine saw between the two revolutions, and to their hugely different outcomes.

One voice that helps define the disastrously different outcome in France, and marks out a position antithetical to De Staël and more extreme than Paine, is that of Jean Paul Marat. Like Paine, Marat is a skilled controversialist, but students should be alerted to the highly inflammatory nature of his rhetoric, far more fervid than Paine's and unlikely to calm an already volatile situation. Marat's argument for a public trial of Louis XVI is founded on the notion that such a trial would expose the abuses of the monarchical system, render a constitutional monarchy impossible, and clear the way for the decisive overthrow of the monarchy and the establishment of some form of representative government. The speech makes it clear that in Marat's mind at least the king has already been tried, found guilty, and executed for treason. And of course, that is exactly what happened, as the Reign of Terror commenced.

Ordinary people also speak here. Students might be asked why so little is usually heard from those for whom the elites in both America and France claimed to act. Neither revolution would have been possible without substantial support from ordinary citizens, and many of these were women. Yet women's rights are completely overlooked in the foundational documents of both revolutions. These concluding excerpts provide an opportunity to reflect again upon the positions of Abigail Adams and Mary Otis Warren on this issue, although in contrast both are upper class. Another bridge between the two revolutions is provided by Fournier L'American's secret journal. Fournier's willingness to defy even constituted revolutionary authorities in the pursuit of radical goals is hard to match in the American experience, even if much of what he has to say seems self-aggrandizing. Of special interest is his attitude toward Lafayette, whom students will probably recall as a trusted lieutenant of Washington and a hero of the American Revolution. Fournier denounces him as a court sycophant who opposes the will of the people and acts to protect the king. The contrasting role of Lafayette in the two revolutions will bear some discussion. In France, his aristocratic status made him suspect to the revolutionists, and his whole-hearted support of the American cause made him equally suspect to the royalists.

Topics for Writing

1. Contrast the revolutionary experience in America and France. Why were the outcomes so different?
2. Join an imaginary debate between Thomas Hutchinson and Thomas Paine on one side or the other.
3. Address the position of women in both revolutions.
4. Contrast De Staël's moderate views with the more radical positions of Adams, Warren, Paine, or Marat.

Further Reading

See also the reading suggestions in the *Anthology*, pp. 2541–42. Two good general histories of the American and French revolutions can be recommended:

Gordon Wood. *The American Revolution: A History*. 2003.

Simon Shama. *Citizens*. 1991.

WILLIAM BLAKE

Songs of Innocence and of Experience

Classroom Strategies and Topics for Discussion

In teaching Blake, as with all lyric poets, you must spend a good deal of time—probably, most of the available time—attending to local effects. But large matters also deserve attention. It is often useful to students (because it provides a kind of orientation that helps in reading individual poems) to point out in advance that Blake's lyrics are marked by their mixture of social and metaphysical awareness. If students have heard this suggestion before they read the assignment, they may be prepared to begin discussion by pointing out specific examples of the combination. (Good ones occur in *The Little Black Boy, The Chimney Sweeper* [both versions], *London*, and *And Did Those Feet*.) Then the class can talk about how Blake achieves this unusual merging of concerns and how successful it is. Such discussion will lead naturally to detailed investigation of individual lyrics. Here are a few useful questions for some of the poems.

Introduction

It is enlightening to consider the *Introduction* to *Songs of Innocence* and that to *Songs of Experience* together, seeking similarities and contrasts between them. Both poems define a poet's role. How does that role differ in the two poems? Worth attention are the poet's subject matter and tone in each case ("happy" songs—the word occurs three times, along with related terms like "pleasant glee," "laughing," "joy"—about a Lamb or about "chear," versus visionary songs from a "weeping" Bard who sings in order to appeal to "the lapsed Soul"); the kinds of communication anticipated (to "Every child" or to Earth and the Soul); the imagined function of poetry (to create emotional effect, to redeem the fall of man). Students might be asked about the differences in the level of diction and syntactical complexity and about the effects generated by these differences. Finally, you might inquire what kind of volume each introduction appears to introduce.

The Lamb

This lyric is useful as a basis for discussing what "innocence" means in Blake's mythology. The lamb, as students should know or be told, is a traditional symbol of Christ. It is also, like the little child, associated with innocence. What is the effect of the childlike diction and repetition in this poem? They create a kind of incantatory effect that almost forces the reader to attend to the speaker's sense of a wondrous universe. The simplest phenomena, to a child's sensibility, can seem astonishing; Blake tries to re-create the feeling of innocent astonishment. Innocence thus becomes a mode of perception—as it appears to be in all the poems of the volume. Discussion can move on in this way to other poems: what is the perspective of innocence in each case? How does it work?

Earth's Answer

The combination of abstract and concrete diction here may interest students. Such phrases as "grey despair" and "Starry Jealousy" (extremely difficult to explicate) exemplify the way that Blake tries to make abstractions part of the physical world. This is a very hard poem to understand. It's valuable, therefore, to show students that they probably understand more than they think they do. You might go through the lyric, stanza by stanza, asking what impression each leaves. Most readers will comprehend the general situation—this is a lamentation by imprisoned Earth. To what does it "answer"? The *Introduction*, just before, ends with an appeal to Earth to "Arise" and participate in a process of redemption. This answer involves Earth's explanation of why she cannot arise—because of emotional, not political, enemies that oppose love and growth.

The Tyger

The poem is convenient to consider in conjunction with *The Lamb* as a transformation of the same sense of wonder into terms of experience rather than innocence. What kind of emotion does it generate in the reader? What is the effect of the peculiar syntax in line 12 ("What dread hand? & what dread feet?")? How does the rest of the poem account for the change in verb in the last lines of the first and the last stanzas ("could" to "dare")?

Topics for Writing

1. One of Blake's characters (e.g., the chimney sweeper, the child on the cloud, or the speaker in any of the poems).
2. What is the city like?
3. Blake's use of nature.

Comparative Perspectives

1. By the eighteenth century, many European writers indicate their disapproval of the colonial oppression of native peoples, but the references are often oblique and fleeting. By the beginning of the nineteenth century, the antislavery movement has gained strength and the tone of these references changes. Compare, as appropriate, Pope's "poor Indian" (*An Essay on Man*, epistle I, line 99), Candide's encounter with the maimed slave who works in the sugar mill (chapter 19), Blake's "*Little Black Boy*." What lessons do we learn about authorial perspective when we set any of these beside the *Narrative of the Life of Frederick Douglass, an American Slave?*
2. What view of nature do we see in Blake's *Introduction* to *Songs of Experience* and in *Earth's Answer?* Who or what seems to be responsible for "the darkness dread & drear" of the world? Compare the reasons in Leopardi's *The Infinite* for declaring "The world is mud."

   [Blake's nature is good; false religion and reason cause its downfall. Leopardi, however, sees nature as the source of sorrow.]

Further Reading

See also the reading suggestions in the *Anthology*, p. 2540.

Frye, N. *Fearful Symmetry*. 1947. Sees Blake as developing a unified myth through his poetry. (See Hirsch, cited in the *Anthology*, for an opposing view.)

Gleckner, R. *The Piper and the Bard*. 1959. Treats *Songs of Innocence* and *Songs of Experience* as dividing naturally into groups organized by common images and themes.

Gleckner, R. F., and M. L. Greenberg, eds. *Approaches to Teaching Blake's* Songs of Innocence and Experience. 1989. Another invaluable collection.

O'Neill, J., ed. *Critics on Blake*. 1970. A work specifically intended for undergraduates. Includes a smattering of criticism from 1803 to 1941 as well as several later essays; its essays concentrate on *Songs of Innocence* and *Songs of Experience*.

William Wordsworth

Classroom Strategies and Topics for Discussion

As some students may know already, William Wordsworth has a special position as the announcer of Romanticism in England (in the preface to Lyrical Ballads). You should probably suggest before they begin reading that they will find in his poetry an even more emphatic stress on nature than Rousseau and Goethe offered, and equivalent attention to the importance of the self and its feelings. Students might also be alerted in advance to the significance of memory and of childhood as Wordsworthian themes. A few suggestions about the two long poems follow.

Lines Composed a Few Miles Above Tintern Abbey

As so often with poetry, it is illuminating to read a passage aloud at the outset and to talk about the effect of the verse form. If students have just been reading Blake, they will hardly be prepared for the leisurely, ruminative rhythms of the blank verse, which by its very movement helps to establish the contemplative tone of the poem. Talking about the introductory section (lines 1–21), you might inquire about the speaker's attitude toward appearances created by human beings as opposed to those of nature. The orchard tufts that "lose themselves / 'Mid groves and copses" epitomize a pattern as the poet subsumes human artifacts into the natural world, making the hedgerows seem like bits of wood, the farmhouse smoke seem like a hermit's smoke, and so on. Observation of this fact prepares readers for the complicated attitude toward the human that develops as the poem goes on. One can trace throughout the poem the ways in which the speaker approaches and retreats from connection with the human: he speaks of acts of kindness and of love, but immediately moves on to something "more sublime"—a mood that enables him to forget the body, become all soul, and see into the life of things. The "fretful stir" of the third section suggests real antipathy to the human. Nourishment comes from the natural ("in this moment there is life and food / For future years" [lines 64–65]); Nature guards the heart and soul and moral being. But the poem is resolved by an address to his sister. The ending is worth dwelling on: Does it in fact resolve the problems the poem has established? What are those problems? One of them, certainly, is the speaker's relation to others of his kind. Another is the loss implicit in growing up (students can be asked to find evidence for this notion). Yet another is the difficulty of preserving in memory what is lost in experience. How does the final section answer these problems? Or does it only evade them? How convincing is Wordsworth's evocation of nature as a moral force? How does his vision of "something far more deeply interfused" (line 96) compare with the evocation of universal "oneness" at the end of the first epistle of *An Essay on Man*?

Ode on Intimations of Immortality

To a considerable extent, the themes of this poem duplicate those of *Tintern Abbey*. Students may find it interesting to begin by trying to locate ideas that the two poems hold in common, going on to analyze ways in which differences in expression and context can alter meaning. Specifically, it may be valuable to compare the sense of past versus present in the poems, and the function of nature, which here appears to be more emotional than moral. The word "glory" (along with "glories" and "glorious") occurs at least seven times in this ode. "There hath past away a glory from the earth," line 18 proclaims. Considering the different occurrences of the word and its cognates, what does "glory" appear to mean here? It cannot be defined precisely, but a group can talk about its associations (with royalty, with divinity, with splendor, beauty, radiance, for example) and about the range of meanings suggested by the word's various uses in the ode. Perhaps hypothesize that the word's value for the poet comes partly from its vagueness and its breadth of association. The poem is trying to articulate something that cannot be precisely located; it tries to make the reader understand this "something" by playing on the reader's feelings. A passage particularly worth paying close attention is the account of human development in stanzas VII and VIII. What does this theory of development involve and imply? It glorifies the preconscious and deprecates maturity; it implicitly argues that human association (the heavy, freezing weight of "custom") contains the seed of the soul's destruction. Compared with the view of *Tintern Abbey*, this seems more extreme, more somber. What about the resolution of this poem? Is it more or less satisfactory than that of its predecessor? Does it solve the emotional problems that have been evoked? Why is the last word "tears"? Does that fact suggest anything about the atmosphere of this ending as opposed to the other?

Topics for Writing

1. Sunshine and clouds in *Immortality*.
2. An impression of the "sister" in *Tintern Abbey*.
3. The morality of *Tintern Abbey* (or of *Immortality*).

Comparative Perspectives

1. How would you compare the view of the city in the selections in Vol. 1 of the *Anthology* with those expressed in Vol. 2 by writers such as Swift (Dublin in *A Modest Proposal*), Rousseau (from book IV), Blake (*London*), and Wordsworth? Each of these writers has a unique perspective on city life. Explore the various dissatisfactions they articulate and think about the way Aeschylus treats Athens in the *Oresteia*, or the Psalmist speaks about Jerusalem.
2. Explain the role of childhood in the theory of poetic inspiration that animates *Tintern Abbey* and *Immortality*. Compare Wordsworth's idealization of youthful percipience with the approach

taken by other writers to the impressionability of the young, including Rousseau, Proust, Pirandello, Faulkner, and Munro.

Further Reading

See also the reading suggestions in the *Anthology*, p. 2543.

Bewell, A. *Wordsworth and the Enlightenment*. 1989. An anthropological approach to Wordsworth and his historical context.

Davies, H. *William Wordsworth*. 1980. A highly readable biography, with splendid plates.

Davis, J., ed. *Discussions of William Wordsworth*. 1965. An exceptionally useful collection of essays that exemplifies many points of view.

Ferry, D. *The Limits of Mortality*. 1959. A study of Wordsworth's major poems that places those included in the *Anthology* in the context of the poet's other work.

Hall, S., with J. Ramsey, ed. *Approaches to Teaching Wordsworth's Poetry*. 1986. Pedagogically invaluable essays.

Noyes, R. *William Wordsworth*. 1971. In the Twayne series. Provides thoughtful criticism as well as a biographical introduction and bibliography.

Dorothy Wordsworth

The Grasmere Journals

Classroom Strategies and Topics for Discussion

There are at least four ways of using Dorothy Wordsworth's *Grasmere Journals* in the classroom, and since they are complementary rather than mutually exclusive, it is worth considering them all. Traditionally, critics have combed through the sister's journals to find insights into her brother's poetry; more recently, feminist scholars have trained on the same materials a psychoanalytic lens; general readers have always been fascinated by the journals as sources of wonderful "inside information" about an extraordinary group of people who changed the course of English literature; and most important, perhaps, as the headnote in the *Anthology* stresses, students of the Romantic era can focus on documents that reveal a remarkable sensibility confronting the issues of mind and nature that lie at the heart of so much Western literature of the early nineteenth century.

Probably the most famous example of William Wordsworth's transmutation of Dorothy Wordsworth's perceptions is *I Wandered Lonely as a Cloud*, in which the daffodils so exquisitely described by Dorothy in her journal entry for Thursday, April 15, 1802, become the subject of one of his best-known poems. William Wordsworth recollects the daffodils in tranquility, musing on the value they impart to him, self-declared "a poet," when he is far from the original scene. If you have read *Tintern*

Abbey with your students, you may want to send them back to that poem to find the reference, in lines 25–31, to the kind of moment when such a memory was important to him.

Dorothy uses her journals, as that word implies, to record the dailiness of experience as it is being lived, generally preferring the "we" to the "I," although she certainly does specify when she alone makes a judgment: "I never saw daffodils so beautiful." Significantly, she looks at them without thinking of the profit she might realize from them, more concerned to render an accurate description of the veritable colony of flowers that she discovers in their own habitat. Yet it is she who invents the famous, witty anthropomorphic characterization of the dancing flowers, "some of whom rested their heads upon these stones as on a pillow for weariness."

In other words, although she often represses the first person singular, Dorothy is far more than the possessor of the "wild eyes" (*Tintern Abbey*, lines 119, 148) on which William Wordsworth grew to rely; she has her own idiosyncratic imagination. She never simply records; she too transforms what she sees. In this case, her imputation of "weariness" to the gay flowers bespeaks her own preoccupation with such exhaustion. No one can read the entries in her journals without noting the frequency of her (and her brother's) headaches, bouts of amnesia, and recurrent, if brief, sieges of (probably dyspeptic?) illness.

You may be surprised by the sympathy that your students will express for these symptoms of anxiety and by how interested they are likely to be by the family story that at least to some degree precipitates them. You may want to point out that the journal entries in the *Anthology* were all written in anticipation of the forthcoming marriage of William Wordsworth to Dorothy's close friend Mary Hutchinson, of whom the brother and sister think at the end of April 15, 1802, the day of the daffodils. The day before, the point at which the *Anthology* picks up the entries, Dorothy is "ill out of spirits—disheartened": Is this because William has just returned from visiting Mary and fixing the day of their wedding (October 4, 1802), an event so traumatizing that Dorothy was unable to attend it, devoted though she was to both the bride and the groom?

Should you choose to dispense information of this sort, you may want also to identify the "Annette" with whom so many letters are exchanged as Annette Vallon, the young French woman who was the mother of William's daughter, Caroline. Before the marriage to Mary took place, Dorothy and William went to Calais to spend about a month with Annette and Caroline. (Originally, Dorothy had expected that William would marry Annette, whom he met during his tour of France in the early 1790s; although it became clear that neither partner wished to resume and formalize their relationship, the Wordsworths remained supportive. Years later, Caroline named a daughter "Dorothy" in honor of her beloved aunt.)

None of this biographical data, however, need be brought into the classroom. Another approach to integrating the life that Dorothy's jour-

nals describe to the poetic enterprise that she shared with Wordsworth
and Coleridge (also an important presence in these excerpts) is simply to
ask your students about the relation between the small events of an apparently uneventful existence to the development of intellectual and
moral consciousness. For one thing, you can use Dorothy Wordworth's
journals to initiate your students into the role that reading literature
plays in writing literature. Once your students have seen these entries
from *The Grasmere Journals*, with their references to Spenser's *Prothala-
mium* (Sunday, April 25) and Milton's sonnets (Friday, May 21), they
should understand why the influence of Milton and Spenser can be detected in Wordsworth's poems.

Even more rewarding is to investigate with your class the way the
blandness of the activities engaged in here nevertheless excited complicated responses. If Dorothy Wordworth's extreme modesty contrasts
with the "egotistical sublime" of her brother, the way she interprets
events is no less compelling than his more self-involved thought process.
For instance, the random encounter with the local population that gives
rise to Dorothy's self-deprecating insight into the shared laughter of the
"two sisters at work" at the expense of the brother and sister with whom
they "had some talk" on April 16, 1802, seems to have no effect on her
brother, intent on finishing his poem.

An extreme example of her habit of internal correction may be seen in
the episode of the beggar who calls her a "fine woman" when she gives
him "a piece of cold bacon and a penny": "I could not help smiling. I
suppose he meant 'You're a kind woman!' " It's worth speculating why
"kind" is easier for her to accept than "fine." Is this a class-based reaction, suggesting that she could not imagine that the beggar might praise
her as a woman? Or is she unwilling to admit so grand a compliment, in
which "fine" would be a moral judgment? Coupled to this suppression of
the self is an instinctive empathy (a sensitivity that she shares with
William) for the solitary figure in a crowd.

Note the entry for June 3, 1802, when she looks at "a thousand buds
on the honeysuckle tree, all small and far from blowing save one that is
retired behind the twigs close to the wall and as snug as a bird's nest."
Here, as in the appreciation for the isolated figure, seen also in the entry for June 1 that speaks of the solitary columbine "sheltered and
shaded by the tufts and bowers of trees," we see her mind at work, linking the comforting image of the nest with the excluded figure. As the
passage on the columbine continues, it is hard to refrain from drawing
an explicit connection between Dorothy's situation and the flower's, a
connection of the sort that she resolutely refuses to make: "It is a graceful slender creature, a female seeking retirement and growing freest and
most graceful where it is most alone. I observe that the more shaded
plants were always the tallest—a short note and gooseberries from Coleridge."

What her prose does do, as in the conclusion of this journal entry, is
imply connections through its use or lack of punctuation. One ponders
the link between solitariness and freedom, between being out of the

light and achieving height, between the contemplation of the lone female and the note from Coleridge. The reference to being beloved cited
in the headnote offers another strange example of this tendency: "My
tooth broke today. They will soon be gone. Let that pass. I shall be
beloved—I want no more" (May 31, 1802). How does she get from teeth
to love? Are they, as Susan M. Levin suggests, symbols of sexual potency? Has she resigned herself to decrepitude? Is she really saying, "I
want everything"?

Whatever one makes of the mysteries of these journals, which were
never intended for the kind of inspection to which they have now been
subjected, we cannot but be grateful for the fineness of the observations
they preserve. Perhaps no better example of this may be found in these
selections than in the entry for Friday, May 14, 1802, a day of a late-
season storm. Early in the day, William seeks "an epithet for the
cuckow." After dinner, Dorothy kneads bread, mends stockings, and
watches the strange night:

> The woods looked miserable, the coppices green as grass which looked quite
> unnatural and they seemed half shrivelled up as if they shrunk from the air. O
> thought I! what a beautiful thing God has made winter to be by stripping the
> trees and letting us see their shapes and forms.

The unexpectedness of the conclusion that she draws from the desolate
scene reveals the modern artist latent in the careful homemaker.
Dorothy Wordsworth's appreciation for the stripped-down shapes and
forms of the created world should help each of us see afresh the surroundings in which we live.

Topics for Writing

1. Keep a journal for twenty-four hours and record with as unblem-
   ished an eye as possible the shapes of what you see and the events
   in which you participate, and then compare your account with one
   of Dorothy Wordsworth's journal entries. How has life changed
   since the beginning of the nineteenth century? What habits of your
   own mind can you discover from your work? What can you now
   appreciate about the details that recommend themselves to Wordsworth's consciousness?
2. Is there such a thing as a feminine sensibility? Citing evidence
   from *The Grasmere Journals*, try to distinguish between observations and preoccupations that derive from the social role Dorothy
   Wordsworth played and those that reflect the quality of her intellect and imagination.

Further Reading

See also the reading suggestions in the *Anthology*, p. 2543.

Homans, Margaret. *Women Writers and Poetic Identity*. 1980. While it
deals primarily with the small number of poems that Dorothy

Wordsworth wrote, this book makes many observations that are useful in regard to her journal writing as well.

Levin, Susan M. *Dorothy Wordsworth and Romanticism*. 1987. Informed by contemporary psychological and linguistic critical insights, this valuable book contains a good bibliography and perceptive comments, some noted above.

Wordsworth, Dorothy. *The Grasmere Journal*. 1987. A beautifully produced edition of the complete journal, richly illustrated with maps and contemporary drawings by artists like Constable, Harden, and Turner. Introduction by Jonathan Wordsworth.

Samuel Taylor Coleridge

Classroom Strategies and Topics for Discussion

Coleridge's poetry is likely to interest students through its capacity subtly to differentiate states of emotion and also compellingly to suggest the nature of an emotional condition. If undergraduates think his tone sometimes overwrought, they often can be brought by close attention to the text to understand the precision of his poetic effects and how richly they are used in poetic structures.

Kubla Khan

Absolutely surefire as a way of engaging student attention is the problem of automatic writing brought up by Coleridge's account of the composition of this poem. You should point out that the footnote calls attention to the dubious authenticity of this account, but then go on to invite speculation about why the notion of the poet as inspired creator is so compelling to the imagination. Why should we like to think that poetry issues from unconscious depths, without effort, discipline, or rewriting? Certainly this view contradicts ordinary experience of what it is like to write anything at all; good writing, most people find, is hard work. It is then valuable to point out how the vision of the poet as natural seer comes into the poem itself. You might inquire about the "damsel with a dulcimer" and how she figures in *Kubla Khan*, and about the "I" at the poem's end and what others are alleged to "cry" about him. What do the final lines ("For he on honey-dew hath fed, / And drunk the milk of Paradise") mean and imply? The poet here emerges as an awe-inspiring figure, set apart from others, mysteriously dangerous, nourished in other ways than ordinary mortals, possessed of essentially magic powers ("And all who heard should see them there"). Another kind of question worth pursuing in relation to this poem is the power of scene to evoke feeling. Students can be asked to specify the various individual scenes summoned up by description and to talk about the kinds of emotion they call forth.

Dejection: An Ode

The poem is worth going through stanza by stanza, to specify what is happening in each stanza and how each relates to its successor. If time forbids such detailed examination, here are a few matters to investigate. What is the relation between the conversational tone of the opening lines and the rhetorical intensity of, say, stanza III? In other words, how does the speaker make plausible his movement from one tone to the other? In effect he documents that movement in the course of stanza I: the casual observation about the weather leads him to think about the prospect of bad weather that would fit with his mood; by stanza II it has become apparent that the remark about the weather was in the first place only an effort to disguise the mood of depression. How is *scene* used in this poem (perhaps in comparison to *Kubla Khan*)? Here too one can trace precise correlations between scene and feeling. Special attention should be paid to the idea that the human experiencer gives meaning to nature, announced at the end of stanza III and the beginning of stanza IV; students might be asked to trace the intertwining of subjective and objective through the poem. What is the meaning of "Reality's dark dream" (line 95)? The speaker seems to have in mind fantasies stimulated by the dark realities around him; the rest of stanza VII specifies such fantasies. What psychic purpose do they serve? They enlarge the reference of the depression that tends to isolate the person who feels it; in the development of the poem, they prepare for the invocation in stanza VIII, which declares the speaker's capacity to concern himself with others. Finally, what is the role of the "Lady" in the poem and how does it compare with the role of the "Sister" in *Tintern Abbey*?

Topics for Writing

Writing topics can develop from any of the questions suggested above; it is also often useful to ask students to write about the function of a single image and how it is developed in the poem. See also "Topics for Writing" for Shelley, below.

Comparative Perspectives

Coleridge claims that the fragmentary *Kubla Khan* resulted from a narcotized state. In *The Tomb of Edgar Poe*, Mallarmé refutes the critical dismissal of Poe's work because it was said to have arisen from "drunken fantasies." Comment on how different uses of inebriation mark different ideas about the nature of poetry and the role of the imagination.

[The headnotes for Coleridge and for Mallarmé provide a helpful overview.]

Further Reading

See also the reading suggestions in the *Anthology*, p. 2540.

Bygrave, S. *Coleridge and the Self: Romantic Egotism.* 1986. A psychologically focused essay.

Hill, J. *A Coleridge Companion.* 1983. Supplies a biographical sketch as well as invaluable background and interpretation for *Kubla Khan* and *Dejection*.

Watson, G. *Coleridge the Poet*. 1966. Concentrates on the achievement of the poems, with considerable analysis of individual texts.

GEORGE GORDON, LORD BYRON

Classroom Strategies and Topics for Discussion

Of these five lyrics by Byron, three are from that part of his production that traces the speaker's or main character's loves, betrayals, and separations. Students are likely to be fascinated by the autobiographical substrata of these poems, and that taste can easily be gratified with reference to the extensive biographical record. Then it would be useful if students would reread these brief poems, seeing their broader application to the vicissitudes of love as experienced by most of humanity. A discussion of the uses and limits of biography in the reading of poetry might follow. We do know a great deal about Byron's life, and what we know should be brought to bear on these poems. But such poems are not a mere reflex of the poet's experience; they are a shaping of that experience in such a way as to become an interface with our own. They are successful not because they are drawn from Byron's singular life but because they are drawn from that life in such a way as to apply to our own.

[Again Deceived! Again Betrayed!]

These five simple a-b-a-b quatrains are probably based on a brief affair Byron had with a servant girl. That said, the interest of the poem is in the nuanced psychological tracing of the experience of betrayal. The speaker begins by ruefully declaring himself a "dupe," a circumstance that teaches an expensive lesson, the more so since he's been taught it "twenty times" before. The lesson? Our lovers are sometimes false and deceive us; as often we are false to our lovers and deceive them. No one has much control over these shifting roles; they are the effects of "wayward Passion." Yet the love involved is "genuine." The speaker is no more (and no less) a victim than a victimizer. His intentions are no more capable of being steadfast than hers. Nonetheless, he can't help wishing the affair had continued.

[Politics in 1813. To Lady Melbourne.]

This poem of three rhymed couplets is a work of sharp political satire. Nonetheless its address to Lady Melbourne—mistress of the Prince of Wales and mother-in-law of one of Byron's lovers—gestures again to a biographical context. For this poem, though, this is only a gesture. The poem is directed to public affairs and appropriately addressed to a semi-public figure, a close friend of Byron's. More exactly, the poem professes "indifference" to public affairs because the choices are so appalling. Student attention might be called to the last line, in which each epithet is recited in the order of the figures and groups anathematized in the second couplet: the mad king, the bad prince, and so on. The king was indeed mad, and had been off and on for years. The Prince of Wales was in consequence the Regent. He and his equally disreputable brothers vied for power; the parliamentary ministry was in disarray. Meanwhile, abroad, the Napoleonic Wars were in their final, bloody, and expensive years. At home the economic distress caused by the war was growing more and more acute. No one in or out of power had the least idea what to do about it.

Stanzas for Music

Byron also wrote a kind of "pure poetry" that stands in the background of some of the French symbolist poets represented later in this *Anthology*. There is no pertinent biographical or historical context for poems of this sort; finally, this poem is about itself, about the music that it makes, about the emotion it describes and evokes. The title appropriately designates it as a lyric to be set to music, which in the aesthetic already under development seemed the "purest" of art, because it was thought to be exclusively self-referential, only about the interrelationships of its own sounds. The commonplace of later nineteenth-century aesthetics—that "all art aspires to the condition of music"—emerges from this perception and will bear application to this poem. Students may resist this line of thought, but it's useful to begin discussing it as early as possible, so that they can be prepared for its full expression later in the nineteenth century and into the twentieth.

Fare Thee Well

This poem's biographical context, detailed in the footnotes to the text, is Byron's divorce, which was complicated by an infant daughter. However, as with "[Again Deceived! Again Betrayed!]," the interest of the poem is the nuanced psychological portrait it draws of its speaker, alternatively forgiving and vengeful, self-pitying, self-revealing, and self-deceiving. Student attention might be called to line 33 and following, where the speaker offers bitter "solace" to his ex-wife, in the shape of their child. A self-pitying aside ("Wilt thou teach her to say—'Father!' / Though she must his care forgo?") carries a sting, but he can still imagine that he "shall bless thee," even while he twists the knife. For if the child should grow up looking like him, she'll be a continuous reminder to his ex-wife of how she wronged him, and his ex-wife will be "yet true to me" in that reminder. Close in-class reading, with student participation, will help fill in the portrait.

When We Two Parted

This poem has no specifically determined biographical reference, though there probably was one. It tells the story of the aftermath of a secret love affair, and again presents a complicated psychological character sketch of the speaker. In retrospect, the poet is ashamed of the affair and yet shares the shame that has fallen upon his subsequently ill-famed lover. He can't explain the attraction that drew him to his lover, and he can't understand her later behavior. In all of these professions, he presents himself as the wronged party, and that alone should elicit among first-time readers some suspicion as to his innocence. That suspicion can be usefully exploited in the classroom.

Topics for Writing

1. Students will have by now read other writers whose work is informed by their biography, so Byron provides an opportunity to write about this phenomenon and its pitfalls.
2. Byron was a brilliant political satirist, as we see in "[Politics in 1813]", as was his friend Percy Shelley, whose "England in 1819" is in this *Anthology*. Write a paper comparing these two poems.
3. Byron and Shelley pioneered the writing of a kind of "pure poetry" in English. Students might need to be supplied with other examples before writing a paper exploring such poetry.

Further Reading

See also the reading suggestions in the *Anthology*, p. 2540.

Leslie Marchand. *Byron: A Biography*. 3 vols. 1957.

The best book on Byron's poetry remains this:

Jerome McGann. *Fiery Dust: Byron's Poetic Development*. 1968.

PERCY BYSSHE SHELLEY

Classroom Strategies and Topics for Discussion

One aspect of Shelley's poetry likely to interest undergraduates is his combination of lyric impulse with political and social passion—a version of the same linkage found in Blake.

England in 1819

This sonnet is a useful place to start discussion—partly because it is likely to contradict any expectations students might come with about Shelley as a poet. In the next to the last line of the sonnet, *graves* become a summarizing image for all the phenomena previously evoked. The point of the grave appears to be that a "glorious Phantom" may burst out of it. But graves are also, above all, places where someone (or, by extension, something) is buried. In what sense can kings, princes, armies, and the rest be said to bury something? In other words, how does the metaphor of graves enlarge or illuminate what has come before? Among other things, all the realities Shelley has evoked seem in his view to represent ends to hope, belief, or possibility; this is one reason his tone is so angry. Before all the early references are summed up as constituting "graves," however, they are also characterized by a wealth of individual metaphors. What are some of these metaphors? Students will presumably mention *dregs, mud, leeches, sword, book, statute*. Do these metaphors have anything in common? Typically, they reduce something human to something nonhuman, thus preparing for the final reduction of everything to the grave. A line that students are likely to find particularly difficult, because of its extreme condensation, is line 10: "Golden and sanguine laws which tempt and slay." (The footnote helps, but not a whole lot.) It is worth spending some time on elucidation here, working out what it might mean to imagine laws as tempting and slaying. Do golden laws tempt and sanguine ones slay? Or are laws in general being imagined as both golden and sanguine? What kinds of laws might tempt? How do they slay? A particular reason for attending to this line is that it is likely to lead to a perception of how relevant Shelley's indictment might be to our own time.

Ode to the West Wind

How does the high value attached to *energy* in this poem compare with the valuing of energy in *Faust*? One might remark, in this connection, the degree to which Shelley attaches the idea of energy to that of *purpose*. What is the relation between the poet's dwelling on description and his apparent belief that the poet can provide "the trumpet of a prophecy"? It might be argued that the luxurious descriptions here exemplify an important aspect of the poet's power: to evoke, to make real, to generate the force of incantation. These are the methods he (or, for that matter, she) can use to inspire and to prophesy.

A Defence of Poetry

How does the emphasis on power in this essay compare with the stress on energy in *Ode to the West Wind*?

Topics for Writing

The exercise on an image suggested for Coleridge would work well here too. Other possibilities:

1. Compare Shelley and Coleridge on dejection.
2. Use the *Defence* as a means of characterizing one of the other Romantic poets.

Comparative Perspectives

1. *Ode to the West Wind* makes frequent allusions to many of the same masterpieces of world literature that appear in the *Anthology*. How many can you identify?

    [Shelley's adaptation of *terza rima* and the poem's opening image of fallen leaves clearly allude to Dante's *Divine Comedy* and the rich epic tradition that the Italian master drew on. The comparison of clouds to a "fierce Maenad" will be appreciated by students who know about the Dionysian sources of Greek tragedy. "I fall upon the thorns of life, I bleed!" invokes Christ's crown of thorns. In turn, in its evocation of seasonal change and tone of desperation, the poem stands as a source for Tennyson's *In Memoriam* and Eliot's *The Waste Land*.]

2. In *A Defence of Poetry*, Shelley admits the possibility of a moral gap between the human beings who write poetry and "that spirit of good of which they are the ministers." As you read the biographical introductions to the writers you are studying this term, do you note any such contradictions? Need an artist be a good person to create good art?

Further Reading

See also the reading suggestions in the *Anthology*, p. 2542.

Chernaik, J. *The Lyrics of Shelley*. 1972. Contains new texts of many Shelley poems and offers thoughtful readings of the lyrics in the *Anthology*.

Duerksen, Roland. *Shelley's Poetry of Involvement*. 1988. Shelley as social commentator.

Hall, Spencer, ed. *Approaches to Teaching Shelley's Poetry*. 1990. Another useful MLA volume.

Reiman, D. *Percy Bysshe Shelley*. 1969. Provides an excellent short general biography and critical introduction, with useful bibliography.

White, N. *Shelley*. 2 vols. 1940. The standard biography, monumental and exhaustive.

JOHN KEATS

Classroom Strategies and Topics for Discussion

If students enjoy poetry at all, they usually like Keats for the incantatory and evocative power of his verse (although they wouldn't put it that way). Class time can usefully be spent on trying to elucidate how he achieves his effects. For example (a few poems):

La Belle Dame sans Merci

This narrative poem begins with a question, a statement of a problem. How is the question finally answered; that is, what, exactly, *does* ail this knight? How has the woman injured him? Or is it his total absorption in love that has damaged him? What about the kings, princes, and warriors who appear to him—what exactly do they warn him about? Such questions will emphasize the fact that one element in the poem's power is the presence of what is *not* said, the suggestions of a narrative behind the explicit narrative, which the reader must figure out. Descriptively, there is considerable stress on seasonal signs of cold and on the contrast with what has gone before (the withered sedge and silent birds call to mind their opposites). How does this technique reiterate the poem's theme?

Certainly the denuded form of external nature echoes the sense of psychic deprivation the knight feels, and it underlines the fact that his deprivations depend on his previously having—or thinking he had—what now he lacks.

Ode on a Grecian Urn

In many ways the representations on the urn appear superior to what real life has to offer. What are some of these ways? One might mention the degree to which art offers stimulus to the imagination (unheard melodies, which must be imagined, are sweeter than those actually heard; and the sequence of questions emphasizes the imaginative inquiry set in motion by the sight of the urn's shapes); the impossibility of disappointment for characters embedded in artistic form; and, most important, the permanence of art, comparable to eternity. Increasingly, the poem stresses this element of permanence and its effect on mortals. What kinds of effect does it have? Specifically, what does it mean that the urn can "tease us out of thought" (line 44)? Perhaps it makes us feel rather than think; perhaps it makes us surpass thought, entering a realm of intuitive knowledge; perhaps, as other lines suggest, it helps us avoid ordinary kinds of thought by removing us from commonplace experience. The ode's final lines can of course supply much matter for debate. The fundamental question here, beyond what it means to identify beauty and truth, is why this should be sufficient knowledge for humankind.

Ode to a Nightingale

What sort of "happiness" is it that creates numbness and heartache? This is a point worth dwelling on, trying to define the sort of emotion Keats here wishes to evoke—by no means an easy matter. What is the poem's attitude toward ordinary human experience (stanza III)? How does the function of art as suggested in this poem differ from that implicit in *Ode on a Grecian Urn*? Art, here, is epitomized by "Poesy" (line 33), whose "viewless wings" carry the hearer of the nightingale's song to imaginative union with the bird. The "dull brain" (line 34) creates obstacles to such fusion, as "thought" appears to generate problems in the previous poem. Here too, then, art enables mortals to transcend their limitations, but by a rather different process from that suggested by *Grecian Urn*. What is the importance of death in the poem? The poet declares himself "half in love with easeful Death" (line 52) and imagines death while listening to the bird as a rich and satisfying experience, but also imagines it as a state of deprivation in which he would "become a sod" (line 60). The bird's power, like that of the urn, comes partly from the possibility of imagining it as free of the threat of death—not, of course, in its own literal body, but because nightingales have always existed and will continue to exist and to become the substance of imagination. So there seems to be a contrast here between two views of death: the literal death that makes people and birds alike into mere pieces of earth, and an imagined kind of death that becomes itself a form of fulfillment. Why is the "self" unsatisfactory in the final stanza? The self seems a being deprived of imagination because existing in isolation, separated from the bird that has enabled the speaker to transcend his own sense of limitation.

To Autumn

In relation to this poem of lush description, possibly the most useful question is the simplest and most obvious: How does it make you feel? If students can specify emotional responses, one can work backward from such responses to their stimuli in the text. It's essential to pause on the personification of Autumn in the second stanza, to inquire how that works in the poem. Autumn becomes a person deeply enjoying the experiences that only this time of year offers: the sense of luxurious ease. The "music" of autumn, specified in the final stanza, has less obvious power than "the songs of Spring" (23). What is attractive about this kind of music? One might wish to mention its multiplicity, both of source and of sound, and the impression it gives of the unity of all nature.

Topics for Writing

1. The function of nature in a single poem.
2. A comparison between a Keats poem and one by Shelley.
3. A single emotion that attracts the speaker—and why.

Comparative Perspectives

1. *La Belle Dame sans Merci* is one in a long line of texts from many cultures and eras that express a masculine fear of a demonic female. Compare Keats's indirect depiction of this creature's power to other treatments of this theme.

   [Possibilities include the Sirens who tempt Homer's Odysseus, the lady in *Sir Gawain and the Green Knight*, and their more recent counterparts, including, perhaps, Phaedra and Hedda Gabler. What relation does the victim or would-be victim have to the seductress? Why is the beleaguered male in any of these examples singled out for attack? What makes him vulnerable?]

2. Keats's evocations of the five senses bring to mind the sensual worlds of Baudelaire, Mallarmé, Verlaine, Rimbaud, and the Surrealists. How does the finish of Keats's full stanzas reflect the all-too-human world, where, beauty notwithstanding, "youth grows pale, and spectre-thin, and dies"? Contrast the fleeting, luxurious details of "a beaker full of the warm South" in *Ode to a Nightingale*, line 15, with an image from the work of one of these poets. What kind of meaning is Keats trying to convey? How and why do the later poets purposely blur the boundaries of the senses?

3. How does Keats's *Ode on a Grecian Urn* (based on his viewing of classical Greek vases) reflect a view of the complexity of human ex-

perience that we recognize from Homer's poems and the shield of
Achilles in particular?

[The two sides of heroic life are present in both poets' works:
peace and war, wedding and funeral.]

Further Reading

See also the reading suggestions in the *Anthology*, p. 2541.

Dickstein, M. *Keats and His Poetry: A Study in Development.* 1971. Supplies a particularly detailed reading of *To a Nightingale.*

Evert, W. H., and J. W. Rhodes, eds. *Approaches to Teaching Keats's Poetry.* 1991. A volume in the MLA series.

Gittings, R. *John Keats.* 1968. Gittings attempts to provide factual sub-
stantiation for every detail of the poet's life; Bate and Ward (cited in
the *Anthology*) offer critical as well as biographical interpretation.

Vendler, H. *The Odes of John Keats.* 1983. Offers brilliant, exhaustive interpretations of all the odes.

Watkins, Daniel P. *Keats's Poetry and the Politics of the Imagination.*
1989. Keats as social commentator.

CONTINENTAL ROMANTIC LYRICS: A SELECTION

This selection of French, German, Italian, Spanish, and Russian lyric
poems greatly expands the pedagogical possibilities for teaching the Romantic period. As is the case with all the selected lyrics grouped
throughout the *Anthology*, these poems may be approached in many different ways. The headnote speaks of the grand Romantic themes that
cross national boundaries; you may select one of them—time, death, nature, or love—for comparative study that will quickly reveal how differently each poet responds to a similar problem. Or you may want to look
at the works of Russian writers of the period (adding the lovely poem by
Bunina to a class on Pushkin), for example, or the Spanish poets (Bécquer and de Castro), with an eye toward teaching some of the work of
their compatriots later in the semester. Equally important is the explicit
way in which so many poets of the nineteenth and twentieth centuries
wrestle with the idea of poetry itself, making it their ultimate subject;
this point is easily made by noting references in these lyrics to nightingales and swans or the song of the wind, all of which represent the spirit
of poetry that Romantic writers seek to incorporate into their very being.

If you have not yet concentrated on the short lyric as a distinct genre,
you should choose a few of the more complex poems in this selection
and work through them with your students in great detail, examining the
way idiosyncratic speaking voices capture the play of mind as they twist
and turn through their subjects. *Et nox facta est* by Victor Hugo, *The
Lake* by Lamartine, *To Sylvia* and *The Village Saturday* by Leopardi, and

Yearning for Death by Novalis would be particularly good choices for this kind of extended treatment. You might also consider using a single poem to complement a narrative that you are studying, either to indicate how widespread certain conventional assumptions were within the Romantic period or to juxtapose works from different periods with each other, to show your students how certain thematic preoccupations may be treated differently in different times and places.

The comparative questions at the end of each entry below will suggest some fruitful combinations; you will doubtless discover more as you plan your course.

Friedrich Hölderlin

Classroom Strategies and Topics for Discussion

As with so many Romantic works, your presentation of these four well-known poems may be facilitated by references to the author's life experience. The headnote explains that the young Hölderlin "found work—not very successfully—as a tutor." In 1796–97, he fell deeply in love with Susette Gontard, the mother of the children he taught in his second such assignment. In this, the great love affair of Hölderlin's life, he found his poetic voice, addressing a number of poems to her as "Diotima" (honor of Zeus). This was a requited affair, and Susette wrote many letters that have been preserved. Herr Gontard fired Hölderlin, not surprisingly. In a two-volume epistolary novel, *Hyperion: Or the Hermit in Greece*, published in 1797–99, many of the dilemmas the young poet faced are explored through his fictional protagonist, Hyperion, a modern Greek who goes to study in Germany in the wake of a failed political revolution in Greece. Hyperion falls in love with a woman called Diotima, and one of the crises he faces is her untimely death. Thus Hölderlin's fascination for the Greek classics and his personal struggles shape his writing career.

The Half of Life

Composed 1803–04, when Hölderlin was thirty-three years old, *The Half of Life* may be compared to the beginning of Dante's *Inferno*, for it is a midlife retrospective. The beauty of the images in the first stanza of the poem (Keatsian in their sensory richness) gives way in the second stanza to the expectation of barrenness to come, a vision of the second half of life, a time of aging and decay. You may want to spend some time discussing the disjunction between the two stanzas, which seem so diametrically opposed to each other, without any transitional gestures linking them. The poem's pessimism is deep (and accurately prefigures the rapid descent into madness that effectively silenced Hölderlin only a short while after this poem was written).

If the first stanza is, as one critic has suggested, about "merging," with the image of the swans, traditional symbols of the soul, dipping their heads in the mirroring water, the second is about "isolation." The coming of winter will erase the natural beauty of youth, replacing it with human artifacts that separate and mute the human observer. "Walls stand / Speechless and cold, in the wind / The weathervanes clatter." You can make much of these images, and the weathervanes in particular cry out for comment. Are we subject to the whims of the elements, turning without control? What good does it do for humankind to measure the direction and velocity of the wind? How do such objects deface the landscape?

Hyperion's Song of Fate

In Hölderlin's novel, Hyperion writes this poem after receiving a letter from the dying Diotima. Recalling ideas as old as Homer about the unbridgeable distance between the mortal and the immortal, the poet ruminates on "the celestials" who walk "up there in the light / on floors like velvet" to the accompaniment of soft winds and a heavenly harpist. In this imagined luxury the gods enjoy their "fateless" existence and flowers never die.

The third and last stanza turns to the tragic human lot; blindness contrasts to the calm gaze of eternal beings. The very shape of the poem, each stanza indented so that it looks like a downward precipice, expresses its meaning, a device that your students will surely want to discuss.

Brevity

This short poem exemplifies its title. The frigid cold that marked the second stanza of *The Half of Life* returns here, as does the quirky imagination that characterizes misplaced effort as "swimming at sundown." The futility of song with which the poem opens is picked up again at its close, with another unusual image: "the annoying nightbird" makes its impression not for any song that it may utter but for its visual intrusion and its pesky motion, flitting and "blocking your vision."

To the Fates

Both *Brevity* and *To the Fates* are strictly Asclepiadean odes, a Greek model that Hölderlin frequently followed. They are characterized by four-line stanzas, with two longer lines followed by two shorter ones, the first two marked by heavy caesuras. One critic speaks of the impact of Hölderlin's "falling rhythms and marked pauses" in these odes, which even in translation can be perceived. As with *Hyperion's Song of Fate*, that sense of fall is powerful. If you have been doing metrical analyses with your students, these are excellent texts for detailed study.

These poems, written in the last two years of the eighteenth century, are haunted by the fear of a man not yet thirty that his time was running out. The classical past burdens his imagination, as does the evanescence of the seasons. Hölderlin seems to see himself as one of those fallen warriors of ancient myth for whom the proper obsequies have been

omitted, so that his soul will not find rest "even in Orcus below." Yet the
poem concludes with a positive thought. Unlike the inhabitants of the
Homeric underworld, or an Orpheus without his lyre, Hölderlin will
have had his godhood if only he can write his poems. It is painful to realize that his days for writing poetry were numbered, and worse, that unlike Keats and Heine and so many other young poets who died young,
Hölderlin suffered from a dementia that left him in just the kind of
"shadow world" he speaks of in this ode, alive but stripped of his sanity
and his music.

Topics for Writing and Comparative Perspectives

1. Discuss the importance of the classical past in Hölderlin's poetry.

    [To focus this more particularly, you might ask your students to
    compare Shelley's *Ode to the West Wind* with Hölderlin's *To the
    Fates*, in terms both of their form and of their attitudes toward
    time.]

2. What is the importance of the way a poem looks on the page?
    Comment on *Hyperion's Song of Fate*.

    [A good juxtaposition would be to compare and contrast the vi-
    sual effects sought by the Dadaists, focusing especially on the se-
    lections in the *Anthology* by Tristan Tzara.]

3. Compare Hölderlin's depiction of the "annoying nightbird" in
    Brevity with Keats's nightingale and discuss the significance of bird
    imagery in lyric poetry.

    [If you have read the medieval lyrics in Vol. 1 of the *Anthology*,
    you may want to revisit some of them, especially the anonymous
    Song of Summer, for their loving evocations of birds and their
    songs.]

Further Reading

Constantine, David. *Hölderlin*. 1988. An excellent introduction for the
  English-speaking reader, written by a veteran teacher who knows how
  to present matters relating to rhythm and form. His analysis of the
  odes is particularly worth reading.

Santner, Eric L. *Friedrich Hölderlin: Narrative Vigilance and the Poetic
  Imagination*. 1986. A sophisticated literary discussion of Hölderlin's
  proclivity for "paratactic composition." See especially the detailed
  analysis of this quality of "side-by-sideness" in *The Half of Life*,
  pp. 81–91.

Unger, Richard. *Friedrich Hölderlin*. 1984. An overview of the life and
  times of the poet, in the Twayne series.

Novalis (Friedrich Von Hardenberg)

Classroom Strategies and Topics for Discussion

Another writer who found his vocation in mourning the loss of a beloved girl and then died young himself, Friedrich von Hardenberg (who became Novalis) typifies the popular image of the Romantic poet. Identified with "The Blue Flower," a symbol of the unattainable that he introduced in his unfinished novel, *Heinrich von Ofterdingen*, Novalis represents a conservative Germanic ideology. If you choose to teach the three German poets in this selection together, you will be able to draw significant distinctions among Heine, Hölderlin, and Novalis. All three were born in the same tumultous decade, but were from different backgrounds; not surprisingly, each developed a unique sensibility and voice. Of the three, Novalis most fixedly pursues the quest for transcendence.

A good way to begin your examination of Novalis's role is by noting the privileged atmosphere in which he was raised. (Hölderlin, whom Novalis knew, was of middle-class origins, and Heine, a Jew and a revolutionary spirit, exiled himself from Germany.) Carefully educated at home, the young Novalis went off to the University of Jena, where in the company of closest friend, Friedrich Schlegel, he frequented the home of August Wilhelm Schlegel and his wife; thus he was, in effect, present at the creation of German Romanticism and knew the leading figures of the movement, including Goethe and the great dramatist Schiller, with whom Novalis studied history at Jena.

Goethe actually visited the deathbed of the young woman to whom Friedrich von Hardenberg had become engaged. In many ways, that doomed courtship shaped von Hardenberg's short life. Like Dante, he fell deeply in love at first glance with a girl who was to become his poetic inspiration. This process began when he saw Sophia von Kuhn in November 1794, when she was not yet thirteen and he was some ten years older. In 1795, their engagement was announced; when she was barely fifteen, Sophia died. As Dante's Beatrice had a richly suggestive name, so did Sophia. As Sophie, she was the youngster whom he adored; as Sophia, after her death she became the symbolic embodiment of the wisdom that is deeply identified with Christian mysticism.

The choice of Novalis for a poetic name also deserves elucidation: the family had an estate named Grossenrode in Hannover, from which they took the name "von Rode." Latinized, this became "de Novali," and "seems to have meant 'one who clears new land'—a pathfinder or a pioneer." The pioneer who chose this name had only three years in which to write the works on which his reputation is based. Sophie died in March 1797; a month later, one of his brothers died. Novalis eventually wrote six Hymns to the Night, of which the poem printed in the *Anthology* is the last. With it, the painful contemplation of death and the loss of Sophia yields to the love of Jesus, "the sweet bride" who will never fail.

The title *Yearning for Death* seems to have been assigned to this poem (the only one of the Hymns written entirely in verse) by Schlegel, after the death of Novalis; its mood is actually more purposefully directed to reunion with Christ. As the poem begins, we are traveling, already embarked for the cool, "everlasting Night." The world is "alien" to human beings, as line 11 indicates: "To our Father's house we would return." Contemplating the past when God was a presence in this world (the German *Vorzeit*, translated here as "the times forgone," occurs three times in rapid succession, beginning with line 18 and then repeated at the head of the two central stanzas beginning at line 19), Novalis sketches the vitality of the primitive world. We are back at the beginning of the universe, it would appear, when man is created in "the lofty image that [the Father] bore" (lines 23–24). This quasi-historical survey of the olden days alludes to scenes of martyrdom, both that of "children toward God's kingdom going / [who] For death and torment strove" (lines 27–28) and that of the savior, "Refusing not the smart and pain, / That it might be our dearer gain" (lines 35–36). Since the world is no longer a place where these sacrifices would be meaningful, "temporal life" is equated with "hot thirst" that cannot be slaked (line 39). Our dead (like Sophie) have been buried; indeed, it is from these dead that the impulse to move on surges:

> Methinks from the far distance sounded
> An echo of our sorrow.
> Perhaps our loved ones likewise longing
> Have wafted us this sigh of longing.

Interestingly, to give oneself over to Jesus one moves downward, the easier direction presaged by the poem's opening lines. One needs only to "sink" to be embraced by God, not to attempt the arduous upward climb prescribed in other visionary verses. By depicting a maternally nurturing Father God who has lived among men and women and offers Jesus to them as a bride, Novalis emphasizes the availability of salvation. To reach it is to "return": nothing needs to be invented to deserve to go home. This sense of return is reinforced in the original German: "the dark earth's womb" of line 1, *der Erde Schoss*, anticipates the last two words: *Vaters Schoss*, the "Father's arms," or more precisely, "the Father's womb," the receptacle in which humankind is formed and comforted.

Topics for Writing and Comparative Perspectives

1. Contrast the significance of up and down in *Yearning for Death* with that expressed in *Hyperion's Song of Fate*. How does the poet's religious vision enter into the sense of movement in each poem?
2. Compare the representation of the great Romantic themes Night and Death in Novalis's *Yearning for Death* with that in Heine's *Ah, Death Is Like the Long, Cool Night*, Hugo's *Et nox facta est*, or Keats's *Ode to a Nightingale*.

Further Reading

See also the reading suggestions in the *Anthology*.

Neubauer, John. *Novalis*. 1980. A volume in Twayne's World Authors series, this informative book covers Novalis's entire career. He was not
only a poet but also a philosopher and a bureaucrat, well educated in
the sciences.

Reynolds, Simon. *Novalis and the Poets of Pessimism*. 1995. An attractive, small volume with a black-and-white reproduction of Franz
Gareis's 1799 oil painting of the long-haired, bright-eyed poet, it includes James Thomson's translation of *Hymns to the Night*, set against
a facing version of the original.

Anna Petrovna Bunina

Classroom Strategies and Topics for Discussion

With Bunina, the tradition of women's poetry in Russia may be said to
begin; at the same time, in terms of her stylistic development, she is a
transitional figure. Her early work was regarded as neoclassical, while
From the Seashore clearly deals in a Romantic idiom. Partly because of
her sex, partly because of the support she received from Aleksander
Shishkov (known as a traditionalist), Bunina earned the scorn of
Pushkin, who, according to Catriona Kelly, derided her work as "a crying
example of the worthlessness of poetry before Romanticism." Bunina
seems to admit as much in a witty poem (not in the *Anthology*) called
Conversation between Me and the Women: in this imaginary dialogue,
the women reprimand her for ignoring their concerns, while Bunina, the
"me" of the poem, admits to having written odes about great men to advance her own career.

In *From the Seashore*, however, a purer voice emerges. You may want
to call to your students' attention the time-honored image of a harmonious cosmos with which this poem begins. The sea and the sky seem
one continuous entity, and the tremulous sense of peace in the landscape seems to travel from one unit of existence to another, from the
shore to the treetops, where the birds nest. This mood is echoed by an
image of domestic tranquility as we move indoors, where children, like
the birds, "nestled / Modestly in the corners."

Ask your students to trace the way Bunina appeals to the different
senses in establishing the calm that is soon to be shattered: from the silence comes the sound of the "golden harp," calling up a specific image
of a middle-class music room in which Lina, a particular woman joins in
another example of harmonious connection. Color is also described in
just enough detail that we feel we are in the presence of a real scene:
from the beautiful sunset of a moonless twilight to the glowing "rose"
flame leaping across the hearth and the "dark silver" smoke, we have a
powerful visual image of rich contentment.

What happens to the fire? How does the sixth stanza transform the particularity of this happy family gathering to a more abstract distillation of heat? How does the seventh turn the flowing liquid sea arid? How does the rippling movement of the opening translate to "heaving"?

This modest poem expresses a keen eye for detail that carefully prepares for its disruptive conclusion. The effortless flowing of sea from sky cannot help the "poor woman," cold and parched, who requires the fire to "flow" and the sea to "churn" if she is to recover the health that has been leached out of her and the poem in its final stanzas.

Topics for Writing and Comparative Perspectives

1. Compare the opening of Bunina's poem with that of *Tintern Abbey*: why do so many Romantic writers attach significance to the apparent connectedness of sea, landscape, and sky?

   [You might want to mention the opening of Genesis as perhaps the archetypal site for this sense of cosmic integration, a state of being into which, significantly, God quickly proceeds to introduce difference.]

2. Many of the great Romantic poems document their authors' various experiences of fatal illness. Compare the tone of Bunina's *From the Seashore* to that of Heine's *Ah, Death Is Like the Long Cool Night* or Rosalía de Castro's *The Ailing Woman Felt Her Forces Ebb*. How explicit are the references to physical suffering? Is the writer accepting or bitter?

3. Compare and contrast the experience of nature and death in Bunina's *From the Seashore* and in Anna Akhmatova's *Requiem*, discussing the way the enormities of twentieth-century politics transform the poetry of personal grief.

Further Reading

Kelly, Catriona, ed. *An Anthology of Russian Women's Writing, 1777–1992*. 1994. The source of the quotation cited above, this groundbreaking volume presents two of Bunina's poems. The introduction discusses the broader topic and may be useful if you plan to teach Anna Akhmatova's poetry as well.

Alphonse de Lamartine

Classroom Strategies and Topics for Discussion

Like so much Romantic poetry, *The Lake* can lead you into a discussion of the relationship between autobiography and art. This poem, based on a specific recollection of time Lamartine spent on Lake Bourget with Julie Charles, was written in August 1817. Julie died in December 1817; although she was already ill when these verses were composed, to read them as a tribute to a lost beloved anticipates the event. In them, the poet seizes on a personal experience and transforms it into a symbolic meditation, as the headnote puts it, "on nature and time." His private suffering is not his primary subject, as the first stanza makes clear. It is rather the human confrontation with eternity, on a boat traversing "time's vast ocean" instead of a real Alpine lake.

Lamartine stands at the very beginning of the French Romantic tradition; the formal characteristics of *The Lake*, regular quatrains of perfect alexandrines, could as easily belong to a neoclassical poem. The poem is famed for its rhythmic and melodious qualities, well caught by the English translator in lines 59–60. Many of its themes, particularly in the four stanzas that begin "O time, suspend your flight! and you, blessed hours, / suspend your swift passage" in which the speaker ostensibly quotes his beloved, have deep roots in the Western tradition. The "voice so dear" echoes Ovid's *Amores*, with the famous cry to the horses that draw the chariot of the night, "*Lente, lente currite noctis equi*," as well as the aubade, in which the lady bewails the coming of the dawn that will drive her lover from her bed.

What Lamartine brings to these conventions is an urgency and a universality of sweep that was enormously appealing to his generational peers. His *Meditations Poetiques*, the short volume of which *The Lake* is the centerpiece, was one of the great best-sellers of French literary history. The poem records the ambivalence with which the Romantics viewed nature. On the one hand, *The Lake* is the most famous Continental example of the "pathetic fallacy," the tendency to attribute human emotions to the natural world; on the other, it presents an alien, if majestic, landscape, a stage set against which the speaker's emotions play themselves out rather than a specifically visualized place.

The first three quatrains establish the landscape frame; the next six (lines 13–36) recall the scene a year before. You might ask your students to contrast the stormy landscape of the metaphysically grand third stanza, with the water breaking against the rocks' "torn flanks," and the calm of the fourth and fifth, in which the speaker and his beloved sail together. The shores (again, as if they were human), prospectively enchanted by her voice, provide an eerie aural accompaniment of "strains unknown to earth" as an undercurrent to Julie's eloquent plea to the night. Her words establish the imagery that the speaker recapitulates in the beginning of the poem and effect the transformation from actual experience to metaphor: the ocean is time.

In the following three stanzas, the speaker challenges the universe, in grand heroic style: note the prevalence of question marks and exclamation points. You could have your students trace the personification of the great abstraction—"jealous," thieving, and indiscriminate time—and the speaker's effort to rally nature to stand for him against time by preserving the memory of happiness. Then, in the last three stanzas, an erotically charged landscape is invoked, as the poet, now using the third person to celebrate "their love," transforms his recollected love affair into an objective value that will be preserved in the lake and its environs, whether in peace or in storm, on "glad slopes" or "savage rocks," and thus transcend both the threat and the promise of the changeable surroundings. Elevated and presumably ennobled by his love, he ends magnanimously, on a note of benediction.

Topics for Writing and Comparative Perspectives

1. In *The Lake*, like Wordsworth in *Tintern Abbey*, Lamartine returns
   to a place where he was once happy. Compare and contrast the two
   poets' reasons for valuing the landscapes of their choice and the
   poetic prayers with which they end their poems.
   [Wordsworth's focus on the imaginative sustenance he derives
   from hedgerows and hills memorializes a poetics of intellectual activity that contrasts with Lamartine's more passionate quest for immortality.]
2. Compare Lamartine's presentation of time in *The Lake* with that of
   Novalis in *Yearning for Death*; of Keats in *To Autumn*; or of Tennyson in *Tithonus*.
   [Note that Julie distinguishes between those for whom time is a
   burden—see lines 25–28—and those for whom it should be pro-
   longed.]
3. Two of the most famous poems in French literature use the image
   of a boat on the water but to very different effect. Compare and
   contrast poetic point of view and/or landscape description in
   Lamartine's *The Lake* and Rimbaud's *Drunken Boat*.
   [Each of these poems defines the sensibility with which it is associated: see the helpful headnote to Rimbaud in the *Anthology*.]

Further Reading

See also the reading suggestions in the *Anthology*, p. 2541.

Levi, Anthony. *Guide to French Literature: 1789 to the Present.* 1992.
Contains a short, informative article about Lamartine.

Heinrich Heine

Of the three German poets represented in this selection of Romantic
lyrics, Heine is the best loved and most frequently quoted, in large part
because his poems seem very simple; a great many of them have been
set to music and generations of German speakers have grown up with
these *lieder*. From our students' point of view, Heine's poems offer a
wonderful introduction to some major nineteenth-century preoccupations because they seem at first so unthreatening, yet yield so much
when discussed at length.

[A Pine Is Standing Lonely]

The spirit of Northern Romanticism breathes through this poem: re-
productions of Caspar David Friedrich's paintings will allow you to present visually the kind of austere, vaguely mysterious landscape captured
here. Asking about the way Heine personifies the pine tree leads you
into a discussion of the idea of nature as a virtually human presence for
so many of the Romantic poets. Why is the pine "lonely"? The bare,
snowbound plateau symbolizes a kind of emotional dormancy very close

to death—the ice and snow, the speaker tells us, "enshroud" him, yet the pine tree is sleeping, not dead, and he dreams of an exotic palm tree, also "lonely and silently mourning."

In eight brief lines, the poet paints an archetypal tragedy. We are all solitary, longing for something quite beyond reach. Diametrically opposed to each other, the two trees can never meet. Note the juxtaposition of Northern and *Eastern*, rather than *Southern*; Heine's poetry abounds in details like this, words or ideas that don't quite match one's expectations and therefore require some thought. There are also many Asian references in Heine's work. Here, a Middle Eastern palm tree may conjure up a cultural divide—perhaps it is not too extreme to read in the gulf separating the pine and the palm something of the cleavage between Heine's Germanic and Judaic heritages.

[A Young Man Loves a Maiden]

It may be helpful to work out the complications of the artless first stanza: A loves B, B loves C, C loves D, and "these two haply wed." The angry B marries E, and poor A is left inconsolable. Notice too that C and D marry "haply"—not "happily." The formula for comedy, boy loves girl, and so on, has no place here; as the last stanza suggests, perhaps the formula was never accurate to begin with. Your students will probably want to talk about this poem at some length. Indeed, the last stanza makes a good argument for the study of literature. The old stories when deeply felt are always new.

[Ah, Death is Like the Long, Cool Night]

Heine is another Romantic poet who suffered terribly from a long, incurable illness; unlike others in the *Anthology* (see especially Bunina and de Castro), he does not see death as a threat. You may want to link this beautiful poem with the more objectified situation of the pine and the palm tree: note the reiterated contrast between cold and hot, between death and sleep, perennial themes to which Heine returns again and again throughout his work.

The slight disconnection between the two stanzas invites the reader to supply the missing link. Mentioned without self-pity, the poignancy of the nightingale singing "in dreams" seems to be the product of the poet's hallucination. Why this gleaming vision should appear to the poet, "tired of light," is left to our imaginations. Working this through with your class should offer a good opportunity to talk about the frequently drawn analogy between lyric writers and nightingales. Why should the capacity to sing be enhanced by the dark? How does that notion fit the Romantic exaltation of the fanciful and irrational?

[The Silesian Weavers]

In addition to the short, deceptively simple songs of the sort cited above, Heine wrote a number of explicitly political poems. Deeply influenced both the events of the day (when he wrote this poem, Heine had established a friendship with Karl Marx) and by the classical past, Heine may well be combining references to two kinds of textile workers in this poem. The dislocations caused by the Industrial Revolution are behind the protests of the Silesian weavers against "intolerable working conditions during June 1844," as the footnote will inform your students. In threatening both God and king, the weavers enunciate Heine's radicalism. They may also evoke the three fates of ancient mythology—the Parcae, who spin, measure, and cut the threads of life. Certainly the heavy rhythms of the poem proclaim that fate will vindicate the brutalized workers.

Yet another meditation on death, this poem predicts the downfall of Prussian tyranny. It also incorporates the odd reversals of expectation that Heine so frequently plays with. The flower, the emblem of life, is "crushed in a day," while the worm, the agent of death, feeds fat "on rot and decay."

In summary then, you can demonstrate to your class that Heine's reliance on simple sentence structure, obvious rhymes, and naïve diction establishes a tension reiterating that implicit in the poem's double consciousness. On the one hand, he appears to offer simple, confident assertions. Yet the confidence is subtly undermined by the implications suggested above. The effort to state simple truths, like the effort to love, is a difficult endeavor, and, like its counterpart, it may finally prove inadequate. Hearing these poems can reinforce an understanding of how the music of the verses actually conveys this double sense. If you or a colleague speak German well, one or two of the shorter poems read aloud in the original will remind your students that many poetic effects are not easily got at through discussion.

Topics for Writing

1. Compare any two lyrics by Heine in their use of imagery.
2. Discuss the concept of death implied in one of Heine's poems.
3. How does the idea of the past figure in Heine?

Comparative Perspectives

1. Although Shelley refers to poets as the "unacknowledged legislators of the World" in A Defence of Poetry, Romantic poets, himself included, often tackle specific political content in their works. How does Heine's use of ballad form in The Silesian Weavers differ from Shelley's use of the sonnet in England in 1819? What other poems that you have read resemble Heine's narratives?
2. Like many of the writers of the Romantic era, Heine often turns his personal experience into poetry. Compare the experiences that apparently underlie both Ah, Death Is Like the Long, Cool Night and Keat's Ode to a Nightingale.

Further Reading

See also the reading suggestions in the *Anthology*, p. 2541.

Brod, Max. *Heinrich Heine: The Artist in Revolt.* 1957. A study of the poet's literary career.

Fairley, B. *Heinrich Heine: An Interpretation.* 1977. Scholarly and thorough.

Kohn, Hans. *Heinrich Heine: The Man and the Myth.* 1959. Short lecture offering suggestive definitions of Heine's characteristics as a poet.

Liptzen, Sol. *The English Legend of Heinrich Heine.* 1954. A lucid account of the shifts of Heine's literary reputation in England.

Perraudin, M. *Heinrich Heine.* 1988. A general critical study.

Roche, M. W. *Dynamic Stillness.* 1987. Treats the importance of quietness as a theme in Heine and other major German poets.

Rose, William. *The Early Love Poetry of Heinrich Heine: An Inquiry into Poetic Inspiration.* 1962. As the title suggests, this work concentrates on analysis of Heine's early lyrics and of their sources.

Spencer, H. *Heinrich Heine.* 1982. A fairly elementary introduction in the Twayne series. Useful bibliography.

Giacomo Leopardi

Classroom Strategies and Topics for Discussion

Petrarch and Leopardi are generally considered the preeminent lyric poets of Italy. Petrarch, of course, is world famous; Leopardi is less well known, partially because Romanticism was never central to Italian culture as was the humanism that we associate with Petrarch. Short-lived, unlucky in love, the celebrator of his regional landscape, Leopardi fits the pattern of the Romantic poet in many ways. In other ways, however, he plays against type: a scholar and intellectual of the first rank, he wrote more prose than poetry (there are only thirty-four poems in the *Canti*, his major work in the genre, from which the selections in the *Anthology* are drawn). Most interesting, perhaps, is his attitude toward nature, which he came to see as the great enemy of human happiness. In *Tintern Abbey*, Wordsworth claims that "Nature never did betray / The heart that loved her" (lines 122–23). The philosophical poetry of Giacomo Leopardi explores precisely the opposite of that sentiment.

The Infinite

This early poem, written in 1819, is set on Mount Tabor in Leopardi's hometown, the northern Italian city of Recanati. Leopardi often climbed this hill, to which he had access from the back gate of his family's garden. Thus the poem begins by acknowledging the habitual affection in

which he holds the spot, so "dear" as is "the hedge which hides away /
The reaches of the sky." But this is no nostalgic reflection on happy
childhood days. With that reference to the hedge, *The Infinite*, unlike
many other lyrics in this selection, posits discontinuity as its point of departure: the human being is isolated in and alienated from a terrifying
universe.

The central lines of *The Infinite* allude to one of the most famous
statements in Pascal's *Pensées*: "The eternal silence of those infinite
spaces terrifies me." Perhaps not yet convinced that this is the fundamental truth about the universe, Leopardi ends the poem with a suspended judgment. The vibrancy of the wind and the live sound of the
present seem to counter "the dead seasons" and the "more than human
silences" that surround him.

TO HIMSELF

The latest of the poems in this selection, *To Himself* was written in
1833, when Leopardi was bitterly unhappy in the aftermath of a deeply
felt but unrequited love. The uncharacteristically short lines and lack of
metaphors express formally the bleakness that the poem describes. The
poet addresses not merely himself but his heart, here considered more a
motor than the locus of love. "Rest, rest, forever. / You have beaten long
enough."

In the following sentence, the word translated as "vacuum" is in Italian *noia*, a recurring and crucial term for Leopardi, akin to, but even
bleaker than, Baudelaire's *ennui*. In its existential inclusiveness, it balances the earthier specificity of the short declaration to which it leads:
"The world is mud." The ending here is Sophoclean in its hard-eyed
sense of the unremitting cruelty of human life: "The only gift / Fate gave
our kind was death." Leopardi is now convinced that nature is the root
of all our troubles—the definitive judgment of the final lines offers no
hope of any kind. "The boundless emptiness" is in the original *l'infinita
vanita*, and thus carries with it a theological force. All is vanity.

TO SYLVIA

It can be rather hard on students to expose them to too much unremitting despair; the two longer poems in this selection offer a slightly
softer view of a still-deplorable situation. *To Sylvia*, written in April
1828, pays tribute to an idealized image of a village girl who died young.
Although her "perpetual song" (line 8) is from the start set against the
insistence in the first stanza on the evanescence of her "mortal lifetime,"
the nostalgic recollections of Sylvia at her "woman's tasks" give us an
image of the teenaged Leopardi turning away from his scholarly labors
in his father's library to listen to her song and look around him at the
beauty of the natural landscape.

The accusation against nature is all the more bitter because of this
sense of disappointed hope: "why / Do you not keep the promises you
gave? / Why trick the children so?" That line deserves full discussion

with your class. From Rousseau on, childhood is a sacred component of the Romantic understanding of life. To violate it is one of the cardinal sins. Time, too, is a villain here, depriving Sylvia of her allotted years: "Before winter struck the summer grass" (line 36), before her natural "flowering" (line 39), she has been deprived of life.

To Sylvia concludes with as many questions as final judgments. If the sadness that the poet feels is not merely a response to Sylvia's premature death, by choosing to focus on her the poet avoids the totalizing vision of *To Himself*. Looking at the original Italian confirms this personalizing, rather than universalizing, of despair. The "stark sepulchre" is *una tomba ignuda*, "an unmarked grave," a sign of Sylvia's individual fate even as it points the way that we all must go.

THE VILLAGE SATURDAY

Written in 1829, during a period when Leopardi had returned home (which he did not leave until he was twenty-four years old and allowed to go to Rome—like Recanati, a conservative place of which his father approved), this sad, lovely poem finds some positive value in the passing of time, for the transition from Saturday to Sunday brings peace to the hard-working inhabitants of the village and happy memories prevail. Woman's archetypal task, spinning, is here undertaken by an old woman (in *To Sylvia*, it is the doomed girl who weaves) who regales her neighbors with stories of time past. The landscape darkens, but illuminated by "the whitening of the moon," the site spells beauty and contentment.

The earlier poems find silence fearful; here, "happy chatter" and the carpenter's almost biblical activity punctuate the Saturday evening as it turns to a Sunday, the welcome seventh day. To be sure, *noia* awaits: this is the word translated as "tedium" in line 39, which predicts the coming return to "habitual travail." And, as in *To Sylvia*, a child is apostrophized. This youngster seems to be enjoying his "flowering time," but the speaker warns of what will inevitably become of "the great feast of life." Yet the poet holds his tongue. The mood is gentler, more accepting, less fierce than in the two shorter poems; the outlook, however, remain bleak.

Topics for Writing and Comparative Perspectives

1. Discuss the significance attributed to sounds and silence in Leopardi's poems.
2. Choose examples of landscape description in Leopardi's poems and explore their relevance to his angry statements about nature, "the ugly force." How would you compare his view of the lonely hill in *The Infinite*, or the darkening shadows in *The Village Saturday*, with the hopeful evocation of the English landscape in Wordsworth's *Ode on Intimations of Immortality* (note the importance of that last word), or of the Swiss lakeside in Lamartine's *The Lake*?
3. What is the young poet's relation to Sylvia? Compare the respect-

ful distance that separates him, on his ancestral balcony, from this village girl with the way Goethe's Faust imposes himself on Gretchen.

4. Discuss Leopardi's depictions of women weaving or spinning. [Compare the classical Fates alluded to in Heine's *Silesian Weavers*, or Gretchen in *Faust*.]

Further Reading

See also the reading suggestions in the *Anthology*, p. 2541.

Carsaniga, G. *Giacomo Leopardi: The Unheeded Voice*. 1977. A reassessment that places Leopardi in his social and historical context.

Grennan, Eamon, trans. *Leopardi: Selected Poems*. 1997. See the helpful introduction by John C. Barnes and the translator's comments. Like those of Casale in *A Leopardi Reader*, these translations are accompanied by the Italian originals.

Nelson, Lowry, Jr. "Leopardi First and Last." In *Italian Literature Roots and Branches*. G. Rimanelli and K. J. Atchity, ed. 1976. Study of Leopardi in relation to his literary predecessors.

Wilkins, Ernest Hatch. *A History of Italian Literature*. 1954. The chapter on Leopardi places the poet in his literary context.

Victor Hugo

Classroom Strategies and Topics for Discussion

As one of the great exemplars of the Romantic movement in Europe, Victor Hugo merits attention not only for the remarkable range of his individual accomplishment but also for his consistent embodiment of the principles of Romanticism. Glorification of imagination (indeed, of consciousness); attention to the phenomena of the natural world; indignation over social oppression; interest in the illuminations provided by detail; an effort to reimagine and resee the everyday—such manifestations of the Romantic spirit appear everywhere in Hugo. Any of them might provide a starting point for investigation of *Et nox facta est*.

Et nox facta est offers an intricate treatment of consciousness. Students will think at first that "consciousness," in this poem, alludes only to Satan's mental states; and indeed Satan's emotional progress provides an appropriate starting point for investigation. If your class has read *Paradise Lost* (in Vol. 1 of the *Anthology*), comparison with Milton's Satan—who, like Hugo's, declares his hatred of the sun—is one way to elucidate the problem. It can be argued that Hugo's defier of God is a more nearly sympathetic figure than is Milton's. At any rate, you might offer this hypothesis to the class and invite them to support or refute it by reference to the text. But the question of how one is invited to feel about Satan can also be considered without reference to Milton. How do such adjectives as "aghast" and "dumbfounded" and "sad" make one feel about Satan? How does one respond to his desperate flight after the dying star? to his "Quiver" at the growing of his "membraned wing," his shivering at the loss of two suns? These instances of apparent invitations to pity must be considered in relation to such terms as "bandit" and "monster" and to Satan's declaration of hatred for God; certainly no case can be made for sympathy or pity as *adequate* responses to this being. Hugo insists that one understand Satan both as victim and as villain and that one reflect about the relation between the two reactions.

Thus the poet invites alternative states of consciousness in the reader. He also tacitly contrasts Satan's state with God's ("absorbed in being and in Life"); the meaning of the perverted archangel depends on awareness of the state from which he has fallen. Finally, providing a complicated retrospect on the entire poem, Hugo's concluding section introduces the question of the writer's consciousness and its meaning. Students should be asked to speculate about the importance of this section (lines 214–31) in the poem as a whole. It calls emphatic attention to the fact that the narrative we have just read is and must be entirely a product of imagination, since it alludes to "Cycles previous to man, chaos, heavens," about which no human being can possibly have direct knowledge. The "sage," the "thinker," the "wise man"—in other words, the poet— undertakes a superhuman moral search, "further / Than the facts witnessed by the present sky." His effort is described in heroic terms. What is the connection between his grand, impossible, necessary undertaking and that of Satan, which the poem has just described? This question cannot be answered with certainty, but speculation about it is sure to prove fruitful in leading to an understanding of the mysterious, dangerous power that the Romantics believed inherent in the poetic act.

Topics for Writing

1. In what respects is Hugo's Satan a heroic figure? Describe in detail how the impression of his heroism is developed through the course of *Et nox facta est*.
2. What is the importance of the white feather in *Et nox facta est*? Consider the allusions to feathers and to wings of various sorts in the poem as a whole; do not rely on the explanatory footnote as a guide to the feather's *significance*.

Comparative Perspectives

Western and Islamic writers return again and again to the figure of Satan, from perspectives as varied as the eras in which they live. Compare and contrast the diabolical figures in, as appropriate, Job, the Koran, Dante's *Inferno*, Goethe's *Faust*, or Milton's *Paradise Lost*, with Hugo's fallen devil. How and why do different historical periods reinterpret this character?

Further Reading

See also the reading suggestions in the *Anthology*, p. 2541.

Grant, Elliott M. *The Career of Victor Hugo.* 1946. A useful literary biography.

Guerlac, S. *The Impersonal Sublime: Hugo, Baudelaire, Lautreamont.* 1990. This treatment of Hugo in conjunction with other important French poets emphasizes his modern aspects.

Houston, J. P. *The Demonic Imagination: Style and Theme in French Romantic Poetry.* 1969. The section on Hugo relates his "demonic imagination" to that of other French Romantic poets.

Porter, L. *The Renaissance of the Lyric in French Romanticism.* 1978. Places Hugo in his immediate literary context and stresses his importance as lyricist.

Swinburne, Algernon. *A Study of Victor Hugo.* 1886. An important English poet reacting to an important French poet.

Gérard de Nerval

Classroom Strategies and Topics for Discussion

Nerval (1808–1855) is a centrally important French Romantic writer. Students may be interested in his biography, which includes a record of bizarre behavior, frequent hospitalization for insanity, and suicide at the end. However, the biography has little or no bearing on the extraordinary lyrics offered in the *Anthology*. In them, he evinces a quiet control over his materials, in which the human and natural worlds interpenetrate and transform one another, and in which time and mutability exercise overpowering dominance. Such materials can be observed throughout the whole range of Romantic writing, in Wordsworth and Hölderlin, for instance, as well as Nerval.

Students may already be familiar with some poetry where the same materials are handled; perhaps they know Keats's *Ode to a Nightingale*. In any event, a general discussion of this area of the Romantic imagination would be a good introduction to a reading of these poems.

NOTRE-DAME

This poem projects the ancient Parisian cathedral into some distant future, outlasting the city itself but finally succumbing to the natural forces of time and decay. Student attention might be directed to the extended metaphor in the first stanza, in which time becomes a wolf and the cathedral a ravaged ox stripped to the bone. Literature is apparently more durable in this future; men will still read Hugo and thus be able to imagine the resurrection of the ruin "just as she used to be." But her collapse and decay, and her gradual return to nature, is inevitable and irreversible. Nothing, the poem says, is permanent except the imagination, not even its realization in art.

AWAKENING IN THE CARRIAGE

This poem demonstrates the interpenetration of the human and natural worlds on a virtually line-by-line basis. Trees become a fleeing defeated army; the road becomes a billowing ocean; steeples become shepherds leading houses that have become sheep; mountains get drunk and rivers become an attacking boa constrictor. This series of interpenetrations and transformations is announced as if perceived: "This is what I saw." Finally, though, they are explained as an effect of penumbral consciousness: "I was in the carriage, having just awoken!" What appeared as irrationally *given* is provided with a rational foundation—a foundation in the liminal stage between sleeping and waking in which perception itself becomes irrational, associative, and unpredictable.

A LANE IN THE LUXEMBOURG

The setting is a park in Paris. The apparitional woman who is the focus of this poem has appeared often in Romantic writing, in many versions. She's gone before she's really been seen; she sings but vanishes before the song has been heard. Nonetheless she might have been the speaker's soul mate. Not even that status can be permanent, however. Everything is in flux, and the vanishing girl is emblematic of all that vanishes: youth, sunshine, good fortune. Student attention might be called to the unheard song, which, as usual in Romantic writing, is all the sweeter for not being heard. The imagined is always better than the actual because it is not subject to time and natural law.

APRIL

This poem also handles the theme of mutability. The first stanza presents an early spring that already looks and feels like late summer or fall, with oppressive sunshine, longer evenings, and reddening leaves. The unspoken fact of this situation is that every early spring is already a fall in potential; human consciousness is always conscious of time. The second stanza attempts to seize the moment of spring, to purge the perception of a potential fall and winter with which it is accompanied. Student attention might be directed to the last lines, where spring is invoked as a "new nymph/ who steps from the water, smiling." Time and its operations are implicit in this image, however muted. Nothing is exempt.

GRANDMOTHER

This touching poem relates the common experience of being unable to produce the expected emotions at the appropriate moment, say at the funeral of a close and much-loved relative. The speaker testifies to feeling only "surprise, rather than sadness," even as everyone else is weeping, and he is told that he, too, "ought" to weep. The crucial turn in the poem is the assertion of the first line of the third stanza: "Vociferous sorrow is soon over." A quieter, less expressive grief, on the other hand, gains strength from time, a notion emphasized in the final lines with the metaphor of a name carved into the bark of a tree. Students might be asked which they find most convincing—the assertion, the counter-assertion, or the metaphor.

Topics for Writing

1. Time and mutability in a few of Nerval's poems.
2. The interpenetration of the human and natural worlds in a few of Nerval's poems.
3. The striking use of metaphor in a few of Nerval's poems.

Further Reading

See also the reading suggestions in the *Anthology*, p. 2542. As the head note states, there is little on Nerval in English. Here are two good books to consult.

Umberto Eco. *Six Walks in the Fictional Woods*. 1994.

George MacLennan. *Lucid Intervals: Subjective Writing and Madness in History*. 1992.

Mikhail Yuryevitch Lermontov

Classroom Strategies and Topics for Discussion

Lermontov (1814–1841) was a young army officer when he was killed in a duel at the age of twenty-seven. This alone has cast about his work a hazy romantic glow, but the work itself is clear-cut and hard-headed. Its themes and attitudes are derived from the stock of pan-European Romanticism, refreshed by wit, irony, and a peculiarly Russian fervor. It might be useful to introduce these five poems with a discussion of Romanticism as an international aesthetic movement with an impact on all media. Its epicenters were Germany and England, from which it spread across the continent, eventually reaching Russia—and finally, the United States. Upper-class Russians were francophiles in cultural sympathies, and so the chief conduits of Romanticism into Russian writing were French. Lermontov composes compact lyrics on the themes of lost love and isolation, especially the isolation of the artist. The rhymed translations preserve some sense of his intricate formal invention.

[13]

This brief poem declares the loss of love and details its aftermath. The "image" of the formerly beloved survives, though the speaker calls it powerless. Students might be asked to what extent they believe this, given the rest of the poem, and especially the final two lines. First, the speaker retains a sense of exclusive possession over the "image." Finally, the "image" is given divine status, however diminished. It is a "fallen god," in a "forsaken shrine," but the speaker still kneels and prays before it. Has he indeed "shed / The weight of longing and remorse"?

[18]

Byron is probably the best-known, virtually iconic figure of pan-European Romanticism. He sedulously promoted himself as an alien-ated, homeless exile, burdened by nameless sins, by social isolation, and by fame and his own genius. Any poem that opens by invoking Byron courts the same iconic identity. Lermontov's speaker distinguishes him-self from Byron; he's a Russian. But otherwise his Byronism is complete, down to the disdain for "the mob" with which the poem concludes. Student attention might be directed to the extended simile beginning in the seventh line, in which the speaker's soul is likened to a shipwrecked, sunken boat. His "broken hopes" are then consigned to the sea, whose "secrets" and "treasures" are inviolable, just like the speaker's thoughts. Students could be asked what these thoughts consist of. If they are the thoughts of a Russian Byron, we already have a good general picture of them.

[19. To *]

This poem is implicitly installed in a dramatic situation, in which the speaker responds to the interrogation of a lover about his past. That past is too terrible and painful—too Byronic, in short—to be revealed. The speaker's refusal of self-revelation is motivated not only by self-interest, but also by his concern for the happiness of his beloved. Students might be asked to weigh these two stated motivations. Which is more impor-tant, or more convincing?

[24]

Students may be familiar with Shakespeare's Sonnet #130, which plays with the threadbare clichés of the Petrarchan tradition. If not, it might be useful to supply them with a copy. Lermontov is involved in an analogous performance. The beloved of this poem does not resemble Venus; no one worships her. A nymph is more attractive. Nevertheless, her exuberance and grace are beyond a cliché's ability to represent them, and even the world-weary speaker finds them irresistible.

THE POET'S DEATH

This is probably Lermontov's most famous poem, written on the occa-sion of Pushkin's death in a duel. Part lament and part a scornful attack on Pushkin's killer, the poem takes the event of Pushkin's death as em-blematic of the hatred which the general culture bears for the artist, of which the killer is simply an aggravated instance. Parts of the culture hypocritically mourn the slain poet, and Lermontov deals with this hypocrisy and its motivation in fear and incomprehension in the first verse paragraph. Students might be asked to identify the referent of the second person pronoun in line nine, just to be sure they are following Lermontov's increasingly bitter rhetoric. The killer is analyzed in the second verse paragraph. Lermontov identifies him with some xenophobia as a foreign adventurer, a mocker of Russian language and the shameless murderer of Russia's greatest poet. Pushkin becomes like a character in one of his own plays in the third verse paragraph: a poet killed in a duel. Lermontov's anger glances momentarily at Pushkin himself in lines thirty-nine to forty-four, for having placed himself in such company and in such a situation. But line forty-five returns to the poem's proper focus, the art-and-artist–hating culture that tortures figures like Pushkin—and of course, figures like Lermontov—by giving praise (laurel wreaths) that wounds in a carnival of insincerity and falsehood. The result is the poet's death and burial, which definitively "sealed his lips and stopped his tongue" (1.56). Again, students might be asked to identify the referent of the third person plural pronoun in line forty-five, just to be sure they are following, and similarly, the second person pronoun in line fifty-seven. With line fifty-seven the poem enters its final movement, in a fury of passionate denunciation. At this point students might be asked how they evaluate the passion and hostility of this poem's rhetoric, and whether it seems to them to be justified.

Topics for Writing

1. Lermontov's loves.
2. Lermontov's Byronism.
3. Lermontov on the artist and society.

Further Reading

See also the reading suggestions in the *Anthology*, p. 2541.

John Mersereau. *Mikhail Lermontov.* 1962.

Paul Paganuzzi. *Lermontov: Autobiographical Reflections in the Poet's Work.* 1967.

Gustavo Adolfo Bécquer

[I Know a Strange, Gigantic Hymn]

I Know a Strange, Gigantic Hymn, the first poem in Bécquer's posthumously published *Rimas*, introduces the poet's themes and "these pages," the volume itself, which (like so much Romantic poetry) is devoted to an impossible task. The challenge is to capture the ineffable. The opening stanza suggests that poetry has a salvific function, bringing light where there has been darkness, and the poet seeks a language that unites human feelings and senses. Immediately, however, the difficulty of his task is acknowledged: human beings cannot get beyond their "impoverished language," for there is "no cipher," no secret code of writing or sign, to accomplish the synaestheic union that will render this great universal truth and speak to the particular beloved. In this brief and elegant set of quatrains, Bécquer announces his preoccupations.

[NAMELESS SPIRIT]

Nameless Spirit, the fifth of the rimas, more fully explores the implications and difficulties of these preoccupations. Here, the spirit of poetry itself, "Espiritu sin nombre," speaks, expressing the age-old tension between forms and ideas first articulated, perhaps, by Plato and Aristotle. The spirit takes many substantial forms from nature. This poem can be read in minute detail with your students, who will be able to delineate the fleeting and brilliantly imagined states in which the poetic spirit can be identified. In the second stanza, the spirit, beautifully voiced, moves in the cosmos; in the third through the fifth, it assumes the shape of many transient emanations of the natural world, from moonlight to cloud, from snow to seafoam.

In the sixth stanza, the spirit seems to move closer to human actions. Appropriating one of the central Romantic images, Bécquer makes this nameless spirit "a note in the lute," without telling us whether there is a musician. This resembles the aeolian harp, the passive instrument through which the wind itself makes music. If perfume resides by nature in the violet, it may also be extracted by human effort; and the tombs and the ruins that flame and ivy momentarily inhabit are by definition built by human hands but at the same time are emblems of human mutability and failure.

Through line 36, the spirit expresses a full range of emotions, again lodged in cosmic and natural entities, coming closer to the world in which we live in the exquisite image beginning on line 37, as it swings, like a spider or even a monkey, between the trees. Evoking the world of classical antiquity and Germanic folklore, the spirit takes on a more literary consciousness as it inspects the overt and covert sites in which mythic creatures have their being. The spirit reasserts its consciousness of human history in looking "for the now obliterated / traces of the centuries" (lines 53–54), training its "pupil" on "the whole of creation" (59–60).

In a triumphant finish, poetry offers itself as the link between form and idea, between Heaven and Earth, and names the poet as its vessel. Rare indeed is the Romantic statement that speaks with such confidence; this exhilarating poem expresses the highest aspirations of an age in love with poetry, nature, music, and the seeing eye, the "pupil" that can read order and beauty in the endless varieties of life.

Topics for Writing and Comparative Perspectives

1. Bécquer wrote a series of prose *leyendas* (legends) as well as the dozens of poems published in Rimas. Find evidence in *Nameless*

Spirit of his awareness of the legends of old and consider why so many Romantic artists were fascinated by mythic visions of natural beings.

[Consider juxtaposing the selections by Bécquer with Goethe's *Faust*, especially the *Study* scene in which Mephistopheles has the spirits serenade Faust, to "dazzle him with dream shapes, sweet and vast." Would Bécquer agree that the poetic visions they conjure are "an ocean of untruth"?]

2. Compare Bécquer's idealistic claims for poetry with those of his Romantic predecessors Shelley (*Ode to the West Wind* in particular) or Coleridge (*Kubla Khan*); or contrast them with the vision of poetry as "disheveled" musicality in Paul Verlaine's *Art of Poetry* or the sense of poetry's limits and powers in the *Lament for Ignacio Mejías Sánchez* by the great Spanish poet of the twentieth century, Federico García Lorca.

3. Elsewhere in his poetry, Bécquer speaks of the power of the "pupil," or eye. Why is the power of sight so important a theme in Romantic poetry?

[A good comparative essay might ask this in connection with Wordsworth's philosophic effort in *Tintern Abbey* to distinguish the work of eye from that of ear; or with the brilliant imagery of Aimé Césaire's *Sun Serpent* and *Day and Night*, which make pure visual sensation primary.]

Further Reading

See also the reading suggestions in the *Anthology*, p. 2539.

Bynum, B. Brant. *The Romantic Imagination in the Works of Gustavo Adolfo Bécquer*. 1993. This useful contextualization of Bécquer's work within the frame of European Romanticism provides a good basic bibliography of critical writings about the period and offers a reading of *Nameless Spirit* on pp. 45–48. Quotations from Spanish primary and secondary texts are not translated.

Turk, Henry Charles. *German Romanticism in Gustavo Adolfo Bécquer's Short Stories*. 1959. Although none of the specific works discussed are in the *Anthology*, Turk's broad introduction considers the degree to which Bécquer's work may have been directly influenced by German philosophical and poetic traditions.

Rosalía de Castro

Classroom Strategies and Topics for Discussion

The opening poem, *As I Composed This Little Book*, sets the tone for this moving series of verses. De Castro was a champion of her native region, Galicia, and her earlier verses were written in Galician. In *Beside the River Sar*, she writes in Castilian, Spain's language of high culture, but likens her work to "the prayers and rituals of belief," verses that children commit to memory and that speak to a popular audience.

Yet the critic César Barja has called de Castro "the most modern of Spanish poets of the nineteenth century," pointing to her "subordination of verse to poetry, to inner rhythm." Keeping this in mind, you might ask your students to notice the shifting line lengths that the translator has been careful to preserve. No rigid metrical pattern is imposed on her poems, which respond to the pressures of thought rather than to the exigencies of form.

[Mild Was the Air]

The first stanza of *Mild Was the Air* offers a particularly striking example of this fluidity: the short, soft opening lines record an inevitable event; the final couplet expands to accommodate the watching mother's painful contrast of the child's peaceful passing with her own bitter response. Note, too, the shifting point of view throughout this poem: third person yields to second, as the speaker addresses both herself and her dead child, working out of her grief in the conclusion to return to the more objective third person, and the shorter final line: there is nothing to be done. "It is the earthly way."

[A Glowworm Scatters Flashes]

Articulating a horror of science that reminds the English-speaking reader of Tennyson's *In Memoriam*, de Castro here cites the brevity of a firefly's glow and the distance of a star, beautiful emanations of the natural world that bring no comfort to the distressed. Like Tennyson, who finds the proto-Darwinian assurance that nature was "careful of the type" of little use to human beings when she was "so careless of the single life" (p. 674), de Castro deplores human ignorance in the face of the profound questions of life and death, scientific advances notwithstanding. Explaining phenomena like glowworms or distant stars is "vain" (line 6), a matter of information rather than knowledge. Her fear is that God is absent in a universe so cold.

In stanza two, she kneels, uncertain of what kind of icon is set before her. What is the "Deity" of which she speaks in the third stanza? The idol that she worships, the "image rudely carved," appears to be the dead child lying in a cemetery surrounded by carved angels in "lofty marble niches," whose flesh she returned to dust in *Mild Was the Air*. The angelic message, however, offers little sympathy. Rather, it accuses her of a virtually pagan insolence for daring to dispute the decisions of an unfathomable God.

[The Feet of Spring Are on the Stair]

A Tennysonian concern for the evanescent individual is heard again in this poem. The celebration of springtime coupling in the opening lines is oddly expressed in the quasi-scientific reference to "atoms," treated here as if they were unique beings. Beginning with a traditional evocation of spring's beauty, this short lyric quickly ends with the harsh certainty that "Summer masters Spring" and heat dries up new life.

[Candescent Lies the Air]

De Castro's treatment of the images of nature so typical of Romantic rhetoric is both subtle and simple. The last poems in the selection take the familiar seasonal theme and give it a surprising twist. As noted above, her praise of spring, like its duration, is short-lived, and again the shifting line lengths seem to echo the swift passage of which the final stanza speaks. As hinted in the poem discussed above, De Castro's summer is cruel, scorching and stifling. The brook turns "noisome," and the insect sounds are "a low death-rattle." Conventional notions of time are undercut: "The midmost hour of day / Is best called night." Winter would be preferable to the "sorry" summer that spells death.

[The Ailing Woman Felt Her Forces Ebb]

Rosalía de Castro died on July 15, 1885, after enduring years of pain. It is hard not to think of her suffering in the intense Spanish summer heat in *The Ailing Woman Felt Her Forces Ebb*, which stresses the incongruity of "the ailing woman," never explicitly identified with the poet herself, dying by inches in an inappropriate season, out of harmony with her own being, it would seem, as with the natural world. In this final poem, the great Romantic themes that she has touched on all come together, reinforcing the sense that all the assumptions that made the nineteenth-century poets worship nature have been violated—time and the seasons are out of joint.

Topics for Writing and Comparative Perspectives

1. Rosalía de Castro's poems treat winter as a kinder time than spring or summer. Explain why this should be so, and compare her view of the connotations of weather changes and the seasons with that of other poets whose work you have studied.
   [Good choices include Shelley in *Ode to the West Wind*; Heine in *Ah, Death Is Like the Long Cool Night*; Lamartine in *The Lake*; or T. S. Eliot in *The Waste Land*.]
2. Discuss the relation of form to content in the poems of Rosalía de Castro. In what sense is she a precursor of the modern attitude toward verse forms observable in the work of twentieth-century poets like Akhmatova or García Lorca?
3. Compare and contrast the portrait of a woman dying in these poems with Flaubert's description of the death of Madame Bovary. How does the difference between the two help us understand the contrast between Romanticism and realism, and between the resources of the poet and those of the novelist?

Further Reading

See the suggestion in the *Anthology*, p. 2540.

ALEXANDER SERGEYEVICH PUSHKIN

The Queen of Spades

Classroom Strategies and Topics for Discussion

One provocative aspect of Pushkin's great story is the way a reader's expectations are systematically manipulated and violated. To trace the ways in which anticipation is generated, only to be thwarted, may help students realize the artistry of this narrative.

What does the opening scene lead one to expect? A story about gambling, perhaps, about winning and losing. Its central character, one might think, will be Tomsky, the only person who speaks at any length and the one who offers judgments on others ("Hermann's a German: he's cautious—that's all"). After he tells the story of his grandmother, none of the responses suggest that those who make them will have any narrative importance. Chapter two in its first section divides the interest between Tomsky's grandmother and the girl Lisaveta, promising a romantic fairy tale on the order of *Cinderella*—the poor abused underling will find her prince. When Hermann reappears, at the chapter's end, we may suspect that he will be the prince, although his intense interest in money already has disturbing overtones. Chapter three begins by suggesting a sexual denouement but ends with the countess's death; the tale has changed direction once more. Chapter four exposes Hermann in his full heartlessness and leads one to expect that this will be a story of complete frustration; no one will achieve what she or he desires. Chapter five turns into a ghost story, focusing our interest on whether the dead countess has revealed the truth; chapter six leaves that question unresolved (has she deliberately named the wrong third card or has she by supernatural intervention switched the cards?). The "Conclusion," contradicting all previous suggestions, gives everyone but Hermann—and Hermann is, after all, the principal character—his or her heart's desire.

Why does Pushkin adopt such techniques of playing with the reader? Students may find it interesting to ask why we have the kinds of successive expectations suggested above. When we try to locate a story's main character on the basis of who has the most to say, when we allow ourselves to expect a romantic story or a sexual one or to focus our attention on exactly how a ghost has dealt with a human being, we demonstrate the degree to which we read every piece of writing in relation to other literary works we have experienced. Not what we know about life but what we know about literature leads us to think that Lisaveta might find her Prince Charming; we may not "believe" in ghosts, but we've all read enough ghost stories to know the kinds of questions one should ask about the operations of such beings. Pushkin, by manipulating our expectations, calls attention to their nature. He thus suggests the possibility that in reading a work of fiction we both expect and want something quite different from what we find in our actual lives. Of course, the characters Pushkin creates also want, within the fiction, something different from what their lives offer them. Everyone dreams of a way of escaping from the dissatisfactions of his or her existence. Hermann—who intentionally calls Tomsky's tale of his grandmother a "fairy-tale"—in his actual confrontation with the old woman says to her, "The happiness of a man is in your hands." His imagination has indeed created for him a world of happiness dependent only on the winning of money; his earlier doctrine that "economy, moderation and industry . . . are my three winning cards" has vanished in fantasy. A young man of "fiery imagination," Hermann exemplifies in extreme form what the story's other characters also reveal—that imagination disguises harsh or boring actuality by projecting into the future the fulfillment of desire. When Hermann entreats the countess "by the feelings of a wife, a lover, a mother" to grant his request, he suggests that even authentic tender feelings can become merely instruments of the imagination's insatiable hunger, words to be invoked rather than emotions to be experienced. Pushkin arouses the reader's desires in various ways only to frustrate them; he assigns satisfactions to his characters in almost random fashion, as though to mock longings for a universe controlled by justice.

This way of investigating *The Queen of Spades* implies that the story has dark social and moral implications. The point, of course, might be argued; you can inquire of students whether they believe Pushkin to be offering a serious social indictment. What human qualities and social arrangements does the story criticize? What evidence does it provide for the author's outrage at, perhaps, human self-deception, self-absorption, heartlessness? or at the maneuverings for wealth and position that society encourages? or at inequities of rank and power? How does Pushkin enforce his attitudes?

Students may find it useful to reflect on the narrator's importance in this fiction—and the reader's. Since the story reveals the emotional and moral inadequacies of all its characters, it in effect makes a hero of the storyteller, who alone demonstrates his awareness of what is really going on in a corrupt society. And this storyteller, through the manipulations of the reader discussed above, brings that reader to comparable awareness. If he denies us the obvious sorts of literary satisfaction, he provides a kind of moral satisfaction by placing us, finally, in a position of superiority to the characters. Our consciousness has been altered; we have been made to understand something. And the narrator's consciousness has guided us to understanding.

The story repays close attention to detail; almost any paragraph can be analyzed as attentively as a lyric poem to reveal its structural relation to the whole. A deceptively simple way of engaging student interest in Pushkin's larger purposes is to concentrate on his use of concrete detail. For example, you might wish to consider the description of the furniture in Lisaveta's bedroom and in the countess's, Lisaveta's clothing and the countess's, or the various allusions to flowers.

Topics for Writing

1. Discuss the importance of Tomsky as a character in the story.
2. How appropriately does the "Conclusion" conclude the narrative? Consider how each of its details has been prepared for in the fiction as a whole.
3. Analyze the character of Lisaveta, making sure to support your analysis by specific reference to the text.
4. Discuss the importance of Hermann's moralizing in *The Queen of Spades* as a whole. Why do you think Pushkin conceives him as a German?

Comparative Perspectives

1. Compare the appearance of the countess's ghost in the midst of Pushkin's realistic world with the intrusion of the supernatural in ancient classical literature. Do we doubt the existence of ghosts in works such as the *Oresteia* or the *Aeneid*? Could the countess be only a figment of Hermann's imagination? In what sense may we view even Hermann himself as a creation of Lisaveta's?
2. Why does Pushkin tell us that Hermann's first letter to Lisaveta Ivanovna is "taken word for word from a German novel"? How is the idea of originality perceived differently in different cultures and eras?
   [It would be interesting to compare the influence of old books on the Christian humanists, for whom imitation was a beloved pedagogical exercise, or on a character like Don Quixote, with the emphasis on originality in the post-Enlightenment West.]

Further Reading

See also the reading suggestions in the *Anthology*, p. 2542.

Barta, P., and U. Goebel, eds. *The Contexts of Aleksandr Sergeevich Pushkin*. 1988. A collection of essays that attempt to place Pushkin in his historical and literary setting.

Lavrin, Janko. *Pushkin and Russian Literature*. 1947. A short study primarily concerned with the historical background and setting of Pushkin's work, this establishes a useful context in which to consider the writer.

Magarshack, David. *Pushkin*. 1967. A biography with emphasis on its subject's literary development.

Petrie, Glen. *The Fourth King*. 1986. Critical exegesis of Pushkin's accomplishment in many genres.

Simmons, Ernest J. *Pushkin*. 1937. A sound biography offering little literary analysis.

Todd, W. *Fiction and Society in the Age of Pushkin: Ideology, Institutions, and Narrative*. 1986. As the title suggests, this study examines the social implications of Pushkin's fiction.

Alfred, Lord Tennyson

Classroom Strategies and Topics for Discussion

The narrative interest of the Tennyson poems included in the *Anthology* should involve student readers. Even *In Memoriam A. H. H.* implicitly tells a story about the domination and then the weakening of grief; the two shorter poems more vividly elucidate narratives of human feeling. *Ulysses*, the more readily comprehensible of the two, is a good place to start.

Ulysses

Students might be asked what they think the purpose of the poem is. The answer most likely to emerge, finally, is that it both establishes and celebrates a particular kind of human character. What seems to be the precipitating cause of Ulysses' monologue? He appears to be at a point of decision about his life; Tennyson's rendering reveals how and why he proposes to change course. What, exactly, do we learn or deduce about Ulysses' character? This is of course the most obvious subject of discussion, but it is a fruitful one, as students find support in the poem itself for their understanding of its central character. Related, and almost equally important, is the question of what makes Ulysses a hero in Tennyson's view. If students have read the *Odyssey* (in Vol. 1 of the *Anthology*), they will remember Homer's version of Ulysses' character and will realize that it only tangentially coincides with Tennyson's. The poem's final line, of course, epitomizes the attitudes here held up for admiration. The contrast with Telemachus (lines 33–43) is worth dwelling on. What, precisely, does Ulysses mean by "his work" and "mine"? How does he make the reader feel about the opposition between them?

In Memoriam A. H. H.

A large question that can focus the entire discussion of the poem is how Tennyson manages to unite public (social, intellectual, theological, scientific) and private concerns in what purports to be an extended record of his grief over a personal loss. (Since the potential selfishness of dwelling on one's own feelings concerns many adolescents and adults alike, the question is one of large interest.) Finally in *In Memoriam*, the dead young man, Hallam, becomes representative of a higher human species approaching realization, but originally his importance comes only from his close friendship with the poet. To trace the stages by which his significance is enlarged, and the correlation between this enlargement of meaning and the diminishment of grief, is probably sufficient enterprise for any class.

A few more local issues that may prove illuminating (and that often can call attention to larger problems): The Prologue purports to be a statement of faith, but in fact it expresses great uncertainty. How is uncertainty conveyed? It is worth noting a sequence of ambiguous verbs: "thinks" (line 11), "seemest" (line 13), "know not" (line 15), "cannot know" (line 21), "trust" (line 23). Also relevant are the contrast between the assertions of faith, or the appeals to God (e.g., "Let knowledge grow from more to more," line 25), and the statements of fact (e.g., "They are but broken lights of thee," line 19; "these wild and wandering cries," line 41). As students attend to the varying rhetoric of this piece of the poem, they should come to see that it establishes a kind of drama, an internal conflict between faith and perception that in fact runs through the poem as a whole (and can be traced, if there's time).

Section 3: Personified Sorrow dominates this section; her "whisper" epitomizes one aspect of the speaker's struggle. Why does the speaker perceive what she says as both sweet and bitter? This allegation suggests that he finds perverse comfort in the notion that all of nature simply duplicates the sense of futility that he himself experiences, given his loss. It is particularly important because it provides one answer to the question of how Tennyson unites small and large concerns; here he demonstrates the psychological pattern by which human beings can make the universe subordinate to their own feelings, turning nature itself into an objectification of personal emotion. What is the effect of the final stanza? It emphasizes the continuing ambiguity of the speaker's responses; he cannot decide whether it is comforting ("natural good") or destructive ("vice of blood") to allow himself this kind of interpretation.

Section 5: This section raises the question of poetry and its function. What *is* its function in this passage? Concealment is emphasized more than revelation: poetry's discipline helps to numb pain and to obscure the intensity of feeling. Why is it "half a sin" to write poetry about this subject? By implication, because it falsifies in being unable to reveal all. Students might be asked to seek other passages in which the poet speaks about the function of poetry.

Section 21: Here the function of poetry comes up again, in relation to imagined responses to it. Why does the poet imagine various others reacting to his poem? Perhaps he is thus suggesting his own doubts about what he is doing. The specific things that are said are worth examining and summarizing: that such dwelling on grief fosters weakness in others, that it constitutes self-indulgence and seeking after fame, that concern with the private has no validity in a time of public upheaval and of dispute over the revelations of science. How is the problem of negative response resolved? The poet claims the spontaneity and naturalness of his song, and his compulsion to sing it; he cannot help himself, as a bird cannot help itself. If students are asked whether this resolution seems adequate, they are likely to say no—and probably they would be right. The weakness of the resolution is part of the continuing structure of doubt; the poet cannot yet fully justify what he is doing.

Section 95: This section contains the moment of revelation that most clearly resolves the problems previously articulated. What is the importance of the natural setting? Earlier, nature in a large, abstract sense seemed to echo the poet's sense of futility; now specific details of nature generate a sense of calm. But it could be argued that the most significant fact here is that the speaker is now able fully to notice what lies outside him; he is no longer locked in his own grief. What is the stimulus to the visionary experience? Looking at the leaves (in the sixth stanza), the poet is reminded of natural cycle and of the fact that even fallen leaves may remain green, as Hallam's memory remains green for him. The speaker thinks specifically of the dead man and of his qualities of character; this leads to the revelation. What does that revelation consist of? The poet announces that it cannot be fully stated in words (yet another glance at the problem of poetry's function), but he conveys a recognition of universal pattern making sense of time, chance, and death, those apparent obstacles to human happiness. Then he returns to the natural scene. Why? The calm continues, but it is a calm involving movement and process; dawn comes to foretell the day, symbolizing the new day of acceptance and possible happiness in the poet's experience.

Topics for Writing

1. Science in *In Memoriam*.
2. An analysis of one section of *In Memoriam*.
3. The use of animals in *In Memoriam*.
4. Water in *In Memoriam*.
5. Tithonus and Ulysses as characters.

Comparative Perspectives

If Arthur Hallam died too young, Tithonus lives to be too old. Compare Tennyson's contemplation of the cruelty of these complementary states with Keats's reflections on death in his odes, or with Rosalía de Castro's treatment of the seasons in *Candescent Lies the Air*, or Heine's in *Ah, Death Is Like the Long, Cool Night*, or with the fierce and specific verses of García Lorca's *Lament for Ignacio Sánchez Mejías*.

Further Reading

See also the reading suggestions in the *Anthology*, p. 2542.

Bloom, H., ed. *Alfred Lord Tennyson*. 1985. Miscellaneous, often provocative essays.

Culler, A. D. *The Poetry of Tennyson*. 1977. Supplies a particularly fine treatment of *In Memoriam*, analyzing the poem's form and thought and giving detailed accounts of specific poetic effects.

Kissane, J. *Alfred Tennyson*. 1970. In the Twayne series. Centers on treatments of the poet's work in various genres: lyric, narrative, and drama.

Tennyson, C. *Alfred Tennyson*. 1949. The standard, thorough biography.

ROBERT BROWNING

Classroom Strategies and Topics for Discussion

The question likely to interest students most in any reading of dramatic monologue is that inherent in the form: How does an imagined character reveal himself or herself without any apparent intention of doing so? The question, in relation to the bishop ordering his tomb, has two obvious aspects: What do we learn of his personal history? What do we learn of his character?

The two matters, of course, are closely connected. From line 3 ("Nephews—sons mine . . . ah God, I know not!") on, the reader is increasingly forced to realize the interdependence of history and character. The fact that the bishop does not know the nature of his relationship to the men around the bed reveals that he has had promiscuous relations with women—a revelation both of character and of experience. As students call attention to the details that show the bishop's nature and uncover his past, you can ask them to think more deeply about the implications of almost any line. The clergyman's lack of knowledge about his children, for instance, speaks of more than his promiscuity: it suggests his lack of concern for human ties in general, in his failure to keep track either of his women or of their offspring.

Lines especially worth attention include line 14 ("Saint Praxed's ever was the church for peace)," an example of a trick frequently repeated in the poem. The speaker appears to declare something he values—"peace"—only to reveal as he goes on that he has done everything possible to contradict this value: he has fought every inch of the way. Then there is the bishop's description of his setting, particularly the columns of "Peach-blossom marble": how does the description reveal him? The conjunction of "Peach-blossom," "red wine," and "mighty pulse" (lines 29–30) suggests the degree to which he attributes vitality to the realm of sensuous satisfaction, conveying more affection for stone than for women (or putative offspring). Lines 56–61, about the frieze the dying man images, are also worth attention: they demonstrate his detailed aesthetic awareness and how that dominates any religious feeling, as religious and pagan references mingle for the sake of an imagined spectacle in stone.

Specific questions about the bishop's character may lead students more deeply into the poem. For example, in what terms does he understand other people? His interpretation of Gandolf and of his "sons" suggests that he can grasp the nature of others only by thinking them like himself. (Of course, the poem offers no evidence that they are *not* like himself: we see only through the bishop's eyes, and through his eyes everyone emerges as grasping and competitive.) What is the bishop's attitude toward language? He appears to be an obsessive talker, but he also thinks about language: for example, "marble's language, Latin pure, discreet" (line 98). Language becomes for him an aesthetic phenomenon like marble itself, and a woman's "talking eyes" (line 96), which speak a nonverbal tongue, seem no more appealing than "Choice Latin, picked phrase" (line 77).

The last line of the poem reiterates line 5; how has its meaning and effect changed, given all that has come between its two occurrences? As we learn more and more about the bishop, we realize that he considers a woman to be merely a piece of lapis lazuli or a statue: her value, too, is purely aesthetic. The only ground for envy he can imagine concerns the possession of aesthetic objects.

At the end of the poem, the bishop appears to have achieved a certain peace, as he rests in "the church for peace" (line 14). What accounts for his apparent emotional shift? He knows that his sons will follow not his will but their own, that he will not have the tomb he desires; he knows that he is dying. But his past aesthetic triumphs continue to comfort him: even if he possesses nothing now to arouse Gandolf's envy, he possesses his past, his perceptions, and the memory of his perceptions. He contents himself at last with what he securely has.

My Last Duchess, which appears to constitute a less complicated narrative, provides a particularly useful focus for discussion because it allows students to tease out meanings from the apparently direct and simple. Questions of character are obviously at issue in this poem. Although a teacher may wish to begin discussion by making sure students understand the situation and the past happenings that have taken place (To whom is the duke speaking, and why? How did the duchess die? What does she look like in the portrait?), such concerns quickly lead to more subtle matters of characterization. What was the duchess like as a person? This obvious question can generate intense classroom exchange, as it leads to the related problem of the duke's nature. Why does the poem emphasize works of art so insistently? Is there any relation between the duchess's portrait and the bronze statue of Neptune (line 54)? Does the word "fair" (line 52) have any special importance by the time the duke uses it here? What is his attitude toward money?

Finally, students may find it interesting to contemplate why Browning would choose to tell his story in verse rather than prose. The narrative could provide the substance of a short story or even, conceivably, a novel. Here, though, the story is told in retrospect and allusively. What are the advantages and disadvantages of such a method? How does the use of couplets contribute to the poem's meaning and impact?

"Childe Roland to the Dark Tower Came," a more obviously difficult poem, also tends to generate lively controversy—usually over the fundamental issue of what the poem is *about*. It probably should be acknowledged at the outset that no definitive answer to this question is likely to present itself: critics have debated for many years whether the poem has allegorical meaning. You might direct discussion by asking students to specify what, exactly, the poem allows its readers to *know* (e.g., we know that someone is looking for something; we know that he has been searching for a long time; that many before him have failed in the quest; that he follows the cripple's advice). Many facts emerge from the narrative; what crucial facts remain missing? Students may decide that they

feel deprived of important information about what the point of the quest is, why so many have undertaken it, what the Dark Tower "stands for." Next they might think about why the poet would choose to omit so much information. In other words, what poetic effects are achieved by the omissions?

One way of trying to define the poem's mood and its effect on the reader is to trace the speaker's uncertainties, which multiply steadily as the poem goes on, from his doubt about whether the cripple lies through his doubt about his own fitness, his questions about whether the horse is alive or dead—on and on. How do these uncertainties affect the reader?

Discussion of the poem's ambiguities may lead to larger issues about the workings of poetry. Students may wish to discuss whether definable meaning is essential to a poem, whether creating a mood is sufficient goal for a poet, what besides clear meaning determines poetic impact.

Topics for Writing

1. The five senses in *The Bishop Orders His Tomb*.
2. The importance of conflict in the poem.
3. Why I admire the bishop.
4. Why I feel contempt for the bishop.
5. Why the duchess's portrait is behind a curtain.
6. The duke's "skill in speech" (cf. lines 35–36).
7. The importance of the title to "*Childe Roland to the Dark Tower Came.*"
8. The similes in "Childe Roland to the Dark Tower Came."

Comparative Perspectives

1. The intense subjectivity of much nineteenth-century poetry reaches an apogee in the dramatic monologues of Tennyson and Browning. Why did the Romantic and Victorian poets excel in monologue but not in drama? Why is this essentially a Western poetic genre? What categories of post-Enlightenment culture produce the egotistical sublime?

   [The intense self-absorption of Browning's speakers makes this a particularly rewarding question to pursue and opens up vistas into the self-reflexive works of the great modernists, notably Proust and Joyce.]

2. What is happening in "*Childe Roland to the Dark Tower Came*"? How would you compare this version of a quest narrative with the medieval poems it imitates and the modern searches it anticipates?

   [If they have read *Sir Gawain and the Green Knight* and portions of Dante's *Inferno*, students may be asked how Browning amalgamates the two but adds a distinctly modern note when he has nature "peevishly" despair of the burnt-out landscape (stanza XI). In the context of Vol. 2 of the *Anthology*, this last reference shares some of Tennyson's Darwinian anguish, but Browning may also be seen here as an experimental anticipator of Robbe-Grillet. Like

The Secret Room, "*Childe Roland*" stretches conventions and rhetorical postures as if to gauge how elastic they may be, without any genuine concern for "meaning."]

Further Reading

See also the reading suggestions in the *Anthology*, p. 2540.

Bloom, H., and A. Munich, eds. *Robert Browning: A Collection of Critical Essays*. 1979. Useful for suggesting varied critical approaches.

Burrows, L. *Browning the Poet*. 1969. Presents itself as an introductory study; it contains a useful detailed reading of *The Bishop Orders His Tomb*.

Thomas, D. *Robert Browning: A Life Within Life*. 1982. A well-written biography.

Frederick Douglass

Narrative of the Life of Frederick Douglass, an American Slave

Classroom Strategies and Topics for Discussion

This personal account of self-discovery, survival, and escape translates into narrative terms the linked concern with the social and the emotional to be found in the work of such poets as Blake and Shelley. Douglass's story has obvious historical interest, but it also generates vivid awareness, still relevant today, of the emotional realities of oppression. Although students may find Douglass's language on occasion uncomfortably high-flown, they will probably be caught up in the drama of his efforts to escape conditions that appear inescapable.

Because the shift to prose narrative constitutes such a startling change from the poetry that surrounds this work in the *Anthology*, it's probably useful to begin by talking about autobiography as a form. Students can be either told or asked about what it means to tell a story of the self. The important point here is that telling such a story involves imaginative activity comparable to that involved in writing a poem. The facts of a life are given, but the appropriate way of imagining the self is not. The autobiographer must decide, consciously or unconsciously, how to present him- or herself—as hero or victim, as unique individual or as representative of a group, as defined principally by childhood experience or as self-creator. Selections must be made among the many events remembered; one cannot set down *everything*. Such self-imagining and such selection form the story. Another way of putting the same truth is to point out that many different stories can be told of any individual; students might be asked to think about how many different life stories they can imagine for themselves.

As for Douglass's story, it divides itself naturally into two teaching units, the first one extending to the beginning of chapter X. It's useful to ask students when they read to try to decide what the center of each chapter is, in terms of narrative or emotional interest. Following are a few suggestions, chapter by chapter, of how classroom discussion might be focused.

Chapter 1

It's worth spending some time on the first paragraph, concentrating on the question of what that paragraph establishes, how it prepares us for the book that succeeds it. Points worth mentioning: the stress on deprivation, on what the narrator does *not* know; the linkage of slaves to the natural cycle (they locate their birthdays by planting-time, etc.); the degree to which the narrator identifies himself with his social class; the mention of contrast between the situation of blacks and that of whites as a source of consciousness; the definition of the narrator as someone who figures things out (his way of estimating his own age). The tone is matter-of-fact, yet emotion permeates the paragraph. Where does it come from? You might comment on the emphasis on the negative (no knowledge, no memory, want of information, "could not tell," not allowed, etc.) and on the explicit reference to early unhappiness. The episode in the chapter receiving the greatest emotional stress is Douglass's concluding account of watching the whipping of his aunt. Why, one might ask, does this episode merit such extended attention? It is directly stated to be "the first of a long series of such outrages"; in other words, it has representative meaning. It announces themes that the rest of the text will reiterate—not only the irresistible power and brutality of white masters but the degree to which sexual issues are intertwined with those of slavery. And it suggests the way in which Douglass as a child felt himself directly implicated in the persecution he saw, not for altruistic but for selfish reasons: "I expected it would be my turn next."

Chapter II

This chapter concerns Colonel Lloyd and his household; its most emphatic detail has to do with the songs the slaves sing. "To those songs," Douglass writes, "I trace my first glimmering conception of the dehumanizing character of slavery." Can we understand why the songs affect him thus? Douglass stresses the mixture of joy and sadness in the songs; the joy is associated with going to the Great House Farm. There is pathos, thus, in the very cause of joy, pathos in the fact that slaves achieve their satisfaction out of such impoverished stimuli. The importance of the invariable undertone of deep sadness is of course primary: Douglass insists that there is no joy without sadness in the slaves' lives, but that in spite of their oppression they manage to find causes for qualified happiness.

Chapter III

The episode of the two Barneys is central here. Why? The arbitrary punishment meted out to them by an unjust master, whose concern is

greater for his horses than for the slaves who care for those horses, epitomizes the dehumanization of slavery.

CHAPTER IV

The series of murders toward the chapter's end best expresses the
theme. It is worth commenting on the relation of chapters II, III, and IV
to one another—a steadily intensifying emphasis on slavery's injustice.
Why, the class might be asked, has Douglass thus far said so little about
himself, except as observer? Obviously, he wishes to insist as forcefully
as possible on his identification with his people: whether or not he is actually murdered, he participates emotionally in the plight of the victims.

CHAPTER V

"I look upon my departure from Colonel Lloyd's plantation as one of
the most interesting events of my life," Douglass writes. Why? He attributes to this event the possibility of his subsequent escape, and he attributes the event itself to the interposition of Providence. Why is this
important? It places the narrative as a whole in a religious context and
suggests in a muted way an issue that will later become explicit: how can
Christians reconcile themselves to slavery?

CHAPTER VI

The key event of this chapter, and perhaps of the book as a whole, is
the abortive reading lessons Douglass receives from his mistress (see the
headnote). Their importance is directly stated in the text and is quite obvious but nonetheless worth discussing. Why does the chapter end with
the story of Mary's mistreatment? Douglass wishes to emphasize that
even in the best possible situation for slaves, injustice and oppression remain, and remain impossible to withstand.

CHAPTER VII

This chapter dwells almost entirely on reading and on the degree to
which learning to read from white children intensified Douglass's consciousness of the intolerable difference of situation between him and his
white contemporaries. The most important theme here is the way the
child moved from consciousness of his particular plight to awareness of
generalizations that could be made about it. Why is the capacity to gen-
eralize perceived as a source of strength? The boy's interest in the term
abolition, his reading of *The Columbian Orator*, even his conversation
with the Irishmen all enlarge his comprehension. The ability to go beyond himself, to understand himself in a social context, is crucial to
Douglass's self-freeing. Students might be asked about the relation between his interest in books and his ability to figure out how to learn to
write. Both aspects of his character declare his capacity to make use of
what lies outside himself, a capacity of enormous value to him.

CHAPTER VIII

This chapter reports Douglass's enforced leaving of Baltimore and of his relatively kind master. Its central episode, however, is the partly imagined story of his grandmother, who, if she now lives, "lives to remember and mourn over the loss of children, the loss of grandchildren, and the loss of great-grandchildren." Douglass goes on to envision, however, her solitary death, and to insist that a righteous God will punish those responsible for such a situation. Why is this episode so important in the narrative economy? Talking about this problem will provide a way of discussing the degree to which this autobiography builds itself up by the use of symbolic events, events not necessarily directly autobiographical. If one tries to describe what kind of person Douglass is (and the effort to do so makes a useful classroom exercise), it is necessary to dwell on the fact that he is a symbol-maker, someone who sees experience in symbolic terms. Just as the whipping of his aunt symbolizes for him one aspect of injustice, the isolation of his grandmother symbolizes another. Her alienation in old age, however, assumes special symbolic importance because, as this book increasingly makes clear, the sense of community among slaves is their greatest resource; isolating the old woman in the woods deprives her of this community. Douglass's way of writing resembles a poet's method of creating events: he uses individual happenings to stand for kinds of happening and to evoke the emotion associated with other events of the same order.

CHAPTER IX

Now Douglass finds himself at the mercy of a hard master. This chapter is very short; at its heart is the matter of Southern Christianity. Why does Douglass linger on this aspect of his culture? He thus finds another way to emphasize the injustice of his situation: it is injustice considered in relation to the human obligation to God as well as that to other people. He is gradually enlarging the scope of his concern and his claim.

CHAPTER X

In this first chapter of the second assignment, the scale of the narrative changes. Chapters X and XI together occupy almost as much space as the nine preceding chapters. All the rest, from one point of view, is background; now the autobiographer moves toward the crucial—the absolutely central—event of his escape, showing what emotional forces made escape feel like a necessity and what contributed to making it a possibility. Chapter X summarizes the narrator's experience with three different masters. Its central episode is the failed attempt at escape, important both in relation to what led up to it (the increasingly intense abuse in Douglass's life) and what it leads to (increased determination to escape successfully). But it is worth asking also about the importance of other events, most notably the "magic root" that protects Douglass from being whipped, the Sabbath school he establishes, and his experience as a caulker in Baltimore. An effort should be made to establish both his intensifying sense of personal integrity and independence and his increasingly emphatic sense of community.

Chapter XI

Now the escape actually takes place, but this chapter, more than any previous one, emphasizes emotional rather than external event—an effect made more emphatic by the author's deliberate suppression of the literal details of his escape. Instead, he talks about his feelings. It's useful to discuss which feelings are most important: the sadness at the thought of breaking the ties of affection with his slave friends, exhilaration at freedom, suspicion of white and black men alike, wonder at the prosperity of the North, excitement at earning his own money. And time can profitably be spent on delineating the relation between these emotions and those earlier evoked in the book—to what extent these feelings confirm or develop from earlier ones.

Appendix

Here Douglass makes most explicit the larger meaning of his narrative. He claims not to be talking about a single life but to be discussing a problem with its bearing on religious professions and practice. Yet the *Narrative* ends with his reassertion of his own name and identity. The large question of how this book integrates its concern with the individual and with the social must be confronted finally—in writing or in class discussion.

Topics for Writing

1. A single episode and how it relates to the whole.
2. What kind of man was Douglass?
3. A way in which this narrative relates to late-twentieth-century problems.
4. The importance of songs and hymns.
5. A single character (apart from Douglass) and his or her importance in the story.
6. What whipping means in this narrative.

Comparative Perspectives

1. While a slave, Douglass witnessed and sometimes engaged in violent action, and his Narrative is a revolutionary document. Does it achieve revolutionary status by advocating violence as a means of transforming an evil system? How do the cruel treatment of his own aunt, described at the end of chapter I, and his conflict with Mr. Covey (chapter X) lead him to an understanding of the nature and sources of violence? How much do the proprieties of his era and the vocabulary at his command permit him to articulate that

understanding? Compare and contrast the depiction of violence in the work of postmodernist writers such as Alain Robbe-Grillet.

2. At the end of chapter II, Douglass says that the "wild songs" of slaves express and relieve their unhappiness. In *A Defence of Poetry*, Shelley proclaims that "Poetry is the record of the best and happiest moments of the happiest and best minds." To what degree is their disagreement resolved if we view "wild songs" and poetry as fundamentally different means of expression? Could one argue that the two forms are similar and that the contradiction suggested in this juxtaposition is more apparent than real? Drawing on the reading you have done this semester, define poetry and song and explain the emotions that seem to produce them.

Further Reading

See also the reading suggestions in the *Anthology*, p. 2540.

Huggins, N. *Slave and Citizen: The Life of Frederick Douglass*. 1980. Offers a short but comprehensive biography for the general reader, with a bibliography of historical sources.

Preston, D. J. *Young Frederick Douglass: The Maryland Years*. 1980. Concentrates on Douglass's youth, with a section on his late-life return to Maryland; Preston provides a thorough, lucid account.

Stepto, R. "Narration, Authentication, and Authorial Control in Frederick Douglass's Narrative of 1845." *Afro-American Literature: The Reconstruction of Instruction*, ed. R. Stepto and D. Fisher. 1978.

and

Stone, A. "Identity and Art in Frederick Douglass's Narrative." *College Language Association Journal* 17. 1973, pp. 192–213. Two essays that explore Douglass's work as narrative and specifically as autobiography.

Sweet, L. *Black Images of America, 1784–1870*. 1976. Places Douglass's thought in the context of intellectual history, with stress on his concept of nationality.

WALT WHITMAN

Classroom Strategies and Topics for Discussion

Song of Myself

The notion of the self as inherently fascinating dominates much literature of the Romantic period. One may think, for example, of the Rousseau of the *Confessions*, or of the character of Faust. Since college students themselves are in a developmental stage of intense self-concentration, concerned with defining and understanding their own identities, they are likely to be readily interested in the problems of what it might mean to write a "song of myself"—and what in fact it *does* mean in Whitman's version. Does any notion of the self emerge from the selections printed in the *Anthology*? Certainly one would have to comment on the idea of the self as infinitely inclusive, not defined by difference (as most of us define ourselves) but by comprehension. It is worth pausing to specify some varieties of comprehensiveness here suggested: geographical, political, vocational, sexual ("I am the poet of the woman the same as the man" [21.4]), emotional. Are these claims of vast inclusiveness equivalent to Rousseau's insistence on his uniqueness? It might be argued that Whitman, on the contrary, tries to unite himself with all the rest of humanity—all the rest, that is, of American humanity. Yet, paradoxically, such an attempt at union underlines the speaker's specialness—he alone has the capacity for such inclusiveness. It might be worth pausing to discuss what the poet's notion of containing all kinds of people within himself really means. It is obviously not literal. Does he, perhaps, mean that he has a large capacity for sympathy and empathy? Is this another way of celebrating the poetic imagination, directed now not toward birds and urns but toward other human beings?

One way of getting at important aspects of *Song of Myself* is to inquire in what ways it might be peculiarly American. Published only five years after *In Memoriam*, it of course reflects a very different sensibility. The difference can be explained in terms of Tennyson's and Whitman's personalities, but also in relation to the divergences between English and American culture in the mid-nineteenth century. Obvious answers to the question about "American" aspects of the poem might begin with the specific geographic allusions that abound. Almost equally apparent are the references to American occupations—planter, raftsman, fancy man, rowdy, and the like. It is yet more illuminating to note Whitman's enormous emphasis on the idea of democracy. This is both explicit ("I speak the pass-word primeval, I give the sign of democracy" [24.10]) and implicit, in the reiterated idea of the equality of humankind. (Why should the "primeval" be associated with democracy? The poet appears to imply that democracy constitutes the natural state of humanity—a favorite notion of the Romantics.) Whitman's diction is often insistently American: "Shoulder your duds dear son" (46.15). (Students might be asked to seek other instances of especially "American" language.) And his verse form deviates dramatically from the developed conventions of English poetry, deliberately risking prosiness, working in leisurely rhythms. Even the idea of unity through diversity, here imagined as epitomized in a single person, can be understood as an American concept, a personalized version of a national ideal.

Out of the Cradle Endlessly Rocking

This extended lyric particularly invites comparison with previous Romantic poetry. An obvious point of connection is Whitman's use of nature. How does the speaker's attitude toward the birds compare with, say, Keats's toward the nightingale? Whitman appears to be more interested in evoking the birds in themselves, imagined in terms of the birds' situation rather than only in relation to the speaker's needs. The bird song, for Whitman, has more specific emotional meaning and more detailed narrative background. The speaker's sense of identification with the bird is more emphatic. The experience he reports has taken place in the distant past; Keats creates the illusion that he speaks of the present. (This is a point worth dwelling on: what differences are generated by the speakers's different locations in time? It is interesting to consider the relative poetic values, and the different poetic functions, of immediacy versus the impression of meditated meaning.) Both poems stress emotional contrast; both stress the melancholy of the birdsong. Death becomes in both lyrics an important issue: what is the difference in their treatment? (It might also be valuable to compare Whitman's musings on death here with Shelley's in *Stanzas Written in Dejection*.) To Whitman, death seems to comprise a kind of literary temptation ("The word of the sweetest song and all songs," line 180), a "delicious" word, the "key" to all poetry—but not even at the level of fantasy an invitation to suicide. Students might be asked to look for the evidence the poem supplies of its speaker's great vitality. He identifies his own energy with that of his impulse to write verse ("A thousand warbling echoes have started to life within me, never to die," line 149), and he defines himself, in Faustian fashion, with infinite wanting ("The unknown want, the destiny of me," line 157; "O if I am to have so much, let me have more!" line 159). Knowledge of death, in his apparent view, is necessary to the capacity for full expressiveness of life. Why does he evoke the sea as "savage old mother," "fierce old mother," "some old crone rocking the cradle"? The idea of the sea as mother of humanity, the origin of all life, is a Romantic commonplace, but Whitman through his adjectives suggests a common source for life and death: the principle of life contains, inextricably mingled, that of destructiveness.

Topics for Writing

1. Whitman's relation to his reader (in a single poem).
2. The personality the poet creates for himself (in a single poem).
3. The importance of a single image from nature.
4. Whitman's optimism.

Comparative Perspectives

1. Explore the ways in which Whitman defines a sensibility that is both indisputably American and inimitably personal in *Song of Myself*. Compare the attitudes and verbal devices that contribute to this definition with the means by which other modern writers create aesthetic philosophies that similarly combine idiosyncratic and national characteristics.

   [Good choices include Baudelaire's *Paris Spleen*, Yeats's *Easter 1916* or *Lapis Lazuli*, or Akhmatova's *Requiem*.]
2. Whitman is hardly the first to associate his own vocation with the song of the solitary bird, as he does in *Out of the Cradle Endlessly*

Rocking; this call is heard by Keats, in *Ode to a Nightingale*. But he may be one of the last to embrace this symbol wholeheartedly. How is Whitman's use of this poetic convention more complicated than that of earlier writers?

[Discuss the emotional complexity that Whitman hears in the "aria" of his "brother." What is the significance of those two words? What is beginning to happen to the age-old sense of nature as a reliable source of beauty and inspiration? Such questions could lead into the study of a modernist such as Rilke, or Stevens, or Yeats, for whom art has a status separable from or superior to nature.]

Further Reading

See also the reading suggestions in the *Anthology*, p. 2543.

Allen, G. *Walt Whitman Handbook.* 1946. Provides useful biographical and critical background.

Asselineau, R. *The Evolution of Walt Whitman.* 2 vols. 1960–62. Consists of a biographical volume subtitled *The Creation of a Personality* and a critical volume on *Leaves of Grass* called *The Creation of a Book.*

Kummings, D. D. *Approaches to Teaching Whitman's* Leaves of Grass. 1990. Stimulating collection representing varied approaches.

Price, K. M. *Whitman and Tradition.* 1990. Study of literary influences.

Waskow, H. *Whitman: Explorations in Form.* 1966. Attempts to "define individual poems by showing how they work, and to define Whitman's poetry by demonstrating the relationship among the various ways of working."

Woodress, J., ed. *Critical Essays on Walt Whitman.* 1983. Includes nineteenth- and twentieth-century responses to the poet and supplies an excellent survey of issues relevant to understanding his work.

Herman Melville

Billy Budd, Sailor

Classroom Strategies and Topics for Discussion

The sheer suspense of this psychological narrative will keep students reading the story, but—like professional critics—they will probably have trouble with its complexities and ambiguities. Such "trouble" can itself supply a source of interest. In any case, it is helpful, before the first assignment (the narrative naturally divides at the end of section 17), to suggest that readers concentrate on trying to fathom the characters of Billy, Vere, and Claggart, and on thinking about the voice of the storyteller, what it's like and what it contributes to the story's effect. The first discussion may well concentrate on just these matters.

The obvious first question for a class, though, is why Melville includes at the beginning the detailed account of the black sailor in Liverpool.

This is, of course, only the first of many "digressions" apparently designed to insist on the broad implications of Billy's story. Billy belongs to a type, the narrator suggests; we should understand what happens to him in relation to the function of that type. The black sailor is the center of his companions' attention; he seems to have an enviable role and to foretell just such a position for the hero of this story. The episode is worth returning to at the end of the discussion of *Billy Budd*, as a good example of Melville's irony.

Subtle and important points can emerge from class conversation based on such apparently simple and straightforward questions as What is Billy like? What is Claggart like? In arriving at a consensus on such matters, it is obviously important not to let the discussion stray too far from the text. Students might wish to talk about the imagery used to characterize Billy. On the one hand, he resembles "a dog of Saint Bernard's breed," or an "upright barbarian"; on the other, he turns out to be the kind of barbarian Adam may have been before the Fall. How does one reconcile the apparently degrading and the apparently exalted metaphors associated with Billy? Is it possible that to be a barbarian or a dog might be a good thing, given the nature of civilized society? In chapter 16, Billy is said to be ignorant, simpleminded, unsophisticated. Such qualities precipitate his destruction. Are they therefore to be condemned? Like all questions associated with *Billy Budd*, these have no definitive answers, but pursuing them will help readers realize the complexity of the narrative.

The characterization of Vere also presents difficulties. What are we to make of the explanation of his being called "starry Vere"? The matter-of-fact account of the epithet associates him with a long tradition of English heroism, but also suggests that the adjective is a kind of joke. Is it a good thing or a bad one that he loves books? (This manifestly unanswerable question is worth raising because his scholarly nature becomes relevant later on.) Students should particularly note the stress on his social conservatism, and the imagery ("a dyke against those invading waters") associated with it.

You should make sure that students understand the nature of Claggart's job on the ship, to which Melville gives considerable stress. It becomes important that he is the officer in charge of discipline. The storyteller suggests that he is impossible to characterize adequately ("His portrait I essay, but shall never hit it"). Why? Worth noting particularly is the emphasis on covert suggestions of "something defective or abnormal" about him, suggestions summed up, on the social level (they are also relevant on the psychological level), by the persistent stories of a criminal past. What is the source of the antagonism Claggart feels for Billy? Speculation about this matter provides much of the substance of chapter 12; does this speculation resolve anything? What would it mean to say that this is the fundamental antipathy of evil for good? Can we believe in this sort of antipathy? Would the Bible support such belief?

The voice of the storyteller in some ways presents the greatest difficulties of all. Passages that should be considered in assessing it include the observation at the end of chapter 2 that Billy is not a conventional hero and his story no romance (What does *romance* mean here? Is the narrator simply claiming realism for his tale?); the apology for digression at the beginning of chapter 4, with the association between digression and sinning (Why? Is this simply a joke? Does it raise questions about the nature of "sin" in the story itself?); and (particularly important) the discussion in chapter 11 about Claggart's antipathy, a discussion that suggests and rejects the possibility of inventing an explanation. This last sequence implicitly insists that the storyteller does not finally have control over his story, and other passages echo the point. It makes a claim of truth for the narrative, and it argues that reality is more "mysterious" than invention. Students should be asked how they respond to such a claim. Does it make them trust or distrust the narrator? It certainly could be argued that the storyteller goes out of his way to hint that he is not a dependable or adequate guide through the intricacies of his own story; why should he do such a thing? Perhaps he is trying to make his readers reflect on the final incomprehensibility of their own experience, and of all human experience, and to tell us that the difficulties of his story correspond to those of life.

The second class should perhaps begin with renewed discussion of the imagery associated with Billy. There is, of course, increasing stress on biblical reference, most of which associates Billy with innocence or virtue. Melville renews his allusions to Billy as child, as barbarian, and as dog; he adds, at a crucial moment (just before the hanging), the singing bird. How does this imagery control or affect our developing impression of Billy? Does it convey the storyteller's clear judgment? Students will be interested in the large moral questions raised by the second half of *Billy Budd*. For example, does Billy receive a fair trial? Both possible answers to this question should be fully explored. If Captain Vere's arguments are taken with full seriousness, the answer will probably be yes; if one believes that morality rather than legality or practical considerations should operate in legal proceedings, the answer will be no. In Melville's account, considerable stress is placed on the influence of Vere's "unshared studies," which, along with his superior intellectuality, differentiate him from the other men. Is the point that Captain Vere's is the more well-thought-out position? If this *isn't* the point, what is?

The problem of the storyteller's role also recurs more emphatically in the second half of *Billy Budd*. For example, he claims not to know what happened in the final private interview between Billy and Captain Vere; he can only "conjecture." This device reiterates the claim of truth for the narrative; it may also renew the reader's uneasiness. It's worth asking once more why the narrator, the inventor of characters and action alike, should disclaim his own authority. Do the questions he implicitly raises about authorial authority extend to other kinds of power? Or does one come to believe in the truth of the story he tells? Another question about the way the story is being told may arise with the "digression" after the hanging: what is the point of introducing these speculations about why Billy's body didn't move? Do they suggest something supernatural about his death? Does the reader find him or herself trying to come up with other explanations? Do we believe that the problem matters at all?

A few more large questions that might prove stimulating: Do the three principal characters conduct themselves in the crisis in ways you would anticipate from their characterizations in the first half? Claggart is the villain, but he alone does not cause Billy's death. Who or what should be blamed? Captain Vere? "Society"? War? Chance? How do you feel about Billy at the end? Is he saint or simpleton? Can you think of comparable instances, in public or in private life, of conflicts between legality and justice that are very difficult to adjudicate?

Topics for Writing

Most of the questions that have been raised here would provide good material for essays, whether or not they have been discussed in class. (Since this work is so richly interpretable, everyone can have individual opinions differing from ones arrived at collectively.) Some other possible topics:

1. Why does the action occur during the French Revolution?
2. Billy as a passive hero.
3. Billy's effect on others.
4. Captain Vere: the tragedy of the educated man.
5. Claggart's motives.

Comparative Perspectives

1. Works as different as *Antigone, Narrative of the Life of Frederick Douglass, The Guest*, and *Things Fall Apart* tackle a question similar to the ones Melville puts here: When should the law be obeyed? What is the relationship between law and justice? How does the tone of the work in question guide us to varying responses to these problems?
2. The British composer Benjamin Britten turned both *Billy Budd* and *Death in Venice* into operas, helping us see that both texts describe the disturbing attraction felt by a quasi-paternal authority figure for a very young man. Compare the emphases of Melville and Mann in dealing with these feelings. Both writers draw heavily on classical and biblical allusions rather than examine these situations in explicitly psychological terms. What difference does half a century make in the presentation of this theme in the two works? How does Freud's effort to analyze "Dora" expose some of the complicated sexual attitudes that may underlie the tensions in these two short novels?

   [If time and context permit, listening to key portions of the leading tenor roles—Vere and Aschenbach—would be a rewarding exercise.]

Further Reading

See also the reading suggestions in the *Anthology*, p. 2542.

Miller, E. *Melville*. 1975. Both biographical and critical, stressing Freudian interpretation.

Parker, H. *Reading* Billy Budd. 1990. Focused on the difficulties of interpretation and their significance.

Stafford, W. *Melville's* Billy Budd *and the Critics*. 1969. Offers an enormous amount of useful information, containing texts of Melville's story and of the play made from it; an essay on the Hayford-Sealts text; and a collection of early and recent criticism from several points of view, including treatments of characters, sources, digressions, tradition, theological implications, and a valuable bibliography.

EMILY DICKINSON

Classroom Strategies and Topics for Discussion

First-time readers of Emily Dickinson typically have trouble understanding why such tiny poems should be taken seriously. Because Dickinson makes no loud claims for herself, because her lyrics do not elaborate their emotional arguments, perhaps even because of their eccentric punctuation, students may make the mistake of thinking these are easy and obvious poems. Your first task, therefore, is to demonstrate how much goes on beneath the surface of apparently simple verse—and for this purpose, there is no substitute for close attention to a specific text. A class can easily spend an hour exploring implications of a single short poem; to do so provides the best way to demonstrate the complexity of Dickinson's achievement.

If time limitations forbid such leisurely analysis, you may use a more general approach. You could point out, for example, that at least five of Dickinson's lyrics here printed deal centrally with death (216, 449, 465, 712, 1564). Beyond this theme, the five poems have little obviously in common. Yet it is illuminating to compare them with one another—say, 216 and 712. Do they share any images? Students might notice immediately that both suggest connections between graves and houses: "Alabaster Chambers," "a House that seemed / A Swelling of the Ground." Are these associations reassuring or disturbing? This question should generate considerable discussion—possibly even controversy. The solidity, beauty, security of alabaster, satin, stone (216, first stanza) might be cited as forms of positive suggestion; and the apparent affinity to nature of the "House" in 712. On the other hand, the fact that the alabaster chambers remain untouched by morning and noon (with the past participle repeated for emphasis) is more ambiguous. One could argue that being untouched by diurnal sequence implies existence beyond time, transcendence—or, with very different emotional tone, that it implies the cessation of experience. Similarly, the "Centuries" that have elapsed since the speaker in 712 set out on her journey with Death may convey the positive associations of "Immortality" or the terrifying possibilities of "Eternity." Does the speaker convey a consistent attitude toward death in each case? The effect of 216 depends on the contrast between the first and second stanzas. Is that contrast mainly between the ignorance of breeze, bee, and birds and the "sagacity" of the dead? Perhaps so—but the sagacity has already "perished," so "the meek members of the Resurrection" in their sleep can oppose no wisdom to the "ignorant cadence" of the birds.

The noun "Resurrection" in 216, like "Immortality" in 712, suggests a Christian view of the afterlife. Does anything else in either poem substantiate this view? The predominant images, in both cases, are secular—in 216, details of tomb, coffin, and natural world; in 712, items of clothing and scenes that recapitulate stages of human life. Why, then, the Christian allusions? Generations of critics have debated this problem, and no definitive answer is likely. Students might, however, find it interesting to think about the degree to which both poems achieve their effects by juxtaposing incongruous points of view without mediating between them. The most obvious example is the imagining of Death as a gentlemanly figure stopping his carriage for a lady and of the journey through eternity as an exercise in civility. To think of gossamer and tulle in relation to death, or of horses and eternity, also strains the imagination by invoking sharply different focuses of perception. The abstractness of "Immortality" contrasts with the concretely imagined scene of two figures in a carriage. To think of the dead as "members of the Resurrection" conflicts with thinking of them in their graves; to turn attention to what happens in the air makes it hard to think simultaneously of what happens underground; and to sum up the dead as having embodied "sagacity" violates the expectations that the poem has established.

The techniques students will discover by trying to figure out the relation of these two poems recur in many others. In other lyrics too they can find unpredictable juxtapositions of abstract and concrete and of opposed perspectives; gaps in meaning that both demand and elude interpretation (What, for example, is the relation, on the narrative level, between the "House" before which the travelers pause in 712 and their continued journey? What does the grave have to do with eternity?) and the shock value of unexpected words (e.g., "omnipotent" in 585, "infirm" in 1129, "enabled" in 1207, "Pangless" in 1564). The effect of the punctuation is worth discussing: often a dash at the end of a poem suspends meaning, implying that a thought or feeling is only interrupted, not completed; often a dash in the middle of a line forces a pause that demands attention for a phrase suddenly made fresh by being perceived as a small, contained unit. And you may wish to call attention to Dickinson's slant rhymes ("away" and "civility," "chill" and "Tulle"). True rhymes in a quatrain structure create effects of finality, order, closure. These near-rhymes, like the dashes, suggest that matters cannot quite be closed off, that no statement comprehends the significance of any phenomenon.

Rhetoric, rhythm, and punctuation reiterate the same implications of open meaning. These poems demand active involvement from their readers. Their predominantly simple language, their way of contemplating the ordinary until it becomes strange (think of the buzzing fly in 465), suggest that everyday experience also invites active involvement, active interpretation—and that all meaning depends on interpretation. One can imagine the dead as buried or as resurrected (or as both at once); one can imagine a train as an animal or a star (585). Such acts of imagination make the world simultaneously comprehensible and mysterious.

Topics for Writing

1. Animal life in Emily Dickinson.
2. A "feminine" aspect of Dickinson's poems.
3. Who is the speaker, and what is she like (in any poem)?
4. Dickinson's sense of humor.

Comparative Perspectives

1. Compare the attitude toward human consciousness and its power or weakness relative to nature in "The Brain—Is Wider Than the Sky—" (632) with Coleridge's *Dejection: An Ode* or Leopardi's *The Infinite*. Which poet is more confident of the mind's ability?
2. How does Dickinson's unsentimental treatment of the familiar imagery of birds (as in 328 or 1084) contrast with the lusher poems of Keats and Whitman discussed above? Does she seem more like the Romantic or the modernist poets in this regard?

Further Reading

See also the reading suggestions in the *Anthology*, p. 2540.

Fast, R. R., and C. M. Gordon, eds. *Approaches to Teaching Emily Dickinson's Poetry*. 1989. An exceptionally useful and varied collection.

Pollak, V. *Dickinson: The Anxiety of Gender*. 1984. Analyzes the life and work with emphasis on her experience as a woman.

Sewall, R. *The Life of Emily Dickinson*. 2 vols. 1974. A thorough, readable, and interesting biography.

———, ed. *Emily Dickinson: A Collection of Critical Essays*. 1963. A group of essays illuminating in their diversity.

The Nineteenth Century: Realism and Symbolism

NIKOLAI GOGOL

The Overcoat

Classroom Strategies and Topics for Discussion

Gogol (1809–1852) is one of the most significant Russian prose writers of the first half of the nineteenth century. *The Overcoat*, published in 1842, is the best known of a cycle of five stories set in St. Petersburg, the capital of czarist Russia. Its chief problems for the first-time reader are its shifting narrative tone—how does the narrator want us to take him?—and its generic instability—what kind of a thing is this? Whatever other tones the narrative voice assumes, the principal one is comic, and whatever other genres the story may gesture toward or veer through, the principal one is social satire. Demonstrating this to students may take some time, but it will be time well spent. Once the comic voice and the satiric aims of the story are established, a first-time reader will have access to the story's other dimensions. The voice can also be alternatively mordant, indignant, clinical, and fantastic. Any short list of the story's other generic possibilities would include realism, spiritual biography, folk tale, ghost story, and farce.

The comic voice can be established if students are encouraged to examine the sequence early in the story in which the protagonist is born and christened. The narrator calmly informs us that the protagonist's surname is Bashmachkin. Then there follows a digression questioning the appropriateness of this name. It is derived, we are told, from the Russian word for "shoe," but all the Bashmachkins inevitably wore boots. The comedy of this can be demonstrated to students by recalling the number of English names derived from objects or occupations: Fisher, Miller, Carpenter. With any luck, students with such names will be in the class, and they can be asked if they or any of their forebears time out of mind follow these occupations. The Christian name is Akaky Akakievich. To a Russian this is immediately funny, punning as it does upon "kaka" (feces). The joke is given its kicker in the next sentence: "Perhaps it may strike the reader as a rather strange and contrived name, but I can assure him that it was not contrived at all." Then the narrator explains that Akaky's mother was offered a number of other names, all ridiculous, out of the ecclesiastical calendar, and decides the child should instead be named after his father. "We have reported it here so that the reader may see for himself that it happened quite inevitably and that to give him any other name was out of the question," the narrator concludes, with the deadpan delivery that is the hallmark of his comic tone. The case for a comic narrator can be emphasized with reference to any number of episodes.

A good one comes near the end of the story where the desperate protagonist solicits the aid of a self-important official in the search for his stolen overcoat. The official blusters at the self-effacing Akaky; he nearly faints, and on his way home without the coat he catches a cold that ultimately kills him. "That's how violent the effects of an appropriate reprimand can be!" is the dryly humorous remark of the narrator. This same episode can also be used to demonstrate the story's frequent engagement with the genre of social satire. The Person of Consequence with whom Akaky has an audience is the epitome of a mid-level functionary, newly elevated and insecure, and thus given to authoritarian displays, and very uncomfortable with those of higher status. In one of the asides that had the potential of getting Gogol into difficulties with the czarist censors, he details the chain of command whereby the Person of Consequence thinks it proper that he should be approached, and then says: "Everyone in Holy Russia has a craze for imitation; everyone apes and mimics his superiors." This is a very palpable hit at the Imperial Court and its attendant and maddening bureaucracy. More generally, the social satire of the story concerns not only the czarist bureaucracy, but St. Petersburg itself, as an avatar of the modern industrial city—soulless, lacking in community or even humanity, vast, impersonal, and deadening. Emblematic of this is the freezing cold which is the typical climate of the story, occasioning the need for the overcoat around which the story turns. Akaky's position in his office and in St. Petersburg is of the lowliest, and his life is compounded of poverty, isolation, and grimly relentless routine. When, in proud possession of his new overcoat, he makes his way across the city to an evening party being held more or less in the overcoat's honor by an upper clerk in his office, the story lays bare the great city's empty heart. This becomes even clearer upon his return to his cheap tenement late at night after the party: "[N]ot a soul anywhere; only the snow gleamed on the streets and the low pitched hovels looked black and gloomy with their closed shutters. He approached the spot where the street was intersected by an endless square, which looked like a fearful desert with its houses scarcely visible on the far side." Of course, this is where he is set upon and robbed of the overcoat, which had momentarily (and pathetically) brought a kind of joy into his life, perhaps for the first time, and certainly for the last. Student attention might also be called to the implicit eroticism with which Akaky possesses the overcoat, and with which it endows him. For this is also a story of attachment and loss, but unlike the case of Little Hans in Freud's trenchant study, Akaky has no means to accommodate loss. His need for the overcoat is desperate; he endures strict privations and strips himself of his small savings to purchase it. Its all-too-brief possession is for him a self-affirming triumph. When he is robbed of it, and in the attempt to recover it encounters the Kafka-esque bureaucracy that presides over such small affairs, to the poor crucially important, the experience literally kills him. Students will also want to discuss the final sequence of the story. Akaky returns from the dead and as a fearsome corpse robs people of their overcoats all over the city, finally being satisfied with the theft of the overcoat belonging to the Person of Consequence who spurned him. In this fantastic sequence, Gogol appears to have arranged some kind of equivocal justice for his much-wronged character. It's satisfying that the Person of Consequence loses his overcoat and gets a good scare into the bargain, but Akaky is, after all, dead, and the grave offers few uses for a warm coat.

Topics for Writing

1. Comic narrative effects.
2. Narrative digression.
3. Social satire.
4. Multigeneric experimentation.

Further Reading

For additional reading suggestions, see p. 2545.

Daniel Rancour-Laferriere. *Out From Under Gogol's Overcoat: A Psychoanalytic Study.* 1982.

William M. Todd. *Fiction and Society in the Age of Pushkin.* 1986.

GUSTAVE FLAUBERT

Madame Bovary

Backgrounds

Madame Bovary is the story of Emma, a young woman living in Normandy in the 1840s. She has received a convent education that has filled her head with romantic dreams of luxury and love. She marries a country doctor, Charles Bovary, an awkward, dull, but honest and loving young man, and bears him a daughter. Quickly disappointed and bored by her marriage, she resists the advances of a shy student, Léon, but then becomes depressed and revives only when Charles manages to move into a larger village, Yonville. There she quickly succumbs to the advances of a dashing landowner, Rodolphe. She wants to elope with him, but he deserts her in the last moment. On a trip to Rouen where she attends the opera, she again meets Léon, now a law clerk, and becomes his mistress. Her clandestine meetings and the luxuries she purchases involve her in debt to a local, usurious merchant. When he presses her and all attempts to get help from her lovers fail, she commits suicide by arsenic poisoning. Only after her death does Charles discover her infidelities.

Flaubert wrote the novel after his return from a trip to the Levant, deliberately choosing a low and commonplace subject and a heroine whose vulgarity he despised. He felt he had to make a new beginning as all his early writings had been lyrical and romantic. He worked assiduously at the novel, describing his slow progress and his "agonies of composition" in letters to his friend Louise Colet.

Flaubert's treatment of sexual encounters, frank for his time, and his description of the ceremony of extreme unction caused an attempt by the government of Napoleon III to suppress the book as obscene. The defense won acquittal on the argument that the story actually shows the wages of sin and even metes out harsh punishment for Emma's adulteries. The success of the book was thus assured. What Flaubert wrote, however, was neither a salacious book nor a warning against adultery but a supreme work of art, which today is generally regarded as the first modern novel, clearly set off by its objectivity from the earlier moralizing novels of writers such as Balzac, Dickens, and Thackeray.

Classroom Strategies

Flaubert divided the novel into three parts, which can be taught in three assignments. If necessary, part 2 may be divided after chapter VIII and part 3 after chapter VI, making five assignments.

The main difficulties of the book come from defining the author's ambiguous attitude toward Emma, which obviously includes condemnation of her lying, her lust, and her improvidence, satire on her romantic illusions, and compassion for her sufferings. As the headnote indicates, Flaubert's point of view is not as detached and completely objective as the reputation of the book may suggest. The story begins in the schoolroom with a teller who speaks of "we" as if he were one of the boys in the class, but then the point of view shifts to omniscience: much that is represented could not possibly have been seen or felt by Madame Bovary. Occasionally Flaubert comments disapprovingly on her "hardhearted and tightfisted peasant nature" or her "corruption." But at the end, in his description of the extreme unction, he solemnly pronounces forgiveness even for her sensuality and lust. One must keep alert throughout for shifts in perspective of this kind. For example, the ball at the castle of the Marquis (chapter VII of part 1) is drenched in the atmosphere of Emma's own dreams and longings. The agricultural fair on the other hand, which has been called "polyphonic" in reproducing the speeches of the pompous officials alternating with the lovetalk of Rodolphe, is viewed not through Emma's eyes but with the satirical and ironic detachment of the author.

Other valuable points for discussion are the satirical picture of the whole society (particularly as represented in the odious pharmacist

Homais, who is the target of Flaubert's dislike of the ideas of progress, science, and democracy) and the character of Charles Bovary, who opens and closes the book and whose final judgment, "It was decreed by fate," is endorsed by the author even though Rodolphe finds it slightly ridiculous.

The technique of building the book around striking pictorial scenes should also be discussed. The ball, the agricultural fair, the ride in the woods, Emma receiving Rodolphe's letter and climbing to the attic, the opera (*Lucia di Lammermoor*) in Rouen, the visit to the Cathedral, the cab ride, the scenes in the hotel with Léon, and finally the suicide print themselves indelibly on one's memory, and it pays to ask by what means Flaubert has accomplished this. Often small details are used almost symbolically, as in the little scene of Charles and Emma having supper, he eating boiled beef, she drawing knife lines on the oilcloth on the table: a scene used by Erich Auerbach in *Mimesis* to stress the novelty of Flaubert's impersonal realism. Or to take another example: the wooden napkin rings of Binet and the whirr of the lathe, which saves Emma from falling to her death. Such details serve to point out the estrangement between husband and wife while emphasizing also the role of little things, the chances of life.

Topics for Discussion and Writing

1. Discuss the character of Emma and the author's attitude toward her.
2. Discuss the social picture and social types of the novel: the husband-physician, the landowner, the law clerk, the pharmacist, the merchant-usurer, the beggar, and others.
3. Discuss Percy Lubbock's statement in *Craft of Fiction* that this is "the novel of all novels which no criticism of fiction can overlook." In comparison with other novels you have read—*The Princess of Clèves*, for instance—what features do you discover in it that might justify Lubbock's praise?
4. Discuss the implied philosophy of life or scale of values. Do you agree with Martin Turnell (*The Novel in France*) that this novel is "an onslaught on the whole basis of human feeling and on all spiritual and moral values"? Think also of the "positive" figures: Emma's father, the pharmacist's apprentice, the old peasant woman at the agricultural fair who got for fifty-four years of service a medal worth twenty-five francs, or of Dr. Larivière, who comes too late to save Emma.
5. Discuss some particularly clearly visualized episodes such as the agricultural fair and the scene in the Cathedral. Both contrast the trivial lovetalk with the pompous rhetoric of an official or a guide. What is the effect of this?
6. Ask how far the story transcends its local setting in time and place and, particularly, how far its scenes, persons, actions, and emo-

tional and mental attitudes may be applied to our own time. Emma is sometimes thought of as a typical dreamer like Don Quixote, but in fact the two are very different. Don Quixote takes action, however foolish, while Emma can only plan a trip to Italy. Homais has become the type of the conventional small-town man who has accepted all the commonplaces of nineteenth-century progress, faith in science, and democracy, and he is, in the last words of the book, rewarded with the order of the Legion of Honor. Do we still find this type today?

Comparative Perspectives

1. Like Flaubert, Molière ran afoul of authority for his depiction of religion.
   a. Compare the treatment of French Catholic mores in *Madame Bovary* with Molière's portrait of Tartuffe. Which do you think poses a greater challenge to ecclesiastical control?
   b. How convincing do you find Molière's defense of the stage in the three prefaces to *Tartuffe*? Compare Flaubert's strategy of speaking not in his own voice, but through the debates between Homais and the Abbé Bournisien in the discussion of theater in part two, chapter XIV.
2. Like St. Augustine, like Rousseau, Emma is deeply influenced by her reading. Describe the fiction and poetry that move her and analyze your own responses to such material. If reading matter can corrupt, is the fault in the text or in the reader?
   a. Note Emma's love of Walter Scott (and the power and limits of her response to the performance of *Lucia di Lammermoor* in part two, chapter XV) and Romantic poetry (see the reference to Lamartine's *The Lake* in part three, chapter III).
   b. One critic has noted Flaubert's attitude toward a "stilted romantic sensibility." Does that mean he rejects Romanticism in all its forms? Discuss some elements of *Madame Bovary* that seem romantic to you and compare them with elements you have observed in your study of nineteenth-century lyric poetry.
3. The death of Emma Bovary and the death of Ivan Ilyich are among the most famous scenes in nineteenth-century fiction. Compare and contrast the kinds of details singled out by Flaubert and Tolstoy, two masters of realism, and comment on the points they make about the nature of the characters who are dying. For a wider-ranging examination of tone, look at some other literary death scenes (of Hector in the *Iliad*, for example, or of Aschenbach in *Death in Venice*). In each case, examine the values implicit in the author's descriptive techniques and show how they guide the audience to make judgments about the deceased.

Further Reading

See also the reading suggestions in the *Anthology*, p. 2545.

Auerbach, Erich. *Mimesis: The Representation of Reality in Western Literature*. Trans. Willard Trask. 1953. "In the Hotel de la Mole" has luminous pages.

Bart, Benjamin F., ed. *Madame Bovary and the Critics: A Collection of Essays*. 1966.

James, Henry. *Notes on Novelists*. 1914. Throws doubt on the choice of subject.

Levin, Harry. *The Gates of Horn: A Study of Five French Realists*. 1963. The chapter "Flaubert" gives a general appraisal of *Madame Bovary*.

Lubbock, Percy. *The Craft of Fiction*. 1921. In chapters 5 and 6, Lubbock stresses the role of telling and the point of view.

Porter, Laurence M., and Eugene F. Gary, eds. *Approaches to Teaching Flaubert's* Madame Bovary. 1995. One of the volumes in the MLA series.

Steegmuller, Francis. *Flaubert and* Madame Bovary. 1939; new ed. 1950. Good on the biographical background and the genesis of the book.

Turnell, Martin. *The Novel in France*. 1950. Criticizes Flaubert from a moral point of view.

FYODOR DOSTOEVSKY

Notes from Underground

Backgrounds

Notes from Underground consists of two distinct parts. First comes the monologue of a lonely, spiteful former clerk who lives in a garret in St. Petersburg and states his hatred of humanity, progress, science, and determinism. Next follows a kind of memoir in which the same man reminisces about events in his earlier life. An attempt at self-assertion has led to his jostling an officer; an intrusion into the company of former schoolfellows has resulted in humiliating altercations and finally in a visit to a brothel. There he in turn humiliates the prostitute Lisa by depicting her future terrible fate. Deeply moved and determined to change her life, she calls on the Underground Man, only to find him engaged in a disgraceful scene with his servant. Newly humiliated, he seeks vicarious revenge by sexually assaulting the girl and forcing money on her. She flees, throwing the money away. The Underground Man remains in his hole, alienated, mortified, disgusted with himself and everything around.

The story, written in 1864, reflects the beginning of Dostoevsky's conversion to a conservative creed. He had, as explained in the *Anthology* headnote, taken part in an underground circle, which the government of Tsar Nicholas considered subversive, but which was mainly a discussion group interested in the utopian socialism of Fourier. Dostoevsky was arrested, tried, taken to be shot, but reprieved at the place of execution to ten years of penal servitude in Siberia. Four years he spent in a stockade in chains and six as a common soldier on the frontier of China. He returned to Petersburg in 1859, a changed man.

Notes from Underground is a departure from Dostoevsky's early manner as a social novelist and anticipates the later great novels beginning with *Crime and Punishment* two years later.

Classroom Strategies

Two assignments or three. Part II can be divided after chapter V, if three are desired.

The first part, the monologue, presents difficulties to students in that it contains a searing attack on the assumptions of their tradition. The whole Enlightenment cherished by the West—including the ideas of perpetual progress, of scientific truth, of a well-organized, rational society "in pursuit of happiness"—is not only questioned but jeered at. Students are apt to discount the whole diatribe because it is put into the mouth of a despicable being, who himself declares that he is motivated by resentment at his failure in human relations. Such a dismissal would be an enormous mistake: the Underground Man is right in Dostoevsky's eyes in asserting human freedom, which seems to him the essential prerogative of our species. He feels that he is robbed of it by deterministic science, which forbids him to argue that two plus two may be five, and by the utopian schemes of socialist world-improvers who would force humanity into an artificial collective paradise. Through the mouth of his unlovely speaker, Dostoevsky attacks all rationalism, all utopianism, all illusions about natural goodness. He does not believe that men and women follow their enlightened self-interest as the utopians hope. Rather, in his view, they are creatures of passion, even senseless and destructive passion. The human species is bloodthirsty, and history is a record of butcheries. Our nature, as history shows, craves chaos and destruction, even suffering and pain. The intellectual position of the Underground Man can be seen as an anticipation of existentialism, which in the writings of Jean-Paul Sartre and Albert Camus asserted indeterminism, the freedom of the will, and choice. It can also be seen as curiously prophetic of the terrifying inhumanities we have witnessed in our own century.

Topics for Discussion

The whole question of optimism versus pessimism about the fate of mankind will properly take center stage. Questions about the brutalities of humankind both past and present will make for exciting debate. Our own modern fear of totalitarianism is raised as the Underground Man revolts at the thought that the individual soul might become a member of an "ant heap," a "mere cipher," a "piano key," an "organ stop" (as he says in many variations).

The second part, in particular, raises psychological questions: Dostoevsky depicts a personality dominated by resentment, who doubts the stability of human personality and who himself oscillates between pride and humility, the desire to humiliate others and the hardly concealed desire of being humiliated. The scenes with Lisa are the best illustrations.

A literary question is raised by the dramatic monologue, which at times is almost like a stream of consciousness, in its relation to the confessions of the second part, which buttress and justify the tone and content of the first part. The parody of the rescue of a prostitute is the most striking example. The whole story, told by an "antihero," may at first strike us as purely negative; yet it is one of the paradoxes of Dostoevsky's art that he uses his most doubtful characters as spokesmen for his most cherished ideas. Though Dostoevsky complained of the suppression of a chapter by the censor, hinting at a religious solution that he found later, we may at this stage of our knowledge of Dostoevsky's writings remain baffled by the blind alley in which the Underground Man has lost himself.

A further point of discussion is raised by the peculiarly Russian setting of the person and events of the story. Dostoevsky considers the Underground Man, in his alienation from society, to be representative of the generation of the forties and the fifties. The story particularly attacks the utopianism of such novels as Nikolay Chernyshevsky's *What Is to Be Done?* (1863), which much later was highly admired by Lenin, and jeers at the materialist progress reflected in the Crystal Palace at the London Universal Exhibition, which Dostoevsky saw in 1862. Polemics against Russian radical critics of the sixties color the speech of the Underground Man. The nature of the reflections on romanticism, which here means "dreaming" or vague "idealism," and the picture of the stratified society (clerks, bureaucrats, military officers, prostitutes) date the story to the same extent as the wet snow and the fog localize it in a St. Petersburg winter.

Topics for Writing

1. Discuss the attack on the idea of progress, on the natural goodness of humankind, on the benefits of science, and on rationalism and optimism generally.

   [Clues to possible answers are suggested in the headnote and in "Topics for Discussion," but may be different for different students.]

2. Discuss the view that humanity's history shows our cruelty: that we *want* to suffer and inflict pain. Do not exclude current and recent history.

   [In psychiatry the term "sadomasochism" would describe this condition. In the story, the scenes with Lisa are perhaps the best examples.]

3. Discuss humanity's "terrifying freedom." Are you convinced by the

argument against determinism and for complete individualism, even caprice? Are you any more convinced by the converse of these views? Why or why not?

4. What does the term "Underground Man" imply?

[In Russian, *podpolie* means "below the floor." The Underground Man is compared to a mouse living in a cellar-hole, but the actual protagonist lives in a garret with a servant. The answer is suggested by the whole tone of resentment, isolation, and alienation.]

Comparative Perspectives

1. The protagonist of Dostoevsky's *Notes from Underground* labels himself an antihero who couldn't resist writing about himself, despite his sense that "a novel needs a hero." What does he mean by this? What neurotic needs drive antiheroic figures? Are such characters peculiar to nineteenth- and twentieth-century art, or can you think of other examples?

[Examine the narrator's own definition of his antiheroic state— being "estranged from life"—to open up many vistas. Achilles arguably fits this definition. What changes is the vocabulary available for analyzing compulsive, self-destructive behavior, not the impulse behind it; in contemporary literature, examples abound. Possibilities include Hermann in Pushkin's *The Queen of Spades*, Gregor in Kafka's *The Metamorphosis*, Eliot's J. Alfred Prufrock, and The Misfit in O'Connor's *A Good Man Is Hard to Find*.]

2. Must two times two equal four? Explain the Underground Man's critique of reason and compare it with other challenges to what seems to him a dead and mechanistic way of dealing with the world.

[Possibilities include Swift's *Modest Proposal* as well as his account of life among the Houyhnhnms; Blake's *Mock On, Mock On, Voltaire, Rousseau*; Tzara's *Dadaist Disgust*; and Borges's *The Garden of Forking Paths*.]

Further Reading

See also the reading suggestions in the *Anthology*, p. 2544.

Carr, Edward Hallett. *Dostoevsky, 1821–1881: A New Biography*. 1931. Sober and factual.

Dostoevsky, Fyodor. *Notes from Underground*. Ed. Robert G. Durgy; trans. Serge Shishkoff. 1969; reprinted 1982. Contains a section of modern criticism.

Frank, Joseph. *Dostoevsky: The Seeds of Revolt, 1821–1849*. 1976.

———. *Dostoevsky: The Years of Ordeal, 1850–1859*. 1984.

———. *Dostoevsky: The Stir of Liberation, 1860–1865*. 1986. The period of *Notes from Underground*.

————. *Dostoevsky: The Miraculous Years, 1865–1871.* 1995.

Jones, Malcolm V. *Dostoevsky: The Novel of Discord.* 1976. A good recent introduction.

Simmons, Ernest J. *Dostoevsky: The Making of the Novelist.* 1940. Provides a reliable digest of Russian scholarship.

LEO TOLSTOY

The Death of Ivan Ilyich

Backgrounds

The Death of Ivan Ilyich is the story of a Russian judge in the 1880s who, from an accidental fall while climbing a ladder to fix a curtain, contracts an illness that leads to a lingering, painful death. In the course of dying, Ivan Ilyich recognizes that he has led a wrong life, yet at the very end he feels he has defeated death. There is a light—symbolizing hope in the form of another life—at the bottom of the black sack into which he is being pushed.

The story was written in 1886, after Tolstoy's "conversion" in 1879. It reflects his lifelong preoccupation with death and dying and his ambition to found a simplified religion, together with his criticism of urban civilization.

In its bald manner of telling, the story differs sharply from Tolstoy's earlier work, including the epic novels *War and Peace* and *Anna Karenina.* Its tone is rather that of a parable: "Ivan Ilyich's life had been most simple and most ordinary and therefore most terrible" (p. 1189).

Classroom Strategies

The Death of Ivan Ilyich is so unified that it is difficult to divide. If you wish to present it in two assignments, use the end of chapter III as a breaking point.

The story is so straightforward that students cannot misunderstand it. It is intended to remind us forcefully of the inevitability of death and the loneliness of every human being when confronted with his or her own death. Tolstoy brings home the contrast between the triviality of the life and activities of the average person (Ivan Ilyich in Russian is the equivalent of John Smith in English) and the sudden, awesome awareness of death and dying. One could argue that he stresses this contrast because he resents the hypocrisy with which the fact of death is usually swept under the rug.

Students may have difficulties with the harsh satire upon doctors, the institution of marriage, and the courts of law. They may also reject as not clearly motivated the final acceptance of death that Ivan achieves. Possibly an explanation of the Russian class system may help to explain details: the bureaucracy sharply divided from the peasantry, of which Gerasim, the assistant to the butler, is the lonely representative. He alone has genuine compassion for his dying master and is able to speak of death, while all the upper-class characters are hidebound in social conventions and hypocrisy.

Topics for Discussion

Compare the attitude to death and dying in the story with representative American attitudes. What do our current substitutions of funeral director for undertaker, casket for coffin, deceased for dead man or woman, and passed away for died have to do with Tolstoy's theme? In Tolstoy the ritual of the Orthodox church—the confession, the display of the corpse in an open coffin, the concern of the widow for the price of the burial plot, but mainly the hypocrisy of the people surrounding the man—is satirized. Also exposed are the annoyance of the family at their own inconvenience (the girl is eager to marry), the callousness of the doctors interested in the diagnosis of the illness (floating kidney or vermiform appendix?) rather than in the suffering of the patient, and the hardly concealed pleasure of Ilyich's supposed friends at the news of his death, since it will vacate a position at court. But Tolstoy wants primarily to convey our need to recognize the majesty of death and the triviality of the life of the average man.

A powerful vein of realism runs throughout this story. Ugly details usually excluded from conventional fiction bring before us the smell of the disease, the processes of elimination, the sound of screaming in excruciating pain. Yet there is also a degree of contrivance almost too neat in the way the characters are typed and in the contrast between their lives at the beginning and at the end. Small satirical details like the creaking of the hassock or the "full bosom pushed up by her corset" of Ivan Ilyich's wife will seem too artful, and the final image of the black sack with the light at its bottom is obviously a symbol with a manifest design on our feelings. Suspense is deliberately eliminated by the title and the first scene of the funeral service.

The story can be seen as a miniature educational novel. Ilyich slowly comes to recognize that what we all know in theory (that human beings are mortal) is going to happen to *him*. He slowly progresses not only to a recognition of the inevitability of death but to a rejection of his former life and finally to a dim hope for transcendence and even redemption.

Topics for Writing

1. What is the attitude toward death and dying of the main character, Ivan Ilyich, and of the author?
   [Clues to an answer are found in the comments above.]
2. What elements in the story are unrealistic?
   [See the comments above.]
3. Trace the main events and changes in Ivan Ilyich's life discussed above.
   [Details of Ivan Ilyich's earlier life appear in the reminiscences he evokes.]
4. Describe the society implied in the story (the group in the law

courts, the family doctors, the servants). What elements appear to you peculiarly Russian or representative of the late nineteenth century? What elements seem universally applicable?

[However blunt Tolstoy's attack on society and its hypocrisy, his main concern is to emphasize the universal truth of man's mortality and the falseness of living without consciousness of the end.]

Comparative Perspectives

1. Dostoevsky's Underground Man was once a "nasty" and "rude" civil servant, while Tolstoy's Ivan Ilyich prides himself on occasionally letting "the human and official relations mingle." In the hands of writers such as Dostoevsky and Tolstoy, the culture of the bureaucracy became one of the great subjects of nineteenth-century European narrative. How does Tolstoy's depiction of Gerasim's relationship to Ivan Ilyich reinforce our understanding of the evils of governmental systems? Compare the degree and nature of irony in diverse texts that deal with the stifling of imagination promoted by such systems. Include, as appropriate, *A Modest Proposal*, *The Metamorphosis* and *Ladies and Gentlemen, to the Gas Chamber*.

2. *The Death of Ivan Ilyich* offers a devastating portrait of a marriage, a topic that preoccupies modern artists much as adulterous love fascinated their medieval counterparts. What social changes are involved in this shift of interest? As appropriate, diagnose the marital difficulties of the Golovíns and compare them with those in *Hedda Gabler*, *The Dead*, *The Barking* or *Walker Brothers Cowboy*. How do differences in taste relate to differences in class and family background, and how much do they contribute to the problems faced by the couples in these works?

Further Reading

See also the reading suggestions in the *Anthology*, p. 2547.

Maude, Aylmer. *The Life of Tolstoy*. 2 vols. 1917.

Simmons, Ernest J. *An Introduction to Tolstoy's Writings*. 1968. Elementary and informative.

CLUSTER: REVOLUTIONARY PRINCIPLES

Classroom Strategies and Topics for Discussion

This section presents excerpts from some of the nineteenth century's most innovative and influential thinkers, whose ideas continue to exercise a profound impact. Involved in pursuits as widely disparate as zoology, political economy, and ethics, at least four of these writers (Darwin, Marx, Engels, and Nietzsche) completely overhauled their own disciplines, and in so doing necessitated foundational revision of not only those disciplines and their adjacent fields but often of entire ways of conceiving and living in the world. All of them remain controversial to this day.

The first writer here represented is Charles Darwin (1809–1882), with excerpts from his two pivotal works, *The Origin of Species* (1859) and *The Descent of Man* (1871). Darwin himself was a cautious and retiring naturalist, ill-suited to public controversy, and the very public execration from pulpits and universities that greeted these two books required others to speak on behalf of his ideas. Nonetheless, there are ample signs in these excerpts that Darwin was perfectly aware of the passions, usually religious in origin, that his work would ignite, and he tried (unsuccessfully) to deflect or forestall what he accurately predicted would be the principal criticism to which his work would be subjected. One general strategy Darwin engaged to counter any attack is a calm, careful, dispassionate, and systematic exposition of the facts ranged in support of his theories. More particularly, he knew that religious prejudice would be especially offended by the notion of the mutability of species over many, many tens of millions of years, flying as it does in the face of the story told in Genesis. Much would be heard, he rightly thought, about dignity, nobility, and godliness—and of debasement and irreligiosity. With this in mind, he writes:

> To my mind it accords better with what we know of the laws impressed on matter by the Creator, that the production and extinction of the past and present inhabitants of the world should have been due to secondary causes. . . . When I view all beings not as special creations, but as lineal descendants of some few beings which lived long before the Silurian system was deposited, they seem to me to become ennobled. . . . There is grandeur in this view of life, with its several powers, having been originally breathed into a few forms or into one; and that, whilst this planet has been cycling on according to the fixed law of gravity, from so simple a beginning endless forms most beautiful and most wonderful have been, and are being, evolved.

Passages of this sort are to be met with frequently in both works. Of course, they failed to deflect religiously informed attacks, but they show that Darwin was thoroughly aware of the inevitability of such attacks. Students also need to be reminded that geology had only recently been placed on a sound scientific footing, with the publication of Lyell's *Principles of Geology* (1830–1833). Until then the enormous stretches of time in which the planet and its flora and fauna exist had not been firmly established or fully appreciated. The Silurian system (mentioned above) was formed about four hundred million years ago. Traditional orthodox Christian thought, derived from an examination of the Old Testament, held that the earth and all life on it was about four to six thousand years old. Those who first peered into this abyss of deep time so newly opened up were sometimes terrified and often recoiled in denial. However, for Darwin and allied thinkers, these vast stretches of time made the operations of evolution possible. Without Lyell's work, Darwin could never have done his own.

Discussion of the continuing debate between "evolutionists" and "creationists"—a debate that appears to be exclusively American—is probably inevitable. Teachers may or may not be well informed on the theory of evolution—either Darwin or post-Darwinian—and so may well feel some trepidation when entering these currently choppy waters. But teachers must certainly be able to discuss with students what scientists mean when they use the word "theory," and that when they use the word it does not simply mean an educated guess, approximately equal in scientific value to any other educated, or uneducated, guess.

Students may also want to discuss the extension of Darwin's ideas into areas where he never intended their application, such as Herbert Spencer's "social Darwinism." Such a discussion can be used as a bridge to Marx and Engels's social theories, from which the next selection is excerpted.

Karl Marx (1818–1883) and his friend and collaborator Friedrich Engels (1820–1895) published *The Manifesto of the Communist Party* in 1848. The more technical analysis of nineteenth-century industrial culture and laissez-faire economics is in Marx's massive *Capital* (1864–1879). However, most of his ideas are already in place in the *Manifesto*. It often seems as if there are two Marxes: one is a rather dry, post-Enlightenment economist; the other an enthusiastic Romantic propagandist. The propagandist's ideas have their foundations in sober economic analysis, but that analysis is walled off from more fervid revolutionary rhetoric. Engels's own work, such as *The Condition of the Working Class in England* (1845), is usually that of a first-rate, independent investigative journalist. The *Manifesto* is their best-known collaboration. In the excerpt printed in this section, they provide a brief but compelling overview of the historical development of political and economic arrangements from medieval feudalism down to bourgeois capitalism. These arrangements develop dialectically, and in capitalism, the proletariat and the bourgeoisie are related as antithesis to thesis. Students may want to explore Marx's historical and materialist dialectic, which he developed through a reading and critique of Hegel. It would be useful to remind them that Marx himself was a bourgeois intellectual who once had academic ambitions, and that Engels came from a family of wealthy industrialists. Their dialectical method of historical analysis produces the "inevitable" downfall of bourgeois capitalism through a proletariat revolution. Students will want to discuss this "inevitability," especially since the collapse of Soviet communism makes it seem as if bourgeois capitalism is permanently triumphant. They can be brought to see that though the prophecy of capitalist collapse was plainly wrong, or at the very best hugely premature, the analysis of the effects of capitalism on the industrial working class is penetrating and accurate. What Marx and Engels failed to take into account was the meliorism and capacity for change that the trade union movement enforced on the market for industrial labor. The ten-hour workday and regulations against child labor were among the first signs of this trend. By the 1950s in the United States, unionized industrial workers made very good livings under markedly better conditions. Students might be asked to reflect on the implications of the relative collapse of the trade union movement in the United States and the outsourcing of many industrial jobs to nonunionized overseas locations for the long-term survival of the new global capitalism of which Marx and Engels observed the beginnings.

The next excerpt is from Emile Zola's open letter on the Dreyfus affair known as "J'accuse" (1898). This searing indictment of militarist corruption, anti-Semitism, and malfeasance won Zola as many enemies as friends. Students will probably not have read any of Zola's novels about the miserable conditions under which the industrial proletariat lived and worked, though they might be familiar with the musical *Les Miserables*. If that is the only way for teachers to connect your students with Zola, use it. Since students will probably have just read Marx and Engels, you can point out that these novels are like a concrete working-out of Marxist theories concerning the dehumanization and alienation of industrial labor. "J'accuse" has other aims as well. Zola wants the French courts and especially its military tribunals to admit their criminal errors and undo the wrongs they have committed. It seems clear that Zola thought of himself as a patriot, and that he regarded the French republic of his day as the legitimate heir of the high ideals of the French Revolution, with the capacity to right wrongs and ensure that justice be done. That is to say, despite the Marxist tendencies of his fiction, in "J'accuse" he writes as a good bourgeois liberal. Zola thought that the power of conservatism, entrenched in the legislature, the judiciary, the military, and the presidency itself could surely be overturned if public opinion could be mobilized against it. Perhaps he was right, but events in France during the century since the Dreyfus Affair give no cause for optimism.

The excerpts by Friedrich Nietzsche (1844–1900) are from *The Gay Science* (1882). In these famous pages, among other things Nietzsche announces the death of God. The deliberate provocations offered by Nietzsche's writing are likely to inspire useful, if passionate, student reaction. In his views on Pauline Christianity's "slave morality," his attack on the philosophy of ethics, his disdain for European nationalism, his contempt for the hypocritical routines of both inherited religious faith and the binding necessities of professional role-playing, there's something to offend everyone. The issue of Nietzsche's blithe atheism can be used to stand for all that is potentially offensive in these brief excerpts, and it provides a good opportunity to look back at some of the earlier excerpts in this section. Darwin's work was hated and feared by many people with religious commitments, and not only those who persisted in reading Genesis with fanatical literalism. Despite his efforts to placate the religious, it's fairly clear that Darwin's own religious views are deist. His deism is of a standard sort; a refusal to accept an interventionist God yields God as first mover, the framer of the laws of nature that then operate according to their own logic. Mankind evolves under purely material conditions. Marx and Engels are openly atheistic, and they regarded religion as one more instrument of ideological oppression. They extend Darwin's scientific materialism into the analysis of social forces and conditions. The most powerful determinant of human social and political arrangements, and ultimately of consciousness itself, are material economic conditions. Nietzsche inherits all of this, though he has little use for Darwin's plodding deistic science, and he regards the communists and and socialists of his own day as frivolous. The news of God's death, announced in his work by a madman, is accompanied by the accusation that we—the culture of contemporary Europe—have killed him. Of course, we refuse to accept responsibility or admit this to be the case, even while the stench of the divine corpse is everywhere. We've killed God through materialist science and political theory, while persisting in sterile ritualism from the notion that God is somehow necessary to social cohesion and to the maintenance of morality. If students can be brought this far, they can perhaps join Nietzsche in the questioning and overturning of all inherited values.

Samuel Beckett, especially in *Waiting for Godot*, begins from the same position, though his attitude is hardly the same as Nietzsche's. For Beckett, the absence of God—a once-comforting presence who provided meaning and purpose to an otherwise meaningless human condition—is the inevitable and undebatable result of the development of human thought. We may not like it much, but it is undeniable nevertheless.

The writer of the last excerpt in this section is probably the least known among these contributors, the British novelist and essayist Mona Caird (1854–1931). Her contribution, from *The Morality of Marriage* (1897), is an attack on the marriage and property laws prevalent at the time. With this selection, the first-time reader will have seen just about every verity and social institution subjected to withering critique: the theory of special creation, bourgeois capitalism and free-market economics, the integrity of the judiciary and of representative democracy, Christian belief as a basis for morality—the list goes on. Caird attacks another basic social institution, marriage and the family. It seems likely that she had read Engels's *The Origins of the Family, Private Property and the State* (1886), but in any event she cannot wait to hasten the current arrangements on their way. Since her time many of the problems she identifies have been ameliorated, in part because of activists like herself. Students need to be asked if these improvements have gone far enough, and what remains to be done.

Topics for Writing

1. Darwin's defense against his religious critics.
2. Marx and Engels and the "inevitability" of the collapse of capitalism.
3. Nietzsche's critique of Christian ethics.
4. Zola's attack on the military judiciary.
5. Caird's attack on the institution of marriage.

Further Reading

There are no general studies embracing all the writers in this section. Studies of nineteenth-century science are usually separate from studies of nineteenth-century social theory or philosophy. In addition to the materials listed in the *Anthology*, the following three books may be of use:

Chadwick, Owen. *The Secularization of the European Mind in the Nineteenth Century.* 1975.

Himmelfarb, Gertrude. *Darwin and the Darwinian Revolution.* 1959.

Ringer, Fritz. *Education and Society in Modern Europe.* 1979.

Henrik Ibsen

Hedda Gabler

Backgrounds

This is the tragedy of a beautiful, proud woman, the daughter of a general (whose picture presides over the scene). At thirty, in straitened circumstances, she marries George Tesman, a scholar studying "the domestic industries of Brabant in the Middle Ages." To further his research, Tesman takes her on an extended honeymoon trip from their Norwegian town (Christiana, now called Oslo) to the Continent. The play begins with their return home.

They have rented a splendid house in the expectation that Tesman will soon be appointed professor, but this turns out to be uncertain. A rival, Eilert Loevborg, has just published a survey of the history of civilization and might thus win in a competition for the chair. Eilert, however, who has courted Hedda in former times, has a drinking problem, from which he has (for the time being) been rescued by a former schoolmate of Hedda's, Mrs. Thea Elvsted, during a stay in the country. When he returns to town, Thea leaves her husband to follow him, fearing his relapse into alcoholism. As soon as Eilert meets Hedda, he begins to court her again passionately and abandons any idea of challenging Tesman for the professorship. He now dismisses his published work as trivial and is absorbed in writing a book on the future of mankind, the manuscript of which he carries with him.

Hedda is violently jealous of Eilert's relationship with Thea and considers the new abstinence a sign of weakness and of subservience to the other woman. A friend of the house, Judge Brack, arranges a drinking party, which Hedda taunts Eilert into joining. The party is a disaster for Eilert: he gets drunk and late in the night goes off to a brothel, losing his manuscript on the way. When Tesman finds it and brings it back to the house, Hedda in her jealousy burns it. It is somehow, she feels, Eilert and Thea's child. This striking scene ends the third act. In the fourth act, we hear that Eilert has not only gotten into trouble with the police but has killed himself with the pistol that Hedda had given him. The Judge, who also has designs on Hedda, threatens to testify that she supplied Eilert with the pistol unless she gives herself to him. Trapped by her marriage, by the prospect (which she scorns) of bearing Tesman's child, and by the fear of local scandal, she shoots herself.

In his youth, Ibsen had written romantic verse plays such as *Peer Gynt*, but established his reputation as a writer for the stage with his social plays. These advocated causes such as the emancipation of women

(*A Doll's House*) or discussed taboo topics such as hereditary veneral disease (*Ghosts*). *Hedda Gabler*, unlike Ibsen's other plays, seems to have no direct social purpose, unless it is to celebrate the dilemma of the rebellious individual who must die to escape societal constraints. The play, extremely effective on the stage, has allowed many famous actresses to display their art.

Classroom Strategies

The play can be taught in two class periods.

The greatest difficulty of the play lies in explaining the character and behavior of Hedda. We must assume that she is desperate on returning home; hating her dull, somewhat obtuse, and even ridiculous husband; and further disgusted by the prospect of bearing a child—in particular, his child. She is not, however, a blameless heroine. Her playing with the pistol in threatening Judge Brack and later giving one of the two pistols inherited from her father to Eilert, thus practically ordering him to commit suicide, forecasts her own final decision. She behaves with cold contempt toward her husband, with callousness and maliciousness toward his harmless aunt, with cattish jealousy toward Thea, and with violent, domineering passion toward Eilert, who has to prove himself in her eyes by drinking and returning "with a crown of vine-leaves" in his hair. When he fails, she quite unconcernedly sends him to his death. At the same time, she is strangely hemmed in by conventions. She yearns for luxuries—a liveried footman, a thoroughbred horse, a grand piano—and has ambitions to play hostess. She is unwilling to commit adultery, though she flirts with Judge Brack, and she is deeply upset by the prospect of a police investigation and a local scandal. Her main trait is a fierce individualism: pride in her family, her beauty, and her independence. The fear that she might have to yield to Judge Brack is the last straw in motivating her suicide. There is something grotesque and a little sick in her insistence that a beautiful death consists of putting a bullet through the temple and that Eilert has bungled his by shooting himself in the abdomen. Still, we are asked to admire her beauty, pride, and yearning for freedom, and to pity her as the victim of the dull, limited, or cowardly people around her.

The only problematic character besides Hedda is Eilert. We must assume that he is something of a genius. Ibsen contrasts what Eilert sees as Tesman's dull, antiquarian subject with Eilert's allegedly brilliant speculations about the future course of civilization. At least in the imagination of Hedda, he is an almost Dionysian figure, whose collapse and ignominious end come as a terrible blow to her.

The construction of the play demands attention. We may notice the deliberately misleading optimism of the beginning. By the end of Act I, Hedda has bested both her husband and his aunt and by hypocritical blandishments extracted the secret of Thea's relationship with Eilert. In Act II, she proves her power over Eilert by inducing him to join the Judge's party. The act ends with Eilert leaving and the two women,

Hedda and Thea, left alone waiting for his return late into the night. Act III is the turning point, the *peripeteia*, which ends with Hedda burning the manuscript of Eilert's new book. Act IV brings a speedy resolution. The story of the horrible end of Eilert, the disappointing recognition that Eilert's manuscript can be pieced together again from notes preserved by Thea and Hedda's own husband, the threat of Judge Brack all add intensity and suspense to the final moment when, playing "a frenzied dance melody on the piano," Hedda ends her life with a pistol shot. The comments of the two survivors, Tesman screaming "She's shot herself! Shot herself in the head! By Jove! Fancy that!" and Judge Brack's commonsensical "But, good God! People don't do such things!" (p. 1281), make a grotesque, almost parodic point.

Comparative Perspectives

1. Hedda's idealized vision of her father deforms her life. How does Ibsen dramatize General Gabler's enduring control over his daughter? How would you compare the relationship between the Father and the Daughter in Pirandello's *Six Characters in Search of an Author*? Even if not related by blood, many of the female characters represented in the *Anthology* experience quasi-incestuous relations with strong paternal figures. Discuss the attitude toward these relationships in, as appropriate, the *Odyssey* (Nausicaa) or Freud's "Dora."

2. Why does Hedda sit down to play "a frenzied dance melody on the piano" as a prelude to committing suicide? Compare the implication that there is heroic beauty in her act with the treatment of suicide in *Madame Bovary*, or with the tragic but differently motivated suicide that ends *Things Fall Apart*.

Further Reading

See also the reading suggestions in the *Anthology*, p. 2545.

Bentley, Eric. *In Search of Theatre*. 1953. Contains a good chapter on Ibsen.

Brustein, Robert. *The Theatre of Revolt: An Approach to the Modern Drama*. 1964. A survey of modern drama containing chapters on Strindberg, Chekhov, Brecht, Pirandello, and others. Chapter 2 deals with Ibsen.

LeGallienne, Eva. "Preface to Ibsen's *Hedda Gabler*." 1953. Praise from a famous American actress.

Northam, John. *Ibsen's Dramatic Method: A Study of the Prose Dramas*. 1953. Concentrates on Ibsen's stagecraft.

GIOVANNI VERGA

Freedom

Classroom Strategies and Topics for Discussion

Giovanni Verga (1840–1922) made his reputation writing romances but is currently highly regarded because of his later style, which alienated his original audience. The story *Freedom*, first published in 1883, is a good specimen of this later style, which Verga called *verismo* (truthful representation). Students may have already read earlier examples of nineteenth-century realism in the *Anthology*, for instance Flaubert's *Madame Bovary* (1856). Flaubert's focus on the everyday lives of provincial French bourgeoisie is much different, but the intention to represent his materials with the strictest accuracy is the same. Flaubert also pioneered a manner of depicting the psychology and points-of-view of his characters, now called "free indirect discourse," which Verga made his own. In free indirect discourse, the narrative moves with little or no authorial commentary among the points-of-view of a story's characters. At any given moment the reader will be regarding the story not from some objective "outside," but from *inside* the consciousness of a given character. Other writers as diverse as Henry James and Proust adopted the same technique, and it offers the literary historical origins of experimental modernism's "interior monologue" in writers like Joyce or Faulkner. Other features distinguish Verga's *verismo*: a stripped-down, stark spareness, an almost complete absence of any narrative commentary on his story's characters or their actions, and an interest in the lowest socioeconomic segments of society. In much of this he resembles his contemporary, the French naturalist writer Emile Zola. *Freedom* displays all these features. It tells the story of a violent peasant uprising and its equally violent suppression with uncompromising harshness.

Because of the numbness induced by our own blood-drenched cinema, students may not be shocked by this story, but its first readers certainly were. It would be worth spending some time exploring student reactions to the first few pages of this very brief story. The body count in the first two hundred fifty words alone is explicitly five, but implicitly much higher: "The smell of blood made them drunk. Sickles, hands, rags, stones were all dripping with it." The manner in which Verga launches his story without explanation or background leaves a first-time reader completely unprepared for the bloody violence that ensues almost immediately. The narrative makes no attempt to secure a reader's sympathy for the murderous mob of peasants, but some hint of motivation is conveyed by the cries of vengeance uttered as the mob goes about its ghastly work. " 'That's for you, rich pig, who grew so fat on the flesh of the people that you can't even run away!' " In fact, Verga lays some emphasis on the aroused mob's irrational fury, which falls upon the authors of its misery and the completely innocent with equal avidity. After the murder of an eleven-year-old boy, son of the local notary, someone yells: "He would only have grown up a lawyer!" If students can be brought to see these events freshly and in all their horror, than the shock-value of Verga's prose can be revived. The aftermath of this rampage falls on a Sunday, and the same men and women who had killed the priest without mercy the night before gather in front of the church for Mass, and grumble when no service is forthcoming. Student attention might be called to the rich irony of this scene. Then the story comes to a head: "Now it was time for them to share out those woods and those fields. Everyone was adding up on his fingers how big his own portion ought to be, and casting hostile glances at his neighbor." For these peasants, "freedom" means the freedom to own land, to break up the estates of the great landholders. Of course, nothing of the sort transpires; the next day soldiers arrive, and some five or six people, chosen more or less at random, are summarily executed. Then judges arrive, and a whole tedious and incomprehensible legal process is set in motion, in which the hapless peasants are enmeshed. Those judged most responsible are led away to the city for lengthy incarceration, equally lengthy trial, and eventual execution. At first the whole village goes with them, but the villagers can't survive in the city. They return to the lives they had lived before the massacre. "The bigwigs couldn't work their lands by themselves, and the poor couldn't live without the bigwigs." The endless, humiliating, and inexorable trial concludes the story, which is ultimately focused upon the futility of the uprising, not its violence. Students might be questioned on this score; the violence is so overwhelming that they might miss its pointlessness in the midst of its cruelty.

Topic for Writing

1. The representation of violence.
2. Narrative point-of-view.
3. The uprising as retribution; the trial as violence.

Further Reading

See also the reading suggestions in the *Anthology*, p. 2547.

Olga F. M. Lombardi. *Social Awareness and Political Awakening*. 2005.

Tullio Pagano. *Experimental Fictions: From Zola's Naturalism to Verga's Verismo*. 1999.

Guy de Maupassant

Hautot and His Son

Classroom Strategies and Topics for Discussion

Guy de Maupassant (1850–1893) was Flaubert's closest disciple and developed a distinguished mastery of short fiction. This story, first published in 1889, shows in its brevity something of what he could do. Maupassant grew up in Normandy, and this is one of the many stories he wrote about Norman country life. Readers of *Madame Bovary* will recognize some of the scenery. The large, prosperous farmstead strongly resembles Emma's childhood home, and Emma's father, Monsieur Rouault, is the literary precursor of old Hautot. Rouen, the local cathedral city, is where both Emma and old Hautot pursue their respective illicit liaisons. Beyond such details, the chief resemblances are stylistic and technical. Maupassant learned from Flaubert a commitment to realism, with minimal authorial commentary, economy and precision of detail, and clarity of narrative drive. This last is especially important in the short story, where so much has to be done in so few pages. There are other specific narrative techniques in which Maupassant was probably instructed by Flaubert. One, free indirect discourse, has had wide influence on other writers as well (see *Instructor's Guide* on Verga). Another can be called counterpoint, a method of narrating simultaneous events sequentially by cutting back and forth between them, and using the juxtapositioning of these events to provide an implicit commentary on and evaluation of them. In *Madame Bovary*, a good example is the scene at the county fair in which Rodolphe and Emma exchange endearments while speeches and prizes are being given. In this story, the scene in which young Hautot visits his father's mistress and tells her of his father's accidental death while she weeps and his little illegitimate half-brother beats him on the shins and kicks his ankles is a carefully prepared and presented example of the same technique. Student attention can usefully be called to this scene. It is the first time young Hautot has met his father's secret family; he had been unaware of his father's mistress until his father told him about her on his deathbed, and he didn't know about his half-brother's existence until he paid his visit. Young Hautot launches into an elaborately circumstantial narration of his father's hunting accident and death, but the woman is too distraught to understand him, and the child, supposing young Hautot to be the source of his mother's distress, attacks him while he speaks. At her request, he repeats the same elaborately circumstantial narration; because she is calmer the child stands next to her and holds her hand.

Students can be encouraged to tease out the evaluative content implicit in these juxtaposed events. These technicalities have their interest and importance, which it would be hard to overemphasize. But of course, they are in the service of the story as a whole. Maupassant swiftly and vividly limns his principal characters, propels their actions, opens up their personalities and their motivations, and drives his story to its conclusion. Like his master Flaubert, his focus is on the provincial bourgeoisie, and although in this story Maupassant is by some measure less witheringly satirical of his chosen subject than Flaubert, he is just as comprehensively understanding. Students can be asked, for instance, how the story evaluates the character of old Hautot. They can be assisted in assembling the materials and evidences for a convincing answer: the initial description, the conversation with his guests and hunting companions, the shooting accident, the conversation with his son on his deathbed, the refusal to confess to the priest before dying. The same exercise might be carried out with regard to young Hautot, but it will be more difficult, as most of the burden of the story falls emphatically on him. The special issue is his relationship with his father's mistress and her child, his young half-brother. Students will probably need to be reminded how equivocal their position is. She has some kind of a job, but it probably doesn't amount to much, and as a single woman and an unmarried mother, let alone the mistress of a prosperous farmer, she is socially beyond the pale. Old Hautot's death leaves her and her son without protection or resources. As an illegitimate child he has no legal claim on his father's estate. The old man could have remediated this in a will, but for reasons detailed on his deathbed (and perhaps others) did not. Students need to see how few alternatives she has, and young Hautot presents himself as one of them, so long as she can overcome her grief and fear, muster her considerable charm, as well as her talents as a cook, and enlist her child in the effort to attract his sympathies and attentions. All of this she is apparently able to do; the offer to him of his father's pipe after the meal is done is a none-too-subtle transfer. A vista of a lifetime of Thursday afternoon assignations opens up before young Hautot. But Maupassant refuses the reader any easy satisfactions; the story is scrupulously open-ended. Students might be encouraged to question the legitimacy of its conclusion.

Topics for Writing

1. Re-tell this story from the point of view of the mistress.
2. Discuss the manner in which this story evaluates its characters and their actions.
3. Argue for or against the propriety and effectiveness of the open-ended conclusion.

Further Reading

See also the suggestions in the *Anthology*, p. 2546.

David Bryant. *The Rhetoric of Pessimism and the Strategies of Containment in the Short Stories of Maupassant*. 1993.

Laurence Gregorio. *Maupassant's Fiction and the Darwinian View of Life*. 2005.

ANTON CHEKHOV

The Lady with the Dog

Classroom Strategies and Topics for Discussion

Short fiction has a very long history, but the short story itself is a modern form. If your students have read some of the ancient and medieval tales in the first volume of the *Anthology*, a good way to begin your discussion of *The Lady with the Dog* is to ask how the genre differs from its ancient precursors. The fantasy of Lucian's *A True Story*, for example, is a lot closer to a work like *Candide* than it is to Chekhov, and densely plotted fabliaux and tales like Boccaccio's do not aim at the kind of psychological subtlety we find in *The Lady with the Dog*. Other short fiction closer in time, like Pushkin's *Queen of Spades*, with its intermingling of irony and the supernatural, or *The Death of Ivan Iliych*, with its moral agenda and visible closure, would make especially good contrasts. Discovering what makes Chekhov's story special will help students deal with the complex conciousness and unresolved plots of many recent short narratives, like those of Alice Munro. Often called "New Yorker stories" after the magazine that has published so much apparently indeterminate and open-ended fiction, these subtle works challenge students. Once it is understood that they portray experience in ways much more like "real life" than do the older fictional forms, your class can get to the heart of Chekhov's accomplishment.

Ask your students, too, how many of the writers in the *Anthology* are represented by selections from two different genres; Chekhov's experience as a playwright explains much about his narrative technique. As a dramatist, he is the least moralizing of storytellers. In both genres, he emphasizes character and action in the expectation that his audience will respond to what it observes and draw its own conclusions. Unlike other dramatists, Chekhov's plays are known, as the headnote in the *Anthology* points out, for their naturalistic scenes and their seeming plotlessness—but plot is there in abundance, waiting to be uncovered in the inner lives of his characters, if not in loud, definitive, stagy confrontation scenes. Students may first think that Chekhov's story similarly lacks form and punch.

He filters *The Lady with the Dog* through Gurov's consciousness without abandoning the objectivity of the third-person narrator and certainly uses physical detail as any conventional narrator would. It is, as always, helpful to ask your students to comment on the implications of character descriptions. *The Lady with the Dog* deals with its secondary characters in this traditional way, with the intellectual pretensions of Gurov's tall wife somehow corroborated by her dark eyebrows, and the servility of Anna Sergeyevna's husband captured by his side-whiskers, bald spot, and badge. We have no difficulty understanding why the protagonists of the story find their marriages unsatisfying. Anna Sergeyevna herself is initially subjected to this reductive descriptive technique: her toque, her lorgnette, even—perhaps especially—her Pomeranian dog tell us that she is seen, and perhaps sees herself, in terms of social images.

Gurov himself is the center of the story, and you will probably want to spend some time on the paragraphs that establish his character as the story begins, when we still see him from the outside: "bored and ill-at-ease in the company of men," he is not particularly interested in his work at a bank. Alone at a seaside resort, he seems a typical man-about-town. His thoughts as he enters Anna Sergeyevna's room for the first time confirm this impression of him, as he idly categorizes the different varieties of women he has known. Thus well into the second section of the story, we see that Anna Sergeyevna does not mean a great deal to him.

Yet as the story develops, and Gurov ceases to be the bored, judgmental sensualist, we recall again the playwright's art. Physical details seem to become symbolic, suggestive in the way that stage effects can be. The scene changes, as in a play, deserve some attention: what is the mood of a seaside resort? Why do casual affairs characterize a place like Yalta? How do the long paragraphs devoted to the roaring of the sea at Oreanda and Gurov's meditation as he watches Anna Sergeyevna's train depart and feels that "he had only just awakened" begin to shift the mood of the story? We realize here, in the reflections that recall so many of the great romantic nature poems that would work well in combination with Chekhov's story, that he is capable of a deep and thoughtful response to the world around him.

Were Gurov just a roué, the return to Moscow would be the end of this liaison. "It's time for me to be going north," he thinks, presumably to a colder, brisker world of reason. But the introduction to part III of the story may upset the reader's expectations; this is a Russian story, and the romance of the snow on the lime trees and birches has a spiritual resonance that undercuts the notion of a return to reality. Only when the lovers are separated do they recognize that something remarkable has happened to them.

When Gurov pursues Anna Sergeyevna in the provincial theater—a place where the playwright rules—they move out of the public eye to stand "on a dark narrow staircase over which was a notice bearing the inscription 'To the upper circle.' " How does that directional sign forecast the higher aspirations toward which their relationship has surprisingly led? How does Gurov's "double life," embarked on once Anna Sergeyevna begins her secret visits to Moscow, begin in the moment of stepping out of the stalls and into the stairwell? Why should her excuse to her husband be that she is being treated by a specialist in "female diseases"? Is this a lie?

Chekhov's story never analyzes why the feelings of these two people change, yet the weight of the transformation weighs upon us as it does on them. Ask your students to try to explain the difference between the first visit to a hotel room, where Gurov rather unfeelingly eats his watermelon, and the one with which the story concludes, in which Anna Sergeyevna weeps as she drinks tea. The parallel actions announce how much has in fact been transformed, a realization that is capped when Gurov glimpses himself in the mirror and discovers the pathos of his and his lover's mortality. The narrator then offers the simile of the migrating birds to reinforce the character's sudden perception. How much does a rhetorical device intended to explain through comparison explain? How are all human beings like migrating birds caught in cages? Why should this figure of speech lead to the information that "they forgave one another all that they were ashamed of in the past and in the present"?

Would this be a better story if it ended by telling us that Anna Sergeyevna ran off with Gurov and that they quarreled? Or that their respective spouses died and they remarried and lived happily ever after? Or that discovery brought shame to Anna Sergeyevna but only a temporary inconvenience to Gurov? Does a transcendent moment of melancholy and pity, such as that experienced by Gurov as the story closes, last? Questions like these will probably elicit a good deal of class discussion, and in effect, that discussion will prove the wisdom of Chekhov's narrative reticence.

Topics for Writing

1. How does Chekhov use seasonal change in shaping his narrative? [If you have also assigned *The Cherry Orchard*, you can expand this topic to cover both works, of course.]
2. Both of the leading characters in this story find themselves taking steps that would have been inconceivable to them when we first meet them. Describe the ways in which Chekhov conveys their transformation. Which do you think undergoes the more profound change? Why?

Comparative Perspectives

1. Compare and contrast Tolstoy's Ivan Ilyich and Chekhov's Gurov. What are their lives initially like? How and why do they change? What is the meaning of each story's ending?
2. Compare Flaubert's novelistic treatment of adultery with Chekhov's in *The Lady with the Dog*.
   a. Look, for example, at the description of Rodolphe's way of placing Emma as one among his many conquests in chapters XII and XIII in part two of *Madame Bovary*. What does Flaubert reveal about the workings of his mind that would make it impossible for him to change, as does Gurov, although he initially "places" Anna Sergeyevna as one type of woman he has known as well?
   b. Or compare the youthful Anna Sergeyevna with the equally inexperienced Emma Bovary. Which qualities does Flaubert underline in his portrait of Emma that make her so easy to corrupt?
3. Comment on the description of Oreanda in section II of *The Lady with the Dog* and compare the treatment of a similar romantic landscape in Lamartine's *The Lake*. How does the sensibility of the scientifically trained Chekhov differ from Lamartine's (as in the reflection that "this continuity, this utter indifference of life and death" holds "the secret of our ultimate salvation")?

Further Reading

See also the reading suggestions in the *Anthology*, p. 2544.

Johnson, Ronald L. *Anton Chekhov: A Study of the Short Fiction*. 1993. One in the Twayne's Studies in Short Fiction series, this book has a good discussion of narrative perspective in *The Lady with the Dog*.

The Cherry Orchard

Backgrounds

Chekhov's plays have the reputation of being plotless, static, a mere string of scenes held together by a mood. But this is not true of Chekhov's last play, *The Cherry Orchard*, which has a clear plot line: Madame Lubov Ranevskaya returns to her estate in the provinces of Russia after an absence of five years. With her are her seventeen-year-old daughter, Anya; a governess, Charlotta; and a footman, Yasha. They are greeted by the brother of Lubov, Leonid Gayev; a maid, Dunyasha; and a merchant, Yermolay Lopahin, who is the son of a serf on the estate, but who has made money—even become wealthy—cultivating poppies. He soon reminds the arrivals that the estate will be up for sale unless they can raise the money to pay the heavy debts. The great cherry orchard will have to be cut down to make room for country houses. It is spring now: the orchard is in bloom, all white, a symbol for Lubov of the innocence of her childhood, which she betrayed when, after the death of her husband and the accidental drowning of her other child, a son named Grisha, she left for Paris with a lover, who has since robbed and betrayed her.

The second act in the open air provides relief in an idyllic setting. The "eternal" student Petya Trofimov, who was the tutor of the drowned boy, courts Anya and grandiloquently talks about the backwardness of Russia and the bright future of humanity. The merchant Lopahin reminds Lubov of the impending sale, which she faces helplessly.

The third act is the turning point. Recklessly, just on the day of the auction, Lubov gives a dance: at the end, Lopahin comes back from town and awkwardly announces that he has bought the estate when another bidder seemed about to acquire it. He has paid ninety thousand rubles for it above the mortgage.

The fourth act returns to the scene of the first, the nursery, where the company assembles, ready to depart. Lubov and her brother have somewhat recovered from the blow of the sale. Lubov is returning to Paris to look after her ill lover, who has been bombarding her with telegrams. Leonid has gotten a job in the local bank. Anya will go to Moscow to study. The house will be locked and eventually demolished. We hear the sound of the axes cutting down the cherry orchard.

Classroom Strategies

The play has four acts; two assignments should suffice.

The most controversial question, still being debated, concerns the pervasive tone of the play. Is it a tragedy or, as Chekhov insisted, a comedy? The headnote in the *Anthology* discusses the issue at length. There is an undoubted pathos in the sale of the estate and in the situation of old Firs being left alone in the abandoned house. (It is possible but not necessary, however, to think of him as dying. We may surmise that Lopahin, who goes off to Kharkov, instructs his clerk Yepihodov to look after the house.) There is also sadness in the passing of the old order, in the destruction of the beautiful orchard, and in the acquisition of the estate by an upstart developer. The end can be seen as an example of the twilight of Tsarist Russia or, more accurately, of its landowning class.

But the economic and social themes are made purely personal and possibly trivial by the passive resignation of Lubov, who feels that she must pay for her sins, and even more by the grotesque fecklessness of her brother, Leonid. Though Lubov can say that without the cherry orchard life has no meaning for her, she accepts the solution. Her brother says that "we all calmed down, and even felt quite cheerful." Lubov, in fact, is sleeping and feeling well and is now off to Paris to live on the money of a great aunt, money that she knows will not last long. There are so many comic and even farcical characters and scenes in the play that the gloom of the main event is considerably lightened.

Anya, a serious decent girl, is the only character not ridiculed. Even Trofimov, the student who courts her and who pronounces famous, grandiloquent speeches on the backwardness of Russia and the need for expiating the sufferings of the serfs in the past, is himself a good-for-nothing who has never done any work. His speech promising a bright future for mankind sounds hollow, as does his pompous assertion of being "above love." Lubov punctures this boast by scolding him: "At your age not to have a mistress!" The relationship with Anya fizzles out.

Lubov's brother, Leonid Gayev, is similarly a figure of fun: effete, limited, even stupid. He drinks and eats and talks too much, telling the waiters quite inappropriate stories of the decadents in Paris. He plays imaginary games of billiards on all occasions, loudly giving commands in the jargon of the game. The adopted daughter of Lubov, Varya, is a poor, awkward spinster who spoils her last chance of marrying Lopahin in a painful scene in which she speaks of a broken thermometer. Charlotta, the governess, performs card tricks, practices ventriloquism, and lugs a nut-eating dog around. The neighboring landowner with the comic double name Simeonov-Pishchik (something like Squealer) is as broke and irrepressible as the owners of the cherry orchard, but is rescued by an Englishman turning up out of the blue to pay him for the lease of some white clay found on his estate. Having swallowed a whole box of pills of Lubov's, he suddenly falls asleep and talks knowingly about Nietzsche's advocating the forging of bank-notes. The clerk, Semyon Yepihodov, is an even more grotesque figure. He is unlucky, constantly knocks over things, finds a cockroach in his drink, and quite irrelevantly drops the name of Buckle, a British historian. The maid, Dunyasha, is a foolish girl in love with the one definitely repulsive character, the valet, Yasha. Firs, the old man-servant who remembers with nostalgia the days of serfdom, is a pathetic figure, hard of hearing, shuffling, ludicrous in his loneliness. One has to conclude that the play is a mixture of comedy and pathos.

Topics for Discussion

1. Consider the picture of Russia at the turn of the century: the play presents the landed gentry with their hangers-on and servants, the new merchant-developers risen from the serf class, and the ineffectual, verbose student intelligentsia.

2. The technique of the play deserves discussion, especially the contrasts of the four acts. These take place during spring, summer, a day in August, and, shortly after, the day of departure. The white bloom of the cherry trees in Act I is juxtaposed against the sound of the axes felling them in Act IV. Action shifts quickly from one speaker to another, and small incidents interrupt any semblance of a continuous argument or mood.

Topics for Writing

1. Is the play a tragedy or a comedy? How does Russia look, as seen in this play? What message is implied, if there is one?

   [Chekhov's attitude is not that of a reformer or revolutionary, but is also not reactionary. It is an attitude of deep human sympathy for almost everybody, coupled with a dim hope for progress. While extravagance is obviously condemned and the merchant, Lopahin, depicted favorably (as Chekhov's letters insist), the playwright also excuses real passion, even guilty passion—or at least shows understanding for it.]

2. Can one define the role of symbolism in this play?

   [The cherry orchard dominates, obviously. More puzzling is the sound of the broken string. This, when it first sounds out of doors in Act III, is explained as possibly caused by the fall of a bucket in a distant mine or perhaps as the cry of a heron or the hooting of an owl, but its unexplained repetition at the very end of the play (p. 1333) has a weird, ominous effect. Attempts have been made to trace it to a childhood memory of Chekhov's or more simply to the general superstition that a broken string, say on a guitar, presages ill luck or even death.]

Comparative Perspectives

1. In setting the scenes for his play, Chekhov kept the cherry orchard out of sight, yet it dominates the stage action. What exactly is threatened and then lost—and what is gained—by cutting down the cherry trees? Literature through the ages presents many other such cherished but often doomed orchards, forests, and fields. As appropriate, compare the symbolic functions of Chekhov's orchard with those of the Cedar Forest in *Gilgamesh*; the Garden of Eden in the Jewish, Christian, and Islamic traditions; the wilderness in *The Bear*; and/or the woods in *Matryona's Home*.

2. Readers (as opposed to spectators) often fail to appreciate the impact that stage music has on a theater audience. The famous

"sound of a snapping string" heard in *The Cherry Orchard* is only one in a pattern of sounds and songs woven throughout. Discuss the different functions of music here and in other plays.

[Possibilities include Greek choral odes and the various musical interludes in *Faust*, *Six Characters in Search of an Author*, and *The Good Woman of Setzuan*.]

Further Reading

See also the reading suggestions in the *Anthology*, p. 2544.

Barricelli, Jean-Pierre, ed. *Chekhov's Great Plays: A Critical Anthology*. 1981.

Chekhov, Anton. *Anton Chekhov's Plays*. A Norton Critical Edition. Trans. and ed. Laurence Senelick. 2005. Contains several useful critical essays.

Hingley, Ronald. *Chekhov: A Biographical and Critical Study*. 1950; 1966.

Magarshack, David. *Chekhov the Dramatist*. 1951; 1960. Has a chapter arguing for the comedy of *The Cherry Orchard*.

Valency, Maurice. *The Breaking String*. 1966. A general study of Chekhov's themes.

CHARLES BAUDELAIRE

The Flowers of Evil *and* Paris Spleen

Backgrounds

His contemporaries would have been amazed to know that Charles Baudelaire, a dandyish Parisian poet and art critic whose disturbing *Flowers of Evil* earned him a court fine in 1857, would continue to inspire writers, critics, and even rock groups for more than a century after his death. Baudelaire's fascination with questions of good and evil, his passion to explore the unknown (especially forbidden topics), his combination of crude realism and escapist dreams, and the insistent sensuality of his tormented love relationships strike chords in readers everywhere. These are not necessarily pleasant chords, despite occasional peaceful and harmonious lyrics, for Baudelaire distrusts prettiness. He tries to shock us into clearer insights by undermining conventional attitudes: addressing his beloved as a potentially rotting carcass in *A Carcass*, or accusing his reader of being—like himself—full of vices and fundamentally hypocritical. Baudelaire's modern appeal, however, derives from more than shock effects. Speaking from his own anguished subjectivity, the poet describes broadly human concerns: the fear of death and decay, the need for love, a painful alienation from others and from society. In response, he desires to create beauty, to understand the relationships between things ("correspondences"), and to find answers. Such themes are reinforced by a precise and disciplined style that coordinates classical meter and rhyme schemes with extraordinarily subtle interrelationships of images, associations, and logically developed argument.

To the Reader functions as a traditional preface, introducing the book's themes and establishing a common ground with its reader; however, there convention stops. This preface is also a direct attack on the reader, who is included—along with the poet—in a lurid sermon on human sin. The catalogue of sins culminates unexpectedly in "BOREDOM," seen as a destructive apathy that is worse than conventional vices because it refuses to become involved and merely "swallows the world in a yawn" (see note 5, *To the Reader*, in the *Anthology*). Images of the devil as scientist in his laboratory boiling off human willpower, or as puppet master controlling our strings, underscore this fundamentally religious vision in which free will is of paramount importance. The riddling eighth stanza launches a long, five-line sentence suggesting that one supreme sin remains to be mentioned. That sin is finally identified as boredom, described literally as a chain-smoking beast. In a line that continues to be quoted to this day, the poet accuses himself and his reader of complicity in this worst of evils.

Correspondences is an anchor point in Baudelaire's work, a classically perfect alexandrine sonnet proclaiming that everything is interconnected (corresponds) at a subterranean level that the poet, a seer, is specially qualified to perceive. Baudelaire insists on connectedness throughout, repeating the French word *comme* ("like" or "as") six times in the two middle stanzas; moreover, he strengthens the impact of this link-work by giving the word two syllables instead of the usual one. (In classical French verse, the mute *e* is sounded separately when it precedes a consonant.)

The sonnet develops its argument in logical stages of hypothesis, explanation, and illustration. At the beginning, nature is seen as quasi-divine, a living temple in which only humankind wanders blindly. In this basic unity of all life, explains the second stanza, the senses—or, more specifically, "scents and sounds and colors"—are fused (literally, "answer one another"). The third stanza offers examples of these five reciprocal senses in perfumes (*smell*) that are fresh as (literally) a child's flesh (*touch*), sweet as oboes (*taste* and *hearing*) and green as prairies (*sight*). The overwhelming tones of youth and immaturity in these images prefigure the maturing of perfume images into rich, overripe ("corrupt"), expansive odors that dizzy and transport the senses. It is this ecstasy of the mind and senses that fascinates Baudelaire, and it is a motif he will evoke in different images throughout his poetry.

In the love poem *Her Hair*, Baudelaire celebrates his mistress's head of hair as another route to ecstasy. The poet's recurrent theme of the *voyage* blends with erotic escapism as Jeanne Duval's tresses become a perfumed sea of ebony, a black ocean whose sensual pleasure invites him to dream of a sea voyage to exotic tropical climes. (Compare the less erotic but similarly ecstatic voyage in *Invitation to the Voyage*.) This richly colorful dream dominates the whole situation, for clearly Jeanne herself—hair, oasis, and gourd of wine—disappears under the weight of the dream-evocation she has inspired.

A *Carcass* intends to shock the reader with its brutal description of an animal carcass swarming with maggots—a carcass, moreover, that the poet ends by comparing with the woman he loves. The contrast of ideal femininity and physical mortality was familiar to the Romantics; Baudelaire is treading familiar paths when he parodies Petrarchan imagery ("star of my eyes," etc.) and the *carpe diem* tradition (claiming in the last stanza that he is "the keeper for corpses of love / Of the form, and the essence divine!"). He has pulled off a surprising poetic gamble, nonetheless, in transforming images of decay into images of new life; the hum of flies and maggots into the more acceptable music of waves, running water, wind, or a thresher winnowing grain. By this transformation, the poet has demonstrated the power of artistic imagination (eighth stanza) before returning to the cruder image of the hungry dog and the final, aggressive emphasis on universal decay—inevitable for all but the art of poetry.

Invitation to the Voyage, written for Marie Daubrun, is celebrated for the musicality of its verse and the peaceful beauty of its visionary trip to an idealized Holland: the Holland of Dutch interiors painted by Vermeer, for example, or the Holland that collected objects of Eastern splendor through its seafaring empire. It is a dream of harmony, as embodied by a woman addressed as "child" or "sister" rather than the erotic images of other love poems. This harmony is also the profound unity of *Correspondences*, in which beautiful sensuous images combine to address the soul in its sweet and secret native tongue.

Song of Autumn I is the first of two short poems written in October 1859; the second poem is a love poem addressed to Marie Daubrun. The scene is Paris; winter approaches, and Baudelaire (who detests cold) hears the customary October delivery of cordwood in the courtyard. Wintry passions will enter his soul. His heart, chilled to a frozen red block by despair and hard work, is compared to a setting sun frozen in its own arctic hell. The poem is especially accessible through the ascending sequence of images based on the sound of falling logs: Baudelaire imagines the regular thumps as the construction of an executioner's scaffold, the blows of a battering ram destroying a tower, or nails being driven into a coffin. Autumn's dull knocking does not announce an arrival; instead, it heralds a departure into winter and, by association, death.

The three *Spleen* poems included in the *Anthology* evoke this same melancholy in an even more concentrated fashion. They may be taught individually or as a group, expressing different facets of the speaker's alienation and despair. You may wish to compare the bitterness of Dostoevsky's narrator in *Notes from Underground*. Like *Song of Autumn I*, each *Spleen* employs both realistic details and larger abstract or fantastic visions, and each depicts a progression of images. The best-known, *Spleen LXXXI*, pursues a series of confinement images from covered pot, dungeon, and barred prison to the enclosures of brain and skull. A series of water-related images dwindling gradually from city to playing cards characterizes *Spleen LXXVIII*, while the first half of *Spleen LXXIX* accumulates images of the dead past to evoke the poet's numb despair at the meaningless passage of time. Before students become too discouraged by the theme of gray misery, remind them that these are virtuoso performances, developments on a theme, just as is the peaceful dream of *Invitation to the Voyage*. Baudelaire considers it a kind of redemption to be able "to produce a few beautiful verses" (*One O'Clock in the Morning*), and he finds in art a counterweight to the boredom and sense of helplessness called *spleen*.

The Voyage assumes a number of familiar Romantic themes, such as the deception of everyday life in a world too petty and cramped for the human spirit, the desire to escape by traveling to exotic and unknown realms, and the lure of the infinite. Although contemporary students may be struck chiefly by its colorful allegories of the human condition, its attack on organized religion (VI, lines 97–100) and on political structures (VI, lines 95–96) was so pointed that the poem was rejected by the journal scheduled to publish it. Writing to his friend Charles Asselineau on February 20, 1859, Baudelaire predicted that *The Voyage* would cause "nature to shudder, and especially lovers of progress."

The poem's eight sections fall into three general movements: the first describing a human craving (felt already in childhood) to voyage toward an intuited ideal realm (I–V), the second depicting the sin and corruption that the traveler encounters everywhere on earth (VI), and the final sequence reiterating the experienced traveler's compulsion to continue—along with the traveler's realization that the voyage leads beyond mortal experience and into the only remaining unknown region, death.

Although there are scattered examples of short poetic works written in prose before Baudelaire, the appearance in 1862 of twenty-one *Little Poems in Prose (Paris Spleen)* by the French poet marked the first time that the genre had been named as such. For Baudelaire, these poems filled a different role from *The Flowers of Evil*: based in everyday experience, they offered a broad range of "impressions of the street, Parisian events and horizons, sudden starts of consciousness, languorous daydreams, philosophy, dreams themselves, and even anecdotes." In his dedication, he envisioned the ideal prose poem as a "poetic prose that would be musical without rhythm or rhyme, supple yet irregular enough to adapt to the lyric movements of the soul, to fluctuations of reverie, to sudden starts of consciousness." The prose poem is no less poetic for not being written in verse; it manifests the same internal rhythm and intricate organization of theme and image that we associate with lyric poetry. In Baudelaire's eyes, this supple and rhythmic prose was uniquely suited to expressing shifts of consciousness. It is easy to see how not only poets but also twentieth-century novelists exploiting stream-of-consciousness techniques (e.g., James Joyce, Virginia Woolf, and William Faulkner) are indebted to Baudelaire's example.

Classroom Strategies

Two days will allow you to give a good sense of what Baudelaire is about and why he has been such a powerful influence on later literature; three days will allow you to look closely at a number of poems. There are several ways to enter the subject, depending on your own and your students' preferences. The autobiographical stance of the four prose poems makes them especially accessible to students who are "afraid of poetry," and they allow easy entry into Baudelaire's characteristic themes. The picture of the harassed poet alienated from a commercialized society (*One O'Clock in the Morning*) is a familiar theme, to be paired with the escape wish in *Anywhere Out of the World* (students appreciate the humorous realism of the hospital image, too). Alternately, you may wish to begin with the longer thematic poems (*The Voyage* and *A Carcass*) and move to a selection of shorter lyric pieces. Another possibility might be to structure the days according to selected thematic contrasts ("Spleen and Ideal," a grouping in *The Flowers of Evil*; or dream and reality, beauty and ugliness, escape and a feeling of being trapped, eroticism and childlike harmony).

Topics for Discussion

1. Baudelaire combines aspects associated with realism and with Romanticism. How far can he be considered as belonging to the age of realism? In what ways may he be considered a Romantic? Discuss this in light of the general introductions to the relevant sections.
2. Discuss the theme of the *voyage* throughout Baudelaire's poetry.
3. Discuss the appearance of an urban (as opposed to rural or pastoral) sensibility in Baudelaire's poetry.
4. Baudelaire is often claimed as the first Symbolist poet, although Symbolism as such did not develop until much later in the century. What elements in his poetry support this claim?
5. Compare and contrast the world represented by Baudelaire's speaker with the world represented by (1) Petrarch's speaker, (2) Pope's speaker in *The Rape of the Lock*, (3) the narrator in *Notes from Underground*.
6. How are women imagined and characterized in the poems you read? What attitude is implied? Is it dual or contradictory? Does Baudelaire give similar weight to the description of men? Compare the picture of women in Baudelaire and in (choose) (1) Pope's *The Rape of the Lock*, (2) Voltaire's *Candide*, (3) Goethe's *Faust*. What definitions of womanliness are depicted, affirmed, or criticized in each work?
7. Discuss the themes of art and of the role of the artist in Baudelaire's poetry. You may wish to compare your findings with similar themes in Wordsworth, Coleridge, Keats, and Shelley.

Further Reading

See also the reading suggestions in the *Anthology*, p. 2544.

Auerbach, Erich. "The Aesthetic Dignity of *Les Fleurs du Mal.*" In *Scenes from the Drama of European Literature: Six Essays.* 1959. Impressive stylistic analysis.

Benjamin, Walter. *Charles Baudelaire: A Lyric Poet in the Era of High Capitalism.* Trans. Harry Zohn. 1973. An imaginative theoretical treatment by a forerunner of deconstructionist criticism. See also the chapter on Baudelaire in his *Illuminations* (1968).

Bersani, Leo. *Baudelaire and Freud.* 1977. An interesting discussion of Baudelaire's poetry, arranged according to Freudian terminology.

Caws, Mary Ann, and Hermine Riffaterre, eds. *The Prose Poem in France: Theory and Practice.* 1983. Studies in the French prose poem from Baudelaire to modern times.

Eliot, T. S. "Baudelaire." 1930. In *Selected Essays.* 1932. A discussion focused on Baudelaire's religious views.

Porter, Laurence M. "Baudelaire's Fictive Audiences." In *The Crisis of French Symbolism.* 1990. Includes psychoanalytic perspectives in a discussion of Baudelaire's attempts to communicate with differently imagined audiences.

Poulet, Georges. *Exploding Poetry: Baudelaire/Rimbaud.* Trans. Françoise Meltzer. 1984. Contains an extended essay on Baudelaire's consciousness or worldview by a major phenomenological critic.

Raymond, Marcel. *From Baudelaire to Surrealism.* 1957, reprinted 1961. A major critical work that contains a discussion of Baudelaire and his influence on modern poetry.

Rees, Garnet. *Baudelaire, Sartre and Camus: Lectures and Commentaries.* 1976. A brief volume of accessible, popularized lectures.

Sharpe, William Chapman. *Unreal Cities: Urban Figuration in Wordsworth, Baudelaire, Whitman, Eliot, and Williams.* 1990. An interesting discussion of Baudelaire and other city-oriented poets of the modern age.

STÉPHANE MALLARMÉ

Backgrounds

Like Baudelaire, whom he admired, Stéphane Mallarmé wrote in a variety of forms: verse and prose poetry, translations of Edgar Allan Poe, and theoretical works that often began as reflections on theater and ballet performances. A sociable man, he composed delightful "occasional" poems for his friends: conversational quatrains written on fans, or composed as a postal address and (successfully) sent by mail. For awhile, he even edited a small fashion magazine. A poorly paid teacher of English, he tried to earn money and gain credit in the French national educational system by writing a book on English words, a manual for the review of English parts of speech, and by translating a mythology manual for the schools. In short—and unlike his Symbolist peers—Mallarmé was embedded in the conventional society of his time: and yet he was also "Prince of Poets" and is remembered today for a small number of finely crafted poems that are the most intellectual, the most impersonal, and the most abstract of Symbolist literature. Life and beauty exist in these poems, but "elsewhere," in a new dimension of interlocking allusions that uses everyday reality only as a point of departure.

Saint, written in the same year that Mallarmé began *The Afternoon of a Faun* (1865), is a deceptively simple and appealing short lyric that hints at coexisting levels of reality. A poem of extreme delicacy, it uses subtly interwoven images to suggest alternately presence and absence—as do many of Mallarmé's poems. It was written as an occasional poem for the saint's day of a friend, Cécile Brunet, and he called it "a little melodic poem composed especially with music in mind." Indeed, it was set to music by Maurice Ravel in 1896. The *Anthology* headnote discusses the poem's remarkable unity (one sentence from beginning to end; two overlapping scenes of contrasting nature) and the fact that the poem's original title ("Saint Cecilia Playing on the Wing of an Angel") is illustrated by the imaginary harp evoked in the third stanza. The play of presence and absence emerges from the ingenious manner in which physical images first appear and then are taken away; the viol described through the first stanza, for example, exists but cannot be seen—it is concealed by the window frame; the gilt on the sandalwood *used* to shine but is now peeling away; a mandolin and flute are mentioned, but only as accompanying the viol in *former* concerts—they also are now absent. The missal's music used to sound (or *flow*, a visual image) at services, but now it is now absent; the harp evoked by the angel's wing at sunset (or by the shape of its cast shadow) exists only in the imagination. The cumulative play of all these images prepares and justifies the otherwise impossible concluding image of a "musician of silences." References to music are not casual in Mallarmé: in *Music and Letters*, major lectures delivered at Oxford and Cambridge in 1894, he explains that the aim of the new French poetry is "the musicality of everything," and adds (alluding obliquely to German idealist philosophy) "Music and Letters are the alternate face . . . of a single phenomenon I call the Idea."

The Afternoon of a Faun, a faun's dimly recalled erotic dream of a passionate pursuit, also treats themes of music, absence, and poetic creation. In dramatic monologue of some density, the italicized passages represent the dream itself, and the body of the poem recounts the faun's attempt to understand his situation. Awakening with troubled feelings and mysterious tooth marks on his chest, he alternately recapitulates his dream and evokes it in a musical solo on the reed pipe (16–22, 42–62). The dream is unabashedly lustful (as in conventional scenes of satyrs and nymphs): the faun remembers cutting reeds for his pipes, coming across two sleeping nymphs, and passing immediately to an attempted double rape. Awake, he lasciviously imagines seeing the nymphs naked once more, sucks the juice from clusters of grapes held high, and, reeling with passion and wine, reaches a peak of desire in which he imagines seizing the goddess of love herself—only to fall back, chastised and sleepy, ready to go back into the dream and find the nymphs again.

Both *The Tomb of Edgar Poe* and *The Virginal, Vibrant, and Beautiful Dawn* are more direct in their evocation of poetic language and the plight of the poet. The *Anthology* headnote and related footnotes cover important allusions in these poems, including a brief explanation of how Mallarmé came to write a tribute to Poe. The Symbolists venerated the American poet as a precursor: they respected his theory of willed, craftsmanlike creation in "The Philosophy of Composition" and his portrayal of beauty, excess, mystery, and death. Unlike most American readers, they also admired the rhythm and melody of his verse. (See also the headnote to Baudelaire.) Poe filled, moreover, a sympathetic role in Romantic and Symbolist tradition as the misunderstood genius, the "accursed poet" scorned by the vulgar crowd. The famous line in the *Tomb* that describes Poe's writing as "bestow[ing] a purer sense on the language of the horde" (using everyday words in combinations that together evoke a different or transcendent meaning) probably fits the Symbolists' concept of poetic language more than it does that of Poe, nonetheless. The figure of an exiled poet reigns in both sonnets; in the first, the poet is the victim of slander; in the second, more abstract poem, the metaphor of a swan represents the poet trapped in his impossible search for perfection. For the Symbolists, and especially for Mallarmé, poetic language achieves perfection through combinations and allusion—through *signs* pointing to each other and to a purer realm. The so-called "swan sonnet" reinforces this emphasis on poetic language when it concludes with a capitalized Swan that (in French) is simultaneously heard as Sign (*Cygne/Signe*).

Classroom Strategies

The four poems printed here are a good introduction to Mallarmé's characteristic play of images and concept of poetic language; you may also enjoy using them in a comparison of selected Symbolist lyrics. *The Virginal, Vibrant, and Beautiful Dawn, Bridges,* and *Moonlight,* for example, present three very different Symbolist landscapes. Rimbaud's *The Drunken Boat* and Mallarmé's *The Afternoon of a Faun,* both longer poems, provide differently focused narratives of poetic creation. Both Rimbaud and Mallarmé believe in the poet's prophetic role; the one ends in silence, the other in brilliant hermetic poems and the paralyzing vision of an all-encompassing Book.

A convenient way to begin is to take one of the short poems as an introduction to Mallarmé's style. *Saint* is a good choice because it is relatively uncomplicated, depending on a straightforward sequence of physical images. You may, however, wish to take advantage of your students' familiarity with Edgar Allan Poe (and all the legends surrounding him) by beginning with *The Tomb of Edgar Poe*.

When you take up *The Afternoon of a Faun*, make sure your students grasp the distinction between the italicized passages (dream memory) and the narrative portion (real time). Once the basic story line is clear, you can focus on such things as the faun's dual nature: on the one hand (and in passionate detail) the classical convention of the faun as a lascivious forest spirit, a part of nature; on the other hand, the faun as an image of the creative artist: preparing his tools (cutting the reeds for pipes), grasping after beauty, seeking meaning through art (the melodies that mingle with the landscape and become fused with the contours of the nymphs), and finally returning to the world of dream to continue his search. It is useful to select a few passages to examine Mallarmé's extended chains of images (partly to clarify those passages, and partly to show that the poet works this way). In lines 4–6, for example, the uncertain faun pursues the labyrinthine branches of his doubt only for them to dissolve into the real branches of the surrounding woods, a return to reality that proves his remembered triumph was only a dreamed (ideal) or poetic counterpart. Wind and water are mentioned, but only as absent (the same technique found in *Saint*); instead, the landscape contains the dryly flowing melody of the faun's flute—a melody that rises to the sky as a visible breath of inspiration and falls back as an arid rain. In both passages, the play of words suggests the mysterious other world that is characteristic of Symbolist imagination.

Topics for Discussion

1. How does Mallarmé use language to "bestow a purer sense on the language of the horde"? What is the "language of the horde," and how is it different when used in Symbolist practice?
2. How might one argue that all Mallarmé's poems have, as their implied subject, poetic or artistic creation?
3. Poetic language, for Symbolists, should approach the condition of music. Does "the condition of music" mean the same thing for Mallarmé and Verlaine? How does each poet represent music in his poetry?
4. Discuss the layering of real and unreal images in Mallarmé's poetry.
5. *The Afternoon of a Faun* has been set to music and also made into a ballet. What qualities in the poem contribute to such settings?

Further Reading

See also the reading suggestions in the *Anthology*, p. 2546.

Porter, Laurence M. "Mallarmé's Disappearing Muse." In *The Crisis of French Symbolism*. 1990. Discusses the poet's gradual exploration of indeterminacy as the only acceptable muse.

PAUL VERLAINE

Backgrounds

For many, *Autumn Song* expresses the quintessential Verlainean persona: a sensitive, melancholy, somewhat passive soul whose moods express alternately yearning and helplessness. While translation can only hint at the melodic delicacy of the lilting French lines, the subtly interwoven images are quite clear. At the beginning of the poem, nature is anthropomorphized and also equated with music; at the end, the speaker is equated with nature. Throughout, the mood is established by an interpenetration of images in which no one category dominates: the initial sound of sobbing (presumably human) is quickly attributed to violins, which are then attributed to autumn. This seasonal sobbing wounds the speaker with a monotonous (single-toned, like a violin string) languor. In the second stanza, a clock chime tells the hour and evokes memories in the speaker, who weeps—echoing the autumn violins. In the third stanza, the initial humanization of nature is reversed as the speaker is first subject to "ill winds" and then equated with autumn's dead leaf. No specific cause is given for this melancholy; as so often in Verlaine, the reference remains open and ambiguous.

One of Verlaine's most famous poems is *Moonlight* (Clair de lune), in which a melancholy mood is established by a dreamlike pastoral masquerade that has been compared with the rococo paintings of similar masquerades (*fêtes galantes*) by the French artist Antoine Watteau (1684–1721). Such tableaux by various artists were popular in the eighteenth century and constituted a recognizable theme and style. Watteau's own masquerades (he had studied with the theatrical designer Claude Gillot) were notable for their overtones of theater and artifice, their ambiguous actors and melancholy clowns. Verlaine himself wrote a one-act pastoral comedy, *The Ones and the Others* (1871), that takes place in a "Watteau park."

Moonlight is a tour de force that begins with a personal address ("Your soul") but shifts into an impersonal perspective immediately after these two words. The change is all the more abrupt inasmuch as the French omits "like": your soul *is* a landscape, not just like one. The landscape, moreover (as the translation indicates), is most likely not found in nature but is a landscape painting, which is populated by the artifice of a masquerade party reenacting pastoral romances. In this dramatic tableau, masked revelers are vaguely conscious of their own alienation. Artifice and discrepancy rule: masks, mummeries, disguises, and uncertain songs about love and happiness that combine with the melancholy half-light of the moon. Despite the charade of love in the first two stanzas, any real eroticism emerges only in the decor of the last two lines with the spurting of the tall fountains. In this play of uncertain identities, the first line's human addressee is effectively lost from sight, replaced by marble statues and ecstatically sobbing fountains at the end.

In *The White Moonglow*, written for his fiancée before their wedding, the same moon reigns as in *Moonlight*, but here the poet tries to evoke a moment of perfection: no doubts about love or happiness, but an exquisite instant of peace and harmony. The short, regular (four-syllable) lines in the French are remarkable for their subtle melody, and the poem creates an enchanted scene as it moves in swiftly noted details from woods to pond and sky, all dominated by the reflected light of the moon. The picture is complete, and some readers will wish to go no further; yet Verlaine includes some puzzling elements that may undermine this completeness. Just as in *Moonlight*, there is a sense of distance and separation, and mournful images appear. Disembodied voices flee; a willow tree (conventionally associated with mourning) is reflected, black, in the pond; the wind weeps; and the tender peace of the last stanza has nothing to do with human beings, but seems to descend from the moonlit sky. Verlaine's fiancée seems remarkably absent, and perhaps the poet is absent too—except that it is his reverie and reflects his unique sensibility.

Wooden Horses strikes a very different tone: it is set at a country fair in Belgium with merry-go-rounds, loud music, carnival crowds out to have fun and—instead of romantic shepherds and shepherdesses—soldiers and fat maids off duty and bent on sex. Driving rhythm and insistent rhymes whirl the poem along ("turn" is repeated eight times in the first [French] stanza), and the desperation of that drive is reinforced by the image of wooden horses galloping round and round without hope of hay. There are hints of an ironic contrast between physical and romantic love: the sudden elegance of the evening sky in its velvet coat buttoned with golden stars and the covert allusion to Plato's dialogue on love, the *Phaedrus* (line 21 is literally "horses of their soul"), come from a different dimension than the cruder lusts of the carnival. (Verlaine did not always write about sensitive souls, and some of his poems are gleefully pornographic.) After his conversion, the poet introduced a disapproving note to counteract the joyous drums at the end: he revised the penultimate line, "Away the lovers go, in pairs," to read "The church bell rings sadly."

The Art of Poetry, which Verlaine wrote in 1874 but published only in 1882, was a witty and humorous manifesto that quickly became a cause célèbre when it drew attack from traditionalists. Pouring contempt on the classical virtues of French poetry—clarity, precision, and intricate rhymes—it was adopted by a new generation of antiestablishment poets who called Verlaine their leader. The *Anthology* headnote summarizes the manifesto's antitraditional recommendations and its call for liberation from conventional metrical, intellectual, and pictorial restraints. The poem itself is full of puns, humor, and surprises: "tipsy," for example (line 7), can also be translated "gray": an in-between color, foreshadowing the next line's advice to join opposite qualities. Line 5's recommendation to make mistakes in word choice not only contradicts classical academic values but implies using wordplay to suggest additional connotations. The critique of rhyme in stanzas 6 and 7 is itself loaded with excessive or grating rhymes. (You may understandably be put off by the phrase in stanza 7 "What crazy negro or deaf child / made this trinket . . ."; one can say only that Verlaine is reaching for obvious rhymes in these lines and finds them in cultural stereotypes that otherwise have no place in his poetry.) In a challenge to its readers, *The Art of Poetry* culminates in elusive images that have nothing to do with literary *form*: poetry should be pure music, or an indefinable something that wings its way toward other skies, or a fresh morning wind scented with mint and thyme. Such poetry is an immediate appeal to the senses. Words are transparent (or at least made to seem that way), and the impression is all. At the time, of course, these words were anything but transparent. The shock of irregular meter, puzzlement over ambiguous images, and the lack of an explicit message all caused contemporary readers to stop and notice the new literary style. Paradoxically echoing the Romantic prejudice against artifice while employing his own counter-canonical artifice, Verlaine opposes the impalpable spirit of *poetry* to academic definitions of *literature*. (The force of this opposition is best understood if we remember that the French Academy, a unique national institution, approved the addition of new words to the language and elected the "best" writers to its society of "Immortals.") Despite Verlaine's later admission that he treasured "irreproachable rhymes, correct French, and good poetry of any kind," the poem's last line has become one of the most famous critiques of canonically "correct" writing in any language: next to the evocation of experience, "all the rest is literature."

Classroom Strategies

These five poems make an eminently teachable cluster and, as a group, they also invite comparison with Rimbaud's different approach to autobiographical themes and imaginary scenes. At the beginning, take advantage of the personal stance of the *Autumn Song* and *The White Moonglow* to interest students in the creation of a poetic mood; then show them two different examples in *Moonlight* and *Wooden Horses*. A good way to move to *The Art of Poetry* is to bring up its last two stanzas and ask your class if the previous poems are apt illustrations. Are they "poetry" or "literature"? How does Verlaine's distinction relate to earlier poetry the class has read? As you discuss the details of these poems with your students, you can mention some of the Symbolist tactics described at the beginning of this section and begin to show how and why Verlaine's poetry is a forerunner of so much modern literature.

Topics for Discussion

1. Discuss *Autumn Song* and *The White Moonglow* as mood poems. How does each poem use natural surroundings? What mood is established?
2. Verlaine calls for nuance and ambiguity in *The Art of Poetry*. To what extent does his own work embody these recommendations?
3. Comment on the role of music in Verlaine's poetry, both his recommendations in *The Art of Poetry* and his own poetic practice.
4. Explain the opposition of "poetry" and "literature" in *The Art of Poetry*. Do you agree? What examples of "literature" and "poetry"

(perhaps of poetics) do you recall from previous reading? Is Verlaine's poetry without artifice?

5. How does Verlaine's work extend familiar Romantic themes? How is it different?

6. How might *Moonlight* and *Wooden Horses* be seen as impersonal evocations of a subjective mood?

Further Reading

See also the reading suggestions in the *Anthology*, p. 2547.

Porter, Laurence M. "Verlaine's Subversion of Language." In *The Crisis of French Symbolism*. 1990. A perceptive discussion of Verlaine's use of language to subvert certainty. The whole book is recommended.

ARTHUR RIMBAUD

Backgrounds

Rimbaud's mythic status may be traced to his image as a scandalous boy-genius and visionary: on the one hand, he is a poet-prophet in the grand tradition of Romantic literature, and on the other, an adolescent rebel who attempts every mode of transgression. Yet Rimbaud's writing would not have had such impact if he had not also been a remarkably adventurous and experimental poet who, in the five years of his teenage literary production, created complex structures out of brilliant hallucinatory images and revolutionized the rhythms of poetic prose.

By the time he was sixteen years old, Rimbaud had run away from home several times, seeking to escape the boredom of small-town life and his mother's strict supervision. Paris was a magnet for would-be writers and artists, and the young poet sent several of his poems to the established poet Paul Verlaine, hoping to attract his attention. During the summer of 1871 he worked on *The Drunken Boat*, an ambitious poem of twenty-five quatrains in perfectly rhymed alexandrines (the classical twelve-syllable line) that was to be his introduction to the Parisian literary world. In September, Rimbaud presented the poem to Verlaine personally. Its saga of adventure on the high seas was a triumph of imagination, and not least because the young poet had never seen the ocean. Rimbaud was a voracious reader, and in *The Drunken Boat* he combines and transforms images taken from (among other sources) novels like Jules Verne's *20,000 Leagues under the Sea* and James Fenimore Cooper's *The Last of the Mohicans*, the poetry of Victor Hugo and Charles Baudelaire (*The Voyage*), and a fanciful travel magazine, *Le Magasin pittoresque*. The poem has been seen as an allegorical account of his abortive attempts to escape Charleville in 1870–71; as a foreshadowing of his poetic career and disillusionment; and as a Symbolist version of the Romantic (and Baudelairean) theme of escape and adventure into the unknown.

It is a voyage of intoxicating liberation, but also one of defeat. Strangely passive at the beginning, the boat is liberated by mysterious natural forces from its ties to land and civilization. Freed of any trace of its former life, and from control of its journey as well (the steering devices and the sight of beacons), the boat plunges into a primal chaos represented by the Poem of the Sea. From this point until the last two stanzas, Rimbaud presents a dazzling display of intertwined visionary images that fuse light, sounds, taste, and touch; exotic scenes and biblical legends; brilliant colors and infinite dark; fantastic fish, animals, and birds; delirious skies and pulsating ocean depths. Violent emotions accompany these clusters of images, from the ecstasy of mystic revelation ("I have seen what men imagine they have seen") to—gradually—fear, yearning, and despair. It is typical of Symbolist writing that, in each image cluster, no one element is the key to the whole. Every set of images (for example, stanzas 7, 8, 10, 12, or 20) evokes a fantastic scene with its own unique combination of emotions and connotations; together, the sequence of scenes makes up a narrative of revelation that gradually turns menacing. Sailing on through beauty now mixed with death " and decay, the boat is tossed into the sky, where it plunges on until, finally overwhelmed, it calls for oblivion and total absorption in the sea (stanza 23) or a return to Europe with its familiar fixed forms (stanza 21). Two diminished futures offer themselves at the end: a return either to childhood as a frail boat drifting in a puddle or to the—now completely rejected—role of commercial ship in a world of authorities and prisons. The formal poem is rounded off—the conclusion echoes the situation at the beginning, except that the boat has lost its indifference— but the speaker's dissatisfaction suggests that his journey is not over.

  A Season in Hell was written between April and August 1873, in diverse locations in France, London, and Brussels (scene of the July gunshot that ended his affair with Verlaine). The only work that Rimbaud himself published, it is a remarkable set of autobiographical but hallucinatory prose poems arranged as a short preface and seven separate sections: *Bad Blood, Night of Hell, Deliriums* with its subsections I: *The Foolish Virgin / The Infernal Bridegroom* and II: *Alchemy of the Word, The Impossible, The Flash of Lightning, Morning,* and *Farewell.* The work is often taken as Rimbaud's farewell to poetry, and in *Alchemy of the Word* the poet makes clear that he has lost hope in his vocation as a poet-prophet: it is now "the history of one of my follies." In *Farewell* he adds, "I must bury my imagination and my memories . . . I who called myself magus or angel, dispensed of any morality, I have come back to the soil . . . Peasant!" Despite his disavowals, *A Season in Hell* is a masterpiece of poetic prose that draws much of its emotional power from the skillful counterpoint of themes and images and from the supple rhythms of language evoking a torturous stream of thought. In addition, the poet continued working on the prose poems of *Illuminations.* Nonetheless, *A Season in Hell* provides a picture of disillusionment that was followed soon after by Rimbaud's abandonment of writing.

  Night of Hell, like the rest of *A Season in Hell,* is written as a monologue set in a hell with all the trappings of traditional doctrine: fire, pitchforks, poison, and Satan (who may well be the voice of his own ironic self-consciousness). The speaker is convinced of his damnation, which he blames both on his own sinful nature and on the fact that he was baptized a Catholic; for without baptism, there would be no heaven or hell. Several themes alternate throughout the section: his misery as a damned soul aware of his condition; his yearning for salvation and happier times (along with a massive skepticism that emerges in various ironic passages); the poet's miraculous creative powers and associated hallucinations. Some critics feel that *Night of Hell* evokes the summer Rimbaud spent in London with Verlaine: the "errors that are whispered to me" would be the words of the older poet (the *bell tower* phrase is actually printed in one of Verlaine's later poems), and the "glimpse of conversion to righteousness and happiness, salvation" may refer to Verlaine's summer return to Catholicism. Whether or not there is such a specific reference, the description of salvation is heavily ironic: "millions of charming creatures, a sweet sacred concert . . . and goodness knows what else." Rimbaud's impatience with insipidity, with conventional thoughts, and with the boredom of a regulated life makes him prefer the stimulation of fire and pitchfork—but it does not alleviate his anguish.

The Bridges and *Barbarian* represent the shorter, visionary prose poems that Rimbaud wrote at the end of his literary career. Most critics accept that *The Bridges* is a transposition of a real scene: the bridges over London's river Thames on a gray day. It has also been suggested that the poem describes an unknown painting. No matter what the source, Rimbaud clearly creates his own painting with words, and moreover informs us that he is doing so. The word-painting begins impersonally with geometric patterns, the angular shapes of the bridges as they appear along the river and contrast with buildings on the shore. Additional details of hovels, masts, and parapets give texture and interest to the scene. Gradually, the description is humanized: musical chords are heard, and "one detects" a note of color—perhaps even musical instruments. A question is asked: What kind of music? Once uncertainty exists, a subjective perspective has entered the picture. It is no longer an impersonal description but now a mental event. Just at this point, a ray of sun pierces the gray landscape and ends the poet's reverie—or, from another angle, the poet reveals and obliterates this game of his imagination.

Both *The Bridges* and *Barbarian* (discussed in the *Anthology* headnote) exemplify Rimbaud's culminating work as *voyant*, a poet-seer who creates transcendent images of reality. Letters written when he was sixteen to his former teacher, Georges Izambard, and to a poet-friend, Paul Demeny, eloquently express the young poet's vision of his nature, his destiny, and the path he must take. He reproaches his teacher for having gone back into "the comfortable rut" of teaching, predicting "you will end up self-satisfied, someone who has done nothing because there was nothing he wanted to do." In contrast:

I want to be a poet, and am working to make myself a *Seer* [*Voyant*]. . . . The sufferings are enormous, but one must be strong, be born a poet, and I have recognized that I am a poet. It is not my fault at all. It's a mistake to say "I think": you should say "I am thought."—Forgive me the play on words.

I is somebody else. So much the worse for wood that discovers it is a violin.

Two days later, a letter to Demeny recapitulates the same ideas in more detail.

For *I* is somebody else. If brass wakes up a trumpet, that's not its fault. This is clear to me: I am present at the birth of my thought: I watch it, I listen to it. . . . I tell you one must be a *seer*, make oneself a *seer*.

The poet becomes a *seer* by a long, immense and reasoned *derangement* of *all the senses*. All forms of love, suffering, madness; he explores himself, he exhausts within himself all poisons in order to keep only their essences. Ineffable torture where he needs complete faith, superhuman force, where he becomes among all the great invalid, the great criminal, the great accursed—and the supreme Scholar!—For he arrives at the *unknown*!

These passages are often used to explain the basic concepts of Rimbaud's poetry: the *voyant* as a mystical or Illuminist seer; the poet as an impersonal force of nature; the artist's need to plumb the depths of human experience; and a concurrent faith that the result of such adventure will be supreme knowledge—the discovery of the unknown. Rimbaud clearly follows in the Romantic tradition of the poet-prophet, especially as it is transmitted through Baudelaire, whom he salutes as "the first *voyant*, king of poets, *a true God.*"

Classroom Strategies

Students are predictably interested in Rimbaud's vision of the poet-prophet or seer, and you can show them how he pursued that vision in three different kinds of writing. Rimbaud may also be discussed as an inheritor of the Romantic tradition of the visionary poet, or as a secular example of mystic or Illuminist literature. You may want to give them passages from his letters (see above) and remind them of Shelley's claim that "Poets are the unacknowledged legislators of the world" (*A Defence of Poetry*). Remaining within Symbolism, you may decide to show connections with the Baudelaire of *Correspondences* and *The Voyage*, or contrast Rimbaud's more impersonal style with the mood poetry of Paul Verlaine. Rimbaud foreshadows modernist style in its ruptured rhythms and rapid shifts of images, and he is also indispensable to understanding the aims and techniques of twentieth-century Surrealist poetry. The easiest way to begin is to emphasize the narrative and implied autobiographical stance of *The Drunken Boat* and, subsequently, *Night of Hell*. If you are using passages from the letters to explain Rimbaud's sense of mission, you can ask what scenes in *The Drunken Boat* illustrate the young poet's claim of making himself a seer.

Topics for Discussion

1. Choose a passage from a letter to Izambard or Demeny (above) and ask students to explain its relevance to *The Bridges* and *Barbarian*. (*The Drunken Boat* is certainly possible, but students may limit themselves to repeating its narrative line.)
2. On March 2, 1950, Balanchine's New York City Ballet performed the world premiere of a ballet based on Rimbaud's *Illuminations*. What is there in Rimbaud's poetry that makes it a candidate for modern ballet? Discuss in relation to *The Bridges* and *Barbarian*.
3. Discuss the play of thematic and pictorial opposites in *Night of Hell*.
4. Discuss Rimbaud's use of irony throughout these poems.
5. In *Night of Hell* Rimbaud states that he is a damned soul. How does he explain this condemnation, and what kind of case does he make for guilt or innocence?
6. Compare Rimbaud's sense of mission with that of his Romantic precursors (Blake, Keats, Shelley, for example). Why does he call Baudelaire "the first *voyant*"?
7. Compare the autobiographical voice in Rimbaud, Verlaine, and Baudelaire.

Further Reading

See the suggestions in the *Anthology*, p. 2546.

Porter, Laurence M. "Artistic Self-Consciousness in Rimbaud's Poetry." In *The Crisis of French Symbolism*. 1990. Includes psychological perspectives in an intricate description of Rimbaud's style as a changing relationship to his implied audience.

CLUSTER: PERSPECTIVES ON EUROPEAN EMPIRE

Classroom Strategies and Topics for Discussion

This section contains excerpts from a wide variety of writers: zealous expansionist European ideologues such as Macaulay and Rhodes; an internationalist visionary, Garibaldi; an intrepid English woman explorer, Mary Kingsley; a resistant African chief, Machemba; and two observers of the Anglo-Boer War, one an English South African, Olive Schreiner, and the other a black African, Sol Plaatje. From their different perspectives they share a common experience: the explosive assertion of European colonial and imperial control, especially in India and Africa, and in Europe, internecine nationalist strife.

Thomas Babbington Macaulay (1800–1859), a well-known Whig historian, man of letters, and politician, was also deeply involved in governing British India. His contribution, an excerpt from his *Minute on Indian Education* (1835) is sublime in its conviction of the patent and demonstrable superiority of all things English over all things Indian. His concern is the choice of a language of instruction for the training of native elites and civil servants. His conclusion? English, of course! Neither of the classical languages of India, Sanskrit and Arabic, are adequate to modern knowledge, and the many vernaculars are hopelessly inadequate. Students might be asked to rehearse and question the reasons Macaulay gives for these assertions. Whoever knows English "has ready access to all that vast intellectual wealth which the wisest nations of the earth have created and hoarded in the course of ninety generations." Beyond this, he offers strong practical reasons of governmental and legal administration and of commerce to recommend English as the language of choice. Students might be encouraged to join the debate Macaulay sketches, so as to evaluate his rhetorically weighted arguments.

Giuseppe Garibaldi (1807–1882), the next contributor, is represented by his extraordinary *Memorandum* (1860), an open letter to all the heads of state in Europe. In it he advocates a single federated European state, devoted to peace and prosperity at home and international trade abroad. Accustomed to internationalist and globalist political rhetoric as students are likely to be, it is important that they recognize how singular an idea this was in the great age of nationalism and militaristic colonialism. Europe is now closer and closer to a federated union, after a century and a half of bloody wars among its nation-states since Garibaldi made his proposal. The *Memorandum* profits from Garibaldi's long experience of war and of foreign military domination. He offers a strikingly different perspective on nationalism, militarism, and empire. Students should be encouraged to contrast his ideas with those of Macaulay and Cecil Rhodes.

Machemba's *Letter to Major von Wissman* (1890?) is a rare artifact out of the colonialist archives, a document of native resistance. Now is the time to emphasize the frequency and violence of such resistance, and how implacably it was crushed. Students will immediately appreciate the dignity and pride of Machemba's refusal to submit to colonial control, and they can be brought to appreciate his diplomatic wile. Ultimately, his efforts at resistance failed, and he was driven into exile. Students might be asked what other outcomes are conceivable.

The next contributor, Cecil Rhodes (1853–1902), is represented by an excerpt from his *Speech at Drill Hall, Capetown* (1899). This provides the purest statement of imperialist ideology in this section. Far from being an apologist for or a critic of imperialism, Rhodes is its enthusiastic advocate. If there is any crack in his confidence, it is his implicit fear of conflict between the various European powers in their race for domination over Africa. His immediate context is the long-simmering conflict between English and Dutch settlers in South Africa. Students might be asked if the race for domination produced any other armed conflicts between Europeans besides the Anglo-Boer War.

Students will probably find the next excerpt, by Mary Kingsley (1862–1900), drawn from her *Travels in West Africa* (1897), immediately accessible and attractive. One of a small troop of Victorian woman explorers, she traveled alone deep into the Congo, armored in corsets and crinoline and followed by porters bearing trade goods. She is always unflappable, always amused and amusing, and always alert to the smallest detail of either the landscape and its flora and fauna, or of local mores and indigenous ways of life. Her sense of confident superiority carries her through swamps and jungles as well as into remote African villages and trading posts. Students might be asked where this otherwise unassuming, middle-class Victorian woman, raised for a lifetime of domesticity, gets the sheer *spunk* she demonstrates in these pages. They might also be asked what face of empire she represents. Traveling as a small trader, a pursuit she shared with many other Europeans in Africa, she was only interested in paying her way, not making a fortune. Her pursuits were those of a naturalist and an ethnographer. How were imperialist aims served by such pursuits?

Two other selections in this section return the reader to South Africa and the Anglo-Boer War. The first is by Olive Schreiner (1855–1920), an excerpt from her *An English-South African's View of the Situation* (1897). This is an attempt to mediate between Dutch and British settlers on the brink of war. A well-known novelist, essayist, and political activist, Schreiner's point of leverage is a "small knot of speculators" (represented in this section by Cecil Rhodes) who deserve the enmity of both groups of settlers. Students might be asked how effective they find this effort to unite the two groups in hostility to a common enemy. Another feature of Schreiner's essay is her persistent appeal to racialist thought. The Dutch are "a people most nearly akin to the English of all European folk," and they share, along with common racial stock, certain laudable traits of racially inherited temperament. Students can be asked to evaluate this appeal to racial heritage and questioned about its sources. They will also probably notice that indigenous peoples are completely unmentioned, and they'll want to know why: they are quite plainly not in Schreiner's frame of reference. But they were (and are) by far the majority population of South Africa. The last selection in this section, an excerpt from the *Mafeking Diary* (1899), is by a black South African contemporary of Schreiner, Sol T. Plaatje (1876–1932). He was present at the siege of Mafeking because he had gone there before the war broke out to work as a clerk and court interpreter (he spoke Afrikaans, English, and several local vernaculars). From his testimony it is clear that the South Africa of his day was rigidly stratified by race. His perspective permits him to distinguish among South Africans from all manner of ethnic groups, not just Dutch and English. As the siege progressed and food grew scarce, the English authorities gave heavy preference in their rationing arrangements to European inhabitants. In the midst of violence and outrage, Plaatje is calmly matter-of-fact. Students may want to compare his attitudes toward the Dutch and English to Schreiner's attempt at mediation.

Topics for Writing

1. Construct a counterargument to Macaulay's, advocating the use of one of India's largest vernaculars, such as Urdu or Hindi, as the language of instruction.

2. Reply to Garibaldi as a European head of state, accepting or rejecting his proposal.
3. As Cecil Rhodes, reply to someone like Machemba, about to be victimized by one of Rhodes's land grabs.
4. Imagine an Olive Schreiner as concerned about indigenous people like Plaatje as she is about Dutch and English settlers, and rewrite her *View of the Situation*.

Further Reading

See also the suggestions in the *Anthology*, pp. 2545–46.

Winfried Baumgart. *Imperialism: The Idea and the Reality of British and French Colonial Expansion, 1880–1914*. 1982.

H. L. Wesseling. *The European Colonial Empires, 1815–1919*. 2004.

The Twentieth Century:
Modernisms and Modernity

INTRODUCTION

It may be useful simply to begin with what your students are already thinking: why is *this* particular period of time—the whole of the twentieth century, all the way back to 1900 or even before—still being called "modern"? After all, your students are thinking, way back then doesn't seem very modern at all. The name just doesn't fit. Calling Model-T's and silent films and Wilbur and Orville Wright's airplane "modern" seems silly to them.

Part of the problem is that modern is just not a very good name for a literary period. Since "modern" is the word we tend to use to describe whatever is happening *now*, whenever that *now* happens to be, its use can be more confusing than descriptive. Nevertheless, we persist in using it—and there's no change in sight. So it is useful at least to mention that the word "modern," as it is being used in this context, doesn't mean "now" or even "recently," but instead has to do with a series of cultural, intellectual, and artistic characteristics that began to dominate Western culture sometime around the turn of the twentieth century—though many had appeared far earlier—and that these characteristics bear similarities that allow us to group them under a name, the Modern, in the same uneasy way that certain observable characteristics of other periods (Romantic, Enlightenment, Renaissance, etc.) allow us to lump large numbers of writers, thinkers, and artists under those names. And it's useful to mention that the dominant set of characteristics and tendencies we persist in calling modern are no longer dominant—they've been replaced by other characteristics and tendencies we have come to call Postmodern, another not very helpful word. Of course, announcing to students that they are living in a Postmodern age does not necessarily lead to greater clarity. If they're unsure about what "modern" is supposed to mean, "Postmodern" becomes even more incomprehensible. In any case, like the Molière character who is amazed to discover he's been speaking prose all his life, students are often surprised by learning they're living in the Postmodern Era, even if they're pleased to discover that the time they're living in at least *has* a name.

The introduction to "The Twentieth Century: Modernisms and Modernity," attempts to describe briefly what those cultural, intellectual, and artistic characteristics of the "modern" are, and how they are related. It begins by noting some of the more important philosophers and social thinkers whose thought both led to and reflected the climate of mind at the end of the nineteenth and the beginning of the twentieth century—Darwin, Comte, Marx, Nietzsche, Bergson, Freud, Saussure, Wittgenstein, and Husserl—and on into the middle of the century with Heidegger, Sartre, and Camus. All of these thinkers challenge, revise, or disrupt the accepted assumptions of preceding centuries, the nineteenth century in particular, and have the effect of making it possible for *everything* to be challenged. Everything must be interrogated, questioned, doubted, whether it is religion, science, social and political relations, human psychology, or the nature of language itself. The kinds of questions these thinkers were most interested in, after all, were epistemological—that is, they are not interested so much in *what* we know, but *"how* we know what we know." And their answers, however massive and complicated their systems might have been, were generally posited as possibilities, without the arrogance of absolute certainty. The first victim of this new climate of thought was Absolute Truth.

Of course, this new environment had recognizable effects on literature and art; or rather, literature and art confirmed and expressed what it was like to live and think in this new world. The Introduction notes a number of the most important of the literary movements of the young century. Expressionism, Dadaism, Surrealism, and Futurism are just a few of the many movements, impulses, and challenges made by writers and artists early in the century, and all of these "Modernisms" register "different ways of expressing the reality of the world."

It is not at all difficult to convince students of the radical nature of this change. If they are having difficulty seeing the difference between a poem by Eliot or Rilke and one by Tennyson, for instance, they will have less difficulty if the teacher presents a Pre-Raphaelite painting and compares it with a Picasso, Braque, Kandinsky, or Mondrian; or a musical composition by Tchaikovsky or Mahler and compares it to one by Schoenberg, Bartok, Webern, or Stravinsky. The paintings, the music, and indeed, the literature of the first half of the twentieth century illustrates, as well as anything can, the "revolution of the mind" that is perhaps the most insistent characteristic of what we mean by the word "modern." The Introduction briefly discusses a whole bevy of writers who are working out of that revolution and whose work constantly interrogates the "conventional images of the world" and the "forms in which reality is represented." In all of them—Pirandello, Conrad, Woolf, Faulkner, Joyce, Eliot, Kafka, Proust, and so on—we find experiments with perspective and style and a tendency to expose a sense of discontinuity. Writers had begun to feel that history itself had become discontinuous, fragmented, broken up—and that they had been left in the position of having to discover an altogether new way of talking about their world. And writers had also begun to believe that perhaps the only place where unity and coherence was still available was in art itself.

Though the tendencies we call "modern" certainly began before World

War I, it was that great catastrophe which, for many, confirmed and so-lidified the arguments of early modernism, and "turned the generations of the early twentieth century against anything inherited from the recent past." The modernist work that came after the Great War was even more insistent on reexamining "the bases of certainty, the structures of knowl-edge, the systems of belief, and the repositories of authority in a society that had allowed such a war to occur."

Sometime around mid-century, after the West had gone through yet another world war, even more devastating and total than the first, mod-ernism began to evolve into postmodernism. Postmodernism, as hard as it may be to define, took an even tougher line against entrenched sys-tems of mainstream thought, including the authority many "high mod-ernists" continued to lend to the "idealist Western tradition reaching back to Homer and the Bible." Where modernists such as Eliot, Mann, Yeats, and many others often expressed a kind of fear and trembling about the fragility or even exhaustion of that tradition, postmodernists accept it as a given, and are able to be much more playful in their rejec-tion of the "depth and profundity" that modernists had worked so hard to locate in a world which to them seemed to have lost the capacity to find it. Modernists were most interested in depth, that which lies below the visible surface, because that is where profundity resides; Postmod-ernists reject depth in favor of a full examination of the surface, because attention to the surface registers their sense that profundity itself is an illusion. A comparison of work by almost any of the early modernists in the *Anthology* with some of the later postmodernists—Beckett, Borges, Calvino, Robbe-Grillet, and Achebe, in their various ways—would no doubt be particularly instructive. And the teacher who has already brought in some paintings and music to demonstrate the differences be-tween late nineteenth-century and early twentieth-century artistic prac-tices might now do well to bring back Picasso and compare his work with the paintings of David Hockney or Andy Warhol, or to play some-thing by Bartok and compare his work with that of Philip Glass or Jimi Hendrix.

JOSEPH CONRAD

Heart of Darkness

Conrad's *Heart of Darkness* is both immensely controversial and im-mensely important. The combination can be deadly for a teacher unpre-pared to deal with the story's complexities and the intense arguments that have been made both for and against it. There is nothing easy or comforting about *Heart of Darkness*. The very structure of its narrative and its often foggy and inflated language create uneasiness and, some-times, confusion in readers. But that is by no means all. The story quite deliberately camouflages its central meanings, even as it seems to assert that its central meanings are inordinately important for us to under-stand. And finally, readers must inevitably ask the kinds of questions posed in recent years by critics who find the story's representation of

Africa and Africans, Conrad's attitude toward colonialism, and his portrayal of women—to name just three of the story's most controversial features—to be, at best, suspect and, at worst, downright dangerous.

Despite this, however, *Heart of Darkness* remains a crucial text in modern literature. In his powerful and influential critical essay on the story, Chinua Achebe attacks it precisely because "Conrad . . . is undoubtedly one of the great stylists of modern fiction, and a good storyteller into the bargain. His contribution therefore falls into a different class—permanent literature—read and taught and constantly evaluated by serious academics. *Heart of Darkness* is indeed so secure today that a leading Conrad scholar has numbered it 'among the half-dozen greatest short novels in the English language' " ("An Image of Africa: Racism in Conrad's *Heart of Darkness*," first published in 1975). Achebe singles out *Heart of Darkness*—and not one or another of the more obvious texts such as Joyce Cary's *Mr. Johnson* or Evelyn Waugh's *Black Mischief*, for instance—because *Heart of Darkness* continues to be taught, continues to be taken seriously, and is therefore, in Achebe's view, the more dangerous because of the power and permanence of its impact.

Despite Achebe's influential criticism, the reasons Conrad's short novel continues to be taught and taken seriously have only solidified since T. S. Eliot referred to it with epigraphic authority in *The Waste Land* and *The Hollow Men*, F. R. Leavis declared Conrad one of only four English novelists whom he considered part of the "great tradition," and Lionel Trilling in 1961 included *Heart of Darkness* as one of the fundamental texts in the serious study of modern literature. In his famous and influential essay, "On the Modern Element in Modern Literature," Trilling supposes that one of the "shaping and controlling ideas of our epoch" is "the disenchantment of our culture with culture itself"— and he, like so many before and since, can hardly find a more developed literary example of that idea than *Heart of Darkness*.

Backgrounds

To begin to understand why *Heart of Darkness* seems to so many to be a crucial text, one must piece together a large number of scattered references, scenes, and details within the text, and then carefully place them all inside a larger literary and historical context. The story often seems to resist this kind of reconstruction, but it is essential work if we are going to get anywhere near the heart of *Heart of Darkness*.

One might take, for instance, one of the most crucial, and arguably the most famous, moments in the story as an example of the difficulty both readers and teachers must face. Just before his death, Kurtz is said to have a "supreme moment of self knowledge"—the kind of epiphanic moment the reader has perhaps witnessed before in stories like *The Death of Ivan Ilyich* or in plays like *King Lear*. Readers know that stories often depend upon such moments; and it is here when they quite rightly expect the story's conclusive meaning to be revealed. But what Kurtz says, "in a cry that was no more than a breath," is: "The horror! The horror!"

It's an extraordinary moment, a moment that calls attention to itself as decisive, but if Marlow does understand the nature of the "the horror" glimpsed by Kurtz, he neglects to tell us precisely what it is. What he tells us instead is that it is "the expression of some sort of belief," "a glimpsed truth," "an affirmation, a moral victory paid for by innumerable defeats, by abominable terrors, by abominable satisfactions," and that Kurtz's capacity to have seen what he saw and to say it causes Marlow to affirm that Kurtz was a "remarkable man" to whom Marlow will remain "loyal to the last."

For the reader hell-bent on conclusive meanings, and most are, this is just not enough. In interpreting this moment, we are left, in some ways, to our own devices—Marlow's understanding of his own experience is too indistinct to tell us precisely, and, in any case, Conrad seems perfectly content to allow readers a way out, to shake our heads in frustration, to stop paying attention, to walk away without fully comprehending the meaning of Marlow's tale.

As already suggested, "our own devices" used to interpret this and other scenes in *Heart of Darkness* had best include an ability to piece together specific scenes, images, and allusions and place them in the historical and literary context, as well as the larger context of the story as a whole.

For Marlow, as for Conrad and so many other modernist thinkers, the most profoundly disturbing thought was that if you poke a forefinger into the human species, you will "find nothing inside but a little loose dirt, maybe." This idea, that there is nothing substantial, lasting, or unchanging at the human core, operates somewhere near the center of a number of major modernist writers and texts—in Dostoevsky; T. S. Eliot; Beckett; Musil; Gide; and even Hemingway, whose dispirited waiter in a "Clean Well-Lighted Place" tells us something Conrad would have understood quite well:

> It was all a nothing and a man was a nothing too. It was only that and light was all it needed and a certain cleanness and order. Some lived in it and never felt it but he knew it was all nada y pues nada y nada y pues nada. Our nada who art in nada, nada be thy name thy kingdom nada thy will be nada in nada as it is in nada. Give us this nada our daily nada and nada us our nada as we nada our nadas and nada us not into nada but deliver us from nada; pues nada. Hail nothing full of nothing, nothing is with thee.

To the extent that there is nothing stable and eternal at the human core, at least not enough to defend against the compulsions of our most basic instincts, the developed restraints of civilization can be seen to be particularly necessary. When our worst instincts find no resistance in their way, civilization emerges as the most effective—and for most of us, the only—stay against communal disintegration. We find this disquieting perception lurking behind Eliot, in particular, but also in Virginia Woolf's *Mrs. Dalloway*; D. H. Lawrence's *Women in Love*; E. M. Forster's *A Passage to India*, where the Marabar Caves serve as the most explicit metaphor for this idea after *Heart of Darkness* itself; and, famously, in the work of Sigmund Freud, whose *Civilization and Its Discontents* is an essential gloss for the reading of Conrad and the other early and high modernists.

For Freud, of course, the function and purpose of civilization is to provide restraints that serve to control the Id's raging compulsion to satisfy its desires. But this comes at considerable cost to human happiness, which after all derives in part precisely from our ability to satisfy those desires. Since civilization is constantly restricting and rechanneling desire, Freud notes that it becomes quite possible to imagine that "what we call our civilization is largely responsible for our misery, and . . . we should be much happier if we gave it up and returned to primitive conditions. . . . Civilized man has exchanged a portion of his possibilities of happiness for a portion of security."

Freud's view in *Civilization and Its Discontents* is that we are overdeveloped apes trying to live like ants—and not doing a very good job of it. We begrudge civilization's restraints, and as a result have taken up an attitude of hostility to civilization itself. But for Freud as for Conrad, "returning to primitive conditions" and living out the Romantic promise of the "noble savage" is a dangerous attraction. For those who must rely on the restraints of civilization rather than an "inner strength" to maintain a sense of order, security, or community, a life unencumbered by restrictions and "external checks" would lead inevitably to a kind of chaos. Still, the attractions of a life without restraints is so powerful that, once fully felt, we, like Kurtz, would find it practically impossible to reject. The struggle between desire and restraint is one we might well lose, and at the first opportunity we might, like Kurtz, attempt to crawl back on all-fours into the jungle of our own "exalted and incredible degradation."

Civilization, for all of its repressive burdens and illusions—including the organized violence of war, imperialism, and colonialism—provides the rivets that hold together the sunken ship of self. You will excuse such an awkward introduction of one of Conrad's metaphors here, I hope, but *Heart of Darkness* is a symbolic tale, and there is very little in it that cannot now be recognized as part of Conrad's symbolic scheme—from the "vast artificial hole" someone has been digging, the meaning of which is "impossible to divine"; to the man who attempts to put out a fire with "a hole in the bottom of his pail"; to the rotten hippo meat stowed on board Marlow's boat; to the rivets Marlow waits for interminably at the Outer Station.

Now, the rivets in the story are meant to be quite literal rivets, of course, but even the lowly rivet takes on symbolic weight in *Heart of Darkness*. The world without "external checks"—those "rivets" that hold us in place, and make it possible to close up the hole at the center of us all—is a world of "utter silence" and "incomprehensible darkness" where "no warning voice of a kind neighbor can be heard whispering of public opinion. These little things make all the great difference." Long before we ever meet Kurtz, Marlow tells us "rivets were what Mr. Kurtz really wanted, if he had only known it." Rivets, then, function symbolically in the same capacity as those "kind neighbors" of civilization, "ready to cheer you on or fall on you," and who compel you to step delicately "between the butcher and the policeman, in the holy terror of scandal and gallows and lunatic asylums"—precisely the "kind neighbors" who are unavailable in the heart of a darkness. The problem is that "when they are gone you must fall back upon your own innate strength, upon your own capacity for faithfulness," and Marlow finds very little evidence, in himself or others, that many of us actually have the "innate strength" required.

To peer into this abyss of self is to begin to understand what Aldous Huxley meant when he said, "Ye shall know the truth and the truth shall make you sick." The effect of this recognition is much like the effect of the rotting "dead hippo meat" in the story. (Nothing, as I said, is without its symbolic weight in *Heart of Darkness*.) Once we have the smell of rot in our nostrils, it is impossible to ignore, and very difficult "not to be contaminated by it." "You can't breathe dead hippo waking, sleeping, and eating, and at the same time keep your precarious hold on existence," Marlow tells us. And so he will go out of his way to make sure that those least prepared for that particular stench, the stench of the revealed human condition, will be capable of continuing to believe that it is something other than it is.

The unprepared include Kurtz's Intended, quite obviously, but to a certain extent it includes all of us. Readers may or may not be prepared to face up to an understanding of human nature that Conrad believes might be devastating. So he takes some care to wrap the story in such a way that the reader, like the Intended, may walk away from it disbelieving or unimpressed, but at least not *necessarily* dispirited. Conrad's narrative technique in *Heart of Darkness* goes some distance in achieving this effect.

Structure

Structurally, *Heart of Darkness* is a box within a box within a box—a frame tale in which an unnamed narrator reports, at astonishing length and astonishing detail, a story told by Charlie Marlow, a fellow seaman for whom, we are told, the "meaning of an episode was not inside like a kernel, but outside, enveloping the tale which brought it out as a glow brings out a haze." Marlow's tale centers around his version of his meeting with the extraordinary and mysterious Kurtz ("Whatever he was, he was not common," Marlow tells us), who is clearly proposed as Europe's symbolic representative, the very best that Europe has to offer. "All Europe contributed to the making of Kurtz," and by European standards he is a "universal genius." Kurtz goes to Africa as an "emissary of light" but, once settled into his post as an ivory-trader for a Belgian company, he so successfully uses "methods" based on "brutal instincts" and "monstrous passions" that he has shaken the more traditional imperialist traders in Africa into a species of fear and envy. Kurtz's success comes from methods they suspect they cannot match, and they are both envious and concerned about them. And, because of the nature of the recommendations that have preceded Marlow to Africa, they believe that he, too, is like Kurtz—one of the "new kind," a member of that "gang of virtue" which is making their already difficult lives in the Congo even more difficult. As a result Marlow is distanced from them by their suspicions of him as well as his distaste for them. All we will ever really know about them comes from snatches of inconclusive conversation and the biased impressions of a storyteller, Marlow, who neither likes nor respects them.

The narrative of *Heart of Darkness*, then, is told by someone we know very little about, who is reporting the story of another man, Marlow, who he—the narrator—finds vague, inconclusive, and perhaps untrustworthy. Marlow himself is describing an experience he fully admits he does not entirely understand, amidst relationships with people he dislikes, distrusts, or finds irretrievably mad, in a world entirely alien to him. When we add to these possibilities for distortion the narrative's ironies, its shifts in tone, and its movement back and forth in time, we can argue that the ugliest and most dispiriting truths the story has to tell are camouflaged by the structural difficulties of the narrative and by its hazy and imprecise language. It is as if Conrad were saying, "You may read this story, but I will give you every reason and opportunity to ignore it." By the time we reach the end of *Heart of Darkness* it is possible for us, like the unnamed narrator on the deck of the *Nellie*, to be unmoved by what we have heard—after all, we might say, it's simply the account of a strange experience of inconclusive meaning passed along by a yarn-telling sailor already known for his inconclusive tales.

We are, in a sense, being protected by the padding of Conrad's narrative from full immersion in the destructive element.

Interpretation and Classroom Strategies

The unnamed seaman who is the narrator of *Heart of Darkness* tells us near its beginning that we are to "hear about one of Marlow's inconclusive experiences." But *Heart of Darkness* may actually be not so much inconclusive as capable of supporting innumerable conclusions. It can, and has, been read in many ways. It can be read as a kind of adventure tale, though the reader who is inclined to read it this way will no doubt be disappointed, if not actually dispirited, by the difficulties presented by the narrative and the inconclusive implications of the story. It can be read as being about late nineteenth-century European colonialism, but the reader inclined to read it this way will find it troublingly ambivalent about the particular kinds of colonial procedures described in the story. And it can be read, as has already been suggested, as a story about the examination of self, a voyage of self-discovery that leads to some shattering results—not only about the nature of Marlow's own self, but about the nature of the human self generally, and the consequent unhappy necessity for, but fragility of, a civilization that acts to provide the checks and restraints the self cannot provide.

Marlow's glimpse into the abyss of self—to use the metaphor Conrad himself uses—reveals an "impalpable grayness, with nothing underfoot." As I have suggested, such a glimpse can be terrifying and debilitating because it discloses the resounding hollowness of us all, a hollowness that, when the chance arises, can be filled by a "wild and passionate uproar" of desire, need, and aggression that is "monstrous and free," an "incomprehensible frenzy" of "brutal instincts" and "monstrous passions"—characteristics that sound to us like nothing so much as Freud's description of the Id. With Kurtz, for instance, "the wilderness had found him out early, and had taken on him a terrible vengeance for the fantastic invasion. I think it had whispered to him things about himself which he did not know, things of which he had no conception till he took counsel with this great solitude—and the whisper had proved irresistibly fascinating. It echoed loudly within him because he was hollow at the core."

Nevertheless, Marlow insists that Kurtz is "remarkable," and he persists in a surprising loyalty to Kurtz, which compels him, finally, to lie to the Intended to salvage her memory of him. Kurtz's remarkableness is only this: he is, for Marlow, a kind of spiritual hero. Kurtz has descended fully into an abyss that Marlow could only peep into, and Marlow has come to "understand better the meaning of his stare, that could not see the flame of the candle, but was wide enough to embrace the whole universe, piercing enough to penetrate all the hearts that beat in the darkness. He had summed up—he had judged. 'The horror!' " Kurtz has recognized his own hollowness, recognized the "abominable terrors" and "abominable satisfactions" that he, like all of us, is heir to. Kurtz is the man who has gone all the way down, close enough to have a full, hard look at the worst, and has at great cost managed—however cryptically—to have told us what he sees. For Marlow, this is a heroic achievement.

Some have suggested that *Heart of Darkness* remains a crucially significant modernist text because it takes up so many of the most characteristic elements of modern literature. "Nothing," says Trilling, "is more characteristic of modern literature than its discovery and canonization of the primal, non-ethical energies" and "the terrible message of ambivalence toward the life of civilization." Conrad confronts both in *Heart of Darkness* and does so some years before any other major modernist writer in English.

Still, the reasons that Postcolonial and feminist critics, not exclusively but in particular, have been concerned about the continued use of *Heart of Darkness* as a major text in the modernist canon are perfectly understandable. One need only to point to Conrad's use of persistent and dangerous stereotypes of Africa and Africans; of African culture and civilization appearing as a ready-made embodiment of "savage" behavior and "primitive" customs; of European civilization, especially British civilization, put into play as the only viable stay against the attractive compulsions of "savagery" for the hollow man; of women depicted as the last bastion of civilized values who must "stay out of it" in order to protect their men from the worst aspects of themselves; of women as innocent believers in an illusion; of women proposed as being so weak and vulnerable to the ugly truths of life that merely to learn of them might endanger their ability to function.

Perhaps the most disturbing questions asked by postcolonial critics come from Marlow's (and we quite rightly suspect Conrad's) seemingly contradictory attitudes regarding Europe's colonial incursions into Africa. Here's the problem: Marlow belittles, even satirizes, the idealized and grandiose arguments of colonial imperialism; he sees it as nothing but "robbery with violence, aggravated murder on a great scale, and men going at it blind. . . . The conquest of the earth, which mostly means taking it away from those who have a different complexion or slightly flatter noses than ourselves, is not a pretty thing when you look into it too much." But at the same time, his uneasiness about the nature of human nature, his profound horror of the hollowness he sees at the center of us all, compels him to admire the restraints provided by civilization—and the civilization Marlow apparently sees as most capable of providing such restraints is specifically European, and even more specifically British, the very civilization that engaged so thoroughly in imperial and colonial enterprises.

Throughout the story, Marlow expresses his contempt and disgust for those who imagine the colonization of Africa as a "noble cause." The European "pilgrims" who surround Marlow at the Outer Station are full of "imbecile rapacity"; they are as "unreal as everything else—as the philanthropic pretense of the whole concern, as their talk, as their government, as their show of work." The Africans unfortunate enough to have come into contact with such "emissaries of light" are merely worked until they are used up, after which they are simply left to die "as in some picture of a massacre or a pestilence." Later, we are introduced to the members of the Eldorado Exploring Expedition, another band of colonial exploiters, whose talk is "the talk of sordid buccaneers . . . reckless without hardihood, greedy without audacity, and cruel without courage." And finally, of course, we are introduced to Kurtz himself, whose "methods" are "no method at all"—he is a menacing grotesque, a "hollow sham" who has nevertheless succeeded in setting himself up as a kind of god among people he has apparently frightened and cowed into submission and complicity; the degree of his mercilessness and viciousness is made even worse, if more effective, by its being entirely unpredictable. If he had "a fancy for it . . . there was nothing on earth to prevent him killing whom he jolly well pleased."

Marlow registers and reports all of these things about the colonial enterprise with apparent disgust. He appears to recognize what is now so widely recognized about the actual nature of colonialism in Africa and elsewhere, and to understand its motivations and justifications far better than many, if not most, of the people of his time. And yet, just when we are settling in to feel comfortable about *Heart of Darkness* as an anti-Imperialist story, one that exposes imperial colonialism in all of its horrors and lies, the story undercuts our expectations, and certainly our comfort, by presenting us with what appear to be contradictory arguments and unsettling qualifications. We want our revulsion toward imperialism and colonialism to be uninterrupted by allowances and hesitations; we do not want to imagine that anything might be said to redeem it. But the story seems to suggest that there is—"What redeems it is the idea only. An idea at the back of it; not a sentimental pretence but an idea; and an unselfish belief in the idea—something you can set up, and bow down before, and offer a sacrifice to."

So what is this "idea," and in what possible way could it "redeem" Marlow's otherwise jaundiced view of imperialist rapacity? Except in the case of Kurtz, who impresses Marlow for other reasons, it is those who can "set up an idol and believe in it" who attract his sympathies and admiration. For Marlow, the idol, the redemptive "idea," appears to be dedication to one's work. The power and necessity of work as a kind of saving activity was a very powerful nineteenth-century notion, and it permeates Victorian literature in a way similar to the idea of evolutionary meliorism, the belief in the gradual but inevitable progress brought about by the operations of civilization, which was a staple of Victorian ideology and a foundational idea in the justification of colonialism. The Victorian idea of the importance of work is expressed perhaps most passionately in the essays of Thomas Carlyle, but the author of *Shooting Niagara* would undoubtedly have been surprised to see it applied to an African "cannibal" who dedicatedly operates the boiler on Marlow's steamship because he believes there's an evil spirit inside it which must constantly be pacified; not to speak of a white, European, "hairdresser's dummy" of an Outer-Station accountant who sports a green parasol and who manages to keep his books and his grooming in "apple-pie order" despite the "great demoralization of the land." "That's backbone," remarks Marlow of the accountant. "His starched collars and got-up shirt fronts were achievements of character." Nothing, even the sick and dying Africans who are everywhere around him, is allowed to interfere with the carrying out of his work.

Marlow's sympathies are with those who can tackle a darkness "properly"—those who meet the truth of their own and the world's incomprehensibility with their "own true stuff," an "inborn strength"; what he can't abide are those who tackle a darkness armed only with the pretence of "superstition, beliefs, and what you may call principles," which are "less than chaff in a breeze." As the examples of the boilerman and the accountant suggest, when men are "tackling a darkness" it does not seem to matter to Marlow just how ridiculous, how callous, how merciless, or how blind this dedication to the work at hand might be, just as long as that dedication remains in place and is not swayed by whatever conditions—social, cultural, or psychological—may happen to present themselves as interferences. Marlow's values are the values of a traditional ship captain, whose job it is to pilot the ship to safety *no matter what* the distractions of sea and crew may be, to save the ship *no matter what* may interfere with the process.

Marlow's ideas are the kinds of ideas no doubt put forward in Towson's *An Inquiry into Some Points of Seamanship*, the antiquated book that he finds in a woodpile on the way downriver. He treasures it because in Towson's book he finds evidence of the seaman's "singleness of intention, an honest concern for the right way of going to work," which has the effect of making Marlow forget the jungle and the pilgrims "in a delicious sensation of having come across something unmistakably real." The boilerman and accountant, too, have a "singleness of intention" that Marlow admires, no matter how much else they may ignore, and no matter how horrifying, unjust, and genuinely disturbing what they ignore may actually be.

For us this is no less than shocking. For an accountant to carry on with his bookkeeping and toilette by remaining callously indifferent to the dead, dying, and enslaved Africans everywhere around him hardly elicits admiration in us; we want him to stop keeping the books for an already illegitimate and vicious enterprise and *do* something about the condition of the people, to attend to their plight. If Marlow were to show the first inclination to bring as much aid as he could muster to the Africans who have been left to die, if he were even to write letters to the company or the press attacking and exposing the colonial project, in fact if he were to do *anything* other than to merely wait for the rivets that will fix his boat, complain about the "papier-mâché Mephistopheles" who works the station, or think about how much he wants finally to meet Kurtz, *Heart of Darkness* would be a much more easily acceptable and accessible work of fiction. Those who want *Heart of Darkness* to be something other than it is have every good reason to want it, but it remains implacably resistant to our turning it into something more immediately approvable.

Achebe's famous 1975 attack on the story may not be entirely adequate *literary* criticism, but it is undoubtedly important social and political criticism. For Achebe, and many others since, Africa in *Heart of Darkness* may well be a "metaphysical battlefield," but its image in the story is simply an indication that "Joseph Conrad was a thoroughgoing racist." Conrad's use of Africa "eliminates the African as a human factor," reducing an entire continent and its people to the status of a backdrop "for the break-up of one petty European mind." In many ways, the crux of Achebe's argument is not that *Heart of Darkness* is not a great story, but that the dangers of continuing to pass on its images of Africa and Africans is hardly compensated for by its greatness. Teachers will be wise to tackle this issue in class. It will, without fail, create an extraordinarily rich occasion for discussion.

Feminist critics have similar problems with *Heart of Darkness*. In the story, it is women, Kurtz's Intended in particular, who embody the precarious fragility of civilization. "They—the women I mean—are out of it—should be out of it. We must help them to stay in that beautiful world of their own, lest ours get worse." For Marlow, civilization—despite its blatant failures and its determined belief in its own lies—is a *necessary* illusion; it must be preserved as a stay against the impenetrable darkness, that sense of nothingness, that may otherwise invade and destroy. Marlow lies to the Intended at the end of *Heart of Darkness* in order to protect her from what he thinks is a truth so devastating that she, like the good Mrs. Moore in *A Passage to India*, might not be able to withstand it.

For Conrad to have embodied these ideas about the fragility of civilization in the image of women opens up *Heart of Darkness* to quite understandable attacks from critics, especially feminist critics, who see that he is merely using persistent and treacherous nineteenth-century stereotypes of women—stereotypes which then, as now, were used to keep women in a subordinate position. Arguments very much like this were used, for instance, to keep women from the vote, and continue to be used by men as a way of marginalizing women in the world of action and power.

Perhaps some of the usual warnings about this kind of criticism may still apply: beware allegorizing characters in literature—interpreting a particular woman as standing for all women, for instance; or accept the fact that in most of his fiction, Conrad's women are rather less women than symbolic figures; or even that Conrad is merely participating in the typical view of women in his time, and so it is unfair to ask him to be prescient in matters of twenty-first-century gender issues. Still, it must be said that current gender criticism seems perfectly correct about the images of women in *Heart of Darkness*, and these images can only be justified, if justification is possible, by arguing that their use by Conrad in this particular case are essential to what he is attempting to accomplish. To make the Intended in *Heart of Darkness* emblematic of a fragile and vulnerable civilization, full of the kinds of illusions necessary to maintain itself—illusions, Conrad thought, that must in any case be protected, even by lies, if necessary—was to create an emblematic figure his contemporary readers would certainly recognize and understand, even if we early twenty-first-century readers might very rightly find them problematic.

But, again, the teacher would be wise to take up these issues and, like the question of Conrad's image of Africa and Africans, the discussion will be very likely be spirited and valuable.

Teaching *Heart of Darkness* is no easy job. In comparison, even the famous difficulties of *The Waste Land* may seem paltry, merely to call out for a teacher who can point knowingly at an allusion. But to do so, with full knowledge of the kinds of literary, historical, social, political, and critical questions it can raise, can be exhilarating and constructive. Give it plenty of time, treat it with the care and seriousness it deserves, and it—and your students—will repay the effort.

Topics for Discussion and Writing

1. It has often been claimed that *Heart of Darkness* is poised between the values, methods, and sensibility of the nineteenth century on one hand, and those of the modernists on the other. Is this so? In what ways?
2. Pick a few paragraphs—you can do so almost at random. Have students make a list of key words, images, and themes in those paragraphs, and then discuss how they are used throughout the story. Pay attention to recurring words and images, their general pat-

terns, and the ways they enlarge and deepen as the story progresses.

3. What is "the horror" glimpsed by Kurtz? Why does his glimpse of it mean so much to Marlowe?

4. Marlowe seems to both admire and abhor Kurtz. How do you ac-count for this?

5. Marlow "admires" very few characters in *Heart of Darkness*. Which ones are picked out for special praise? What similarities, if any, do they share?

6. Why does the structure of the story offer a way for the reader to ig-nore its implications?

7. Why does Marlowe lie to the Intended, Kurtz's fiancée?

8. Is Conrad, as Chinua Achebe has said, a "thoroughgoing racist"? What is his attitude toward Africa and Africans in *Heart of Dark-ness*? Similarly, what is his attitude toward European colonialism? It is likely that a powerful argument can be made against any sin-gle conclusion you or your students may draw. What does this sug-gest about the nature of *Heart of Darkness*?

9. Hand out appropriate passages (or read in full) from Postcolonial and feminist criticism of *Heart of Darkness*. Have your students ar-gue both sides of the questions raised.

Comparative Perspectives

Chinua Achebe's *Things Fall Apart* was in great part written to correct the version of Africa and Africans we find in stories like *Heart of Dark-ness*. No matter how significant Conrad's work is for an understanding of some of the central questions and concerns of modern literature, his treatment of the condition of Africans under colonial rule and his de-scription of African life (insofar as there is one) appears to confirm the kinds of sophomoric and racist versions popularized in Eurocentric his-tories of Africa, in popular fiction, and in bad movies. Unfortunately, these Saturday matinee ideas about Africa—"savage," "uncontrolled," "uncivilized," "cannibalistic," and so on—became such staples of West-ern thought about Africa and such foundational ideas in the West's con-struction of justifications for colonialism that African writers such as Achebe (not to speak of Wole Soyinka, Ngugi Wa Thiong 'O, and others) have found it necessary to combat such ideas in much of their work.

Things Fall Apart is far and away the most important work in the *An-thology* to teach in conjunction with *Heart of Darkness*. The logistics of this are not as difficult as they would immediately seem. Teachers of *Heart of Darkness* will no doubt want to use it as an opening gambit in their discussion of modernism, which is not only appropriate but per-haps even necessary. And although *Things Fall Apart* was written over fifty years later, and using it in conjunction with *Heart of Darkness* may seem to be well out of chronological order, Achebe's novel takes place in a period approximately contemporary with the time frame of Conrad's story and serves to "fill in" precisely the kinds of information about aspects of African life and civilization that are absent in Conrad.

Though the teacher of *Heart of Darkness* may well wish to point out that Conrad's version of Africa is in many ways simply the standard Western view held in Conrad's time (and for long after), it at least should be pointed out that there were correctives to that view already available. Montaigne's sixteenth-century essay *Of Cannibals* is such a corrective. When Montaigne points out that men call barbarism whatever is not their own practice, and that we have no other test of truth and reason than the example and pattern of the opinions and customs of the country we live in, he is warning about the distortions caused by Eurocentrism and offering a set of ideas it took the West another four hundred years to comprehend, if they have been comprehended even yet. Any excuse to read more Montaigne is a good one. If nothing else, he demonstrates to students that ideas just as "modern" and progressive as theirs have been around for a long time.

Finally, much has been said above about the insights and concerns of Sigmund Freud in *Civilization and Its Discontents* and their connection with the insights and concerns of Conrad in *Heart of Darkness*. Teachers should plan to discuss the implications of Freud's ideas in the context of their discussion of Conrad's story. It does not matter much that Freud, in general, has been discredited. No one can discredit the fact of Freud's impact on modern thought, or that the kinds of concerns he evidences in *Civilization and Its Discontents* were concerns that both predated and postdated his work. The simple fact is that what Freud spells out in *Civilization and Its Discontents* is very similar to what so many writers and artists were then thinking. We can decide they were all thinking wrongly, but we cannot ignore the fact that they were thinking it.

CLUSTER: CIVILIZATION ON TRIAL

In his influential essay "On the Modern Element in Modern Literature" (1961), Lionel Trilling argued that the "characteristic element of modern literature" and "one of the shaping and controlling ideas of our epoch" was "the disenchantment of our culture with culture itself." In the essay, Trilling proposes a syllabus—his syllabus—that would provide the student with both a historical and an intellectual context as well as some illustrious examples from twentieth-century literature as a focus for an exploration of modern literature's "bitter line of hostility to civilization." It includes Sir James Frazer's *The Golden Bough*, Nietzsche's *The Birth of Tragedy* and *The Geneology of Morals*, Conrad's *Heart of Darkness*, Mann's *Death in Venice*, and Freud's *Civilization and Its Discontents*; then it moves back again to Diderot's *Rameau's Nephew*, Dostoevsky's *Notes from Underground*, Tolstoy's "Death of Ivan Ilyich," and two plays by Pirandello. Along the way Trilling references Eliot's *The Waste Land* and "The Hollow Men." It should be noted that the teacher of the *Norton Anthology of Western Literature* has much of this material immediately at hand and is in a particularly advantageous position to discuss with students the many ways that artists and thinkers expressed their disenchantment with and hostility toward civilization.

As the introduction to the "Civilization on Trial" cluster suggests, in the nineteenth century there was an emphasis on what most writers and thinkers thought was the gradual, but inevitable, ascent of civilization (or at least Western civilization) toward a kind of pinnacle—"Better fifty years of Europe than a cycle of Cathay," as Tennyson declared. For these writers, the problems of civilization were the problems that *confronted* civilization, those yet unresolved difficulties that continued to present obstacles to civilization's forward progress. But somewhere around the turn of the century, and certainly after World War I, civilization itself came to be seen as the problem. The "problem" of civilization was, of course, viewed differently by different writers and thinkers. The selections included in the "Civilization on Trial" cluster mean to present some of those different perspectives, and the teacher's selective use of other texts in the *Anthology* (any of the selections mentioned by Trilling, but also poems by Baudelaire and Rimbaud, Cavafy's *Waiting for the Barbarians*, Yeats's *The Second Coming*, and Kafka's *The Metamorphosis* come immediately to mind) would certainly provide students with a splendid sampling of exactly what Trilling meant when he argued that hostility toward civilization itself was the "characteristic element of modern literature."

In pedagogical use of the "Civilization on Trial" selections, it might be best to begin with the article from the eleventh edition of the *Encyclopaedia Britannica* (1911), which is as sunny a view of the virtues of civilization as one could possibly want. Its unshaded optimism raises the ante even on nineteenth-century expostulations on the glories of civilization's unabated progress. But it is very difficult to find any literary examples willing to follow the lead of the *Britannica*'s utopia-is-on-its-way view. The *Anthology*, certainly, will provide none. Writers and thinkers were already more concerned with the problems presented by civilization, rather than the soon-to-be-surmounted glitches that might impede it.

Max Weber's arguments in the excerpts from *The Protestant Ethic and the Spirit of Capitalism* (1904) take up some of those problems. Weber, with Marx at his back, sees that the economic organization of the industrial West is redefining civilization in such a way as to institutionalize a kind of spirit-numbing asceticism, an asceticism we do not *choose*, as Christian ascetics once chose it, but instead as something we are *forced* to do. The result, he argues, is that the economic order has created for us a kind of "iron cage" that strips civilized life of its religious and ethical meaning and turns it into a kind of competitive sport. Gregor Samsa's position in relation to his employers in *The Metamorphosis* would be one good literary example a teacher might point out, but the most suggestive might be something like Charlie Chaplin's film *Modern Times*—the first thirty minutes of which are not only some of the funniest minutes in film history but are also a marvelous example of what Weber means when he talks about the "mechanized petrification" of life in which spiritless economic acquisition is the goal, not the by-product, of civilization's development.

Though it is not taken up specifically in the "Civilization on Trial" cluster, another important and easily demonstrable early twentieth-century attitude emerged about the problem of civilization itself: an absence of vitality. Early in the century, before World War I, and perhaps taking a cue from Nietzsche, there was a powerful sense that civilization had somehow refined away cultural and individual vitality, leaving us limp with civilization. We see this expressed in all of those writers, artists, and thinkers who declare that civilization has lost its nerve, and especially in the early twentieth-century interest in "the primitive," as it was then called. I am talking now about artists like Henri Rousseau, the paintings of Picasso or the German Der Blaue Reiter group, or the music of Igor Stravinsky. There are obvious traces of the idea even in speculative novels like H. G. Wells's *The Time Machine*. Some, like the painter Paul Gauguin or the novelist D. H. Lawrence, for instance, left Europe in personal searches for new sources of vitality. They went wherever they thought they could still find it; Gauguin, for instance, went to Tahiti, and Lawrence to Australia and New Mexico.

At the outbreak of World War I, writers as different as the German poet Rainer Maria Rilke and the English poet Rupert Brooke actually welcomed the war as a way out of this kind of world-weariness:

> Now, God be thanked Who has matched us with His hour,
> And caught our youth, and wakened us from sleeping,
> With hand made sure, clear eye, and sharpened power,
> To turn, as swimmers into cleanness leaping,
> Glad from a world grown old and cold and weary . . .
> —Brooke, from "Peace," 1914

> Now your unsettled plans have been taken off your shoulders by a settled common destiny—I can imagine that this is an unforgettable joy, thus all at once to be involved in One power and One emotion, especially after the many-minded times that have long since confused and wearied all of us.
> —Rilke, letter to T. F. von Munchhausen, August 15, 1914

The idea also finds its way into the work of C. P. Cavafy and André Gide, and—in their sometimes violent rejection of tradition and embrace of the irrational (another source of vitality)—the writings, paintings, and manifestoes of the Expressionists, Futurists, Surrealists, and Dadaists.

During and after World War I, when the most "civilized" nations in the world spent four years doing everything they could to destroy each other, attitudes toward the problem of civilization hardened, deepened, and became much more pervasive. The old nineteenth-century attitudes—let alone those presented in the eleventh edition of the *Encyclopaedia Britannica*—were now practically impossible to maintain. Even as solid a representative of Western civilization as Henry James was moved to a kind of despair:

> The plunge of civilization into this abyss of blood and darkness . . . is a thing that gives away the whole long age in which we have supposed to be, with whatever abatement, gradually bettering, that we have to take it all now for what the treacherous years were all the while really making for and meaning is too tragic for any words.
>
> —Henry James, letter to Hugh Walpole, 1915

And Rainer Maria Rilke, whose letter in August 1914 applauds the salutary effects of the war, discovers in less than a year that the "common destiny" of civilization will be quite different from what he originally imagined:

> Shall we not later also, and for always, as now we are learning to do, postpone all knowledge, deem humanity's plight inextricable, history a primordial forest whose bottom we never reach because it stands finally, layer upon layer, on piles of wreckage, a mirage on the back of ruination?
>
> —Rainer Maria Rilke, letter to Princess Marie von
> Thurn und Taxis-Hohenlohe, July 9, 1915

The change registered in Rilke's letter is echoed later by Paul Valéry (see the selection in the *Anthology*) as well as many other writers:

> There died a myriad,
> And of the best, among them,
> For an old bitch gone in the teeth,
> For a botched civilization,
>
> Charm, smiling at the good mouth,
> Quick eyes gone under earth's lid,
> For two gross of broken statues,
> For a few thousand battered books.
> —Ezra Pound, from *Hugh Selwyn Mauberley*, 1920

> What is that sound high in the air
> Murmur of maternal lamentation
> Who are those hooded hordes swarming
> Over endless plains, stumbling in cracked earth
> Ringed by the flat horizon only
> What is the city over the mountains
> Cracks and reforms and bursts in the violet air
> Falling towers
> Jerusalem Athens Alexandria
> Vienna London
> Unreal
> —T. S. Eliot, from *The Waste Land*, 1922

The remaining selections in the "Civilization on Trial" cluster in the *Anthology* were all written after World War I, and, whatever the differences in their interpretations of civilization's problems and discontents, all bear the mark of having been through that catastrophic period in Western history.

Of these, Oswald Spengler's *The Decline of the West* (1919) is perhaps the most thoroughly pessimistic analysis of the situation of Western civilization in that it posits no possibility at all for recovery. Civilizations, he proposes, have a predictable life cycle, and Western civilization is spinning ineluctably toward its conclusion. Spengler differed from most Western historians in that he placed the death throes of modern European civilization in the context of a global history, where, he notes, many non-Western civilizations had passed through the same cycle with the same result.

W. B. Yeats's ideas about history, best illustrated in the *Anthology* by *The Second Coming*, are strikingly similar to Spengler's, both in their shape and their pessimism. For both, civilizations began to decline when the original sources of their energy began to be less powerfully operative, and complete collapse was inevitable when those sources were entirely exhausted. For Spengler, the very fact that a Civilization, as opposed to a Culture, exists is the sign that it is on its way toward disintegration. The outward-looking tendencies of civilization (Imperialism, for example) reveal its sickness; it is the inward-looking intensity of a Culture that signifies its health. For Yeats, if not Spengler, the disappearance of one source of energy inevitably gives rise to another, very likely its shadow-self, its opposite. So as the West turns and turns in the "widening gyre," when "things fall apart" and the "center cannot hold," a new civilization is emerging—a "rough beast, its hour come round at last, slouches toward Bethlehem to be born."

Students may never have thought about it before, but probably all of them have some notion about the shape of history. Many probably still retain the nineteenth-century notion of evolutionary meliorism, the idea that developments in science and thought mean that we are gradually but inevitably, bettering ourselves. Others will hold a cyclical view, similar in some ways to that of Spengler, but more similar—probably—to the viewpoint of later historians such as Arnold Toynbee. Still others will hold with Aldous Huxley, who proposed that history was just "one damn thing after another." In any case, when talking about Spengler (or a number of the other writers in the *Anthology*) it might be useful and interesting to ask students to at least think about the concept of history they actually hold.

The excerpt from Paul Valéry's *The Crisis of the Mind* opens with the recognition of the fragility of civilization. Like other great civilizations that have risen and fallen, Valéry reminds us (as Eliot does in *The Waste Land*) that the great civilizations of his time—France, England, Russia, and he certainly could have mentioned Austria, a nineteenth-century power that had collapsed like a cold soufflé—could just as easily disappear. "We see now," he says, "that the abyss of history is deep enough to hold us all." For Valéry, the crisis is one of intelligence. The Western mind had poured all of its power and energy into making war, and all the knowledge and wisdom accumulated throughout the preceding centuries had been unable to stop it—"the illusion of a European culture has been lost, and knowledge has proved impotent to save anything whatever."

The European mind, then, was unable to cope with the circumstances of the war. Valéry proposes the reason for this is very like what Rilke, in the first letter quoted above, called the "many-minded times that have long since confused and wearied all of us." There was, Valéry argued, the "free coexistence, in all her cultivated minds, of the most dissimilar ideas, the most contradictory principles of life and learning." This 'many-mindedness' was, for Valéry, the very characteristic of a *modern* era—that is, it was not something one could just *will* away. We were modern and there was nothing for it. Consequently, the efforts of the thinker seem futile, if not downright dangerous, and we stand like the melancholy Hamlet looking out over a domain that is no longer his, and which no longer needs him.

Finally, we have two excerpts from Sigmund Freud (published in 1927 and 1929). Civilization was, for him also, an illusion, but a necessary illusion. Both of these excerpts were written some years after the Great War (World War I) ended but, once again, the mark of having lived through that experience is everywhere apparent. Freud's major concern in *Civilization and Its Discontents* is human aggression, a reasonable subject to take up after the war, but its central argument is that for us human beings, the very act of living in civilization is inevitably to create neurosis. As the *Anthology*'s introduction says, civilization's very purpose is to provide a "set of restraints" so that the community and the individual might survive and prosper. But human beings are, in Freud's view, instinctively hostile and competitive, and accept such constraints with great reluctance. Happiness exists when desires are fulfilled, and civilization works toward the restriction of fulfilling instinctual desires. In order to live and work within the constraints of civilization, then, human beings must repress desire, and that repression creates, in its turn, neurosis. It's not a happy view, and Freud's outlook for the future of civilization is by no means optimistic. Still, though he understands perfectly well why we may be hostile to civilization, he refuses to reproach it for "trying to eliminate strife and competition from human activity." Civilization's restraining measures are, after all, indispensable for the continued stability and security of the human community, which would, without them, eventually disintegrate.

Certain useful literary "matches" for the selections in the "Civilization on Trial" cluster have been made throughout. I will list them here for easy reference, though teachers will no doubt find other equally useful examples in and out of the *Anthology*.

Sigmund Freud: Conrad, *Heart of Darkness*
Max Weber: Kafka, *The Metamorphosis*
Paul Valéry: Eliot, *The Waste Land*
Oswald Spengler: Yeats, *The Second Coming*

CONSTANTINE CAVAFY

Backgrounds

The critic Edmund Keeley declared Constantine Cavafy to be "the most original and influential Greek poet of this [twentieth] century." This claim reflects Cavafy's ability to blend imagination and history together in his work. In Cavafy's poetry the material facts of the historical record blend with the poet's imagined re-creation of the way people felt and lived in the distant past. His themes of desire are offered in a language suggestive of dreams that would be all too nebulous were it not for the hard, descriptive detail that fills so many of his poems. This blend of sharp descriptive prose-like diction set in dreamscapes loaded with desire make Cavafy's work unique in the pantheon of twentieth-century poetry; no one else has his ability to bring the ancient world so fully realized into the emotional and political life of the present.

His greatest innovation is the flat, stark diction that is as palpable in the original Greek as it is in these translations. His simple, everyday language, according to C. M. Bowra, who is familiar with the original Greek version of the poems, had no precedent before Cavafy's work. Says Bowra: "neither Greek nor Western European models" can be found for his kind of diction. Therefore, the unusual conjunction of spare language, ancient topics, and modern sensibilities must be understood as emerging from Cavafy's own "natural instinct for words." In more recent years, South African Nobel Laureate J. M. Coetzee has even appropriated the title of one of Cavafy's poems for his own strange parabolic novel, *Waiting for the Barbarians*.

Waiting for the Barbarians

Along with *Ithaca*, this is Cavafy's most famous poem. It took years, however, for it to become well known to Western readers. It was originally composed at the end of the nineteenth century and published only in one of the poet's rare private editions in 1910. In any event, the poem should not be read or taught as a literal rendition of historical fact. Adhering to poetry's claim on imagination and symbol, the poem speaks more generally and universally to the problem of Otherness, of the foreign, and the unknown among human societies.

To read the poem simply as a fully imagined rendition of a historical episode would be to miss this larger philosophical issue about the all-too-human distinction made between an "us" and a "them." Put simply, in this poem the established Roman community has defined itself entirely through comparison with what it is not—the Barbarians—and found itself boring in that comparison. The same conundrum was discussed by Hegel in his famous discourse on masters and slaves, and again by Marx. That discussion aside, the poem opens the door as did both Hegel and Marx to the problem of essentialism.

For if any sense of community is dependent on some other existing community, is it fair to say that there is any such thing as an essence to any one community? Is any nation or state fully itself in some mysterious way or are all communities defined simply by their relationship to some other entity? The best class discussion of this poem will occur if this question becomes the focal point for understanding this poem.

The City

Like *Waiting for the Barbarians*, this poem was first published in the private 1910 edition of Cavafy's poems. And like that poem, it is best understood from a philosophical, imaginative, dreamlike perspective rather than from a materialist one that would focus on real cities and real places. In other words, this poem is best read as a parable rather than a report.

The heart of the poem has to do with the burdens and problems that plague us all. In the mid-nineteenth-century, the great American poet and philosopher Ralph Waldo Emerson in his essay *Self Reliance* made much the same point as Cavafy does in this poem when he said, "My giant goes with me wherever I go." In his poem, Cavafy touches on an insight particularly common in Anglo-American literary culture: namely, that one's own interior mental life, one's own interior imagination, one's own inner sensibility, is always primary. Outer forces, according to this view, have far less impact and consequence than inner forces. Like Nietzsche, to whom one might refer for comparison, Cavafy makes happiness the primary goal of human life. Therefore, if one is not happy, one had best search for the cause inside rather than outside.

The American poet Robert Frost makes a similar point when he distinguishes between "inner" and "outer" weather. It works best to teach both this poem and *Waiting for the Barbarians* as parables. If one does, they work in conjunction with similar parables in the included selections from Nietzsche, Freud, Rilke, and Kafka.

Sculptor of Tyana

Unlike the previous two poems, this poem requires the reader to begin from specific facts and a historical context. One should take the references seriously and allow them to work symbolically as a portrait of the artist. In other words, the art work described in this poem can be shown in class to reveal the interior life of the artist. By understanding this sculptor's references, one has a better sense of the sculptor. The poem, then, becomes a canny portrait of the sculptor and manages, through these references, to reveal the man's erotic, political, and religious views.

Robert Browning's *My Last Duchess* would be a wonderful poem to read in conjunction with *Sculptor of Tyana*. As it happens, Cavafy was much taken by Browning's poetry, work he had become familiar with as a student in England during his youth. A fun in-class assignment would be to have students describe themselves only through a variety of their possessions.

Ithaka

Addressed to Odysseus and referring explicitly to the famous journey as told by Homer in *The Odyssey*, this poem is better read as a parable in line with *Waiting for the Barbarians* and *The City* rather than as another version of Homer's epic. When read as a parable, both Odysseus and Ithaca become symbols in a larger pattern applicable to any life at any time. Where *The City* suggests that one's inner life dominates one's destiny, this poem takes the opposite tack and probes the influence and importance of outer events on one's life. Ithaka becomes symbolic of any life goal and as a result the *road* to that goal, rather than the goal itself, is what requires the most attention. One might compare Robert Frost's *The Road Not Taken* to this poem.

Classroom Strategies

One or two class periods can be devoted to all or just a few of these poems. One strategy would be to take just two or three of the poems at a time and develop commonalities between them. For example, students might begin with *The Sculptor* and, using the notes provided in the *Anthology*, they might develop a portrait of the artist from the many references. Then, using *In the Evening, Kaisarion,* and *The Next Table,* they could develop a portrait of the narrator or persona from details provided in those poems. In so doing, students would see how poetry even at its seemingly most detached actually tells us a great deal about the secrets of the inner life.

Another issue for a full class period is the conflict between free will and essentialism, which circulates throughout so many of these poems. Students might debate this problem in relation to *Ithaka* and The City. Do these poems endorse or mock the idea of free will?

Another issue worthy of a single class period is to explore the idea of art as it is described in these poems. *Kaisarion* would be the most helpful starting place for such a discussion.

Topics for Discussion and Writing

1. Choose one of Cavafy's poems and, juxtaposing it with Kafka's *The Metamorphosis*, explain why a parable differs from a poem or story in the typical use of those generic terms.
2. Compare one poem each from Cavafy, Rilke, and Stevens. In what ways do they differ? Do they differ at all?
3. What is Cavafy's view of love? Choose one or two poems and discuss.
4. What is Cavafy's view of art? Choose one or two poems and discuss.

Comparative Perspectives

A number of other writers—in and out of the *Anthology*—might be useful in putting Cavafy into a literary context:

1. His use of the ancient world in his poems might be compared to Ezra Pound and H. D., among many others.

2. Emerson and Nietzsche have already been referenced when talking about the primacy of the "inner life" in Cavafy's work. But this is, of course, a central idea for most of the early twentieth-century Modernists. We find it in Rilke, Stevens, Kafka, Woolf, D. H. Lawrence, Joyce, Proust, and Strindberg, and most everyone else. It might be useful to examine the different ways in which some of these writers try to reveal the "inner life"—for example, dreams or "stream of consciousness."

Further Reading

Bowra, C. M. *The Creative Experiment.* 1949.

Jusdanis, Gregory. *The Poetics of Cavafy.* 1987.

Keeley, Edmund. *Cavafy's Alexandria.* 1976.

Liddell, Robert. *Cavafy: A Biography.* 1976.

Rochelle, Christopher. *C. P. Cavafy.* 1990.

William Butler Yeats

Backgrounds

We continue to read W. B. Yeats because he wrote incontestably great poetry of widely differing types for over fifty years; because the various phases he passed through mirror the course of modern poetry as a whole; and because his work both charms the unsophisticated reader and challenges the sophisticated. He is the modern poet who most forcefully suggests to students something of the possibilities of poetry. The poems selected here are among the most famous and most representative of his work.

When You Are Old

When You Are Old is one of the five love poems that Yeats copied out in manuscript and presented to Maud Gonne, who inspired many of his poems and much of his imagery. The central themes of the five poems have to do with threats to love—pity, tears, exhaustion, death, and, in the case of *When You Are Old*, age.

The poem is relatively straightforward until the last stanza, when the speaker of the poem presents the figure of Love pacing upon mountains and hiding "his face amid a crowd of stars." Here, the figure of Love has fled from the physical realm to the Olympian—the realm, that is, of poetry. Like other poems of Yeats's, this one features the sad recollection of the physical passion of youth from the perspective of wise age, which must replace sweet but fleeting passion with the eternal beauty of art. *Sailing to Byzantium* raises similar issues, as does Keats's *Ode on a Grecian Urn*.

The author expects us to see that he has based his poem on a poem by the sixteenth-century French poet Ronsard, but with a difference. Whereas the speaker in Ronsard's poem stresses the fast-fading joys of youth to strengthen his argument that the beloved should yield to him now, Yeats takes the argument to an entirely different plane of feeling, with a love that has fixed itself forever among the stars.

Easter 1916

To convey the state of mind—and of Ireland—out of which this poem rises, it may be useful to hand out copies of Yeats's *September 1913*, in which the poet insists that the money-minded middle class (the paudeens) have so completely taken over that the romantic spirit of the Irish revolutionaries is dried up: "Romantic Ireland's dead and gone / It's with O'Leary in the grave."

By the time of *Easter 1916*, an appropriate time of year for thoughts of rebirth, Yeats's views have changed. The Irish spirit and what Yeats refers to in *September 1913* as "all that delirium of the brave" have revived with the Easter Rebellion. And for Yeats, all has "changed, changed utterly: / A terrible beauty is born." The first stanza of the poem delivers an Ireland reminiscent of *September 1913*—it seems a fool's country, meaningless, a "casual comedy" in which all heroism is dead. The second stanza enlists a number of Yeats's friends and acquaintances who played prominent roles in the Rebellion—Con Markiewicz, Patrick Pearse, Thomas MacDonagh, even John MacBride (the estranged husband of Maud Gonne)—to suggest how the meaningless Ireland of *September 1913* has been transformed utterly.

The third stanza is truly extraordinary. It contrasts mutability with stasis, the living stream and the seasons with the "stone" that the poet associates with the fatal revolutionary purpose of his friends. The imagery of the stanza seems governed by the compelling forward motion of the changes these friends brought about. The stanza surges with activity, plunging forward with increasing speed and power, dazzling the ear. The whole of the natural world participates in this motion, enchanted into action, so to speak, by the single-mindedness of the revolutionary vision—perhaps in the same way that a stone in a stream generates ripples, eddies, even cascades.

But the single-minded passion necessary to create such an active transformation can "make a stone of the heart." In the fourth stanza Yeats raises the questions that must be asked about the consequences of any passionate action, especially revolutionary action. Where will it end? Was it necessary? Was it excessive? Was it worth the cost? Yeats raises the questions, but—and we can be thankful for this—declines to answer them. That, Yeats says, "is Heaven's part, our part / To murmur name upon name" and to "know their dream; enough / To know they dreamed and are dead." Yeats's response to the Easter Rising is, then, complex. The last lines of the poem, the refrain, shift from a comparatively simple celebration of change into something celebrative but simultaneously deeply ambivalent. The words "terrible" and "beauty" in the refrain have picked up important new connotations; they are now as highly charged with apprehension as with celebration.

The Second Coming

With the possible exception of *Sailing to Byzantium*, this may be Yeats's most famous poem. To expound its implications fully it will be necessary to introduce a brief description of Yeats's theory of history, which is discussed in the headnote. But this introduction should be kept brief and pithy, or the poem will get lost in the theory. It is enough to say that here Yeats implies a second coming is at hand, not literally the coming of the Antichrist but of a new era that will have characteristics opposite to those of Christianity—an era that Yeats imagines beginning around the year 2000. The first stanza describes the disintegration of the Christian era, which has lost coherence, unity, order. The "centre cannot hold; / Mere anarchy is loosed upon the world"; the falcon whirls beyond the control of its master. At the end of this era, then, the order and ceremony of Christianity will be reversed. Lines 5 and 6 suggest an explosion of violence—an inverted baptism, with inverted results; the innocent will be drowned in their own blood.

The second stanza declares the meaning of this incoherence: "Surely some revelation is at hand; / Surely the Second Coming is at hand." As a symbol of the new era Yeats imagines a kind of Sphinx, a "shape with lion body and the head of a man," which is just beginning to move as "indignant desert birds" reel above it. Their presence recalls the uncontrolled falcon that begins the poem, and thus confirms the link between the end of the old era and the beginning of the new. The poet's ability to visualize this new beginning then ends: "The darkness drops again." But he knows what he has "seen," and he knows its meaning. The new pitiless cycle of history has been waiting its turn, "vexed to nightmare" by the twenty centuries of the Christian era. Its time now has come; and Yeats leaves us with his final question: "what rough beast, its hour come round at last, / Slouches toward Bethlehem to be born?"

There is no definitive answer, of course. There is no more poem. But the implications of *The Second Coming* are that the new order will reverse the values of the exhausted Christian era; the new era will be violent, "blank and pitiless," where only "the worst" will have the intensity to carry out their convictions. And since the traditional answer to the riddle of the Sphinx has always been "man," the "rough beast" may be humanity itself. Yeats doesn't like the look of what he sees.

Leda and the Swan

The Second Coming deals with the end of the Christian era and the beginning of a new one. *Leda and the Swan* deals with the beginning of the classical era that preceded the Christian, but a classical era that many take to be a metaphor for our own. As the descent of the dove upon Mary announces a scheme of things that in *The Second Coming* is nearing the end, so the rape of Leda by the swan announces a scheme of things that includes the Trojan War (fought for Helen, one offspring of this union) and the murder of Agamemnon by Clytemnestra (another of its offspring). You may well find that your students are concerned by this mythologized glorification of what is, in fact, the rape of a terrified girl. The powerfully sensual description of that rape is pursued right up to the last two lines, when attention is directed to a more abstract issue: did she foresee the future? How far in *this* instance did the divine suffuse the human? The combination of these two aspects can be a strong catalyst for class discussion.

Sailing to Byzantium

Again, with the possible exception of *The Second Coming*, this may be Yeats's best-known poem. Except for Eliot's *The Love Song of J. Alfred Prufrock* and one or two of Robert Frost's pieces, it is perhaps the best-known modern poem in English. Although *Sailing to Byzantium*, like *The Second Coming* and *Leda and the Swan*, requires some knowledge of Yeats's personal mythology to be fully understood, you must again be on guard against losing the poem amid symbolic baggage.

A reading of the poem is best begun by comparing "that" country which the speaker is leaving (Ireland, perhaps) with the place to which he is going—Byzantium. Both are symbolic places, and idiosyncratically so, since the meaning Yeats means to give them is true only insofar as we accept the poet's claims for them. They cannot be better understood by reading more about Byzantium or the mating habits of the early-modern Irish; they can be understood as symbols only by reading more Yeats. "That" country is the country of the young, the passionate, the fertile; it is a place "caught in the sensual music," a place of generation and, therefore, of the inevitable decay that comes with mortality. Byzantium, on the other hand, is a city of the soul, especially of the artist's soul; it suggests changelessness and immortality. It is that place where the spiritual and secular meet in art.

The second stanza establishes the poem's speaker as an "aged man" who must "sing louder," that is, insist on the primacy of spirit over body as he becomes older. And since the spirit is best represented in art, the speaker has "sailed the seas" to reach Byzantium. Once there, in the third stanza, he asks the city's "sages" to instruct him, to become the "singing-masters" of his soul, to gather him into the "artifice of eternity" that only art can make.

In the last stanza, the speaker makes known his desire—that he shall never again take bodily form except, perhaps, as a work of art, a golden bird upon a golden bough who will sing "To lords and ladies of Byzantium / Of what is past, or passing, or to come." Thus if the poem concentrates on the speaker's desire to leave the world of mortality in order to achieve an immortality of the spirit through art, the last line suggests its opposite—the world of mortality, the very world the speaker has renounced. (So likewise in *Lapis Lazuli*, the Chinese elders look out upon a world in turmoil from their secure place in art, and their glittering eyes are untroubled, tranquil, gay.) The last line echoes "Whatever is begotten, born, and dies" in the first stanza and thus serves to remind us, as Yeats always reminds us, that when something is gained, something is lost. *Sailing to Byzantium* looks back at earlier poems such as *The Stolen Child* and *The Dolls* (both of which might usefully be handed out to students), and ahead to *The Circus Animals' Desertion*, in which Yeats insists that the ladder of his vision, and of all art, starts in the "foul rag-and-bone shop of the heart." Like Keats in *Ode on a Grecian Urn*, Yeats recognizes that the immortality of art is cold; it derives from and serves life—the one thing it cannot be. *Sailing to Byzantium* can very easily be read as being "about" the desire of the aged to transcend the decay of the body in favor of the eternality of art, but the ambiguity of the poem should not be ignored.

Among School Children

This poem, like *Sailing to Byzantium*, begins with the question of old age, the contrast between current decrepitude and remembered youth, and then moves to a consideration of how age and final decay come to everyone, no matter how wisely one has worked to find an ideal world to pit against the imperfections of reality. Plato, Aristotle, and Pythagoras, like the speaker and the rest of us, become old scarecrows—"Old clothes upon old sticks to scare a bird."

As if to mock humankind's inevitable decay and to put off thoughts of it, "nuns and mothers worship images"—nuns worship religious icons as mothers worship idealized versions of their children. The invocation of these visions (both icons and fantasies are a kind of art) leads Yeats to his final stanza. Here Yeats again insists on the necessity of combining real and ideal, mortal and immortal, life and art. The ideal worlds of Plato and Aristotle are achieved only by denying an important part of what life is; they bruise the body to "pleasure soul." Instead, Yeats appears to say, images and theories cannot be separated from life itself—"How can we know the dancer from the dance?"—and the actual world and the visionary world, the worlds of mortal imperfection and artistic perfection, must exist in concert. The "comfortable kind of old scarecrow" and the child he once was are one thing, much as the chestnut tree is always its past and future as well as its present, a synthesis of leaf, blossom, and bole.

Byzantium

In this poem Yeats stresses particularly the mutual dependence of the changeless, perfect world of Byzantium and the mortal world of "all that man is . . . The fury and the mire of human veins." *Byzantium* exploits the same contrast as its predecessor, but what existed as a rather ambiguous implication in *Sailing to Byzantium* becomes the central issue here.

After four stanzas that describe the spirit world of Byzantium and how the mortal becomes immortal, Yeats gives the final stanza over to images, as one critic puts it, "not only of the eternal world, but also of the world of nature which is feeding it." In this poem, then, the natural and spiritual are inseparable; one can never be entirely abandoned for the other.

Students will find Yeats's imagery—the dolphins, the mummy, and so on—significantly more difficult here than in *Sailing to Byzantium*, but most of their troubles will be addressed in the footnotes.

Lapis Lazuli

When *Lapis Lazuli* was written, in 1936, Europe was both emerging from an economic depression and heating up for war. Hitler and Mussolini were gaining power in Germany and Italy, and the Spanish Civil War was running its course toward Franco. It was not just "hysterical women" who must have told Yeats that they were sick of art, or that he should use his considerable powers for political purposes. In these years, public affairs were intruding on private visions so forcefully that almost all of the important younger British poets and novelists of the period (Auden, Spender, Day Lewis, MacNeice, Isherwood, Orwell, Warner, and others) were engaged in writing books that were emphatically political. Poetry, especially as it was being written by High Modernists, was seen as a kind of luxury, too obscure and resistant to the needs and desires of the public to do the work in the world that these writers, and Yeats's "hysterical women," thought needed to be done. *Lapis Lazuli* constitutes Yeats's answer to them.

The first stanza presents the accusation: art is no longer enough. Commitment is needed, because "if nothing drastic is done" war will break out. Yeats's use of a popular seventeenth-century ballad to describe war has enticed some critics to claim that Yeats was ignoring political realities. Indeed, the scornful phrase "King Billy bomb-balls" does have the effect of deflating the seriousness of what might, and did, happen. But Yeats surely intended this deflation, because it serves to place the war to come in the larger context of all wars, in the larger context of the rise and fall of civilizations (many of which are now remembered or understood only through, and because of, their art), a subject with which Yeats, like Eliot and Pound, was much obsessed.

The second stanza suggests that in the play of civilizations even the greatest of actors do not betray the tragic parts they play, though they and we know they are participating in tragedy. Instead they retain a "gaiety" that "transfigures all that dread." They commit themselves but remain themselves. They empower the play they are in and, at the same time, transcend it by displaying the proper heroic reaction to catastrophe. And these "actors," Yeats suggests in the third stanza, are the ones who make civilizations. Their work may fall, may not last out the day, their "wisdom" may go "to rack," but "All things fall and are built again, / And those that build them again are gay."

The fourth and fifth stanzas locate that transcendent gaiety in one seemingly unspectacular work of art, a piece of lapis lazuli "carved by some Chinese sculptor into the semblance of a mountain with temple, trees, paths, and an ascetic and pupil about to climb the mountain." In it, Yeats discovers all their civilization, now available only through art. He imagines them seated between mountain and sky, surveying "the tragic scene" below. And their "ancient, glittering eyes, are gay." They have, through art, survived, immortalized, and thus transcended the civilization from which they emerged. Through them, through art, their civilization retains the only meaning left to have. If King Billy's bomb-balls are pitched in, if Yeats's civilization is "beaten flat," his art—if it is really art—will remain, preserving its world for the instruction and delight of future men and women, perhaps even "A young girl in the indolence of her youth, / Or an old man upon a winter's night" (*On Being Asked for a War Poem*, lines 5–6).

The Circus Animals' Desertion

The Circus Animals' Desertion was written in the last year of Yeats's life, and it serves as a kind of final survey of his career, a map of his imagery and thinking, and a declaration about the source of his art. The "circus animals" are, of course, the images that Yeats has used throughout his poetic life, during that "winter and summer till old age began." Here again are all the "stilted boys" of his imagination: Oisin, Niamh, Countess Cathleen, Cuchulain, the various faces of Maud Gonne, "Lion and woman and the Lord knows what." In his insouciant litany of his "masterful images," Yeats admits—a bit sadly, one feels—that it was the images themselves that finally enchanted him, not "those things that they were emblems of."

In the final stanza, Yeats speculates, as he had so often in his earlier work, about the source of his art. And he discovers it, as we knew he must, in the "mound of refuse," the noisy and filthy thing, that life is. No matter the heights to which imagination may climb, the ladder of vision necessarily stands planted in the mire of earth. And now that the ladder is gone, he "must lie down where all the ladders start, / In the foul rag-and-bone shop of the heart."

Classroom Strategies

If you plan to teach all nine of the poems, you should probably allow at least two—better yet three—days for the purpose. Yeats's poems tend to build on themselves, the meaning and imagery of one informing the meaning and imagery of the next. Hence it is wise to keep them in their chronological order, though it will be difficult not to make *Sailing to Byzantium* and *Byzantium* into a matched pair.

Should you choose to teach a representative sample of the poems, I would recommend *Easter 1916, The Second Coming, Sailing to Byzantium, Among School Children,* and *Lapis Lazuli.* The middle three poems here are among his most famous as well as his best and introduce some of his most persistent poetic concerns, while providing a kind of unity to your students' experience of his work.

The most difficult immediate problem for students will lie with the "allusive imagery and symbolic structure" of Yeats's work, especially his best work. Not only are many of his most suggestive images and symbols derived from sources well out of the mainstream of Western thought—occult texts, Irish myths and legends, personal friends and unrequited lovers, and so on—but they are also filtered through Yeats's own fertile imagination and given their applicable meanings *only in the context of Yeats's own work.* That is to say, the only way students can fully understand Yeats's images and symbols is to read more Yeats, though as suggested in the critical discussions above, these can be understood and appreciated without plunging deeply into Yeats's personal mythology. A brief description of his most important mythical structure—Yeats's cyclical model of history—appears. Yeats's historical "gyres," or spirals, in the headnote might best be represented in the following way:

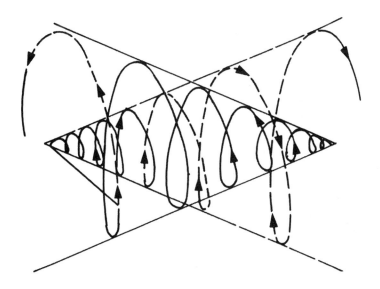

It is important to notice that the gyres interpenetrate, that a new one begins only as its opposite concludes, that each gyre represents a cycle of history covering approximately two thousand years, and that—though one is always dominant—the opposing gyres exist simultaneously, one always implying the other. (His "Byzantium," therefore, exists at that midpoint—1000 C.E.—of the gyres' interpenetration.) Yeats's use of this model, as well as his related use of the "phases of the moon," is personal in the extreme, but can be related to other cyclical versions of history, such as those of Vico, Spengler, and Toynbee.

To get students in the mood to discuss such matters, it is useful to point out that all of us have and maintain versions of history, whether we realize it or not. To mention some of them—the Christian version; the "wave"; evolutionary meliorism, or the idea of progress; the strictly linear (Aldous Huxley's "one damn thing after another")—will always evoke discussion and soften up the doubters. Teachers who wish to know more about Yeats's particular version should consult *A Vision*, surely one of the most arcane and, in some ways, difficult books ever seriously offered by a major writer.

Students will very likely recognize Yeats's technical prowess after they are advised of it, but they are unlikely to respond to it on their own. Yeats himself once said that poems should be "packed in ice or salt," meaning that they should retain traditional, formal structures. Like Frost, he felt that writing poems without formal complications was like playing tennis without a net. It should come as no surprise, then, that each of the poems here is highly structured.

Sailing to Byzantium uses four stanzas of eight lines apiece, and each stanza maintains a rhyme scheme of *a b a b a b c c*. This very tight formal structure is at the same time relaxed in the sense that it is almost invisible; it seems not to intrude at all on the development of the poem's meaning. Each stanza suggests a movement in space, from "that country" to "Byzantium," which corresponds to the speaker's movement of mind, from engagement in nature to engagement in spirit. The first stanza, one of Yeats's most memorable, is as rich and sensual as the natural world it observes. The phrase "those dying generations" calls up one of the central issues of the poem—that in the world of nature whatever is born must inevitably die, in fact is always in the process of dying. This phrase, and the notion it suggests, is immediately called up again by the "salmonfalls," which salmon climb to spawn and die. The richness of organic life, "fish, flesh, or fowl," reechoes in a phrase summarizing its rich but also limiting processes: "Whatever is begotten, born, and dies." And this is echoed again, with extended meaning, in the last line of the poem. Thus the first stanza describes the "sensual music" of the natural world while it sings the very music it describes.

In *Among School Children* (eight stanzas of eight lines each with a rhyme scheme of *a b a b a b c c*), the formal structure of the poem again reflects its interwoven thoughts and images. The movement of the thought is supported by recurring imagery—the scarecrow, Leda (and swans), history, Plato, "image," and "dream." Thesis and antithesis (age/youth, reality/dream, mortal/immortal) finally achieve synthesis. The assurance of Yeats's formal structure gives a certain credence to the assurance of the poem's final resolution.

Topics for Discussion and Writing

1. In what ways is *When You Are Old* like *Sailing to Byzantium?*
   [See "Backgrounds," *When You Are Old*.]
2. What is Yeats's attitude toward the Easter Rebellion of 1916 and the people who were involved in it? Are his feelings mixed? How do we know?
   [See "Backgrounds," *Easter 1916*.]
3. How do the images in stanza three of *Easter 1916* relate to the poem as a whole?

[See "Backgrounds," *Easter 1916*, third paragraph.]

4. How does the second stanza of *The Second Coming* answer the first stanza?

   [See "Backgrounds," *The Second Coming*.]

5. What are gyres? What have they to do with Yeats's idea of history? How are they used in the poem? Does Yeats seem to think that the coming era will be better or worse than the last? How do we know?

   [See "Backgrounds," *The Second Coming*, and the third and fourth paragraphs of "Classroom Strategies."]

6. What is going on in the first stanza of *Leda and the Swan*? How long does it take to realize that Yeats is alluding to a classical myth? What use does he make of that myth? What do the last two lines mean, and why is the beak finally "indifferent"?

   [See "Backgrounds," *Leda and the Swan*.]

7. What is the crucial difference between "that" country and Byzantium? Why does the speaker wish to sail to Byzantium in *Sailing to Byzantium*? What does he want to do once there?

   [See "Backgrounds," *Sailing to Byzantium*.]

8. Through what details does Yeats conjure up the natural world in the first stanza of *Sailing to Byzantium*? Why these details? What are his feelings about the world of "sensual music" that he renounces? From what evidence in the poem do we infer these feelings?

   [See "Backgrounds," *Sailing to Byzantium*, and the seventh paragraph of "Classroom Strategies."]

9. How are Keats's *Ode on a Grecian Urn* and *Ode to a Nightingale* similar to *Sailing to Byzantium*?

   [Both contrast the sensual, temporal world with a world of immortality and timelessness. Both use a bird as a symbol of that immortality.]

10. What is Yeats's point in *Among School Children*? How are the images worshiped by "nuns and mothers" similar? What other poems by Yeats help us to understand this one?

    [See "Backgrounds," *Among School Children*, as well as the last two paragraphs of "Classroom Strategies." *Leda and the Swan*, *Sailing to Byzantium*, *Byzantium*, and *The Circus Animals' Desertion* can all be usefully related to *Among School Children*.]

11. How does *Byzantium* answer *Sailing to Byzantium*?

    [See "Backgrounds," *Byzantium*.]

12. What would Yeats's answer be to those who want him to write poems about present-day concerns? What does Yeats mean by "gaiety" in *Lapis Lazuli*? Doesn't Yeats take the possibility of war seriously?

    [See "Backgrounds," *Lapis Lazuli*.]

13. In what ways is *The Circus Animals' Desertion* a review of Yeats's poetic career? Where does it locate the source of art?

    [See "Backgrounds," *The Circus Animals' Desertion*.]

14. What are the major thematic concerns in Yeats's work? Is he consistent in the positions he takes on matters that concern him? Where can apparent contradictions be found? Is he ambivalent about many of these matters? Should Yeats be consistent or certain?

Comparative Perspectives

See comparisons suggested to the poems of Victor Hugo, Walt Whitman, and Rainer Maria Rilke.

Further Reading

See also the reading suggestions in the *Anthology*, p. 2556.

Archibald, Douglas. *Yeats*. 1983. An overall study, but especially interesting on Yeats's work with regard to politics and public life.

Bloom, Harold. *Yeats*. 1970. Yeats's achievement discussed and judged in the context of the Romantic tradition, especially the work of Blake and Shelley.

Diggory, Terence. *Yeats and American Poetry*. 1983. The impact of individual poems on the "tradition of myself" in American poetry. Poets discussed include Eliot, Stevens, Tate, Ransom, Warren, MacLeish, Roethke, and Robert Lowell.

Donoghue, Denis. *William Butler Yeats*. 1988; 1971. A fluent, generalized thematic discussion of Yeats's relationship to European Romanticism, exploring ideas of self, imagination, will, action, symbol, history, world, vision, and self-transformation.

Ellmann, Richard. *Yeats: The Man and the Masks*. 1948; 1978. A very fine, short critical biography.

Finneran, Richard J. *Editing Yeats's Poems: A Reconsideration*. 1990. A scholarly companion to Finneran's 1989 revised edition of Yeats's *The Poems*, containing new material.

Henn, T. R. *The Lonely Tower*. 1950. A thorough and influential study of all of Yeats's work.

Kinahan, Frank. *Yeats, Folklore, and Occultism: Contexts of the Early World and Thought*. 1988.

Longenbach, James. *Stone Cottage: Pound, Yeats, and Modernism*. 1988. Situates Yeats inside the Modernist movement.

Lynch, David. *Yeats: The Poetics of the Self*. 1981. A more specialized psychoanalytic study emphasizing the analysis of the self practiced by Heinz Kohut.

Stallworthy, Jon. *Between the Lines: Yeats's Poetry in the Making*. 1963. Displays various drafts of Yeats's work in process.

Stanfield, Paul Scott. *Yeats and Politics in the 1930s.* 1988. Another discussion of Yeats's relation to politics.

Timm, Eitel. *W. B. Yeats: A Century of Criticism.* Trans. Eric Wredenhagen. 1990. A survey of Yeats criticism structured according to early, middle, and late works that describes critical tendencies and approaches and includes debates over specific works.

Zwerdling, Alex. *Yeats and the Heroic Ideal.* 1965. Yeats's vision of heroism and its expression in his poetry.

Luigi Pirandello

Six Characters in Search of an Author

Backgrounds

Pirandello's plays are so important to modern drama as a whole that it is almost impossible to imagine what it would have been like without him. His theoretical concerns—the inability of language to say what one most wants to say; the difficulty a person has in establishing germane communication with another; the variability of personality; the relation of life illusion to stage illusion; the relativity of perception to time, place, mood, personality, and even the state of one's digestion—anticipated almost every important development of the modern theater. He is humorous, exasperating, fascinating, profound—a true genius of the theater.

Six Characters is about fictional and dramatic "characters." These differ from human beings in that they are embodiments of feelings, ideas, or overpowering emotions and are trapped in their embodied roles. Unlike human beings, they are also possibly immortal; "whoever has the luck to be born a character," says the Father in *Six Characters*, "can laugh even at death. Because a character will never die." Thus characters have a life of their own—they live on eternally but only so far developed as their creator has made them. Our six characters, having been abandoned by their author, are so overpowered by emotion that they are compelled to come to the theater and plead with the professional actors (who are rehearsing Pirandello's play *The Rules of the Game*) to reenact their drama. The Father says: "The play is in us: we are the play . . . the passion inside us is driving us on." The characters have been created but left stranded, with no play or novel to house them; their vitality has no context in which to live. They can reach their completion only as parts of a play.

Discovering a ready-made setting for their "existence," they insist that their tragedy is more important, more urgently in need of expression, than the Pirandello play being rehearsed. The drama of their lives is simple enough, though complicated at the end by the question of what has happened as opposed to what is happening. What has happened takes up almost the entire first act and can be outlined as follows: the Father is a rationalist who married beneath himself. He notices the interest that his secretary takes in his wife and that it is returned. It is a platonic relationship, but the Father senses their love and sends them off together, though he keeps his young Son with him. The wife obediently leaves with the secretary, and they raise three children of their own. The abandoned Son grows up resentful and arrogant; he has been raised away from his father by a wet nurse. The Father keeps up with his wife's new family, even going so far as to watch the Stepdaughter as she comes and goes from school. The secretary eventually takes his family and leaves town. Years pass and the secretary dies. His wife and children, destitute, move back to their original town, but they do not contact the Father. The Mother gets a job with Mme. Pace, a dressmaker who runs a call-girl ring from her shop. Mme. Pace lures the Stepdaughter into her service. The Father patronizes the establishment and unwittingly ends up in the arms of the Stepdaughter, only to be interrupted by the screams of the Mother ("just in time," according to the Father; "almost in time," according to the Stepdaughter). The Father is horrified and reunites the family under his roof. His own Son opposes the reunion and becomes excessively bitter toward all of them, especially his Mother. There is an explosion of emotions in the house; the Mother agonizes over her Son's bitterness, and the Boy—the wife's middle child by the secretary—despises being what he sees as a charity case.

But this is not all. To this point, we know the history of the family by watching it filled in, piece by piece, by the characters. The inner action now merges with the outer action of the play (Act Three) when the wife's youngest child falls into a garden fountain and drowns, and the Boy, who watches in horror as it happens, draws a revolver and shoots himself. Because this last event takes place after the actors and the Producer (who were rehearsing the Pirandello play) have prepared the scene for the play the characters want to perform, the question of what is "real" and what is "illusion" becomes even more tenuous. The characters "perform" the final acts of their history, but when the shot rings out confusion reigns; the Boy lies on the ground while some of the actors cry, "He's dead!" and others claim, "It's all make-believe. It's a sham!" The Father rejoins: "What do you mean, make-believe? It's real."

The play deals with various planes of "reality" and does so in such a way as to place the entire notion of reality under suspicion. That the theater is an illusion is not at issue here, although the degree to which the theater is simply unable adequately to reflect reality certainly is. When the actors, who have adopted conventional stage mannerisms, attempt to act out the parts the characters have provided for them, the characters—whose "real" drama is about to be enacted—can hardly recognize themselves; they laugh satirically.

FATHER [*Immediately, unable to restrain himself.*] Oh, no!
[*The* STEPDAUGHTER, *watching the* LEADING ACTOR *enter this way, bursts into laughter.*]
PRODUCER [*Furious.*] Shut up, for God's sake! And don't you dare laugh like that! We're not going to get anywhere at this rate.

STEPDAUGHTER [*Coming to the front.*] I'm sorry, I can't help it! The lady stands exactly where you told her to stand and she never moved. But if it were me and I heard someone say good afternoon to me in that way and with a voice like that I should burst out laughing—so I did.

Pirandello is suggesting the wide gulf that inevitably separates life from its re-creation on stage. Robert Brustein has pointed out that when the "Producer transforms the sordid, semi-incestuous happening in the dress shop into a romantic and sentimental love scene between the Leading Man and the Leading Lady . . . the Father understands how the author came to abandon them—in a fit of disgust over the conventional theatre."

But if one of Pirandello's central concerns is the theater's inability to catch reality as it is, an even more central concern is his seemingly paradoxical notion that theater is "truer" than life. He expresses this by contrasting the fixed reality of literary characters with the ever-changing reality of human beings. Fictional characters are "less real," perhaps, "but truer." It is the characters' tragedy that they are fixed within immutable bounds, often in one disastrous moment of their lives, or that, like the Boy and the Little Girl in *Six Characters*, they may have personalities and histories that are barely developed. Still, though they may be frustrated by their ineffective attempts to extend their fixed identities, they do not—like the human beings they imperfectly imitate—have to experience the yet more frustrating attempt to unify the multiple aspects of their personalities. As the Father tells the Producer in the play:

> But [our reality] doesn't change! Do you see? That's the difference! Ours doesn't change, it can't change, it can never be different, never, because it is already determined, like this, for ever, that's what's so terrible! We are an eternal reality. That should make you shudder to come near us.

The Father's argument here is also Pirandello's: human beings—unlike the imaginative creations of human beings—are merely a series of moods, impressions, beliefs, idiosyncrasies, and social masks that can never be fully integrated. The human tragedy—and comedy—is that we keep trying to unify these disparate elements and are disconsolate at our failure.

Many of the most important of Pirandello's works, including *Six Characters*, were written during the most insecure and troubled period of the writer's life. His wife's insanity began in 1903, after the birth of their third and last child and the loss of the family fortune. Pirandello refused to institutionalize her. She remained at home torturing the family with her insane rages while Pirandello suffered in silence, his wife beating at his door while he wrote. Among other things, she accused him and their daughter of incest, an accusation that so unsettled the daughter that she attempted suicide.

It is not difficult to imagine why artifice held such attraction for him, or why it struck him as being so obviously different from reality. His writing was his only release. Pirandello once wrote to a friend that he would sometimes sit in his study all day "at the service of the characters of my stories who crowd about me, each one wanting to come to life before the others, each one with his particular unhappiness to make public." His "madmen" characters provided a way to shout and revolt at his predicament. *Six Characters* is one of many plays that reveal Pirandello's torment as well as his genuine pleasure in the immortal fixity of his creations, creations that would not cringe at his wife's accusations and that could strut, immortally undemoralized, out the door and into an eternal future.

Two of the most significant influences on Pirandello were Henri Bergson (1859–1941), with his theory of "psychological" time and his emphasis on the mutability of personality, and Henrik Ibsen, with his grasp of the inner life. More interesting, perhaps, is the degree to which Pirandello himself has touched subsequent dramatists and fiction writers. Only Shakespeare and Ibsen, it has often been said, have been more influential. Anouilh, Sartre, Camus, Beckett, Ionesco, Giraudoux, O'Neill, Pinter, Stoppard, Albee, Wilder, Wesker, and Genet all show Pirandello's influence in one way or other.

Classroom Strategies

Because of the peculiar problems of *Six Characters*, it may need to consume two class periods and, for best effect, should be taught in tandem with other self-reflexive works.

Like the stories of Borges, John Barth, or Robert Coover, Pirandello's play will be a fascinating puzzle to some and a positive headache to others. It will be important to establish the context of *Six Characters* before discussion of its theoretical implications swamps the class. We have "real" actors putting on a "real" play in a "real" theater, interrupted by "fictional" characters who want to act out their "real" "fictional lives," or to have them acted out by the "real" actors. The melodrama of these characters' lives can, and should, be outlined for the students—perhaps in a handout distributed at the first class. During the first day of discussion, this melodrama—what we have here called the "inner action" of the play—should be established. Since the characters' story is mainly revealed in Act One, you may wish to limit discussion to that act on the first day. Acts Two and Three will provide discussion of the "outer action" of the play, with the theoretical and philosophical implications it raises. Although there are many possible approaches, the central theme of reality and illusion—in part because it is so thematically central to much modern drama—will probably be the most fruitful. The last few paragraphs of "Backgrounds" are intended to suggest some of the most significant theoretical questions raised by Pirandello.

It may be difficult to persuade students of Pirandello's humor, in part because it does not translate very well and in part because students are unlikely to be amused when they are confused. The notion of humor was basic to his writing (he wrote an essay on the subject in which he insists on its importance in comprehending and coping with suffering) and will be basic to students' enjoyment of the play. You should read appropriate passages or, perhaps more effectively, have students take parts and do a reading in class. There is a fifty-two-minute videotape available from Films for the Humanities, a compressed but lively version of the play, which would be extremely useful for students to see.

Topics for Discussion and Writing

1. In the original stage directions Pirandello says of the characters: "A tenuous light surrounds them, as if radiating from them—it is the faint breath of their fantastic reality." In the revised edition he states that in order for the six characters to be distinguished from the actors of the company, the characters should wear semi-masks: "The CHARACTERS should not appear as ghosts, but as created realities, timeless creations of the imagination, and so more real and consistent than the changeable realities of the ACTORS."

   Why did Pirandello make this change? What does it have to do with his theory of characters and his notions about human personality? In what ways can a character achieve independence from its author? Is this just a literary notion or does it have some application to everyday life?

   [Characters are fixed while human beings are not, and it is human beings who feel cheated and disappointed at their predicament.]

2. In what way is the play about the problem of illusion and reality? What is "real" in the play? Are there *degrees* of "reality" in *Six Characters*?

   [See "Backgrounds" for discussion.]

3. What purpose does the "play-within-the-play" serve? What other plays use this technique?

   [This device is a daring move on the playwright's part, since it exposes the artificiality of the medium. Students may be familiar with Shakespeare's critique of dramatic styles in *Hamlet* or *A Midsummer Night's Dream* (not in the anthology).]

4. What do you make of the end of the play? Is the Boy dead? In what ways is he dead? In what ways is he not dead?

   [We cannot, perhaps, definitively resolve the question of the Boy's death. We can say that he is dead insofar as the play ends, that he is not dead insofar as the play may be put on again.]

Comparative Perspectives

Discuss the contrast between the aggressively "realistic" opening and the appearance of the Six Characters in masks and under special lights. Compare the moments when Brecht's characters directly address the audience. Why do Pirandello and Brecht not draw a clearer distinction between realms of being? What are the roots of this ambiguity?

See also comparisons suggested to Goethe's *Faust* and Ibsen's *Hedda Gabler*.

Further Reading

See also the reading suggestions in the *Anthology*, p. 2553.

Bishop, Thomas. *Pirandello and French Theater*. 1960. Contains a helpful chapter, "Ideas in Pirandello's Theater."

Brustein, Robert. *The Theatre of Revolt*. 1964. An illuminating and cogent discussion of the play.

Giudice, Gaspare. *Pirandello: A Biography*. Trans. Alastair Hamilton. 1975. A good, short biography.

Lorch, Jennifer. "The 1925 Text of 'Sei Personnaggi in Cerca d'Autore' and Pitoëff's Production of 1925." *Yearbook of the British Pirandello Society* 2 (1982): 32–47. Gives a detailed discussion of Pitoëff's innovative production of *Six Characters* and its impact on later versions of the play (see introduction).

Oliver, Roger. *Dreams of Passion: The Theatre of Luigi Pirandello*. 1979. Discusses *Six Characters* and four other plays, as well as Pirandello's aesthetics.

Stone, Jennifer. *Pirandello's Naked Prompt: The Structures of Repetition in Modernism*. 1959. Discusses Pirandello's plays in relation to modernism and especially cubo-futurism.

Vittorini, Domenico. *The Drama of Luigi Pirandello*. 1957. A thorough study, first published in 1935, that Pirandello approved.

MARCEL PROUST

Swann's Way

Backgrounds

In the eyes of many, twentieth-century writing after 1913 is merely a footnote to Marcel Proust. It was Proust's massive novel, *Remembrance of Things Past*, that gave literary definition to the concept of "human time"—a subjective or *bodily* experience of living in time that would represent human existence far more accurately than the "clock" time of exterior, scientific measurement. Proust shows his narrator, Marcel, carefully building a picture of his "whole" self out of layers of buried memory. Each glimpse of an earlier "Marcel" brings with it a forgotten world of experience and makes clear the emotional and intellectual links between past and present identity. The detailed description of sense perceptions (the smell of a book or stairway, the taste of a small cake and tea) becomes a key to uncovering a past that is actually a series of layers creating the present. Proust's ability to convince us of the reality of these experiences derives in large part from his use of concrete details—

details that follow a stream of psychological association and seem to es-
pouse the rhythms of the remembering consciousness itself. Both the
richly remembered scenes and the example of the narrator's associative
memory have provided a compelling example for later writers, themselves haunted by the question of knowing the self and the difficulty of
representing it in language. The extraordinarily complex architecture of
this multivolume novel, and its complex symmetry of themes and
metaphors, has also proved a fruitful example for modern novelists who
emphasize organization by themes or mental associations rather than by
linear or chronological construction. While the appreciation of Proust's
aesthetic constructions will take more than one reading, students usually feel—often to their surprise—a strong identification with his description of sensuous memory, and with the search for the past as a way
of giving meaning to the present.

The title *Overture*, introducing a book whose title translates literally
as "In Search of Lost Time," sets the tone for a chapter that examines
the meaning of memory itself. Marcel's process of associative memory is
at stake, from the beginning where he talks about the state of half-
consciousness and blurred perceptions when he is going to sleep, to the
end where he describes the successful recall of his childhood world.
Marcel is attempting to recompose his "self's original features," and he
finds that the memory of physical sensations is an indispensable part of
this process. His dreams and confused memories are shaped by the
physical position of his limbs in bed; later on, it will be the taste of
madeleine soaked in tea that calls up a world the conscious mind has
forgotten. "My body . . . faithful [guardian] of a past my mind ought
never to have forgotten . . ." allows the narrator to recapture scenes,
events, and emotions that were otherwise lost to consciousness.

After the introduction, in which the older narrator recalls (among
other things) his childhood experience of going to sleep, we move into
the years at Combray when Marcel's bedtime hours were dominated by
his Mamma's goodnight kiss. The child Marcel appears as a sensitive,
highly nervous boy whose devotion to his mother is coupled with a lively
imagination and the need for reassurance and familiar surroundings: he
is disturbed by the way the slide-projected story of Golo and Geneviève
de Brabant becomes superimposed on the appearance of his familiar
bedroom, and confused by the way Golo's cloak or face seems to share
the reality of down-to-earth objects like the doorknob.

The initial description of the narrator's ambivalent state of consciousness now moves to a series of embedded stories that center on themes of
love and loss: Marcel's anxious wait for Mamma's kiss, and Swann's similar anxiety during his earlier love for Odette (a piece of information
known to the older Marcel, and alluded to here as he narrates events in
full perspective). The narrative center of these tales is the dinner party
from which Marcel is sent to bed without his accustomed goodnight
kiss—a dinner in which Proust's famous capacity for character sketches
and social satire emerges especially strongly in the portraits of the two
sisters, Flora and Celine, and their inability to thank Swann directly for

his present of a case of Asti wine. Throughout the evening, Marcel undergoes alternating hope and despair as he appeals to his mother through a message carried by Françoise, is humiliated when she refuses to respond, decides to stay up for her no matter what the cost, and is unexpectedly allowed her company for the night when his indulgent father recognizes the child's real misery. The *Overture*, however, is not merely a story of Marcel's successful attempt to obtain his goodnight kiss. The sequence of memories also culminates in Marcel's first realization that his mother is excusing him as a "nervous" child, not truly responsible for his actions and psychologically flawed. This realization, which is accompanied by feelings of guilt at having thus "traced a first wrinkle upon her soul" but also by Marcel's determination to enjoy the evening's unrepeatable indulgence to the hilt, forms a climax after which there is a sudden break, and the narrator concludes with a meditation on the role of memory.

The picture of Proust that remains in the mind is of an extraordinarily sensitive aesthete and intellectual who lived most of his adult years shut up in a heated, cork-lined room in Paris because he suffered from asthma. The disease that attacked him at the age of nine sharply limited his activities; nonetheless, he was able to transform personal experience—seaside vacations at Cabourg, country visits to Illiers and Auteuil, a year's military service at Orléans, participation in Parisian salon society, protests during the Dreyfus affair, and his relationship with Albert Agostinelli—into a complex panorama of Parisian society around the turn of the century.

Many readers like to compare Proust and the philosopher Henri Bergson, author of the influential *Essay on the Immediate Data of Consciousness* (1889). Bergson stressed the importance of "duration," or lived time, as the direct intuition of consciousness—to be valued over the sterile mathematics of measurable "clock time." While the comparison is often illuminating because of the similarity between Proust's and Bergson's rejection of positivist explanations of human experience, it remains a comparison rather than a causal link.

Classroom Strategies

Your students will enjoy Proust more if you devote two class periods to the *Overture*—one discussing the psychological drama of Marcel's going to bed, another examining the famous Proustian style that calls up buried memories. Since Proust is traditionally associated with the project of recapturing forgotten layers of memory, we recommend using this aspect as an opening wedge. Here there are two easy approaches: examining a short but significant passage as a "laboratory sample," and asking students to think about the processes of memory—their own and those described at the beginning of the book.

You may find it useful to start with the last sentence and read aloud the famous description of the Japanese flowers that are only crumpled bits of paper until they expand in water and become a miniature landscape. Some students may have seen these flowers, and those who have not can still appreciate the gradual unfolding of the description as the bits of paper become wet, and then "stretch and bend, take color and distinctive shape, turn into flowers, houses, human figures." You may then wish to read back into the preceding page, taking up the episode of the madeleine and its contrast between the "memory of the intellect" that preserves "nothing of an old past" and the memory of the senses—"smell and taste"—that enables one to call up buried worlds.

Another possibility is to examine the description of consciousness and memory at the beginning, asking students to compare their own experiences with the narrator's account, and pointing out the use of this relaxed or open consciousness to link different stages of life: "I had effortlessly returned to a period of my early life . . . the sense of existence as it may quiver in the depths of an animal . . . [I] gradually recomposed my self's original features." Once you have established the role of involuntary (bodily, sensuous) memory in calling up past experience, you are ready to describe the rest of that experience: Marcel's adoration of his mother, his misery as he ascends the staircase, his alternate hope and despair as he waits for her kiss, and the rest.

A number of passages lend themselves well to discussion: the magic lantern, the dinner party, the sending of the letter via Françoise, Marcel's mixed feelings as his father tells his mother to stay with the boy, the descriptions of the grandmother (her love of the outdoors, her relationship to the great-aunt, her choice of books).

The chief difficulty that students encounter is the length of the sentences and paragraphs. Perhaps they should be reassured that the long sentences are not a quirk of translation but an integral part of Proust's style—a style that consciously sets out to imitate the rhythms of a mind caught up in its many memories. Encourage them to read fast and to read aloud. They should not stop and wonder about each image and allusion (on first reading, at least), but read quickly through the sentences and paragraphs to get the drift of the whole. Once they realize, for example, that the first two pages are a series of associations by a mind drifting in and out of sleep, they will be more comfortable about the shifting, digressive pattern of the prose. Only then should each image be taken up for what it contributes to the whole picture.

A second difficulty may come with Proust's habit of embedding stories within stories. Students may be confused by what seems constant digression from the topic, and they should be encouraged to read quickly through to the end of the passage where the digression finally makes thematic sense. You may wish to meet the problem head-on by examining the embedding or associative technique with the class. Two useful examples come in the passage where Marcel's anguish is compared with that of Swann's unhappy passion for Odette (which then becomes a generalized description of unrequited love in Parisian society), and the description of the grandmother's character in the midst of a scene in which Marcel's mother reads him a book.

Topics for Discussion and Writing

1. What are the two kinds of memory, according to Proust, and how do they work?

   [The "voluntary" or intellectual memory and the "involuntary," spontaneous memory associated with the senses. See the first and second paragraphs of "Backgrounds."]

2. In what sense is Marcel a "nervous" child? How does his account of the evening illustrate this quality? Will he outgrow it?

   [See the third and fourth paragraphs of "Backgrounds." "Nervousness" in this sense is the quality of being high-strung and over-imaginative. It appears in Marcel's sensitivity to colors and smells and in his anxiety over the ambivalence of reality and fantasy in the magic-lantern picture on his wall, as well as in his anxious dependence on his mother. The adult Marcel—our narrator—seems equally sensitive to sense perceptions and the nuances of memory.]

3. Comment on Proust's use of digression.

   [See the fifth and sixth paragraphs of "Classroom Strategies." Digression is not only a technique of the associative memory but also an excellent way to introduce short sketches of intrinsic interest that add to our knowledge of characters or situations.]

4. From what point of view is the story told?

   [See the third paragraph of "Backgrounds." Proust blends the still-naïve experiences of the younger Marcel with the informed perspective of the older Marcel who is narrating the novel.]

5. Are there any comic elements in the story?

   [See the fourth paragraph of "Backgrounds." In addition to the almost caricatural pictures of the two sisters, students may note the constant frustration of any conversational thread, and the way the grandfather is thwarted in his desire for gossip.]

6. Compare Proust's associative technique with that of other writers known for use of the "stream of consciousness." (In this anthology, the selections by Joyce and Faulkner provide examples.)

Comparative Perspectives

1. In the years of his youth, according to Marcel, middle-class people of the older generation took "almost a Hindu view of society, which they held to consist of sharply defined castes." What errors do Marcel's great-aunts in particular fall into because of their rigid sense of class distinctions? Compare Proust's attitude toward social rank with that of other authors whose work you have read this term. Why have so many writers been so preoccupied by the different manners and attitudes with which it is associated? How important do you think social background really is?

   [If appropriate, start with Voltaire's witty dissection of Cunégonde's brother in *Candide*, or Dorine's acid comments on the social background of Tartuffe. Other good candidates include *The Queen of Spades, Hedda Gabler, The Cherry Orchard*.]

2. Toward the end of the *Overture*, surprised by his father's unexpected kindness, Marcel likens him to "Abraham in the engraving after Benozzo Gozzoli." Explain the application of the biblical story of Abraham, Isaac, and Sarah to the events here recalled, and comment on Proust's reason for introducing it through an involuntary visual memory.

3. Like Jean-Jacques Rousseau, Marcel has very early memories of a parent reading to him. Why is this such a primal experience for children? What role does family intimacy play in such recollections? Why do children want to have the same books read and reread? How would you compare the importance of the spoken word in oral culture to the role played by books read aloud in these two works of memory?

[This is a particularly open-ended inquiry, obviously; but it should help students identify some of the elemental components of literary experience.]

Further Reading

See also the reading suggestions in the *Anthology*, p. 2553.

Bloom, Harold, ed. *Marcel Proust*. 1987. More general than but with some overlap from Bloom's collection *Marcel Proust's* Remembrance of Things Past; it contains some useful essays.

Bowie, Malcolm. *Freud, Proust, and Lacan: Theory as Fiction*. 1987. Discusses and compares the theories of knowledge underlying each writer's work.

Deleuze, Gilles. *Proust and Signs*. Trans. Richard Howard. 1972. Poststructural, semiotic criticism of the novel as a "machine producing signs of different orders."

Ellison, David R. *The Reading of Proust*. 1984. A more specialized theoretical discussion of the narrative self, questions of readability and influence, and Ruskin's influence on Proust.

Fowlie, Wallace. *A Reading of Proust*. 1963; reprinted 1975. A useful guide.

Painter, George. *Marcel Proust: A Biography*. 1959; new edition, 1989. A readable, anecdotal biography.

Poulet, Georges. *Proustian Space*. Trans. Elliot Coleman. 1977. A study of Proust's fictional worldview in terms of time and space.

Proust, Marcel. "On Reading." Trans. and ed. Jean Autret and William Burford. 1971. Proust's views on the psychological experience of reading.

———. *Selected Letters*. Trans. Ralph Manheim; ed. Philip Kolb. 1983.

Zurbrugg, Nicholas. *Beckett and Proust.* 1988. An interesting source of comparative topics for discussion, despite a rather mechanical organization of ideas.

Thomas Mann
Death in Venice

Backgrounds

Thomas Mann often used the figure of the artist in society as a vehicle for examining cultural crisis, and *Death in Venice*—describing the fall of writer Gustave von Aschenbach—is a complex tracery of political, artistic, psychological, and ethical issues. Published two years before the beginning of World War I, portraying a cosmopolitan Europe that is already collapsing under the weight of economic and political rivalries, the novella describes in realistic detail a particular moment of European society. Yet this historical aspect fades into the background before larger themes: the role of art, the role of the artist, and the balance that human beings must preserve between reason and impulse, discipline and spontaneity, conscious and unconscious life. Mann himself noted that an important turn in his work had occurred with the writing of *Death in Venice*. Works after this period regularly incorporate a dual meaning-structure, a system of entwined references that endow characters and events with both psychological and broad historical or mythic significance.

Mann wrote *Death in Venice* in 1911, shortly after he had taken a brief vacation in Venice to recover from nervous exhaustion. Correspondence with his older brother, the already established Heinrich Mann, shows that he was frustrated at being unable to finish a series of planned works, much less the masterwork of which he felt himself capable. Obsessed by his image of the artist's tormented but prophetic role, struggling to define his own lofty concept of art over and against contemporary stress on innovative form, Mann produced the story of a writer many of whose anxieties are close to his own. Yet Aschenbach is not a hero, and while Mann sympathizes with his predicament, he also criticizes him for several kinds of betrayal.

The Gustave von Aschenbach who is introduced at the beginning has earned his respected position (and the honorific *von* before his name) by hard labor at his craft, by a search for dignified expression, and by the repudiation of uncontrollable depths—that is, the fatal knowledge and profound emotions of the "abyss." (Compare Baudelaire's *The Voyage*, in which the true artist plunges "to the bottom of the abyss" to find something new.) Mann's ironic description of the way this "master of his trade" has fought his way to a conventional, uninspired style in a quest for perfection prepares the ground for a shattering reversal. Challenged by the sight of a pugnacious traveler outside the mortuary chapel, the exhausted Aschenbach starts thinking about a foreign vacation to reinvigorate his creative powers. He imagines escaping from the monotonous, confining routine of his European life and sees that escape in Eastern landscapes with lush swampland, tigers, and bamboo thickets. Venice, finally, is the place to which he retreats: "half fairy tale and half tourist trap," combining East and West, past and present, art and commerce, all with an odor of corruption—an "impossible destination, forbidden to him" that "enchanted him, relaxed his will, made him happy)."

The happiness that Aschenbach encounters in Venice is accompanied by complete disorientation that begins on the initial ferryboat ride when he feels "that things were starting to take a turn away from the ordinary, as if a dreamy estrangement, a bizarre distortion of the world were setting in." He beholds with horror a garishly painted and bewigged old man among a crowd of young excursionists—yet he himself will later undergo a similar cosmetic rejuvenation when he pursues the Polish youth Tadzio.

Aschenbach's relationship with Tadzio fuses two main themes: erotic love and the artist's worship of beauty. He is drawn to the youth's classic beauty, which recalls the perfection of Greek sculpture and especially busts of Eros, the god of love. Gradually, as Aschenbach watches Tadzio on the beach and in the dining room, the references to godly beauty increase; so, too, does his attraction, which he now defines as a "paternal kindness . . . the attachment that someone who produces beauty at the cost of intellectual self-sacrifice feels toward someone who naturally possesses beauty." Only when the writer is accidentally prevented from leaving Venice does he realize that he is in love with Tadzio. It is worth noting that Mann does not criticize Aschenbach's love itself but rather his response to it. The writer accepts doom for himself and for others rather than separation from Tadzio and a return to a life of humdrum toil; even after discovering that plague has stricken the city (and that the authorities are concealing it), he does not warn Tadzio's mother. His obsession with Tadzio also leads him to define a despairing view of art—and a personal submission—that precisely negates the Platonic position he appears to adopt.

References to Greek culture permeate *Death in Venice*, partly because they express Aschenbach's traditional German admiration for Greek art and philosophy and partly because the web of allusions supports the development of other themes in the novella. Eros (the Roman Cupid), god of love; Hermes, patron of travelers and "soul-summoner"; Semele, who perished in the flames of her lover Zeus, king of the gods; Helios, fiery god of the sun that "turns our attention from intellectual to sensuous matters"; the boatman Charon, who ferries souls to the world of the dead; Narcissus, who drowned in his own reflected image; Hyacinthus, doomed object of Apollo's love; Dionysus, the "stranger god" whose orgiastic revels drive out reason; Eos; Pan; Poseidon; and others all have symbolic roles in Aschenbach's journey toward death. The allusions become more significant toward the end, as he seeks to understand his attachment to Tadzio in terms of Greek homosexual love (the *pederasty* that is literally the love of an older man for a youth, generally with implications of leading the youth toward adulthood) and especially Platonic views of art.

Aschenbach's discourse on love and the artist, in which he imagines himself speaking to the young Phaedrus of the Platonic dialogue, derives from several sources. The most obvious reference is clearly the *Phaedrus*, in which Socrates counters a speech on love by the sophist Lusias with two of his own. Another well-known Socratic speech on love occurs in Plato's *Symposium*—a much-annotated copy of which was found in Mann's library after his death. The philosopher Arthur Schopenhauer, whose discussion of the artist's nature greatly interested Mann, linked both dialogues with Plutarch's *Erotikos (Dialogue on Love)* in the forty-fourth chapter of his *The World as Will and Representation*. Despite apparent similarities, however, there are sharp differences between Socrates' address to Phaedrus and that of Aschenbach. Where one talks about the artist, the other talks about knowing the beautiful. Aschenbach focuses on the necessary "self-debauchery" of the artist, who is doomed by a knowledge and understanding that sympathizes with the abyss through intoxication with sensuous beauty. Socrates, conversely, interprets physical beauty as a sign of the ideal and describes how love of a beautiful youth can draw the mind to contemplate concepts of ideal beauty and moral perfection. Aschenbach's despairing conclusion in *Death in Venice* is that the world of the senses will inevitably lead the artist astray. It is a conclusion prefigured by his earlier dream of a Dionysian orgy, when his last effort of will is insufficient to protect him against the onslaught of the Stranger-God, "the enemy of the self-controlled and dignified intellect." From then on, he is enslaved by the world of earthly experience, submitting to the barber in an attempt to make himself more attractive and pursuing Tadzio wherever he goes. Aschenbach dies in his beach chair with the ambiguous image of Tadzio-Hermes before his eyes, trying vainly to follow the "pale and charming psychagogue" into the immensity before him but sinking back into mortality and death.

Mann employs a series of leitmotifs and oppositions to organize thematic patterns throughout *Death in Venice*. There are smaller recurrent themes, such as the leitmotif in Tadzio's "twilight-gray eyes," the reddish hair and snub nose that belong to an obscurely menacing character, or Aschenbach's repeated eating of strawberries that, shortly before the plague strikes him down, are "overripe and soft." More prominent themes include the figure of a traveler-guide, beginning with the traveler by the mortuary and continuing in the ship's purser, the Charonlike gondolier, and the various references to Hermes. There are also individual passages that echo each other, such as the description of the painted old man on the ferry and Aschenbach's transformation by the barber; or the writer's return to the little square where he rests again on the edge of a fountain; or his early "affinity for the undivided, the immeasurable" echoed in the ending scene, in which he recognizes Tadzio-Hermes beckoning him into "an immensity full of promise." Yet the broadest and most persistent contrast is that of Apollo and Dionysus as opposed rational and irrational forces—a famous opposition that Mann would have known from Friedrich Nietzsche's *Birth of Tragedy*. Reinforcing this contrast is a second thematics, of East and West, in which the West is associated with order and discipline, with bourgeois habits and dignity, and with Apollo as the god of light and rationality. Conversely, the "stranger-god" Dionysus comes from the East (as is clear in Euripides' play *The Bacchae*, which Aschenbach's dream recalls). Death also comes from the East; the plague afflicting Venice is an Asiatic cholera originating in the Ganges delta. *Death in Venice* is a highly structured composition that demonstrates Mann's desire to create, in prose, a "musical complex of associations."

Classroom Strategies

Death in Venice can be taught in two or three days, depending on how thoroughly you wish to explore its thematic patterns. It is probably easiest to begin by considering Aschenbach the man—his dedication to his work, ambition, the willpower and self-control (and repression) that have come to dominate his life—before moving into questions of literary style and its implied moral choices. Once students have a good picture of what Aschenbach has become, and what he has sacrificed to reach that pinnacle, you can ask them if they have any predictions about what will happen to him, and whether his "moral resoluteness" indeed signifies "a reduction, a moral simplification of the world and of the human soul and therefore also a growing potential for what is evil, forbidden, and morally unacceptable." Get them to talk about their ideas of art (e.g., its moral and social function, the importance of form, the relative importance of spontaneity and discipline) and you will be launched into the second strand: Aschenbach the writer, who has devoted his life to a certain concept of beauty.

It may be interesting at this point to broaden the discussion with references to other works in the volume, comparing different styles and concepts of art (see the introductions to "Realism, Naturalism, Symbolism" and "Contemporary Explorations" for discussions of realism, naturalism, symbolism, modernism, and postmodernism). At this level, it is not merely Aschenbach's concept of art that is relevant, but Mann's own practice: his psychological realism, use of myth, almost musical organization of themes and motifs, *and* critical distance from Aschenbach himself.

The stages of Aschenbach's infatuation with Tadzio are relatively clear. What remains to be explored is the degree of self-knowledge (or delusion) the writer attains, and also the secondary mythic plane of interpretation created by classical allusions having to do with human nature and the search for absolutes. Students may find the picture of Aschenbach repellent, but they should recognize that he constantly attempts to deal with fundamental issues. They may find the opposition of Dionysus and Apollo oversimplified, too (one hopes); this in itself is another subject for discussion.

Since Mann is such a complex writer, it will be helpful to focus on certain key passages as microcosms of intertwining themes. The most obvious possibilities are the Dionysian dream and the final "Phaedrus" soliloquy. The latter may be difficult for students to follow without guidance, not only for its philosophical distinctions but also because they may be expecting a more direct description of Aschenbach's death from plague at that point. There are, in addition, many useful passages or symbolic scenes throughout the novella, some of which are mentioned in the last paragraph of "Backgrounds."

Topics for Discussion

1. Why is it important that Aschenbach see Tadzio first as an incarnation of ancient Greek sculpture?
2. How does Mann bring out the *successive* stages of Aschenbach's infatuation with Tadzio?
3. Do you agree that the artistic form has "two faces," that it is "moral and amoral at the same time"? How does this concept determine Aschenbach's career as a writer?
4. What are several reasons for Aschenbach's unwillingness to tell Tadzio's mother about the plague?
5. Describe and contrast the two "Phaedrus" passages.
6. Discuss the importance of mythological references for an understanding of *Death in Venice*.
7. How does Mann's description of Venice make it an appropriate place for Aschenbach's downfall and death?
8. Where else have you seen the concept of "abyss" used in reference to art?
   [See "Backgrounds," third paragraph.]
9. Describe the combination of psychological realism, historical detail, and symbolic allusions in *Death in Venice*.
10. How does the contrast of East and West, Dionysus and Apollo, underlie issues in *Death in Venice*?
11. Discuss the theme of the traveler throughout *Death in Venice*; in what sense does Hermes preside over Aschenbach's journey into infatuation and death?

Comparative Perspectives

1. Aschenbach's illicit sexual desire is linked to the onset of plague. How does Mann's treatment of this connection compare with Boccaccio's introduction to the *Decameron* or Chaucer's *The Pardoner's Tale*?
   [After the stark realism of Boccaccio's opening pages, the plague recedes from view. If feasible, a comparison between Mann's novella and *The Pardoner's Tale* would allow for some surprising parallels. In

each case, the protagonists search for death. The Pardoner, who may without knowing it be expressing his own anxieties in his depiction of the doomed rioters, must confront his own confused sexuality in the Host's angry expostulation in the epilogue. Aschenbach undergoes a similar confrontation, couched in modern rather than medieval terms.]

2. Contrast the imagery and tone of the vision that seizes Aschenbach with "hallucinatory force" in chapter 1 of *Death in Venice* with the imagery and tone of the scene described in stanza VII of Wallace Stevens's *Sunday Morning*. How does each writer challenge the modern Western pose of separation from such antiquated, distant ritual practices?

Further Reading

See also the reading suggestions in the *Anthology*, p. 2552.

Bloom, Harold, ed. *Thomas Mann*. 1986. Twenty-one essays on themes, texts, and techniques in a range of Mann's work, including two pieces on *Death in Venice*.

Ezergailis, Inta M., ed. *Critical Essays on Thomas Mann*. 1988. Fourteen essays on a range of broadly focused topics.

Hatfield, Henry. *From* The Magic Mountain: *Mann's Later Masterpieces*. 1979.

Jonas, Ilsedore B. *Thomas Mann in Italy*. Trans. Betty Crouse. 1979. A discussion of Mann's use of Italy and his depiction of Italians throughout his work.

Lesser, Esther H. *Thomas Mann's Short Fiction: An Intellectual Biography*. 1989. The stories read individually and as part of Mann's intellectual development.

Lukács, Georg. *Essays on Thomas Mann*. Trans. Stanley Mitchell. 1965; reprinted 1979. Important essays by a major twentieth-century critic.

McWilliams, James R. *Brother Artist: A Psychological Study of Thomas Mann's Fiction*. 1983. Especially relevant to the theme of the artist in Mann's work.

RAINER MARIA RILKE

Backgrounds

Rilke's exceptional lyric gifts make him the most prominent German poet of our century. His work, *The Duino Elegies* especially, speaks to the modern sense of a fragmented universe with "all that was once relation so loosely fluttering hither and thither in space"—a universe in which communion constantly gives way to solitude. Yet Rilke's vision is redemptive as well as tragic. Sharing with Joyce a highly developed sense of the artist's mission, he sees art as a way to combat chaos by lending shape to the invisible, and to transform suffering and unify life and death in the context of eternity.

Archaic Torso of Apollo

Apollo is just one of the statues in Rilke's poetic museum, but as god of poetry and light he assumes pride of place. *Archaic Torso of Apollo* displays for the first time the typical Rilkean sonnet form: *abba abab cddc cdcd eef gfg.* The volume it begins is dedicated to Auguste Rodin, and in fact it can be said that the poem aspires to the condition of the statue it describes—seeking heft, palpability, the power to confront its observer directly and irresistibly (its second-person form of address at the close has this effect) and to move him out of complacency: "You must change your life." The maimed statue embodies both the incompleteness of human art and its transcendence in spite of all: "We cannot know his legendary head / with eyes like ripening fruit. And yet his torso / is still suffused with brilliance from inside, like a lamp."

Light, Apollo's attribute and imperium, endows this stone with being. The glow of life, of animal warmth and sexual heat, irradiates the poem, shining from breast bone and shoulder, from the center of procreation (at the poem's physical center), its exuberance finally breaking out "from all the borders of itself" and spilling beyond form. Such is the role of art, creating a beauty whose impact reaches beyond its own formal boundaries.

In connection with *Archaic Torso of Apollo* it is important to remember Rilke's long association with Rodin, who served as patron, employer, friend, and exalted example. Rodin's enormous industry and initiative provided a model that Rilke—plagued as he was with an impossible double hunger for solitude and love, barraged by the shapes of his fevered imagination—could not hope to match. The sculptor, according to one of the characters in Rilke's story "The Last" (not in the anthology), enjoys special mastery:

> A song, a picture you notice, a poem you like—all have their significance and value, the same, I think, for him who first creates it as for him who re-creates it. The sculptor creates his statues only for himself: but . . . he also creates space for his own statue in the world. . . . Art raised man to God.

Rilke's poem can be said to re-create the sculptor's creation. To it belongs the joy of renewing the triumph of light (form, life) over chaos.

Other influences on Rilke include Poe (particularly his linkage of terror and beauty, as seen in the opening of the first elegy) and Baudelaire (see the headnote in the anthology). Rilke also admired the lyrics of Hölderlin and translated Valéry. Impressionist painting—Cézanne's work in particular—affected his way of seeing as well as his energies. Of Cézanne he wrote:

> I notice by the way Cézanne keeps me busy now how very different I have grown. I am on the road to becoming a worker, on a long road perhaps and

probably only at the first milestone. . . . This consuming of love in anonymous work, which gives rise to such pure things, probably no one has succeeded in doing so so completely as old Cézanne.

The Panther

This poem, written in Paris in 1902, provides an excellent example of the "new kind of literary and artistic inspiration" (see headnote) that Rilke gained there. A favorite of Rilke's among his own works, *The Panther* demonstrates the power of intense visualization through which he found the means to objectify his art and go beyond the cultivation of sensation that typifies the Romantic lyric. Beginning with the panther's exhausted gaze, so concentrated on the bars that entrap him, the poem seems to merge the observer and the panther as they enter into each other's visual fields. Deeply empathizing with the pacing animal, the poet makes him into an image of ritual. Circular movement becomes a dance, an art form that takes its energy from the animal's "mighty will" even in paralysis.

The poem makes of this double seeing an engagement between audience and object when "the curtain of the pupils / lifts, quietly." As if in the theater, the observer glimpses the reality behind the façade and the panther, like an actor, seems to absorb the observer's interest. So profound is this exchange that the image of the human being outside the bars "enters in"; and, removed from the scene, readers may feel that they merge spiritually with the powerful, entrapped animal, whose situation can be interpreted as a metaphor for our own lives.

The Swan

Ask your students to count the number of lines in *The Swan*, which is a truncated sonnet: the opening sequence of the poem, as in any sonnet, introduces a proposition that will lead to some kind of turnaround in the concluding sestet. At the start, where we expect quatrains, the last lines drop off and Rilke leaves us with two tercets instead, as if to mimic the swan's uncompleted labors. The swan out of water, the proverbial ugly duckling, is like the poet who has not yet achieved his vision. The release into the medium in which he flourishes is, tellingly, likened to giving in to death.

The fully articulated sestet embodies the poet's mastery of form as it records the swan's majestic command of his true element. A rich comparison can be drawn to an image of swans in *The Half of Life* by Hölderlin, whose work Rilke admired. Found in the anthology, that poem links the "gracious" movement of the swans to youth and life; Rilke's swan represents "the interpenetration of life and death" discussed in the headnote, a state of quiet triumph rather than loss.

Spanish Dancer

Titles are important in Rilke's work. One needs the title of this brilliant poem to make sense of the daring introductory image, which, much like the extended similes of ancient epic, takes on a life of its own before it reveals its relevance to the subject at hand. Note the footnote explaining the derivation of the term *flamenco* from the verb meaning to flame and have your students work through stages in the life of the flame described here as a metaphor for the creative work the dancer is engaged in—and perhaps for human life itself. How does Rilke's use of imagery here resemble that of the Surrealists? How many meanings can we ascribe to the act of extinguishing with which the dancer concludes her performance?

Classroom Strategies

It would be helpful to start with *Archaic Torso of Apollo*, not only because it is first chronologically but because its relative compactness and formality make it most manageable. This poem can serve as a convenient introduction to Rilke's conceptions of the artist and of art. Students who are able to read the original German text should be encouraged to read aloud to the class and to comment on any effects (rhythmic, verbal, imagistic) that they find specific to the German original.

Topics for Discussion and Writing

1. What is the role of light in *Archaic Torso of Apollo*?
   [See "Backgrounds" for further discussion.]
2. Why does Rilke choose to emphasize the sexuality of the statue?
   [In a letter to Kappus, Rilke says that "artistic experience lies so incredibly close to that of sex, to its pain and its ecstasy, that the two manifestations are indeed but different forms of one and the same yearning and delight." See "Backgrounds" for further discussion.]
3. What does *Archaic Torso of Apollo* say (and demonstrate) about the role of art?
   [See "Backgrounds" for discussion.]
4. How should we interpret the famous command at the end of *Archaic Torso of Apollo*?
5. If you read German, you may wish to read aloud or compare passages from the translation with the original poem. Students may also be encouraged to try reading the original text on their own and to comment on the way the translation has or has not succeeded in grasping the German original. Some of the bolder ones may attempt their own translations, which will bring them closer to the text at the same time that it induces a healthy respect for the difficulties of translation.

Comparative Perspectives

1. Compare the high expectations of art that inform Rilke's celebration of the "archaic torso of Apollo" with García Lorca's tragic rec-

ollection of the "marble torso" of Ignacio Sánchez Mejías. If Rilke's poem is by definition an Apollonian view of art, does García Lorca's horror at the blood of the fallen toreador offer a Dionysian view? Where would Yeats's meditation, in *Lapis Lazuli*, on the art that finds beauty in flawed stone fit in this continuum?

2. *The Spanish Dancer*, *The Swan*, and *The Panther* make meaning out of the special way that their subjects move; in *Archaic Torso of Apollo*, the statue seems full of motion. Compare and contrast the qualities attributed to each and consider Rilke's sensitivity to motion with the predilections shown by other poets for other sensory details.

   [Note, for instance, the significance of stasis in Wordsworth's lyrics and of light in Dickinson's verse, and try to define the writers' different poetic sensibilities in terms of these attractions.]

3. Compare and contrast the terrifying visions of created life embodied by Rilke's panther and Blake's tiger.

4. Swans, like nightingales, are interpreted by poets in a number of ways. Comment on the different uses to which these two avian metaphors for poetry are put, and compare Rilke's vision of the almost mystical swan with that of Hölderlin in *The Half of Life*, or perhaps with the figure of the bird imagined in Yeats's *Leda and the Swan*.

   [Nightingales, from Ovid onward, seem to be associated with the idea that expressive beauty comes from a tragic wound. By contrast, despite the popular image of "the dying swan," the poets cited above develop ideas about the grace and the power of the swan.]

Further Reading

See also the reading suggestions in the *Anthology*, p. 2553.

Lehnert, Herbert. "Alienation and Transformation: Rilke's Poem 'Der Schwan.'" In *Rilke: The Alchemy of Alienation*, eds. Frank Baron, Ernst S. Dick, and Warren R. Maurer. 1980. An excellent discussion of *The Swan*, alluded to in the comments above.

Mandel, Siegfried. *Rainer Maria Rilke: The Poetic Instinct*. 1965. A useful introduction to Rilke's work.

Mason, Eudo C. *Rilke, Europe, and the English-Speaking World*. 1961. Mason discusses both Rilke's view of the English-speaking world and its views of him.

Shaw, Priscilla W. *Rilke, Valery, and Yeats: The Domain of the Self*. 1964. Shaw discusses the relationship between self and world in Rilke, with particular reference to his view of the body and the world of objects.

WALLACE STEVENS

Backgrounds

Stevens is a poet of the drama of the mind, which is caught in its "double fate of self and world." He can be difficult, arcane, and even precious, but at his best he is elegant and resonant. He makes use of images, parables, anecdotes, lectures, dialogues, monologues, aphorisms, and so on, to promote the life of the imagination. As Northrop Frye has said: "His poetic vision is informed by a metaphysic; his metaphysic is informed by a theory of knowledge; his theory of knowledge is informed by a poetic vision." But always, in Stevens, we come back finally to "poetry itself, the naked poem." It is the poet's responsibility, as he sees it, to renew a world under the constant threat of imaginative impoverishment, and he fulfills that responsibility in poems of extraordinary range and speculative brilliance.

Sunday Morning

Sunday Morning is Stevens's most famous poem and perhaps his best. It is a poem of contrasts—the female subject of the poem confronts two opposing views of paradise, neither of which is immediately satisfying: the earthly paradise, which she finds decadent and empty, and the mythological, religious paradise, to which she cannot commit herself. The woman, in whose highly civilized rooms we find ourselves, is too sensitive to content herself with the decadent pursuit of earthly pleasure and too sophisticated to accept the religious idea of heaven. Her meditation on the matter, Stevens tells us, "is anybody's meditation."

The first stanza contrasts a luxuriously sensual natural world with "silent Palestine." But the objects of the sensual world—"late coffee," "pungent oranges," the "green freedom of a cockatoo"—"seem things in some procession of the dead." She is unable, emotionally, to commit herself to the physical or to the spiritual. The second stanza develops the questions raised in the first. What does the natural world offer that can be "cherished like the thought of heaven"? The answer is that "Divinity must live within herself," through her experiences, and the memory of those experiences, in the natural world.

But if the Earth—the natural world, the world of physicality—is to be, as the third stanza puts it, "all of paradise that we shall know," she must then wonder what is to happen when the world of nature passes, to remain alive only in memory and desire. The sky may seem "friendlier" if paradise is invested in Earth, but she still feels "the need of some imperishable bliss."

The sixth stanza reconsiders the traditional view of paradise in a way that recalls Keats's *Ode on a Grecian Urn*. In this view, paradise is static, a "cold pastoral" (Keats's term), where rivers "seek for seas / They never find." It lacks beauty because it lacks death, and "Death is the mother of Beauty." Without death there can be no passionate pleasure.

In the last stanza, the woman relinquishes her desire for the paradise promised by religion; she finds that "The tomb in Palestine / . . . is the grave of Jesus, where he lay"—nothing more. We, however, must continue to live in "an old chaos of the sun," where death makes for beauty and sponsors the only paradise available to us, a place where:

> . . . in the isolation of the sky,
> At evening, casual flocks of pigeons make
> Ambiguous undulations as they sink.
> Downward to darkness, on extended wings.
>
> (lines 117–20)

Peter Quince at the Clavier

Stevens wrote *Peter Quince at the Clavier* during the same period in which he wrote *Sunday Morning*, and both poems evidence concern with the cyclical process of life and death in the natural world. In this poem, however, physical beauty becomes immortal not only through the memories of the living but also by its transubstantiation into art. "Music is feeling," not mere sound, and it is music that in the first stanza brings the speaker to desire. The speaker compares his awakened desire for an unidentified woman of his memories to the "strain / Waked in the elders by Susanna," a "strain" that made their thin blood "pulse pizzicati of Hosanna." The second and third stanzas recreate the biblical story in a way reminiscent of paintings by Rembrandt and Tintoretto.

The last stanza recognizes that the passionate throbbing brought on by such beauty must, inevitably, die: evenings, gardens, seasons, maidens—all die. "Susanna's music touched the bawdy strings / Of those white elders; but, escaping, / Left only Death's ironic scraping." But in memory, as in art, Susanna's music—her beauty and the desire it awakens—is immortal, and "makes a constant sacrament of praise."

Anecdote of the Jar

Anecdote of the Jar can be, and has been, interpreted in two mutually exclusive ways. One view of the poem finds that the jar represents the imposition of form by intellect and that its introduction onto the hill destroys the "natural beauty" of the surrounding wilderness. Another view, perhaps less dedicatedly Romantic, notes that the wilderness is "slovenly" at first, but that the jar—which has form and is therefore representative of art—takes "dominion" and establishes order where before there was merely "wild" chaos. This second interpretation of the poem has the advantage of having a basis in Stevens's aesthetics—his insistence that art, because it has form, produces order and beauty in a world where flux and chaos otherwise predominate.

Both interpretations, however, assume that Stevens means to evaluate the wilderness, as well as the jar, either positively or negatively. Through the introduction of form, however undistinguished ("The jar was round upon the ground" hardly seems to suggest a particularly significant form), our perception of nature is inevitably altered.

The Emperor of Ice-Cream

With the cold-blooded assurance of the child, the speaker of *The Emperor of Ice-Cream* registers the meanness and finality of death and urges the reader to recognize that "the only emperor is the emperor of ice-cream." The ministrations over the dead become a kind of ugly carnival, the attempt at decorum is exploded by the recognition that it is, after all, merely empty formality—a pathetically inadequate illusion unappreciated by the one for whom it is being performed. Death is final, the hands that once embroidered fantails are still, the horny feet are cold. Death should be the end of the charade: "Let be be finale of seem."

The Idea of Order at Key West

The Idea of Order at Key West illustrates the ascendancy of the poetic mind over the chaos and strength of the natural world, represented here by the sea. As in *Peter Quince*, music is related to the desire to impose order upon the world. In *The Idea of Order*, however, the female singer creates the world in which she exists through her song and, more important, changes the world significantly for those who hear her. Nature attains a higher order of reality when it is organized by the artist, who speaks to and for her audience.

In the first line of the poem, it is apparent that the singer has powers greater than those of the sea. The sea possesses no ordering imagination; it moves and makes sounds, but they are movements and sounds without direction. It is the woman's song—not the "grinding water and the gasping wind"—that commands the speaker's attention. In comparison, the sea becomes a mere backdrop, a "place by which she walked to sing." The fourth stanza further emphasizes the idea that nature, without the creative imagination to order it, is beautiful but meaningless. Her voice gathers together not only the sea, but all that the sea apportions.

> It was her voice that made
> The sky acutest at its vanishing.
> She measured to the hour its solitude.
> She was the single artificer of the world
> In which she sang. And when she sang, the sea,
> Whatever self it had, became the self
> That was her song, for she was the maker.
>
> (lines 34–40)

Because the singer is the "single artificer" of her world, the sea becomes, both for the singer and for her audience, her particular vision of the sea. There is no "world for her / Except the one she sang and, singing, made."

When the singing ends, the speaker finds the world arranged, organized, gorgeous, in such a way as to be beyond the understanding of the aesthetician ("Ramon Fernandez"). The last stanza is a coda that pays tribute to the "rage for order" and to the inspirational quality of the art such a rage produces.

The Man on the Dump

Once again, the central interest in *The Man on the Dump* is art—specifically the creation of poetry, and the problems of the poet as he imaginatively creates his world. "The dump is full / Of images," but these images are mainly exhausted, timeworn, obsolete, laughable; the poet sits atop the mound of the tradition's imagery and takes inventory—sifts, mocks, rejects. If the moon is going to come up at all in a poem, it will have to come up "as a moon" (not as a stale image of the moon) in an "empty sky" (a sky swept clean of all the trash the poet must reject). The process of rejection, the sloughing off of the trite, purifies and renews the imagination, and the poet is able to begin a new cycle of creativity. He beats "an old tin can" in order to create a fresh version of reality: "One beats and beats for that which one believes."

The poem ends with a series of questions that ask, essentially, why the poet has rejected certain images and why he continues to sit among them. The answer, if there is one, appears in the last line: the discarded images that now "torture the ear" were once fresh, once a direct apprehension of reality, the truth—the thing itself. It is still the poet's job of work to find or refind the image that offers the thing itself—"The the"—and reorder the world into beauty.

Classroom Strategies

The six poems can be covered in two class periods. The most difficult aspects of Stevens's aesthetics and poetics are contained in *Sunday Morning* and *Peter Quince*, so it would be useful to concentrate on these two during the first class meeting. If you can spend only one class period on the work, *Sunday Morning* and *The Idea of Order at Key West* are the most representative, significant, and telling poems to discuss. *The Emperor of Ice-Cream*, however, is perhaps the most accessible.

Stevens's work offers both concrete imagery and abstract speculation, and the abstractions will cause most of the difficulty for students, who will want a definite meaning assigned to lines such as "Let be be finale of seem," phrases such as "The the," and images such as the jar in Tennessee. The more elusive these things are (and are intended to be) the more the student will insist on an assigned meaning—and decide, in its absence, that the poems are "not worth the trouble." This tendency will be exacerbated because of Stevens's continual use of art itself as his central subject. Some students find this fascinating, but many tend to doubt that it is an important enough subject for a poem, finding in it a certain self-absorption and an illusory self-importance. A discussion of literary language—tending as it does toward multiple meanings, as opposed to scientific language, which tends toward a sole meaning—can be useful in this context. So can the fact that Stevens worked as a successful insurance executive. Students find this duly surprising, but admirable. If a hardheaded businessman thinks poetry is so important, then . . .

Students might be directed to notice that quite often in Stevens's work a line in the poem presents a truth demonstrated by the poem as a whole. In *Peter Quince*, for instance, the speaker's claim that "music is feeling, then, not sound" is confirmed by the poetic music that envelops each of the poem's characters. The coarse elders, for instance, are characterized by coarse poetic rhythms and images ("A cymbal crashed, / And roaring horns") or else pizzicati plucking intended to suggest their glandular excitement. The simpering Byzantine maids come and go with "a noise like tambourines." Susanna's music, however, is as "clear and warm" as she is.

In *The Idea of Order at Key West*, visual and auditory imagery fortify Stevens's notion that the natural world, however beautiful, remains meaningless without the ordering power of the artistic imagination. The sea can only cry, grind, and gasp until it is transformed by the woman's song. Once again, the poem demonstrates its own claims.

Topics for Discussion and Writing

1. What kinds of contrasts can be found in *Sunday Morning*? What purpose do they serve? How does Stevens exploit the traditional activities of a Sunday morning?
   [See "Backgrounds" for discussion.]

2. How does music function in *Peter Quince at the Clavier*? What is meant by "music is feeling, then, not sound"? How is this thought demonstrated in the poem as a whole?
   [See "Backgrounds" and the third paragraph of "Classroom Strategies."]

3. What aesthetic position is suggested by *Anecdote of the Jar*? What other poems suggest a similar aesthetic position?

4. Both *The Emperor of Ice-Cream* and *Sunday Morning* concern themselves with death. How do they differ? Have they any similarities?

5. How does *The Idea of Order at Key West* illustrate the artist's ability to order the natural world? Do you believe any of this? Can you name any examples of art that has caused us to reperceive the nature of the world? What did Oscar Wilde mean when he said that "Nature imitates art"?

6. Why does the poet in *The Man on the Dump* need to discard used-up images? Why do they become exhausted? Why would Stevens insist that it is important to discover new, fresh images?

7. Why does Stevens make such use of contrast? Locate and discuss examples of contrasting images, voices, settings, and points of view (see especially *The Idea of Order at Key West*, *Sunday Morning*, *Anecdote of the Jar*, and *The Man on the Dump*).

Comparative Perspectives

1. Compare the contemplation, in *Anecdote of the Jar*, of a simple object and its impact on its surroundings with similar meditations in Rilke's *New Poems*.
2. Although Stevens gives *The Idea of Order at Key West* a contemporary setting, the poem conjures up images of the ancient Greek world, and virtually any historical period or cultural tradition offers examples of the "rage for order" described here. Reviewing the reading you have done this semester, discuss a text in which you see the human mind struggling to make sense of experience. Do you find art as successful at imposing order as this High Modernist vision implies it to be?

    [Works that challenge that assumption may be proposed for students to analyze. Good choices from the modern period include Freud's frustrated efforts to make sense of Dora's experience, Kafka's *The Metamorphosis*, Beckett's *Endgame*. If appropriate, consider selections from Vol. 1 as well, including but not limited to Job and the essays of Montaigne.]
3. Discuss Stevens's idea of the poet as creator of reality in light of Baudelaire (see especially *One O'Clock in the Morning*, *Windows*, *A Carcass*, *Her Hair*, and *Correspondences*).

Further Reading

See also the reading suggestions in the *Anthology*, p. 2555.

Bloom, Harold. *Wallace Stevens: The Poems of Our Climate*. 1977. Intriguing commentary on his work, noting the "anxiety of influence" caused by similarities to Emerson, Whitman, Tennyson, Shelley, and others.

Doggett, Frank. *Stevens's Poetry of Thought*. 1966. Clear, straightforward discussions of the poems.

Morse, Samuel French. *Wallace Stevens: Poetry as Life*. 1970. An extended critical biography.

Pearce, Roy Harvey, and J. Hillis Miller, eds. *The Act of the Mind: Essays on the Poetry of Wallace Stevens*. 1965. The essays by Morse, Pearce, Vendler, and Macksey are particularly useful.

Stevens, Wallace. *Letters of Wallace Stevens*. Ed. Holly Stevens. 1966. Interesting letters that also contain observations on Stevens's own poetry.

———. *The Necessary Angel: Essays on Reality and the Imagination*. Ed. Holly Stevens. 1951. Stevens's own discussions of poetry and poetics.

Vendler, Helen H. *On Extended Wings: Wallace Stevens' Longer Poems*. 1969. A discussion of poetic and critical attitudes for and against Romantic norms.

James Joyce

The Dead

Classroom Strategies and Topics for Discussion

This long short story demonstrates the fullness of vision that a focused episode can take on when described by a master writer. Every detail counts; every reference expands beyond its immediate relevance. While *The Dead* would repay intensive word-by-word scrutiny, you will do better to choose a few key moments to highlight without exhausting your students. Beginning with its title, one useful approach is to examine how *The Dead* simultaneously evokes and embraces opposites: life and death, the present and the past, the individual and the community, Ireland and the world.

A natural place to start is with the community gathered in the opening section of the story. The Misses Morkans' annual dance is, on the one hand, a ritual celebration, a New Year's revel. On the other hand, the specter of death hovers over the party, and the jollity is in fact rather forced. As several critics have remarked, the aunts' quite genuine hospitality issues not only from the goodness of their hearts; the party also serves as an advertisement for Mary Jane's music school. Who are the members of the family? Much may be made of the dominance here of the elderly maiden aunts living in a "dark gaunt house." Ask your students why, as the headnote points out, Joyce should have changed the married state of the Misses Morkans' real-life prototypes.

The group of characters collected here are of course the most prosperous of Dublin's bourgeoisie. This information is provided by the street names in the second paragraph of the story: note that most of Mary Jane's students live in a fashionable part of town. Ask your students how this piece of information subtly contributes to our understanding of the role class plays in *The Dead*: how has the Morkan family changed since the days of Johnny the millhorse? What has happened to the people who still work in the mills? It may be helpful to explain at this point that except for enclaves such as these, Dublin in Joyce's day was an exceedingly poor city that had not participated in Ireland's rising economy: one-third of the inhabitants in the central part of the city lived in slums, and only one in five workers had a full-time job.

Early in your discussion, you will also want to sensitize your students to the way the narration incorporates different characters' points of view, moving from the community to the individual. From whose perspective does the opening paragraph show us the world of the Misses Morkan? It is presumably Lily's voice being echoed, with its use of "literally" when "figuratively" would be the more accurate word choice. Critics have pointed also to Joyce's decision to name the caretaker's daughter Lily, a flower with funereal associations; alert your students to the significance of names in Joyce's fiction, most dramatically demonstrated in the final sequence.

Gabriel Conroy, the first man to enter the story, is eagerly awaited by his aunts; the expectations that eagerness may have raised in the reader are somewhat deflated as we observe his difficulty in finding the right tone in which to address Lily and his self-conscious concern that he has offended her. Moreover, he is wearing galoshes: punctilious, nervous, anxious Gabriel hardly provides the anticipated virile masculine presence. (Note his position in his nuclear family; the favored nephew, he is nevertheless the second son of his demanding mother, who gave her children imposing names. Gabriel's elder brother bears the name Constantine, the first Roman emperor to convert to Christianity. Like "Gabriel," to be discussed further below, it sets a high standard for a child.) In fact, none of the men at the annual dance seems particularly prepossessing. Freddy Malins, drunk and self-indulgent, who has failed to button up his fly, looks and acts rather like a big baby, rubbing his eye with his knuckles and giggling before he reaches the punchline of his own story. Likewise, the formidable Mr. Browne has been a trial to the aunts, "laid on here like the gas" as Aunt Kate complains—again, a whiff of death enters the story.

After the opening glance through Lily's eyes, we see most of the rest of the story through Gabriel's—that is, from the perspective of an individual who lacks the ability to get along easily with others. His insistence on wearing galoshes like everyone "on the continent," which amuses his wife, takes on new importance in his encounter with Miss Ivors, the champion of Ireland's indigenous Gaelic culture (only Gretta, born in the West of Ireland herself and demeaningly labeled "country cute" by Gabriel's mother, calls this brusque, amused, and well-educated woman by her comfortable, unpretentious name, Molly). It is worth pausing at this point in the story to review the crisis of Irish politics embodied in the conversation between G. C., the author of literary reviews for a conservative paper, and Molly Ivors, who takes him to task for neglecting his own country. Joyce here fastens on issues that still divide compatriots around the globe and that deeply affected his own life. What are the sources of personal authenticity? Must an individual represent a community? Your students will probably have strong feelings about whether or not one should define oneself primarily as a product of race, religion, or national affiliation. What have been the consequences of "identity politics" in the twentieth century? How does the choice of the place to spend one's summer vacation dramatize the conflict between Gabriel and Miss Ivors?

Gabriel finally has the limelight all to himself in his much-prepared-for after-dinner speech. Working through this speech carefully, you can show your students how Joyce uses Gabriel's remarks to organize many of the oppositions so central to *The Dead*. He praises life-affirming, positive qualities—the generous array of food (so sensuously described by Joyce); the hospitality of his aunts; the beauty of their music; the traditions of his country. Yet each affirmation is undercut by details mentioned elsewhere, details that bring the dead of the title before the reader and rob the present of its superficial vitality. Irish hospitality is also demonstrated by the monks of Melleray, who supposedly sleep in their coffins, music is no longer as well performed as it used to be; Ireland is riven between Celtic roots and European sophistication.

The way Joyce handles these points of contention may be most easily exemplified by the constant presence of music in the story: Aunt Julia's triumphant singing of Bellini's aria, a coloratura showpiece, is only one of the story's many containers of the theme of death in life. Although her voice still rings true, she has aged perceptibly, and her closeness to death is emphasized by the contrast between her person and the music she chooses (*Arrayed for the Bridal* is an ebullient expression of the virginal hopes of the heroine of Bellini's opera *I Puritani*). The joy in the music sung by the heroine, Elvira, functions ironically both in the opera, for she is about to go mad, and in Joyce's knowing use of it. (Joyce was an opera lover and once famously took second prize in a singing competition that the great professional Irish tenor, John McCormack, won.) And the brilliance of Aunt Julia's performance, so unexpected in one so old, makes all the more fierce Aunt Kate's anger at the pope's decision "to turn out the women out of the choirs that have slaved there all their lives and put little whipper-snappers of boys over their heads."

This theme of displacement echoes throughout *The Dead*. In the second of the three phases of the story to which the anthology headnote refers, the anecdote about Johnny the millhorse encapsulates many complex attitudes toward Ireland and the condition of its people. Your students should have no trouble elucidating the significance of Johnny's "tragic" experience once you call it to their attention: Patrick Morkan's pretensions to grandeur cannot survive the force of habit and the call of the past that led his workhorse to circle the statue of "King Billy" rather than conduct his owner to join with "the quality [at] a military review in the park."

Art and music provide the transition that links the powerful third section of *The Dead* to the story's initial stages and sets up the culmination of all its themes in the hotel room to which Gretta and Gabriel Conroy repair as the night draws toward day. The artist in Gabriel sees his wife listening intently to Bartell D'Arcy's voice in the next room as he sings "The Lass of Aughrim." The tenor (unlike Aunt Julia) is not in his best voice; he is separated from his audience, and the sight of Gretta in the shadow, straining to hear him, suggests itself to Gabriel as a painterly composition that he would call *Distant Music*. "He asked himself what is a woman standing on the stairs in the shadow, listening to distant music, a symbol of." The clumsy syntax of that sentence conveys the workings of Gabriel's mind, a mind that feverishly reviews moments of intimacy between husband and wife as the Conroys approach the hotel. When they reach their room, Gabriel's expectations as lover and artist are overturned.

The Dead ends with Gretta's revelation of her past intimacy with Michael Furey, in a brilliant coda that fully exposes Gabriel's inherited snobbishness and debilitating sense of inadequacy. Bristling at his wife's recollection of a former romance, he at first goes on the attack: "—What was he? asked Gabriel, still ironically." Used to dealing with others in terms of occupation and status, Gabriel is properly humiliated by Gretta's simple answer. The seventeen-year-old Michael Furey "was in the gasworks," here a pathetic reference that offsets Aunt Kate's exasperated mention of the gaslike pall that Mr. Browne has cast over the Christmas holidays.

Your students should have no difficulty hearing the pun in Michael Furey's last name; those who are familiar with the archangels Gabriel and Michael should be able to explain the contrast between Gabriel, the angel of the annuciation charged with conveying a difficult message to a young woman, and Michael, the leader of God's armies. Michael Furey, eternally young and passionate, stood in the rain for a last glimpse of Gretta; Gabriel Conroy, declining into middle age, does not venture out into snow without galoshes.

Moving toward the Joycean epiphany in the final paragraphs, however, Gabriel appears to achieve a sensitivity to the feelings of others of which he has not shown himself capable until now. The narrative takes us into Gabriel's mind processing the events of the day as he tries to sleep. His awareness of his own ridiculousness and pomposity is mitigated by the "generous tears" that fill his eyes, and we remember that Gretta had quite sincerely praised his generosity, thinking better of him for lending Freddy money than he himself does in the internal monologue that precedes her comment.

The oppositions that are everywhere to be found in *The Dead* typically complicate its conclusion. He will be making a journey "westward": is he foreseeing his death, or will he be revisiting the sources of Irish identity? Is he recognizing a common humanity as he muses (in another example of odd syntax) on the "snow that was general all over Ireland" or do the chill images of dissolution and mortality symbolize the final destruction of a self that was none too sturdy to begin with? Is the "swooned" of the final sentence a token of authorial sentiment or is it a vocabulary choice meant to mark the limitations of Gabriel's late-Victorian aesthetic? In debating unanswerable questions such as these, today's readers can still test their own sensibilities by looking into the vistas opened up by one of the great modernist writers.

Topics for Writing

1. How does the seasonal setting of the Misses Morkans' annual dance mirror the thematic concerns of *The Dead*? Does the party celebrate an end or a beginning? How does the falling snow add to the mood and development of the story?
2. Discuss the importance of music in *The Dead*.
   [If you have access to a tape of John Huston's 1987 movie version, your students can hear the melodies and grasp the way music permeates the story. You can also ask your students to note ways in which the movie distorts the story; one is by having Aunt Julia sing in an off-key, wavering voice.]
3. How does the story of Johnny the horse express Joyce's conviction

that Dublin is the "centre of paralysis"? What other evidence is there of that problem in *The Dead*?

Comparative Perspectives

1. What kind of character is Gabriel Conroy? Compare him to the protagonists of other modernist works, such as Eliot's J. Alfred Prufrock or Mann's Gustav von Aschenbach.
2. Compare and contrast Joyce's view of Irish politics in *The Dead* with those expressed in the poems of Yeats.

Further Reading

See also the reading suggestions in the *Anthology*, p. 2551.

Leonard, Garry M. *Reading* Dubliners *Again: A Lacanian Perspective*. 1993. Densely argued, with interesting close readings.

Williams, Trevor L. *Reading Joyce Politically*. 1997. A materialist interpretation that offers close analyses of the text in terms of power structures and economic difference.

VIRGINIA WOOLF

A Room of One's Own

Classroom Strategies and Topics for Discussion

This wonderful, totally idiosyncratic work, a landmark of twentieth-century cultural criticism, can serve a variety of purposes in your course. You might begin by asking students to what genre *A Room of One's Own* belongs. Is it a lecture? Is it an essay? Is it fiction? That one can say yes to each of these suggestions, without excluding the others as equally valid designations, immediately should establish the fluidity of Woolf's prose and the way it mirrors human thought. *A Room of One's Own*, like so many of Virginia Woolf's novels, breaks down conventional boundaries and in its own elusiveness embodies one of her core perceptions— that consciousness is neither fixed nor static.

Woolf herself would probably have been amazed by the changes wrought by *A Room of One's Own*. This witty and heartfelt analysis of (among other things) the influence of gender and poverty on human creativity has transformed the literary canon in English. Generations of university women have responded to the lecturer's exhortation to the young women of Newnham and Girton and in fact recovered poets and even playwrights who wrote alongside Shakespeare. Their existence takes away nothing from the bravura of Woolf's imagined tragedy of Judith Shakespeare; in fact, the recovery of these writers is one proof of the power of Woolf's fiction.

The array of women writers with which the anthology concludes may suggest that the material preconditions for art that Woolf lays out here have finally been achieved. It would be worth pursuing this hypothesis:

outside of Proust, how many writers have ever had the benefit of "soundproof rooms"? If women are no longer laughed at when they proclaim a desire to write, have they ceased to be the looking glass that reflects and enlarges the image of the men to whom they are attached? (We live in an era when a political spouse may be male rather than female, yet it is the rare husband of the candidate or office holder who sits in photogenic, wide-eyed wonderment as his wife speaks.)

Certainly the very presence of women students in your own academic institution bears witness to how the world has changed since Woolf wrote, but the prose in which she captured the world has not grown stale. Woolf is such a keen observer of quotidian detail that you might ask your students to sharpen their own eyes and look around themselves: "London was like a workshop. London was like a machine." The pace of the modern city has accelerated since 1928, when Woolf wrote these words, but the sense of rupture with the past implied by those terse sentences fuels much of her work and is one of the marks of the modernist movement. At a time when New York's Museum of Modern Art has had to give up drawings by Van Gogh and Manet on the grounds that these works have ceased to be "modern," you could anchor an inquiry into the meaning of "modern" and "modernism" in a discussion of *A Room of One's Own*. In what ways are Woolf, Joyce, and Proust more "modern" than many of writers of the very late twentieth century whose novels turn up on the best-seller lists? (Most popular fiction of the day treats readers like consumers by providing them with detailed inventories of characters' possessions and thus tends to be much closer, at least in this attention to the external world, to ninteenth-century realism.)

There is no question that *A Room of One's Own* mirrors its own time—a time when a writer could speak of Mussolini without having a political ax to grind, or complain about having to work for a living without acknowledging a worldwide depression (which began in 1929, a year after Woolf delivered her lectures, and lasted in many cases until 1939). It may, in fact, be helpful to review some of the history of Europe between the wars with your students: ask whether anyone can identify Mussolini (1883–1945), who was much admired at the time Woolf wrote *A Room of One's Own*. By 1920, Mussolini had established a fighting force called a *Fasci di Combattimento*, using the ancient Roman symbol of authority, the *fascinae*, to anchor his party's claims to lead the Italian people to greatness. As the first Fascist dictator in a fractured Europe, Mussolini was credited with "making the trains run on time." In the 1930's, of course, Mussolini began on a program of imperial conquest and collaboration with Hitler. He would not then have been casually mentioned by Woolf, who writes in her diaries of the horror of the Fascist bombardment of England and feared the consequences of a Nazi invasion, a real threat in the early years of World War II.

Yet *A Room of One's Own* also transcends its historical context and even its declared subject, for what Woolf described here is a quest as relevant at the end of the twentieth century as it was at the end of its third decade: she looks for the "pure fluid, the essential oil of truth." She understands that anger, like any emotion, colors and distorts truth. As the English publisher of Freud's works and a woman painfully self-aware of the way childhood shapes the adult consciousness, she knows firsthand how being laughed at "in his cradle by a pretty girl" may have twisted the professorial mind so that it is incapable of arriving at an objective view of experience. For all this sophistication about the impact of forgotten irritants on the way we think and feel and the concomitant implication that nothing stable exists outside the mind of the beholder, the selection in the anthology suggests that the essential oil can be found in the greatest art, represented here by the "incandescent" mind of Shakespeare. Readers of Shakespeare may wonder about the meaning of that "incandescent," and many artists and critics would challenge the apparent implication of a single standard of art or truth. Especially if you are going on to read writers such as Beckett or Robbe-Grillet, you may want to use Woolf's text to prepare your students for current doubts about the existence of immutable, objective truth.

Woolf's "evocations of states of mind," as the headnote describes them, have lost none of their innovative freshness. The long paragraph that dominates chapter two is a good laboratory for scrutinizing the transitional strategies that create a rhetorical unity out of so apparently random a sequence. Beginning in the library, reflecting on the anger of the professors who write books about women, the would-be lecturer goes off to lunch, where she comes upon an abandoned newspaper. Have your students look closely at the headlines that lead her to announce that "this scattered testimony" demonstrates that "England is under the rule of a patriarchy." What is it about topics ranging from The Shamelessness of Women to the dangling film actress, from a scene of violence in a cellar to the sports score that bespeaks masculine dominion? Sitting in a lunchroom and staring out the window, the narrator reflects in an elliptical way on the sources of masculine power. Throughout these chapters, she prefers ironic obliquity to direct attack, but the scorn for male chauvinist pretension is not hard to track: "How much thinking those old gentlemen used to save one!"

Not until she pays her check does a new paragraph begin: it is money that frees her from the power of patriarchy. Her aunt who "died by a fall from her horse when she was riding out to take the air in Bombay" seems almost an antidote to the Hollywood actress suspended in air. For this woman died exercising her independence, not acting out a film producer's fantasy of female daring. (Perhaps Judith Shakespeare, who "let herself down by a rope one summer's night" makes a third female acrobat seeking freedom at great cost to herself.)

Woolf's walker through the city returns to the question of patriarchy with her brilliant suggestion that "Anon . . . was often a woman". She draws a line between the male ego and the female "desire to be veiled" that culminates in a remarkable equation drawn between British imperialism and men's quest of fame. As in her insistence that social class makes a difference—"genius like Shakespeare's is not born among labouring, uneducated, servile people", Woolf does not shrink from separating persons by race and gender. In a sentence that calls for analysis of her attitudes toward race, class, and gender, those three central categories of contemporary critical discourse, Woolf's narrator dryly notes: "It is one of the great advantages of being a woman that one can pass even a very fine negress without wishing to make an Englishwoman of her". (It would be interesting to teach *A Room of One's Own* in close proximity to Ingeborg Bachmann's *The Barking*, another reflection on connections between patriarchy and the social aberrations it breeds. Writing a generation after Virginia Woolf, Bachmann sees egotistical masculine behavior as an arbitrary social form and an implicit cause of fascism.)

Today's critics have pursued the significance of similar passages, questioning the extent to which this daughter of privilege (if not of great wealth) understood the crushing social and economic pressures that continue to deprive human beings of the ability to realize their talents. As influential as Woolf's work has been, it is important to point out that she was also deeply influenced by her contemporaries. The most obvious contemporary influence on Woolf was Marcel Proust, whose *Remembrance of Things Past* was, perhaps, her favorite book. Although she is often linked with Joyce, she did not—at least in her public statements—much like his work, which she called "indecent." Joyce was mainly interested in using stream-of-consciousness techniques as a way of exploring the conscious mind; Woolf was interested in life below the level of consciousness, emotional life, and she used all of her considerable creative powers to render and articulate that life. Woolf was also influenced by Henri Bergson's discussions of the immediate data of consciousness as it exists outside of clocktime. Dorothy Richardson, whose experiments in stream-of-consciousness predated Woolf's, and Katherine Mansfield, whose sensibility and insight made Woolf envious, were also significant influences.

Woolf was at the center of what was perhaps England's most influential group of intellectuals during the 1920s and '30s—the Bloomsbury group. It has often been noted by biographers of the group and its individual members that their principles were derived from the Cambridge philosopher G. E. Moore, who argued, among other things, that "aesthetic enjoyment and the pleasures of human intercourse include *all* the greatest, and *by far* the greatest, goods we can imagine." Woolf went some distance in expressing these principles in life as well as in literature.

Topics for Writing and Comparative Perspectives

1. Find evidence in *A Room of One's Own* of Virginia Woolf's novelistic talents. Can this text be categorized as fiction?
2. How does the lecturer use irony and humor as devices to advance an argument?

   [If you wish to expand this topic, you might have your students compare the argumentative strategies of Sor Juana in the other great feminist treatise in the anthology, the *Reply to Sor Filotea de la Cruz*: how does each writer use autobiographical detail? How would you characterize the tone of their respective attacks on male dominated societies?]

3. Show how Woolf makes the case that women express themselves in ways that are natural to them and not available to men. Do you agree with her?

   [Compare Dorothy Wordsworth's style in her *Grasmere Journals*.]

4. Compare ideas about opportunities for women to create fiction explored by Leslie Marmon Silko in *Yellow Woman*. How do their cultural situations contribute to Woolf's and Silko's understanding of their own freedom to create?

Further Reading

See also the reading suggestions in the *Anthology*, p. 2556.

Bell, Quentin. *Virginia Woolf: A Biography*. 1972. The definitive biography of Woolf, written by her nephew (the son of Clive and Vanessa Bell). It has been criticized for being too sympathetic with the Bloomsbury sensibility, but no one knows more about Woolf than Quentin Bell.

Colburn, Krystyna. "Women's Oral Tradition and *A Room of One's Own*." In *Re:Reading, Re:Writing: Re:Teaching Virginia Woolf*, eds. Eileen Barrett and Patrick Cramer. 1995. An explanation of the choice of "Mary Beton," "Seton," and others that derive from "The Ballad of the Four Marys," an old folk song.

Duisinberre, Juliet. *Virginia Woolf's Renaissance: Woman Reader or Common Reader?* 1997. Although there is little of direct relevance to *A Room of One's Own* in this book by a well-known feminist critic of Shakespeare and his contemporaries, it brings together Woolf's various comments about Renaissance figures like Montaigne, and forms a background against which one can better appreciate the genesis of Woolf's searing vision of Judith Shakespeare.

Gordan, Lyndall. *Virginia Woolf: A Writer's Life*. 1985. This biography moves back and forth between the life and the work, with special attention to the latter.

Woolf, Virginia. "Mr. Bennett and Mrs. Brown." In *Collected Essays*, vol. I. 1966. An extremely important essay for understanding Woolf's approach to character in fiction, especially insofar as it differs from the English Edwardian realists.

Franz Kafka

The Metamorphosis

Backgrounds

Even now, some ninety years after *The Metamorphosis* was written, students find it as fresh and contemporary as the latest story by David Foster Wallace, and as baffling and troubling as the last stories of Jorge Luis Borges. What still interests and excites contemporary readers and writers about Kafka is his ability to force us to look beyond the seemingly calm surface of the story for a symbolic or allegorical meaning, along with his persistent refusal to deliver such a meaning. As soon as we try to nail down Kafka, he gets up and walks away with the nail. Kafka frustrates our expectation that there is a final, unequivocal meaning to be found anywhere. Nevertheless, students will find Kafka's prose precise and objective, and they will find it especially enchanting because it appears to be in service to the inner life—dreams, fantasies, unconscious fears and desires—without straining their ability to understand what is being said. As baffling as Kafka often seems to be, he manages in his best work to present his world with the humanity, humor, and power that we expect from great writers of any era.

To say that someone is "like" a vermin, an insect, a giant bug—or to feel "like" that ourselves—is to say something we all understand, metaphorically. The metaphorical basis of Kafka's tale is rather simple; it is Kafka's matter-of-fact, almost journalistic, insistence on the *reality* of the metaphor that strikes us as being curious. In *The Metamorphosis* Gregor Samsa has been transformed into a metaphor that states his essential self, but this metaphor in turn is treated as an actual fact. Gregor does not just call himself a giant bug; he wakes up to find himself one. Kafka has transformed the metaphor back into fictional reality, and this counter-metamorphosis becomes the starting point of his tale. Such a fictional act seems simple enough, but it is extraordinarily radical, one of the most radical beginnings of any story anywhere.

Kafka confirms his intention to insist on the *fact* of Gregor's metamorphosis by his use of absolutely ordinary language, a language purged of surprise, to describe it. The first two paragraphs of the story tell us a great deal about Kafka's method in *The Metamorphosis*. In the first paragraph, Gregor is introduced already transformed—but he is introduced by a narrator who seems absolutely unsurprised by what has taken place, a narrator who presents this extraordinary moment with the cold objectivity and precision of a visiting zoologist. In the second paragraph, we notice that the narrator remains separate from Gregor's consciousness (and is thus able to make factual comments such as "Samsa was a traveller"), but still identifies almost completely with Gregor, sees through his eyes and ears, removed only slightly farther away from things than the character himself. Such a narrative stance makes it impossible for us to read the story as if it were merely a hallucination or a dream. As importantly, and more intriguingly, the narrator seems curiously unhurried to explain what we are most interested in. When the narrator *does* evidence astonishment, it is not over Gregor's transformation at all, but instead over a vaguely erotic picture, from an illustrated magazine, that hangs on the wall of his room. "It showed a lady in a fur hat and boa, sitting up straight and holding out an enormous fur muff that entirely concealed her forearms." The narrator refuses to be impressed by the same things we are, and the frustration of our expectations—expectations we probably did not know existed—is curiously humorous.

The Metamorphosis is also a family drama, a drama about the relationship between Gregor and his sister, his mother, and—especially—his father. Indeed, if we forget for a moment that Gregor is now a monstrous insect (although Kafka clearly doesn't want us to forget), his behavior resembles nothing so much as that of a monstrous infant, struggling unsuccessfully to establish a functional identity in an environment with which he is unequipped to cope, and in a family situation that continually reconfirms his lack of status. Gregor's family depend on him for their welfare, but as a "father"—the breadwinner, the one economically responsible for the family's welfare—Gregor feels himself to be a failure. He is such a minor functionary in his company that he can be mercilessly assailed by its chief clerk who arrives at the Samsa home only a few minutes after Gregor should have arrived at work. The chief clerk berates Gregor "on behalf of your parents and your superior"—the two sources of authority, and therefore of punishment, in the story—in full view of his family, accuses him of doing unsatisfactory work, implies that he may have stolen money from company funds entrusted to him, and reminds him how easily he could be fired. He treats Gregor like the vermin that Gregor has, in fact, become and exposes Gregor's sense of vulnerability and guilt.

The world of officials and the world of fathers appear to be essentially the same. Both worlds have authority and use that authority to punish Gregor, whose guilt attracts their attention and their desire for power. This is exacerbated by Gregor's own sense of insufficiency, which has stultified him spiritually long before his physical transformation. His literal imprisonment—in the body of a giant insect, locked in his room, with employers and family members as jailers—is made even more intolerable by his horrible awareness of it. It has been suggested that Gregor's acceptance of his metamorphosis occurs because he recognizes that his present status as insect is about the same as his former status as human being.

In *The Metamorphosis*, every weakening of the son's position results in the strengthening of the father's. In the end, one will triumph, the other will die. Gregor makes three forays out of his room and into the world of his family, and these three forays constitute the central events of the three sections of the story. In part I, Gregor struggles to open his door with his jaws, but when he emerges from his bedroom, he frightens away the manager and is finally driven back by his infuriated father, who wields a walking stick and a newspaper and stamps the floor in anger. In part II, Gregor is overtaken by the desire to see his mother, but when his angry and exultant father, now wearing a uniform that suggests his new-found authority and power, discovers him outside his room, he drives him back by pelting Gregor with apples. In part III, the starving, wounded Gregor comes out while Meg—the only one in the family who has shown anything resembling sympathy for his plight—is playing the violin. He is entranced by the music, but is driven back this time by a different, and more devastating, kind of attack: the stark indifference of his family. His mother is now fast asleep, and Meg, who has had enough of tending her brother, locks his door behind him and cries, "At last!" Gregor dies alone, to be discovered in the morning by the charwoman. His father delivers Gregor's epitaph: "Thanks be to God."

Gregor's treatment by his family—especially his father—is progressively more violent, fueled by their increasing disgust and annoyance at having to put up with such a creature in their house. In many ways, they become as monstrous, as parasitical, as Gregor looks. As long as Gregor filled the role of breadwinner, the family (especially the father) was moribund, but as soon as Gregor is reduced to a bug, the family comes alive. In fact, Gregor's diminishment is in direct proportion to his family's advancement. For the family to thrive, Gregor must die. After his death, the family—suddenly and happily free of the burden that was their son—decide to leave the apartment, which is "something they had not done for months," to take the tram excusion into the country. The last paragraph of the story is written in Kafka's most lilting cadences. It is springtime; the tram is "full of warmth and sunlight"; they are free; and Meg, under the admiring gaze of her mother and father, demonstrates her own metamorphosis. Like a butterfly emerging from a cocoon, she has "blossomed into a beautiful, full-blossomed girl." Mr. and Mrs. Samsa come to the conclusion that "the time was also coming when they must start looking round for a nice husband for her. And they saw it as a sort of confirmation of their new-found dreams and good intentions when, at the end of the journey, their daughter was the first to stand up, stretching her young body."

It is easy, perhaps too easy to read the central metaphor in *The Metamorphosis* as Gregor = giant bug = modern man and to insist that it is a parable about the human condition in the modern world. In many ways such a reading is perfectly justifiable; in other ways it extends the story's implications beyond what it can reasonably be expected to suggest.

Kafka's inability to assert himself, his overwhelming sense of shortcoming and consequently of guilt mark everything he ever wrote. Although he was a brilliant graduate in law, he never practiced, taking instead a position as a civil servant in the Austrian government. He was engaged several times and had several affairs (his meeting with Felice Bauer led directly to his writing *The Metamorphosis*) but could never bring himself to marry. Kafka even asked that his unpublished writings be destroyed upon his death. Fortunately for us, Max Brod, his literary executor, published them anyway.

Any analysis of Kafka's work must take into account the peculiarly poetic and tormenting character of Prague. As all biographers of Kafka agree, his Prague was perfectly suited to reflect his disposition—a place of Slavonic melancholy, weighed down by its history, where different traditions and tongues competed and where desire for the unequivocal is persistently met by recognition of its impossibility. Because Kafka was a German-speaking Jew living in Prague, he felt even more powerfully the burden of his separateness, which reveals itself also in the very form of his stories. In his work—as in the Jewish tradition—time is a dimension that fuses past and present, eternity and the instant, just as it fuses the extraordinary and the mundane, the ultimate and the immediate. Authority is not represented by fathers alone, but also by Gentiles, who may turn from allies to enemies at any given moment. For Kafka's characters the world of authority—of Law—is closed but ambiguous, and nothing can be finally resolved. In the Jewish tradition, full resolution can take place only with the decisive return of the Messiah; until that time everyone lives in the middle of an inconclusive history. We find this same "in the middle" effect in Kafka, where the story typically begins *after* the decisive event has taken place, where characters go through a gradual shifting of states of being but are never granted a conclusive resolution to their problems.

The Metamorphosis was written in late 1912. It is one of the very few stories that apparently satisfied Kafka to the point that he wanted to see it published. Though it would be a mistake to interpret the story merely as a coded autobiographical document, *The Metamorphosis* does, of course, have personal significance for its author. It quite evidently reflects his sense of personal inadequacy in comparison to his father—a strong-willed, self-made authoritarian—who, as we know from reading Kafka's *Letter to His Father*, once likened his son to an insect. Kafka's tenderness toward his sister, Ottla, can be felt in his depiction of Meg, as can his frustration over his mother's inability to deal with his psychological difficulties.

After Kafka wrote *The Judgment* in 1912, a few months before he began *The Metamorphosis*, he wrote in his diary, "Thoughts of Freud, naturally." And it *was* natural: Kafka was intensely aware of the work of Freud and others working in the developing field of psychoanalysis, and he sometimes claimed that "the therapeutic claims of psychoanalysis" were an "impotent error" and that he was "nauseated" by them. Kafka had read some of Freud's work, had heard him discussed in various intellectual circles, and was personally acquainted with Otto Gross, a member of Freud's inner circle. The impact of Freud is evident in the importance Kafka attaches to the images of his inner life (as well as his talent for portraying them), his extraordinary interest in childhood experience and in the Oedipal situation in particular, and his awareness of his own neurotic symptoms.

The climate of thought that made his work possible is also evident in expressionism, one of the most influential aesthetic movements of the early twentieth century. Its central tendency is to distort or magnify the shape of reality in order to suggest a higher order of emotional reality beneath the surface. It assumes, like many of the major movements of modern art and literature, that art based predominantly on visible reality is inadequate. If Robert Wiene's film *The Cabinet of Dr. Caligari* (1919) is available, it might be useful to screen it for the class, since it quite dramatically and enjoyably reveals a number of German Expressionism's essential features: the distortion of surfaces, the obsession with the inner life, and the relationship between individual and authority (especially the conflict between fathers and sons).

Classroom Strategies

The Metamorphosis can be taught in as few as two class periods. The first discussion of the story could emphasize the nature of its narrative, while the second might concentrate on the relations between Gregor and his family, his feelings of guilt and inadequacy, the ambiguity of self-knowledge and values, and the relationship between the individual and authority.

The narrative of *The Metamorphosis* exploits the gap between a reader's expectations and his or her findings. Inevitably, then, students will find Kafka's narrative curious or even unacceptable. Though they may not know exactly why they find it so (they often accept events far more outlandish in a science fiction story), a close examination of the events described and of the tone the narrator uses will allow them to move beyond their initial confusion. In order to press the point home, it might be useful to read from other writers who use similar narrative strategies—Beckett, Borges, Donald Barthelme, Robert Coover, or Peter Handke, for instance. But perhaps the most telling comparison might be made between Kafka's narrative and everyday newspaper reports, which often describe the most extraordinary events in a tone of detached, journalistic objectivity. The cool, detached quality of such reports on unlikely events makes them bleakly humorous. In *The Metamorphosis*, the effect of such a narrative is first to establish the fictional reality of the metaphor: Gregor is a giant bug. But like the newspaper stories, it also delivers humor, deriving, for the most part, from the apparent disjunction of the tone of the narrative from the events it describes. Teaching humor, beyond insisting that it's there, is very difficult, perhaps impossible; but there are particular moments in the text that might be used to establish Kafka's humor: Gregor's difficulty over getting up for the first time after his transformation and feeling anything but fresh or sprightly, along with his attendant worry over lying idle in bed and getting behind in his work; Gregor's attempts to speak, which come out in "a distressing squeak"; the chief clerk's lecture on the nature of business; the three lodgers, who behave like performers in a vaudeville routine; or the cleaning woman, who appears to respond to Gregor as if he were nothing more than a ridiculous obstacle to completing her work.

Henri Bergson—with whose work Kafka was familiar—has claimed that "we laugh every time a person gives us the impression of being a thing" and that the comic produces "something like a momentary anesthesia of the heart," which is brought on by "looking at life as a disinterested spectator." In *The Metamorphosis* Kafka meets these requirements, and our response is precisely what Bergson might have expected. Invariably, Kafka's grotesquely extravagant vision of people enmeshed in the sad absurdity of the universe evokes in us an uneasy laughter.

Topics for Discussion and Writing

1. How does Kafka use his central metaphor in *The Metamorphosis?* In what ways is his use of it different from what we might expect to find?

   [Kafka's central metaphor, Gregor = giant bug, is insisted upon as being literally true. The metaphor is treated as an actual fact. To get the response he evidently wants, Kafka exploits the gap between what the reader expects and what he finds. The reader's objections to Gregor's transformation into a monstrous insect are undermined by the literalness, the journalistic objectivity, of the narrative.]

2. How does the apparent disjunction between tone and event create humor in *The Metamorphosis?*

   [See the second paragraph of "Backgrounds" and the second and third paragraphs of "Classroom Strategies."]

3. What is the relationship between Gregor and his family? What clues in the story suggest that his relationship with his family, particularly his father, is unsatisfactory?

   [See "Backgrounds," from the fourth paragraph through the seventh. Besides the many evidences of Gregor's indifferent treatment in the story, students should note details such as his father's use of a newspaper (something we typically use to squash bugs) and a walking stick (a traditional symbol of paternal authority) to drive Gregor back into his room during their first confrontation. It is also worth noting that Gregor apparently feels it necessary to lock his room in his own home.]

4. Discuss the central events in each of the three sections of the story. In what ways do these events suggest that the weakening of Gregor results in the strengthening of the family as a whole?

   [See "Backgrounds," the sixth and seventh paragraphs.]

5. What significance is attached to food in *The Metamorphosis?*

   [Kafka often uses food as an image of spiritual, psychic, or artistic fulfillment in his stories, just as he uses hunger and starvation to suggest unfulfillment. *The Hunger Artist* is the most famous example of his use of this formula. In *The Metamorphosis*, Gregor is first offered fresh food, which does not satisfy him. His sister, "in the goodness of her heart," then tries to satisfy Gregor by offering him half-decayed food from the family table. As his family becomes more indifferent, his sister merely shoves "any old thing into his room with her foot," then clears it out "with a whisk of her broom," heedless of whether it has been tasted or left untouched. Soon after, Gregor eats almost nothing while, by contrast, his family and the three boarders stuff themselves with meat and potatoes and make much of their satisfaction. Gregor thinks: "I do feel like eating . . . but not these things. The way these lodgers stuff themselves—and I'm starving." On his last foray out of his room, Gregor trails "thread, hairs, and scraps of leftover food" to listen to his sister play the violin. The music affects him greatly, and he feels "as if he were being shown the way to that food he had so longed for." But it is too late. When Gregor's flat and dry corpse is discovered, the rotting apple thrown by his father still imbedded in his back, Meg says, "Just look how thin he was. . . . The food used to come out exactly as it had gone in."]

6. What is the significance of the minor characters in the story—the chief clerk, the three lodgers, and the cleaning woman?

   [See the fourth paragraph of "Backgrounds." Note that the family feels itself independent enough to dismiss the three lodgers, and their demands, only after Gregor's death.]

7. What is the importance of the final scene in the story, the family's trip to the country? Why is it written so lyrically in comparison to the rest of the text?

   [The lyricism of the last scene reflects the family's new dispensation, the revival of their prospects. Gregor's death allows them their release, and the language of this final scene embodies their new hopes. See the seventh paragraph of "Backgrounds."]

8. *The Metamorphosis* has been read and interpreted in many ways—as an example of existentialist philosophy, a depiction of humanity's condition in the modern world, a presentation of psychological neurosis, and a theological parable. Discuss these various interpretive possibilities.

Comparative Perspectives

1. In *Notes From Underground*, part II, chapter I, the Underground Man announces that "every decent man of our time is and must be a coward and a slave." To what extent does this description fit Gregor Samsa before he turns into a giant bug? Is it true of him in his metamorphosed state? Is it true of his entire family? How many other protagonists of the modern period could be similarly characterized? What sets of circumstances are involved in each case?

   [Consider, among others, Prufrock metaphorically transformed into an insect, "formulated, sprawling on a pin."]

2. Listening to his sister play the violin, Gregor—who had not particularly appreciated music before—is deeply affected. "Was he a beast to be so moved by music?" This difficult sentence makes us reread it: it seems to ask whether a dung beetle could have this capacity to respond to high art and therefore to throw Gregor's identity into question once more. What sensibilities are ascribed to animals in Rilke's *The Panther* for instance. Why is it easier to ac-

cept the idea of a powerful animal's alertness to his surroundings?

3. What other texts in the anthology might bear significant comparison to *The Metamorphosis*?

   [One might usefully compare *The Metamorphosis* with *The Death of Ivan Ilyich*. In both works we are told of a character who moves toward death; in Tolstoy that death is redemptive, and it provides the central meaning of the text, but in *The Metamorphosis*, Gregor's death is remarkable precisely because it is without redemption. Comparisons also can be drawn between *The Metamorphosis* and *Notes from Underground*, especially with regard to the depiction of a psychological condition that suggests self-hatred. In *Endgame* we experience the same discrepancy between extreme unreality and the dry precision of its presentation, and we laugh with a similar uneasiness. In *The Love Song of J. Alfred Prufrock* the title figure sings of his own insufficiency. And texts as different as *A Modest Proposal*, *Candide*, and *The Garden of Forking Paths* all use a similar kind of narrative strategy to provoke the reader's response. It is important to note, however, that Swift and Voltaire both assume a firm and commonly understood series of values against which they measure their irony, whereas Kafka has no such center and no such certainty.]

Further Reading

See also the reading suggestions in the *Anthology*, p. 2551.

Anders, Gunter. *Franz Kafka*. Trans. A. Steer and A. K. Thorlby. 1960. A well-known analysis of *The Metamorphosis* that examines Gregor's transformation as an extended metaphor for Kafka's view of the world "as it appears to a stranger."

Anderson, Mark, ed. *Reading Kafka: Prague, Politics, and the Fin de Siècle*. 1989. Useful study of Kafka's relation to his time.

Benjamin, Walter. "Franz Kafka. On the Tenth Anniversary of His Death." In *Illuminations*, ed. Hannah Arendt, pp. 111–40. 1968. Benjamin describes clusters of related images, gestures, and motifs in order to suggest the nature of Kafka's world.

Bernheimer, Charles. *Flaubert and Kafka: Studies in Psychopoetic Structure*. 1982. Employs contemporary critical theory to describe aspects of Kafka's work.

Corngold, Stanley. *The Commentators' Despair*. 1973. A useful annotated bibliography of works on *The Metamorphosis* (up to 1972).

———. *Franz Kafka: The Necessity of Form*. 1988.

Deleuze, Gilles, and Felix Guattari. *Kafka: Toward a Minor Literature*. Trans. Dana Polan. 1986. An important study of Kafka's many-sided alienation from his linguistic and social context.

Gray, Ronald. *Franz Kafka*. 1973. Useful brief studies.

Koelb, Clayton. *Kafka's Rhetoric: The Passion of Reading*. 1989. Employs critical theory to describe aspects of Kafka's work.

Lawson, Richard. *Franz Kafka*. 1987. Biographical study.

Robert, Marthe. *As Lonely as Franz Kafka*. Trans. Ralph Manheim. 1982. Psychoanalytic criticism.

Robertson, Ritchie. *Kafka: Judaism, Politics, Literature*. 1985. Describes Kafka's emerging sense of Jewish identity.

Sandbank, Shimon. *After Kafka: The Influence of Kafka's Fiction*. 1989.

Stern, J. P., ed. *The World of Franz Kafka*. 1980. Contains portraits and photographs.

Stric, Roman, and Yardley, J. C., eds. *Franz Kafka (1883–1924): His Craft and Thought*. 1986. Collected essays.

Thiher, Allan. *Franz Kafka: A Study of the Short Fiction*. 1990.

Udoff, Alan, ed. *Kafka and the Contemporary Critical Performance*. 1987. Collection of essays.

T. S. ELIOT

T. S. Eliot is probably the best-known and most influential twentieth-century poet who wrote in English. He believed that great writers represent their time, and his own poems, plays, and criticism have given modern Western society a characteristic voice. When we read *The Love Song of J. Alfred Prufrock* we find ourselves engaged with a vulnerable, self-conscious presence that has become so central to twentieth-century literature that it is hard to imagine the modern consciousness without him. *The Waste Land*, with its insistent depiction of a civilization in fragments and its dramatic litany of the symptoms of the collapse, is, for many, the central statement of modern culture's obsessions and fears. Eliot did not stop, however, with the bleak vision of these earlier poems. *Little Gidding*, from the *Four Quartets*, attempts to redeem the earlier despair; it is a redemption conjured out of the language itself, grave and endlessly fascinating. The range of Eliot's vision and the power of his language make the poet a dominating presence in modern literature.

The Love Song of J. Alfred Prufrock

Backgrounds

The opening three lines of *The Love Song of J. Alfred Prufrock* raise significant questions as to just exactly what kind of poem it is. The "I" of the first line does not at first present any particular problems; it appears to be the shadowy, wispy figure of J. Alfred Prufrock. The "you," however, is a different matter. Is it the reader? If so, then the poem is a monologue: the speaker alone, addressing an audience of readers. The monologue depends on its honesty, because we tend to believe that what the speaker has to say, especially about himself, is true.

But perhaps the "you" is another person in the poem, someone whose silent companionship calls forth Prufrock's poetic speech? If so, then the poem is a dramatic monologue, and we are invited to look beyond the spoken words for sources of psychological motivation. In such a case we are dealing not with a private self but instead with a self on public display, subject to the usual distortions and camouflages associated with the social self. But who then is this "you"? Eliot himself said that it was an unidentified male companion. But it has also been suggested, with considerable plausibility, that the mysterious "you" is simply Prufrock's public self, which can be differentiated from the sensitive, thinking, inward Prufrock who is the "I" in the poem.

In any case, what we clearly have in the poem is a central figure driven by a psychic unrest toward action (to break away from a meaningless life? make a proposal of love? upset the universe?), yet dissuaded from action by a psychic terror of the unfamiliar, the new, the upsetting. So the poem dramatizes in its narrative, its images, even its rhythms, a tug of war between impulses of restlessness, anticipations of a movement toward a goal, enticements vaguely erotic and sexually arousing (like light brown hair on the woman's arms), and impulses of escape through anesthesia (the etherised patient), through acceptance of defeat ("And would it have been worth it, after all"), and through nostalgia for more primitive states characterized by uninhibited instinctual drives. In one part of himself, Prufrock longs for the fatal interview with its moment of truth; in another part of himself he fights it with every ounce of his rational and rationalizing brain. Such a sketch is far too simplistic to contain the poem, but it may serve usefully as a scaffold for approaching it.

Prufrock's world has three main features. It is trivial and full of trivialities like marmalade and tea. It is in part a metaphor or symbol of Prufrock's own frustrated interior consciousness. And it is, in addition, a sort of Dantesque Inferno. The Dantesque qualities are not to be overlooked. The epigraph (and we should always pay close attention to Eliot's epigraphs) is from *The Divine Comedy* and suggests the degree to which the landscape of the poem is to be seen as hellish and the speaker of the poem as one of the damned. From the first stanza, with its sinister litany of "half-deserted streets" and "sawdust restaurants with oystershells," through the feline "yellow smoke that slides along the street," and so on, we are aware that the modern city has become one of the circles of Hell for Prufrock—as in the poetry of Baudelaire, whose Paris is also a derivative of Dante's Hell.

If the first few stanzas of *Prufrock* use a modern cityscape to mirror interior psychic states, the remaining stanzas elaborate the triviality of Prufrock's existence in that setting. It is a setting shorn of heroes; Prufrock is "not Prince Hamlet, nor was meant to be." Should he rise from the dead, like Lazarus, the response would be indifference. He not only cannot answer the "overwhelming question," he cannot even ask it.

Questions of real depth can lead only to speechless ellipsis. In an environment where the only great issues are issues of etiquette ("My necktie rich and modest"), who would dare "disturb the universe?"—and what would "they" say if someone did? Since the women "in the room" can reduce even so extraordinary a figure as Michelangelo to a subject of tea-party conversation, he can guess what short work they would make of *him.*

Shrunk to the dimensions of the world that up to now has contained it, Prufrock's life is "measured out" with "coffee spoons"—has become a meaningless round of meaningless activity; after "tea and cakes and ices" he wonders if he has the "strength to force the moment to its crisis." The "crisis," we suspect, is *any* moment of significance, but Prufrock seems to situate it specifically in a proposal to a woman. Somewhere in this suffocating void, then, there is a woman whom Prufrock wishes to approach, perhaps seriously—for this is a "love song," after all. But the possibilities of success are almost nil. Prufrock's prospects are dimmed by his own shyness, by his morbid consciousness of "them," and by the ways of a world over which he cannot even presume to have control. His fantasies and desires, his vision of the romantically heroic self that he longs to be, are inevitably intruded upon by the "real world," a world in which he grows old and wonders if he dares to "eat a peach." In his fantasies, he may have "heard the mermaids singing." He cannot, however, "linger in the chambers" of his romantic wishes for very long before "human voices"—the voices of the world he actually inhabits—drown him and his fantasies together.

Eliot wanted, as he once said, "an expression of *significant* emotion, emotion which has its life in the poem and not in the history of the poet." The way emotion could be born inside the poem, without turning loose what were merely personal—and therefore idiosyncratic and trivial—emotions, was through an "objective correlative":

> The only way of expressing emotion in the form of art is by finding an "objective correlative"; in other words, a set of objects, a situation, a chain of events which shall be the formula of that *particular* emotion; such that when the external facts, which must terminate in sensory experience, are given, the emotion is immediately invoked.
>
> —*Hamlet and His Problems* (1919)

Prufrock, especially, presents Eliot's use of this method to good advantage.

Eliot quite consciously left few biographical clues behind him. Until recently, we had no published collection of letters, and there are no diaries, memoirs, or autobiographical writings to work from. Hugh Kenner has called him "the invisible poet," and Eliot himself was pleased to be called "Old Possum."

We do know that he was, from the first, much disturbed by the conflict between his supersubtle and refined intelligence and what he apparently felt were the demeaning distractions of his physical life. Similarly, he felt the sanctuary of the inward self to be under constant stress from the insistent social and material facts around him—shabby streets, sickness, the social round, the dance of courting. He was inhibited and perhaps afraid when in the presence of women; yet he desired them, and the resulting struggle often left him feeling inadequate, irritated, and distressed. All of these impressions find their way into *The Love Song of J. Alfred Prufrock* and suggest some of the reasons for the poem's tonal interplay of self-mockery and despair.

In the poem we find adaptations of Dante, Baudelaire, and Jules Laforgue, whose presentations of interior landscapes of atomized consciousness were particularly important to Eliot during the period in which he wrote the poem. He was also influenced by the dramatic monologues as well as the crisis-ridden personae of Browning and Tennyson. Henri Bergson's notion of life as a succession of psychological states, memories, and roles has possibly left its mark on the poem, as have Dostoevsky's portrayals of characters with significant psychological disabilities, and Henry James's analysis of the unlived life, especially in *The Beast in the Jungle* and *Crapy Cornelia*. Influences from the seventeenth-century English metaphysical poets (particularly John Donne) and the nineteenth-century French symbolist tradition may likewise be traced.

Classroom Strategies

The Love Song of J. Alfred Prufrock will take a full class period, since you will likely be inclined to discuss not only the poem but the characteristics of modern poetry generally. Even if other modern poets—from Baudelaire through Rilke and Stevens—have been covered, you may feel the need to review or qualify earlier remarks and make direct applications to Eliot. Beginning with *Prufrock*, in which some of the problems of reading Eliot appear in reasonably simple form, seems the best approach to take, no matter whether you teach all three poems or not.

When approaching *The Love Song of J. Alfred Prufrock*, familiar though that poem has now become to most teachers, it is worth remembering that early readers of the poem often found it obscure and incoherent. Arthur Waugh, father of Evelyn Waugh, reviewed it with the verdict that "the state of Poetry is indeed threatened with anarchy which will end in something worse even than 'red ruin and the breaking up of laws.' " Most students coming to Eliot for the first time are "early readers." For many, establishing the "I" and the "you" will be the most helpful step. Although it can plausibly be argued that Prufrock has no fixed identity and, additionally, that the entire poem takes place not in the real world but in his tormented subconscious, students will grasp the poem more clearly on a first reading if they view the speaker of the poem as a middle-aged man named Prufrock and the "you" as the reader. The first line then becomes an invitation to go with the speaker on his outward and inward journey. The point that what we "see" in the poem has more to do with Prufrock's consciousness than with any material facts can be established on a second reading by the implications of lines 2 and 3. The evening is "like" an anesthetized patient because Prufrock himself is "like" one. Students are likely to understand this poem long before they comprehend it. With a bit of help they will enjoy it immensely.

Topics for Discussion and Writing

1. What kind of poem is *The Love Song of J. Alfred Prufrock*? Is it a monologue? A dramatic monologue? An inner monologue? What difference does such an identification make?
   [See the first three paragraphs of "Backgrounds."]
2. How is description—especially of the cityscape—used in *Prufrock*?
   [See the fifth and sixth paragraphs of "Backgrounds."]
3. What sort of person is Prufrock? What does his full name suggest about him? What is he afraid of? In what ways is his life trivial or meaningless? To what extent is the title of the poem ironic?
   [See "Backgrounds" and "Classroom Strategies."]

The Waste Land

Backgrounds

Experience shows that students attempting to cope for the first time with the flurry of allusions, the imbedded meanings, the tone, and the structure of *The Waste Land* are soon out of their depth. You will be well advised to read as many of the commentaries listed below as you have time for.

Underlying myth. It is important, first, for students to understand a background that the poem takes for granted. The following summary by Cleanth Brooks of the myth that underlies the poem is perhaps the clearest to be had:

> The basic symbol used, that of the waste land, is taken . . . from Miss Jessie Weston's *From Ritual to Romance*. In the legends which she treats there, the land has been blighted by a curse. The crops do not grow and the animals cannot reproduce. The plight of the land is summed up by, and connected with, the plight of the lord of the land, the Fisher King, who has been rendered impotent by maiming or sickness. The curse can be removed only by the appearance of a knight who will ask the meanings of the various symbols which are displayed to him in the castle. The shift in meaning from physical to spiritual sterility is easily made, and was, as a matter of fact, made in certain of the legends.

Eliot once remarked of Joyce that his use of the *Odyssey* as background in *Ulysses* gave him "a way of controlling, of ordering, of giving a shape and a significance to the immense panorama of futility and anarchy which is contemporary history." Where Joyce used Homeric myth as a parallel, Eliot used anthropology (Jessie Weston's book, behind which lies Sir James Frazer's immensely influential *The Golden Bough*) as well as a succession of key works in the Western literary tradition. In this way he transforms the original anthropological vegetation myth into one that has symbolic application to the modern world.

Voices. Eliot's original title for the poem was taken from Dickens—"He Do the Police in Different Voices." And, indeed, there are many different voices in the poem, many different speakers. Some have names (Tiresias, Madame Sosostris), most have not—but are clearly "characters" in the poem. There is the sledding "I" of lines 8–18; the grave "I" of lines 27–30; the "hyacinth girl" (lines 35–41); the friend of Stetson (lines 60–76); the nervous speaker and her respondent (lines 111–38); Lil's friend and advisor, who tells her story (lines 142–72); the Spenserian/Marvellian speaker (lines 173–201); the object of Mr. Eugenides's desire (lines 207–14); the "typist" (line 252); the visitor to the church of St. Magnus Martyr (lines 257–65); the three "Thames daughters" (lines 292–95, 296–99, 300–305); and the (apparently) single voice of section V.

All of these different voices are, however, absorbed into the one comprehensive voice of the poet, through which the other voices speak. Eliot himself named Tiresias (who clearly speaks lines 215–56) as the "most important personage in the poem, uniting all the rest. . . . What Tiresias *sees*, in fact, is the substance of the poem." It is a good choice: Tiresias—witnessing prophet, seer of past, present, and future, with experience as both man and woman—connects the fragments of a civilization scattered through time and space. In Tiresias (see the *Odyssey* X and XI and *Oedipus the King*) past and future are always present, contained in a single consciousness. Had Eliot left the matter open he would have allowed us to assume that the all-comprehending voice in the poem was his own, an idea that he probably thought presumptuous.

Tone. Despite the competing voices of the poem, it sustains a singular tone—urbane, grave, dry, abrupt, poignant, slightly sinister, and suffering, vibrant with something very like Old Testament prophetic despair. This is the tone of the poet in the poem, who does not take lightly what he sees.

Structure. The poem means to appear as disjointed as the world it describes, and we are left to put the pieces together, to make sense of them, just as we are in the "real world." Most poetry, like most fiction, is linear: one stanza leads to the next with a kind of inevitability, and the poet usually takes pains to lead the reader from one part of the poem to the next. Words and stanzas rush—and then, and then, and then—to an inevitable conclusion. The "meaning" of *The Waste Land*, on the contrary, is lodged in the spaces between the lines, where the suggestions of the poet and the responses of the reader mix to make sense of the material at hand. The central theme of the poem is the breakdown of civilization, the resulting death-in-life that is a consequence of that breakdown, and the difficulties of cultural regeneration from this death-in-life. Each of the five sections (or movements) of the poem cleaves closely to this theme.

Section I, "The Burial of the Dead," introduces the reader to the underlying myth of the poem, presents the first image of the waste land, offers the controlling images of water and dryness, explores the difficulty of being aroused from death-in-life, and suggests the false avenues—such as the occult—that might be taken to establish meaning in an otherwise meaningless world.

Section II, "A Game of Chess," again gestures toward the notion of death-in-life, but this time by exploring the failure of love due to emotional impotence; the emptiness of marriage, shown especially through the rejection of offspring; and the suggestion that nature itself has become perverted or artificial.

Section III, "The Fire Sermon," again presents the failure of love, but this time by emphasizing the emptiness of sexual relationships outside of marriage; it explores the automatism of lust, and the "mind-forg'd manacles" (see Blake's *London* [pp. 547–48]) that debase societies and individuals alike.

Section IV, "Death by Water," though extremely brief, enforces the notion that the forces of life (water) easily become the forces of death (by drowning). We are left uncertain whether the death is regenerative or sterile; whether it is real or an image reflecting the speaker's longing for oblivion.

Section V, "What the Thunder Said," continues to insist on the harsh, stony, wasted landscape of the present, but also offers the prospect of regeneration and inner peace through the avenues of giving, sympathy, and self-control. The incantatory "Shantih shantih shantih," which comes directly after the thunder speaks, literally *means* something like the "peace that passeth understanding," but it has also been thought to suggest the sound of the much-desired rain.

The comparison of past and present. Past and present in the poem are meant to be simultaneous; they are both contained in the poem's central consciousness. Eliot, like Yeats, was aware in his work that present experience is merely the sum of past experiences. Thus the past may allude to a similar condition in the present, serving as a prophetic warning to contemporary readers:

> What is the city over the mountains
> Cracks and reforms and bursts in the violet air
> Falling towers
> Jerusalem Athens Alexandria
> Vienna London
> Unreal
>
> (lines 372–77)

Or the past may emphasize the comparative decadence of the present. Eliot uses direct quotations, half-quotations, parodies of well-known texts, and allusions through tone, rhythm, and imagery to register the existence of a once vital tradition that has been either corrupted, forgotten, or ignored in the modern present. A few significant examples of various kinds follow:

Lines 1–7: lines meant to bring to mind the vital, regenerative April and the pilgrimage to a holy place in the *General Prologue* to Chaucer's *Canterbury Tales*.

Lines 31–34, 42: from Wagner's opera *Tristan and Isolde*, a story of tragic passion, the lines evoke a kind of passion no longer available in the modern world, and also, however, an enhanced awareness of the aridity of *mere* passion, which is further suggested by the image of desolation and emptiness in line 42.

Lines 60–68: Baudelaire's "unreal city," Dante's souls awaiting transport to the various circles of Hell, Joyce's Dublin graveyard scene in *Ulysses*, and Blake's vision of London in his poem *London* are used here to suggest the infernal quality of modern life in the modern city.

Lines 77–110: the opening is a parody of Enobarbus's speech describing Cleopatra in Shakespeare's *Antony and Cleopatra* 2.2, and it registers a comparison between a gloried past and a tawdry present. In Shakespeare, the queen is a kind of magical goddess, and her barge and the surrounding seascape suggest harmony with the natural world. In Eliot, the scene is a sexual and natural waste land; the woman can muster no magic without the most artificial aids, and she is surrounded by painted images of rape and violence. Yet here too a melancholy hint remains of the destructive capacities of passion and of the *likeness* of that world to ours.

Line 172: Eliot's use of Ophelia's mad farewell in *Hamlet* 4.5 makes even more sinister the pub story told about Lil and Albert and provides ironic commentary on the "sweet ladies" involved.

Lines 173–84: Spenser's image in his *Prothalamion* of the "sweet Thames" covered with flower petals for an impending double marriage stands in stark contrast to the modern Thames described by the speaker.

Lines 266–78, 279–91: again, Spenser's *Prothalamion* is invoked in order to contrast the sweating, polluted river of the present with the sparkling "sweet Thames" of the past.

Lines 306–311: these lines combine the words of St. Augustine, recalling his youthful days of "unholy loves," with those of the Buddha, denouncing desire in his *Fire Sermon*. Carthage, like London, was a commercial center and was, as London might be, destroyed. Conceivably, Virgil's *Aeneid* is also suggested here: Carthage was the site of Dido's funeral pyre, again a monument to passion that ends in death.

After reading *The Waste Land*, one of Eliot's friends declared that it was his "autobiography." But the autobiographical elements of the poem are so deeply imbedded, and we know so comparatively little about Eliot's life, that to unearth what is strictly personal in the poem will probably take years of rather difficult excavation.

Some personal facts are relevant. During the final period of the poem's composition, Eliot's troubled marriage with his first wife, Vivien, was collapsing. She suffered one of her many nervous breakdowns in 1921, and her crises, combined with the strain of his monotonous clerk's job at Lloyd's Bank and a persistent lack of funds, drove Eliot to a breakdown of his own later in that year. He wrote much of the poem during a period of recuperation at Margate ("On Margate Sands. . . . I can connect / Nothing with nothing" [lines 300–02]) and in Lausanne. Vivien had suffered from bouts of mental illness ever since their marriage in 1915. They had been married under rather mysterious circumstances and without the blessing of his pious and still influential parents. Contemporary rumor suggested that Eliot, in the "awful daring of a moment's surrender / Which an age of prudence can never retract" (lines 404–05), had "compromised" Vivien and then felt obliged to marry her, but this has never been verified. Whatever the case, Vivien's behavior, especially during her bouts of nervous illness, alarmed Eliot and others. One account describes her this way: "She gave the impression of absolute terror, of a person who's seen a ghost, a goblin ghost, and who was always seeing a goblin in front of her. Her face was all drawn and white, with wild, frightened, angry eyes. . . . Supposing you would say to her, 'Oh, will you have some more cake?' she'd say, 'What's that? What do you mean? What do you say that for?' She was terrifying." Very possibly her accents can be heard in lines 111–38 of the poem.

Like all other Europeans and a large number of Americans, Eliot found World War I and its exhausting aftermath a sign that civilization as it had been lived for five hundred years or so was collapsing. Images from the war, or having to do with war, infiltrate *The Waste Land* at every point: the dehumanization of the people of London, the continued references to collapsing or inverted towers and bridges, the "rats' alley" (a term used to describe the trenches as well as urban blight), the allusions to the Russian Revolution in lines 367–77, and the vision of the waste land itself. The Great War had changed everything, and Eliot's poem registers that change and suggests its effects.

In a 1920 essay on Philip Massinger, Eliot writes: "Immature poets imitate; mature poets steal; bad poets deface what they take, and good poets make it into something better, or at least something different. The good poet welds his theft into a whole of feeling which is unique, utterly different from that from which it was torn; the bad poet throws it into something which has no cohesion." Though these comments may be self-serving, there is no doubt that Eliot's own use of his predecessors is transformative.

The direct influence of Ezra Pound on the final version of *The Waste Land* must not go without mention. In January 1922, Eliot showed the manuscript of the poem to Pound, who remarked that it was impressive enough "to make the rest of us shut up shop." Even so, he felt it could be improved; he slashed out whole sections of the poem, tightened others. The poem we have is, in fact, so heavily indebted to Pound's editorial skills that it is almost a collaboration. Eliot's dedication of the poem to Pound, *il miglior fabbro* ("the better craftsman"), is as justified a dedication as ever appeared on a work of literature. The nature and extent of Pound's editing can be viewed firsthand in the *Facsimile and Transcript of the Original Drafts* of the poem, edited by Eliot's second wife, Valerie.

Classroom Strategies

The Waste Land will take a minimum of two class periods. Students will not follow Eliot's poems effectively without your aid and generosity—generosity in establishing the general meaning (without sounding pedantic) of individual allusions, lines, images, and symbols. *The Waste Land*, especially, can be turned into a kind of poem-encyclopedia—a great off-putting puzzle—if you do not keep the whole poem continually in focus.

How do you teach *The Waste Land*? Two warnings may be useful:

- Do not attempt to go through the poem line by line, allusion by allusion, reference by reference. Students will be impressed by Eliot's knowledge, and no doubt by yours, but they will miss the poem altogether and worry overmuch about which of Eliot's allusions is to appear on their next exam.
- Do not pretend that the poem is simple once one has some sort of "key," or that there *is* a key. Eliot once told a group of students at Harvard that *he* thought everything about it was pretty clear. He was reportedly disturbed by their laughter.

Some suggestions of procedure may also be helpful:

1. Begin with *Prufrock*. Some of the difficulties of Eliot's poetic method in *The Waste Land* clear up in advance on students' encounter with this poem.
2. Place *The Waste Land* in the context of modern thought and writing—its major themes, images, techniques—already encountered by the student in previous assignments. Useful contextual remarks on the modern era will be found in the headnote, which students should be asked to review.
3. Make sure the underlying myth of the poem is understood (see "Backgrounds": *Underlying myth*). If you are well grounded in the Arthurian legends you will find they buttress the discussion, since students usually have some knowledge of these legends and of quest narratives in general, owing to the proliferation of films and books such as J. R. R. Tolkien's *Lord of the Rings* or Frank Herbert's *Dune*. Easily called up too are the many quest narratives students have met with earlier in the anthology: the *Odyssey*, *The Divine Comedy*, *The Canterbury Tales*, *Don Quixote*, *Gulliver's Travels*, *Candide*, and *The Death of Ivan Ilyich*, to mention only a few. The particularities of the myth as used by Eliot will be new to the class, but not the basic form of the quest.
4. Emphasize that the poem's "voices," however numerous, belong to a presiding, comprehending consciousness (which may be called either Tiresias's or Eliot's) and that the story told by each voice contributes to Eliot's overriding theme.
5. Analyze briefly the way the fragments of the poem hang together

and make its central themes resonate. Since each section of the poem emphasizes something different, yet contributes to the emotional and intellectual effect as a whole, it will be wise, early on, to discuss what each section individually is about, but without going into detail.

6. At about this point, if time permits, it pays to let the class hear the poem in Eliot's own rendering of it (on CDs or cassette tapes), with its grave Anglo-American twang. This will not only enhance the fascination of the poem but it will also register unforgetably the myriad interconnections of sound and sense within the poem and provide a dramatic background for the next procedure.

7. Pick one section for extremely close examination. Section II, "A Game of Chess," is perhaps the easiest to deal with in this way. Section III, "The Fire Sermon," also offers comparatively easy opportunities for close scrutiny. Section I, "The Burial of the Dead," and the concluding section V, "What the Thunder Said," generally strike students as the most difficult.

8. Discuss the range and character of critique within the poem. The way that Eliot manages the devaluations of the present by implicit comparisons with the past can best be demonstrated by looking at lines 77–105 in section II, lines 173–202 in section III, and lines 266–91 in section III. To convince students of the persuasiveness of this technique, you might consider invoking the way politicians imply a decline in the current conditions by evoking past stabilities, or the way teachers condemn present educational standards by comparing them to the standards in place when they were in school. The point is not that any of these speakers, including the poem's speaker, expects to recapture the past. It is simply that the past, seen as golden, makes a persuasive point of reference for inciting improvements in the future. In *The Waste Land*, however, one must remember also that the past functions as evidence that basic human frailties do not greatly change.

Topics for Discussion and Writing

1. What is the underlying myth of *The Waste Land*? Where does it come from? In what other works do we find it? How does the poem use it to comment on our world?
   [See "Backgrounds": *Underlying myth.*]

2. Discuss the use of different speakers in *The Waste Land*. How does their use mirror the disjointedness of modern experience? In what way is Tiresias important?
   [See "Backgrounds": *Voices.*]

3. How does Eliot compare past with present in the poem? To what purposes?
   [See the appropriate section in "Backgrounds" and suggestion #8 in "Classroom Strategies."]

4. Describe the controlling images of *The Waste Land*: water and dry-

ness, the seasons, and so forth. How do they interrelate in the poem?

5. Define the attitudes toward love and sex expressed in the poem. How do they relate to a waste land?

The Hollow Men

Backgrounds

This is one of T.S. Eliot's most intriguing poems because it was composed in the period just after *The Waste Land* (1922) and before his famous conversion to the Anglican faith in 1927. In other words, it is a transitional poem on his road to conviction. In 1927 he famously declared that he was "royalist in politics, classicist in literature, and Anglican in religion." Prior to that his work, particularly *The Waste Land*, had stood as the ultimate twentieth-century expression of tragic doubt and loss of faith and conviction.

The Hollow Men, coming as it does between the poetry of doubt and the poetry of faith, has often been a critical lightning rod. Some read the poem as the most pessimistic, nihilistic poem Eliot ever wrote, the nadir of his spiritual quest, while others see in it the first glimmer of a redemptive path that will eventually be associated with a notion of the Christian salvation that finds its fullest expression in Eliot's *Four Quarters*.

To teach *The Hollow Men*, you should know that the five sections of the poem may be read as a journey into a heart of darkness; this would explain the allusion to Conrad, and it would also ask you to read the ending as a discovery of emptiness and nihilism. On the other hand, you can also read the poem as a journey toward the possibility of faith and redemption. In this reading, critics assume that the "We" of Section 1 is modern humanity. The section is then read as a poetic lament—as close to absolute despair as poetry can come. This lament is exacerbated in Section 2, which moves to the specific fact of relationships only to suggest that no loving relationship is possible. The redemptive reading, then, depends entirely on Sections 3 through 5. These in fact are the sections that generate the greatest controversy.

The problem could be presented to students as follows: Does the language in these sections become ever more despondent or do the images of "Lips that would kiss / Form prayers to broken stone" suggest room for faith? As far as this issue is concerned, and it is a crucial one, good class discussions can arise from close attention to these particular stanzas.

As a further note to the competing readings of this poem, you might add that the reason for the extended date on this poem's publication, 1924–1925, has to do with the poem's tortured publication history. Eliot evidently struggled with the poem, publishing various versions beginning with one titled *Doris's Dream Songs* in 1924. He then radically changed that poem and published it as *The Hollow Men* in the magazine he himself edited, *The Criterion* of January 1925. Even then he felt compelled to continue revising, and with much adding and subtracting he published the poem in yet another version, also called *The Hollow Men*, in the prestigious New York literary magazine, *The Dial* (March 1925).

Classroom Strategies

You could teach either the nihilistic or the hopeful readings, or both—if you and your class are adventurous—since both readings are supported by the poem's imagery, symbolism, and other poetic and prosodic elements. A good class discussion strategy, then, would be to encourage students to form groups and take a particular side and then have the class argue the various sides from one or the other perspective.

Four Quartets: Little Gidding

Backgrounds

As with each of the *Four Quartets*, *Little Gidding* is written in a form that its author liked to think of as analogous to Beethoven's late quartets. It has five movements: an introduction and a statement of theme, a lyrical development of that theme with a meditation on it, a metaphorical journey that suggests the theme of exploration, a shorter lyric, and a summary of the whole that echoes the opening movement.

The first movement is set in midwinter at Little Gidding, a seventeenth-century Anglican religious community. The time of year suggests the coldness of old age and oncoming death, a time when the "soul's sap quivers." But the first movement emphasizes the possibilities of renewed life, a springtime that, for the speaker, must take place outside of time—it is "not in time's covenant." Pentecostal fire gleams in the poem in the same way the "brief sun flames the ice." Little Gidding, where the eternal ritual of prayer and worship persists and remains valid, becomes symbolic of a place outside of time, a spiritual realm that is "the intersection of the timeless moment," is "England and nowhere," "never and always." It is the place, the speaker suggests, where all travelers must come and that will "always be the same." Little Gidding exists in an order of reality beyond the world.

The second movement begins with three rhymed stanzas that suggest the hopelessness of mere earthly existence by lyrically detailing the death of the four Heraclitean elements—air, earth, water, and fire—and the civilization that these earthly elements make up. These are followed by a long narrative section in which the speaker, walking in the "waning-dusk" on fire patrol during the London blitz of World War II (during which the poem was written), encounters "a familiar compound ghost / Both intimate and unidentifiable." This "ghost" both is and is not the speaker; it is himself and everyone. The meeting is much like that of Dante the pilgrim's meeting with Virgil in *The Divine Comedy*. Thus, the ghost in *Little Gidding* has the "look of some dead master" and is the speaker's guide and kindred spirit. This kindred spirit rehearses the futility, isolation, and guilt that, in the end, are all that life has brought him.

He has found that what he once took for "exercise of virtue" came to nothing but the "bitter tastelessness of shadow fruit" because his work and life were not in service to spiritual values.

The third movement attempts to establish a set of values alternative to those cited by the "ghost." Those who once lived these alternative values are our inheritance; they have become for us a "symbol perfected in death," and we, like Little Gidding itself, can be united with them in a common spiritual present.

The pentecostal experience is the central theme of the two-stanza lyric that makes up the fourth movement. It is about the gorgeous terror of being "redeemed from fire [Hell] by fire [the pentecostal flame]." The movement insists that such an experience consumes like love, a love that surrenders all to a spiritual principle beyond us.

> We only live, only suspire
> Consumed by either fire or fire.
> (lines 212–13)

The final movement echoes all the previous themes and images and attempts to reconcile them. Here, the past is reconciled with the present, the poet is reconciled with his work, "the fire and the rose are one." All takes place in symbolic Little Gidding on "a winter's afternoon, in a secluded chapel" where "History is now and England." The poem, like the life of the spirit, finds that

> . . . the end of all our exploring
> Will be to arrive where we started
> And know the place for the first time.
> (lines 242–44)

Little Gidding contains what many find Eliot's best poetry and his most profound and generous thought. The poem finds life in death, spring in winter, the flame in the ice. And it was the last major poem that Eliot would write—finding, perhaps, that the end *was* his beginning.

Eliot was received into the Anglican Church in 1927, an answer to his own despair in *The Waste Land* and the basis for his work in *Little Gidding*. The conflict between the life of the spirit and the life of the body found its resolution in *Little Gidding* and in the other *Four Quartets*.

Little Gidding is, as we might expect, soaked in the Anglican liturgy, its images and its rhythms. Beyond that, there are explicit references to Dante (especially in the second movement), to the mystical visions of Dame Julian of Norwich, and to the anonymous fourteenth-century *Cloud of Unknowing*. The influence of W. B. Yeats is evident throughout, most notably in sections having to do with the decrepitude of old age. The major accents in the poem, however, apart from the liturgical ones, come from Eliot's own earlier poems, particularly *The Waste Land* (see *Little Gidding*, lines 64–71, 80–89, and 100, for instance), which quite understandably were at the back of his mind during the writing of *Little Gidding*.

Classroom Strategies

Little Gidding will require at least one class period. You might find it useful at the beginning of your discussion of *Little Gidding* to consider it in relation to *The Waste Land*, since what Eliot despaired over in *The Waste Land* is resolved in *Little Gidding* through his acceptance of the spiritual life—which in the earlier poem is seen as only a remote, perhaps unattainable, possibility. His vision of a civilization in decline, his insistence on the importance of the past as a comment on the present, his sense that the past and present exist simultaneously—all are found in *Little Gidding* just as they are in *The Waste Land*. The speaker's encounter with the "compound" ghost can almost be seen as the Eliot of *Little Gidding* talking with the Eliot of *The Waste Land*. What needs to be pointed out, of course, is Eliot's change of attitude: the state of civilization may be precarious, but it can be redeemed. The past cannot be reclaimed entire:

> We cannot revive old factions
> We cannot restore old policies
> Or follow an antique drum.
> (lines 187–89)

It can, however, be reclaimed in our lives by our participating in its best values. In *The Waste Land* Eliot's attitude is one of revulsion; in *Little Gidding* he experiences revulsion, but moves beyond it toward acceptance and love. *Little Gidding*, unlike *The Waste Land*, wants to be a generous poem.

Topics for Discussion and Writing

1. Why does *Little Gidding* take place in midwinter? How does the opening remind us of *The Waste Land*? In what ways does *Little Gidding* constitute an "answer" to *The Waste Land*?
   [See the second paragraph of "Backgrounds" and "Classroom Strategies" for discussion.]
2. Who is the "compound ghost" in *Little Gidding*? Of what elements is he "compounded"?
   [See the third paragraph of "Backgrounds."]
3. Why is the historical Little Gidding an appropriate setting for this poem?
   [See the second paragraph of "Backgrounds."]

Comparative Perspectives

1. *The Waste Land* probes the mixture of "memory and desire," a preoccupation that applies well to the writing of many other European modernists. Try to characterize the distinctive understanding of memory that motivates Eliot and, as appropriate, the writing of Proust, Joyce, or Freud.

2. *Little Gidding* takes its name from an English village and seems deeply rooted in local soil. At the same time, as in *The Waste Land*, Eliot's familiarity with non-Western sources leaves an imprint on the poem that lifts it into a "timeless moment" beyond parochialism. Drawing on your reading of other religious poetic texts in this anthology, discuss the "intersection" (line 54) of mystical themes that transcend specific rites and suggest a common human longing for union with the divine.

Further Reading

See also the reading suggestions in the *Anthology*, p. 2550.

Ackroyd, Peter. *T. S. Eliot: A Life*. 1984. A full-length biography.

Behr, Caroline. *T. S. Eliot: A Chronology of His Life and Works*. 1983.

Bloom, Harold, ed. *T. S. Eliot's* The Waste Land. 1986.

Boernstein, George. *Transformations of Romanticism in Yeats, Eliot, and Stevens*. 1976. Describes similarities and differences in relation to Romantic norms.

Brooker, Jewel Spears. *Reading* The Waste Land: *Modernism and the Limits of Interpretation*. 1990.

———. *Approaches to Teaching Eliot's Poetry and Plays*. 1988. Published as part of the MLA series "Approaches to Teaching World Literature."

Brooks, Cleanth. *Modern Poetry and the Tradition*. 1939. Chapter 7 contains Brooks's clear discussion of the underlying myth in *The Waste Land*.

Davidson, Harriet. *T. S. Eliot and Hermeneutics: Absence and Interpretation in* The Waste Land. 1985.

Eliot, T. S. *Selected Essays*. 1950. "Tradition and the Individual Talent" remains a crucial essay for understanding Eliot's work.

Eliot, Valerie, ed. The Waste Land: *A Facsimile and Transcript of the Original Drafts Including the Annotations of Ezra Pound*. 1974. An indispensable aid to understanding *The Waste Land*.

———, ed. *The Letters of T. S. Eliot*. 1988.

Gardner, Helen. *The Composition of* Four Quartets. 1978. An important aid to understanding *Little Gidding*.

Gish, Nancy. The Waste Land: *A Poem of Memory and Desire*. 1988.

Gordon, Lyndall. *Eliot's Early Years*, 1977, and *Eliot's New Life*, 1988. One of the few detailed biographical studies of Eliot.

Harding, D. W. "Little Gidding." In *T. S. Eliot: A Collection of Critical Essays*, ed. Hugh Kenner. 1962. Pp. 125–28. The best short discussion of *Little Gidding*.

Kenner, Hugh. *The Invisible Poet: T. S. Eliot.* 1959. Particularly interesting on tone and language.

————, ed. *T. S. Eliot: A Collection of Critical Essays.* 1962.

Longenbach, James. *Modernist Poetics of History: Pound, Eliot, and the Sense of the Past.* 1987. Draws on contemporary philosophical approaches (Gadamer, Nietzsche, DeMann).

Menand, Louis. *Discovering Modernism: T. S. Eliot and His Context.* 1987. Discussion of Eliot in the context of modernism.

Schwartz, Sanford. *The Matrix of Modernism: Pound, Eliot, and Early Twentieth-Century Thought.* 1985. Systematically describes the relationships between twentieth-century philosophers and modernist poets to construct an intellectual-historical model of modernist thought.

Smith, Grover. *T. S. Eliot's Poetry and Plays.* 1956. A highly detailed and thorough investigation of the work, particularly useful on influences and sources.

Spender, Stephen. *T. S. Eliot.* 1976. A readable short introduction to Eliot, written by another poet of considerable accomplishment.

Sultan, Stanley. *Eliot, Joyce and Company.* 1987. Contains a discussion of *The Love Song of J. Alfred Prufrock* and *The Waste Land* as "exemplary shapers" of English modernism.

Tramplin, Ronald. *A Preface to Eliot.* 1988. Gives a full overview and interpretation.

ANNA AKHMATOVA

Requiem

Backgrounds

Anna Akhmatova (pronounced Ahk-*mah*-tova) is one of those writers who testify, who bring to light a painful dimension of social reality in the twentieth century and impel us to a deeper understanding of that era. Like T. S. Eliot denouncing the loss of values in *The Waste Land,* or Kafka portraying the dehumanization of industrial society in *The Metamorphosis*, the Russian poet mourns the death of individual freedom and the negation of family ties during the most famous political purges of modern totalitarian society. For each writer, modern society is sick or wounded. Akhmatova's testimony, however, strikes a personal note from the beginning, unlike the more distanced and often symbolic perspectives of Kafka, Eliot, Mann, Brecht, or Beckett. Her readers are immediately confronted by a subjective "I" speaking throughout, whether in individual short poems or in a longer cycle like *Requiem.* There are clearly historical reasons for the subjective "I" in *Requiem,* for the cycle refers directly to the poet's own experience during the purge. However, this "I" whose mounting emotions reach out to the reader is not exclusively Akhmatova's own, for it is gradually equated with the voice of her people. Like Dostoevsky and Tolstoy in the last century and Solzhenitsyn in this, Akhmatova is part of a Russian tradition that expects its major authors to be more than subjective individuals and ultimately to bear witness for the national conscience.

Requiem took its current shape over more than twenty-five years. The central (numbered) poems appear to be the first ones written, as if to express her immediate personal shock at the arrest and imprisonment of her husband and son. The first numbered poem is dated 1935 and describes her husband's arrest that year. Numbers V and VI are dated 1939, the year after her son, Lev, was arrested for the second time and then imprisoned for the seventeen months Akhmatova mentions in the "Preface." Number VII, which announces the son's condemnation, is dated Summer 1939. The following invocation to Death is dated August 19, 1939 (from their home in Fontanny Dom), and number IX, which describes her mad despair, is dated May 4, 1940. The year 1940 is when Akhmatova began to cast her personal tragedy in larger terms, for the "Dedication" and the two epilogues, all of which link her fate to that of her people, are dated March 1940, and the tenth numbered poem ("Crucifixion"), which invokes a religious parallel and consolation, is dated 1940–43. Akhmatova herself gave the dates for these poems and for the prose "Preface" (April 1, 1957) and introductory epigraph (1961), as if to reaffirm the historical authenticity of what she says. Nonetheless, she has not forgotten the inner constraints of poetic form, for it seems likely that other poems—written later but reflecting situations earlier in the cycle—were left undated so as not to contradict the sense of chronological development from one stage to another.

In the years when the first poems were written, life was precarious indeed. Manuscripts were often confiscated and examined by the secret police for indications of subversive thinking, and Akhmatova reportedly destroyed the manuscripts of individual stanzas of *Requiem* after they were committed to memory. Political censorship had existed for decades and writers did not stop writing, but they often turned to scenes from history, mythology, or the Bible in order to be able to comment obliquely on situations that could not otherwise be addressed. Thus Akhmatova in the thirties wrote an "Armenian" fable in which she took the role of a bereaved ewe asking the shah (and any image of a ruler would evoke Stalin) "Have you dined well? . . . was my little son / To your taste, was he fat enough?" *Requiem*, however, was too open in its condemnation to be published or even acknowledged in Stalin's lifetime, and in fact, the subject of the Stalinist regime was such a sensitive topic that the entire cycle was not published in the Soviet Union.

The epigraph and "Preface" to the cycle introduce Akhmatova to us in three ways: as a person who refused to seek refuge in other countries (she sharply criticized those who did), as a woman waiting numbly outside prison for news of a loved one inside, and as a writer asked by her fellow-sufferers to bear witness to what happened. As the poet begins to speak in the "Dedication" and "Prologue" she evokes their common situation but still sees herself as an individual, a person separate from "my chance friends / Of those two diabolical years." It will take the development of the poem itself, and a crisis of mounting personal agony that cannot be faced alone, for the speaker to identify herself with other sufferers in Russia and throughout history.

Religious and patriotic images are present from the beginning. The women waiting before the prison rise each morning "as if for an early service"; other religious references appear in the icon kissed in the first numbered poem, the invocation to "Say a prayer for me" in the second, the swinging censers in the fifth, the transcendent cross in the sixth, and the culminating projection of the bereaved mother's plight onto a biblical level in the last numbered poem, "Crucifixion." A broad sense of Russian history and culture provides another framework transcending current events: age-old "innocent Russia" is the true victim of the present regime ("Prologue"), contemporary tyrannical murders have an historical precedent (the 1698 execution of the Streltsy in the first poem), and a projected image of the Russian people of "folk" underlies the lilting melancholy of the second poem, which echoes both the simplicity and metrical form of a Russian folksong. Shattering as their individual experiences may be, these women are not alone in either divine or human history.

Classroom Strategies

Requiem can be taught in one period. You may help your students focus their reading if you suggest ahead of time that they read the numbered poems as the diary of a mother who is grieving—perhaps to the point of madness—over the arrest of her son. In class, this personal focus can be situated in the larger perspective of the public poet through examining the "Preface" and, later, the frame of "Dedication" and epilogue. *Requiem* takes its place in the stream of literary works that evoke a moment in history, such as works by Dostoevsky or Chekhov in the preceding section, or by Mann, Kafka, Camus, and Solzhenitsyn in the modern section. You may wish to comment on the way the Russian authors especially take it upon themselves to speak for their country, and to ask whether students can think of American authors who do the same. It may bring the poem painfully alive if you draw parallels with the vigils of bereaved mothers in Argentina during the military dictatorship: the thousands of women called simply "The Mothers," who gathered each week in the large public square of Buenos Aires, holding the photographs of the "disappeared": their husbands, children, and grandchildren, who were taken by the secret police.

While students will probably be drawn by the image of the grieving mother and imprisoned son, they may have some trouble in linking the perspectives in the "story" poems of the core section. Part of the poem's interest, of course, lies in the rich variation of lyric forms in the different parts, but at the beginning it is probably best to emphasize that these shifting and fragmented perspectives are so many glimpses, over time, into the mind of a woman who is greatly shaken by grief and fear. The "Prologue" and the first numbered poem are spoken in the first person, using a relatively objective style to describe painful events. In the second numbered poem, however, the pain has apparently dominated the speaker to the point that she is no longer capable of using the subjective "I," but imagines a scene in which she is seen only from outside, part of a strangely alienated landscape. That such alienation is real becomes apparent in the following poem, which returns to the "I" but claims incredulously "No . . . it is somebody else who is suffering." In the fourth poem, the "I" restored to her full sense of self looks back on her early carefree life, and compares with it her current misery as she waits outside prison on New Year's Day. In the next two poems she is increasingly fearful as she addresses her son; tinges of madness enter, in her confessions of mental confusion, and in images of the stars staring down like predatory hawks. By the seventh poem, sentence has been passed, and she speaks in frantic contradictions of the need to adjust, to kill memory, or to live, before moving to the eighth poem's invocation to Death, and images of the swirling Yenisey River and glittering North Star. She sinks openly into madness in the ninth poem, but only for a moment: madness means forgetting, and it is clear from the poignant images of the latter half of the poem that the speaker cannot and will not forget. The tenth poem, however, marks another significant break in perspective as the poet ceases to speak in subjective terms and withdraws personally from the scene, which is now transformed into a biblical drama. As the epilogues show, the speaker's development throughout the cycle has purged her of a purely separate subjective identity and united her with all those who suffer.

Each poem in the cycle also has its own formal and thematic unity, usually involving the development of a particular dramatic scene. A close reading of two or three individual poems will allow you to discuss them as independent works and will give students a sense of how Akhmatova varies her style. For example, the "Prologue" is a brief evocation of a historical period whose horror is emphasized through images of contradiction, madness, or inverted proportions. The first numbered poem is more intimate and focuses on a poignant domestic scene, as did Akhmatova's early work. The second numbered poem uses simple folktale imagery and folk rhythms to present a landscape of alienated identity. The seventh poem, "The Sentence," conveys a state of shock through the speaker's alternating and contradictory moods. You will find your own favorite examples, which may also serve to explore more fully a particular issue.

Most students will have some sense of the secret police systems in dictatorships and totalitarian countries, but they will probably not be acquainted with the geographic references coordinating the setting of *Requiem*. It may be useful to bring or sketch a map of the former Soviet Union in order to situate references to Leningrad and the Neva River, and to the Royal Gardens at Tsarskoe Selo close by; to Moscow (home of the Kremlin), to the Don River, to the Yenisey River in Siberia, where many concentration camps were located, and to the Black Sea.

Topics for Discussion and Writing

1. Why does the woman in the "Preface" ask Akhmatova, "Can you describe this?" Why is she happy at the poet's response? What aspect of Russian literary tradition is involved in both question and response?

   [See "Backgrounds," the discussion of the second epilogue and the tradition of the writer as national conscience.]

2. How does the figure of the narrator change over the course of the cycle? Does she lose or gain a sense of identity (or both)?

   [See the headnote in the anthology, and "Backgrounds" for the poet's identification with the community of suffering women and with the biblical mother of Christ.]

3. What coherence do you perceive in the numbered poems taken as a group? What themes or strategies hold them together?

   [See "Classroom Strategies" for a discussion of the fragmentation of narrative perspective.]

4. To what extent do the individual poems stand on their own, as independent pieces?

   [See discussion in "Classroom Strategies."]

5. Why does the tenth numbered poem suddenly present a biblical scene? What previous elements prepare this shift in setting?

   [See the headnote and the discussions of religious imagery and narrative perspective in "Classroom Strategies."]

6. Does the United States have "national writers"? Regional writers? Are American writers and artists expected to act as a "national conscience"? In what way?

   [Answers will vary.]

7. How are frame and core related in the cycle? Does one develop into the other, or were both conceived at once? Explain.

   [See the headnote and "Backgrounds" for a discussion of the chronological development of the cycle. This question assumes you will have mentioned that most of the inner poems were composed before the "Dedication," "Prologue," and epilogues of 1940.]

8. How effective do you find the poem as a political protest? *Requiem* was not published until well after the purges were over and Stalin was dead; is it, then, totally lacking in influence?

   [Answers will vary. Some students will be content with intrinsic aesthetic value, while others may find the poem too specific and therefore dated. You may wish to suggest—in line with traditional "masterpiece" values—that as long as situations of repression and political censorship exist anywhere, such a poem is potentially explosive in its assertion of civil rights and human values; and that it witnesses movingly to feelings that are timeless as long as children die and mothers grieve, even in a world of perfect freedom.]

Comparative Perspectives

1. Poets frequently claim to lack the words they need, yet in the face of more personal punishment than that experienced by most of the

writers in the anthology, Akhmatova replies "Yes, I can," when asked, "Can you describe this?" How does she use poetry to objectify her experience and thus relieve her suffering even while recording it? How would you compare this approach to pain with that of Tennyson in *In Memoriam A. H. H.*, or García Lorca in *Lament for Ignacio Sánchez Mejías*?

2. In the second epilogue Akhmatova makes poetry a political testament; because "the list has been confiscated," her statement seems all the more necessary. Compare the spare means she chooses to voice her outrage with the different rhetorical strategies chosen by other politically committed poets in the anthology. Consider, for example, the way Césaire adapts the imagery of Baudelaire and the French surrealist tradition or the way Yeats uses classical and historical allusions.

Further Reading

See also the reading suggestions in the *Anthology*, p. 2548.

Akhmatova, Anna. *Poems*. Trans. Lyn Coffin. 1983. The introduction is written by Joseph Brodsky, who knew Akhmatova.

Contemporary Poetry and Poetics. Fall 1988. Several papers from a symposium on Akhmatova appear in this issue (pp. 7–44).

Driver, Sam. "Directions in Akhmatova's Poetry since the Early Period." *Russian Language Journal*, Supplementary Issue: *Toward a Definition of Acmeism* (Spring 1975): 84–91. Notes as a "new thematics" Akhmatova's increasing sense of "nostalgia for European cultural history." (Note that Russian citations are not translated.)

Ketchian, Sonia. "Metampsychosis in the Verse of Anna Akhmatova." *Slavic and East European Journal* 25, 1 (1981): 44–60. Examines the complex layers of reference in Akhmatova's poetry as coordinated with a theme of metempsychosis or the transmigration of souls.

Ketchian, Sonia, and Julian W. Connolly, eds. *Studies in Russian Literature in Honor of Vsevolod Setchkarev*. 1986. In "An Inspiration for Anna Akhmatova's *Requiem*" Sonia Ketchian argues that the aspects of a Requiem by Armenian poet Hovannes Tumanian influenced Akhmatova's poem.

McDuff, David. "Anna Akhmatova." *Parnassus: Poetry in Review* 11, 2 (Spring—Summer 1984): 51–82. Provides a perceptive, focused, and well-documented overview of Akhmatova's work in the context of political, personal, and literary events.

Rosslyn, Wendy. *The Prince, the Fool, and the Nunnery: The Religious Theme in the Early Poetry of Anna Akhmatova*. 1984. A discussion of Akhmatova's early religious poetry.

KATHERINE ANNE PORTER

Flowering Judas

Backgrounds

Katherine Anne Porter, one of the most brilliant literary stylists in American literature, is at once dazzling and resonant. A highly personal writer, she was disgusted by work in which, as she saw it, "poverty of feeling and idea were disguised, but not well enough, in tricky techniques and disordered syntax." Her own techniques are not tricky and her syntax is not disordered, and she may strike students as traditional. But, like that of other modernists, her work was intended to achieve "order and form and statement in a period of grotesque dislocations in a whole society when the world was heaving in the sickness of a millenial change."

As the title suggests, betrayal is at the center of "Flowering Judas." Braggioni, the fat, self-pitying revolutionary, appears to have betrayed the earnest ideals of the movement he leads through his love of luxury and his indifference to his fellow revolutionaries. Laura, the repressed, virginal *gringita*, has betrayed Eugenio—first by refusing his offer of love, then by delivering to him the drugs he uses to commit suicide. She has betrayed the children she teaches; even though she tries to love and take pleasure in them, they "remain strangers to her." Most important, perhaps, she betrays herself by rejecting "knowledge and kinship in one monotonous word. No. No. No" and by disguising her sexual coldness as earnest revolutionary idealism. Laura is afraid; she cannot live; she is "not at home in the world." It makes her, finally, a "cannibal" of others, a "murderer" of herself. When she eats the "warm, bleeding flowers" of the Judas tree in her nightmare vision, she symbolically participates in a sacrament of betrayal.

Porter establishes everything in deft, economical flashes. Braggioni (whose very name suggests his nature) "bulges marvelously in his expensive garments," his mouth "opens round and yearns sideways," he "swells with ominous ripeness," his ammunition belt is buckled "cruelly around his gasping middle." Braggioni as revolutionary is so completely savaged by this portrayal that it is difficult to take sufficient note of his continuing importance in the movement, and his necessary emphasis on the movement as a whole over mere individual members of it. The reader must be aware of the extent to which Braggioni is portrayed in the story from Laura's perspective, and although her perspective undoubtedly reveals an important slice of the truth, it is nevertheless distorted by her own ascetic idealism and her nagging fear of what he wants to offer. For Laura:

> the gluttonous bulk of Braggioni has become a symbol of her many disillusions, for a revolutionist should be lean, animated by heroic faith, a vessel of abstract virtues. This is nonsense, she knows it now and is ashamed of it. Revolution must have leaders, and leadership is a career for energetic men. She is, her comrades tell her, full of romantic error, for what she defines as cynicism in them is merely "a developed sense of reality."

It is important, then, to notice that the very traits which have led to Braggioni's lewdly obese insolence—vanity, arrogance, self-love, malice, cleverness, love of pleasure, "hardness of heart"—are precisely those that have made him a "good revolutionist." He is, on the other hand, a man capable of certain sorts of love; he can sacrifice himself and accept sacrifice from others. He is capable of both revolutionary and amatory action. His ability to love begins with himself and oozes over those with whom he comes into contact.

Laura, however, lives paralyzed, in a wasteland of self-repression. Her ideals remain intact, though she must sometimes struggle to maintain them. Her own taste requires fine handmade lace, a revolutionary heresy since "in her special group the machine is sacred, and will be the salvation of the workers." And she is still, significantly, engaged by the faith of her childhood.

> She was born a Roman Catholic, and in spite of her fear of being seen by someone who might make a scandal of it, she slips now and again into some crumbling little church, kneels on the chilly stone, and says a Hail Mary on the gold rosary she bought in Tehuantepec.

Yet caught between her revolutionary sympathies and the sympathies of her own past, she finds the experience "no good" and ends by merely examining the tinseled altar and its presiding doll-shaped saint, whose lace-trimmed drawers "hang limply around his ankles."

Laura's revolutionary activity is equally unfulfilling. She takes messages to and from people living in dark alleys; attends fruitless union meetings; ferries food and cigarettes and narcotics to sad, imprisoned men; she "borrows money from the Roumanian agitator to give to his bitter enemy the Polish agitator." She is found to be comforting and useful, but her revolutionary ardor is of little use when it comes to leading the revolution—for that, Braggioni is needed.

It is only in Laura's dream at the end of the story, a dream brought on by her recognition that by betraying Eugenio she has betrayed herself, that she comes to a horrifying understanding of her condition: her fear of love, of life. She awakes trembling at the sound of her own voice, "No!," and is afraid to sleep again. Porter ends the story here; we do not know if Laura's realization will save her from what she has become. Her dream, which as Robert Penn Warren says, "embodies but does not resolve the question," tantalizes us with its implications.

Porter once said that "everything I ever wrote in the way of fiction is based very securely on something real in life." "Flowering Judas" is modeled on an incident that happened to a friend of hers, Mary Doherty, during the Obregon revolution in Mexico. In an article Porter wrote in 1942, she said:

> The idea first came to me one evening when going to visit the girl I call Laura in the story, I passed the open window of her living room on my way to

the door, through the small patio which is one of the scenes in the story. I had a brief glimpse of her sitting with an open book in her lap, but not reading, with a fixed look of pained melancholy and confusion in her face. The fat man I call Braggioni was playing the guitar and singing to her.

In a later interview (1965), she added more information:

There was a man (you would know his name if I mentioned it, but I rolled four or five objectionable characters into that one man) who was showing Mary a little attention. . . . Goodness knows, nothing could be more innocent. But you know, she wasn't sure of him; so one day she asked me to come over and sit with her because so-and-so was going to come in the evening and sing a little bit and talk. She lived alone in a small apartment. The way I described the place was exactly as it was. There was a little round fountain, and what we call a flowering judas tree in full bloom over it. As I passed the open window, I saw this girl sitting like this, you see, and a man over there singing. Well, all of a sudden, I thought, "That girl doesn't know how to take care of herself."

Critics of the story have often noted that the background facts concerning Laura are distinctly similar to those in Porter's own experience: the Catholic upbringing, Porter's having been a teacher in Mexico, her involvement in revolutionary causes there, a stubbornly aesthetic sensibility. It is by no means difficult, then, to establish a biographical basis for *Flowering Judas*, but it would be a mistake to lose sight of the degree to which Porter has transformed the raw data of her experience into fiction.

Classroom Strategies

Students will be so absorbed by Porter's beating Braggioni about the head and shoulders that they will be likely to miss the fact that he is eminently successful—in every way—when compared with Laura. If she seems heroic to students, uncorrupted in comparison with Braggioni's corruption, they will not understand the significance of the final dream sequence or the reasons for her vision of self-betrayal.

Pointing out her resistance to Braggioni will not, by itself, be enough to suggest Laura's sexual coldness and her inability to love. Given the nature of Braggioni, what woman wouldn't feel as she does? It will be important, then, to point out that she is unable to perform as a lover in any sense: as a divine lover in the Christian sense; as a collectivist lover of her fellow human beings in the revolutionary sense; or as an erotic lover. This last can be effectively suggested by noting her rejection of no less than three suitors, including her hasty retreat after upsetting the horse of a "gentle" admirer who has approached her with "noble," if direct, simplicity; and the thoughtless tossing of a Judas blossom at a "brown, shock-haired youth [who] came and stood in her patio one night and sang like a lost soul for two hours."

Porter's exquisite and immensely suggestive prose style is hardly a problem; students who will understand nothing else will recognize its brilliance and clarity. Robert Penn Warren's essay, *Irony with a Center*, contains a wonderful close reading of a passage from *Flowering Judas* (the paragraphs beginning with "Braggioni catches her glance" and ending with "you will know that Braggioni was your friend"), which will be of splendid aid in suggesting to students how Porter's prose works.

Topics for Discussion and Writing

1. In what ways is Braggioni a failed revolutionary? In what ways is he successful?
   [See paragraphs 2–3 of "Backgrounds" for discussion.]
2. What's wrong with Laura? What is the significance of her dream at the end of the story? What has she betrayed? Why is the dream, like the story, bursting with Christian symbolism?
   [See paragraphs 2–6 of "Backgrounds."]

Comparative Perspectives

The rejection of a limiting and debilitating asceticism, or at least some severe suspicions about it, is available in any number of writers in this anthology—from Rabelais to Blake to Rilke. On the other hand, it might be interesting to compare the way Porter uses religious symbolism to emphasize that rejection with the way T. S. Eliot uses such symbolism to support it.

Further Reading

See also the suggestions in the *Anthology*, p. 2553.

Warren, Robert Penn, ed. *Katherine Anne Porter: A Collection of Essays.* 1979.
    The essays by Warren (*Irony with a Center*, mentioned above) and Welty, and the interview by Lopez are of particular interest.

West, Ray B. "Katherine Anne Porter: Symbol and Theme in 'Flowering Judas.'" *Accent* 7 (Spring 1947), pp. 182–87.
    An influential essay that emphasizes Christian imagery in the story.

ALFONSINA STORNI

Backgrounds

The poems in the anthology illustrate well the evolution of Storni's work outlined in the headnote. Students should have little difficulty with the first few; having become familiar with Storni's idiom and concerns, they will be able to work through the longer, more complex late poems with your assistance.

Squares and Angles

There should be no problem identifying the kind of world this witty poem depicts. You might want to ask why the geometric architectural forms described here are identified with the modern world. Although Storni is hardly a contemporary, *Squares and Angles* has lost no currency in today's world of modular housing. What were the economic and ideological reasons for the cookie-cutter shapes embraced by so many early modernist architects? Why does Storni reject the presumably egalitarian ethic of the squares and angles that typify the kind of twentieth-century design that she turns into a metaphor for lazy stereotypical thinking? Today's students speak of "nerds" while earlier generations spoke of "squares." You might ask what those words mean, and ask how they relate to "Ideas in a row / And an angle on the back." If your classroom facilitates board work by students, you might invite someone to draw the shape that typically represents a tear and then elicit from your students why its ovoid contours suggest greater depth and human emotion than the square tear that Storni conjures up here in mock horror.

You Want Me White

This poem starts with an indignant survey of similes (white as dawn, foam, pearl, snow) typically used to signify passive female chastity. It then progresses to a more vigorous representation of masculine debauchery based on actions accomplished:

> You have held all the wineglasses
> In your hand,
> Your lips stained purple
> With fruit and honey

and so on. In the last long stanza, the tables turn, and the speaker throws out a challenge to the man who has kept only his "skeleton . . . intact." The woman who cannot regenerate her virginity is no worse than the man who has lost his connection to nature. Implicit here, it appears, is an accusation of sterility and bad faith. Let this man renew the vital earthiness that ought to accompany the human experience of love, a richer contact with sensuality than the hypocritical playboy's entanglement "In all the bedrooms." Not until he can achieve this miracle and integrate flesh, body, and soul does he have a right to demand her miraculous conversion.

Little-Bitty Man

This short poem shows the power of repetition. The title issues another one of Storni's challenges: one is used to hearing about "the little woman." What is the effect of calling a member of the male sex "little bitty man"? How many meanings circulate in the familiar figure of the bird in the cage? As in *You Want Me White*, the female speaker ends up in a surprisingly strong role in an age-old debate. A standard complaint ("you don't understand me") becomes an affront to the male ego: "Nor do I understand you." Nor does she seem to want to; it's traditional to hear of men who seduce and abandon, but here the woman has had her fill of the man and seeks her freedom. Half an hour has been enough for her.

Ancestral Burden

Addressed to her mother, this poem makes a good companion piece to *Little-Bitty Man*, for it is another one of Storni's statements of essential female strength. Despite the conventional characterization of women as "weak," they have learned to carry the burdens of emotional stress that men have been taught to hide. Storni describes her mother's tear as a poison drink—all the more potent because it is the distillation of the pain that men apparently diffuse by projecting it onto women.

This poem may initially seem difficult to your students, but the headnote provides the necessary clue to understanding. As a woman's poem, *The World of Seven Wells* upsets the masculine tradition of Petrarchan compliments to the lady. For example, in Ariosto's *Orlando Furioso*, Alcina's facial beauty is described in typically decorative terms:

> Her serene brow was like polished ivory, and in perfect proportion. / Beneath two of the thinnest black arches, two dark eyes—or rather, two bright / suns; soft was their look, gentle their movement. . . . Below this, the mouth, set between two dimples: it was imbued with native cinnabar. Here a beautiful soft pair of lips opened to disclose a double row of choicest pearls. (Canto 7)

By contrast, the grotesque imagery of Storni's poem sets the body within the cosmos and the natural world. The perspective is oddly off-center; "There above" suggests a low vantage point, and a certain tenuousness is communicated by "on the neck, / is balanced the world / of the seven doors," as if the neck might not be strong enough to support so monumental a burden. We begin with "two planets" and a nucleus, apparently the two lobes of the brain. The scalp and hair are bark and forest.

While the description of the eyes with their "tender doors" and marine blue glance seems far more inviting, the prospect in which they are situated remains disturbing. A broad seascape over which "butterflies and insects hover" may call up halcyon days at the seashore. But who wants butterflies and insects hovering above their eyes? Similarly, the elegance of "snails of mother-of-pearl" associated with the ear is undercut by references to "antennae" (as of hovering insects or technological appurtenances:) and "catacombs," which lead to the convolutions of the middle and inner ear ("tubes located to the right and to the left"), intricate mechanisms that even the most fervent lover is unlikely to include in an admiring catalogue of female charms.

The perspective keeps shifting without any clear sense of a line to connect the views. How do we get from the distant "mountain / over the equatorial line of the head" to "the wax-like nostrils" that promote olfactory perception of pretty "flowers, branches, and fruit," and then back off again to contemplate what sounds like scorched terrain that gives the lie to all verbal pretensions:

> And the crater of the mouth
> with raised edges
> and dry chapped walls:
> the crater which spouts forth
> the sulphur of violent words,
> the dense smoke which comes
> from the heart and its turmoil. . . .

The struggle within the head of beast and angel is too much for poet to control, "and the human volcano erupts."

The last stanzas are marked by a peculiar incongruity that undermines what seems at first a return to convention. Praising a rosy complexion, instead of the traditional damasked roses we confront "mossy cheeks"; and instead of a beauteous forehead, "a white desert, / the distant light of a dead moon." The cheeks seem about to metamorphose into some vegetable form and the forehead to radiate not saintly intellect but a lunar catastrophe. For the sublunary reader, the effect is foreboding.

Portrait of García Lorca

The World of Seven Wells is a kind of puzzle that students can usefully take apart and examine; although its images are, to say the least, unorthodox, its method of producing them is intelligible. At any point in the poem, one knows which of the head's orifices have been reached. The poem signals a profound change in Storni's use of imagery that becomes even more pronounced in her *Portrait of García Lorca*, which soon abandons any pretense of linear logic. This portrait too starts at the top of the head, but the tour of a face is almost immediately obscured: "a curtain of death is drawn," and in moving down from forehead to eyes to cheekbone to mouth to throat, the poem superimposes disconnected, often threatening scenes on the facial contours it ostensibly portrays.

A tribute from one Spanish-speaking artist to another, with its references to violence and death, it brings to mind the Surrealist films of a third such figure, Luis Bunuel, and the earlier traditions of the Spanish Baroque. The famous image of an eyeball being slashed in Bunuel's *Un Chien Andalou* is evoked in the mind of the reader by the horrific fifth and sixth stanzas; but in the spirit of Surrealist experimentation, there is nothing personal about the imagery in the movie or in Storni's poem. The effect is more to alienate than engage. At a moment when modernists were getting inside the heads of their characters through stream-of-consciousness narration, Storni is writing poems that literally get inside the heads of her subjects.

The poem seems at its conclusion to cast García Lorca as a titan of Renaissance exploration, bridging Atlantic and Pacific with his eyes "like lost ships" sailing an endless ocean. His intellectual power seems perversely to precipitate the ominous suggestion to "Let the head fly / (only the head)." Perhaps the animal references that link García Lorca's brilliant energy to that of powerful birds and animals of prey prepare us for the paradox that the poem seems to explore: so great a figure can only realize his transcendent gifts by a violent separation from the material world.

This poem makes a fascinating companion piece to García Lorca's *Lament for Ignacio Sánchez Mejías*, for both offer homage to a heroic being who unites past and present through his creative powers. The classical references here include the suggestion of "Grecian eyes," perhaps as in ancient statuary, and the vision of him acting in some undefined theatrical ritual, with "the mane of the satyr . . . on the face / of an ancient mask." His facial bone structure connects him to the Andalusian hills and valleys. The very traits for which García Lorca praised Sánchez Mejías are praised here: a deep evocation of a primal Spain, an outsized embodiment of antique virtues. García Lorca, however, is writing out of tremendous personal and national pain, mourning the death of a beloved celebrity; Storni had met García Lorca, but she was not an intimate of his. Moreover, *Portrait of García Lorca*, as the headnote in the anthology informs your students, is visionary rather than reactive. It was written two years before García Lorca's murder.

Departure

This is another poem with an eerie prophetic force, since it seems to prefigure Storni's suicide. Yet *Departure* does not speak of despair. In fact, the images of "golden dust" and coral brought up from the sea may owe something to the optimistic spirit of Shakespeare's last plays. Storni knew these works well, having written a farce called *Cymbeline in 1990* that transposes this redemptive romance to a modern setting. In the original, of course, the long-lost brothers of Imogen sing the beautiful dirge that includes a famous couplet:

> Golden lads and girls all must,
> As chimney-sweepers, come to dust.

Death seems beautiful here, as it does in Ariel's song in the second scene of *The Tempest*:

> Full fathom five thy father lies;
> Of his bones are coral made;
> Those are pearls that were his eyes:
> Nothing of him that doth fade
> But doth suffer a sea-change
> Into something rich and strange.

Perhaps it is not too far-fetched to hear an echo of these sentiments in Storni's *Departure*, a poem full of light and air, in which the sea elevates rather than immerses.

Certainly, there is a sense of mystical elation in this poem. *Departure* shares the Surrealistic impulse that becomes so prominent in *The World* of *Seven Wells* and *Portrait of García Lorca*, but it presents a landscape of dream rather than nightmare. By concluding with the spinning spindle enveloped by the rays of the sun, Storni remakes the classic female image of the distaff into an emblem of ecstasy. If there are hints of opiates administered to a body in pain in the references to poppies and "the sky [rolling] through the bed / of my veins." the overall effect nevertheless is exhilarating. The departure seems clearly to bring the speaker to a better place.

Topics for Discussion and Writing

1. Identify some of the images traditionally associated with women in Storni's poems and discuss her use of them. Is she using them in conventional ways?
2. As her poetic style evolves, Storni depicts the world as a place of dislocated parts. What is the emotional impact of her references to the body and the landscape?

Comparative Perspectives

1. Compare the color schemes of Darío's *Sonatina* and *Leda* with the values ascribed to white, red, and black in Storni's *You Want Me White*. In what ways do Darío's poems reflect a masculine perspective that Storni rejects in her poem?
2. Compare *The World of Seven Wells* with Emily Dickinson's poem 632 ("The Brain—is wider than the Sky—") or Virginia Woolf's depiction of the mind at work in *A Room of One's Own*. Are their concerns with the process of human consciousness marked in any way as gender-related?
3. Describe some of the dislocations of scale and imagery in *The World of Seven Wells* or the *Portrait of García Lorca*, and compare the impact of these incongruities with those encountered in Canto 4 of *The Rape of the Lock* or in *Gulliver's Travels*. How do the eighteenth-century satirists' descriptions of freakish bodies in inappropriate roles comment on their own societies? Do you think that Storni is writing satire in these poems?
4. Compare Storni's *Portrait of García Lorca* with Lorca's *Lament for Ignacio Sánchez Mejías*. How does Storni's invocation of the "wild animal" that "snarls in [García Lorca's] face / trying to destroy him / in its rage" contrast with García Lorca's portrait of the bull that gored Sánchez Mejías?

Further Reading

See the reading suggestions in the *Anthology*, p. 2555.

DADA-SURREALIST POETRY: A SELECTION

Backgrounds

Dada-Surrealism is now situated as the most radical element in twentieth-century modernism, even though its rebellious founders rejected the possibility of becoming part of a canon. It is in fact two movements, the one more performance-oriented and revolutionary and the other—after a bitter break with Dadaism—emphasizing the consistent exploration of the "revolution of the mind" in any medium. Single or double, Dada-Surrealism takes many modernist themes and techniques to the edge of possibility, emphasizing the role of antilogic and the unconscious in performance as well as in written and artistic form. Most readers find Dada-Surrealism fascinating and even familiar, nonetheless, since the tactics of oddly juxtaposed images, rapid unexplained shifts in point of view, sequences patterned by emotions and not logic, and the will to shock or at least startle the audience form such a large part of contemporary film, TV, advertising, and avant-garde writing and theatrical performance. To make the point that Dada-Surrealism is part of an evolution rather than a completely alien phenomenon, one has only to bring in the reproduction of a Surrealist painting (René Magritte or the early Salvador Dalí, for example) and compare it with major earlier works. It is likely that the Surrealist painting, with all its distortions or startling perspectives, will seem part of contemporary culture in a way that the earlier stylized realism is not.

Tristan Tzara, the best-known figure of Dadaism, is often identified with his *Seven Dada Manifestoes* (1924). His later work extends beyond Dada polemics, however, and includes a major poem, *Approximate Man* (1931), whose nineteen sections explore, in subjective and lyrical tones, the uncertainty of language and personal identity. Poetry and polemics are represented equally in the works printed here. Both the *Proclamation without Pretention*, given complete, and *Dadaist Disgust*, the culminating section of the *Dada Manifesto 1918*, are manifestos issued in 1918, and both use poetic effects as part of their attacks on art and society. *Dadaist Disgust* is more broadly aimed and attacks all the icons of conventional society in the name of spontaneity, vitality, and intense feeling. The *Proclamation without Pretention* focuses on conventional art—or, more precisely, professional formulas for the production and appreciation of "the Beautiful." It is worth remembering that the Dadaists' disgust is historically quite specific: reacting against the "Papa's Europe" that brought on World War I, they reject what they see as its arrogantly destructive mindset. If family, morals, money, logical systems, social hierarchies, respect for the past, faith in progress, and the individual's duty to society are all shibboleths of nineteenth-century respectability, the *Dada Manifesto* will pour scorn on them in the name of individuality, equality, intensity, spontaneous and even contradictory emotions, immediate experience, freedom, and, finally, LIFE.

In the passages leading up to the final paragraph, which is titled

Dadaist Disgust, Tzara justifies his distrust of scientific and moral pronouncements by saying "everyone has danced according to his own personal boomboom. . . . Logic is always false. It draws the superficial threads of concepts and words toward illusory conclusions and centres." It "asphyxiates independence," while morality "infuses chocolate, into every man's veins." Tzara protects himself by not accepting any predetermined values: "I am against systems; the most acceptable system is that of having none on no principle."

The very form of these manifestos demonstrates the Dadaist's break with conventional patterns: the *Dada Manifesto 1918* includes scribbles as part of the text, and both manifestos play merrily with typographical conventions; contraries and contradictions are gleefully thrown in the reader's face or glide suddenly into bizarre and disproportionate images. Yet there is a certain cumulative pattern to each piece. Rapid shifts of subject and tone gradually establish their own alternating rhythm and reinforce the work's rebellious tones. Coming at the end of the manifesto, *Dadaist Disgust* pulls together themes from previous passages (*rejection* of family, compromise and sociability, logic, hierarchies of any kind, knowledge of the past, authority and progress; *approval* of shock, spontaneity, word associations, individuality, contradictions, anarchy, intensity, and living in the present) in a condensed summary that races on, through increasingly vivid capitalizations, to its shouted conclusion: "shrieking of contracted pains, intertwining of contraries and all contradictions, grotesqueries, nonsequiturs: LIFE." *Proclamation without Pretention* is even more traditionally organized, in two parts: an attack on professional artists (the "druggists" who assemble their works calculating the rules and prescriptions of pretentious experts) and the proclamation of a natural "antiphilosophy" that is nihilist, vital, spontaneous, gaily contradictory, whimsically illogical, and full of dynamic images that escape academic control. The poem-manifesto ends in a final (boldface) dig at the druggist-artists as narcissistic runts who are still staring at their navels.

As the headnote states, Dadaism was a decentered movement whose adherents often disagreed violently over ideology and action. Kurt Schwitters, for example, once proposed joining the Berlin Dada circle but was rejected by its leader, Richard Huelsenbeck, because he was "too aesthetic" and not sufficiently active in politics. Schwitters is often considered on the outskirts of Dada because he never joined an active Dada group and spent most of his life in Hannover producing artworks that usually took the form of collage (the *Merz* pictures) or gigantic constructions that grew by accretion. While he is usually known as a visual artist, he also composed remarkable sound poems (combinations of sounds organized as pieces of music) and wrote a collection of prose and poetry, *Anna Blume*, which is known chiefly for the title poem, printed in the anthology. (There are, in fact, several *Anna Blume* collections, for the first edition of 1919 caused a sensation and Schwitters published various sequels; later, he and the Dadaist poet Raoul Hausmann even collaborated on a proposed novel.)

Schwitters's writing style evolved as much as his collage art and constructions; the lyrical *Anna Blume* is still close to the expressionist poetry he produced in his youth, predating the abstract word poems of subsequent years. It can be and is usually read as a love poem—unlike two pieces in the later, retitled collection *Blume Anna* that print the alphabet backward (one in capital letters, the other lowercase; the poet insisted on German pronunciation). Huelsenbeck attacked the lyrical *Anna Blume* because it *could* be read as a bourgeois love poem, "a typical idealist product prettified by craziness." Nonetheless, Schwitters's own crisp, chilly readings of the poem show that he considered it an experiment with rhythm and sound patterns as much as anything else.

Anna Blume is most easily approached as a humorous, ecstatic, happily illogical expression of love. The five senses of normal experience are multiplied to twenty-seven (not a specific allusion, but simply a joyful expansion), and grammar soon falls by the wayside: "I love your!" Here the English *your* should not be interpreted as an adjective for which we can imagine a following noun (such as *eyes*): the German text fractures grammatical logic with a declined form of the pronoun (*Dir*). Schwitters's English adaption, *Eve Blossom Has Wheels*, proposes "thine!," which appropriately startles the grammar-conscious reader and leads into grammatical forms of *I* and *you* until they propose a merger as "*We?*" (*Wir*, rhyming with *Dir*). Puns and free association achieve a subconscious meaning that coexists with surface nonsense: the "uncounted female," for example, is a play on the German *Frauenzimmer*, a familiar term for woman that includes the word *room* (*zimmer*). Rooms have numbers, Anna is unique or unnumbered among women, and thus the phrase offers a tribute that seems, on the one hand, totally gratuitous and, on the other, validated by a play on words. Mocking common sense—in the color contradictions ("Blue is the colour of your yellow hair"), in the image of Anna walking around on her hands, in the prize question's parody of a syllogism—and using increasingly sensual images that are anchored in Anna's name, Schwitters manages to express the delirium of love and also an unwillingness to subordinate its spontaneous emotion to any regulation or restraint.

The simple vocabulary and emotional directness of poems by Paul Éluard make him the most intuitively accessible Surrealist poet. From his early experiments with automatic writing to his Resistance poetry during World War II, Éluard emphasized primary emotions and the elemental power of *sight*. "To see is to understand, to judge, to distort, to forget or forget oneself, to be or to disappear." His poetry is charged with visual images that interpret the world of experience, whether it be love, sadness, confusion, or anger—and love is almost uppermost. Like Rimbaud, he believes in the artist as *voyant* or seer: poetry is "a lesson in things," and *seeing* (here he refers to visual artists) bridges the gap between the material world and human experience and also between individual human beings. "The role of the artist," he says, is "to teach how to see"; it is a "nostalgia for total light." The mystic overtones of these assertions correspond to the descriptive style of Éluard's poetry, in which everyday scenes are *not* reproduced realistically. Instead, these scenes are reconfigured into dreamlike settings that expose the poet's emotions—perhaps his relationship to a woman—and, throughout, his experience of the world at that precise moment.

Woman in Love (1923) begins with a shocking image ("She is standing on my eyelids") that is typical of such transfiguration. The picture is painful or grotesque unless one interprets it as a metaphor for the poet's obsessive dreaming about his beloved. Such a realistic explanation may be useful, but it also loses the force of the original picture, which is pursued throughout various images of overlap to evoke the absolute fusion of two lovers. Much of Surrealism's appeal depends on this ability to evoke startling, impossible, but subconsciously meaningful images. The *First Manifesto* quotes Pierre Reverdy's 1918 definition of a desirable image as "bringing together two more or less distant realities. . . . The farther they are away yet still connected, the stronger the image." In the second stanza, the sequence of images that describe this apparently dominant woman ("Her eyes are always open," for example) culminates in another impossible but powerful scene: her dreams overcome daytime reality, dissipating plural suns (*plural* demonstrating the continued dominance of dream) rather than being dissipated in broad daylight. The last two lines, however, break the illusion and return it to the poet's control as he comments on his emotional state and the nonsense he has just uttered: speaking "without anything to say."

The three shorter poems pursue similar themes of love and mingled identity, but they also introduce elements of pain and loss. Éluard had married his first wife, Gala, in 1917, and their relationship was not simple: in 1929, she left him for the painter Salvador Dalí. The epigraph to *Dying for Not Dying* (1924, included in *Capital of Pain*) refers to the volume as "his last book," and Éluard took a boat for Tahiti the day before publication. Some felt that he intended to follow Rimbaud's example and abandon literature; others claimed the influence of Breton's poem *Let Everything Go!* Less literary explanations have been found in Gala's affair that year with the artist Max Ernst; months after Éluard's departure, she located the poet in Singapore and brought him back to Paris. The poems are deceptively simple: brief, spare scenes delineated by spare yet precise images. This simplicity encloses complex and poignant emotions, whether it be a sense of cosmic interconnectedness in the lover's gaze, his fearful glimpse of her damaged and damaging nature, or his utter desolation as he watches himself lose a dreamed-of ideal partner.

Vision is emphasized in the other two poems: the first set in an ordinary restaurant where the poet is torn between two dimensions of life, and the second using images of time as a mirror (or mirrored time) to raise questions of appearance and reality. In the restaurant, the poet annoyedly denies his difference from other people—his special acquaintance with mystery—and tries to discard the fragments of his dreams; at the same time, he is pulled toward the rich "inward language" of sleep and wonder, to which he finally submits, as the ending series of visionary implosions shows.

André Breton employs a more measured, even logical framework in his poetry. *Free Union* takes its point of departure in the traditional *blason* form, in which a person or object is described (positively or satirically) through a list of qualities: one of the most popular was the "blason of the feminine body." The modern poet presents an encyclopedic list of associations, some of which are easily visualized ("mist on the windowpanes," "thoughts like flashes of heat lightning"), while others are responses to intuition ("eyes of water to be drunk in prison") or word associations ("a neck of impearled barley": pearl barley; pearls in a necklace). Each image implies a perspective or emotion ("with the back of a bird in vertical flight"), and the detailed list builds through its own series of internal associations to culminate in the picture of his wife as an embodiment of all nature.

Vigilance is structured as an autobiographical narrative, but a strange narrative in which the speaker turns out to be asleep and describing his journey into a further dimension of dream. Breton moves from relatively familiar images at the beginning—the tower's reflection in the river Seine—to large abstract images of "the heart of things" at the end. Differing from Éluard's more intuitive approach, he adopts a logical perspective to explain his vision's separate stages. As a dream figure, the narrator sets fire to the bed in which he is sleeping, and burns away all vestiges of cooperation with the everyday world (compare the oceanic purge in Rimbaud's *The Drunken Boat*). Dual images emphasize the shift from one to another dimension of reality, as the bedroom furniture metamorphoses into animals: chairs into lions, sheets into white-bellied sharks, imagined flames into the beaks of ibises (the hieratic bird of the Egyptian *Book of the Dead*). Like Éluard in *To Be Caught in One's Own Trap*, the narrator leaves behind the "passersby" of everyday life, "whose shuffling steps are heard far off," to pursue a larger mystery. The lace shell in the shape of a breast reminds us that the experience of "mad love" (undiluted passion) was among the Surrealist's favored routes to inner vision and the state they called the "sublime point" or "the marvelous."

Aimé Césaire and Joyce Mansour, poets a generation after Breton and Éluard, make use of Surrealist perspectives and techniques in their own very different ways. Césaire's connections with Surrealism are confined to the 1940s and linked to a concurrent exploration of black Caribbean identity, an exploration to which he subsequently devoted himself in plays, poetry, essays, and the celebrated *Discourse on Colonialism*. In 1945, however, an essay by Césaire, "Poetry and Knowledge," published in his journal *Tropiques*, clearly echoes themes and images familiar from Surrealism—some of them evident in the Breton and Éluard poems printed here. Summarizing his views in a series of concluding "Propositions," Césaire states: "Poetry is that attitude that by the word, the image, myth, love and humour places me at the living heart of myself and of the world" and "On the marvellous contact of the interior totality and exterior totality, perceived imaginatively and simultaneously by the poet, or more precisely within the poet, marvellous discoveries are made." The ending "Corollary" asserts: "The poet is that very old and very new, very complex and very simple being who—within the lived confines of the dream and the real, day and night, between absence and presence— seeks and receives, in the sudden unleashing of internal cataclysms, the password of complicity and power." Whether in the automatic writing of *Day and Night* or the more focused and coordinated address of *Do Not Have Pity* and *Sun Serpent*, these poems show an eagerness to use Surrealist tactics of free association, startling juxtapositions, and reversals to liberate thought processes and enable a fresh look at the world of the Caribbean. The tropical landscape of these poems differs sharply from the sketched-in symbolic settings in Éluard and even from the proliferating but intellectualized cosmos of Breton's *Free Union*. Césaire's poet is barely distinguishable from a landscape that undergoes upheaval and revolution, rediscovering its relationship to a basic "ancestral heritage / the invincible zeal of acid in the flesh of / life—sea swamps—."

Mansour's poetry returns to an inward and personal vision, one that uses but radically subverts core Surrealist themes of mad love, absolute freedom, dream life, the search for the marvelous, and transfiguring experience. Where the early Surrealists emphasize male love for a woman who is per se a route to the marvelous, Mansour asserts a female perspective and predatory fantasies that turn romantic love on its head and point to more difficult emotions. *Men's Vices* approaches parody in its picture of the predatory female—the femme fatale of male iconology— who revels in the power given her by men's own fantasies. *I Opened Your Head* is a far cry from Éluard's *Woman in Love*, whose structure it nonetheless recalls. Instead of the earlier poet's tender, even abstract picture of inseparable lovers, Mansour gives the scene in visceral, impossible physical details that evoke a brutal will to dominate one's partner. It does not really matter whether the victim is male or female (in her plays, Mansour sometimes destabilizes gender identity by giving the same attributes to both male and female characters), but rather what kind of emotional or existential plight is being defined. For it *is* a plight: the agony of the shared nightmare in *I Saw You through My Closed Eye*, or the symbolic vision of *Empty Black Haunted House*, in which rooms are crowded with unfinished visions and objects beyond reach. Mansour's scenes remain rooted in mundane interpersonal reality even when they are most fantastic and dreamlike. She does not take the prescribed Surrealist route of escaping to the *marvelous*, but accepts the reality of "eternal inedible bread" and opens herself to the night.

Classroom Strategies

The Dada-Surrealist poetry presented here present selections from six different writers but may easily be treated as the development of a single evolution in art and literature. As previously suggested, one way to introduce this evolution is to bring in examples of Surrealist painting and contrast them with earlier works, including the covers of the anthology. You may want to lead off discussion of the poetry by looking at the turn away from previous practice in Tzara's *Dadaist Disgust* and examining the Dadaists' specific attacks of the society of their time (whose mind-set and conventions they blamed for World War I). Tzara's *Proclamation without Pretention* is an amusing parody of pompous proclamations that satirizes the claims of conventional Great Art to immortality and the Beautiful, and it sets the stage for writing that looks to different goals. Schwitters's sensuously lyrical, absurdist *Anna Blume* is an appealing example of this differently oriented poetry, and it also leads into the following Surrealist love poetry. Links are easily made between Éluard and Breton, and then continuities and contrast appear in the differently focused poets of the next generation, Césaire and Mansour.

Not to be overlooked, however, is the opportunity to introduce selections from these poets in other periods: for example, the rebellion of Tzara's *Dadaist Disgust* with Heine's *The Silesian Weavers* or Shelley's *England in 1819*; or, in love poetry, the fusion of woman and nature in Éluard's *Woman in Love* and Lamartine's *The Lake*. Breton called Surrealism the "prehensile tail of Romanticism," and Surrealism's visionary qualities suggest comparisons with Romantic and Symbolist literature as well as with modernist avant-garde techniques.

Topics for Discussion

1. Both Dadaists and Surrealists point to Rimbaud as a precursor. Which work or works by the earlier poet explain their interest?

   [The easiest responses for Dada will be found in *A Season in Hell*, for Surrealism in the *Illuminations* or *The Drunken Boat*.]

2. Dada is a movement of pure revolt, and Tristan Tzara sums up the themes of that revolt in *Dadaist Disgust*, the conclusion to his *Dada Manifesto 1918*. What specific elements in contemporary society did the Dadaists find disgusting, and why? What political impetus for that disgust in suggested by the date of the manifesto and the fact that the original Dadaists gathered in Zürich, Switzerland, between 1916 and 1918?

3. Dada has been described as simultaneously "Art and anti-art." How does Tzara's *Proclamation without Pretention* describe the weakness of conventional or canonized art, and what does he wish to put in its place? Is his own *Proclamation* devoid of artistic techniques?

4. Discuss the love poems by Kurt Schwitters, Paul Éluard, and André Breton; what image of the beloved do they propose, and how is that image rejected in poems by Joyce Mansour?

5. An ideal Surrealist image will bring together two distant realities that are somehow felt to be connected (or are shown, by the poet, to be connected). In what way do Breton's *Free Union*, Éluard's

Woman in Love, and Césaire's *Sun Serpent* illustrate this principle? [Note: any one of these poems can be used in itself.]

6. How do Éluard's *To Be Caught in One's Own Trap*, Breton's *Vigilance*, and Mansour's *Empty Black Haunted House* evoke a sense of supreme mystery, each in its own way?

7. Breton's *Free Union* and Aimé Césaire's *Sun Serpent* and *Day and Night* are crammed with wide-ranging, almost encyclopedic details. What function do these details fill in each poem? How is it the same, and how different?

Further Reading

See also the reading suggestions in the *Anthology*, p. 2550.

Bradley, Fiona. *Surrealism*. 1997. Offers a useful, illustrated short introduction to Surrealist art that includes the contributions of women.

Camfield, William A. *Max Ernst: Dada and the Dawn of Surrealism*. 1993. Sheds light on early Dada.

Chadwick, Whitney. *Mirror Images: Women, Surrealism, and Self-Representation*. 1998. Presents an interesting perspective on the situation of women in Surrealism.

Elderfield, John. *Kurt Schwitters*. 1985. Discusses the artist's work with some attention to his writing.

Hubert, Renee Riese. *Magnifying Mirrors: Women, Surrealism, & Partnership*. 1994. Presents another interesting perspective on the situation of women in Surrealism.

Naumann, Francis. *New York Dada 1915–23*. 1994. Sheds light on early Dada.

Richardson, Michael, and Kryzysztof Fijalkowski, eds. *Refusal of the Shadow: Surrealism and the Caribbean*. 1996. Assembles contemporary essays chiefly by Caribbbean Surrealists that demonstrate Surrealism's impact and its relation to colonialism in the Caribbean.

Schmalenbach, Werner. *Kurt Schwitters*. 1967. Discusses the artist's work with some attention to his writing.

Suleiman, Susan. *Subversive Intent*. 1990. Chapters offer valuable theoretical insights into the role of Surrealist women writers in relation to the French avant-garde.

WILLIAM FAULKNER

Like other great moderns, Faulkner hungered for a mythology. He was content to construct *his* from his home country of north Mississippi, creating a region so firmly rural, so adamantly uncosmopolitan, that a child could be named Wall Street Panic Snopes in vague recognition of

the world of big doings, of business and wars and interminglings of nations—a world utterly foreign to characters wrapped up entirely in their
own country: enduring it and dying into it. His achievement was to create a fictional world for the American South—Yoknapatawpha, a land
both real and imagined, encompassing an Indian past and a black past
and present, the fading gentility of the Compsons and the thriving crass-
ness of the Snopes, the eternal soil and rivers that coil and uncoil their
histories, together with the wilderness and its legend of bear.

It was perhaps precisely because in the twenties the fixity of Southern
life—its reliance on a set caste structure, its unwavering gaze backward
to a time of glory—was beginning to waver, that the literary renaissance
centered around Faulkner was possible. For Faulkner, the Southern past
exercised a compelling influence, yet he was enough at odds with his
heritage to be able to step outside, take its measure, and commit its conflicts to literature.

Barn Burning

Backgrounds

Barn Burning was originally conceived as the opening chapter of *The
Hamlet*. Perhaps because it appears to contradict, or at least qualify, a
major theme of that novel—the inexorable rise of Snopesism—it was
dropped from the novel, but it soon took up residence, complete in itself, as a short story.

The story has for center the conflict between family, with its "old
fierce pull of blood," and a new version of order, a "peace and dignity"
separate from and untouched by the tawdry, graceless malevolence so familiar to the story's young protagonist. The conflict is embodied in Sarty
Snopes, a boy trapped in a recurrent family history: the family sets up as
tenant farmers, some offense is committed, they are accused, they react
by burning a barn, a trial ensues, they are sent packing, they go to another part of the state and set up again as tenant farmers, and so on,
endlessly. Sarty's father is Ab Snopes, the clan's patriarch, a man of mechanical rigidity, with the "impervious quality of something cut ruth-
lessly from tin, depthless, as though, sidewise to the sun, it would cast
no shadow," a man who has set a lifetime of puny, "niggard blazes" for
his family but who, when crossed, is capable of setting other men's property furiously ablaze.

Sarty is held tight to his father and his family by the ties of blood, the
only ties Sarty knows or can know. When his father thinks Sarty might
have betrayed the family while on the stand in the trial that opens the
story, he strikes him and says:

> You're getting to be a man. You got to learn. You got to learn to stick to your
> own blood or you ain't going to have any blood to stick to you.

Like his cringing mother, his older brother, his bovine sisters, the wagon,
the gaunt mules, the battered stove, the broken clock, the worn broom,

Sarty is inextricably tied to the never-ending, destructive round of his family's life, carted about when they move, present when the barns burn.

When Sarty and his father go to the plantation house of Major de Spain, however, the boy forgets "his father and the terror and despair both," as he encounters a world of people who are safe from his father's rigid malevolence:

> People whose lives are a part of this peace and dignity are beyond his touch, he no more to them than a buzzing wasp; capable of stinging for a little moment but that's all; the spell of this peace and dignity rendering even the barns and stable and cribs which belong to it impervious to the puny flames he might contrive. . . .

For Sarty, the house registers a world of decency beyond his world; for his father the house registers a world that only humiliates him, and his response to humiliation is, as it always has been, to defile and destroy. His rug ruined, Major de Spain demands compensation, the Justice of the Peace supports him (though hardly to the worth of the rug), and Ab prepares to answer his humiliation in the way he always has. The family cycle has begun its inexorable motion.

This time, however, Sarty warns Major de Spain of his father's intentions. As Sarty runs from the scene, he hears gunshots, and believes his father dead. Sarty has broken free of the clan's cycle of recurrence, but grief and despair overwhelm him; he is alone now in a world where only the "slow constellations wheeled on." He walks away through the dark woods, whippoorwills registering the dawn of a new day, and does not look back.

Although our response to Ab Snopes should be measured first against Sarty's developing sense of decency, the story nevertheless suggests that Ab's iron rigidity and his pyromaniac malevolence have a basis in the social structure of Yoknapatawpha. Ab has a deep sense of "the preservation of integrity," a strong conviction of the rightness of his actions. He cannot tolerate any humiliation that comes from the direction of those in authority, especially when that authority is maintained by systematically subordinating others. As Ab leaves the great house, after having tracked horse dung on the Major's rug, he tells Sarty: "Pretty and white, ain't it? . . . That's sweat. Nigger sweat. Maybe it ain't white enough yet to suit him. Maybe he wants to mix some white sweat with it." Undeniably, Ab has a ferociously unlovely notion of integrity, but his single-minded rejection of authority nevertheless suggests that he is in some measure another of those figures of resistance who criticize the existing social structure by attempting to destroy it. That Barn Burning allows for this view of Ab Snopes might have been another reason for Faulkner's dropping it from The Hamlet, since in that book, and the subsequent books that trace the rise of the Snopeses, Snopesism is to be understood as a purely diabolical version of evil.

Classroom Strategies

Barn Burning can be taught in one class period, as can *Spotted Horses*. If you are able to teach both, *Barn Burning*, because it is less obviously a "set piece," should probably be taught first.

The central issues of *Barn Burning* will be evident to most students on the first reading. Any problems will probably have to do with the story's narrative technique. As always in Faulkner, the design of the story is the design of its telling. *Barn Burning* is told from a third-person limited point of view, the central consciousness being Sarty's. Sarty therefore becomes the measure of what we know in the story even when what he thinks is not necessarily the case. Sarty, for instance, thinks his father has been shot by Major de Spain; as we discover from later books in the Snopes saga, this is not so. That Ab was not shot, however, should not diminish our response to Sarty's grief and terror at the story's end; Sarty *assumes* his father's death and his responsibility for it, and this is what the reader must respond to.

Faulkner's narrative allows him to move rapidly in both space and time; periodically, present and future appear simultaneously. We hear Sarty's voice as a boy in all of its colloquial vigor, both in dialogue and in interior monologue ("ourn! mine and hisn both!"). But we are also allowed to hear a version of the mature Sarty, a Sarty who can look back on the events of the story in an attempt to understand their significance: "Later, twenty years later, he was to tell himself, 'If I had said they wanted only truth, justice, he would have hit me again.' "

The opening paragraph of the story offers a splendid display of Faulkner's narrative gifts; we are able to visualize the country store in which the Justice of the Peace holds court, but we are simultaneously so far inside Sarty that we share in his raging hunger as well as his fear and despair. Faulkner manages this through the use of synesthesia, the merging together of various senses:

> from where he sat he could see the ranked shelves close-packed with the solid, squat, dynamic shapes of tin cans whose labels his stomach read, not from lettering which meant nothing to his mind but from the scarlet devils and the silver curve of fish—this, the cheese which he knew he smelled and the hermetic meat which his intestines believed he smelled coming in intermittent gusts momentarily and brief between the other constant one . . .

The end of the story places Sarty in an environment that is again fully realized in realistic terms, but which serves as an almost Dantesque symbolic setting for his grief and loneliness. He is in a "dark woods," alone in the natural world with the wheeling constellations and whippoorwills, severed entirely from both his family and the peace and dignity represented by the house of Major de Spain. Faulkner uses the traditional imagery of regeneration in this last paragraph: it is spring, day is breaking, and Sarty has no option but to walk down the road toward a new life—one quite different, we have been led to suspect, from the one he is leaving.

Topics for Discussion and Writing

1. What kind of narrative technique is Faulkner using in *Barn Burning*? What is the point of view? What difference does it make to our understanding of the story that Faulkner uses Sarty as the central consciousness? What would the story be like if Ab or Major de Spain were the central consciousness?

   [See paragraphs 1–3 of "Classroom Strategies" for discussion.]

2. What is the central conflict in *Barn Burning*? What is Sarty's family life like? How do we know?

   [See "Backgrounds" for discussion.]

3. How is Ab's rigid, mechanical quality suggested? Is there any justification for his behavior?

   [See paragraphs 2 and 6 of "Backgrounds" for discussion.]

4. What does Major de Spain's house symbolize? Is its symbolic meaning clear?

   [See paragraph 4 of "Backgrounds" for discussion.]

5. Why does Sarty warn Major de Spain at the end of the story? Is his action justified?

   [See paragraphs 4–5 of "Backgrounds" for discussion.]

6. Does it matter that, in later books, we find that Ab was not, as Sarty thinks, shot by Major de Spain?

   [See paragraph 2 of "Classroom Strategies" for discussion.]

Spotted Horses

Backgrounds

Spotted Horses, a story that was later incorporated in revised form into *The Hamlet*, apparently has its origins in a horse auction witnessed by the young Faulkner from the porch of a boarding house in the village of Pittsboro, Mississippi. The horses up for sale were so wild they were tied together with barbed wire. The story also partakes of a number of traditions, all belonging to the American tall tale as descended from earlier practitioners such, as Longstreet and Mark Twain. First of all, it is *told*—not just narrated—by a witness not directly involved in the action, in this case an honest (perhaps too honest for his own material good) sewing machine salesman named Ratliff. The teller uses his own highly colorful vocabulary and idiom. He exaggerates shamelessly, taking things to the edge of natural possibility and just beyond, leaving them in the miraculous for a long breath before setting them back on earth. (Faulkner served as one inspiration for the magical realism of Gabriel Garcia Marquez, another member of a traditional society beginning to dissolve.) The telling renders the narration dramatic, as when one of the passel of ponies encounters a wagon containing the sleeping Tull family:

> They waked up when the horse hit the bridge one time, but Tull said the first he knew was when the mules tried to turn the wagon around in the middle of the bridge and he seen that spotted varmint run right twixt the mules and run up the wagon tongue like a squirrel. He said he just had time to hit it across

the face with his whip-stock, because about that time the mules turned the wagon around on that ere one-way bridge and that horse clumb across one of the mules and jumped down onto the bridge again and went on, with Vernon standing up in the wagon and kicking at it.

Tull said the mules turned in the harness and clumb back into the wagon too, with Tull trying to beat them out again, with the reins wrapped around his wrist. After that he says all he seen was overturned chairs and womenfolks' legs and white drawers shining in the moonlight, and his mules and that spotted horse going on up the road like a ghost.

The story balances action against inaction; Mrs. Armstid sitting all day in her wagon "as if carved outen wood," against the pony who bursts into Mrs. Littlejohn's house "like a fourteen-foot pinwheel." Thus contrasted, both motion and stillness take on a cartoonlike ferocity.

Closely tied to this contrast is one between predictability and capriciousness; the Texan man tirelessly eating gingersnaps and then looking carefully into the empty box, Henry Armstid doggedly insisting "I bought a horse," Eck Snopes's son's unfailing luck under the hooves of the spotted horses, who are the very embodiment of chaos—violating the well-ordered world of Mrs. Littlejohn's boarding house and turning the peaceful countryside into a scattering of cries of "Whooy. Head him!"

The story's human embodiment of unpredictability is the notorious Flem Snopes. He appears in the first sentences ("Yes, sir. Flem Snopes has filled that whole country full of spotted horses") as a transformative agent of chaos. He is that common feature of the tall tale, the trickster: a creature so wily that he is never caught in the act, but performs his tricks secretly, at one remove, profiting from anything, but most of all from the predictable foolishness of his fellow humans. Flem is a special, hardy breed of trickster: one who is never tricked, never gets his comeuppance. His secret power, as explained by Ratliff, lies in the ambivalence he inspires. He is a repulsive cheat and a crook, but such a good one that he draws admiration even from his prey: "Why, that fellow could make a nickel where it wasn't but four cents to begin with. He skun me in two trades, myself, and the fellow that can do that, I just hope he'll get rich before I do; that's all." Perhaps because of his rare ability to transcend his circumstances (among other things, to transform himself from store clerk to store owner), Flem is a constant source of pride for his community. What Ratliff believes, and the story demonstrates, is that it is very absorbing to watch just what and how much Flem can get away with.

Classroom Strategies

Once students have become accustomed to Faulkner's prose style, *Spotted Horses* will not seem as difficult to follow, and it will show them that pure, risible joy is among the satisfactions that masterpieces can supply.

The colloquial vigor of *Spotted Horses* overrides whatever minor confusion may be caused by its highly colorful dialect. Students may, however, find some of the attitudes displayed by the characters difficult to comprehend. Why are Mr. Armstid and the other men so smitten with spotted-horse mania, since it is obvious that the horses are good for nothing but stirring up dust? Why does Mrs. Armstid bow to her husband's bad judgment (and to Flem Snopes's chicanery)? It can be pointed out that the ponies, arriving from a mythical and impressive Texas, bring with them excitement and a certain glamor—along with the surefire attraction, imparted by the Texas man, of a *bargain*. In contrast to the long-suffering, hang-dog Mrs. Armstid we have Mrs. Littlejohn: a woman fairly bursting with indignation over the folly of menfolk, who defends her domain from the horses by splitting a washboard over one of their foreheads, and who takes capable charge of the wounded Mr. Armstid.

Topics for Discussion and Writing

1. How does description contribute to characterization in *Spotted Horses*?
   [See particularly the descriptions of Mrs. Littlejohn and Mrs. Armstid in Section VI of the story.]
2. Discuss the contrast Faulkner creates between male foolishness and female steadiness in *Spotted Horses*. Does it have basis in fact? (This is guaranteed to raise the temperature of the discussion.)
3. Is the Texas man the same breed of con man as Flem Snopes? Why or why not?
4. The editor at Scribner's, where *Spotted Horses* was originally published, described it as "a tall tale with implications of tragedy." What are these implications?

Comparative Perspectives

It is difficult, actually, to make easy comparisons between Faulkner and any of the other writers represented in the *Anthology*. There are, of course, stylistic and structural similarities to be found among Faulkner, Joyce, Proust, Conrad, and Woolf, but perhaps the best comparison is with Gabriel García Márquez. *One Hundred Years of Solitude* is not included in this anthology, but many students may well have read it. In any case, García Márquez's creation of a complete fictional world, Macondo, is similar to (and influenced by) Faulkner's creation of Yoknapatawpha County.

Further Reading

See also the suggestions in the *Anthology*, p. 255.

Blotner, Joseph. *Selected Letters of William Faulkner*. 1977.
    A useful selection of the letters, basic to an understanding of Faulkner's life.

Bradford, M. E. "Family and Community in Faulkner's 'Barn Burning.' " *Southern Review* 17 (April 1981): 332–39.
    Explores Sarty's ties to his clan.

Ruppersburg, Hugh M. *Voice and Eye in Faulkner's Fiction.* 1983.
    A discussion of narrative perspective in Faulkner, with concentration on the major novels.

Vickery, Olga. *The Novels of William Faulkner: A Critical Interpretation.* Rev. ed. 1964.
    An early but useful general study.

Volpe, Edmund. *A Reader's Guide to William Faulkner.* 1964.
    A cogent examination of Faulkner's works.

Warren, Robert Penn, ed. *Faulkner: A Collection of Critical Essays.* 1966.

CLUSTER: FREEDOM AND RESPONSIBILITY AT MID-CENTURY

It is not surprising that after the unprecedented slaughter and horrifying discoveries of World War II many people would, with Hannah Arendt, feel tempted to say they were "ashamed of being human." The withered and absurd world offered in the work of many writers after the war—Beckett, Camus, Sartre, Cioran, Vonnegut, and Heller, to mention just a few—derives from a new and terrible knowledge about what it means to be human. Burdened by such knowledge, attitudes and ideas about freedom, responsibility, guilt, human connectedness and disconnectedness all had to be rethought and reexamined. How could the war have happened? How could the Holocaust have happened? How could some of the most sophisticated cultures in the world, with centuries of art, philosophy, and organized law at their back, have fought two ruinous total wars in a matter of a little over thirty years? How could such things happen? And, given that such things *have* happened, how must we now view the human condition?

The three essays in this cluster try to make some headway with these immense questions. Though they may not reveal any absolute truths, all of them insist that we must always confront ourselves with as much truthfulness as we can muster. At the same time, we must vigilantly protect against forces that might overrun our ability or our willingness to look at ourselves and speak truthfully about what we see—whether those forces are political, socio-economic, or psychological and philosophical self-delusion and self-justification.

George Orwell is the kind of writer who is generally understood to be crucial in times of crisis, especially during wartime, when clear-headed arguments relatively uncorrupted by cultural bias or wishful thinking are particularly necessary. His work is what we call, among other things, good reporting. But it should also be pointed out that it is in precisely such times of crisis, especially during wartime, that independent writers like Orwell are often least welcome—by the government and often the general public—and are most likely to be the target of those forces that conspire to "turn the writer, and every other kind of artist as well, into a minor official, working on themes handed to [him] from above and never telling what seems to him to be the whole truth."

Orwell has been called the conscience of his generation because he refused to be turned into that kind of writer. Though he recognized that cultural and ideological bias operated in him just as strongly as it did in others, his awareness of that fact made it possible for him to put aside such biases and respond freshly to events. His work appears to defy the usual tendency to nudge what he sees into conformity with what he *wishes* to see, or what his ideology tells him he *ought* to see.

In "The Prevention of Literature," Orwell argues that the forces that constantly threaten a writer's intellectual liberty—the ability to write accurately about what one sees, hears, and feels—come from two directions. First, there are the theoretical enemies (which in Orwell's time were the "apologists for totalitarianism"); second, there are the more elusive practical enemies, the champions of "go along, come along," who function inside the "general drift of society" rather than participate in active persecution. The essay proposes to concern itself mostly with these practical enemies, but the excerpt is mainly taken up with Orwell's arguments against the theoretical enemies—specifically the Communists of his own time who closed their eyes to the actual situation of the Soviet Union under Stalin and chose to believe that the USSR was realizing the promise of a Marxist classless society. Orwell, an uneasy Socialist for most of his life, was able to distinguish between the promise of Socialism and its quite different reality in the form of Stalin's Soviet Communism.

But Orwell's major point is a simple and still important one. Whatever forces might cause the writer to "write lies or suppress what seems to him to be important news" are forces that will in the end destroy freedom of expression. Without such freedom, the writer's "creative faculties dry up," and, very possibly, prose literature—which, unlike poetry, Orwell clearly associates with truth-telling—will "*come to an end.*" Literature, Orwell argues, "is doomed if liberty of thought perishes," and he insists that "any writer or journalist who denies the fact . . . is demanding his own destruction."

The excerpt from Sartre is tougher sledding. Simply put, insofar as Sartre's ideas can be put simply, humans find themselves alone and disturbingly free, because we are without the comforting direction of a God or a political, philosophical, or religious system that answers all of our questions and gives meaning and purpose to our existence. Though we would much prefer to have answers handed to us, and to submit to a greater authority that would relieve us of the difficulty of making decisions, we are "condemned" now to accept the burden of our own freedom. It would be much easier to live and act in a world where we did not have to recognize that we, alone, are responsible for *everything*. We are free all right, but being free is hard. We may not like it, but that's the way it is.

For Sartre, only the individual is responsible for what happens to him. To declare that anything or anyone else is responsible—the State, God, parents, economic situation—is to deny the truth of one's condition. Sartre would quite obviously disagree with Orwell because—though Orwell does recognize the importance of the individual's not giving in to the demands of the State—his argument is essentially *with* the state, especially the totalitarian state. Sartre would no doubt say that Orwell's concerns are misplaced, and that he should instead be emphasizing the necessity of the individual's facing up to his own responsibility. "It is . . . senseless to think of complaining since nothing foreign has decided what we feel, what we live, or what we are."

It is also Sartre's claim that the individual's responsibility extends far beyond the self, that the individual is also responsible for "the world." One must take responsibility even for the worst of situations: "If I am mobilized in a war, this war is *my* war; it is in my image and I deserve it. I deserve it first because I could always get out of it by suicide or by desertion; these ultimate possibles are those which must always be present for us when there is a question of envisaging a situation. For lack of getting out of it, I have chosen it. . . . For it depended on me and by me that this war should not exist, and I have decided that it does exist." For Sartre, the individual who chooses to participate in war is as profoundly responsible for it "as if [one] had declared it [one's self]."

Sartre would argue that this conclusion is inevitable if one accepts his premises. Still, it will not likely seem logical to students; at the very least it will seem counter-intuitive. There is good reason for this—the fact is, whether one accepts Sartre's premises or not, it is hard to accept the extraordinary weight Sartre places on subjectivism and to then connect it with the world outside the individual. In other words, why does it follow that, even if individuals recognize their responsibility for their own choices and actions, they must also recognize that they are equally responsible for the kind of world they live in?

In all likelihood, the teacher will have to rely on information outside of this excerpt to help students make sense of this difficult concept. A thorough discussion of Sartre's notion of the *"pour-soi"* ("for-itself"), outlined in the introduction, as well as Sartre's related notions of authenticity and engagement, may be useful in this regard. Within the excerpt, teachers might invite a close examination of the second paragraph, which is perhaps Sartre's most direct clarifying sentence about this problem. "He [the individual] must assume the situation with the proud consciousness of being the author of it, for the very worst disadvantages or the worst threats which can endanger my person have meaning only in and through my project; and it is on the ground of the engagement which I am that they appear."

Here Sartre appears to assert that for each individual the world exists and has meaning only through the consciousness and choices of that individual. The idea may not be entirely alien: students may recognize it from their reading of the Romantics, from related—but philosophically thin—ideas such as Ayn Rand's "objectivism" or American libertarianism, or because they are still familiar with solipsistic notions that often dominate childhood.

The excerpt from Hannah Arendt will come as a relief to students after the difficulties of dealing with Sartre. Like Sartre, she insists that "men must assume responsibility for all crimes committed by men and that all nations must share the onus of evil committed by all others." But she comes at the problem from another direction and with other emphases.

For Arendt, the "precondition of any modern political thinking" is to realize "in fear and trembling . . . of what man is capable." It is of little use to put the responsibility for what happened in World War II and the Holocaust on "the German national character," or on "madmen," or on individual fanatics or adventurers such as Hitler or Goering. In fact, Arendt insists, the "great criminal" of the century was the good "family man," the bourgeois who worries only about "his pension, his life insurance, and the security of his wife and children," but who, under significant economic, social, and political pressure, will "sacrifice his beliefs, his honor, and his human dignity." It was on such men that the German "machine of destruction" depended. Such men would "never do harm to a fly" on their own, but, when offered the opportunity to be "fully exempted from responsibility for [their] acts," served "the machine of destruction without opposition."

This is hard on the bourgeoisie, of course—those "normal" men and women who seem at first the least likely to be agents of evil. Arendt points out in this excerpt, as well as in her other essays and books, that it is precisely those who are capable of saying "It was just my job, I was just a functionary," even when their function is to operate a machine of organized murder, who bear the closest watching—precisely because they seem so unthreatening. But, even more than the bourgeoisie, Arendt is arguing against docility, complacency, and self-delusion—just like Orwell and Sartre.

Orwell, Sartre, and Arendt, in very different ways, are all insisting upon a rigorous reexamination of our ideas of responsibility—whether because we as individuals can do no other than to accept it, or because we now know too much about the evil potentialities in humans to ignore it, or because our freedom depends upon it. All three recognize the connection between freedom and responsibility, and an emphasis on this connection will carry the teacher of this cluster through most of the difficulties these three excerpts might present to students.

BERTOLT BRECHT

The Good Woman of Setzuan

Classroom Strategies and Topics for Discussion

With Ibsen, Chekhov, Strindberg, and Pirandello, Brecht belongs on any list of influential modern playwrights; like Chekhov and Pirandello, Brecht, a talented poet and writer of fiction, worked in more than one medium. His reputation, however, rests on his dramatic innovations, deriving not only from his own practice as a playwright but also from his theoretical writings on theater. Many of the best young dramatists working today consciously emulate Brecht, seeking to further their social and political goals by distancing audiences from the staged performance that manifests the importance of these goals. With a leading character whose plight could bring an audience to tears in the hands of a more traditional dramatist, *The Good Woman of Setzuan* vividly demonstrates the paradox inherent in the Brechtian mix of ideological engagement and emotional alienation (see the headnote).

Today's students may be familiar with contemporary plays that break the fourth wall, in which actors step out of character and speak directly to the audience; they will surely recognize these techniques from many popular television series in which the leading character (Jerry Seinfeld, for example) offers ironic commentary on the events just "imitated." This breaking of dramatic illusion is a typical modernist device, most easily recognized in theater or the visual arts. You might show your students a reproduction of Picasso's famous painting *Les Demoiselles d'Avignon*, which introduces multiple perspectives and transforms human faces into African-masklike visages, to demonstrate the way an artist purposely set about fracturing the single-point perspective that was the artistic legacy of the West. One of the challenges in reading (as opposed to seeing) a play by Brecht is to watch how the planes of reality shift before our eyes and ultimately to articulate what this shifting of planes achieves.

Like so many modernist techniques, Brecht's playing with perspectives has ancient roots in other periods and cultures. Originally published in a volume called *Two Parables for the Theatre*, *The Good Woman of Setzuan*, and *The Caucasian Chalk Circle* were inspired by a fourteenth-century Chinese play *The Chalk Circle*, by Li Hsing-tao. The play retells an old Chinese folk tale that resembles the biblical story of the judgment of Solomon (1 Kings 3.16–28). Each of two women insists that she is the mother of a child. To choose between these contesting maternal claims, the judge threatens the child; the real mother gives up her claim rather than see her baby killed. One of the rivals in the Chinese play is a prostitute named Chan Hai-tang: in her goodness, this character inspired Brecht's Shen Te.

The Chalk Circle was richly produced by Max Reinhardt in a German adaptation by Klabund in Berlin in 1924; it was done in an English translation in London in 1931. In 1932, in reaction to the saccharine quality of the Klabund version of *The Chalk Circle*, a writer named Friedrich Wolf wrote a play about the Chinese revolution, *Tai Yan Wakes Up*, set in modern Shanghai and enacted in a spare modern production by Erwin Piscator. Wolf's technique, however, was to engage the audience's sympathy.

Equally dissatisfied with the synthetic sweetness of Klabund's adaptation of the old play and the intense dramatic engagement of Wolf's modern response, Brecht went on to write two of his most popular and influential plays. Both *The Caucasian Chalk Circle*, mainly through its plot, and *The Good Woman of Setzuan*, primarily in its leading character, draw upon the six-hundred-year-old Chinese *Chalk Circle*. In both plays, Brecht is intent on demystifying what Western bourgeois audiences might perceive as its Oriental charm by resetting it in a shabby twentieth-century Asian locale.

Even before his visit to Moscow in 1935, where Brecht saw authentic Chinese theater (see the headnote), he had been exploiting anti-illusionist devices: in 1931, for example, his *A Man's a Man* used masks to demonstrate a character's personality change. Some devices may have been suggested by Meyerhold's revolutionary theater; others are already part of early Western tradition. The direct address to the audience, interpolated songs, and masks to indicate identity appear in Greek and Roman comedy (see the selections by Aristophanes and Plautus in Vol. 1). Ancient theater also employed mechanical stage devices: if your students have studied Greek tragedy, you will want to remind them that when the gods remove themselves from Setzuan in a "cloud," as Brecht's stage directions specify, they occupy a *mechane* very much like the one in Euripides' *Medea*. Nonetheless, Brecht's recent exposure to the stylized drama of traditional Chinese theater, with its masks, songs, and the amazing adaptability of the actors to a variety of roles (including gender impersonation by the celebrated Mai Lan-fang), clearly made its mark on *The Good Woman of Setzuan*.

The modern "half-Westernized city of Setzuan" is the scene for our play. The choice of Setzuan, properly a province rather than a city, indicates that we are in a geographical limbo rather than a historically specific site: the real location is "wherever man is exploited by man." Ask your students what Brecht gains from juxtaposing Eastern and Western motifs here. Would the visit from the gods work as well if the play were set in a contemporary, fully Westernized city? How does his habitual choice of nonrealistic stage pictures of exotic or premodern geographical locations contribute to the distancing effect that Brecht works to achieve in the theater?

You will probably want to return to the question of locale every time the scene shifts. This is easily done if you spend some time discussing *The Good Woman of Setzuan*'s episodic structure, which is again typically Brechtian. Why does he purposely avoid a fluid, chronologically seamless presentation of events? Here is another means by which Brecht constantly jolts the audience out of complacency. Notice in particular the subsidiary skits attached to several scenes (3a, 4a, etc.); having your students identify and explain these additions would be a good preparatory assignment to accompany a first reading of the text, since the students should have no trouble discerning their function.

The prologue, in which Wong speaks directly to the audience and greets the itinerant gods, is in effect the first of these anti-illusionist commentaries. Moving in and out of the action of the play, Wong serves as the audience's ambassador. He is equipped with two props worth some discussion: the cup with the false bottom and the carrying pole. Ask your students to interpret the stage image of his balancing the pole with one hand, his other having been smashed by the irate barber's curling iron. Literally single-handedly, throughout the play, Wong mediates the action, trying to put the best face on human failings when the gods accost him and to persuade them to reconsider the demands of orthodoxy: "Maybe a little relaxation of the rules, Benevolent One, in view of the bad times."

The prologue resembles also the opening chapters of the Book of Job (see Vol. 1) and the *Prologue in Heaven* to Goethe's *Faust* (this volume), in which divine powers question the sustainability of human virtue. The larger texts then proceed to test that virtue, as does *The Good Woman of Setzuan*. By setting his play in a semimythical, semi-Westernized China, Brecht can allude to the Judeo-Christian tradition (which includes, as the headnote indicates, the angelic visit to—and the ultimate destruction of—the corrupt cities of Sodom and Gomorrah in Genesis 18–19) without directly impugning the ways of God to men. The three Chinese gods pictured here are infirm and old-fashioned when the play begins and, despite Wong's excellent advice to them when they appear to him later in dreams, increasingly out of touch with reality. (When the Father in *Six Characters in Search of an Author* speaks of the "disaster it is for a character to be born in the imagination of an author who then refuses to give him life," Pirandello, like Brecht, presents the audience with a devastating image of divine impotence.)

The argument of the atheists that confounds the gods lies at the heart of Brecht's ideology: " 'The world must be changed because no one can *be* good and *stay* good.' " The gods don't want to be bothered, but only change will save the world. Wong himself, a beleaguered water seller, exemplifies the economic roots of human suffering. *The Good Woman of Setzuan* examines the failures of the capitalist system by focusing on the effort to support oneself by the sale of commodities; in this case, water and tobacco. Students will easily understand the contrast between the two, one essential to life, the other a narcotic. An extended discussion of the way each figures in the play can help you organize many of the ideas Brecht examines here.

The opening lines of the play lay out the law of supply and demand ("When water is scarce, I have long distances to go in search of it, and when it is plentiful, I have no income"). Only half-Westernized, Brecht's Setzuan does not boast a modern system of water supply. Wong lives in a "den in the sewer pipe down by the river," the site of the five dreams in which the gods appear to him. Civil engineering is sufficiently advanced to channel wastes that pollute the river, but indoor plumbing has not yet been provided for Setzuan. At the end of scene 1, Shen Te already sees how little refuge her tobacco shop will offer her and tellingly uses a watery image to express her consternation: "The little lifeboat is swiftly sent down / Too many men too greedily / Hold on to it as they drown." In scene 3, she meets her suicidal pilot on a rainy day in the park; using another watery metaphor, Yang Sun explains his friends' lack of concern:

> They don't want to hear I'm still unemployed. "What?" they ask. "Is there still water in the sea?"

There are too many mail pilots for them all to be employed, and illustrating the same universal law of oversupply, Shen Te weeps, adding water to the rainy day. Wong wanders through the park to sing "The Song of the Water Seller in the Rain," complaining that no one wants to buy water in the rain. Shen Te's goodness, however, compels her to buy a cup for Yang Sun, who has fallen asleep by the time she reaches him with this sustenance. And the audience has observed a series of lessons elucidating the economic imbalances that drive human beings to theft and suicide.

The tobacco shop thrives, however, once Shen Te's alter ego, Shui Ta, comes to stay. You may want to ask your students why Brecht chose tobacco and explore with them the reasons it sells better than life-sustaining water. Note how many of the stage directions indicate who smokes what, and how: no sooner has Shen Te opened her shop than the Unemployed Man comes to beg for a cigarette butt, scandalizing the wife of the "family of eight" listed in the dramatis personae, the parasitical past owners of a tobacco shop who will contribute the sacks of (apparently) stolen tobacco that ultimately make Shui Ta's fortune.

> WIFE   What nerve, begging for tobacco. [*Rhetorically.*] Why don't they ask for bread?
> UNEMPLOYED MAN   Bread is expensive.

In "The Song of the Smoke," sung by members of this greedy family of former tobacconists, the insubstantiality of smoke stands for the vacuity symbolized by the commodity they sold and the impossibility of being good in a world where there are no options for intelligence or goodness to succeed.

When Shui Ta arrives, in scene 2, he puts himself on the right side of the law by informing on the petty theft of baked goods by the son of the family of eight, magnanimously looking on while the policeman takes two cigars and puts them in his pocket. Shui Ta's ultimate success is signaled by his smoking of a cigar, a simple act with which an inventive actor can stop the show. In other words, tobacco products affirm social status and have long served as props on which self-doubting or self-aggrandizing smokers equally rely. More fundamentally, of course, you may analyze their addictive properties and the profound social dislocations they cause, exemplified here by the Unemployed Man's predicament.

Students today are likely to perceive the shadow of illegality that hovers over Shen Te's shop more quickly than Brecht's first audiences, for whom smoking had a carefully nurtured romantic aura. Ask your students what roles cigarettes play in films of the 1930s and '40s. Think of the uses of celebrities in advertising campaigns for cigarettes in the 1950s. Smoking has similarly been associated with artistic creativity (note the prominent cigar in Brecht's hand in Rudolf Schlichter's portrait of 1926, reproduced on the cover of *The Cambridge Companion to Brecht*). Nevertheless, *The Good Woman of Setzuan* clearly links tobacco with criminality. When the Husband and Wife of the family of eight drag in the sacks that they ask Shen Te to hide for them, they do so "furtively" and "cryptically," according to the stage directions. It is interesting to note that when Brecht adapted the play for a possible production in the United States, he changed the contents of these sacks to opium. In today's antitobacco climate, it should be easy for your students to see that the play, even in its original version, treats tobacco as a drug, a source of different fetishes and fascinations, the sort of item that an unscrupulous capitalist can turn to profit.

Once you have set up this conceptual background, you will probably want to talk about character, the dramatic element toward which students most naturally gravitate. You might begin by noting the perennial challenge that Brecht's protagonists present to audiences and performers. Despite his ability to imagine outsize theatrical personalities, his theoretical aim is to deflate them, to keep us from sympathizing with them. In his early sketches for *The Good Woman of Setzuan*, he is preoccupied with the pitfalls that await the actor who assumes the title role: "the girl must be a big powerful person," he writes, fearful that impersonating Shen Te as a delicate Chinese beauty will undercut his efforts.

Ask your students to give their opinions of the love story of Shen Te and Yang Sun. What is the attitude toward women here? Why does Shen Te fall in love with a suicidal pilot? How does Brecht use this kind of masochistic relationship, a staple of conventional romance narratives, to further his political agenda? Yang Sun's brutal explanation of his power over Shen Te is the cause of Shui Ta's momentary dropping of the mask in scene 5. He seems to be a total cad, and he will become a willing capitalist functionary in the tobacco factory (see "The Song of the Eighth Elephant"). Yet Brecht allows him to express just enough sentimental concern for Shen Te to keep her love for him from seeming utterly ridiculous. He claims to have bought two tickets to Peking, for example, at the abortive wedding celebration, but he is not above paying court to the landlady on behalf of the tobacco factory. Then again, he threatens to blackmail Shui Ta since his "interest in this young woman has not been officially terminated," but he speaks in Shui Ta's defense when he testifies that he has not killed his cousin, since he has heard Shen Te sobbing in the back room.

How genuine is Yang Sun's attachment to Shen Te? Brecht does not wish to portray complex, psychologically coherent characters; Yang Sun is full of contradictions, and different productions could show diametrically different versions of his romance with Shen Te. At no point, however, are we allowed to lose sight of the pilot's primary concern, which is for himself. Like every other human being—except the good half of the good woman of Setzuan—Yang Sun is ruled by his own self-interest.

Although Brecht did not live long enough to produce *The Good Woman of Setzuan* with the Berliner Ensemble, and therefore to tackle firsthand the paradoxical nature of the double character of Shen Te/Shui Ta, the list of actresses who have taken the role is impressive. In 1956, Uta Hagen and Peggy Ashcroft, two highly intelligent players with a wide emotional range, each a famous Desdemona but capable of tough and unsentimental acting, put their imprint on the role in the first productions in New York and London, respectively. Interestingly, Brecht did not consider casting the role with a man, in the style of the Chinese theater, although that might be an ideal solution to the dilemma he foresaw.

In order not to sentimentalize Shen Te it is helpful to remember what her occupation is. To the commodities for sale in the play, one must add the female body. Shen Te's goodness is not automatic, since before she can offer hospitality to the gods, she has to get rid of a client. And Wong's recommendation of Shen Te is, of course, a joke. She's a prostitute; "she *can't* say no." When she falls in love with Yang Sun, she has to put up with the casual insults that spring to his lips, even as he is about to throw a rope around the tree to hang himself. She enters the park as one of three whores to walk through it while the pilot seeks privacy; she has to insist that she has avoided the occupational hazard of being bowlegged and to defend herself against the charge of nymphomania:

YANG SUN   What do you know about love?
SHEN TE   Everything.
YANG SUN   Nothing. [*Pause*] Or d'you just mean you enjoyed it?

Prostitution for Brecht is just one more metaphor for life in a capitalist society. When the landlady, Mrs. Mi Tzu, talks of Shen Te with Shui Ta, she is about to call her a prostitute when the "cousin" intervenes: "Pauper. Let's use the uglier word." That word explains why persons—of whatever sex and in whatever manner—prostitute themselves. Brecht wants Shen Te to be a "big powerful person," a woman who can impersonate a man, not a tragic whore with a heart of gold. Remind your students of the significance of the play's German title, which is not gender specific: the title character in *Der Gute Mensch von Sezuan* endures the compromised existence that any person caught in the essential contradictions of the capitalist West must deal with. Presumably to inoculate the role against the threat of prettiness, Brecht has Shen Te immediately act on the suggestion of the hardened Husband and Wife that she has to learn to say no and that the easiest way to do that is to invent "some relative who insists on all accounts being strictly in order."

This device allows the playwright to have his cake and eat it too. It makes Shen Te/Shui Ta a virtuoso turn for a major actor, but splitting her/him into two halves runs the risk of obscuring the character's struggle. Shen Te, "The Angel of the Slums," whose name means *divine virtue*, is also the hard-nosed businessman, Shui Ta, whose name means *flood tide*. The image again is of water, here as a symbol of fate. As Shakespeare's Brutus says,

> There is a tide in the affairs of men
> Which, taken at the flood, leads on to fortune;
> Omitted, all the voyage of their life
> Is bound in shallows and in miseries.
> (*Julius Caesar* 4.3.216–20)

To succeed, one must be an opportunist. The Angel of the Slums is an opportunist; but because she puts on a mask that allows her to express the opportunistic side of her character as if it were someone else taking advantage of others' ill fortune (as Shui Ta does with the sacks of contraband tobacco), Brecht makes possible the very prettifying of Shen Te and divine virtue that he ostensibly sets out here to unmask.

Divine virtue is literally on trial in the final episode of *The Good Woman of Setzuan*. Courtroom scenes always make for good theater, and you may want to ask your students why this is so. In a way, the trial epitomizes Brecht's dramaturgy: out of the conflicting testimonies of accuser and accused, truth should emerge—and the observers must make a judgment. In Setzuan, as elsewhere, justice is easily bought and sold. Wong expresses delight when he sees who the new judges are, thinking that the power of the political establishment has been quelled now that the gods replace the pillars of the community whom Shu Fu and Shui Ta have corrupted. Note that Shui Ta is about to "open twelve super tobacco markets"; if you are so inclined, you may encourage your students to reflect on the recent decisions in suits brought against the major tobacco companies in the United States. Who profits? Who ultimately pays? How are strong rulings diluted when appeals courts review them? How do lobbyists influence tobacco legislation? Analyzing judicial and legislative politics would be an eminently Brechtian exercise.

Within the play itself, corruption is not so easily expunged. The divine judges have their own biases. To be sure, they show their independence of the ruling classes when they discount the rich barber's testimony in favor of the defendant:

SHU FU   Mr. Shui Ta is a businessman, my lord. Need I say more?
FIRST GOD   Yes.

But when the court is cleared and Shui Ta tears off his clothes and his masks and becomes Shen Te, the gods refuse to hear or understand or help her. Brecht insists that it is up to us to fix the problems that conventional bourgeois religion and politics sweep under the rug. Directly addressing the audience in the epilogue, Shen Te bluntly asks if the world can be changed.

> You write the happy ending to the play!
> There must, there must, there's got to be a way!

Topics for Writing

1. Brecht called *The Good Woman of Setzuan* a parable, the formal genre that Jesus used for teaching his disciples. How would you characterize the theological content of *The Good Woman of Setzuan*? What kind of religious questions does Shen Te's life raise?
2. Why does Shen Te fall in love with Yang Sun? Do her feelings for him demonstrate her essential goodness?

3. What view of women emerges from the splitting of the good person of Setzuan into male and female halves? How would you compare Shen Te to the other female characters in the play?
4. Discuss the songs in this play, explaining how they relate to the scenes in which they are sung.
5. Give as many examples as possible to demonstrate the view of capitalism expressed in this play. Do you think Brecht fairly presents the workings of a modern economic system?

Comparative Perspectives

1. Compare the descriptions of poverty offered in Swift's *Modest Proposal* and Brecht's *Good Woman of Setzuan*, and the solutions proposed in each. How do you think each writer would react to the other's work?
2. Compare the trial scene in *Billy Budd* to that in Brecht's play. How is Melville's approach to his material fundamentally different from Brecht's? How is judicial practice represented in each case? What definitions of goodness are at stake?

Further Reading

See also the reading suggestion in the *Anthology*, p. 2549.

Bartram, Graham, and Anthony Waine, eds. *Brecht in Perspective.* 1982. A collection of thirteen essays on historical, literary, and theatrical perspectives, including a discussion of Brecht's legacy for German dramatists and the English theater.

Brecht, Bertolt. *Collected Plays.* Annot. and ed., John Willett and Ralph Manheim. 1970 and continuing. In the English edition, published by Methuen, volume 6.i (1985) contains *The Good Person in Szechwan* (not the translation in use here). The introduction and notes differ somewhat from those in the American edition; sparse but extremely valuable, they are worth seeking out.

Brustein, Robert. *The Theater of Revolt.* 1964. The chapter on Brecht is particularly well written and enlightening.

The Drama Review 12, 1 (Fall 1967). A special Brecht issue.

Eaton, Katherine Bliss. *The Theater of Meyerhold and Brecht.* 1985. Considers Brecht's relationship to "epic theater" and twentieth-century experimental theater techniques.

Fuegi, John. *Bertolt Brecht: Chaos, According to Plan.* 1987. Provides a general view of Brecht's work with actors in concrete theatrical situations.

Gray, Ronald. *Bertolt Brecht.* 1961. A good short introduction.

Kiebuzinska, Christine Olga. *Revolutionaries in the Theater: Meyerhold, Brecht, and Witkiewicz.* 1988.

Lug, Sieglinde. "The 'Good' Woman Demystified." *Communications from the International Brecht Society* 14, 1 (November 1984): 3–16. Uses a feminist approach in discussing three plays by Brecht.

Pike, David. *Lukács and Brecht.* 1985. Discusses the famous Brecht-Lukács debate over experimental versus conventionally realistic form.

Willett, John. *The Theatre of Bertolt Brecht: A Study of Eight Aspects.* 1959. Very good on theatrical influences and stage practice, with a useful discussion of Brecht's use of music.

———. *Brecht in Context: Comparative Approaches.* 1984. Diverse interdisciplinary topics.

Witt, Hubert, ed. *Brecht as They Knew Him.* Trans. John Peet. 1974. Short memoirs of Brecht.

Wright, Elizabeth. *Postmodern Brecht: A Re-representation.* 1989. A valuable study that rejects period-oriented views of Brecht's career and demonstrates the continuing importance of his theoretical pieces and early works.

FEDERICO GARCÍA LORCA

Lament for Ignacio Sánchez Mejías

Backgrounds

The most internationally famous Spanish writer since Cervantes, Federico García Lorca is a poet of myth, of emotion, of rhythmic language, of the earth. His visionary poetry and his death at the hands of Franco's militia have already made him a symbol of the artist's opposition to the sterility of the modern industrial West and to the impersonal repressions of the fascist police state. Lorca's imaginative roots reach into the past and the countryside: into the folklore and folk imagery, gypsy legends, ballad rhythms, and pastoral landscape of his native Andalusia. He maintains the mysterious life of nature and the subconscious in the midst of a highly civilized—perhaps overcivilized—society and seems to speak directly from the life of his dreams and personal emotions. To a reader of Spanish, Lorca's lyric rhythms and the dense network of his allusive imagery compose a poetic voice unique in modern literature.

Death is the central theme in *Lament for Ignacio Sánchez Mejías*, as it is in all of Lorca's work. One critic calls him "the poet of death" and notes that Spain has an ancient popular tradition of the "culture of death," which Lorca continually, and naturally, exploits. The bull has long been the characteristic symbol of death in Spain—as in other Mediterranean cultures—and in the *Lament* it possesses the terrors of darkness that gather around the finality that everyone must face. The confrontation with death is, for Lorca, at its most impressive and spectacular in the bullfight: the "greatest poetic and human treasure of Spain" and "the most cultured pastime in the world today; it is pure drama . . . the only place where one can go and with certainty see death surrounded by the most astonishing beauty."

In *Lament*, bulls and bullfighting, death and the spilling of blood permeate every passage, and Sánchez Mejías's death takes on the power of a religious sacrifice. In section 1, "Cogida and Death," the bull invades Sánchez Mejías's body ("a thigh with a desolate horn. . . Now the bull was bellowing through his forehead") and the images of the bull ring merge with those of the hospital ("the bull ring was covered in iodine") in which Sánchez Mejías lies dying. In section 2, "The Spilled Blood," Lorca invokes the bulls of Guisando, "partly death and partly stone," which bellow "like two centuries / sated with treading the earth." Later in the same section, as the moment of the goring approaches, "secret voices" shout to "celestial bulls." Overseeing all is the "cow of the ancient world"—mother of bulls, mother of men—who passes her "sad tongue / over a snout of blood / spilled on the sand."

For Sánchez Mejías, as for Lorca, the bullfight is like a religious ceremony in which priest and congregation alike take part: he has gone "up the tiers / with all his death on his shoulders" and spilled his blood before "a thirsty multitude." The blood—always a symbol of vitality and passion in Lorca's work (the "nightingale of his veins!")—is the medium of sacrifice, a blood so marvelous and potent "no chalice can contain it."

In section I, the poet encounters the moment of death at the instant of its happening. Section 2 presents his rejection of it ("No. . . . I will not see it!") and his simultaneous attempt to universalize it: to give it a meaning beyond itself. In section 3, "The Laid Out Body," the poet attempts to come to grips with death, to accommodate its finality. The section is calmer, more resigned, less hyperbolic. The poet encounters the niggardly meanness of death and asks for answers. There are none, and his final claim—"even the sea dies!"—is cold consolation.

The elegiac occasion gives full play to Lorca's mythmaking, surrealistic imagination. That he called it a lament assures us, says one critic, that it will depend heavily on Lorca's personal emotions. And indeed, though Sánchez Mejías is always at the center of the poem, forever praised, its most powerful presence is the despairing and urgent voice of the speaker. It is through the speaker's impassioned response and poetic insistence, his ability to involve the bullfighter in a larger drama of universal feeling, that Sánchez Mejías will be remembered. He may well have been "a great torero in the ring" and a "good peasant in the sierra," but only the poet can make his strength "like a river of lions" and his blood sing "along marshes and meadows." In section 4, "Absent Soul," Lorca recognizes the oblivion to which death consigns us, how in death we are forgotten "in a heap of lifeless dogs." And so the poet must sing in an effort to defeat oblivion, even though he knows that his song will be but "a sad breeze through the olive trees."

Ignacio Sánchez Mejías was severely gored in Manzanares on August 11, 1934, and died two days later in Madrid. He was one of the most eminent bullfighters in Spain at the time and a man of surprising

talent as a dramatist. His intellectual interests were wide-ranging, a fact
that no doubt contributed to Lorca's powerful sense of loss upon his
death.

The bullfight—in which the bullfighter quite literally faces death in a
mounting sequence of dangerous ritual actions—and the *cante jondo*,
the traditional music of Andalusia, are the primary cultural influences
on *Lament*. In one of the most famous of his essays, Lorca attempted to
find the essence, the "marrow of forms," of successful art in the "dark
sounds" of what the Andalusians call *duende*, the "spirit of the earth,"
the "mysterious power that everyone feels but that no philosopher has
explained":

> The *duende* is a power and not a behavior, it is a struggle and not a concept. I
> have heard an old guitarist master say: "The *duende* is not in the throat; the
> *duende* surges up from the soles of the feet." It is not a matter of ability, but
> of real live form; of blood; of ancient culture; of creative action.

It was in his native culture, in its traditional forms and feelings, that
Lorca located the *duende* he wanted to infuse into his own verse.

Classroom Strategies

Lament for Ignacio Sánchez Mejías can be taught in one class period.
You may wish to compare Lorca with other poets—Rilke, Stevens, and
Baudelaire come to mind—to suggest the range of modern poetry and
poetics. Students who are able to read the original Spanish passages
printed in the text should be encouraged to read aloud to the class and
to comment on any rhythmic effects or verbal associations that they feel
are lost in translation.

In general, American students will have little understanding of the bullfight as such. The bullfight is *not* a sport; it is a ritual. For Lorca's poem, it
is the basis from which the action starts, like the appearance of the ghost
in *Hamlet* or Agamemnon's sacrifice of his daughter Iphigenia in the
Oresteia. Students will be impressed with the play of Lorca's imagination
over the event. They will also be impressed by the way the poem follows
the stages that psychologists say all of us go through when we encounter
death: recognition, refusal, questioning, resignation, and acceptance.

They may not always be able to "follow" the language line by line.
Lorca's use of archetypal and Spanish imagery in the loosely connected
way associated with surrealism will be especially obscure for many. But
one of the extraordinary powers of surreal imagery is that it becomes
more effective as it accumulates. Surrealism exists to locate and make
articulate that place where the conscious intellect cannot go. Lorca's
surrealism works in the sense that it soaks in before it is questioned.

Because each section of the poem is different in form and tone, it
helps to discuss them separately. With the refrain of section 1 students
will be on familiar ground, not necessarily from Andalusian gypsy ballads, but from contemporary popular music, where again the refrain

serves as a kind of "hook" to arrest the listener's attention. Section 2 is probably for most students the most immediately accessible; Lorca's refusal to "see" his friend's spilled blood is simultaneously poignant and insistent. For students who are having difficulty with the poem, concentration on section 2 will help define its tone, demonstrate its emotional power, and clarify its surrealistic mode of meaning.

Topics for Discussion and Writing

1. Why is the death of a bullfighter a particularly appropriate occasion for Lorca's lament about death in general?
   [See the second paragraph of "Backgrounds" and the Lorca head-note.]

2. How does Lorca use images of bulls in the poem? What do they suggest? What other important images are connected with bulls?
   [See the third and fourth paragraphs of "Backgrounds." You might also wish to point out the way Lorca associates the moon (traditionally female, like the "ancient cow" of section 2, and connected with notions of fate) with bulls. Critics have noticed that the moon, its crescent shape perhaps suggesting the bull's horns, presides "with a fatal glow" over Sánchez Mejías's death.]

3. Is any logical organization apparent in the poem? If so, what is it? How does it bear upon the central theme of death?
   [See the second paragraph of "Classroom Strategies" as well as the headnote.]

4. What are the conventions of the elegy in poetry? In what ways is this a traditional elegy? In what ways does it differ from the traditional elegy?

5. What is *duende*? Does this poem have it?

6. Compare Lorca's attitude toward death with that of García Márquez in *Death Constant beyond Love*.

7. If you read Spanish, you may wish to read aloud or compare passages from the translation with the section of the original text given in the anthology. You may also encourage students to try reading the original text on their own and to comment on the way the translation has or has not succeeded in grasping the original. Some of the bolder ones may attempt their own translations, which will bring them closer to the text and, at the same time, induce a healthy respect for the difficulties of translation.

Comparative Perspectives

From the beginning of time, poets have sought ways to come to terms with violent death. García Lorca's poem may usefully be compared to early epics, like *Gilgamesh* and the *Iliad*, in which the death of an exemplary friend fuels passionate mourning and desperate action. What issues that concern Gilgamesh and Achilles obsess the speaker here as well? By what means does the modern poet distill such intensity of feeling into 221 lines?

See also comparisons suggested with Tennyson's *In Memoriam A. H. H.*, Rilke's *Archaic Torso of Apollo*, and Akhmatova's *Requiem*.

Further Reading

See also the reading suggestion in the *Anthology*, p. 2552.

Adams, Mildred. *García Lorca: Playwright and Poet*. 1984. Fuller general study.

Allen, Rupert C. *The Symbolic World of Federico García Lorca*. 1972.

Binding, Paul. *Lorca: The Gay Imagination*. 1985.

Colecchia, Francesca. *García Lorca: An Annotated Bibliography of Criticism*. 1979. A guide to reference material before 1979.

Cannon, Calvin. "Lorca's 'Llanto por Ignacio Sanchez Mejias' and the Elegiac Tradition." *Hispanic Review* 31 (1963): 229–38. Demonstrates the *Lament's* place in the tradition of the classical elegy.

Davies, Catherine, and Garry Marvin. "Control of the Wild in Andalusian Culture: Bull and Horse Imagery in Lorca from an Anthropological Perspective." *Neophilologus* 71, 4 (October 1987): 543–58.

Gershator, David, ed. *Selected Letters*. 1983.

Londre, Felicia Hardison. *Federico García Lorca*. 1984. Fuller general study.

Lorca, Federico García. "Theory and Function of the *Duende*." In *The Poetics of the New American Poetry*, ed. Donald M. Allen and Warren Tallman. 1973. One of Lorca's most important prose statements, it provides great insight into what Lorca is after in his work.

Lorca, Francisco García. *In the Green Morning: Memories of Federico*. Trans. Christopher Maurer. 1986.

Loughran, David K. *Federico García Lorca: The Poetry of Limits*. 1978.

MacCurdy, Grant G. *Federico García Lorca: Life, Work and Criticism*. 1986. Brief overview.

Morris, C. Brian. *"Cuando yo me muera . . .": Essays in Memory of Federico García Lorca*. 1988. Collects seventeen papers from a symposium on Lorca; the essays are chiefly in English while the poetry is cited in Spanish.

Oppenheimer, Helen. *Lorca, the Drawings: Their Relation to the Poet's Life and Work*. 1986. Reproduces drawings from different periods in the poet's life along with valuable commentary on their historical context and personal significance; appendixes contain Lorca's slide lecture entitled "Thoughts on Modern Art" and a film script.

Rees, Margaret A., ed. *Leeds Papers on Lorca and on Civil War Verse*. 1988.

Salinas, Pedro. "Lorca and the Poetry of Death." In *Lorca: A Collection of Critical Essays*, ed. Manuel Duran. 1962. Pp. 100–107. Discusses Lorca and the Spanish "culture of death."

Stanton, Edward. *The Tragic Myth: Lorca and the Cante Jondo.* 1978. See pp. 46–51 for a short but persuasive discussion of bulls, bullfighting, and native Andalusian traditions as mythic elements in Lorca's work, especially *Lament.*

JORGE LUIS BORGES

The Garden of Forking Paths

Backgrounds

Borges is perhaps the most extraordinary labyrinth-maker in contemporary literature. For him everything—the nature of time, of space, of knowledge, of the self, of literary form—is problematic. He looks at the world as a "puzzle" that compels examination even while it resists solution. Nothing can be proved, but nothing can be disproved. Borges combines his immense narrative skill with the qualities of a metaphysician, fantasist, scholar, detective writer, theologian, and ironist. He is very much like the metaphysicians in one of his own fictional places, Tlön, who "seek neither truth nor likelihood; they seek astonishment." In all of his major stories, Borges is intent upon making a coherent fictional world almost entirely out of his intelligence and out of his imagination playing over other intelligences.

The Garden of Forking Paths is a detective story, but one in which the reader, finally, is the detective and time is the solution of the mystery. On the level of plot, the story is reasonably simple: Yu Tsun, a Chinese spy grudgingly working for the Germans during World War I, has to transmit an important message to his chief in Berlin. Since Yu Tsun's identity has been discovered by the British, he must transmit the message before he is caught, and he must do so without letting the British know he has done it. He travels to a suburb of London, to the house of a sinologist named Stephen Albert. Yu Tsun and Albert discuss the nature of a manuscript written by Ts'ui Pên, one of Yu Tsun's ancestors, and then Yu Tsun shoots Albert, who dies instantaneously. In the last paragraph we discover the reason for Yu Tsun's actions: the message he must convey to Berlin is the name of a French city the Germans must attack. The city's name is Albert, and by killing a man of that name Yu Tsun both fulfills his mission and condemns himself to be captured and, ultimately, hanged.

The story, however, is full of coincidences, analogies between characters, and resonances and suggestions of ideas that are more important than the simple plot. The central idea of the story is the labyrinth, which is both the story's subject and its structure. The labyrinth is presented in a number of ways: an actual labyrinthlike walk through English suburban life that Yu Tsun takes on his way to Albert's house; the literary labyrinth constructed by Yu Tsun's ancestor, Ts'ui Pên; and the formal labyrinth of Borges's story itself. The implications of all three are the same: to suggest the infinite possibilities—the "various futures"—of any human action in time, and the consequent shrinkage in the importance of that action when we think of it as just one possible outcome among many. Borges presents a fictional reality that has as its center the death of Stephen Albert at the hands of Yu Tsun, but he implies that there are other conceivable centers, other possible dimensions, other possible times. As Albert tells Yu Tsun, "We do not exist in the majority of these times; in some you exist, and not I; in others I, and not you; in others, both of us. In the present one, which a favorable fate has granted me, you have arrived at my house; in another, while crossing the garden, you found me dead; in still another, I utter these same words, but I am a mistake, a ghost." The story refutes the notion of present time as the only one that contains "reality" and, therefore, the only significant time.

The Garden of Forking Paths effectively blurs most of the categories we use to "know" the world—especially the distinction between reality and fiction. The story begins with Borges blurring the traditional distinctions between author, narrator, and character. We are told in no uncertain terms by someone who appears to be the author of a historical essay that on "page 22 of Liddell Hart's *History of World War I*" we will read about a particular military attack, "planned for the 24th of July, 1916," which had to be postponed until the morning of the 29th because of "torrential rains." The scholarly authority of the voice in this opening passage—the voice of the historian—suggests that the information delivered belongs to the world of fact, outside of fiction altogether. Further, the matter-of-fact authority of this narrative voice tends to make the sections that follow, consisting entirely—except for a footnote—of Yu Tsun's narrative, into a revelation important only in that it "throws an unsuspected light" on the postponement of the battle. The "author" of the "essay" reveals no interest whatsoever in the extraordinary qualities of Yu Tsun's narrative.

If we look at Liddell Hart's book, we find that what our "scholar" says is not what Liddell Hart reports: there was such a battle, but there is no mention of its postponement, and the torrential rains did not fall until November. The "author," then, is as much a fiction as Yu Tsun, Stephen Albert, Captain Richard Madden, Ts'ui Pên, or any other character in the story. Even the "editor," presumably the "editor" of the "journal" that published our "author's" scholarly revelation, is exposed as simply another character in Borges's story when he is offended by Yu Tsun's version of Viktor Runeberg's death and then proceeds to comment authoritatively on the "real" events behind that death. The language is heavily loaded: on the one hand, the German agent is identified as a "Prussian spy" who "attacked with drawn automatic," and his opponent is identified both as "Captain" and "the bearer of a warrent" acting in self-defense; moreover, he did not actually kill Runeberg but merely "inflicted a wound" that led to death. Who is to say whether Yu Tsun or the editor is closer to the truth? What we have, then, is a fictional editor taking offense at a fictional account of a fictional death of a fictional spy in a footnote to a fictional historical essay called *The Garden of Forking Paths* written by a fictional author who was created by Jorge Luis Borges in a piece of fiction called *The Garden of Forking Paths*.

The ramifications of Borges's story lead us back to the relation between historical events and historical narratives of those events, that is, between reality and fiction. Borges suggests that Liddell Hart left out something important when he rendered the battle of July 24, 1916, in his history of World War I. And of course he did. Liddell Hart, like any historian, must leave out more than he puts in; he must make selections based on his own fallible interpretation of what is significant and what is not in the series of events he presents as historical "fact." Historians, then, are writers of fiction who use their intelligence and imagination to create a coherent narrative based on reality. The "reality" of that battle ended when it ended; what is left of it is in books like Liddell Hart's or further emendations like Yu Tsun's tale and even a biased footnote. The disorder and contingency of reality have been replaced by fiction.

Unlike that of almost all of the other major writers of Latin America—Gabriel García Márquez, Pablo Neruda, Carlos Fuentes, Alejandro Carpentier, Cesar Vallejo, and so on—Borges's work appears to be adamantly apolitical. (This despite the fact that Borges was briefly a cause célèbre in the 1940s because of his public opposition to Peron.) His life was devoted to books, to writing them, reading them, even cataloging them, and since his early years—when he was much interested in Argentina's past and its folk literature—his mind has taken up residence in a country without national boundaries. In *The Argentine Writer and Tradition*, Borges argues that the real Argentine tradition is "all of Western culture. . . . Our patrimony is the universe."

Although Borges's reputation in Argentina stresses his poetry rather than his fiction, his influence on contemporary fiction has been exceptional. Almost every postmodernist writer is in some way in Borges's debt.

Classroom Strategies

You will probably want to begin by disentangling the plot and Borges's narrative strategy, and then proceed to disentangle the implications of the plot and the implications of that narrative. At some point, you might draw a "tree" formation on the board (which mathematics and linguistics students will immediately recognize) to illustrate how various alternative possibilities can exist simultaneously. Students usually enjoy hearing the ancient Chinese riddle about the man who dreamed he was a butterfly dreaming he was a man—who woke up. The question then follows: who is he? Is he a butterfly dreaming he is a man (who was dreaming he was a butterfly) who has just awakened, or . . .

The Garden of Forking Paths is the kind of story that can make students' heads hurt. Encourage them to see its playing with reality as part of modern literary techniques as in Kafka's *The Metamorphosis*, for example, or Pirandello's *Six Characters in Search of an Author*. You may want to draw comparisons with later modern works, such as Julio Cortázar's *Hopscotch*, in which the reader is invited to rearrange the order of chapters, or John Fowles's *The French Lieutenant's Woman*, which includes different endings from which the reader may choose. Emphasizing the detective-story qualities of the piece, or noting that it bears significant resemblances to many science-fiction stories (stories about parallel times or alternate worlds, for instance), will also help your students enjoy *The Garden of Forking Paths* before they begin to worry about whether they have completely understood it. On the other hand, one of the things that differentiates Borges's piece from a typical piece of science fiction is the economy and complexity of the narrative. Only a few pages long, the story nevertheless dizzies the reader with continually expanding implications and suggestions. You will find that an exploration of the way Borges uses analogies—between events and between characters—makes his narrative economy more evident. The various kinds of labyrinths suggested by the story have already been noted, and the analogies between them should be obvious. The following are also worth noting:

1. Ts'ui Pên was murdered by a stranger, just as Stephen Albert, the only person to decipher Ts'ui Pên's novel, will be.
2. Ts'ui Pên closed himself up for thirteen years in the Pavilion of Limpid Solitude to write his novel, and Stephen Albert greets Yu Tsun by saying "I see that the pious Hsi P'êng persists in correcting my solitude."
3. Albert reads a section from Ts'ui Pên's novel that has to do with armies marching to battle. He also tries to explain the implications of the novel by describing a scene in which a stranger calls at a man's door and, in one possible outcome, kills him.
4. Stephen Albert—a Westerner who is ostensibly Yu Tsun's enemy— restores the good name of Yu Tsun's ancestor, while Yu Tsun—an Easterner who teaches the languages of the West—kills Albert to prove to his Chief that "the innumerable ancestors" who merge within him are worthy of respect. "I wanted," says Yu Tsun, "to prove to him that a yellow man could save his armies."
5. Yu Tsun, like his ancestor Ts'ui Pên, is faced with transmitting a message. Both must do so through indirection. Paradoxically, Ts'ui Pên invents something traditionally made for the many—a novel— that can be decoded by only one, while Yu Tsun invents for one— the Chief—by addressing the many through the newspapers.
6. Yu Tsun and Richard Madden are paired as spy and counterspy, but both are distrusted aliens who must prove themselves to their chiefs.

Borges and I

Ideally, students will come to this story in a unit on "postmodernism," "the avant garde," or "experimental fiction." Regardless, the story depends on a reader's familiarity with a basic premise about fiction: the author and the author's character are distinct. The author is a real person in the real world while the character is a made-up artificial construct. This story plays devilishly with that basic premise. The "I" of the story *is* the author but he is also just another character, too. In other words, the story plays a mind-game with readers when it asks readers to take seriously the idea that all personae—even so-called autobiographical ones—are just characters in a fiction. If one were to pursue that line of thought, one would have to ask: What if the author was himself just another character? What if every time the author wrote "I" he was, in fact, giving life to a new being? What if, in fact, authors were like the ancient Greek and Roman gods, giving life to their creations even when those beings carry their own names? The "I" in this story is the first-person entity that Borges has all his life employed in his writing, but this time it has at long last come to consciousness specifically in order to rebuke its master.

Profound questions arise from this simple story-puzzle. First, is it possible to say that one's "writing self" is different from one's "talking self"? Contemporary psychoanalytic theory says that the answer is yes. Second, is there such a thing as a soul, a detached essence that might be different from our conscious sense of self? Similar questions are asked in Cavafy's poetry.

Classroom Strategies

Have the students discuss the philosophical issues here with regard not just to Borges but to any of the writers read in the past few class sessions. Most intriguingly, discuss the way in which it is possible for a story to have a life of its own outside an author's intention. We all know it is possible for a story to mean something an author does not intend, but does that mean the story has a personality—a soul? What might identity *be* for an artist?

Topics for Discussion and Writing

1. Discuss the ways Borges uses the labyrinth as the central idea and image of *The Garden of Forking Paths*.
   [See the third paragraph of "Backgrounds."]
2. Discuss the implications of Borges's narrative technique in *The Garden of Forking Paths*. Who is the narrator? In what guise does he present himself? How does Borges blur the traditional distinctions between author, narrator, and character in *The Garden of Forking Path* and "*Borges & I*?
   [See "Backgrounds" as well as "Classroom Strategies." for both stories.]
3. Discuss analogies between characters and between events in *The Garden of Forking Paths*.
   [See the third paragraph of "Backgrounds" as well as "Classroom Strategies."]

4. What kinds of questions does Borges raise in *The Garden of Forking Paths* about the nature of time?

    [See the third paragraph of "Backgrounds."]

5. What relationship between reality and fiction is suggested in *The Garden of Forking Paths*? What conclusions might we draw about the writing of history?

    [See the fourth, fifth, and sixth paragraphs of "Backgrounds."]

6. What clues are given at the beginning of *The Garden of Forking Paths* and how are we misled by them?

    [The name of the person "capable of transmitting the message" is usually interpreted as the name of another agent. The single bullet in Yu Tsun's revolver may suggest that he will commit suicide if captured. Generally overlooked is the fact that the Chief in Berlin spends his time "endlessly examining newspapers" while waiting for his agents' reports.]

7. How does Borges base *The Garden of Forking Paths* in observable documentary facts in order to lend solidity to the idea of alternate worlds?

    [See, in addition of Liddell Hart's book, the following references: the actual town of Albert, located on the Ancre River (near the Somme) and therefore close to the bloodiest battles of World War I; the existing counties of Staffordshire (western England) and Fenton (eastern England); the German writer Goethe (see the anthology); the Latin author Tacitus; a famous Chinese novel, the *Hung Lu Meng* (*The Story of the Stone*); *The Thousand and One Nights* (Vol. 1 of the anthology); recognized pottery styles and a real (though lost) encyclopedia from the Ming Dynasty; physicist Isaac Newton and philosopher Arthur Schopenhauer.]

8. Discuss the questions raised in the last paragraph of the first section of *Borges and I*.

Comparative Perspectives

1. Dr. Yu Tsun arranges his complicated exploit "to prove . . . that a yellow man could save" the armies of a "barbarous country" that held his "race" in contempt. Within this brilliant parody we hear a serious note that links Yu Tsun to many characters in the anthology who are painfully conscious that others consider them inferior beings. How would you compare Yu Tsun's announced motive to that of Sor Juana or of Frederick Douglass? Compare the moral vantage points from which these different writers address the fact of cultural difference.

2. Stephen Albert's elucidation of the novelistic method he discerns in Ts'ui Pên's "garden of forking paths" is more than a witty postmodernist conceit. Over the past few years, hypertext fiction has put exactly such forking paths at the fingertips of computer-using readers who choose the turns they wish to take and thereby determine the outcome of the story, allowing it to mutate constantly at

their wills. Similar experiments have been made with films that viewers control from handsets embedded in the arms of the seats in theaters. Read the opening of Lucian's *A True Story* (in Vol. 1 of the *Anthology*), if possible, or Paul Eluard's *To Be Caught in One's Own Trap*. How do such texts prefigure these technological devices? Why are the tales of *The Thousand and One Nights* also mentioned in Borges's story? What perceptions concerning the nature of reality may make authors shrink from exercising too much "authority" over their creations?

Further Reading

See also the reading suggestions in the *Anthology*, p. 2549.

Alazraki, Jaime. *Borges and the Kabbalah*. 1988. A collection of essays on various aspects of the writer's fiction and poetry.

Balderston, Daniel, ed. *The Literary Universe of Jorge Luis Borges: An Index to References and Allusions to Persons, Titles and Places in His Writings*. 1986.

Bell-Villada, *Gene H. Borges and His Fiction*. 1981. A particularly useful discussion of Borges's use of simultaneous times in *The Garden of Forking Paths*. See especially pp. 93–96.

Bloom, Harold, ed. *Jorge Luis Borges*. 1986. Fifteen essays by different scholars and a chronology.

Borges, Jorge Luis. *Other Inquisitions, 1937–1952*. Trans. Ruth L. C. Simms. 1964. Discussions of *The Garden of Forking Paths* will be aided by reading *A New Refutation of Time* and *The Argentine Writer and Tradition*.

Burgin, Richard. *Conversations with Jorge Luis Borges*. 1969. A useful discussion of Borges by Borges.

Foster, David William. *Jorge Luis Borges: An Annotated Primary and Secondary Bibliography*. 1984.

di Giovanni, Norman Thomas. *In Memory of Borges*. 1988. Seven essays, including a 1983 address by Borges on his work and an anecdotal essay by di Giovanni as Borges's translator.

Rimmon-Kenan, Shlomith. "Doubles and Counterparts: Patterns of Interchangeability in Borges' 'The Garden of Forking Paths.' " *Critical Inquiry* 6, 4 (Summer 1980): 639–47. An interesting discussion of Borges's use of analogies between characters and between events in the story.

Rodriguez-Monegal, Emir. *Jorge Luis Borges: A Literary Biography*. 1978. The only full-length biography of Borges in English.

PABLO NERUDA

Backgrounds

Pablo Neruda was an extremely prolific poet and he had a remarkably wide range of subjects and styles. If there is one consistent note throughout his work, it is in the wild abundance of the things that he sees and can describe in totally unorthodox and original ways. Several critics have pointed to Neruda's admiration for Walt Whitman. Certainly, he shares with Whitman a penchant for cataloging everything as well as an endlessly inventive management of the poetic line. Both their openness to all experience and their transcendence of academic form may be understood as profoundly democratic. These traits also pose a tremendous challenge, to Neruda as to Whitman and ultimately to the reader. Our goal is to find coherence in this abundance by defining the sensibility that notices and celebrates so much, so often seemingly at random. It will be important to reassure your students that they need not "get" every word, or even every line. Probably Neruda himself would have been hard-pressed to deliver a lucid exegesis of every one of his poems. Better to try to identify in each piece where the speaker has situated himself and why he notices the things of which he writes. Finally, even in English translation, readers should allow themselves to be swept up in the flow of imagery and sound, to feel as well as think. (Indeed, this advice should be a constant in our efforts to teach verse.)

Tonight I Can Write

Your students will probably be familiar at this point in the semester with the Romantic arguments about the relative claims of art and nature. This early poem finds the speaker caught between his one-time love for a woman he has lost—his natural feelings—and his artistic curiosity about how to write verses about that love. Can one separate the lover from the poet? The poem begins with the writer's preoccupation: "Tonight I can write the saddest lines." What are the saddest lines? Only by trying them out can be discover. How about "The night is shattered / and the blue stars shiver in the distance"? The love lost has a cosmic significance, we gather, and approximately, nature plays a dominant role in the poem: the endless sky has been shattered: the night wind sings; there are trees.

The poem veers between lines that capture the immensity of night, the backdrop for this love, and other lines in which the speaker seems to be taking his own emotional temperature. "I loved her, and sometimes she loved me too," he says, but then he tries again: "She loved me, sometimes I loved her too." The pain, however, seems less compelling than his effort to write about it. "I no longer love her, that's certain, but how I loved her." His "soul is not satisfied that it has lost her," yet poetry nurtures: "the verse falls to the soul like dew to the pasture."

The form mimics the speaker's tense indecisiveness in its elegant structure, which forestalls the luxury of sustained self-inquiry. It begins with a stanza of one line, then two, then another single line, before settling into its pattern of unrhymed but intricately patterned couplets that keep going back to the original premises, slightly altering them with each repetition. Nevertheless, the poem finds its conclusion: however unsatisfied his soul may be, he will move on. If she will be "Another's," these will be the last verses that he writes for her.

Walking Around

After the slender elegance of the first poem, we move on to new terrain. Here is twentieth-century man in a state of urban fatigue, rejecting the modern bourgeois world of tailor's shops and barber shops. Instead of the romantic night of *Tonight I Can Write* we have the mundane reality of merchandise, elevators, and shoes. The third and fourth lines announce a poetic crisis. The speaker is desiccated. Far from the symbolic equivalent of a shapely white bird, he is a simulacrum made of cheap materials: "a felt swan." Far from skimming a reviving sea, he is "navigating on a water of origin and ash," a densely packed image that recalls the stuff of which man was made in Genesis 2: life leads inevitably to ashes and dust, and highfalutin poetry cannot change that. (One translator captures that sense of poetic irrelevance by rendering this line "awash on an ocean of therefores and ashes.")

The speaker's malaise is more than that of a bored *flaneur*, strolling in a boring cityscape. It goes to the root of his art and his physical being. Everything is ennervating:

> It happens that I am tired of my feet and my nails
> and my hair and my shadow.
> It happens that I am tired of being a man.

For all that, in the delightful fourth stanza (the first of three six-line stanzas in a poem basically built of quatrains), the speaker is capable of relishing the idea of affronting the bourgeoisie. There is a Surrealistic touch to the deliberately provocative imagery here. A notary becomes a symbol of dull legalism: lacking a sense of beauty, "a cut lily" would scare him, as organized religion, in the person of a nun, could be knocked out with "one blow of an ear." Imagining himself on a rampage "through the streets with a green knife," the speaker takes comfort in the inherent menace of vital ("green") life in the face of the moribund surroundings he deplores.

The next stanzas, however, return to the hopelessness of his natural state: he imagines himself in downward motion, "a root in the dark . . . in the wet tripe of the earth," a tomb as well as a root, "a cellar full of corpses." Monday is singled out, the day that starts the week (ask your students if they ever cheerfully reflect. "Thank God it's Monday"). As the speaker conjures up grisly images of the quotidian city, you may want to mention J. Alfred Prufrock's depressed view of the cityscape he crosses as he moves toward—and then retreats from—the overwhelming question that he fears.

> And it [Monday] shoves me along to certain corners, to certain damp
> houses
>   to hospitals where the bones come out of the windows.
>   to certain cobblers' shops smelling of vinegar.
>   to streets horrendous as crevices.

Neruda's walker in the city ends with two long stanzas that describes an increasingly disgusting place. Passing hospitals confirms his "fury" and "forgetfulness." All around him he sees evidence of human weakness and bodily decrepitude that only affirms his previous disaffection with the feeble efforts people make to keep themselves functioning. Neruda presumably refers to the way tradespeople signal prospective customers with "birds the colour of sulphur, and horrible intestines [one translator says "tripe"] / hanging from the doors of the houses which I hate." This is the semiotics of shop owners who need no poetic vocabulary to advertise their wares. There are brilliant sequences in these stanzas, mixing categories and crossing boundaries of animate and inanimate, normal and grotesque. You should ask your students to explain the goads to "shame and horror" encountered on the speaker's stroll: "umbrellas all over the place, and poisons, and navels" or "orthopaedic appliances" and intimate laundry weeping "slow dirty tears." The speaker seems furious with himself for somehow being complicit with all the tawdry devices on which human dignity relies: after all, he is wearing shoes.

I'm Explaining a Few Things

The point of view in *I'm Explaining a Few Things* is chillingly clear. The arresting opening lines dare the reader to complain that the poem doesn't seem poetic: "where are the lilacs?" Now the bourgeois images that engendered disgust in *Walking Around* become gauges to measure what has been lost in the first attacks of Franco's forces on the innocent people of Republican Spain. Neruda's virtuosic management of form—the varying length of stanzas, the strategic placement of half lines, the incantatory voice—all converge to make this a fiercely powerful political and moral statement. The deceptively calm description of suburban life, "with bells, / and clocks, and trees," with wonderful markets and flowers all around, is shattered in the sequence that begins "And one morning." Nor is this a merely personal response; Neruda here speaks as a poet among poets, the artistic conscience of a nation betrayed. He speaks to "Raul" Gonzalez Tunon, to "Rafael" Alberti, and to "Federico" García Lorca, anti-Fascist comrades, the second of whom had been exiled, the third of whom was to be executed.

It would be a good idea to examine a copy of Picasso's *Guernica* and ask your students to compare Picasso's visual depiction of the aerial bombing of Spanish cities with Neruda's furious apostrophe to the "Treacherous generals" who are worse than jackals. The Surrealistic quality of the painter's and the poet's images deserves detailed discussion. Traditional verse forms break down in the face of this enormity. Out of the death of children, a terrible retribution is sure to come:

> from every socket of Spain
> Spain emerges
> from every dead child a rifle with eyes
> and from every crime bullets are born
> which will one day find
> the bull's eye of your hearts.

The simple repetitions of the final stanza would overwhelm anyone with a conscience. But the wrong people were listening.

General Song: The Heights of Macchu Picchu

This meditation on a lost civilization was written in August and September, 1945—in the aftermath of the bombing of Hiroshima and Nagasaki. Neruda actually made the ascent to the heights of Macchu Picchu described here in the fall of 1943. The opening lines of the selection follow him up "the ladder of the earth," a literal description of the incised steps that ascend the cliff. The term may also be a deliberate reminder of Dante's climb out of the Inferno, for we are on a visionary journey to weigh the sins and the accomplishments of the past. (Note that Dante and Virgil pull themselves up by grasping the hair of Lucifer "as a ladder" in a poem divided, like Neruda's, into Cantos [*Inferno.* Canto XXXIV.119].)

Macchu Picchu was a pre-Columbian fortress, but it was more than a military redoubt. The Inca site was built in the mid-fifteenth century and escaped the Spanish Conquest that began in 1532. An architectural symbol of a complex culture, it was raised "like a chalice in the hands / of all" (VII.23). While you are studying Neruda's poem, it would be interesting to have your students read a few excerpts from the *Popol Vuh*, a document produced by the inhabitants of another high citadel that did not escape conquest. Neruda's imagination of the making and inhabitation of Macchu Picchu echoes many of the terms of the Quiche epic. Neruda begins with a kind of creation myth, as does the *Popol Vuh*:

> This was the dwelling, this is the site:
> here the full kernels of corn rose
> and fell again like red hailstones. (VI.13–15)

Life in these early South and Meso-American cities blended ritual and sacrifice, agriculture and war. These interwoven activities capture the imagination here:

> Here the golden fiber emerged from the vicuna,
> to cloth love, tombs, mothers,
> the king, prayers, warriors. . . .
> I behold vestiments and hands. . . . (VI.16–18, 25)

The speaker's Whitmanesque greeting to his "brother" in Canto XII recalls the work of the artisans who are the gods of the Maya "Bible"— "Maker, Modeler . . . Bearer, Begetter" (in Dennis Tedlock's translation) and who were engaged in the same crafts that Neruda salutes:

> laborer, weaver, silent herdsman:
> tamer of the tutelary guanacos:
> mason of the defied scaffold:
> bearer of the Andean tears:
> jeweler with your fingers crushed:
> tiller trembling in the seed:
> potter split in your clay . . . (XII.9–15)

Where the Maya epic celebrates the arts and crafts by attributing to the multiple Quiche gods the talents of their local craftsmen, Neruda, from the vantage point of twentieth-century politics, speaks of the cost to the human beings who wrought their arts and crafts for the terrifying rulers of Macchu Picchu. He declares his solidarity with "Juan Stonecutter . . . Juan Coldeater . . . Juan Barefoot," the common ancestors of "American love" (VIII.I).

> Bring me back the slave that you buried!
> Shake from the earth the hard bread
> of the poor wretch, show me
> the slave's clothing and his window. (X.29–31)

The call for social justice, however, is not the sum of this remarkable poem. In *The Heights of Macchu Picchu* Neruda confronts the powers of nature, the cosmic setting that he invoked in his early love poetry too. Images pour out of the speaker as he looks around him, inviting the great rivers of the Andes (Urubamba and Wilkamayu) to help him penetrate to the creative core of this magnificent ruin. Like William Blake wondering at the sinister perfection of the tiger, Neruda wants to understand how vegetable life came to exist among the stones ("the void of the grapevine / the petrous plant, the hard wreath" [VIII.5–6]). Where is the language that can explain the mysteries of Macchu Picchu? We can only read the stones, for the Incas were a people without writing.

> Who seized the cold's lightning
> and left it shackled in the heights,
> dispersed in its glacial tears,
> smitten in its swift swords,
> hammering its embattled stamens,

borne on its warrior's bed,
startled in its rocky end?

What are your tormented sparks saying?
Did your secret insurgent lightning
once journey charged with words?
Who keeps on shattering frozen syllables,
black languages, golden banners,
deep mouths, muffled cries,
in your slender arterial waters? (VIII.23–36)

The creative energies of the individual and of the universe provoke a
paean to love, but there is great danger. Canto VIII ends with a cryptic
reference to what may be a stone altar where the sun worshipers of the
Incas made their sacrifices. Built in sacrifice in part to isolate a place for
sacrifice, Macchu Picchu fascinates not only the man who approaches it
up the ladder in the cliff, but also the scavenging birds that fly above it:
"And over the Sundial the sanguinary shadow / of the condor crosses
like a black ship" (lines 63–64).

In 43 separate lines, Canto IX enumerates myriad ways of capturing
the essence of Macchu Picchu, finding words to which its builders and
inhabitants had no access. The entire range of sense experience and the
variety of the created universe come together here—eagle, mist, and silver wave, somehow fused with the manmade work of Macchu Picchu—
"entombed ship" (8) or "patriarchal bell of the sleeping" (21) and the
symbols of the South American gods—"Andean serpent, brow of ama-
ranth" (31–32). This extraordinary roll call is simultaneously exhilarating and daunting. You might ask your students to think of the way some
documentary films survey a massive structure like a Gothic cathedral,
lingering lovingly on a gargoyle here, then a segment of a stained-glass
window there, without attempting to link the individual splendors on
which it focuses. There is no verb in Canto IX to render a judgment or
suggest a way of connecting these disparate views of a dead city that still
lives in the dazzling facets that flash before the eye of the poet's mind.

The following Cantos, already mentioned above, turn to the human
beings who suffered and built. The splendor of the structures and the
headiness of the heights cannot keep the poet from looking down as
well.

Give me your hand from the deep
zone of your disseminated sorrow.
You'll not return from the bottom of the rocks. (XII.2–4)

How many people plummeted from those heights accidentally? How
many were thrown over the cliff? How many were offered at the cruel
altar? In sympathy with these lost workers, the speaker bares his own
breast to the knife, pledging what a poet can. In single separated lines
that emphasize the equality of the transaction between the living artist

and the dead who inspire him, Neruda in effect promises the poem that he has just concluded:

> Give me silence, water, hope.
>
> Give me struggle, iron, volcanoes.
>
> Cling to my body like magnets.
>
> Hasten to my veins and to my mouth.
>
> Speak through my words and my blood. (XII.41–45)

Ode to the Tomato

This charming final selection from Neruda's massive oeuvre takes us from the sublime to the delicious. Here, too, the knife looms and will assassinate. Yet the victim of this attack is only a tomato, and if red pulp is spilt, there will be progeny to come: the tomato "beds cheerfully / with the blonde onion." The very short lines here deserve some comment. Is this really a prose poem? What is the impact of separating these salad ingredients out so that each component commands our attention on its own terms? How refreshing to realize that the sensuous voluptuary can revel in "convolutions / canals and plenitudes" that do not stand in for the eternal feminine, but are adored for themselves. Even this deliberately simplified poetic mode gives us one more example of Neruda's gift for evoking the riches of the earth.

Topics for Discussion and Writing

1. The headnote proposes multiple designations of achievement: "Love poet, nature poet, political poet, and poet of common things." Discuss the ways in which Neruda's poems demonstrate his various interests. Comment on the ways in which *The Heights of Macchu Picchu* may be read as uniting all these poetic personae.
2. What is wrong with being "a felt swan / navigating on a water of origin and ash": How does *Walking Around* enlarge the poetic vocabulary and suggest the limitations of classical references?
3. In what ways may *Ode to the Tomato* be considered a love poem?

Comparative Perspectives

1. What view of the city emerges from *Walking Around*? Compare the selection of details that arouse the speaker's disgust with the details that J. Alfred Prufrock notices as he makes his way through the insidious streets.
2. How is Walt Whitman a presence in Neruda's poetry? Discuss the contribution made to Neruda's developing style by the fluidity of

line lengths, the poetic persona, and the range of imagery in *Leaves of Grass*.

3. Many poems in the anthology concern the ruins of the past. Compare and contrast this aspect of *The Heights of Macchu Picchu* with the views of a lost culture in a variety of poems, including Eliot's *The Waste Land*, and Walcott's *Omeros*.

4. Compare the questions posed in Blake's *The Tyger* with those articulated in Canto VIII of *The Heights of Macchu Picchu*. What assumptions does Blake make about the creator that Neruda seems unable to make?

   [Blake seems to know the answer to his question—"Did he smile his work to see? / Did he who made the Lamb make thee?" Neruda seems unsure that there is any articulate presence behind the majesty and cruelty of the rivers of Macchu Picchu: "Who keeps on shattering frozen syllables, / black languages, golden banners, / deep mouths, muffled cries, / in your slender arterial waters?"]

Further Reading

See also the reading suggestions in the *Anthology*, p. 2553.

Gugelberger, Georg M. "Blake, Neruda, Ngugi wa Thiong'o: Issues in Third World Literature." *Comparative Literature Studies* 21 (1984): 463–82. Suggests that Neruda's translating of a few of Blake's socially radical poems (*Visions of the Daughters of Albion* and *The Mental Traveler*) in 1935 may have contributed to his move away from French symbolist influence and toward the engaged poetry of his later years.

Samuel Beckett

Endgame

Backgrounds

Beckett's world is the world of last things—stark, bare, gray from pole to pole—in which characters are bitterly self-conscious and the activity of life is reduced to mere waiting and game-playing. As Tom Stoppard has said, Beckett redefined the minima of theatrical validity. His world is refrigerated and tends toward silence, yet he wrote an extraordinary number of plays, novels, short fictions, and poems that examine such silence in a language as suggestive and penetrating as the language of any writer of his time.

The headnote to Beckett (pp. 1915–18 in the *Anthology*) points out almost all of *Endgame's* central obsessions: the dead world inside, the deader world outside; the four barren characters absolutely restricted in both time and space; the notion of life as a game that cannot be won, only cruelly played; the master/slave relationships of the characters, the struggle of body and soul within each of them.

In *Waiting for Godot*, Vladimir and Estragon play games to endure;

game-playing structures the time they spend waiting. In *Endgame*, game-playing, or the game itself, becomes the central metaphor for existence. Games have no meaning outside of themselves (except indirectly); they are morally and practically superfluous, rule-governed, repetitive, independent of the immediate satisfactions of wants and appetites, dependent on the virtuosity of the players (some of whom dominate while others are dominated), confirmative of role and the stabilizing of position. Games create a world of meaning that is entirely self-reflexive, a dead end. One of the most elaborate of all human games is the play, the drama, which provides an actively present metaphor within the larger metaphor of *Endgame*.

Endgame is aware of itself as a text performed in a theater, and the characters are aware of themselves as characters onstage; they flaunt their consciousness that the whole business is a performance. Their essential traits are those that have been devised in previous plays: Hamm, whose name recalls the term referring to a bad actor, is also Hamlet, who, to quote Hugh Kenner, is "bounded by a nutshell, fancying himself king of infinite space, but troubled by bad dreams." He is also Prospero, but one whose kingdom is without magic, except perhaps the magic of power. Hamm's relationship with the other characters is one of domination and cruelty. He is the hammer to Clov's nail; the Prospero to Clov's Ariel *and* Caliban; the king to Clov's knight; the master to Clov's dog. Both Hamm and Clov continually suggest that they are on stage, alive, only because they have roles to perform in a play, a dramatic game— roles that they cannot stop playing because there is no alternative but to play them. When Clov threatens to leave Hamm, he asks, "What is there to keep me here?" Hamm replies, "The dialogue" (p. 1938). Hamm, Clov, Nagg, and Nell say what they say as if they have said the same things many times before. (Note particularly Hamm's story [pp. 1935–37] and Nagg's joke about the English tailor [p. 1926].) The characters are burdened with a blinding self-consciousness, an awareness of the eternal, repetitive monotony of being trapped in their roles in a game that, when there is nothing outside from which to differentiate it, is meaningless.

When the curtain (if there is a curtain) rises on *Endgame*, it is as if all the characters are just waking up—preparing themselves for another day (another performance), which they hope will soon be finished. The furniture is covered in sheets, suggesting both storage (for the night, between performances) and the covering of the dead. Clov opens the play by performing his ritual actions (he must, according to the script, do this *every* performance) until Hamm removes his personal curtain and announces that he is ready "to play." The stage is their shelter and their gameboard; it is the space in which they do their "living."

In this space there is no future, since the future can be only a mere repetition of the present. Nor can there be a past, except as it persists in memory—the memory, that is, of a life "outside" the stage, a life that seems only disturbingly ironic when compared with present circumstances. The characters live in the hell of an eternal present, but outside is the "other hell." The waves of the sea are like lead, the sun is "zero," there is "no more nature" except the characters' natural tendency to grow old and dwindle toward a death that neglects to come.

> HAMM But we breathe, we change! We lose our hair, our teeth! Our bloom! Our ideals!
> CLOV Then she hasn't forgotten us.

The "little round box" of the universe was once full, perhaps, but now is empty.

Any suggestion of life outside Hamm's kingdom (the flea, the rat, the small boy) terrifies and thrills for the same reason: "humanity might start from there all over again" (p. 1930). Clov, at least, can conceive of a renewal, regeneration, a new play with new roles. But he, like Hamm, can also imagine that new life would mean only a continuation of life as it now exists, a life so checkmated that "a world where all would be silent and still and each thing in its last place, under the last dust" (p. 1938) offers itself as a desirable end, the final "pain-killer" to the prison of endless time the characters now inhabit.

Beckett is rumored to have remarked that in *Waiting for Godot* the audience wonders whether Godot will ever come, while in *Endgame* they wonder whether Clov will ever leave. The "small boy," if there is one, intensifies the question, suggesting both the horror and potentiality of new life. At play's end, Clov is "dressed for the road," suggesting the possibility that he intends to carry out his threat and leave Hamm, perhaps to take in the small boy (as Hamm, apparently, once did) and play Hamm's role himself. Or perhaps Hamm dismisses Clov because he himself intends to take in the small boy, a new player in his game, making Clov no longer necessary. In any case, Clov (who can imagine both "I'll never go" and "I open the door of my cell and go") is still there at the end, "eyes fixed on Hamm." Hamm's final two monologues (pp. 1941–42 and pp. 1946–47), with all of their rhetorical flourish again suggesting scriptedness, are derisive parodies of Jesus' words: they suggest both death and regeneration. Whether regeneration can come in a form other than the play's being enacted again, tomorrow night, is left ambivalent. Hamm finishes where he began, his bloodstained handkerchief over his face, motionless—waiting, perhaps, for the curtain to rise once more.

It has been suggested, by Lionel Abel among others, that Hamm is based on James Joyce—the almost-blind master for whom Beckett worked as a secretary in the late 1920s—and that Clov is based on Beckett himself. Indeed, Joyce (like Hamm) was working on an interminable story, *Finnegans Wake*, during the time Beckett worked with him, and Beckett (like Clov) was very much under Joyce's influence and in Joyce's debt during those years. Even if there is some truth to the claim, however, the play can by no means be read merely as a thinly disguised examination of the conflict between a literary master and his gifted pupil.

Commentators on Beckett often locate him in a tradition that includes Dostoevsky, Gogol, Goncharov, Andreyev, Musil, and Kafka, writers interested in the "marginal self" and who find modern human beings eaten up by consciousness. Dramatically, he has long been included in the "theater of the absurd" with Eugene Ionesco, Jean Genet, and Fernando Arrabal, who certainly belong in such a context, and Harold Pinter, who perhaps does not but who avails himself of many of the techniques we find in Beckett and the others.

Ruby Cohn has outlined a number of evident allusions, parodies, and influences in *Endgame*. She notes Beckett's use of the Bible, especially the Gospel of Saint John; James Joyce, the labyrinth-maker and word-man who may have been a model for Hamm; Shakespeare's *The Tempest* and *King Lear*; Baudelaire, whom Hamm quotes at the end of the play; and Tiresias and Oedipus, blind prophets of suffering.

Classroom Strategies

Endgame can be taught in two class periods. The first should probably examine the thematic implications of the play by exploring the various plausible interpretations that offer themselves to the reader. The second might concentrate on the richness of Beckett's wordplay, his humor, and the way his language lends itself to multiple readings.

You might begin by discussing the implications of the stage setting. It is depressingly bare, enveloped in gray light; the offstage scene is brutally excluded except for the two small windows so high that they can be reached only by ladder. There will be no entrances by persons unknown; only Clov can use the door, which in one production was so narrow that the actor playing the part of Clov thought of himself as a rat squeezing into its hole. The stage certainly appears to be symbolic, though precisely what it symbolizes is a matter of considerable debate. The headnote discusses a number of the possibilities: the stage as the inside of a skull, suggesting that Hamm and Clov are two aspects of a single personality, while Nagg and Nell are suppressed earlier selves; as a last refuge of those who have survived an unnamed catastrophe (perhaps a deluge or nuclear holocaust), making Hamm—to quote Katharine Worth—"lord of the ark of survivors, with his human family and a selection of animals"; as a metaphor for the twilight of civilization, in which Nagg and Nell's ash cans come to represent the dustbin of modern civilized values; as an image of purgatory or purgatorial consciousness; as a womb, from which the characters are eternally hoping—and fearing—to emerge. Beckett has said of his imaginings of life in the womb:

> Even before the fetus can draw breath it is in a state of barrenness and of pain. I have a clear memory of my own fetal existence. It was an existence where no voice, no possible movement could free me from the agony and darkness I was subjected to.

Hugh Kenner adds another possibility, describing the stage as a chessboard and the characters' actions as a game of chess, in which Hamm is the king, Clov the knight, and Nagg and Nell are pawns. The point here is that Beckett has constructed his play so brilliantly and ambiguously that, as Kenner has said, "The play contains whatever ideas we discern inside it; no idea contains the play."

Beckett's refusal to assign a definite meaning to his evidently symbolic characters, setting, and dramatic "action," combined with his denial of the rich inner life that students have come to expect from traditional drama, makes some students uneasy. But this uneasiness can be turned to your, and the play's, advantage. Just as we recognize the terrifying sense of no exit, we are—like Clov—drawn almost irresistibly to see out, to make the laborious climb up the ladder of vision to a world less claustrophobic, fresher than the one Beckett's characters inhabit. Students may resist the notion that there is "an absence of meaning at the core" of the world. They can, however, imagine it, and with their imagining comes a shock of recognition. The game metaphor is of particular use here: any game that has no reference to anything outside itself, that is life rather than a recreation in it (or re-creation of it), can be imagined as a kind of purgatory—repetitive, monotonous, endless.

Students need to be aware of Beckett's extraordinary wordplay as well as his humor. Certain scenes might be read out loud in class, with students taking the parts, in order to emphasize these qualities. The pace of the repartee, which sometimes—though not as often as in *Waiting for Godot*—approaches a vaudeville routine, will become immediately accessible. The opening dialogue between Hamm and Clov (beginning with Clov's "I've just got you up," and ending with his "There's nowhere else") will serve you well. Also useful is the repartee beginning on p. 2213 (Hamm: "Every man his specialty") and ending on p. 2214 (Clov: "Something is taking its course"); Nagg and Nell's dialogue (pp. 2215–17), which includes Nagg's joke; and Hamm and Clov's discussion on pp. 2221–28 beginning with Clov's "Why this farce, day after day?" and ending with Hamm's long, bitter speech.

Topics for Discussion and Writing

1. What is the significance of the stage setting? What does it symbolize? Why doesn't Beckett certify any particular interpretation?
   [See the second paragraph of "Backgrounds" and the second paragraph of "Classroom Strategies."]

2. Why is the play called *Endgame*? What do games have to do with it? How does Beckett use play (including "drama" as "play") in *Endgame*?
   [See the headnote and the second, third, and fourth paragraph of "Backgrounds" for discussion.]

3. Characterize the relationship between Hamm and Clov; among Hamm, Nagg, and Nell. Why is Nagg called "accursed progenitor"?
   [See the headnote and the second paragraph of "Backgrounds."]

4. If "waiting" is the controlling verb in *Waiting for Godot*, what is the controlling verb in *Endgame*?
   [Ending? Gaming? Playing? Finishing?]

5. In what ways does *Endgame* suggest the ending of things? In what ways does it suggest a possible beginning? Can it suggest both?
   [See "Backgrounds."]
6. How is Prospero a useful analogue for Hamm? How is King Lear? The biblical Ham? James Joyce?
   [See "Backgrounds."]

Comparative Perspectives

1. "Ask my father if he wants to listen to my story," Hamm instructs Clov as he launches into a long narrative excursion. While the words the characters speak may be difficult to fathom, the rhythms of Beckett's dialogue represent intergenerational conversations that we all can recognize. How well do family members listen to one anothers' stories in "real life"? Compare *Endgame's* postmodernist dramatization of parental indifference and obsessive childhood memories to the treatment of these concerns in some of the family-centered works in this volume.
2. During his lifetime, Beckett exercised total control over the production of his plays. Now that he has died, his executors have sued directors who have deviated from his detailed and specific stage directions and prescribed scenic designs. How central do you think such physical circumstances are to the success of this play? What would happen if Nagg and Nell were not housed in their ash cans, for example? Discuss the role of stage setting and action in other plays you have read this term, including, if appropriate, Molière's *Tartuffe*, Chekhov's *The Cherry Orchard*, and Brecht's *The Good Woman of Setzuan*. Which playwrights seem to place the greatest premium on precisely defined production techniques? Why?
   [See also comparisons suggested by Stevens's *The Idea of Order at Key West*.]

Further Reading

See also the reading suggestions in the *Anthology*, p. 2549.

Ben-Zvi, Linda, ed. *Women in Beckett: Performance and Critical Perspectives.* 1990. Although not specifically related to *Endgame*, this collection is interesting as a particular examination of Beckett's dramatic work. It contains twelve interviews with actresses from seven different countries (part I: "Acting Beckett's Women") and nineteen essays using modern critical approaches, arranged in order from fiction to drama and radio/television (part II: "Reacting to Beckett's Women").

Bloom, Harold, ed. *Samuel Beckett's* Endgame. 1988. Assembles a range of essays on the play.

Brater, Enoch. *Why Beckett.* 1989. A brief illustrated biography with 122 illustrations, chiefly photos.

Burkman, Katherine H., ed. *Myth and Ritual in the Plays of Samuel Beckett*. 1987. Eleven essays, including a study by Susan Maughlin based on anthropologist Victor Turner's concept of liminality: "Liminality: An Approach to Artistic Process in *Endgame*."

————. *Just Play: Beckett's Theater*. 1980. A thorough study of the dramatic works, particularly interesting on Beckett's language.

Esslin, Martin, ed. *Samuel Beckett: A Collection of Essays*. 1965. Contains a particularly fine essay on *Endgame*, "Beckett's Brinkmanship," by Ross Chambers.

Kalb, Jonathan. *Beckett in Performance*. 1989. An excellent dramaturgical discussion of actual performances as interpretations; includes interviews with eight actors and directors.

Kane, Leslie. *The Language of Silence: On the Unspoken and the Unspeakable in Modern Drama*. 1984.

Pilling, John. *Samuel Beckett*. 1976. A general study, useful on the intellectual, cultural, and literary background to Beckett's work.

Sheedy, John J. "The Comic Apocalypse of King Hamm." *Modern Drama* IX (December 1966): 310–18. A close analysis that suggests both comic and apocalyptic dimensions in the play.

Worth, Katharine, ed. *Beckett the Shape Changer*. 1975. Worth's essay, "The Space and Sound in Beckett's Theatre," is illuminating on *Endgame* and his other plays.

RICHARD WRIGHT

The Man Who Was Almost a Man

Classroom Strategies and Topics for Discussion

Originally published in the magazine *Harper's Bazaar*, this brief, powerful story has many affinities with the outer stories of initiation contained in the anthology, but Wright here manages the difficult task of making articulate the emotions of an inarticulate youth. By using dialect and taking us into Dave's mind, Wright scrupulously records his protagonist's limits. As the headnote and the title suggest, this is a coming-of-age story in which the hero fails to come of age. Its poignancy stems from the truncation of the natural arc of development that the reader expects from such a story, a literary embodiment of Dave's lack of options.

Your students should have little difficulty understanding the means by which Wright captures his protagonist's personality and dilemma. The story, divided into three sections, begins and ends with the boy on the move: Dave's restlessness determines his fate. In the first part, with great economy Wright shows us Dave's sense of inadequacy. The men with whom he works are bigger than he is and "talk to him as though he were a little boy"; his mother and father treat him as one too, as does the white storeowner, Joe: " 'You ain't nothing but a boy. You don't need a gun.' "

That the gun functions as a phallic symbol is quite clear—Dave sees it as the validator of his manhood, fondles it as he awakes in the morning, and ties "it to his naked thigh while it was still loaded." Hoping to achieve through it a virility he cannot yet claim, Dave ultimately finds that he has instead been betrayed on all sides. Joes sells him a virtual antique, too heavy and erratic for an inexperienced seventeen-year-old boy to manage. In the classic Oedipal scene, Dave seductively persuades his mother to give him money for the gun. This hard-pressed woman sees only an immediate use for the catalog her son brings to the house ("We kin use it in the outhouse"). Against the odds, Dave seems to be asserting his masculine powers in this encounter with the dominant figure in the household. The reader recognizes, however, that Mrs. Saunders relents only when she satisfies herself that the gun will really be for her husband. And later on, trying to get her hapless son to confess the truth, she will reveal his secret and expose him to his father's fury and the laughter of the crowd.

Note what Wright does not include in his narrative: he fastens on Dave's humiliations rather than his successes. We do not see the acquisition of the gun, for example, nor do we hear how he tells the story of Jenny's that is at least tentatively accepted. The harrowing central section of *The Man Who Was Almost a Man* concentrates instead in the mule's suffering, and in the last section of his narrative, Wright carefully draws the connection between Jenny and Dave: "They treat me like a mule, n they they beat me" (p. 2248). If in some recesses of his subconscious mind Dave seeks to exert his authority over the one creature he can command, Jenny the mule, when he raises his gun the shots rebound in more ways than one. He makes himself even more the laughing stock of the community he hoped to impress; he not only "bought a dead mule" (p. 2248), but also, in some subtle way, perhaps, destroyed himself. In an odd reversal of the sexual imagery traditionally associated with the shooting of a gun, Dave takes his own innocence when he opens the bloody hole in the flank of the desperate mule. Many initiation stories revolve around the youthful protagonist's first kill; *The Man Who Was Almost a Man* may be read at least in part as a bitter parody of romantic accounts of that epic encounter. Still not mature, Dave fantasizes about making an impact on the world after he has fired the gun with such horrendous consequences; significantly, we learn his full name only in the course of these thoughts: "Ah'd like t scare ol man Hawkins jusa little . . . Jusa enough t let im know Dave Saunders is a man" (p. 2249).

The mule's terrified galloping after the gunshot seems one more symptom of Dave's restlessness; it is perhaps significant that Wright evokes the sound of the train bearing down on the railroad tracks at the end of the story by writing "*hoooof-hoooof*," as if to suggest some equation with the animal. In tones very much like those he has used in condescending to Jenny in the woods before shooting the gun, Dave impatiently awaits the train: "Here she comes, erron the ben . . . C mon, yuh slow poke! C mon!"

The headnote comments on the haiku that Wright was working on in his last years; in 1998, some four hundred of these poems were first published. Even in this early story, we can see evidence of the delicate observation that we associate with Japanese verse. Ask your students to watch the way in which Wright bathes the grim reality of Dave's plight in a transfiguring light. *The Man Who Was Almost a Man* begins in "paling light" (p. 2241); the next section starts in "the gray light of dawn" (p. 2244); the last begins "It was sunset" (p. 2246) and ends when Dave digs up the buried gun in "silence and moonlight" and pulls himself onto a railroad car traveling the rails "glinting in the moonlight" (p. 2249). With such descriptions, Wright stresses the gap between the boy's constricted circumstances and the radiance with which an indifferent universe illuminates them.

The glamor of that last image, however, and the sense that the boy is "getting on with his life," may delude students into seeing Dave's leap onto the train as a triumphant conclusion. Ask them to consider the indeterminacy of Wright's last sentence and the import of the story's title: where is the "somewhere where he could be a man"? What are the boy's prospects? Can we run away from the problems that we create for ourselves?

Topics for Writing

1. Why does Dave want a gun? Discuss the connection between the gun and his relationship with his mother and father.
2. How do the whites in this story treat Dave? How large a role does Wright give to racial tensions in his descriptions of Dave's problems?
3. Discuss the significance of Dave's final decision. Will he be better off because he runs away from home? Is he liberating himself, or will his life be more difficult when he is on his own?

Comparative Perspectives

1. Compare and contrast Frederick Douglass's description of his struggle with a recalcitrant team of oxen in chapter X of his *Narrative* with Dave's disastrous encounter with Jenny in *The Man Who Was Almost a Man*. What does each scene tell us about the contest between a young man and an animal that has been trusted to his care? How is the character of the protagonist revealed by the way he conducts himself?
2. Explain how Dave convinces his mother to let him buy a gun and compare the tensions in his family role to those experienced by other fictional sons in this volume, including Marcel in *Swann's Way* and Gregor in *The Metamorphosis*.

Further Reading

See also the reading suggestions in the *Anthology*, p. 2256.

Hoeveler, Diane Long. "Oedipus Agonistes: Mothers and Sons in Richard Wright's Fiction." *Black American Literature Forum* 12,2 (1978): 65–68. This article makes no direct reference to *The Man Who Was Almost a Man*, but it provides a useful contact for discussing Dave's relationship with his strong mother.

Loftis, John E. "Domestic Prey: Richard Wright's Parody of the Hunt Tradition in 'The Man Who Was Almost a Man.'" *Studies in Short Fiction* 23 (1986): 437–42. A neat comparison between Ike Mc-Caslin's coming of age in Faulkner's *The Old People* (published in late 1940) and Dave's failure to do so in Wright's story (published in the beginning of that year). In other words, Loftis does not argue for any explicit influence of one on the other, but his discussion accentuates the differences between the two boys and their communities: where Ike is supported, Dave is thwarted.

ALBERT CAMUS

The Guest

Backgrounds

Camus is known as the great "moralist" of twentieth-century French letters: "moralist" in a very special French sense that describes a philosophical writer who examines the everyday ethical and moral implications of what it means to be human. Despite the technical brilliance of his work in novels, plays, short stories, and essays, Camus is usually remembered first for his pictures of human beings struggling to understand themselves and the critical circumstances in which they exist. Two elements complement each other in his moral vision: the consciousness of the "absurd" (the discrepancy between our desire for meaning and the actual nonsense of material reality) and a subsequent voluntary "engagement" or devotion to liberty and justice "as if" the world made sense. From the starkly brilliant images of *The Stranger* to the labyrinthine half-dialogue of *The Fall*, Camus's fiction asserts an aesthetic dimension that goes far beyond the philosophical and political frameworks often chosen to discuss it. Nonetheless, his enormous popularity with students continues to be based on his moral insight, a context in which they find him vital and even ennobling.

The Guest is one of Camus's most successful short stories and contains a number of ideas that obsessed him in all his work. Daru lives alone in a vast landscape that suggests a total physical and moral isolation. In many ways, it is similar to Beckett's empty landscapes—absurd, stony, inimical to man—but, unlike Beckett's, it is strikingly beautiful. It is, in any case, the only landscape in which Daru does not feel himself an exile. But into this landscape come men, with their "rotten spite, their tireless hates, their blood lust," their political and cultural ties and assumptions. It is these ties that cause Daru the difficulty he must confront in the story.

Balducci brings the Arab to Daru on the assumption that, since Daru is European, he will complete the process of justice set out by Europeans for Arab offenders. The attitude of the gendarme toward Daru is one of condescension, the kind of condescension that comes with assumed cultural bonds. Balducci calls Daru "son" and "kid" and simply commands the schoolteacher to act as desired: " 'And you will deliver this fellow to Tinguit. He is expected at police headquarters' " (p. 2255). Daru is clearly sympathetic to the natives of his area (he teaches them, speaks the language, distributes food during the drought, and will treat the Arab as a guest), and it is not his job to deal with prisoners. But, as Balducci says, " 'If there's an uprising, no one is safe, we're all in the same boat' " (p. 2256). His demands of Daru, however friendly, are based on the assumption that Daru will act as a European, that he is obliged to accept the prisoner because cultural bonds are stronger than any individual objections Daru may reasonably have. And when it comes down to it, Daru *is* obliged, he *is* a European: the four rivers of France on the map in his schoolroom are the appropriate backdrop for his actions as well as his moral quandary. Balducci sees his world as *us* and *them*, and so does Daru (" 'Is he against us?' " [p. 2256]), although his feelings about *them* are mitigated by his sympathies and his own desire not to be complicit in taking action against them.

When Daru tells Balducci that he will have no part in turning in the Arab, it is not because he thinks the Arab has been unjustly treated (he is, apparently, guilty of a murder), but because Daru does not want to act in a way that will appear to be *for* the Europeans and *against* the Arabs. Essentially, Daru doesn't want to have to commit himself to any course of action, since any such course will suggest to others that he has political sympathies that he does not, in fact, have.

Daru's situation is impossible: though he hopes to evade misunderstanding, he is bound to be misunderstood no matter which option he chooses. The world he lives in guarantees it. Daru attempts to make a choice *not* to do anything, to let the Arab choose freedom or prison for himself; Daru wants to wash his hands of complicity one way or the other. But a man living in a world of "rotten spite" and undeniable allegiances must discover that even not choosing constitutes a choice. Daru has responsibility for the Arab's fate because of his birth and circumstance. He cannot disclaim it.

The end of the story is usually interpreted as an unfortunate misunderstanding, but this interpretation does not do justice to the complexity of Camus's tale. Those who scrawled " 'You handed over our brother. You will pay for this' " (p. 2262) understand Daru perfectly well, though they do not, and cannot, fully appreciate his position. What they understand is that Daru handed over their brother when Daru was born—that the message is written on the map of France confirms why they feel as they do. Daru's solitariness at the end of the story, then, is the solitariness of a man trapped in a universe in which no act is without its moral implications and in which there is no way to elude complicity.

Daru's position may be impossible, as is the Arab's, but this does not mean that he cannot treat the prisoner well as long as the Arab is his guest. Something like brotherhood and a "strange alliance" is established between them, but Daru must recognize that he lives in a world in which brotherhood can simultaneously mean betrayal. Still, the brotherhood developed between Daru and the Arab is necessary and heroic. However small a gesture, it is perhaps all that can be done; like the Sisyphus of Camus's essay (*The Myth of Sisyphus*) one must willingly—even joyously—push the boulder up the mountain knowing full well that it will roll back down again.

Camus was born to European parents in Algeria, then a colony of France, and lived and worked there exclusively until he was twenty-seven. Friends and family continued to live in Algeria throughout his life. His interest and concern in the Algerian Question, as it was then called, are perfectly understandable. What wasn't understandable to many French intellectuals, including Jean-Paul Sartre (with whom Camus had had a spectacular public quarrel in 1952) and Simone de Beauvoir, were Camus's consistent calls for tolerance and understanding and his refusal to back wholeheartedly any movement that called for either violent rebellion or the restriction of individual freedoms. During the Algerian conflict, Camus was hardly silent—in 1956 he flew to Algiers in order to address both French and Muslim citizens although he was constantly under threat of his life—but he adopted the comparatively safe position of concentrating on the effort to spare innocent civilians: "Truce until it is time for solutions, truce to the massacre of civilians, on one side and the other!" Camus, like Daru, clearly hated having to be put in the position of taking sides. And because he was without question the most powerful Algerian-born voice capable of being heard in France, his position carried with it enormous responsibilities, responsibilities that both those on the Left and those on the Right felt he was shirking or misusing. *The Guest* appears to be, in part at least, an attempt to express the personal difficulties he felt in judging the Algerian situation.

Camus often insisted that he was not an existentialist, and he and Sartre were reportedly surprised, and sometimes disturbed (especially after 1952), at seeing their names constantly linked. At one point they jokingly agreed to sign a statement claiming that neither could be held responsible for the debts incurred by the other.

Classroom Strategies

The Guest is teachable in one class period and can be linked with a number of other texts in which characters must make difficult moral choices: *Medea*, *Billy Budd* (Captain Vere).

The major problem that students will have with *The Guest* is selling the story short. Daru's "quiet heroism" is evident, so students will tend to see him as a quiet hero, severely misunderstood and unjustly accused by the Arab rebels at the end of the story. They will compare him with Balducci, clearly a man involved—though not happily—in a master/slave relationship with his prisoner, and find him heroic in comparison. It is more difficult to see him as heroic when we realize that his heroism is not nearly enough. He goes far enough with Balducci to satisfy the letter of the law and far enough with the Arab to satisfy the demands of his sympathies. He is not heroic because he sets the prisoner free. In the first place, he doesn't free him—he only gives the Arab the chance to take his freedom. Second, the Arab's crime is not a political crime—it is a murder, which Daru (as well as Balducci) finds repellent; it is much to Camus's credit that he hasn't made the prisoner's guilt or innocence an issue. Third, he is complicit, whether he likes it or not, in the system that, perhaps justly, has ensnared the prisoner, but that also, perhaps unjustly, has also ensnared the prisoner's countrymen. Daru is heroic not through heroic action but by suffering the inevitable fate that awaits human beings in an absurd universe—and doing it with civility, sympathy, and the desire to be nice.

Students will by no means always understand why the prisoner does not escape during the night, or why he chooses the road to prison rather than freedom at the end of the story. One reason is given in the headnote: the "host's humane hospitality has placed a new burden and reciprocal responsibility on his guest." (p. 2253) There are, however, other possibilities. One has its basis in the master/slave relationship that even a night of humane treatment cannot erase: the Arab simply cannot believe that a European *really* means to set him free. We must remember, as the prisoner no doubt remembers, that Daru still has his gun, just as he still has the power to give or deny freedom at a whim. We know, but the prisoner doesn't, that Daru is uneasy with such power; that he has it whether he wants it or not is, however, undeniable. Teachers may find their position in the classroom analogous to Daru's position. We do not always want the power we have; we may even seek to diminish or deny it. But we give A's and F's and Incompletes, and as long as we stand in front of the classroom we are collaborators in an entire structure of evaluation that is impossible to disregard.

Another plausible reading is that the prisoner takes the road toward prison because prison is precisely what he deserves. He is, after all, a murderer. If Daru, in his role as a teacher, is interested in "conveying to a fellow human being the freedom of action, which all people require," the Arab may very well be capable of learning it. To freely choose to be punished for a crime he has committed is just as admirable, and perhaps more admirable, than eluding the punishment that is due him.

Topics for Discussion and Writing

1. Why does Camus set the story on a remote outpost in Algeria, just after a freak snow has isolated it even more profoundly than usual?

How does Camus use descriptions of the landscape to confirm Daru's isolation? Do the descriptions of the landscape suggest its beauty? Why?

[See "Backgrounds."]

2. What is the point of Balducci's rather long conversation with Daru? Why does Balducci think he can leave the prisoner with Daru? Why does Daru keep him? Why does Daru say he will not take him to prison? What is Balducci's attitude about this?

[See the third, fourth, and fifth paragraphs of "Backgrounds" and the third paragraph of "Classroom Strategies."]

3. Why does Daru give the Arab the opportunity to escape? Why doesn't he escape? Why doesn't he take the road to the Arab lands at the end of the story?

[See the fourth and fifth paragraphs of "Backgrounds" and the fourth and fifth paragraphs of "Classroom Strategies."]

4. In what ways is the Arab treated as a guest by Daru? In what ways is Daru a guest in Algeria?

[See the seventh paragraph of "Backgrounds."]

5. How can this story be seen as an expression of Camus's personal position on the Algerian Question?

[See the eighth paragraph of "Backgrounds."]

Comparative Perspectives

1. Daru is frustrated by the Arab's reluctance to seize the opportunity he gives him to escape. Compare Candide's frequent escapes in Voltaire's satire, for instance. What kinds of cultural situations produce narratives in which chase and escape figure so prominently? What kinds of personality traits are required for a successful escape? What accounts for the tonal differences in the way escape is treated in each of these works?

2. Camus's story of Algeria and Melville's *Billy Budd* revolve around a dilemma faced by an intellectual. Compare the kinds of responsibility with which these intellectuals are charged and the different ways in which they defy their orders. How may these stories reflect their creators' conceptions of the moral efficacy of the scholar in an immoral political situation? How is each story a product of a particular philosophical disposition as well as of a specific political moment?

Further Reading

See also the reading suggestions in the *Anthology*, p. 2250.

Amoia, Alba della Fazia. *Albert Camus*. 1989. An introductory study with a short biography and discussion of individual works organized by genre.

Bloom, Harold. *Albert Camus*. 1989. A selection of critical essays.

Cruickshank, John. *Albert Camus and the Literature of Revolt*. 1959. Reprinted 1978. A useful general study.

Ellison, David R. *Understanding Albert Camus*. 1990. A perceptive, readable overview of Camus's work that describes individual works (*The Guest*, pp. 194–99) and interprets according to structure, historical context, and themes.

Sprintzen, David. *Camus: A Critical Examination*. 1988.

Suther, Judith D., ed. *Essays on Camus's* Exile and the Kingdom. 1980. "The Symbolic Decor of 'The Guest' " by Paul A. Fortier and Joseph G. Morello is on pp. 203–15.

Thody, Philip. *Albert Camus*. 1957. A short but cogent study of the works, including a discussion of *The Guest*.

ALEXANDER SOLZHENITSYN

Matryona's Home

Backgrounds

Solzhenitsyn's work centers on the ways that modern Soviet society affects its citizens. Many of his characters, Matryona among them, are good people victimized by their society, who manage to rise above their predicament and demonstrate an endurance and personal integrity that cannot be destroyed by circumstances. Awarding Solzhenitsyn the Nobel Prize for Literature in 1970, the committee recognized Solzhenitsyn for the "ethical force [with] which he has pursued the indispensable traditions of Russian literature." The choice of the word *Russian* is significant here, since Solzhenitsyn is infinitely more Russian than Soviet. He has condemned the Soviet system from the outset of his career, just as he has condemned what he sees as the corrupt values of the decadent West. In a letter to the Soviet Writer's Union, from which he was expelled in 1969, he wrote: "Literature that does not warn in time against threatening moral and social dangers—such literature does not deserve the name of literature." His unwavering concern for truth and his earnest unwillingness to compromise his beliefs—both maintained at great personal cost—define his reputation as a major literary presence in the last half of this century.

Matryona's Home involves a favorite Solzhenitsyn theme—the righteous person forced to deal with corrupt and difficult circumstances. Matryona is an illiterate peasant who nevertheless faces her circumstances with an almost saintly wisdom. She becomes, in Solzhenitsyn's hands, a testimony to the good that survives in the best of human beings.

Readers of Tolstoy's *The Death of Ivan Ilyich* will have seen something of Matryona's kind of simple wisdom in the servant Gerasim. Other readers may be able to compare Matryona to Dostoevsky's Prince Myshkin in *The Idiot*, Jaroslav Haahasek's Good Soldier Schweik, or Isaac Bashevis Singer's Gimpel the Fool. Solzhenitsyn's story will not bear, or need, a great deal of analysis. In form it is a hagiography—the story of the life of a saint. Like all saints, Matryona is unappreciated, misunderstood, belittled, bedeviled, taken advantage of, and abandoned. She dies while sacrificing herself for others. Her story is told with understated directness by a narrator who, we must understand, knows something about suffering and patience. But even he comes to recognize the spiritual greatness of Matryona:

> . . . the righteous one without whom, as the proverb says, no village
>   can stand.
> Nor any city.
> Nor our whole land.

Matryona does not need material comforts beyond those necessary for survival, and she makes her home available to all the creatures of the earth—itinerant schoolteachers fresh from prison camp, lame cats, mice, cockroaches. Her home is *open* to the natural world and, as always in the pastoral tradition, at her death the natural world mourns her passing. "The mice had gone mad. They were running furiously up and down the walls, and you could almost see the green wallpaper rippling and rolling over their backs."

She owns no suckling pig because she would have had to nurture it only to kill it. She owns no cow because she could not have fed it well enough. Her pathetic and filthy goat suits her needs, and she does not ask for more. She is supremely competent at the business of survival, though that competence is entirely unappreciated. She weathers sickness, physical hardship, bureaucracy, and the age of machines with uncomplaining dignity. The narrator is in search of "deepest Russia" and in Matryona he finds its very core.

Two other central concerns of Solzhenitsyn are evident in *Matryona's Home*: the inefficiency and callousness of the Soviet bureaucracy, especially the cooperative farm system, and the inability of the "machine age" to fulfill the essential needs of human beings. The Soviet system is the target of Solzhenitsyn's narrative wrath on a number of occasions in *Matryona's Home*. The lack of peat, which Matryona must have for fuel during the insufferably cold Russian winter, is particularly suggestive, because it forces the old women of the village to gather their courage and steal it from the bogs—where it is being kept for more privileged members of the Soviet classless society. Matryona's vain and exhausting attempts to get her pension (" 'They shove me around, Ignatich. . . . Worn out with it I am' ") reemphasizes the point, as does her experience trying to get train tickets.

Solzhenitsyn's disgust with the "machine age" takes a number of forms in the story, but the most effective and suggestive is the manner of Matryona's death, which is an antimachine parable. Matryona is so afraid of trains that they have a demonic kind of horror for her: " 'When I had to go to Cherusti, the train came up from Nechaevka way with its great big eyes popping out and the rails humming away—put me in a regular fever. My knees started knocking. God's truth I'm telling you!' "

It is ironically appropriate then, that she should be killed by a train, literally dismembered, as she helps her rapacious and callous relations cart away the pathetic fragments of her own home. The machine she so despised is the agent of her death: "When it was light the women went to the crossing and brought back all that was left of Matryona on a hand sledge with a dirty sack over it. They threw off the sack to wash her. There was just a mess . . . no feet, only half a body, no left hand."

Matryona's death is a testament to the inevitable destruction of the simple values that she embodies and that we are being asked to embrace. Her body, like her life, ends in pieces. The blossoming "red-faced girl clasping a sheaf" cannot survive a system and a way of life that can no longer appreciate her virtues. Once, the narrator insists, "there was singing out under the open sky, such songs as nobody can sing nowadays, with all the machines in the fields."

Like the narrator of *Matryona's Home*, Solzhenitsyn spent time (eight years) in a Soviet prison camp. He had been exiled there in 1945 for creating anti-Soviet propaganda and agitation, after a letter in which he made remarks critical of Joseph Stalin was intercepted by a government censor. After he was released, Solzhenitsyn, again like the narrator, took a job as a schoolteacher in rural Ryazan, near Moscow. During his tenure in Ryazan, Solzhenitsyn apparently became friendly with a person who was the basis for Matryona. The train accident that appears in *Matryona's Home* is said to be based on what happened to that friend.

Matryona's Home was one of the very few works by Solzhenitsyn actually published in the Soviet Union. On its publication, the story was attacked on the grounds that it misrepresented Russian peasants. They were not, said the critics, greedy and rapacious as are Matryona's relatives in the story. They were, instead, as cooperative as members of a collective farm are supposed to be. Solzhenitsyn was denied the Lenin Prize, for which he had been enthusiastically nominated, and his novel *The First Circle* was rejected. (The novel was finally published in the West, as were all of his subsequent works.)

Classroom Strategies

Matryona's Home can be taught in one class period, though you may need to stretch that period if you provide much background information on the Russian Revolution and the nature of the Soviet Union under Stalin. You may wish to compare Solzhenitsyn's picture of Stalinist society with the more urban and personal experience described in Akhmatova's *Requiem*.

The major problem here will not be to convince students of the "truth" of Solzhenitsyn's tale, since they will more than likely be all too happy to accept it as "truth." Because the story answers most of the myths and preconceptions Westerners already have about Soviet life, the problem will be to make sure that students read it with the same degree of resistance with which they would normally confront any other piece of fiction. Students may well find some of Solzhenitsyn's operating notions—the saintly peasant and the evident superiority of the pastoral life, for instance—difficult to swallow once these themes are disassociated from his more explicit condemnations of the Soviet system. It will need to be pointed out that for Solzhenitsyn the universal problems of greed, indifference, misunderstanding, and the desire for unnecessary luxury do not by any means disappear beyond the boundaries of the Soviet Union.

Topics for Discussion and Writing

1. The narrator tells us that he wishes to find "deepest Russia." Does he? In what ways?
   [See the third and fourth paragraphs of "Backgrounds."]
2. What constitutes Matryona's goodness? Would the virtues she exhibits serve her in an urban or technologically sophisticated environment? Does Solzhenitsyn appear to be suggesting that we should return to a life of rural simplicity?
3. How is irony used in the story? What is ironic about the nature of Matryona's death? What is ironic about the things people say about her after her death?
   [See the sixth and seventh paragraphs of "Backgrounds."]
4. How is narrative understatement used in the story? Is it effective? What would be the effect of writing about such a saintly woman in inflated language?

Comparative Perspectives

1. Solzhenitsyn treats the railroad as a malign mechanical intrusion on the natural Russian landscape in *Matryona's Home*. Compare and contrast the image of the railroad in Solzhenitsyn's hands with its functions in stories as diverse as *The Garden of Forking Paths*, *The Man Who Was Almost a Man*, and *Ladies and Gentlemen, to the Gas Chamber*.
   [Emphases include, in the order of the stories listed above, the railroad car as a place of social interaction, the rails as a symbol of adventure, and the transport car as an instrument of dehumanization.]
2. Analyze the symbolic significance of the tearing apart of Matryona's home. For what original purpose had the top room been built? Compare the use of architecture and setting in other texts, including *The Cherry Orchard*, *The Secret Room*, *The Old Chief Mshlanga*, and *Things Fall Apart*.

Further Reading

See also the reading suggestions in the *Anthology*, p. 2554.

Burg, David, and George Feifer. *Solzhenitsyn*. 1972. Discusses *Matryona's Home* as purely documentary, perhaps underrating the fictional elements of the story.

Curtis, James M. *Solzhenitsyn's Traditional Imagination.* 1984. Literary traditions and individual writers (Russian and non-Russian) that influenced Solzhenitsyn's novels.

Labedz, Leopold. *Solzhenitsyn: A Documentary Record.* 1970. A collection of comments, reports, reviews, and extracts of documents and interviews. Interesting for Solzhenitsyn's own comments.

Moody, Christopher. *Solzhenitsyn.* 1973. Contains a short but informative discussion of *Matryona's Home.*

Scammell, Michael. *Solzhenitsyn: A Biography.* 1984. Comprehensive and detailed.

Solzhenitsyn, Alexander. *November 1916: The Red Wheel: Knot II.* Trans. H. T. Willets. 1999. The protagonist of this novel appears to be a thinly disguised portrait of the author.

DORIS LESSING

The Old Chief Mshlanga

Backgrounds

Lessing is one of the most intensely committed of contemporary writers in English. Individual freedom and fulfillment return over and over again as her chief themes, together with a concern for social justice. Only when human beings are full members of society, she suggests, will human society be truly harmonious—or sane. These concerns pervade not only the novels and stories set in England but also the African stories, in which black and white characters alike are molded by their position in society. Lessing's own point of view, she notes, emerges from her experience as the daughter of white settlers in Rhodesia, and her African stories describe different facets of the blocked (or budding) consciousness of that socially privileged class.

Although there is a clear historical context for these stories, they demonstrate the *functioning* of colonialism rather than specific locations, people, or events. Lessing writes about a "Zambesia" that is a "composite if various white-dominated parts of Africa and, as I've since discovered, some of the characteristics of its white people are those of any ruling minority whatever their colour." Her British characters are typically alienated from the Africa they colonize: they cling to their British or European identity, and to the habits of their homeland, as an anchor of security in the midst of a country that remains remote and strange. Now and again there are friendships (e.g., between Tommy and Dirk, Mr. Macintosh's bastard son in *The Antheap*) or inconclusive attempts by newcomers to set things right (Marina Gile's effort to reprove her neighbors and reform her servant Charles in *A Home for the Highland Cattle*), but these relationships are psychologically demanding, often frustrated, and invariably complicated.

There is a harsh economic history behind the social relationships and final conflict of *The Old Chief Mshlanga*. In many ways, the story encapsulates the successive stages of European colonization. In the typical pattern of colonial invasion, commercial companies moved in to an area and established *de facto* dominance before their overseas government took official control (sometimes in apparent response to glaring abuses of power). Southern Rhodesia was administered until 1923 by a British Chartered Company that divided all land into "alienated" property (owned and occupied by white settlers, or occupied by Africans who paid a tax to the settler and to the Company) and "unalienated" African property (which could be appropriated by whites if the Company approved). There were native "Reserves" on "unalienated" land, and the African who lived on such Reserves also paid taxes to the Company. The Company yielded control to the British government's Land Apportionment Act, which effectively reiterated the old distinctions by establishing areas called "Native" and "European." Africans continued to be pushed off "European" land into "Native" country, and in 1956 Lessing wrote after revisiting Southern Rhodesia that only 46 percent of the land was still owned by Africans. The figure of the Old Chief Mshlanga thus telescopes a moment of history: at one time ("not much more than fifty years before") he ruled the whole region inside which the Jordan farm occupies a small portion, but now he is reduced to presiding over a single village. Subject to alien laws and a foreign economic system, he and his people are finally pushed off the last segment of their ancestral territory, which will be "opened up for white settlement soon."

Lessing's view of African politics is clearly grounded in a European perspective, as she herself recognizes. The focus of her story—despite the title image of Chief Mshlanga—is the evolving experience of a young British girl growing up on an African farm. The protagonist's attitude toward European and African traditions, her confused discomfort as events contradict expectations, and her progressive awakening to the beauty of the African countryside may all be compared with Achebe's picture of African life in *Things Fall Apart* (included in this anthology).

Like so many stories of adolescent coming-of-age, *The Old Chief Mshlanga*, is structured by the various stages of the young girl's gradual insight. At the beginning, she is presented as totally removed from the African landscape and its people; she lives in a fairy-tale world of medieval castles, oak trees, snow, and Northern witches. The hot African countryside is unreal and its people an amorphous, faceless mass, "as remote as the trees and rocks." Even the narrative perspective is external, presenting the protagonist in the third person as "a small girl," "a white child," and a "she" who teases and torments the natives as if it were her inborn right. Mr. Jordan's young daughter is insulated from any contact that might arouse insecurity or fear; she " 'mustn't talk to natives,' " and she walks around fortified by two dogs and a gun.

Change and a series of more personal encounters are signaled by an abrupt introduction of the subjective "I." In her own voice, the protagonist tells how she encountered a dignified old man and was put to shame by his pride and courtesy. Chief Mshlanga, she learns later, used to rule the entire country; this extraordinary fact awakens the girl's interest in her surroundings, and she begins to experience the African countryside first as a physical reality and second as a heritage to be shared between her own people and the blacks. "It seemed quite easy"—too easy, as she finds when wandering beyond the farm to visit the Chief in his village. Suddenly the landscape is unfamiliar, even menacing, and she is intensely afraid. The women and children of the village do not respond to her questions, she herself does not understand why she has come, and the Old Chief and his attendants are not pleased by her intrusion. Returning home through the newly hostile landscape, the little Chieftainess can no longer pretend to be an innocent bystander; as the land seems to tell her, she is one of the destroyers.

The end of the story comes quickly and painfully. After an argument over crops trampled by the Chief's goats, her father confiscates the animals and threatens the Chief with the police when he complains that the tribe will starve. Proudly reminding Mr. Jordan that the farm and indeed the whole region have been usurped from the tribe, Chief Mshlanga walks away, followed by his son, who has been Jordan's cook. Pride, however, is a less tangible commodity than the settler's acquaintance with the local authorities, and the Chief and his tribe are soon uprooted and moved to a Native Reserve. The young girl's reaction is not fully visible at this point; she merely reports the quarrel and its aftermath and, a year later, visits the decaying village. The people are gone; their houses are mounds of mud topped with rotting thatch and swarms of ants. Conversely, the land is a riot of triumphant colors and lush new growth. The tone of the final paragraph has changed, voicing an older and more distanced perspective that may or may not be that of the narrator—yet it still views the African landscape from outside, and still with a buried question.

Classroom Strategies

The Old Chief Mshlanga can be taught in a single period. The easiest way to coordinate discussion is to begin with the familiar narrative pattern of "coming-of-age"; in this case, the evolution of the main character toward increased understanding of her African environment. The first page sets up the contrast between a European heritage that is jealously cherished (she reads European fairy tales, medieval romances, and archaistic Victorian literature) and an actual African setting that appears to be—both people and landscape—quite unreal. "The black people on the farm were as remote as the trees and the rocks. They were an amorphous black mass . . . who existed merely to serve." At this point, you will want to introduce some historical background on European colonization of the eighteenth and nineteenth centuries. This background can be as broad as you wish, with examples from Africa, India, both Near and Far East, and the Western hemisphere, but an especially useful tactic is to describe Lessing's "Zambesia" in terms of the actual history of Southern Rhodesia (reminding students that Rhodesia is now Zimbabwe). The split between European and African, black and white, that is so much a part of this story has demonstrable roots, and the familiar theme of coming-of-age is paired with a poignant description of *what* the child comes to sense: her own cultural alienation, and the irreparable damage done to "her" country by colonization and the forced resettlement of an occupied people. Two comparisons are appropriate here: Albert Camus's *The Guest* (included earlier in the *Anthology*), for another example of the colonial predicament seen through European eyes, and Chinua Achebe's *Things Fall Apart* (included later) as a black African perspective on the same conflict. And of course the teacher should make use of the excerpts by Ménil, Fanon, and Achebe in the "On Being a Cultural Other" cluster.

The writing in *The Old Chief Mshlanga* is definitely from a European perspective, as brought out by the contrast between the title image of the African "Old Chief" and the experience of a young settler girl recounted in the narrating. The presence of the Old Chief is crucial but (in terms of the story) only as a symbolic figure who crystallizes questions the girl is beginning to ask. Ask the students to imagine how the story would seem if told from the perspective of the corresponding (somewhat older) child: Chief Mshlanga's son, who works in the Jordans' kitchen.

You may want to take advantage of recurring themes when you examine significant passages with your class. Lessing has clearly used different descriptions of landscape for symbolic purposes. There is the cold and snowy Northern landscape to which the child escapes in her reading, contrasted with Africa's "gaunt and violent" scenery; the contrast of the Jordans' farm and the well-kept, colorful African village; the bigness and silence of Africa with its "ancient sun," "entwined trees," lurking animals, and "shapeless menace"; and the final scene, in which nature has taken over and erased the village after its inhabitants have been sent away. These settings are also linked with different stages of the young girl's awareness. At the beginning, she is armored against fear by her two dogs and the gun she carries; later, she is panic-stricken and lost when walking alone in the immense and alien landscape. The African landscape tells her, "You walk here as a destroyer," as an integral part of the colonial presence; it teaches her that she cannot "dismiss the past with a smile in an easy gush of feeling." The ending paragraph brings out this sense of impalpable loss in its direction of the "unsuspected vein of richness" that persists, buried, in the deserted ancestral ground in the Old Chief's village.

Topics for Discussion and Writing

1. Why is the story titled *The Old Chief Mshlanga*? In what sense is the story both *about* and *not about* the chief?
2. The narrator mentions "questions, which could not be suppressed" and "questions that troubled me." What might be some of these questions, how and by whom are they suppressed, and at what points in the story do they come to the fore?
3. Discuss the various references to fear in the story and the way that they are associated with the narrator's awareness of her surroundings.

4. How does Lessing establish the dignity and importance of Chief Mshlanga? Cite several passages.
5. What does the loss of the goats mean to Chief Mshlanga? to Mr. Jordan? What is implied when Mr. Jordan says "Go to the police, then"? Why is there no further discussion?
6. Describe Lessing's use of symbolic landscapes.
   [Note the contrast of North European and African landscapes in the opening paragraphs; the untouched landscape during the child's trip to and from Chief Mshlanga's kraal (its beauty and strangeness, the sense of menace); the Jordans' farm with its "harsh eroded soil," twisted trees, and migrant workers' compound that was "a dirty and neglected place"; the harmony of the African village with "lovingly decorated" huts and the "enclosing arm" of the river; the final scene of the abandoned kraal.]
7. What signs of colonial government are included in the story? Why are they not given more prominence?
8. Discuss the implications of the last scene: the "festival of pumpkins," the exceptionally flourishing plants, the area's "unsuspected vein of richness." What is this richness? Whose point of view governs the ending paragraph? Can you tell?

Comparative Perspectives

1. The moment when the fourteen-year-old Jordan daughter takes control of the narrative of *The Old Chief Mshlanga* is marked linguistically by her use of the first-person pronoun and socially by her possession of a rifle. As she matures, her need for the gun changes: "I used it for shooting and not to give me confidence." Compare and contrast the relation of protagonist and gun in this and other stories of initiation in the anthology (Dave Saunders in *The Man Who Was Almost a Man*, for instance), and comment on the significance of Lessing's having her story center around a girl, rather than a boy, with a gun. What kind of knowledge does Lessing's female narrator gain? What do boys with guns learn?
2. At the end of the twentieth century, many artists have tried to come to terms with genocidal assaults on despised cultural communities. Compare and contrast the view of the oppressor and the oppressed in stories such as *The Old Chief Mshlanga*, *The Guest*, *Ladies and Gentleman, to the Gas Chamber*, and *Things Fall Apart*. What kind of dominance is sought? To what degree do the victims collaborate in their own destruction? What kind of future do the literary works in question seem to predict?

Further Reading

See also the suggestions in the *Anthology*, p. 2552.

Bloom, Harold, ed. *Doris Lessing*. 1986 A collection of essays, arranged chronologically, that discusses Lessing's novels as well as broad issues of ideology and philosophy. In contrast, the editor's introduction sharply criticizes Lessing for emphasizing issues and lacking stylistic mastery.

Gardiner, Judith Kegan. *Rhys, Stead, Lessing, and the Politics of Empathy.* 1989. Discusses concepts of identity in Lessing's short fiction; contains an interesting analysis of gendered rhetoric used to describe the child in *The Old Chief Mshlanga.*

Knapp, Mona. *Doris Lessing.* 1984. An informative general introduction to Lessing's works, arranged chronologically. Describes individual works and offers a chronology.

Tadeusz Borowski

Ladies and Gentlemen, to the Gas Chamber

Classroom Strategies and Topics for Discussion

This powerful short story may be approached as an inquiry into the human desire to impose form on experience. In many ways, *Ladies and Gentlemen, to the Gas Chamber* is a typical initiation story, one of the staples of modern short fiction. But where the narrator of such stories usually ends up gaining knowledge and self-understanding, the narrator here works to repress such insight.

Careful discussion of the opening of Borowski's story will help you establish the kinds of ironies with which the piece records the totalizing dehumanization that is its subject. The polite locution of the title mocks the activity that the story describes even as we are actually shown the elegantly accoutred Nazi guards in strange moments of politesse, as in their exchanging the Fascist salute with each other as they await the arrival of the transport. Without comment, the narrator notes that the sound of the church bell can be heard in the distance. Even before that, we are admitted to the sociable world of the "Canada" veterans, companionably feasting together, friends of a sort, although they often do not know each other's names. The forms of civilized life, even of the sacred, somehow persist, making the enormity of the concentration camp and the entire Nazi program even more obscene, if that is possible.

Borowski's narrator is a deadpan as he can manage: he wants to avoid offering judgments. The details he supplies, however, evoke the horror that he tries to ignore. With the story's very first sentence, we are reminded of the reversal of all human norms in the camps. As one critic notes, nakedness is our Edenic state; indeed, as they march through the camp, the laborers have a surreal vision of a paradisal landscape: "the apple and pear trees . . . the exotic verdure, as though out of the moon." But this is emphatically a postlapsarian world. For one thing, the linguistic chaos is described as "the babel of the multitude." The notion that human beings might work together in purposeful concert has been squelched, as in the story of the Tower of Babel; worse, the human has become the animal. In fact, as the headnote suggests, delousing is a metaphor for the whole story: Birkenau (Auschwitz II or Auschwitz-Birkenau, where Elie Wiesel, of whom your students may know, was sent) was an *extermination* camp. The vermin are being expunged.

Ladies and Gentlemen, to the Gas Chamber makes it clear that the Nazis did not dedicate themselves to a merely negative project, extermination. Borowski shows us, through the narrator's first experience with "Canada," that the death camps had a "positive" goal as well: they were moneymaking operations, through the use of forced labor and by the collection of gold and jewels that we watch so scrupulously pursued. The profit motive is grotesquely exemplified here in the ravenous feeding of the waiting laborers. Since what they eat comes from those who will be exterminated, they are really feeding on humanity. The contents of the transports, "the goods," are listed indiscriminately: "lumber, cement, people . . ." The laborers fear that they will "run out of people." Those who ingest human flesh ought to sicken, but with time, the digestive system is trained. The Greeks " 'gobble up everything they lay their hands on,' " as if they were somehow untouched by the horror all around them; yet the narrator has earlier noted that "like huge, inhuman insects they move their jaws greedily." Though they eat, they still share the insectlike existence of all the camp inmates, and Borowski's narrator predicts that " 'half of them will die tomorrow of the trots.' " His body still betrays the feelings he will try to conquer: his vision blurs, his mouth dries. Later, having seen death and human suffering in the railroad cars from which he has unloaded food and goods, the narrator will himself retch. The beginner cannot yet control his sympathetic nervous system.

Fighting off nausea is one way of coping with the reality of what he is engaged in. To survive in the extermination camps, one had to become callous. Annoyed by the sound of a rabbi's "loud and monotonous lament," the narrator's companions virtually blame the suffering of the Jews on their religion: " 'If they did not believe in God and in a life beyond they'd have wrecked the crematorium long ago.' " But they themselves will take no such action, unbelievers though they are. The easy hypocrisy of the Frenchman described here as "a communist and a *rentier*" is merely a symptom of the contradictions that had to be embraced in order to live.

Probably the narrator's most consistent way of protecting himself from his surroundings is, as noted above, to refuse all editorial comment. In one remarkable paragraph, what sounds like another voice offers us the hindsight of history, placing these events in context: "When the war is over, the cremated will be counted. There will be four and a half million of them," and so on, until the "accomplishments" of the perfected Nazi machine have been tallied. This documentary overview, curiously inserted in midstory, is like a marker in the narrative, followed by a paragraph that begins, "The cars are already empty." Perhaps because his most painful task is to describe what happens to the persons pouring out of the cars, the narrator needs to pull back in the midst of it.

From the mixture of tongues comes one word of Yiddish: "Mamele!" This is the voice of the child whose mother has reached for a handbag and been trampled for her pains. The fate of the women and children dominates the narrative; those who are weak or unable to work are packed off to the left, into the trucks. From the infant corpses, the maddened, and the maimed, Borowski gives us one searing image after another. Perhaps the hardest to place is the frightened mother brought to the point of denying her child. Infuriated by this apparent moral depravity, a drunken Russian sailor curses her Jewishness and brutally throws her on the truck. Applauded by the SS-man, his action demands a more complicated response of the reader.

In this episode we see one of the reasons the Nazis were able to exterminate so many members of hated minorities. Stripped of all their own resources, the Nazis' victims gained some measure of superiority by denying their human connection with other victims. This determined isolation of the Other, is, of course, the means by which all prejudice thrives and the root of the mentality that allows the narrator and his comrades to survive: Henri explains this self-defensive mechanism in answer to the pathetic question "are we good people?"

The one moment when the narrator allows himself to make eye contact with the human cargo he is unloading shakes him profoundly and alters the moral equation that Henri expounds. The beautiful blonde-haired young woman who asks "Where are they taking us?" reminds him of a girlfriend who has a watch like hers. Knowing the answer to her own question, the young woman "boldly . . . ran up the steps into the nearly filled truck," defiantly going to the death that she could have avoided for at least a time. Here, for a moment, we see a human being not yet corrupted by the system of the camps, making a tragic choice to maintain dignity even though it means death.

Ladies and Gentlemen, to the Gas Chamber does not end with this small moment of heroism, however. Pointedly, it moves deeper into infernal imagery, as the narrator crawls under the rails. A little girl runs mad, a dead hand clutches his—he vomits, and the story's pace shifts again. Stopping for another impersonal documentary look at what will happen to the people herded off the train, the action then draws to its conclusion. The narrative, like classical tragic drama, has taken precisely a day to unfold. Smoke rises with the dawn: as in ancient rites, the sacrifice has been offered up. Order returns, but it is the malign order of the Fascist state: "*Ordnung muss sein.*" The troops march. Borowski's story, like so much twentieth-century literature, is antitragedy. Little is ennobled, nothing is affirmed.

Topics for Writing

1. By suggesting the kinds of defense mechanisms that deadened human responses to horror, *Ladies and Gentlemen, to the Gas Chamber* helps us understand how the Nazis managed to dominate so much of the world for so long. Choose an example of such defensive behavior to analyze.

2. Discuss the use of animal and insect imagery in this story.

3. Do you sympathize with any of the people described here? Explain your reactions.

Comparative Perspectives

1. That "the systematic dehumanization of the camps" mentioned in the headnote succeeded for so long has often been ascribed to the unthinking obedience to which workers in an increasingly bureaucratized Europe had become habituated. Discuss the relationship between the dehumanizing behavior of lawyers and physicians described in *The Death of Ivan Ilyich*, or the office mentality in *The Metamorphosis*, and the administration of the extermination camps here.
2. "Look here, Henri, are we good people?" Goodness is a category explored in a number of twentieth-century texts. Explain why goodness is problematic in *Ladies and Gentlemen, to the Gas Chamber* and in other modern and contemporary works, such as *The Good Woman of Setzuan*, and/or *Matryona's Home*. If goodness can be defined in these texts, of what does it consist? If not, is the impossibility of achieving goodness due to social or personal shortcomings?

Further Reading

See also the reading suggestions in the *Anthology*, p. 2549.

Langer, Lawrence L. *Versions of Survival: The Holocaust and the Human Spirit*. 1982. A helpful analysis of the "world of choiceless choice" and Borowski's way of forcing readers to reevaluate their assumptions about life and art.

ALAIN ROBBE-GRILLET

The Secret Room

Backgrounds

Robbe-Grillet is one of the most influential postmodern novelists and theoreticians. His fiction and theory have influenced French writers such as Nathalie Sarraute, Claude Simon, and Michel Butor; American writers such as John Barth, William Gass, and Donald Barthelme; the Austrian Peter Handke; and a host of others. Reading his work requires us to rupture all our previous assumptions about what fiction "means" and to participate in a nonreferential world of pure fictionality. Yet this fictional world is not at all "unreal," in Robbe-Grillet's view. Instead, it reflects an understanding of the real opaqueness and contradictions of the world in which we live. As Robbe-Grillet says, "If the reader sometimes has difficulty getting his bearings in the modern novel, it is the same way that he loses them in the very world where he lives, when everything in the old structures and the old norms around him is giving way."

It is appropriate that Robbe-Grillet should link a sense of dislocation in the modern novel with the same dislocation in everyday life. The challenge that his works represent to literary criticism is akin to the challenge they pose to contemporary norms and cultural habits, much as it may seem that the enormous technical intricacy of his fiction removes it from real-life considerations. In fact, once students realize that the elaborately shifting scene of *The Secret Room* replays themes that would be called sadistic or pornographic if published in a newspaper, they may have real questions about the significance of this story and the nature of Robbe-Grillet's work. One way of addressing this problem is to begin by discussing the experimental innovations of new-novel technique, and then to consider the ways in which this revolutionary technique causes us to reexamine not just the way we *see* the world, but also the way we think and act in it. The "new novelists" are proposing a metaphysical and social argument, as well as a revolutionary aesthetic strategy. Robbe-Grillet's 1961 essay *New Novel, New Man* describes preparing the citizen of the future by clarifying that most basic level of social relationships: literally, how we "look at things."

Traditional modes of literary analysis are paralyzed when we come to Robbe-Grillet, and that is precisely the way he wants it. Following a linear plot or the protagonist's psychological development will not help us in *The Secret Room* as it would, for example, in *Death in Venice, The Dead,* or *The Old Chief Mshlanga.* To understand Robbe-Grillet's fictions, we must turn to his theories and especially the essays collected in *For a New Novel* (from which the following quotations are taken).

Robbe-Grillet makes one basic assertion everywhere in his theoretical writing: that the conventions we ordinarily find in fiction are, in fact, conventional ways of looking at the world, derived from a worldview we no longer share, a world that "marked the apogee of the individual" and in which "personality represented both the means and the end of all exploration." Such a world required that all the technical elements of narrative—"systematic use of the past tense and the third person, unconditional adoption of chronological development, linear plots, regular trajectory of the passions, impulse of each episode toward a conclusion, etc.—tended to impose the image of a stable, coherent, continuous, unequivocal, entirely decipherable universe." Fictions, indeed words themselves, "functioned as a trap in which the writer captured the universe in order to hand it over to society."

For Robbe-Grillet, there are two problems with this conventional mode of literary representation. First, it is not true to our contemporary understanding of reality, and second, it does not help bring about a new order. The contemporary world is "no longer our private property." Nor is it appropriate any longer for human beings to *impress* themselves upon nature, to mold and shape it in their own image. The modern world is "less sure of itself, more modest perhaps, since it has renounced the omnipotence of the person." Where the traditional language of fiction assumed a "nature," and our superior place in it, we can now make no such assumption. For Robbe-Grillet, the world is not "moral." It is neither "significant nor absurd. It *is*, quite simply." This new reality must be explored, but traditional modes of representing reality are ill-suited to the task. Robbe-Grillet's new-novel techniques aim to reflect the *is*-ness, the quiddity, of things. He wants to "record the distance between the object and myself, and the distances of the object itself," for this kind of narrative aims to show that "things are here and that they are nothing but things, each limited to itself." Linked to this recognition that things "are" in themselves, separate from us, is the realization that we still *perceive* them from our own angle of vision: hence Robbe-Grillet's emphasis on shifting perspective of what *is*, reminding us that any perceiver is limited and that point of view changes in time. The writer is free to invent, without preconceptions. "What constitutes the novelist's strength is precisely that he invents quite freely, without a model."

The political implications of Robbe-Grillet's position are important. In a world that is no longer "stable, coherent, and continuous," traditional modes of operation—including the ways we relate to others, to things, and to institutions—must be revised. Consequently, the writer revises expectations throughout his career and especially in later work that destabilizes any attempt to find a constant center. The beginning of *The House of Assignations* (1965) announces contradiction as its theme and thereafter provides merging but contradictory versions of events: different people are given identical defining traits or are made to speak identical lines, and short passages frequently do not quite fit into the tentatively established storylines. *Action in Project for a Revolution in New York* (1970) sometimes progresses by verbal echoes, or anagrams of a few key words (*rouge* connected with *rogue, urge, roue, joue*) rather than by logical plot sequence; the narrative persona may shift in the midst of a passage, and that same shift indicates (in French) a sudden shift of gender, too—*he* becoming *she*, for example. *Project for a Revolution in New York* is not a political tract, despite its title, but an experimental revolution of "revolving" nightmare scenes that could almost be taken from pulp novels depicting the depersonalized violence of the modern city—the "New York" of popular mythology.

On the technical side, this increasingly impersonal juxtaposition of elements suggests artistic collage processes. Robbe-Grillet was well acquainted with avant-garde artists Robert Rauschenberg and Roy Lichtenstein, and he produced collages himself and also collaborated on a 1978 text with Rauschenberg (*Suspect Surface Traces*). *Topology of a Phantom City* (1975) and *Memories of the Golden Triangle* (1978) display collage assembly techniques, coordinating a series of texts (some printed elsewhere and by other people) with new prose links, or setting them in patterns of mathematical repetition. *Memories of the Golden Triangle* may be read as any one of several overlapping stories, and each newly chosen protagonist will suggest a different slant on the same events (like interactions in "real life"). Less technical or impersonal are the underlying themes of all these works: the murders, rapes, torture, anxious pursuit, and general violence portrayed throughout variations on the basic detective-story form. Here the political significance is more ambiguous. On the one hand, these sado-erotic fantasies (already present in *The Secret Room*) can be interpreted as the aggressive free play of an author's libidinous imagination; on the other, as parodic recognition of similar pervasive themes in contemporary culture, whether in fiction, advertising, newspaper reporting or television.

The "new novel," then, reflects this new state of affairs. It reflects the *is*-ness of things since it is by firmly establishing their *presence* that "objects and gestures establish themselves." The only reality we can discuss, without becoming complicit in an outmoded system of explanatory references ("whether emotional, sociological, Freudian, or metaphysical"), is a reality that simply *is*. In his work Robbe-Grillet wants only to "record the distance between the object and myself, and the distances of the object itself (its *exterior* distances, i.e., its measurements), and the distances of objects among themselves, and to insist further that these are *only distances* (and not divisions)." He wants to do this because this kind of narrative establishes that "things are here and that they are nothing but things, each limited to itself." Linked to this recognition that things "are" in themselves, separate from us, is the realization that we still *perceive* them from our own angle of vision: hence Robbe-Grillet's emphasis on shifting perspectives of what *is*, reminding us that any perceiver is limited and that point of view changes in time.

The most obvious influences on *The Secret Room* are films, paintings, and popular fiction, especially thriller fiction. Robbe-Grillet's associations with filmmaking and filmmakers (particularly Alain Resnais) are many and obvious. The images of *The Secret Room* are snapshots, and *Snapshots* is the title of the 1962 collection in which *The Secret Room* appeared, but they are snapshots given movement by their juxtaposition, creating a kind of montage effect. One critic has noted that whereas traditional fiction "renders the illusion of space by going from point to point in time," Robbe-Grillet's fiction—like a film—renders time "by going from point to point in space." The overall effect of the cinema on Robbe-Grillet's fiction is clarified by thinking of his narrative point of view as a camera eye, which captures what there is to see without necessarily linking what it sees in space *or* time. Readers will recall the extent to which Eliot, Joyce, and Beckett use similar techniques.

Robbe-Grillet's "verbal art" also emulates "painterly style," and *The Secret Room* pays artistic homage to the symbolist painter Gustave Moreau. Robert Rauschenberg, Jasper Johns, and René Magritte have also strikingly influenced his recent fiction, and one senses that Marcel Duchamp's success in transforming our perceptions of objects by revising their context equally left its mark. The painterly notion of collage is evident in *The Secret Room* and elsewhere in his fiction. Finally, the notion that a single "scene" may be presented from a number of perspectives simultaneously, or almost simultaneously, was one of the crucial discoveries of painters such as Cézanne, Braque, and Picasso. It also finds its way into writing by, for instance, André Gide, Gertrude Stein, Wallace Stevens, Jorge Luis Borges, and Lawrence Durrell.

The Secret Room begins as a painterly description from which human characteristics are absent; the stain is a "rosette" and not blood, and it stands out against a "smooth pale surface," not a body. It is a theatrical setting, and "space is filled" with colonnades, an ascending staircase, and a mysterious silhouette fleeing in the distance. The body itself—when finally recognized—is described with excessive surface detail, as if the painter's eye registered only the shapes and textures of flesh, hair, velvet, and stone. Human emotions are depicted as compositional elements: the victim's mouth is open "as if screaming," while the murderer's face reveals a "violent exaltation." Thus far, the scene is a static tableau about which the reader receives progressively more and more information, but Robbe-Grillet invests it with puzzling movement by describing the victim as both wounded and intact and the caped figure in four different, incompatible poses. First seen near the top of the stair and facing away, the murderer has next moved several steps back and appears on the first steps, turning to look at the body. Later he appears standing only a yard away from her, looking down, and finally he is kneeling close to the woman as she breathes convulsively, is wounded, and dies. It is as though time has moved backward, reviewing the stages of the murder and flight before they become fixed on the artist's canvas. Beginning and ending as a painted scene, *The Secret Room* extends the spatial reality it describes by attributing movement and different positions to figures on the canvas. One of Robbe-Grillet's earlier works, it already demonstrates the writer's ability to offer the most precise details within a calculatedly ambiguous and disturbing perspective.

Classroom Strategies

Despite the complexities noted above, *The Secret Room* can be taught in one class period, though its implications—once discussed—might require more time to examine. Students will have problems, to begin with, because they won't understand what to expect on the basis of the initial painterly description. None of the usual clues are present: no indication of plot, no character interaction, no hints about the direction of the story. (You may wish to contrast the informative beginning of *The Guest*.) Try pointing out that this *lack* is precisely the point: the sole focus is a minutely described, yet mysteriously evocative *setting*—the "secret room" of the title. What secret does it hold? How well does it keep its secret?

By the third paragraph it is clear that someone has been killed in this room. The following paragraphs describe the murderer fleeing the scene, and the scene itself is more fully described. Still, there is an uncanny emphasis on physical details and a lack of information about the deed itself or the motive for it. At this point you might ask the students to imagine a murder scene, with the caped figure as murderer/torturer and the woman as victim, just as Robbe-Grillet has presented it. Then have them imagine that the entire action has been filmed from beginning to end. Next ask them to suppose that someone selects four frames from that film, places them side by side without regard to chronology, enlarges each so that we can see every detail, and then paints equally large pictures—identical to the cinema frames—on canvas. Finally, this someone describes in prose what those paintings look like, without telling us until the very end that he or she is describing a series of paintings, not the "real" murder scene itself. This strategy is not particularly fair to the sophistication of Robbe-Grillet's narrative technique, but the analogy makes his method less alien to some students.

Short though the story is, the implications of *The Secret Room* will require some reference to the author's literary theories. If you are unaccustomed to discussing theory in class, you may well be surprised at how interesting it can be to students, especially when combined with a short example of that theory (successfully? unsuccessfully?) put into practice. Besides, the implications of what Robbe-Grillet has to say extend prose fiction to politics, social assumptions, psychology, and personal relations—aspects of experience that students, late in the term, often tackle with some eagerness. In any case, students are usually quite willing to have their assumptions questioned, since it is during their college years that they are questioning the assumptions of everyone and everything around them. Ignoring Robbe-Grillet's theories while teaching *The Secret Room* can turn out to be more confusing, and considerably less interesting, than offering them for student consideration.

One of the more interesting topics for discussion will be the degree to which the story seems to depart from the theories. Insofar as Robbe-Grillet means to turn our attention toward the object, he certainly succeeds, but if we understand that he believes in creating "objective literature"—in the sense of creating a literature that is impassive, impartial, and entirely uncluttered by subjectivity—he just as certainly fails. A couple of examples might illustrate this point: in the story's third paragraph we are told that the victim's body "gleams feebly, marked with the red stain—a white body whose full, supple flesh can be sensed, fragile, no doubt, and vulnerable." Later we are told of her "full buttocks, the stretched-out legs, widely spread, and the black tuft of the exposed sex, provocative, proffered, useless now." Not only is this material blatantly sensational, it is also filled with subjective judgment and evaluation. How would a fully "objective" narrator know that the flesh was "supple," "fragile," or "vulnerable"? And who, exactly, "senses" these things? The phrase "no doubt" immediately suggests the possibility that there might *be* a doubt, even as it registers that the narrator's opinion is contrary to such a possibility. To whom, exactly, is the victim's exposure "provocative"? And who judges that her sex is being "proffered" or decides that it is "useless now"?

The point here is not so much that Robbe-Grillet's theory is not really "objective," however, as that a fully "objective" narration is always impossible. And that it is impossible is something that Robbe-Grillet knows perfectly well. How, then, are we to interpret the nonobjective "objectivity" of *The Secret Room*: as unconscious self-betrayal, as a parody of thriller novels and film noir, as an exposure of sexual and erotic stereotypes, or as simply another layer of representation?

Topics for Discussion and Writing

1. How does this story differ from conventional narrative fiction? Contrast with a story of your choice.
2. What is Robbe-Grillet's theory of fiction? How does it apply to *The Secret Room*?

    [See paragraphs 2–6 of "Backgrounds" for a discussion of theory, then paragraphs 7–8 of "Backgrounds" and paragraphs 3–5 of "Classroom Strategies" for application to *The Secret Room*.]
3. What four stages (or scenes) can you discern in the course of the story? Do they make any logical sense? What impression is made *on the reader* by having events presented in this sequence? How would the effect be changed if a single version of events was presented in chronological order?
4. In what ways is the narrative technique of the story affected by cinematic techniques? Painting techniques?
5. Why does Robbe-Grillet use such loaded images of sexual victimization and violence—images that remind us, moreover, of scenes from popular films and fiction? To what extent do you believe that this sensationalism is intentional?
6. How far can one proceed in interpreting this story? Is there a point at which simultaneous interpretations become possible?
7. *The Secret Room* is dedicated to Gustave Moreau. Discuss the painterly qualities you notice in Robbe-Grillet's description. On the basis of this story, can you visualize the picture as Moreau might have painted it?
8. Edgar Allan Poe stated that a good short story should achieve a "unity of effect or impression" or "a certain unique or single *effect*." To what extent has Robbe-Grillet succeeded in this task?

Comparative Perspectives

1. The opening of *The Secret Room* depicts the fascination with which a voyeur looks at a bloody body. Compare and contrast the perspectives brought to bear on similar scenes in other modern texts, such as Lorca's *Lament for Ignacio Sánchez Mejías* (especially in "2. The Spilled Blood") or Dave's efforts to stanch the bleeding hole in the side of Jenny the Mule in *The Man Who Was Almost a Man*.

    [For Lorca, the blood is a badge of heroism; for Dave, a sign of both his own loss of innocence and his ineptitude. Robbe-Grillet eschews moral or psychological perspectives for a purely aesthetic response.]
2. In an interdisciplinary context, pursue the discussion of Robbe-Grillet's affinity with modern artists and painters by asking your students to analyze and compare the peculiar spatial details of *The Secret Room* with the treatment of space in paintings by De Chirico or Magritte. Link this to Baudelaire's *A Carcass*, perhaps, and the languid odalisques of a painter like Gérôme, to see the

evolution of a continental obsession with monumental architecture and sculptural feminine bodies.

Further Reading

See also the reading suggestions in the *Anthology*, p. 2554.

Bogue, Ronald L. "The Twilight of Relativism: Robbe-Grillet and the Measure of Man." In *Relativism and the Arts*, ed. Betty Jean Craige. 1983.

————. "A Generative Phantasy: Robbe-Grillet's *La chambre secrete*." *South Atlantic Review* 46, 4 (November 1981):1–16.

Gibson, Andrew. "One Kind of Ambiguity in Joyce, Beckett, and Robbe-Grillet." *Canadian Review of Comparative Literature/Revue Canadienne de Littérature Comparée* 12, 3 (September 1985): 409–21.

Heath, Stephen. *The Nouveau Roman: A Study in the Practice of Writing*. 1972. The chapter on Robbe-Grillet discusses the relationship between author and reader.

Nelson, Roy Jay. *Causality and Narrative in French Fiction from Zola to Robbe-Grillet*. 1990. Contains a discussion of Robbe-Grillet's narrative technique.

Oppenheim, Lois, ed. *Three Decades of the French New Novel*. Contains several essays on different aspects of Robbe-Grillet's work as well as a roundtable discussion on the new novel, in which the author participated.

Robbe-Grillet, Alain. *For a New Novel: Essays on Fiction*. Trans. Richard Howard. 1963. A crucial set of essays, extremely clear and concentrated, for understanding Robbe-Grillet's work.

Stoltzfus, Ben. *Alain Robbe-Grillet: Life, Work and Criticism*. 1987. A brief introduction.

————. *Alain Robbe-Grillet: The Body of the Text*. 1985. A discussion of the erotic and sadistic aspects of Robbe-Grillet's writing that recapitulates and develops the writer's own views.

ITALO CALVINO

Invisible Cities

Backgrounds

Fantasy, imagination, pleasure: these are key words to employ in any class devoted to the work of Italo Calvino. From the late 1950s until his death, Calvino used his realist style combined with a flair for poetic description to tell impossibly delightful stories where boys live full lives confined only to treetops and where knights carry out their tasks without a body.

In teaching these stories, it is useful to mention that before writing them Calvino had left Italy and moved to Paris. There, he met a group of experimental writers intent on rescuing fiction from worn-out formulas, techniques, and plotlines. Established by the French writer Raymond Queneau and including such marvelously inventive and imaginative writers as Georges Perec and the American Harry Mathews, the Society for Potential Literature, OuLiPo (Ouvroir de Littérature Potentielle), was dedicated to inventing new forms and tapping into new zones for the creative writer's imagination. Each work of the OuLiPo group is designed around a strict, formal structure that often referred directly to some mathematical principle or formula. Perec's *La disparition* (translated into English as *A Void*), for instance, was written without the use of the letter E. (The translation, miraculously, follows the same rule). OuLiPo's experimental structures usually remain invisible to the reader but they also act as control devices for the writer's imagination, which then requires the writer to explore narratives in entirely new ways.

The story included here comes from Calvino's OuLiPoean novel, *Invisible Cities*, published in Italian in 1972. There is a tight structure governing the form: the book has nine chapters, and each has two dialogues printed in italics at the beginning and end of each chapter. Following the first dialogue one finds sets of cities, each description categorized as "Cities and Names," "Cities and the Dead," and the like. Over the course of the nine chapters one finds that these descriptions divide into sets of tens and fives for a total of fifty-five cities described. One also notices another rule: each city has the name of a woman. Each city, moreover, is placed in a group; if one were to map them, it would have to be done in such a way as to exactly replicate a mathematical correspondence in a formula.

For all this exactitude of structure, however, the very purpose of a structure—to get a better hold on reality, to control one's imagination— is itself undercut by the book's story. The section reprinted here comes from the end of Chapter Eight and playfully alludes to the hidden structure governing the book itself. This allusion comes when the Khan insists on finding order in Polo's cities by replicating them as pieces on a chessboard. What the Khan wants, above all, is knowledge, and he realizes that knowledge can come only from a complete understanding of the order of things. The genius of the book, and of this chapter, is to question that basic assumption about the relationship between knowledge and order.

Ultimately, then, this excerpt pits order and knowledge against the imagination and a sense of chaotic wonder. Calvino's interest in fantasy, imagination, wonder, and the marvelous all come out of his deep skepticism with regard to the importance of order and logical structures as a key to truth. Therefore, for all of Calvino's interest in new forms of order, and for all of his association with OuLiPo, it is also important to recognize Calvino's belief in and commitment to the fable as *the* crucial literary form.

One of the most discerning critics of Calvino's work, Sara Maria

Adler, argues that the structure of the fable appealed to Calvino's goals for all his literary endeavors. She notes that fables are told from a child's perspective, depend on the child's sense of wonder and mystery, and concern a basic conflict between a character, often the child, and the environment more generally. Calvino's innocent narrators, often children, return in this book in the form of the young Marco Polo. Here Marco relates his adventures in a strange environment to an aging king in search of wisdom. More marvelous still, however, is that the book, *Invisible Cities*, becomes all the more modern as it progresses—despite its taking place purportedly in the thirteenth century. By the time readers arrive at this excerpt from Chapter Eight it is becoming clear that Calvino is proposing the notion that cities themselves might well be fables of mental, emotional, and other psychological states of being.

Classroom Strategies

This chapter is best suited to one day. A useful classroom strategy would be to take any one of the five cities and ask the students to read it as a fable about some particular place they may recognize. To do this, one might start with the Khan's realization at the conclusion of the story. He is amazed that Marco Polo can see so much meaning in a mere square of wood on his chessboard. How much better must Polo be able to understand each *actual* city. Therefore, taking what details the five descriptions offer, and reading those details along with the title, have the students identify the emotive traits suggested by each city. From the details and the title, is the location funny, happy, sad, or what? Why? What words suggest which emotions? Put the words on the board and ask the students if a contemporary city they have experienced might be associated with them. Then, you might ask what mental states, what emotional states, and what psychological character states might be associated with the list generated on the board. Given that each of the five cities is named after a woman, a person, might these be human rather than inanimate characteristics? The goal of such a strategy should be to gain insight into the power of fable, metaphor, and the small detail to open up vast insights into the human experience.

Topics for Discussion and Writing

1. How does the metaphor of the chess set relate to the tale of these five stories?
2. Does this story have a single, particular theme? What might it be? How does this theme relate to the fractured, divided form?
3. Given that Calvino was so interested in fables, and given that fables tend to have morals, what might be the moral of this fable?

Comparative Perspectives

1. Compare this story to "Borges and I" by Borges. What view of the teller of tales emerges from the "I" in Borges and Marco Polo here?

2. Compare the view of cities presented here with the view of cities found in T.S. Eliot's *Waste Land*. What is the difference? Why does it matter?

3. Does any other work read this semester lend itself to being read as a fable? Which one? Why?

Further Reading

Adler, Sara Maria. *Calvino: The Writer as Fablemaker.* 1979.

Francese, Joseph. *Narrating Postmodern Time and Space.* 1997.

Hume, Kathryn. *Calvino's Fictions: Cogito and Cosmos.* 1992.

Olken, Irene. *With Pleated Eye and Garnet Wing: Symmetries of Italo Calvino.* 1984.

INGEBORG BACHMANN

The Barking

Backgrounds

The Barking comes from Bachmann's second collection of short stories, *Three Paths to the Lake* (in German, *Simultan*), published in 1972 and written over the same years that she was working on the novel cycle *Ways of Death* (*Todesarten*). Characters from *Ways of Death* reappear in *Three Paths to the Lake*, and cross-references between the stories make it clear that Bachmann intended to provide a panorama of modern Austrian society from a perspective that questioned social relationships of gender and power, and the role of language in establishing identity. The consummate skill that she had brought to her earlier hermetic poetry reappears in the later prose fiction, with its oblique and terrifying pictures of human beings—especially women—unable to express or recognize themselves as complete individuals. The generally bleak picture of personal relationships in a covertly fascist society does not go unchallenged; it is criticized either by implication or occasionally by example. For Bachmann, the writer has both a role and a responsibility to effect social change. In a 1971 interview, she commented that "society could be brought to a new form of consciousness by a new kind of writing. Of course one can't change the world with a poem, that's impossible, but one can have an effect on something." Her influence on later German-language writers and her growing international reputation attest to the impact of Bachmann's "new kind of writing," a consciously modernist style that articulates the twentieth century's "new experiences of suffering."

Readers exploring Bachmann's work may be puzzled by references to the second story collection under different titles: *Simultaneous* and *Three Paths to the Lake*. The 1989 English translation of *Simultan* takes its title from the last (and longest) story in the book, *Three Paths to the Lake*, rather than from the first, *Simultaneous*. *Simultaneous* ("Word for

Word" in English translation) describes the spiritually dispossessed situation of a simultaneous interpreter named Nadja. Nadja exists in a linguistic limbo, an empty space of exchange in which she transmits equivalent meanings for other people's words while living "without a single thought of her own." Another projected title for the collection was *Women from Vienna*, reflecting the fact that all five stories describe different middle-class Viennese women who are, as Mark Anderson says, united "by what is missing from their lives." In one way or another, these women represent an alienation from reality that contrasts sharply with the precise description of apparently trivial details in their daily lives.

These are not isolated cases: instead, all five stories are linked by scattered references to figures appearing in other stories (and in *The Franza Case*) so that a broader pattern of social repression and inarticulate suffering begins to emerge. (This technique of cumulative cross-reference is found in novelist Honoré de Balzac's great nineteenth-century panorama of French society, *The Human Comedy*.) Beatrix, the narcissistic protagonist of *Problems, Problems*, who lives to sleep late and visit the beauty parlor, resents her cousin Elisabeth Mihailovics, whose murder by her husband is described in *Three Paths to the Lake*; she also asks the beauty parlor attendant about young Frau Jordan—seen characteristically not as an individual but as "the wife of that Jordan." In *Three Paths to the Lake*, a successful news photographer named Elisabeth Matrei recalls the different (complex and disheartening) aspects of love in her life; we hear at one point that one of her lovers mentioned living with "a woman from Vienna, an unbelievably ambitious woman, a simultaneous interpreter," and elsewhere that another character worshiped the actress Fann Goldman (a character in the *Ways of Death* cycle). Elisabeth herself feels deprived of speech, a spectator at the events she reports, unable to say what she really feels: "hasn't it ever occurred to anyone that you kill people when you deprive them of the power of speech and with it the power to experience and think?"

Such themes of loss and alienation are already present in Bachmann's earlier prose: the title story of her first collection, *The Thirtieth Year*, presents a narrator who reviews a life of spiritual passivity as he enters his thirtieth year and recovers from an automobile accident. Formerly "everything he did was on approval, on the understanding that it could be cancelled," but now he is no longer on the threshold of unlimited possibilities. "He casts the net of memory, casts it over himself and draws himself, catcher and caught in one person over the threshold of time, over the threshold of place, to see who he was and who he has become." The route to self-discovery dissolves in ambiguity for the narrator of *Malina* (1971), the only completed novel in the cycle *Ways of Death*. *Malina* is narrated until near the end by a writer who has a complicated relationship with two men who are conceivably also aspects of her artistic personality. Ivan is her lover and emotional reference point; Malina, dryly analytic, shares an apartment with her and encourages her to analyze her feelings. By the end of the novel, the narrator has lost Ivan and simultaneously her anchor in concrete reality. She disappears "into the wall," and the novel concludes with Malina's denial of her existence. What has happened? "An I tells its story to the end" ("Ein Ich erzählt sich zu Ende").

A complicated pattern of discovery and loss of identity is similarly visible in *The Barking*. The two protagonists share a mutual discovery in the course of their conversation about Leo Jordan: discoveries about each other, about themselves, and about Leo. Franziska (the diminutive of Franza) comes to question her husband, Leo's behavior toward his mother, toward his cousin Johannes, and eventually toward herself as she recognizes that she too is afraid of him. It is a very cautious questioning and only the beginning of judgment, for Franziska (like old Frau Jordan) is taught to believe that "Leo was just too good to her." First, she is merely amazed and hurt that Leo, a psychiatrist "whose very profession obliged him to uphold a neutral and scientific attitude toward homosexuality . . . could go on and on about this cousin as though he had somehow, through his own negligence, fallen prey to works of art, homosexuality, and an inheritance to boot." Even later, when she hears that old Frau Jordan gave away her cherished dog, Nuri, because Leo didn't like it, she accuses both herself and Leo of cruelty: "What kind of people are we?" We never see the results of her growing comprehension, for Leo has forestalled her and the couple will soon part: "other things came to pass, events of such hurricane force that she almost forgot the old woman and a great many other things as well." Unlike Franziska, old Frau Jordan does not allow herself to analyze or judge her experience. She cherishes the memory of another child, Kiki, but she represses painful recollection of Leo's childhood behavior. On the surface, she constantly effaces herself while praising her exceptional son; random thoughts, however, tell another story, of a vindictive and grasping man who has abandoned his mother, is incapable of close relationships, and may have sent an inconvenient relative to the concentration camps. Old Frau Jordan is incapable of openly judging the contrast between her own sacrifices and Leo's blatant neglect and defends herself from disillusionment by insisting that "Leo is just such a good son!" When the pressure becomes too great, she recedes into hallucinations of barking dogs that blot out her real-life anxiety. Yet her buried resentment surfaces in different ways: in an implied criticism when Elfi replaces Franziska ("how many wives was that now anyway. . . . The barking was so close now that for an instant she was certain that Nuri was with her again and would jump at him and bark"; in self-abasing comments ("your dumb old mother can hardly read anymore anyway"; in our discovery that her accusing Frau Agnes of having taken ten schillings probably displaces an earlier incident she tries to forget ("the day when the last ten schillings had disappeared and Leo had lied to her").

Throughout the story, the indirect focal point is Leo Jordan. Bachmann has very cleverly shown (rather than merely stated) how thoroughly these Viennese women are defined by the invisible priority of the men on whom they depend. Leo is the subject of all their conversations and a dominant figure without ever being present. His destructive impact is clearly connected with Bachmann's equation of patriarchy and fascism; Leo's authoritarian use and intimidation of others for his own purposes, his alienation from human relationships that would imply equality, and his scorn of women and homosexuals are all reminiscent of Nazi beliefs. Bachmann evokes the Nazi connections especially strongly in the passages concerning Leo's homosexual cousin, Johannes, and the study of the concentration camps. Leo Jordan's attacks on Johannes (like his criticism of his first wife) have a suspicious and even guilty air. Johannes had paid for Leo's education, but "Leo was reluctant to be reminded of his mother and his former wives and lovers who were nothing to him but a conspiracy of creditors from whom he would escape only by belittling them to himself and others." We learn from old Frau Jordan's "roundabout way of saying things" that Leo very likely denounced his cousin either out of spite or to protect himself. When his mother learns that Dr. Jordan has written a book on "The Significance of Endogeneous and Exogenous Factors in Connection with the Occurrence of Paranoid and Depressive Psychoses in Former Concentration Camp Inmates and Refugees," she is worried and recalls a mysterious "other thing" that turns out to be Johannes's detention in a concentration camp for a year and a half. Simultaneously, she notes that her son "knows how to defend himself" and that "it meant a certain amount of danger for Leo, having a relative who . . ." Franziska, ironically, interprets the old woman's statement as referring to the wartime danger of having a relative in a concentration camp; more likely (especially given the references to barking that begin at this point), Leo had protected himself by denouncing his cousin. Does Johannes have a "paranoid and depressed" suspicion that such might be the case? If so, it would be important for Dr. Jordan to put such psychoses in scientific perspective.

One of the pleasures of reading *The Barking* lies in its indirect, enigmatic discourse and the opportunity it offers to reconstruct different characters from a variety of clues. Although the headnote in the anthology refers to a fuller picture of Dr. Jordan in *The Franza Case*, it is more rewarding to read *The Barking* in terms of the information given by the story itself. We know, for example, by the end of the story, that both women are dead, but we do not know precisely when or how they died. We can only guess why Leo and Franziska separate; Leo may be involved in another affair that has become serious, or he may be irritated by Franziska's signs of independent thinking. The language itself provides clues to the characters' psychological identity. Thoughts reported in a stream-of-consciousness style reveal not only information but also attitudes and anxieties: Franziska, secretly purchasing a radio for her mother-in-law, reassures herself that she "broke into the meager savings she had set aside for some sort of emergency which would hopefully never arise and could only be a minor emergency at any rate."

Students are sometimes puzzled by the last paragraph, which seems to have little to do with the plot except to make sure that the Pineider taxi service is paid. Yet this paragraph serves as a kind of pendant to the rest of the story. It is not necessary to know that Dr. Martin Ranner (according to *The Franza Case*) accompanied his sister to Egypt, where she died in a paroxysm of self-reproach after being raped by strangers; or that her feeling of self-worth, already severely damaged by Dr. Jordan's insidious attacks, was completely destroyed by this last assault. The last paragraph does not provide this information, but it does complete several themes and acts as a partial counterbalance to the bleak picture of old Frau Jordan's increasing paranoia and death. We learn several things: first, that Franziska is dead and her brother has a strong reason never to see Leo Jordan again; second, that Leo Jordan's destructive example is not the only way of life in contemporary society: Dr. Ranner values human relationships and assumes ethical obligations beyond what is strictly necessary (this may be Bachmann's "utopian" side, although it is diminished by the fact that only the men survive); and third, that Leo Jordan had probably acted true to form by refusing, over several months, to pay the taxi bill incurred by his former wife on his mother's behalf.

Classroom Strategies

The Barking can be taught in one class period. If your students have read the story carefully and have no immediate questions, you may want to move directly to a discussion of the barking itself and its function as a psychological barrier between old Frau Jordan and a reality she cannot face. Some students may well ask you about the last paragraph—which leaves you starting at the end, with a description of the underlying themes that come together at this point. It may be easiest, however, to begin at the beginning, with the description of old Frau Jordan and what we learn about the other characters through her eyes. As soon as her relationship to Franziska is established, it will be useful to introduce the various discovery patterns that are developed throughout the story. The image of Leo Jordan can then be brought out as the hidden, yet dominant, reference point that illustrates Bachmann's attack on the damage done to women and other marginalized figures by a patriarchal (or fascist) society. There are a number of useful themes or passages to consider with the class: the various examples of old Frau Jordan's self-criticism, humility, fear (and buried resentment) of her son; the several stages of Franziska's recognition that the "Leo she came to know through the old woman was a completely different Leo from the man she had married"; the enigma of Leo's relationship to Johannes and his study of concentration-camp psychoses; Leo's personality as an embodiment of fascism; the various passages describing dogs and barking. Discussion should be easy to elicit throughout this story, whether as comments on individual passages, on the differing reaction of Franziska and old Frau Jordan, on Bachmann's view of patriarchy and fascism, or on the recent rise of political groups with neo-Nazi sympathies.

Topics for Discussion

1. What is the significance of the barking? What function does it serve for old Frau Jordan? When (and in what context) does she

first mention hearing dogs barking? How does Nuri fit into the context?

2. Why is the story titled *The Barking* and not *Old Frau Jordan* or *The Jordan Family*? Give some examples of barking in the story and relate them to the plot.

3. Discuss the ways in which the characters' language (especially unspoken thoughts) reveal their psychological attitudes.

4. Discuss Leo Jordan's relationship to his cousin Johannes.

5. Discuss Bachmann's equation of patriarchy with fascism, using examples from the story.

6. Is Leo Jordan a good psychiatrist, in your opinion? Explain.

7. What responsibility—if any—does old Frau Jordan bear for her own fate?

8. Describe the various ways in which Franziska tries to help her mother-in-law. How do these attempts put her into conflict with her husband?

9. How does Franziska come to see her husband in a different light? (Cite and discuss specific examples.)

Comparative Perspectives

1. Compare the narrative attitudes toward maternal figures in *The Barking, Matryona's Home,* and *Walker Brothers Cowboy.* Is the point of these stories to make us feel sorry for unhappy mothers? Is there any sense in which old Frau Jordan, Matryona, and Mrs. Jordan are complicit in their own fates? Did Frau Jordan have options in life that she should have explored in order to free herself from her tyrannical son? How seriously do you view Ignatich's remark that Matryona "was forever meddling in men's work" when he explains how she died? Why does Munro's Mrs. Jordan have headaches?

   [Bachmann criticizes Leo more than she blames old Frau Jordan, and Ignatich's moments of annoyance with Matryona serve only to emphasize her selflessness. Munro's attitude is more complex.]

2. Compare Bachmann's use of the dog Nuri's barking with other instances of similar narrative shorthand. When a pet offers testimony that helps us understand human behavior, what view of the animal world seems to prevail?

   [This favorite device, which students will recognize from vampire films if from no other source, seems specific to Western authors, who tend to sentimentalize alert animals as inhabitants of a separate realm. Pets, inarticulate but expressive of their owner's inner lives, differ fundamentally from the talking, clever animals of African, Native American, and Asian storytelling. Consider, if appropriate, the information about character provided by Argos, the ancient dog who recognizes the disguised Odysseus in book XVII of

Homer's *Odyssey* or the repeated references to lapdogs in *The Rape of the Lock*.]

Further Reading

See also the reading suggestions in the *Anthology*, p. 2548.

Achberger, Karen. "Introduction" to *The Thirtieth Year*. 1987. Situates Bachmann in twentieth-century German literature; concise discussion of the short stories.

Frederiksen, Elke, ed. *Women Writers of Germany, Austria, and Switzerland: An Annotated Bio-Bibliographical Guide*. 1989. Includes a brief discussion of Bachmann's work.

Frieden, Sandra. "Bachmann's *Malina* and *Todesarten*: Subliminal Crimes." *The German Quarterly* 56, 1 (January 1983): 61–73. Considers Bachmann a precursor of German "inner-directed" novels; discusses the psychoanalytic overtones of her style.

Gabriel García Márquez

Death Constant beyond Love

Backgrounds

We read García Márquez for the sheer pleasure of his inventiveness, the explosiveness of his language, the lushness of his imagination. His short fiction often has the magic and energy of a good children's story, and he creates in his readers something that very few writers, even good ones, manage: wonder.

Senator Onésimo Sánchez sells illusions. He has made the same illusory promises every four years in the "illusory" village of Rosal del Virrey, a town so dreary and sordid that "even its name was a kind of joke, because the only rose in that village was being worn by Senator Onésimo Sánchez himself." As in all his previous campaign visits, he brings with him the illusory props of political promises: rented Indians to swell the crowds, music and rockets, cardboard facades of make-believe red-brick houses, an ocean liner made of colored paper, artificial trees with leaves made of felt, rainmaking machines, oils of happiness that will make things grow in the sterile landscape of the village. But this time, Onésimo Sánchez can only go through the motions. His awareness of his imminent death outweighs all other considerations. When he meets himself in the darkness of his own self-knowledge (in part derived from Marcus Aurelius), Sánchez recognizes that *"whether it's you or someone else, it won't be long before you'll be dead and it won't be long before your name won't even be left."* He finds himself unable to sympathize with the rented Indians, barefoot on the saltpeter coals of the blistering village square; he looks upon the villagers with disdain because they are still willing to believe in his carnival of illusions, his fictional world. What

Sánchez now realizes is that his marvelous world of illusions, even though it is backed by the forces of money and political power, cannot defeat the reality of death, of nature, of the absolute and final solitude of every man.

On this final visit to Rosal del Virrey, Senator Sánchez encounters Laura Farina, who appears to him wearing a "cheap, faded Guajiro Indian robe," and though her face is "painted as protection against the sun," it is such that "it was possible to imagine that there had never been another so beautiful in the whole world." She embodies the elements that he uses to fend off the pressure of reality: beauty and love. Like the rose that he has carried with him to that sordid village, Laura's beauty promises to defeat the sterility of the landscape; her love promises to defeat death itself. But nature, and death, cannot be eluded. At the story's end, Senator Sánchez holds her "about the waist, sank his face into woods-animal armpit, and gave in to terror. Six months and eleven days later he would die in that same position, debased and re-pudiated because of the public scandal with Laura Farina and weeping with rage at dying without her." The controlling notion of *Death Constant beyond Love* is suggested by the blunt insistence of its title, which reverses the claims of Quevedo's *Love Constant beyond Death* and acts as a kind of newspaper headline announcing the final discovery of Senator Onésimo Sánchez.

One's first impression of *Death Constant beyond Love* is that it functions very close to allegory—Death, Nature, Love, Beauty, and Illusion seem to be functioning in the upper case—while at the same time it retains some qualities of the tall tale. Though both of these elements are certainly present, the story's method is in no way easy to describe. García Márquez's characteristic style—magical realism—provokes something that all good fiction provokes, a recognition of the infinite suggestibility of language, but does so in particularly observable and enchanting ways. García Márquez has said that everything he writes has its source in something that actually happened and that fiction is "reality represented through a secret code." One of the most observable tendencies of García Márquez's magical realism is to use the "secret code" of his language to lead the reader—within a sentence, from sentence to sentence, from paragraph to paragraph—to places that no reader could have expected to be. He has said that his "real inclination is to be a conjuror," and indeed, the effect of his writing is to levitate the reader, to lift the reader out of the world of prior expectations and let him or her float giddily for a moment before finding ground again.

Death Constant beyond Love demonstrates García Márquez's use of the techniques of magical realism. We can see how García Márquez suggests possible stories beyond the one he is telling, while at the same time he deepens our understanding of the central character:

> Senator Onésimo Sánchez was placid and weatherless inside the air-conditioned car, but as soon as he opened the door he was shaken by a gust of fire and his shirt of pure silk was soaked in a kind of light-colored soup and he felt many years older and more alone than ever.

This we might break down as follows:

> Senator Onésimo Sánchez was placid and weatherless inside the air-conditioned car,

[In what way can someone be weatherless? The word certainly suggests calm, but it is a calm that is almost unnatural, almost artificial. This "weatherlessness" could be attributed to the air-conditioning, but it further suggests that Sánchez is, by his own choice, unaffected by the unpleasant world of hot weather and, by implication, shabby poverty through which it is his duty to ride. The suggestion is that to be "weatherless" is to be somehow separated from life in Rosal del Virrey. The opposite, then, would also be true—to enter into the weather suggests a fundamental connection with life there.]

> but as soon as he opened the door he was shaken by a gust of fire

[We expect "hot air" or its equivalent here; we get "fire," perhaps because it is more elemental and attacks our own senses more aggressively. The word "shaken" first suggests a physical response, but by the end of the sentence it can be seen to suggest an emotional or spiritual response as well.]

> and his shirt of pure silk

[He is rich; he shines in the blistering heat. The shirt suggests that the senator is used to separating himself from the conditions in which his constituents pass their lives.]

> was soaked in a kind of light-colored soup

[The weather attacks him; it has a life of its own, its own magical properties and effects. The word "soup" is particularly suggestive. The peculiar pungency and viscosity of "soup," in this context, compels the reader to participate in Sánchez's sensations. If we assume that this "soup" is *caused* by the weather, rather than being an aspect of the weather itself, we immediately translate "soup" into "sweat." But to say "Onésimo Sánchez sweated profusely" would hardly suggest the energy with which García Márquez wishes to endow the atmosphere of Rosal del Virrey.]

> and he felt many years older and more alone than ever.

[Sanchez's feelings appear to derive from his transition from "weatherlessness" to his immersion in the hot, soupy, and sordid world of Rosal del Virrey—that is, from rose to Rosal, from illusion to disillusion. These feelings of age and solitude are inescapable for Sánchez in his life just as they are inescapable in this sentence.]

Magical realism, in the hands of García Márquez, is a wonderfully supple kind of writing. It penetrates objective reality to reveal the mysterious and poetic qualities that underlie the daily lives of the people and communities it describes. His characters have an aura of woeful futility combined with a wonderful innocence that lends them much of their essential charm and virtue as fictional creations.

Death Constant beyond Love is, like all of García Márquez's fiction, very much a story of Latin America. The geographical, historical, cultural, political, and climatic texture of Latin American life is central to any discussion of García Márquez's work; it is only necessary to compare his work with that of Borges to note the extent to which this is true. It might even be said that magical realism, as a mode of writing, is inextricably bound to Latin America, where the influence of French and Spanish surrealism combined with a desire to use the magical myths of an indigenous tradition to reexamine, indeed transform, an imperfect "colonial" reality.

García Márquez's political concerns are manifest in *Death Constant beyond Love*, just as they are in almost all of his work, including *One Hundred Years of Solitude* and, especially, *The Autumn of the Patriarch*. He is a very active socialist, but one who insists on a socialism appropriate to the cultural and historical conditions of Latin America. "I think the world ought to be socialist," he has said,

> that it will be, and that we should help this to happen as quickly as possible. But I'm greatly disillusioned by the socialism of the Soviet Union. They arrived at their brand of socialism through special experiences and conditions, and are trying to impose in other countries their own bureaucracy, their own authoritarianism, and their own lack of historical vision. That isn't socialism and it's the great problem of the present moment.

Many of the traditional concerns of socialist writing—the exposure of political corruption and oppression, the condition of the common man, the effects of power and money, among others—are evident in García Márquez's work.

Almost everyone who has read García Márquez has noted the affinities between his work and that of William Faulkner. There is the epic creation of an entire fictional world—García Márquez's Macondo and Faulkner's Yoknapatawpha—complete with geography, history, and whole populations of extraordinary characters; there is the lyrical magic of their language, including the tendency to become excessively lyrical. García Márquez has said that he found Faulkner's world, the southern United States,

> was very like my world, . . . created by the same people. . . . When I traveled in the southern states, I found evidence—on those hot, dusty roads, with the same vegetation, trees, and great houses—of the similarity between our two worlds. One mustn't forget that Faulkner is in a way a Latin American writer. His world is that of the Gulf of Mexico.

García Márquez has also said, however, that Faulkner's influence was "really screwing me up" and that his problem was "not how to imitate Faulkner but how to destroy him." Although García Márquez couldn't "destroy" Faulkner, he could move in his own direction: his style is now entirely his own.

García Márquez claims that he "began to long to write," and in fact did write his first stories, under the influence of Kafka's *The Metamorphosis*. Certainly, García Márquez's use of metaphor and his tendency to insist that his metaphors be taken literally, and our sometimes befuddled attempt to discover an absolute "meaning" beneath the text, remind us of Kafka.

Classroom Strategies

Death Constant beyond Love can be taught in one class period. Students will probably experience it as a kind of dessert after a term full of main courses. If students have any particular difficulty with the story, it will very likely have to do with their resistance to taking it seriously. García Márquez's stylistic conjuring combined with his insouciance will probably distract those students who persistently struggle to find "meaning" in the text. The "meaning" is, of course, there—but it emerges like a rabbit out of a magician's hat. Students who resist magic will resist *Death Constant beyond Love*.

To break down this resistance it might be useful first to discuss García Márquez's magical realism and to emphasize its difference from fantasy, from the tall tale, and from surrealism. Reminding students of Kafka's *The Metamorphosis*—with its apparent discrepancy between narrative tone and the extraordinary events being described—might aid them in resolving their problems with the techniques of magical realism.

You might then emphasize Onésimo Sánchez himself: as a would-be dictator, in full control of the means by which the illusion of his benevolence can be foisted on his public, who is nevertheless foiled by death (the allusions to Marcus Aurelius might be useful here); as a human being not unlike ourselves, who must face the knowledge of his own imminent death; as a man who attempts, and fails, to reduce the terror of self-knowledge through erotic passion. Budding Freudians in the classroom will want to play with the clear suggestion of Thanatos here, García Márquez's merging of Sánchez's movement toward death with his desire for passion—especially since the object of his passion is Laura Farina, the very embodiment of earth.

Topics for Discussion and Writing

1. What is the importance of the title? What does it tell us about the story's central thematic concerns?
   [See the third paragraph of "Backgrounds."]
2. García Márquez has said that everything he has written has been about solitude. In what ways is *Death Constant beyond Love* about solitude?

[See the second and third paragraphs of "Backgrounds."]

3. What is the symbolic importance of the rose, the chastity belt, the campaign props, and Laura Farina herself?

[The rose, campaign props, and Laura Farina are discussed in "Backgrounds." The chastity belt worn by Laura Farina would appear to suggest, ironically, that Sánchez's final attempt to find love, and to fend off death, extracts a literal price. The route to beauty and love, then, is blocked by a padlock—a padlock that can be removed only when he turns one of his heretofore illusory promises into a reality.]

4. What similarities and differences can be found between García Márquez's fictional techniques and those of William Faulkner? Franz Kafka? Charles Dickens? How are these techniques similar to those found in the *Odyssey*? How can magical realism be characterized?

[See the fourth through the eleventh paragraphs of "Backgrounds."]

5. How does García Márquez link death with nature and illusion with beauty in the story?

[See the second and third paragraphs of "Backgrounds."]

Comparative Perspectives

1. "We are here for the purpose of defeating nature," Senator Onésimo Sánchez declares in his standard campaign speech, but he speaks, as the narrator of *Death Constant beyond Love* informs us, "against all his convictions." What is wrong with this statement? Why is it worth telling us that the Senator has an honors degree in metallurgical engineering?

[An engineer may modify nature; but no one can defeat it, as the senator's death sentence emphasizes.]

2. Compare the interplay of politics and nature in some other works you have read this semester: is the effort to transform (or even defeat) nature always presented with the irony of García Márquez, or do other writers see any ways in which public policy and human effort may genuinely ameliorate and improve the natural world?

[The Enlightenment is a good point at which to begin a review of these questions. Compare Swift's serious proposals for improving human nature (for example, "curing the expansiveness of pride, vanity, idleness, and gaming in our women") and Pope's assertion in *An Essay on Man* that "Presumptuous Man" should leave nature to its own devices. Discuss Romantic views of nature—Leopardi's, for example, or Wordsworth's.]

3. García Márquez relies on his audience to understand the references to Marcus Aurelius in *Death Constant beyond Love*. Like Eliot and Borges, he weaves echoes of past literary accomplishments into all of his work and, like Eliot and Borges, has himself become a major influence on other late twentieth-century authors.

What is the irony of the quotation from Marcus Aurelius? How are artists remembered?

Further Reading

See also the reading suggestions in the *Anthology*, p. 2552.

Apuleyo Mendoza, Plinio. *The Fragrance of Guava.* Trans. Ann Wright. 1983. A series of interviews with García Márquez.

Bell-Villada, Gene H. *García Márquez: The Man and His Work.* 1990. A general description aimed at a broad audience.

Bloom, Harold, ed. *Gabriel García Márquez.* 1989. Collects eighteen essays on style, themes, and cultural contexts; chronology and bibliography.

Books Abroad. The Summer 1972 issue is dedicated to García Márquez.

Byk, John. "From Fact to Fiction: Gabriel García Márquez and the Short Story." *Mid-American Review* 6, 2 (1986): 111–16.

McGuirk, Bernard, and Richard Cardwell, eds. *Gabriel García Márquez: New Readings.* 1987. Twelve essays plus the 1982 Nobel Address.

McMurray, George R., ed. *Critical Essays on Gabriel García Márquez.* 1987. Fifteen reviews plus fourteen articles and essays on a range of García Márquez's work.

McNerey, Kathleen. *Understanding Gabriel García Márquez.* 1989. A useful introduction with comments on the different works; includes a short biography stressing cultural context and a bibliography.

Minta, Stephen. *Gabriel García Márquez: Writer of Colombia.* 1987. An introduction.

Ortega, Julio, and Claudia Elliot. *Gabriel García Márquez and the Powers of Fiction.* 1988. A general collection that includes five essays and the 1982 Nobel lecture.

Shaw, Bradley A., and Nora Vera-Godwin. *Critical Perspectives on Gabriel García Márquez.* 1986. Nine essays on a wide range of topics, with considerable textual analysis.

Williams, Raymond L. *Gabriel García Márquez.* 1984. An introductory study.

———. "The Visual Arts, the Poetization of Space and Writing: an Interview with Gabriel García Márquez." *PMLA* 104, 2 (March 1989): 131–40.

Derek Walcott

Omeros

Backgrounds

Each of the excerpts included here comes from the long three-hundred-page book-length poem, *Omeros*. While it is recommended that the sections excerpted from that long poem be taught together in one unit, any of the individual excerpts could also be taught separately. The teaching notes that follow will fit either strategy. If you wish to teach all of the excerpts, two 45–50–minute class days are recommended.

In the first day, the idea of epic—at least as it is distinct from lyric—should be discussed. The origins of the category in the Western tradition going back to Homer should be addressed. The continuation of that tradition in Roman culture with Virgil should be mentioned, as should the great Christian epic, Dante's *Divine Comedy*. Walcott's contemporary epic alludes both to Homer and Virgil. One should mention that Walcott's rhyme scheme and meter are based on Dante's terza rima that Dante himself invented for *The Divine Comedy*. It is a triple rhyming stanza meant to suggest the trinity. But if Walcott takes his prosody from Dante, he takes his structure, the very story of a journey, and many of the names from Homer. In short, the book is a mélange of the Western epic tradition and you can teach this fact simply by discussing the poem's formal structure.

It is recommended that you begin teaching this poem with the final excerpt from Book Seven. Beginning with this section has several benefits. First, it offers an accessible biography of the central character, and it sets up the story. Second, it enables you to proceed through each of the remaining excerpted sections with a concrete story already in place. Therefore, you can trace the way various images and themes develop. In particular, you might attend to a number of important themes that flow out of this particular story: identity, time, the meaning of home, and so on.

Classroom Strategies and Topics for Discussion

From Book One

From Chapter I

II

In these sixty lines, Achille makes his boat. A teacher should attend to the many metaphors at play in these lines and explain how, once related, the many metaphors establish a set of themes to trace in subsequent excerpts. For example, the boat comes from a tree, which in turn is part of the natural environment. That environment and the boat are blessed by a priest but they also suggest more pagan religious associations. The suggestion is that there is a set of metaphors pertaining to Christianity as well as a set of metaphors pertaining to a pagan sense of spirituality latent in all creation—birds, trees, and others.

The boat, however, is also named after a slogan found on American money, and, in turn, that slogan is misspelled. These sixty lines, then, bring together the many different ways by which one makes meaning: two religious systems, pagan and Christian, join with two value systems, economic and cultural. The cultural value system here refers specifically to the native population of indigenous people, the Arawak. Also there are references to the current Caribbean dialect, the patois spoken by the main characters. Within all these systems of meaning and value, however, Achille expresses his own individuality. In his mind, which this excerpt allows us to access, he carves for himself a boat of meaning. Discussing the various systems included in this densely packed opening section could easily take up a class period.

A final set of meanings has to do with literary allusion—the allusions to Homer's *Iliad* and *Odyssey* so present in the names of the characters, Achille and Hector, and in the very idea of the larger poem, the journey. Such an allusion, after all, suggests that Walcott's story of Achille is as universally significant as the tale told of Odysseus in ancient Greece.

From Chapter VIII

To understand the story told in these hundred lines, the reader must recognize that by this point in Book One, Achille is deeply in debt and his beloved, Helen, no longer has much interest in him. Metaphorically, this is also a chapter in which Achille is descending to the underworld, much as Odysseus does in the *Odyssey*. On a more literal level, the story is this: desperate to win back her love, Achille decides that the local legend of a sunken treasure ship will be the source of his salvation. In this excerpt, we see Achille, at night, poring over his bank book which only tells him how much he owes to others. He believes, however, that his debt to the love of and for Helen is even more powerful. Against all scientific evidence to the contrary, Achille begins privately diving to the wreck in search of treasure that he plans to give to Helen to win back her love. In the second section, he sees the supposedly nonexistent wreck—but it vanishes before he can reach it. Ever after, though, he searches for it, hoping it will solve the problems he is having with his beloved Helen.

As with the first excerpt, in this one from Chapter VIII, students should pay particular attention to the many metaphors and relationships they invoke. For example, why does Achille, who named his own boat after the slogan on American money, believe that money from a shipwreck will win back his lost lover? What is the association here between love and money? Why is his quest for love a search *downward* into watery depths? What does it mean that the ship he looks for is a legend, a vision that he can never actually touch or discover?

FROM BOOK THREE

From Chapter XXV

In these 137 lines, Achille has a dream in which he leaves the Caribbean and ventures forth to his ancestral land of Africa. In this chapter, he navigates the Congo in Africa and eventually meets his long-lost father, Afolabe. The chapter ends with an extended dialogue between Achille and his father. As with other excerpts, the metaphors here offer the best access to the chapter's central themes: time and memory.

Although both themes are fundamental to the entire book of *Omeros*, they come to the forefront in this chapter. Achille confronts his past not only through his own father and his homeland, but also through the metaphor of language and, in particular, the power of proper names. What might it mean that Achille does not remember what his name means, and that his father does not remember the name he had originally given his son? Also notice the many words, images, and symbols that refer to "time" in this passage. What might this chapter be saying about time?

From Chapter XXVI

I

In these thirty lines, which follow directly from the theme of return to one's origins mentioned above, Achille learns the stories of his tribe, his ancestors, and even of the local gods. At the end of this excerpt he even says the names of the gods. Again, names become a central motif and suggest that one's very identity depends on a particular association of language, ethnic group, and place of origin. This idea of identity should be discussed in terms of the overall pattern in these sections of *Omeros*.

III

Once he says the names of his own people's gods, the names of his spiritual past, he is prepared to understand his present. In this excerpt, then, Achille is still in Africa, in the hut he has been given by his father's tribe, and dreaming of his Caribbean home. When he awakens to the fact that he is still in Africa and sees a local ceremony, however, he is amazed at its resemblance to ceremonies on his home island. He now has a better sense of connection to the rituals he had long taken for granted. The question this section provokes is, What is home? What does the term "home" really mean or imply?

FROM BOOK FOUR

From Chapter XXXV

Now in Georgia, in the United States and in the present moment, the narrator—a fusion of Derek Walcott himself (section I) and an unnamed Native American man (section II)—recount the Trail of Tears from the 1830s when Native Americans were forcibly removed from the southeastern United States to Oklahoma. This expulsion is meant to parallel the Middle Passage that brought Africans to the Caribbean. These seventy-five lines ask students to connect the story of the Trail of Tears to the story of the Middle Passage. Issues pertaining to identity in the Caribbean are here brought home to the United States as well.

FROM BOOK SIX

From Chapter LII

II

Although this excerpt is little more than a list of items—detritus from the British empire—spilled forth from a tea-chest, it offers nonetheless a rich cornucopia of imagery, symbol, and metaphor. A good question to ask concerning this section might be, Given that all of the items in some way pertain to colonialism and empire, how might they be significant to the story of Achille as told in the other sections of the poem excerpted here?

FROM BOOK SEVEN

From Chapter LXIV

I

This is from the conclusion of *Omeros*, and relates Walcott's own view of the character, Achille. Toward the end of this section note that Walcott himself so identifies with his own character that the language suggests he himself has become Achille and the poem is in some way the canoe that Achille carves in Book One.

CLUSTER: ON BEING A CULTURAL OTHER

On Being a Cultural Other offers a wide-ranging set of excerpts held together by a series of related ideas: those with power and authority, for different reasons and with different consequences, tend to define those without power. Those without power are often silenced or unheard in their attempts to establish a definition of themselves when it differs from the one established by those in power. Those in power usually assume that they represent the "norm"; therefore, those without power are defined in terms of their difference from the "norm," their "Otherness." And often, the definition of the "Other" developed by those in power actually becomes the definition accepted by the "Other" himself or herself.

With the exception of Simone de Beauvoir and Audre Lorde, the writers in this cluster are either representatives of a colonized culture or postcolonials writing about what it means to be a cultural "Other." It might be useful for the teacher to begin with them.

After centuries in which Westerners wrote with apparent authority about cultures from everywhere else in the world, the last fifty years or so have seen an amazingly rich, varied, and crucially important rush of literature, commentary, and analysis emerging from those same cultures. It was never, of course, that writers from ex-colonial places had just begun to write; it was that now, having gained independence from their colonial masters, their voices had a far better chance of being heard, and that Western publishers began to realize that there was an interest on the part of their public to listen to them.

The public discovered reasonably quickly that these were some of the most interesting voices on earth. Salman Rushdie once called this literary explosion *The Empire Strikes Back*, and it is, perhaps, the most interesting, exciting, and idea-changing development in Western literature in hundreds of years. It is difficult now to imagine the literature of the last fifty years without Chinua Achebe, Wole Soyinka, Leopold Senghor, Aimee Cesaire, Ngugi Wa Thiong 'o, Salman Rushdie, R. K. Narayan, Derek Walcott, Edward Said, V. S. Naipaul, Samuel Selvon, or Edward Kamau Brathwaite, to name but a few—almost all of whom write primarily in English or French.

Most of the excerpts in this cluster explore some of the major concerns of these writers and suggest some of the reasons they have become such important voices for our time.

René Ménil's short piece establishes the most important idea running through all of these excerpts: in power relationships, when there is a Master and a Subordinate, the Master's way of seeing affects all aspects of the Subordinate's life, including the way the Subordinate sees and defines himself or herself. The Subordinate sees himself or herself as the *Other*, "at a distance," and uses the terms and attitudes of the Master to do so. Ménil is here writing particularly of the effect of colonialism on the colonized. Noting the versions of self emerging from his own island and his own people in poetry and painting, he asserts that the "fundamental characteristic of human existence in colonial society is separation from oneself, exile from oneself, alienation from oneself. . . . I am 'exotic-to-myself' because my view of myself is the view of the white person having become mine after three centuries of colonial conditioning."

Simply put, it is not just that those in power have the power to write the histories and define in their terms the nature of those subordinate to them—something, as Frantz Fanon notes, self-analytical and self-critical Westerners have themselves recognized for a long time—but a more important and perfidious effect is that the subordinate "Others" take on the version of themselves established by the Masters and begin to see themselves as their Masters see them. Students might be reminded of how easily this kind of dynamic can take place, and how pervasive it can become, by calling up the version of themselves established by people who have had power over them—parents, teachers, peers—and the extent to which they began to define themselves as these others saw them. Let them then imagine what the effect of colonial occupation would likely be.

Ménil identifies the problem; Frantz Fanon proposes a solution—to rehabilitate the past and to struggle, violently if necessary, in the present. The first battlefield is the passionate search for a national culture, a precolonial culture with a "dignity, glory, and solemnity" that the colonial masters have devalued to such an extent that the effect, "consciously sought," was to "drive into the natives' heads that if the settlers were to leave, they would at once fall back into barbarism, degradation, and bestiality." The colonial did not seek, then, to be considered by the native as a "gentle, loving mother who protects her child from a hostile environment, but rather as a mother who unceasingly restrains her fundamentally perverse offspring from managing to commit suicide and from giving free rein to its evil instincts."

Among the past events that Fanon is most interested in rehabilitating, and speaking about and for from the "native's" point of view, are those previous acts of revolt and resistance that were crushed. They are important to revisit because they were portrayed by the colonizer as annoying and dangerous insubordinations, and then passed down to the colonized as instances of failure and futility. But now, says Fanon, things are different: "As for we who have decided to break the back of colonialism, our historic mission is to sanction all revolts, all desperate actions, all those abortive attempts drowned in rivers of blood."

Rehabilitating a more accurate—or at least less one-sided—version of one's national culture, then, is crucial to the act of establishing a nation's legitimacy, and therefore crucial for those who take up arms to defend that legitimacy. But Fanon also recognizes that this rehabilitation cannot, in Africa at least, be *specifically* national. "The native intellectual who decides to give battle to colonial lies fights on the field of the whole continent." The colonial, "who has not bothered to put too fine a point" on discriminating between various national or tribal cultures, merely sees Africa as a "haunt of savages, a country riddled with superstitions and fanaticism, destined for contempt, weighed down by the curse of God, a country of cannibals—in short, the Negro's country. Colonialism's condemnation is continental in its scope."

Fanon is pointing out here that colonialism's attitude toward its African holdings was informed by an unabashed racism, and so the rehabilitation of national cultures has to take a different and more expansive course: what must be demonstrated is that "a Negro culture exists." The concept of negritude, then, is the "emotional if not the logical antithesis of that insult which the white man flung at humanity."

In his excerpt, Chinua Achebe takes a gentler and more inclusive view, something he has been criticized by some for doing since his first major work, *Things Fall Apart*, was published in 1958. Achebe uses his personal experience of growing up in a colonized society, where being bilingual and, to a certain extent, bicultural, was expected and accepted. It is not surprising that Achebe, who was raised a "thorough little Christian" and taught in English-run schools, would, like most children, accept what he was taught with a certain degree of steadfastness. What perhaps is surprising, however, is Achebe's capacity to function without "undue distress" in both the imported culture of his colonial masters and his indigenous Igbo culture. It was not until quite late, when he was studying literature and history in Nigeria at University College in Ibadan, that he fully realized the extent to which African life and history was distorted in British imperial literature. And the problem was not just British literature, which had at its base the usual simple-minded and racially biased version of Africa, motivated by ignorance and ill-will, but even those works of literature that were apparently well-meaning, such as Joyce Cary's *Mister Johnson*. One is reminded here of Albert Schweitzer's famous comment to the effect that Africans were his brothers, yes, but they were his *junior* brothers.

At Ibadan, Achebe realized that if he were going to write, the "story we had to tell could not be told for us by anyone else no matter how gifted or well-intentioned." In his work, Achebe attempts to fashion a version of English that uses Igbo vocabulary and speech patterns—a specifically African version of English—that would be "at once universal and able to carry his particular experience." English, after all, is the language most capable of reaching the readers he is most interested in informing. *Things Fall Apart* (available in full in the *Anthology*) remains a prime example of what Achebe set out to do, and succeeded in doing.

Edward Said's excerpt deals with some of the same problems described above, but in a different place, in a different way, and on a different scale. He begins by noting that from the beginnings of Western literature, Europe has presumed to speak for "Asia." Western literature "articulates the Orient" and in that articulation Asia is always being converted "from something into something else"; it is important only in that it represents something *in relation* to Europe. To this day, Westerners speak of the Near, Middle, and Far East, rarely noticing, one suspects, that these designations are geographically accurate descriptions only to Europeans, and that they come from a version of the East that is entirely Eurocentric.

In the West, the Orient is taken seriously (unlike, for instance, Africa), but only as a mysterious and attractive opposite to what seem to be "normal" values. In creating this version of the Orient, the European writer, Said argues, does not act as a "puppet master" for whom the Orient is simply to be manipulated, but instead as a "genuine creator" for whom Oriental mysteries are taken seriously "not least because [the mysteries] challenge the rational Western mind to new exercises of its enduring ambition and power."

The effect, of course, is to make Europe look greater—just as the victor in a conflict is always seen to be greater when challenged by a significant and formidable opponent. In the Western mind, the Orient has become a *complementary* opposite, and in this opposition Europe is seen as the rational alternative to "Eastern excesses." The West demonstrates its strength by being able to resist the Orient's "tempting suggestiveness" and its capacity for "entertaining and confusing the mind."

In particular, Said points to the military and cultural collision between Christianity and Islam, and the misconceptions of Islam based on false analogies between it and Christianity. It was important for Christian Europe to tame and condescend to Islam, because "for Europe, Islam was a lasting trauma"—in great part because of Islam's conquest of Persia, Syria, Egypt, Turkey, North Africa, India, Indonesia, China, Spain, Sicily, and parts of France. Until the end of the seventeenth century the " 'Ottoman peril' lurked alongside Europe to represent for the whole of Christian civilization a constant danger."

How did these versions of the Orient come about? Said suggests that much of the responsibility falls on Western "Orientalists," professional scholars whose business it was and is to define the Orient for the Westerner. In their "insensitive schematization of the entire Orient," he says, Orientalists "made the Orient a stage on which the whole East is confined . . . a theatrical stage affixed to Europe." In Said's view, the Orientalist became a kind of dramatist, using particularly useful items as props and characters for his drama, pressing "ideological myths into service, even as knowledge seemed genuinely to be advancing."

To the Westerner, then, largely because of the information delivered by the professional "Orientalists," the Orient was always to seem *"like some aspect of the West"*—only inferior and dangerous.

The short excerpt from Trinh T. Minh-Ha takes on the question of the implications of the term and idea of the Third World. The colonies may be gone, but, as the *Anthology's* editor says in the introductory notes to the piece, "the vocabulary and images of the dominant West permeate global culture and continue to influence the way in which people represent themselves."

She notes that though the term "Third World" once meant, and to a certain degree still means, something derogative—"undeveloped," "underprivileged," even the home of "savages"—it now means something else as well. The Third World is nonaligned, refuses to accept Western domination, and has turned this refusal into an "empowering tool." Though there is no "unified unaligned Third World bloc"—the Third World "dwells on diversity" just as the First World does—it still represents a threat to Western ideas of itself. "The Master is bound to recognize that His Culture is not as homogeneous, as monolithic as He believed it to be. He discovers, with much reluctance, He is just an other among others."

Nevertheless, as her description of a supposed Western-style celebration of diversity—the Chinese New Year parade in San Francisco's Chinatown—demonstrates, this new mingling of cultural worlds is often still dominated by assumptions and patterns of power held over from an earlier time.

The excerpt from Salman Rushdie is particularly meaty, and should be of great interest to students—if for no other reason than its having been written since 9/11 and that it uses that event as a constant reference point—who perhaps (incorrectly) imagine that many of the problems raised by Ménil, Fanon, Achebe, and Said are now solved.

Students of course will benefit from hearing something about the specifics of Rushdie's own situation as it was in the late 1980s and 1990s, and how being the object of a *fatwa* might have informed his point of view. The teacher would be advised to have a look at Rushdie's particular case and the controversy which then surrounded it.

His excerpt begins with what it means to cross borders, especially those of language, and the kinds of mistakes often made by those who do. He is, of course, talking about translators, but also about those—like Said's "Orientalists"—who attempt to write about other cultures. To begin his discussion, he uses Vladimir Nabokov's "three grades of evil [that] can be discerned in the strange world of verbal transmigration": (1) making obvious errors due to ignorance or misguided knowledge; (2) skipping words or passages that are not understood or which might seem obscure or obscene to his readers; and (3) vilely beautifying the original text or culture "in such a fashion as to conform to the notions and prejudices of a given public."

The problem with all this, and especially the third of these, is that "the way we see the world affects the world we see." If we see the world in a skewed or misconceived way, then when "the creatures of our imagination crawl out from our heads . . . and become actual," these creatures may well be monstrous. This brings Rushdie to his discussion of the events of 9/11, which he calls a "monstrous act of the imagination."

Teachers will need to make a close examination of Rushdie's take on 9/11, because students almost certainly will. What will be most noticeable, and perhaps disturbing, to them is that Rushdie looks at 9/11 in a way quite different from the standard rhetoric of the U.S. political administration and American newspapers, not to speak of the general public, which has for the most part adopted this rhetoric.

Students will probably react immediately, and not positively, to Rushdie's description of the attack on the World Trade Center as a "monstrous act of the imagination," his claim that "murder was not the point," and that the planners of 9/11 behaved like "perverted, but in another way brilliantly transgressive, performance artists." Students will not like words like "imagination," "brilliant," and "artists" being associated with Al Qaeda or other enemies of the United States.

Rushdie registers the degree to which the attack on New York was imaginative and "shockingly successful" from the terrorist point of view because the terrorists made their point, they *created a meaning*: one could strike at the very heart of a seemingly invulnerable high-tech world using, if necessary, low-tech means to do it, and by doing it, create and cross a new borderline.

Rushdie has little sympathy for the terrorists—"people for whom there are no limits at all, people who will, quite literally do anything"—but he insists that the worst thing we can do is to "dehistoricize," "depoliticize," and "depersonalize" them by simply calling them "evildoers" or madmen and then pretending that such talk goes any distance at all in dealing with the questions they have brought into such dramatic view. In this, Rushdie is seconding what Hannah Arendt had to say (in her excerpt from *Organized Guilt and Universal Responsibility* in this anthology) about the danger of imagining the problem with the Nazis was that they were simply "evildoers" or "madmen." Such simplistic views "let the terrorists off the hook" because they reduce the terrorists' responsibility for their acts. "The world is real," Rushdie insists we remember, "There are no demons. Men are demonic enough."

One of the questions raised by excesses as violent and complete as those of 9/11 is the question of limits. And this question, as Rushdie (who himself crossed a line and was threatened with death for doing it) knows as well as anyone, is an awkward one for artists and writers. It's awkward because of their adherence to an ideology of the "frontierless-ness" of art, their "adherence to, and insistence upon, a no-limits position" in their own work. Rushdie recognizes that the artistic impulse to shock and keep on shocking, to go "further and further," may sometimes "become the worst kind of artistic self-indulgence." And so now, he asks, "in the aftermath of horror, of the iconoclastically transgressive image-making of the terrorists, do artists and writers still have the right to insist on the supreme, unfettered freedoms of art?"

There are certainly those who think they do not, and Rushdie outlines with considerable seriousness the arguments of Anthony Julius to the effect that "the aesthetic potential of the transgressive has been exhausted." But, finally, he disagrees with Julius. For Rushdie, the problem is that Julius's position can give the upper hand to "cautious, conservative political and institutional forces" and social groups that are "deliberately fostering a new, short-fuse culture of easy offendedness" where more and more kinds of speech are "being categorized as transgressive." But insofar as "the freedoms of art and the intellect are closely related to the general freedoms of society as a whole," to restrict those freedoms— even in response to so barbaric an assault as that of 9/11—is to undermine civilization itself. In this, Rushdie aligns himself with the arguments of George Orwell (in his *The Prevention of Literature*, also in this anthology), though he ranges much further and, of course, incorporates much fresher threats to artistic freedom.

For Rushdie, how we comport ourselves in this "frontier time" is all-important. "Will we," he asks, "give the enemy the satisfaction of changing ourselves into something like his hate-filled, illiberal mirror-image, or will we, as the guardians of the modern world, as the custodians of freedom and the occupants of the privileged lands of plenty, go on trying to increase freedom and decrease injustice?" Rushdie hopes we pass the test.

It may be easy for students to recognize the "rightness" of Rushdie's point of view if discussion is limited to condemning the "thought policemen" of totalitarian and tyrannical states, or to criticizing religious restrictions carried out by religions that are comparatively unfamiliar, or of rejecting social and political values different from theirs. But discussion will become much hotter (and more interesting) if the teacher drives the discussion toward an examination of restrictions and instances of censorship in their own culture, which, of course, emanate from their own values and assumptions. If bold and secure enough, the teacher could discuss *any* kind of censorship or any kind of restriction—from movie ratings and CD warnings to hate speech and other blatantly transgressive and possibly dangerous acts.

The spirit of Rushdie's essay practically demands that the teacher do exactly that.

At approximately the same time writers from colonies or ex-colonies began to be heard, women began *systematically* to challenge and change the ideas and attitudes both men and women had about women.

Of course, there had for hundreds of years been plenty of writing by women available to Western readers, just as there has been plenty of writing by working-class writers, minority writers, and gay or lesbian writers. What has been different, however, about the writing of the last half-century is the insistence of these writers on identifying themselves in terms of gender, class, or sexual orientation, and writing about themselves in terms of being the "Other." The excerpts from Simon de Beauvoir and Audre Lorde manage, in one way or another, to take up a number of gender, class, and sexual orientation issues and to discuss them in terms of "Otherness."

Beauvoir's *The Second Sex* is a crucial text in the history of feminist politics. In it, she not only identifies and aligns the situation of women with the situation of the "Other" in many other kinds of master/slave relationships, but she also exposes a number of the myths that have been particularly useful in men's attempts to dominate women.

Feminine "mystery" is perhaps the most important and pervasive of these myths. It has, Beauvoir says, been a very "profitable illusion . . . firmly anchored in masculine hearts." Individual *men* may be "mysterious," but *man* is never understood to be, in essence, a "mystery." But as long as women can be conceived of as mysterious in essence, their arguments, claims, emotions, or demands may be ignored or deflected on grounds that they are simply impenetrable, having their source, after all, in a mysterious complex of ideas and emotions that resists reason and understanding.

Beauvoir rejects the notion of feminine "mystery" and notes that "if man fails to discover that secret essence of femininity, it is simply because it does not exist." And she asks men to reject it as well. "To recognize in woman a human being is not to impoverish man's experience: this would lose none of its diversity, its richness, or its intensity if it were to occur between two subjectivities. To discard the myths is not to destroy all dramatic relation between the sexes, it is not to deny the significance authentically revealed to man through feminine reality; it is not to do away with poetry, love, adventure, happiness, dreaming. It is simply to ask that behavior, sentiment, passion be founded upon truth."

She recognizes that this will not be easy; the myth of feminine "mystery" has been too useful for too long, and, besides, there is a "legion of women who see through men's eyes" and who believe that to be a true woman "she must accept herself as the 'Other.'" Beauvoir also recognizes that "it is more comfortable to submit to blind enslavement than to work for liberation." But she hopes that men will eventually and unreservedly "accept the situation that is coming into existence" because "only then will women be able to live in that situation without anguish." And only then will woman be free to "regain her place in humanity."

Audre Lorde is female, black, working class, lesbian, feminist, social-ist, middle-aged, and a partner and mother in an interracial couple, and writes from a perspective extremely attuned to ideas of the "mythical norm" in a society in which any and all of these attributes can make one the "Other." This is particularly true in a society "where the good is de-fined as profit rather than in terms of human need," where the economic system requires "outsiders as surplus people"; and Lorde usually finds herself part of some group "defined as other, deviant, inferior, or just plain wrong."

It is not enough, says Lorde, to point out human differences in sim-plistic opposition. For instance, feminist arguments concentrate on dif-ferences between men and women, but often exclude equally important discussions of class and race; arguments surrounding racism concen-trate on racial differences but often exclude equally important discus-sions of sexual orientation and "Third World people." The problem, Lorde argues, is that all of us have, "somewhere on the edge of con-sciousness," an idea of the "mythical norm," and even those who stand outside the norm—women, people of color, artists, gays and lesbians, among others—often identify their difference from the norm in only *one* way, and then assume that that *one* difference is the "primary cause of all oppression, forgetting other distortions around difference, some of which we ourselves may be practicing."

Lorde insists that all differences must be recognized, and that the op-pressions and exclusions that result from the "distortions which have re-sulted from the ignoring and misnaming of those differences" will never cease until the "old blueprints of expectation and response" are elimi-nated. "The old definitions have not served us. . . . The old patterns . . . still condemn us to cosmetically altered repetitions of the same old ex-changes, the same old guilt, hatred, recrimination, lamentation, and suspicion." Until we stop using the oppressor's tactics and definitions, we will never fully eliminate the oppression of the "Other": "The mas-ter's tools will never dismantle the master's house."

Teachers will have noticed certain recurring notions, themes, and words that run through all of these excerpts: historical and representa-tional distortion; the idea of the "norm" or "the normal"; the persistent use of "profitable illusions" in the maintenance of power; persistent mis-naming, simplifying, and mythifying. Teachers will find that the discus-sions that emerge from the issues made available in this cluster will be particularly rich and heated. They will also find that their discussion of specific literary texts in terms of these issues will make for a more ex-pansive, vigorous, and insightful discussion as long as the literary texts are not taken only as sociological documents or representative examples of political or ideological issues.

CHINUA ACHEBE

Things Fall Apart

Backgrounds

"Literature, whether handed down by word of mouth or in print, gives us a second handle on reality." Achebe's belief in the social importance of literature emerges clearly in this sentence from the polemic essay *What Has Literature Got to Do with It?* Literature for him is not an ornamental fringe benefit of civilization; to the contrary, it provides a necessary critical perspective on everyday experience. By illuminating contexts and choices, literature—both traditional oral literature and the modern printed text—educates us about the meaning of our own actions and offers greater control over our social and personal lives. Achebe continues: literature works by

> enabling us to encounter in the safe, manageable dimensions of make-believe the very same threats to integrity that may assail the psyche in real life; and at the same time providing through the self-discovery which it imparts a veritable weapon for coping with these threats whether they are found within our problematic and incoherent selves or in the world around us.

Thus far, Achebe's description of the educational role of literature could be attributed to many writers in the realistic tradition: Flaubert, Dostoevsky, Ibsen, Solzhenitsyn, or Freud. Nor would his point of view be alien to other writers for whom literature expresses a kind of knowledge: the poet William Butler Yeats, for example, whose description of cultural disintegration ("things fall apart; the centre cannot hold") is borrowed for the title of Achebe's first novel. Yet the particular reality that Achebe describes is located at a specific point in history: a modern Africa whose rich variety of ethnic and cultural identities is further complicated by the impact of European colonialism.

Since the publication of *Things Fall Apart* (1958), Achebe has assumed a leading position as representative and interpreter of African culture at home and abroad. To a European audience that was accustomed to stereotypes of primitive savages in "darkest Africa" (e.g., the murderous Kali-worshipers or loyal servants of Kipling's *Gunga Din*), he has emphasized the complexities of a different society with its alternate set of traditions, ideals, and values. Achebe was enraged that *Time* magazine would call Joyce Cary's *Mister Johnson* "the best novel ever written about Africa" when Cary depicted Africa as a stagnant and impoverished culture whose "people would not know the change if time jumped back fifty thousand years. They live like mice or rats in a palace floor; all the magnificence and variety of the arts, the learning and the battles of civilisation go on over their heads and they do not even imagine them" (cited by Achebe from *Mister Johnson*). He was dismayed that Africans themselves would internalize this kind of attitude and emulate a supposedly superior white European civilization. In *The Novelist as Teacher* (from *Morning Yet on Creation Day*), Achebe reports how a student used European seasons to describe African weather, writing about "winter" when he meant the period in which the harmattan wind blows. If he didn't use the European terms, the student explained, everyone would call him a "bushman"! Achebe's mission, therefore, is to educate African as well as European readers, reinstating a sense of pride in African culture "to help my society regain belief in itself and put away the complexes of the years of denigration and self-abasement."

This educational mission is not a simple one, and Achebe has not hesitated to explore the complexities and contradictions of modern African—specifically Igbo—society. Indeed, he has found himself in conflict with several other writers who prefer a narrower or more militant perspective aimed at reconstituting an essentially "African" identity. For Achebe, this quest is ideal rather than practical, and modern African society must recognize that it has been irrevocably marked by the colonial era. He mistrusts absolutes and generalizations about "African identity," no matter how useful such concepts may temporarily be. "You have all heard of the African personality, of African democracy, of the African way to socialism, of negritude, and so on. They are all props we have fashioned at different times to help us get on our feet again." Perhaps the most famous disagreement between Achebe and his peers concerns the debate over the African author's choice of language. Should African writers use the "colonizer's language" (e.g., English or French) or should they use only their tribal tongue in order to build up an indigenous literature and reject any vestiges of colonial influence? James Ngugi stopped writing novels in English and, as Ngugi wa Thiong'o, began to write in his native Gikuyu (these novels are then translated into English for a Western audience). Achebe has a different attitude. His language is an "African English" expressing a particular cultural experience, and he sees

a new voice coming out of Africa, speaking of African experience in a worldwide language. *So my answer to the question Can an African ever learn English well enough to be able to use it effectively in creative writing?* is certainly yes. *If on the other hand you ask: Can he ever learn to use it like a native speaker?* I should say, I hope not. . . . The African writer should aim to use English in a way that brings out his message best without altering the language to the extent that its value as a medium of international exchange will be lost. He should aim at fashioning out an English which is at once universal and able to carry his peculiar experience.

(*The African Writer and the English Language*, 1964)

In addition to writing the five novels for which he is best known, Achebe has traveled widely and been an active representative of African letters. In 1962 he became the founding editor for Heinemann Books' publishing line called the African Writers Series, and he has founded and edited two journals: *Okike: An African Journal of New Writing* (1971) and the bilingual *Uwa ndi Igbo: A Journal of Igbo Life and Culture* (1986). Two books of essays, *Morning Yet on Creation Day* (1975) and *Hopes and Impediments* (1988), collect major statements such as *The Novelist as Teacher, The African Writer and the English Language, Colonialist Criticism, Chi in Igbo Cosmology, Africa and Her Writers, What Has Literature Got to Do with It?* and *An Image of Africa,* as well as occasional pieces stemming from debates over African culture. Achebe's conviction concerning the importance of literature in creating a national identity led him and poet Christopher Okigbo to envisage a series of children's stories that would offer African children a better sense of their cultural heritage. Their Citadel Press was discontinued after Okigbo was killed in the Biafran war, but the novelist has nonetheless written *Chike and the River* (1966), a novella told from the point of view of an eleven-year-old boy, the animal fable *How the Leopard Got His Claws* (1972, with John Iroaganachi), and various adaptations of traditional tales for children. In fiction, poetry, essays, and lectures, Achebe returns to basic themes of human freedom and dignity, for, as he says in an essay written during the Biafran war, "if an artist is anything, he is a human being with heightened sensitivities; he must be aware of the faintest nuances of injustice in human relations."

Things Fall Apart demonstrates this concern for the quality of human relations on both an individual and a societal level. Whether describing Okonkwo's family, interactions between neighbors and villages, the evolution of traditional Igbo society in response to internal and external pressures, or the arrival of British missionaries and colonial administrators, Achebe has a sharp and often ironic eye for the shifting balances of human relationships. His characters are strongly drawn but they are never simplified, from the briefly mentioned couple Ndulue and Ozoemena, whose mutual devotion amazes Okonkwo, to the complex character of the hero himself. Okonkwo is introduced at the beginning as a powerful and ambitious man who stammers under strong emotion and has recourse to his fists; he is arrogant and even a bully, yet he has an unadmitted tender side that appears in his relationship to his wife Ekwefi, his caring for Ezinma during her fever, and his attachment to Ikemefuna, whose death at his hands shatters him for days. Achebe prepares the reader to understand the contradictions in Okonkwo's personality by his extended description of the hero's shiftless father, Unoka, in the very first pages. Humiliated by Unoka's laziness, shameful death, and lack of title, compelled early to support the entire family, Okonkwo struggles desperately throughout the novel to root out any sign of inherited "feminine" weakness in himself or his son Nwoye.

This insistence on warlike masculine valor corresponds to traditional Igbo values, and Okonkwo rises high in his clan as long as these values are predominant. Nonetheless, things are already starting to fall apart. Internal pressures are at work and point to change. Obierika disapproves of the expedition to kill Ikemefuna, and he later starts to question the exposure of twins; the *osu* (outcasts) are not content with their status and will be quick to convert to Christianity; Nwoye is unhappy under Okonkwo's bullying, and he will never forget that his father killed his foster brother, Ikemefuna. The process is only hastened and distorted by the arrival of British missionaries, administrators, and the new trading stores with their flow of money. Traditional social and religious values—as well as the authority of the villages to govern themselves—are on their way out. In the first two-thirds of the novel, Umuofia's elaborately harmonious society has been clearly established; in the last third, Achebe provides a contrasting description of the invasive colonial presence. These portrayals are scathing. Mr. Smith, who succeeds a more accommodating minister in the church at Umuofia, enforces a harsh and rigid view of Christianity: "He saw things in black and white. And black was evil." The British administrators rule over a populace whose language and customs they do not even try to understand and that they see as a kind of exotica about which one writes scientific books. They establish a system of "court messengers" to convey orders, and the court messengers become a second layer of corruption by using their borrowed authority to cheat and exploit the common people. The District Commissioner lies to get the village leaders in his power and throws them into jail until the villagers have paid an exorbitant fine. Okonkwo's passionate resistance to this exploitation and deceit makes him even more of a hero—or would, if his society had not changed. The Igbo community is afraid of defying raw power (the same power that has jailed their leaders), and when they meet they cannot decide how to respond. At this point, Okonkwo is ready to act alone, separate from the community that has provided context and reference point hitherto. His enraged execution of the imperious court messenger isolates him completely from the community he has just endangered, and it leads him to commit suicide. Suicide is a shameful or taboo death, just like his father's, and this abomination further separates "one of the greatest men of Umuofia" from the clan. On the last page, Obierika's emotional tribute to his friend contrasts bleakly with the suggestion that this tale of flawed epic heroism will be buried in the annals of colonial history as a "reasonable paragraph [in the District Commissioner's book] *The Pacification of the Primitive Tribes of the Lower Niger*."

Language

Certain aspects of Achebe's "African English" are worth mentioning here. The presence of untranslated Igbo words reminds Western readers of the presence of another linguistic culture that has its own frames of thought and separate words for things. Words such as *egwugwu* or *iyi-uwa* are used repeatedly without translation, but their meaning is clear from the context, and their very presence in the English text is a constant reminder of the blend of two cultures.

On a less obvious level, there are also Igbo names whose meaning subtly reinforces themes in the story: a buried, yet real, level of significance that is available to those who take the trouble (as the District Commissioner does not do) to inquire about the African language. Footnotes here explain some of these buried meanings: the name of Okonkwo's lazy father, Unoka, means "Home is supreme"; the doomed

Ikemefuna is named "My strength should not be dissipated"; and Nwoye's name (built on the nongendered root *Nwa* or "child," and discussed in the headnote) contrasts with Okonkwo's name, which combines stereotypical attributes of masculinity (Oko) and a non-Christian Igbo heritage (he was born on Nkwo, the third day of the four-day Igbo week). Ikemefuna, taken from his family and later killed by Okonkwo, whom he considers his father, sings his favorite song about "Nnadi"— whose name, pathetically, means "Father is there" or "Father exists."

Finally, Achebe integrates into his narrative a characteristic aspect of Igbo speech: the common use of proverbs. As he explains in the conversation between Unoka and Okoye, "proverbs are the palm-oil with which words are eaten." (Okoye, leading up to asking for his money, "said the next half a dozen sentences in proverbs.") Proverbs such as "he who brings kola brings life" or "the sun will shine on those who stand before it shines on those who kneel under them" or "if a child washed his hands he could eat with kings" are inserted into the narrative so appropriately that their nature as proverbs may be overlooked, but in the aggregate they illustrate a characteristic aspect of Igbo thought and speech.

Most of the names in *Things Fall Apart* are pronounced basically as they would be in English (e.g., Okonkwo as *oh-kon´-kwo*), once we exclude the fact that Igbo is a tonal language using high or low tones for individual syllables. (Igbo itself is pronounced *ee´-boh*.) Nonetheless, certain pronunciations, where the stress or number of syllables might be in question, are approximated below.

Agbala (*ag´-ba-la*)
Ajofia (*ah´-joh-fyah*)
Chielo (*chee´-ay-low*)
Ezeani (*ez-ah´-nee*)
Ezeugo (*e´-zoo-goh*)
Ikemefuna (*ee-kay-may´-foo-na*)
Ikezue (*ee´-kay´-zoo-eh*)
Kwenu (*kway´-noo*)
Ndulue (*in´-doo-loo´-eh*)
Nwakibie (*nwa´-kee-ee´-bee-yay*)

Nwayieke (*nwah´-ee-eh´-kay*)
Nwoye (*nwoh´-yeh*)
Obiageli (*oh-bee-ah´-gay-lee*)
Ofoedu (*oh-foh´-eh-doo´*)
Okoye (*oh-ko´-yeh*)
Onwumbiko (*on´-wum-bee´-koh*)
Ozoemena (*oh-zeh´-meh-na*)
Umuofia (*oo´-moo-off´-yah*)
Unoka (*oo´-no-ka*)

Classroom Strategies

Things Fall Apart may be taught in three days; more, if you wish to include related cultural material. You may want to begin by giving some sense of recent African history, perhaps starting with a map of contemporary Africa and comparing it with a map of Africa in 1939, a map that shows colonial protectorates covering almost all the continent. Photographs or African art objects (masks, statuettes, cloth, bowls, metalwork, decorated calabash gourds) provided by you or your students will also help to convey the artistic presence and vitality of another culture— a culture opposed, in *Things Fall Apart*, to a European or "progress-oriented" system that is presumably more familiar to your class. As you evoke the particular African society that is about to "fall apart," the novel's title will acquire more and more significance. Comparisons to Yeats's view of modern European history are certainly appropriate, but it may be even more interesting to ask why a Nigerian writer discussing the African colonial experience would find it useful to draw upon a masterwork of English literature.

Things Fall Apart is Okonkwo's story, and students will be fascinated from the beginning by this combative, contradictory, and passionate character. Yet he is very much a member of his community, accepting its laws and struggling to achieve greatness according to traditional values. Achebe's hero does not define himself as a rebel *against* society, as do the heroes of so many European and American novels, from *René* to *The Catcher in the Rye*. In order to understand his character, therefore, and the poignancy of his ultimate isolation, you will find it useful to consider the values of traditional Igbo society as they are introduced at the beginning of the novel. What are the customs and cultural expectations of Umuofia? How does one succeed in this society, and who is left out? What are the important crops? What is the role of war, of religion, and of the arts? How are decisions made in Umuofia, and who makes them? What differing roles do men and women play? What do we learn from the kola ceremony about hospitality and the taking of titles? The dramatic description of Okonkwo's success and Unoka's failure in the first section incorporates a great deal of information about the many dimensions of Igbo society.

Okonkwo is usually presented as a tragic hero, surmounting obstacles that would crush a weaker person, eventually defeated by the same qualities that sustain his greatness. His impoverished beginning as Unoka's son, the complete failure of his crops when he has just borrowed seedcorn from Nwakibie, and his unexpected exile for seven years after an inadvertent manslaughter are all challenges he manages to overcome. Yet there are other challenges to which his response is more ambiguous: his fear and rejection of the gentleness he associates with failure and, most specifically, the killing of his foster son Ikemefuna (when the latter runs to him for help against the villagers) because he is afraid of being thought weak. Students notice how Okonkwo resorts to violence to solve problems, and they are disturbed when he beats his favorite wife, Ekwefi, and narrowly misses shooting her. If they give Okonkwo credit for caring for Ezinma in her illness and for loving Ekwefi, they also recognize that his son Nwoye converts to Christianity (taking the name Isaac) chiefly because he seeks the security and approval that his father has withheld. Okonkwo's courage and readiness for action are prized in the old Umuofia, which sought supremacy among the neighboring villages, but this brand of warlike heroism is obsolete in the new era and certainly ineffective against the power of the colonial government. Time has passed by both Okonkwo and Umuofia: the former dies by his own hand because he is unwilling to change, while the latter is caught unprepared, weakened from within, and unable to do anything but submit.

Ironically, it is the District Commissioner's book title, *The Pacification of the Primitive Tribes of the Lower Niger*, that provides the last words. Only in the larger context of this book—by the Igbo Chinua Achebe—is the account rebalanced.

Topics for Discussion

1. Why does Achebe introduce the colonial presence only in the last third of the novel?
2. What motives does Nwoye have for converting to Christianity, and why does he take the baptismal name of Isaac?
3. How does Achebe create an "African English" in this novel?
4. How does the relationship of Okonkwo to Unoka help determine Okonkwo's conduct throughout the novel?
5. What function do the *kotma*, or "court messengers," fill in the new society?
6. What strengths and what weaknesses does Achebe show in traditional Igbo society?
7. Discuss Okonkwo's relationship to his wife Ekwefi and his daughter, Ezinma.
8. In what way does Obierika represent a transitional figure between the old and new Igbo society?
9. How are the elders of Umuofia shown to be more "civilized" than the District Commissioner or Mr. Smith, the missionary?
10. Discuss Okonkwo's status as "one of the greatest men of Umuofia." How does he represent his society, and what is the significance of his isolation at the end?
11. Compare the two white missionaries, Mr. Brown and Mr. Smith, in their relationships to the villages of Umuofia. Is Mr. Brown's approach without danger?

Comparative Perspectives

1. All civilizations seem to look with particular horror at the father who kills his child, and many of the narratives in the anthology offer variations on this theme. Explore Achebe's treatment of this motif: how does he give psychological credence to Okonkwo's filicidal acts? Compare, as appropriate, Frederick Douglass's suspicions about his father's identity, and his discussion of the slave master's treatment of his own children (chapter I); the suffering and death of Melville's Captain Vere, likened (in chapter 22 of *Billy Budd*) to Abraham on the verge of sacrificing Isaac; the hostility toward Gregor demonstrated by Mr. Samsa in Kafka's *The Metamorphosis*.
    [See also the related discussion of this motif under "Comparative Perspectives" for Proust's *Remembrance of Things Past*.]
2. The diverse realms of the Igbo gods perturb the Christian missionaries, but they resemble the pantheons of most non-Western cultures. What functions do they serve, and how would you compare

their responsibilities to other systems of divinity about which you
have been learning?

[Compare the Sumerian gods in *Gilgamesh* and/or the Greek
and Roman gods.]

3. Why is the term "female murder" used of Okonkwo's crime? Why
is this ironic? How does it reflect attitudes toward women in
Achebe's novel? How does the author distance himself from his
protagonist's views in this matter? How would you compare the
view of women in *The Dead* or *The Metamorphosis*?

Further Reading

See also the reading suggestions in the *Anthology*, p. 2548.

Achebe, Chinua. *Morning Yet on Creation Day: Essays.* 1975.

———. *Hope and Impediments: Selected Essays, 1965–1987.* 1988.

Okoye, Emmanuel Meziemadu. *The Traditional Religion and Its Encounter with Christianity in Achebe's Novels.* 1987. Discusses Achebe's
representation of traditional Igbo religion (including the *chi*), along
with other writers' accounts and occasional disagreement.

M. A. Onwuejeogwu. *An Igbo Civilisation: Nri Kingdom and Hegemony.*
1981. An anthropologist's detailed account of a strongly hierarchized
Igbo political, religious, and social system; useful in understanding
the traditional Igbo society of *Things Fall Apart.* Drawings, photographs, and maps usable for classroom illustration.

Ubahakwe, Ebo. *Igbo Names: Their Structure and Their Meanings.* 1981.
A sociolinguistic explanation of the complex meanings of names in
Igbo society and of the social importance of naming.

ALICE MUNRO

Walker Brothers Cowboy

Classroom Strategies and Topics for Discussion

There is no better place to start a discussion of *Walker Brothers Cowboy* than its beginning, which eschews all the formalities of narrative
introduction and involves the reader at once in a conversational relationship with the young narrator. Using the present tense, as she does
throughout except for one or two significant lapses, she quotes her father's cryptic, quirky question and immediately indicates that there are
no easy certainties available in her fictive world: is the Lake still there?
By the time the story ends, we come full circle back to the Lake but not
to comfort, for the sky above it is perpetually overcast.

This classic story of a child's initiation into some of the mysteries of
life has an almost mythic opening. Family tensions are palpable if unspoken. The narrator clearly prefers her father to her mother, who tries

to make the daughter into a replica of her own wounded gentility, cutting her old clothes down to fit her child. Because it is summertime, the tailoring leaves the girl "sweaty, itching from the hot wool, ungrateful." This sense of discomfort is reinforced a few pages later, when we see the girl dressed up for a shopping trip, her mother's unwilling "creation." As *Walker Brothers Cowboy* starts, the girl has already separated herself from her overly punctilious mother; by the time it ends, she recognizes her distance from her genial father as well.

You will probably want to spend some time on the father's geology lesson, which simultaneously teaches how influence imprints itself upon us (the Great Lakes come from the mark left by the ice on a flat plain) and how faint are the signs of the influence (mimicking the ice's encroachment on the plain, the father's fingers make hardly any impression at all, prefiguring the faint, unreadable mark that Nora will make on the dusty car fender as the story draws to its conclusion).

Munro knows how to weave such hints through the web of details that your students will probably recognize by now as the fabric of modern realistic fiction. The cracks in the sidewalk that the child's imagination sees as "spread out like crocodiles into the bare yards" prefigure her effort to imagine the plain before the Ice Age, with "dinosaurs walking on it." Between the mentions of the crocodile and the dinosaur, Munro inserts a sense of something primal and dangerous that could reemerge at any time as she describes their progress out of town by saying "the sidewalk gives up." Included in the catalog of details that marks the end of civilization as they move toward the water are "grain boats, ancient, rusty, wallowing." Time takes its toll throughout this story.

Munro's way of constructing her story also deserves consideration. Ask your students how Munro's description of her own way of reading, as quoted in the beginning of the anthology's headnote, may apply as well to her way of writing *Walker Brothers Cowboy*. The opening pages of the story apparently ramble—the habitual evening walk taken by father and mother does not open up to any clear-cut narrative event. The story stops after the geology lesson and seems to start in earnest when we read, "My father has a job, selling for Walker Brothers," but that opening takes us down yet another road.

The central plot of the story—the action that leads up to the visit to Nora Cronin's home—begins with the still-unnamed Ben Jordan's taking his children off for an afternoon while their mother rests. Ask your students what difference it would make if that incident had been left to stand alone: why do we need to learn about the narrator's separate excursions with her father and her mother in order for the visit to Nora to make a difference to us (and to her)?

You might point out to your students that (like the opening chapters of Genesis) *Walker Brothers Cowboy* begins with the introduction of two quite different creation stories that establish the complex world of the piece and thus bring meaning and artistic coherence to the "diversions" that take us from Tuppertown to memories of Dungannon, then out of Ben Jordan's territory, and finally back to the Lake and to Tuppertown.

The father teaches his daughter a lesson cosmic in scope in his discourse on the origin of the Great Lakes. The mother, by contrast, works on a personal scale as she tries to create her child in her own image. Exiled from the fox farm, they live in a fallen world; Mrs. Jordan wants her daughter to feel the loss of their family Eden as intensely as she does herself.

Only after several pages marked by the persistent use of the present progressive, the tense for habitual, repeated actions, do we move in to the focused and singular encounter with Nora and her blind mother. For this excursion, "No roads paved when we left the highway." Enigma rules; witness the architectural phenomenon the daughter ponders as they drive along: what do those second-story doors open onto? This is uncharted territory that Ben Jordan tries to make familiar to his children with his songs. These songs too are worth investigating with your students, for Ben is a kind of artist shaping recalcitrant material as best he can to hold back the dark, to keep "the wolf from the door."

The headnote speaks of Munro's predilection for masks. How many masks does Ben Jordan wear as he tries to cheer his children—and himself? His comic routines are his way of transforming the indignities he daily encounters and of shielding the children from the bitterness of their disappointed mother. You might ask your students whether they have any friends or acquaintances who always make jokes. Does that mean that they are incredibly happy people? And you might have them think about what it must feel like to be a traveling salesman, having to convince people that they lack something in order to make a living. How much easier to be, in today's euphemistic phrase, "an associate" employed in a shop, catering to customers who come in quest of merchandise. Walker Brothers Cowboys are like strolling players who may end up with tomatoes or eggs in their faces (if not the contents of a chamber-pot).

Much of the poignancy of this story comes from seeing, through the eyes of his discerning but not yet fully comprehending daughter, the deflation of Ben Jordan's natural buoyancy. In her understated, oblique way, Munro gives a glimpse of an everyday tragedy wrought by religious difference. Why should Munro have Ben Jordan sing a song about invisible Baptists as he drives by the Vacation Bible Camp? What significance does religious denomination have for the people of Tuppertown and environs? How does the narrator grasp the meaning of the picture on Nora Cronin's wall? What phrase echoes in her mind as she takes in the scene in the kitchen?

Your students should have no trouble delineating the contrast between the woman Ben Jordan married and the woman he could not. Why does Nora dance with the little girl? Why can Ben Jordan not follow suit when he is invited to do so? It's probably worth spending some time having your students explain the symbolic import of dancing in a time and place so straightlaced that for two people to hold each other in their arms while music played was practically equivalent to illicit sex.

The significance of narrative point of view may be emphasized by a close look at the story's four-paragraph coda. You might raise this topic by asking your student why Munro gave Nora Cronin a blind mother. Who in *Walker Brothers Cowboy* has the gift of sight? The daughter sees infinitely more than her younger, more practical brother, who "knows better" than to sound the horn when his older sister goads him on and who can be counted on not to remember anything of their visit. Intent on counting rabbits on the road, he will not give away a secret that he has not understood. The father who took his children to see the sweetheart he could not marry knows them well; his son has not seen anything worth talking about, and his daughter will not talk about what she has seen. She would not tell her mother about "the whisky, maybe the dancing."

But there are deeper insights that are not so easily categorized or captured. One needs an artist working at the level of the divine creator to know why the impression of so delicate a handprint on a flat and colorless landscape changes it forever. The child's sense of discovery is tempered by her lack of total comprehension. Her epiphany defies precise description: it is telling that Ben Jordan has no songs left for the return drive, for the human artist can never make permanent sense of the infinitely changeable weather in which we live.

Topics for Writing

1. The importance of time and place: would this story have the same impact if it were not set during the Great Depression of the 1930s, in a remote Canadian area?
2. How does the family unit function in *Walker Brothers Cowboy*?
3. How insightful is Munro's narrator? Find examples of points that she understands and those that bewilder her. Would an omniscient narrator be able to tell this story as well?

Comparative Perspectives

1. Alice Munro's world seems comfortable and knowable, but it is full of mysteries. Compare Stephen Albert's observation at the end of *The Garden of Forking Paths* with Munro's treatment of time and space as exemplified by the father's description of the Great Lakes: "In contrast to Newton and Schopenhauer, your ancestor did not believe in a uniform, absolute time. He believed in an infinite series of times, in a growing, dizzying net of divergent, convergent and parallel times."
2. Compare and contrast the opportunities available to talented daughters described in this volume, including, as appropriate, Munro's narrator; Sor Juana; Hedda Gabler; Shakespeare's sister as imagined in *A Room of One's Own*; and Ezinma, in *Things Fall Apart*.

Further Reading

See also the reading suggestions in the *Anthology*, p. 2552.

Carscallen, James. *The Other Country: Patterns in the Writing of Alice Munro.* 1993.

Martin, W. R. *Alice Munro: Paradox and Parallel.* 1987. This study offers a helpful reading of the discussion of the Great Lakes.

Redekop, Magdalene. *Mothers and Other Clowns: The Stories of Alice Munro.* 1992. Jargon-filled but useful in its tracing of the "paternal and maternal images of reproduction" that it identifies in *Walker Brothers Cowboy*.

Leslie Marmon Silko

Yellow Woman

Backgrounds

The two Western Keresan dialects, Laguna and Acoma, are mutually intelligible and their communities adjacent. Relatively small in area and in population, the Laguna and Acoma communities have produced no fewer than three of the most prominent figures in the Native American literary renaissance: Silko, of Laguna; Paula Gunn Allen, also of Laguna; and Simon J. Ortiz, of Acoma. Allen, a novelist and poet, is much better known as a critic. Ortiz, a sometime writer of fiction, is often cited as the most gifted Native American poet of the late twentieth century. The three writers have long been supportive of one another; Allen has published perceptive, appreciative criticism of Silko in *The Sacred Hoop* (1986) and her own retelling of the Yellow Woman tale in *Spider Woman's Granddaughters* (1989).

In a narrow but useful sense, Silko's *Yellow Woman* may be seen as a miniature version of her novel *Ceremony* (1977)—with the sexes reversed. In the first instance, a young woman identifying herself with the mythic Yellow Woman leaves home and is profoundly affected by a sexual relationship set in a distant landscape. Her lover she imagines as a kachina, a spirit connected to the land. In the second case a young man named Tayo, whose name also appears in Laguna mythology, leaves home and is profoundly affected by a sexual relationship, again set in a distant landscape. His lover is a woman who disappears in winter and is young in spring. Critics have paid attention to the names used by Silko, and indeed they are evocative. The kachina-lover in *Yellow Woman* is named Silva ("the forest trees of a region or country," according to *Merriam Webster's Collegiate Dictionary*). In *Ceremony* the young man's lover has the familiar Spanish surname Montaño (cf. Spanish *montaña*, "mountain," or, in Mexican Spanish, "forest"—Francisco J. Santamaría, *Diccionario de Mejicanismos*).

The traditional stories of marriage, or sexual liaison, between human and nonhuman are not confined to Laguna mythology or even to the

Southwest. They are prominent throughout the native lore of North America and even of Central and South America. Often the nonhuman spouse is an animal (such as a deer or a buffalo), sometimes a plant (most often corn). The sexual bond therefore establishes a valuable in-law relationship between the human community and its source of live-lihood. In one of the old Yellow Woman stories from Laguna, the abductor is a buffalo in the form of a man; at the close of the tale, when Yellow Woman has been reunited with her human husband, the husband finds that buffalo, as if magically, gather around his wife, allowing him to hunt with ease.

In an interview, Silko was asked if the Yellow Woman tales might pos-sibly have arisen from the ordinary woman's yearning to escape social and sexual domination. Silko's answer was an emphatic no: "That's not what it's about." Readers fortunate enough to be steeped in the entire lore may readily agree. But what is the gift, or power, that Silko's heroine brings back to the earthly community? Not food, certainly. (The Jell-O, already being made as she arrives home, is not of her doing.) According to one persuasive line of criticism, the gift is more subtle and decidedly Silkoesque: it is the gift of a new story. One must keep in mind that for Silko stories are a community's most precious possession. Only through stories can the old traditions remain alive. And our modern Yellow Woman, whether we fully approve or not, has brought home a new ver-sion.

Classroom Strategies

Yellow Woman is rich enough to fill a class period. Students tend to have strong personal reactions to the heroine's adventure and may not be hesitant to express them. Are the women's points of view different from the men's?

An effective way to begin the discussion is by showing in its entirety or in part the videotape *Running on the Edge of the Rainbow: Laguna Stories and Poems*, a twenty-minute presentation by Leslie Silko. Avail-able separately, the tape is the sixth part in an eight-part series called *Words and Place: Native Literature from the American Southwest*, di-rected by Larry Evers, distributed by Norman Ross Publishing, New York. Silko's charismatic personality is well displayed as she reads from her work, discusses the importance of storytelling, and tells how what passes for ordinary gossip at Laguna (a neighbor woman runs off with another man) may in fact be a new version of an old tribal narrative.

Topics for Discussion

1. Is the landscape merely a setting for the story, or does it play a stronger role? Note the name Silva and its English-language defini-tion. How does Silva's presumed connection with the remote forest (" 'Can you see the pueblo?' 'We're too far away' ") and the endless mountains (" 'From here I can see the world' ") elevate the story

from the category of a prose idyll or light romance? The *Anthology* headnote mentions that Silko once studied law with the intention of filing land claims; and you might keep in mind that land, for the Native American—as with civil rights for the African American—is the one overriding political issue. Is it possible to read a political interpretation into *Yellow Woman*?

2. What do the stolen beef and the Jell-O have in common? How do these elements break the prevailing mood?

   [Both are nonnative.]

3. Silko has written dismissively of nonnative poets and writers who weave Native American material into their own work. In so doing, "they deny their history," she observes, intimating that they would do better to "create a satisfactory identity for themselves" by incorporating their own heritage instead of someone else's. If this seems a fair criticism, consider making a short list of traditional ethnic materials that might profitably be reworked by Anglo, African, Asian, or other contemporary American writers. Choose a familiar folktale and prepare a brief, original plot summary that touches upon both the traditional story and modern experience. Or take a well-worn example, such as the Cinderella theme, and compare it to the Yellow Woman theme.

Comparative Perspectives

1. The narrator of *Yellow Woman* imagines the conversation about her absence taking place at home: "Where did she go?—maybe kidnapped." Has she been kidnapped? Why does she not immediately return to her people when she has the chance? How much psychological insight does Silko give us into her heroine's thought patterns here? How would you compare the presentation of the young explorer in *The Old Chief Mshlanga*? Are Lessing and Silko writing about the same phenomenon?

   [See the account in "Backgrounds," above, of Silko's emphatic rejection of a feminist reading of her story. Silko's use of traditional material emphasizes mythic patterns rather than self-discovery.]

2. Although Silko's narrator protests to Silva that Yellow Woman stories "couldn't happen now," the stories that her grandfather told her prepare the ground for her encounter with Silva. How much does our readiness to embrace experience depend on our ability to assimilate it to preexisting emotional and intellectual categories? How does the traditional material upon which *Yellow Woman* draws distinguish Silko's storytelling from the narrative strategies employed in other works that subject their protagonists to strange events, including *Gulliver's Travels* or *The Metamorphosis*?

   [One might argue that Silko's narrator can go home again because she knows how to tell her story. This return is problematic, if not impossible, for Swift's and Kafka's protagonists, whose experiences lack narrative precedents that cushion the absurd. Presumably, this tells us something about the contrast between cultures that prize tradition and those that pride themselves on innovation.]

Further Reading

See also the reading suggestions in the *Anthology*, p. 2554.

Ellis, Florence Hawley. "Laguna Pueblo." In *Handbook of North American Indians*, ed. William C. Sturtevant, vol. 9 (Southwest, ed. Alfonso Ortiz). 1979. Concise introduction to Laguna history and culture.

Hobson, Geary, ed. *The Remembered Earth: An Anthology of Contemporary Native American Literature.* 1979. Includes Silko's essay *An Old-Time Indian Attack Conducted in Two Parts*, her scornful critique of Anglo writers who pose as shamans.

Velie, Alan R. *Four American Indian Literary Masters: N. Scott Momaday, James Welch, Leslie Marmon Silko, and Gerald Vizenor.* 1982. Velie compares Silko's novel *Ceremony* to the Grail legend.

Index